Brahms and His World

A Biographical Dictionary

Peter Clive

The Scarecrow Press, Inc.
Lanham, Maryland • Toronto • Oxford
2006

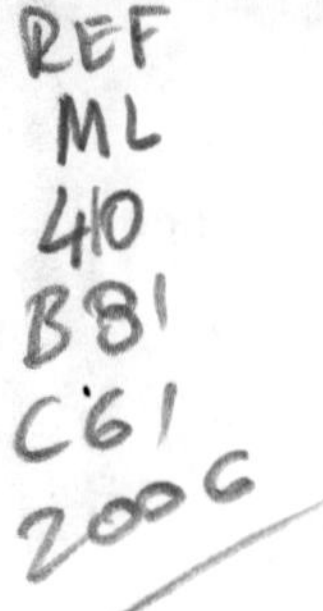

SCARECROW PRESS, INC.

Published in the United States of America
by Scarecrow Press, Inc.
A wholly owned subsidiary of
The Rowman & Littlefield Publishing Group, Inc.
4501 Forbes Boulevard, Suite 200, Lanham, Maryland 20706
www.scarecrowpress.com

PO Box 317
Oxford
OX2 9RU, UK

British Library Cataloguing in Publication Information Available

Library of Congress Cataloging-in-Publication Data

Clive, H. P.
Brahms and his world : a biographical dictionary / Peter Clive.
p. cm.
Includes bibliographical references and indexes.
ISBN-13: 978-0-8108-5721-6 (hardcover : alk. paper)
ISBN-10: 0-8108-5721-9 (hardcover : alk. paper)
1. Brahms, Johannes, 1833-1897—Friends and associates. 2. Composers—Germany—Biography—Dictionaries. I. Title.
ML410.B8C54 2006
780.92—dc22

2005037516

∞™ The paper used in this publication meets the minimum requirements of American National Standard for Information Sciences—Permanence of Paper for Printed Library Materials, ANSI/NISO Z39.48-1992.
Manufactured in the United States of America.

Contents

Preface

This biographical dictionary provides information on more than 430 persons associated with Johannes Brahms: relatives; friends and acquaintances; physicians; fellow musicians; composers whom Brahms particularly admired and in the editions of whose works he was involved; certain conductors, instrumentalists, and singers who took part in notable (especially first) performances of his compositions; poets whose texts he set to music; publishers; artists; and also the rulers of certain German states with whom he had significant contact. Two articles, "Debussy" and "Wallisch," though not falling into any of those categories, are included for special reasons, which should quickly become evident.

The information has been derived from an extensive consultation of primary sources, as well as from a critical examination of a very considerable number of publications. As far as the latter are concerned, a select list of this printed material is given in the bibliography (but see also the introductory note to that section).

At the end of most articles some pertinent printed sources (in particular, publications referred to in the articles or from which quotations are presented) are cited in abbreviated form, full details being given in the bibliography. However, in order to avoid constant repetition, no mention is normally made there of two works that have had to be consulted in almost every case, namely Max Kalbeck's (1976) biography of Brahms and Margit L. McCorkle's (1984) *Johannes Brahms: Thematisch—bibliographisches Werkverzeichnis. . . .* For the same reason, no reference is normally made among the sources cited to articles in standard encyclopedias on music and on art, such as *Grove's Dictionary of Music and Musicians*, *Musik in Geschichte und Gegenwart*, Riemann's *Musik-Lexikon*, *Schweizer Musiker-Lexikon*, or Thieme and Becker's *Allgemeines Lexikon der bildenden Künstler von der Antike bis zur Gegenwart*, the *Grove Dictionary of Art*, and Saur's *Allgemeines Künstlerlexikon*. It may be assumed as a matter of course that due account has been taken of the relevant articles in those reference works.

Acknowledgments

Above all, I wish once again to record my profound appreciation for the quite invaluable assistance provided by Callista Kelly and her colleagues Al MacLennan, Louise McGreal, Laurie Pollock, Karen Robertson, Robert Smith, and Christine Taylor of the interlibrary loans section at Carleton University, Ottawa. I would also like to express my particular gratitude to Otto Biba and Ingrid Fuchs (Gesellschaft der Musikfreunde, Vienna), Renate and Kurt Hofmann (Lübeck), Hubert Reitterer (*Österreichisches Biographisches Lexikon*, Vienna), Michael Struck (Brahms Gesamtausgabe, Kiel), and Stefan Weymar (Brahms-Institut, Lübeck), whose help and advice have been extremely valuable. Finally, I wish to record my indebtedness to all the archivists, librarians, and other staff members of numerous public and private institutions in Austria, France, Germany, Great Britain, and Hungary, who have kindly supplied information or have generously helped in other ways; and also to Gerhard Behrens, G. M. Behrens, James Behrens (all of London), Paul Filotas (Carleton University, Ottawa), Georgette Gruner (Aix-en-Provence), Gordon Harris (Stockport, England), Myra Mackay (Royal Scottish Orchestra, Glasgow), Jim Peschek (Uppingham School, Uppingham, England), Antje Ruhbaum (Berlin), and Christiane Wiesenfeldt (Lübeck).

Reader's Notes

Work numbers are used in the dictionary strictly for the purpose of clarity and are therefore usually omitted where there is no risk of confusion. Thus, designations such as "First Symphony" and "*Magelone-Lieder*" are considered adequate identification without the addition of the opus numbers, whereas the latter are clearly necessary in a case like "Piano Quartet op. 60," since Brahms wrote two other such quartets.

When a person's name appears in boldfaced type in an entry of the dictionary, it indicates that he or she is the subject of a separate entry. Only the first appearance in an entry is bold.

For quotations, unless otherwise indicated, all translations from German and French are my own.

Ranks of nobility have been rendered by the most closely corresponding English terms (e.g., *Freiherr* by *Baron* and *Graf* by *Count*).

Chronology

This chronology presents a selective record of interesting events in Brahms's life. It is primarily intended to enable anyone consulting this dictionary to view some of the relationships and incidents described against a broader background.

1833 **7 May** Birth in Hamburg of Johannes Brahms, second child (after Elise, born 11 February 1831) of Johann Jakob Brahms, a musician, and Johanna Henrica Christiane Brahms, née Nissen, a seamstress. The family is then living at 24 Specksgang (later 60 Speckstrasse) but will change lodgings repeatedly during the next nine years.

1835 **26 March** Birth of the couple's third child, Friedrich [Fritz].

1839 Brahms enrolls at Heinrich Friedrich Voss's elementary school.

1840 In the winter of 1840–41, Brahms, who has already been taught to play several musical instruments by his father, begins to study piano with Otto Friedrich Willibald Cossel; the lessons will continue at least until 1843.

1841 The Brahms family settles at 29 Dammtorwall.

1843 Brahms makes his first appearance as a pianist at a private concert. Eduard Marxsen succeeds Willibald Cossel as his piano teacher (and will later also instruct him in musical theory).

1844 Brahms becomes a pupil at a private secondary school run by Johann Friedrich Hoffmann, which he will attend until 1847.

1846 Brahms begins to earn money playing piano in some local establishments.

1847 **Summer** Brahms spends the summer at Winsen-an-der-Luhe as guest of Adolph Heinrich Giesemann and his wife. While there, he gives piano lessons to their daughter Elise and also conducts a men's choir, for which he writes some compositions. **20 November** Brahms makes his first public appearance as a pianist, playing Sigismond Thalberg's *Fantasia* on themes from Bellini's opera *Norma* at a concert given by violinist Carl Birgfeld at the Apollo-Saal in Hamburg. **27 November** He plays a composition for two pianos by Thalberg with Therese Meyer at her recital.

1848 11 March Brahms attends a performance by Joseph Joachim and the Hamburg Philharmonic Orchestra of Beethoven's Violin Concerto. He will not meet Joachim in person until 1853 (see 1853). **Spring** Brahms stays again at Winsen-an-der-Luhe. **21 September** Brahms, at his own first concert, plays music by Jacob Rosenhain, Theodor Döhler, Bach, Marxsen, and Henri Herz. Among the other artists taking part are singers Franziska Cornet-Kiel and her daughter Adele.

1849 Brahms begins to write potpourris for music publisher August Cranz under the pseudonym G. W. Marks, and performs at some concerts given by other musicians (at Theodor Wachtel's on 1 March, Wilhelm Hollmann's on 23 March, and Rudolf Lohfeld's on 5 December). **14 April** Brahms presents his own second concert, at which he plays Beethoven's Waldstein Sonata, Thalberg's *Fantasia* on Mozart's *Don Giovanni*, a piece by C. Mayer, and his own *Fantasia* on a popular waltz; Cornet-Kiel and her daughter again participate.

1850 Brahms continues to perform at recitals given by other musicians (violinist Hanke's on 14 January, violinist Antoine te Kloot's on 4 March). **March** Brahms takes advantage of the presence in Hamburg of Robert and Clara Schumann, who perform at various concerts there between 16 and 23 March, in order to seek Schumann's observations on certain of his own compositions; however, Schumann lacks the time to look at the manuscripts.

1851 Spring Brahms stays once more with the Giesemanns at Winsen-an-der-Luhe. **5 July** At a private concert celebrating the silver wedding of Hamburg piano manufacturer Christian Heinrich Schröder, Brahms plays some compositions by Karl Würth (Brahms's other pseudonym).

1852 February Brahms plays his Scherzo op. 4 for Henry Litolff, who praises it warmly. (This encounter may have taken place in December 1851.)

1853 January According to a later statement by Eduard Reményi, it is at this time that he first meets Brahms. **April–May** On 19 April Brahms and Reményi leave Hamburg for a joint concert tour, which starts with two concerts at Winsen-an-der-Luhe. On 21 April they arrive at Hanover, where they call on Joseph Joachim, whom Reményi knows from his student days in Vienna. They subsequently give a concert at Celle on 2 May, two concerts at Lüneburg on 9 and 11 May, another one at Celle on the 12th, and two at Hildesheim. **June** On 4 June Brahms and Reményi reach Göttingen where they once more meet Joachim, who arrives there on the same day in order to attend lectures at the university. On 8 June they perform at the Hanoverian court; two days later Reményi is expelled from Hanoverian territory because of his alleged activities during the Hungarian revolution. By mid-June he and

Brahms are at Weimar, where Brahms makes Liszt's acquaintance. **July–late August** Parting company with Reményi, Brahms leaves Weimar at the beginning of July to join Joachim at Göttingen, and he spends most of the summer with Joachim there. During his stay he frequently visits Arnold Wehner. **26 August** From Mainz, Brahms sets out on a walking tour along the Rhine, which finally takes him on 2 September to Mehlem, where he stays for a time with Wilhelm Ludwig Deichmann and his wife. At the Deichmanns, he has an opportunity to acquire a more extensive knowledge of Schumann's music. **30 September or 1 October** Brahms meets Robert Schumann at Düsseldorf. **1 October** Brahms plays some of his compositions for Robert and Clara Schumann, on whom his personality and musical talent make a profound impression. That day Schumann notes in his *Haushaltbuch*: "Visit from Brahms (a genius)." **October** Brahms spends the entire month at Düsseldorf, and during his stay he frequently calls on Robert and Clara Schumann and makes music at their house. On the 9th Schumann begins writing an article, "Neue Bahnen," in praise of Brahms; it will appear in the *Neue Zeitschrift für Musik* on the 28th. During his stay in Düsseldorf, Brahms also makes the acquaintance of Albert Dietrich, and together with Schumann they compose a violin sonata in anticipation of Joachim's visit to the town at the end of that month, Schumann contributing two movements and the others one each. When Joachim plays the sonata with Clara, he correctly identifies the composer of each part. **November–December** After leaving Düsseldorf on 2 November, Brahms spends some two weeks with Joachim in Hanover, and subsequently makes two trips to Leipzig, staying a week in November and some three weeks in December. While there, he manages to arrange for the publication of some of his compositions (opp. 1, 3, and 6 appear in December). He also meets Liszt again and makes a number of new acquaintances, among them Heinrich von Sahr, Julius Otto Grimm, and Hector Berlioz. At a concert on 17 December he plays his Piano Sonata op. 1 and the Scherzo op. 4.

1854 January After spending Christmas in Hamburg, Brahms rejoins Joachim in Hanover. There he meets Hans von Bülow. **1 March** Bülow plays the opening movement of Brahms's Piano Sonata op. 1 at a concert in Hamburg, thus becoming the first pianist other than Brahms himself to perform one of his compositions in public. **March–October** Learning of Schumann's suicide attempt on 27 February and his removal to the clinic at Endenich, Brahms hurries to Düsseldorf to lend Clara moral as well as practical support. Except for a brief period in August, he remains at Düsseldorf until the autumn. During his stay there he meets Julius Allgeyer. **October–December** As Clara sets out on a lengthy concert tour in Germany, Brahms returns to Hamburg. They meet again at Harburg in early November and from there travel to Hamburg, where Clara makes the acquaintance of his parents. Before her departure she accedes to his request that she should address him with the familiar "Du" (but not until the spring of 1856 will he, in his turn, use the intimate form consistently). By Christmas both are back at Düsseldorf, where Brahms now occupies a room in the Schumanns' flat.

1855 **11 January** Brahms for the first time visits Schumann at the Endenich clinic. **January–March** During Clara's absences from Düsseldorf (15 January–10 February for concert appearances in Holland, and 19 February–22 March for further engagements in Germany), Brahms looks after her household. On the first occasion he joins her briefly, to her great surprise, at Rotterdam, where he meets Johannes Verhulst, among others. **April** Brahms and Clara travel to Hamburg in order to attend a performance of Schumann's *Manfred* conducted by Georg Dietrich Otten on 21 April. **May** At the Lower Rhine Music Festival at Düsseldorf Brahms makes the acquaintance of Eduard Hanslick. **November** Brahms gives two concerts at Danzig, together with Clara Schumann and Joachim, and performs Beethoven's "Emperor" concerto at Bremen as well as in Hamburg. **December** Brahms spends Christmas again at Düsseldorf.

1856 **January–February** Brahms continues his concert activities, playing Beethoven's Fourth Piano Concerto at Leipzig, compositions by Beethoven and by himself at Kiel, Mozart's Piano Concerto K466 in Hamburg, Beethoven's "Eroica" *Variations* and a *Toccata* by Bach at Altona, and Beethoven's Violin Sonata op. 96 and other pieces with Joachim at Göttingen. In February, at Hanover, he makes the acquaintance of Anton Rubinstein. **March** Brahms begins to exchange counterpoint studies with Joachim. **May** At the Lower Rhine Music Festival at Düsseldorf, Brahms meets Julius Stockhausen. At the end of the month Brahms and Stockhausen give a joint concert at Cologne. **July** Brahms is present at Clara Schumann's final meeting with her husband at the clinic at Endenich on 27 July. Schumann dies two days later. **Mid-August** Brahms and Clara Schumann leave Düsseldorf for a six weeks' holiday in Germany and Switzerland with her sons Ferdinand and Ludwig and Brahms's sister Elise. **21 October** Brahms moves back from Düsseldorf to Hamburg. **25 October** Brahms performs Beethoven's Fourth Piano Concerto at a concert in Hamburg, conducted by Otten. **22 November** Brahms takes part in a concert at Hamburg devoted to Schumann's memory, playing the Piano Concerto and some pieces with Joachim. **December** Brahms returns to Düsseldorf at Christmas.

1857 **Early months** Brahms remains at Düsseldorf, even during Clara Schumann's repeated absences owing to concert engagements elsewhere. **31 May** Brahms arrives at Detmold for a week's stay, during which he regularly plays at court. At one concert he is the soloist in Beethoven's Fourth Piano

Concerto and takes part in a performance of Schubert's "Trout" Quintet. **September** Clara Schumann moves from Düsseldorf to Berlin. **October–December** Brahms stays at Detmold, where he has been engaged to teach one of the princesses, conduct a small choir, and perform at concerts.

1858 **January** Brahms travels back to Hamburg. **30 March** Brahms tries out his First Piano Concerto at Hanover, with an orchestra conducted by Joachim. **August–September** Brahms stays at Göttingen, where Clara Schumann also resides during a large part of this period. He falls in love with Agathe von Siebold, who returns his feelings. **October–December** Brahms has again accepted a contract to spend this period at Detmold.

1859 Brahms spends the first week of the year at Göttingen. If they did not already do so the previous September, he and Agathe von Siebold now exchange rings as tokens of their love. However, Agathe will some time later break off contact with him after he has expressed his unwillingness to marry her. **January** From Göttingen Brahms travels to Hanover, where the First Piano Concerto receives its first public performance on the 22nd with himself as soloist and Joachim as conductor. A further performance of the work, conducted by Julius Rietz, takes place at Leipzig on the 27th, with Brahms again as soloist; it is badly received. **24 March** Brahms plays the concerto with the Hamburg Philharmonic Orchestra under Joachim, to great acclaim. **6 June** Brahms conducts the first practice session of the Hamburg Women's Chorus (HFC). Among the members of the chorus is a young Viennese, Bertha Porubszky. Later, in Vienna, Brahms will enjoy a close friendship with Bertha and her husband Arthur Faber. **October–December** Brahms once again spends these months at Detmold, except for a brief trip to Hamburg where, on 2 December, he plays Schumann's Piano Concerto and conducts the women's chorus in two of his own compositions at one of C. G. P. Grädener's concerts. He is offered, but refuses, a further contract at Detmold for the following year.

1860 Brahms spends the year mainly in Hamburg where he resumes his connection with the women's chorus and performs at several concerts. Thus, at a concert of the philharmonic orchestra on 10 February, he again plays Schumann's Piano Concerto and also conducts the first performance of his Serenade op. 16. On **20 April** he plays his own First Piano Concerto at one of Otten's concerts. **Spring** Brahms and Joachim prepare a manifesto against the "New German School," for which they enlist the support of various friends. After it is prematurely printed in the Berlin journal *Echo* on 6 May, signed only by Brahms, Joachim, Julius Otto Grimm, and Bernhard Scholz, it draws a sarcastic response from the *Neue Zeitschrift für Musik*.

1861 Brahms spends the year in or close to Hamburg (in July he moves to Hamm, near Hamburg). He makes numerous concert appearances, some of them together with Stockhausen (on 27 April they perform Schubert's *Die schöne Müllerin*, on 30 April Schumann's *Dichterliebe*) and with Clara Schumann (on 15 January they play concertos for two pianos by Bach and Mozart; on 16 November, Mozart's Sonata for Two Pianos, and Clara takes part in a performance of Brahms's Piano Quartet op. 25; and at a philharmonic concert on 3 December she plays his First Piano Concerto, which he conducts).

1862 **January–May** Brahms spends this period mostly at Hamm, except for a few trips. Thus he plays Schumann's Piano Concerto and, with Joachim, Beethoven's "Kreutzer" sonata at Münster on 19 January; he takes part in another concert with Joachim at Celle on 14 February; and he performs Beethoven's Fourth Piano Concerto at Oldenburg on 14 March. Four days later he plays Schumann's *Études symphoniques* and, with Leopold Auer, the "Kreutzer" sonata in Hamburg. **June–July** In June, at the Lower Rhine Music Festival in Cologne, Brahms meets Louise Dustmann-Meyer, who will become a good friend. Subsequently he visits Clara Schumann at Münster am Stein and from there sets out on a short walking tour with Albert Dietrich, Heinrich von Sahr, and Woldemar Bargiel. After stops at Karlsruhe, Baden-Baden, and Frankfurt, he returns to Hamm. **Mid-September** Brahms arrives in Vienna, where he will reside until the following spring. He soon makes contact with the leading Viennese musical circles. **9 November** Brahms attends, as a guest, the performance of Handel's *Messiah* presented in celebration of the 50th anniversary of the foundation of the Gesellschaft der Musikfreunde. **11 November** He is invited to a banquet that is given, as part of the celebrations, at the entertainment establishment "Zum Sperl" (on which occasion Johann Strauss and his band provide the musical fare). **16 November** Brahms presents himself to the Viennese public as pianist and composer, playing the piano part in his Piano Quartet op. 25 at a concert of the Hellmesberger Quartet. **18 November** In a letter to Clara Schumann, Brahms expresses his profound disappointment at having been disregarded by the board of the Hamburg Philharmonic Society, which, as he has been informed by Theodor Avé-Lallemant, has decided to offer the positions of conductor of the Hamburg Philharmonic Orchestra and of the Singakademie (which will both fall vacant the next year) to Stockhausen. (See April 1894.) **29 November** At his own first concert in Vienna, Brahms plays his *Handel Variations* and music by Bach and Schumann, as well as the piano part in his Piano Quartet op. 26; also appearing at the concert are singers Adele Passy-Cornet (see 1848) and Emil Förchtgott. **December** Brahms helps in the copying of the orchestral parts of excerpts from Richard Wagner's operas in preparation for Wagner's concerts in Vienna on 26 December, and 1 and 8

January 1863 (all three of which Brahms will attend). It is almost certain that Brahms meets Wagner himself at this time. Among other persons recruited to assist with the copying are Peter Cornelius and Carl Tausig, with whom Brahms is soon on very cordial terms. In fact, Max Kalbeck will describe the *Paganini Variations*, on which Brahms works during the winter of 1862–63, as "a lasting memorial" to his friendship with Tausig. **7 December** Johann von Herbeck conducts Brahms's Serenade op. 11 at a concert of the Gesellschaft der Musikfreunde. **20 December** Brahms takes part in a concert given by Adele Passy-Cornet, playing two pieces by Schumann and, with Joseph Hellmesberger, Bach's Violin Sonata in E Major.

1863 6 January Brahms gives his second concert in Vienna, at which he plays his Piano Sonata op. 5 and compositions by Beethoven, Bach, and Schumann, and accompanies Marie Wilt in some of his own songs. **March–April** Brahms takes part in several more concerts in Vienna. **May** Brahms returns to Hamburg. Later that month he is elected chorus master of the Vienna Singakademie in succession to Ferdinand Stegmayer, who died on 5 May; he accepts the position in a letter dated 30 May. **10 June** Brahms attends Joachim's wedding with Amalie Schneeweiss (stage name: Amalie Weiss) in Hanover. He will enjoy very good professional and personal relations with the bride. **Late September** Brahms begins rehearsals with the Vienna Singakademie. **15 November** At his first regular concert with the Singakademie, Brahms presents works by Bach, Beethoven, and Schumann, as well as his own settings of some German folk songs. **November–December** Brahms takes part in a number of concerts in Vienna as pianist, playing his own works as well as those of other composers. In addition, his Serenade op. 18 receives its first Viennese performance at a concert of the Hellmesberger Quartet on 27 December.

1864 6 January The program of Brahms's second regular concert with the Singakademie includes works by Bach, Beethoven, and Mendelssohn, as well as German folk songs in his own arrangements. **11 January** Brahms conducts the Singakademie in a program consisting of smaller choral works, including his own Quartets "Wechsellied zum Tanze" and "Neckereien" (op. 31/1–2), the latter of which is receiving its first known public performance. Among the singers is Ottilie Hauer (later Ebner), with whom Brahms will remain in close contact for many years. **6 February** Brahms visits Richard Wagner at the villa that Wagner is renting at Penzing, a suburb of Vienna (now its 14th district). (For an account of the visit, see Gustav Schönaich's article in the Viennese daily newspaper *Reichswehr* on 4 April 1897.) **20 March** The third regular concert of the Singakademie features the first Viennese performance of Bach's *Christmas Oratorio*. One of the soloists is Ida Flatz, whose husband, Franz Flatz, was one of the persons responsible for Brahms's election as conductor of the chorus. **17 April** A concert of the Singakademie conducted by Brahms offers an all-Brahms program consisting of a number of choral pieces (several of which are receiving their first public performances on this occasion), the Sonata for Two Pianos op. 34 bis (played by Brahms and Tausig), and the String Sextet op. 18 (performed by the augmented Hellmesberger Quartet). This is the last concert of the Singakademie conducted by Brahms, who, although unanimously reelected as chorus master, resigns at the end of the season in order to have more time for composition. **Mid-June–end of July** Brahms stays in Hamburg. His parents separate. **August–early October** Brahms stays at Baden-Baden (where Clara Schumann bought a house in October 1862, of which she took possession in April 1863) and at Karlsruhe. He sees a good deal of Julius Allgeyer and of Hermann Levi. **October** Brahms returns to Vienna for the winter.

1865 **2 February** Brahms's mother dies. **May–early October** Brahms spends most of this period at Baden-Baden/Lichtental, where he occupies rooms at Clara Becker's house. He will rent accommodations there again on several additional occasions and will work on some of his major compositions—for example, the First and Second Symphonies, Piano Quintet op. 34, String Sextet op. 36, Requiem, and *Alto Rhapsody*—while staying there. (The house is now known as the "Brahmshaus" and contains a small Brahms museum.) **Mid-June** Brahms pays a visit to Basle where, on the 16th, he is among the invited guests at a performance of Bach's St. Matthew Passion and, on the 17th, takes part in a concert, playing the piano part in his Piano Quartet op. 25. **19–29 November** Brahms performs at concerts in Basle, Zurich, and Winterthur. In Zurich he makes the acquaintance of Theodor Billroth, Wilhelm Lübke, and Otto Wesendonck, who arrange a private concert so that they can hear the First Piano Concerto and the Serenade op. 16. **December** Brahms plays in concerts at Karlsruhe, Mannheim, Cologne, and Detmold.

1866 **January** Brahms performs at two concerts at Oldenburg, and then spends some three weeks in Hamburg. **End of January** Brahms arrives at Karlsruhe, where he stays with Julius Allgeyer for several weeks. **22 March** Brahms's father marries Karoline Schnack, née Paasch. **Mid-April** Brahms stays for several weeks with Jakob Melchior Rieter-Biedermann at Winterthur. **June–mid-August** Brahms stays at Fluntern, near Zurich. He forms a close friendship with Friedrich Hegar, whom he has met previously, and makes the acquaintance of Gottfried Keller. **Mid-August–mid-October** Brahms again rents rooms in Clara Becker's house at Baden-Baden/Lichtental. **20 October** Brahms leaves Baden-Baden with Joachim for a concert tour in Switzerland. **End of November** Brahms arrives in Vienna for the winter.

1867 Mid-February–end of April Brahms gives concerts at Graz, Klagenfurt, Pressburg (Bratislava), and Budapest (where, on this first of his numerous visits to the Hungarian capital, he performs on 22 and 26 April). **First half of August** Brahms vacations with his father, mostly in Styria and the Salzkammergut. **November** Another concert tour with Joachim, this time in Austria. **1 December** At a Gesellschaft der Musikfreunde concert, Johann von Herbeck conducts the first performance of the first three movements of Brahms's Requiem, with baritone Rudolf Panzer as soloist in the third movement. Both Brahms and Joachim are present. **7–10 December** Brahms performs at concerts in Budapest, on the 7th and 10th with Joachim, and on the 9th with the Grün Quartet.

1868 Mid-January Brahms travels to Hamburg, where he stays for a month. **Mid-February** Brahms begins a concert tour with Julius Stockhausen that takes them from Hamburg to Berlin, Dresden, Lübeck, Kiel, and Copenhagen, where they give their final concert on 24 March. Subsequently Brahms plays at concerts in Bremen and Oldenburg. **10 April** Brahms conducts the first performance of the Requiem (still without its later fifth movement) at Bremen Cathedral, with Stockhausen as soloist. Joachim and his wife take part in the concert. In the audience are Brahms's father, Clara Schumann, and a great English admirer of Brahms, John Farmer. **27 April** A further performance of the six-movement Requiem is conducted at Bremen by Karl Reinthaler in Brahms's presence. **May** Brahms announces the completion of a further movement for the Requiem to Rieter-Biedermann, who will publish the work. **June–July** Brahms spends most of this period at Bonn. **September** Brahms visits Switzerland with his father. By the 20th they are both in Hamburg, where Brahms spends the following weeks. **End October–mid-November** Brahms performs, together with Clara Schumann, at Oldenburg, and with Stockhausen in Hamburg. **20 November** Brahms arrives in Vienna.

1869 18 February Carl Reinecke conducts the first performance of the complete (7-movement) Requiem at the Leipzig Gewandhaus. **February–April** Brahms performs with Stockhausen at several concerts in Vienna and Budapest. **May–October** Brahms stays at Baden-Baden/Lichtental. **22 September** Clara Schumann's daughter Julie, for whom Brahms feels a deep but undeclared affection, marries Count Vittorio Amadeo Radicati di Marmorito. **6 October** Hermann Levi conducts a private performance of the *Alto Rhapsody* (soloist: Amalia Boni) at Karlsruhe, in the presence of Brahms and Clara Schumann. **End October** Brahms returns to Vienna. **Early December** Clara Schumann arrives in Vienna for a lengthy stay, during which she gives several concerts, in one of which (5 January 1870) she accompanies, together with Brahms, his *Liebeslieder-Walzer*.

1870 3 March Pauline Viardot, whom Brahms has repeatedly met at Baden-Baden during the 1860s, sings in the first public performance of the *Alto Rhapsody*, conducted by Ernst Naumann. **July** Brahms attends in Munich performances of *Die Walküre* and *Das Rheingold*, conducted by his friend Franz Wüllner. **Summer–Autumn** After Johann von Herbeck retires as artistic director of the Gesellschaft der Musikfreunde at the end of the 1869–70 season, the position of conductor of the society's orchestral concerts is offered to Brahms. On 8 October he informs his father that he has "had to decline it for several reasons," adding that he may take it next year. For the 1870–71 season, the direction of these concerts is now entrusted to Joseph Hellmesberger, while Ernst Frank is appointed chorus master of the Singverein. (The proposed separation of the two positions, both of which Herbeck had occupied simultaneously, is in fact one of the reasons for Brahms's refusal. They will once more be combined when Anton Rubinstein takes over for the 1871–72 season and will remain so under Brahms's eventual tenure of the artistic directorship.)

1871 22 January At a philharmonic concert conducted by Otto Dessoff, Brahms plays his First Piano Concerto in what is apparently its first performance in Vienna. **5 March** At a Gesellschaft der Musikfreunde concert, Brahms conducts the first Viennese performance of the complete Requiem. **19 March** Ernst Frank directs the first Viennese performance of the *Alto Rhapsody* by the Akademischer Gesangverein and Henriette Burenne. **Late March** Brahms travels to Germany where, during the following weeks, he will perform at concerts at Lübeck, Oldenburg, and Bremen. **May–October** Brahms stays at Baden-Baden/Lichtental. Here he completes the *Triumphlied*, inspired by the Franco-Prussian War of 1870–71; it will be dedicated to Emperor Wilhelm I. **October** Brahms returns to Vienna. **December** Brahms accepts the position of artistic director of the Gesellschaft der Musikfreunde, which he will hold for three years (1872–75). **End of December** Brahms moves into rooms at 4 Karlsgasse, which will remain his address until the end of his life.

1872 February At the beginning of the month Brahms arrives in Hamburg, where his father is suffering from terminal cancer; he will die on the 11th. A few days later Brahms returns to Vienna. **May–mid-September** Brahms stays at Baden-Baden/Lichtental. **5 June** Brahms attends Hermann Levi's farewell concert as court Kapellmeister at Karlsruhe prior to Levi's move to a similar post at Munich. The program includes Beethoven's Eighth Symphony, Schumann's Piano Concerto played by Clara Schumann, songs by Schubert sung by Julius Stockhausen, and the first complete performance of Brahms's *Triumphlied* conducted by Levi with Stockhausen as soloist. **10 November** Brahms's first concert as artistic director of the Gesellschaft der

Musikfreunde. On the program: Handel's "Dettingen" *Te Deum* (with the Singverein), Mozart's concert aria *Ch'io mi scordi di te?* (sung by Marie Wilt, accompanied by Julius Epstein), a cappella pieces by J. Eccard and H. Isaak (performed by the Singverein), and Joachim's arrangement of Schubert's *Grand Duo* (D678). During the current season (November 1872–April 1873), Brahms will conduct further Gesellschaft der Musikfreunde concerts on 15 November, 8 December (the program features the first Viennese performance of his *Triumphlied*), 5 January, 28 February, 23 March, and 6 and 8 April.

1873 **May** In Munich Brahms makes the acquaintance of Paul Heyse. **Mid-May–mid-September** Brahms vacations at Tutzing, near Munich. (In August he attends the Schumann Festival at Bonn.) **2 November** At a philharmonic concert in Vienna directed by Dessoff, Brahms conducts the first performance of his *Haydn Variations*. **December** Brahms is made a knight of the Bavarian Maximilian Order for Science and Art. **November 1873–April 1874** Brahms conducts Gesellschaft der Musikfreunde concerts on 9 November, 7 December, 25 January, 2 and 31 March, and 19 April (including *Schicksalslied*).

1874 A busy year during which, in addition to his activities with the Gesellschaft der Musikfreunde, Brahms performs and conducts his compositions in various cities in Germany and Switzerland. **11 January** Franz Liszt performs at a charity concert in Vienna in which Brahms takes part. **End of January** Brahms arrives at Leipzig for a week's concerts. At the final one, on 5 February, Amalie Joachim is soloist in the *Alto Rhapsody*. During his stay in Leipzig, Brahms forges close relations with Heinrich and Elisabeth von Herzogenberg. **March** Brahms performs at two concerts in Munich. **April–May** Brahms appears at concerts at Bremen, Kassel, and Cologne. At the Lower Rhine Music Festival in the latter, he conducts the *Triumphlied* (24 May) and makes the acquaintance of Sir George Henschel. **June–mid-September** Brahms spends the summer months in Switzerland where, after two concerts at Basle, he vacations at Rüschlikon on the Lake of Zurich. On 11 July, at the house of Hermann Goetz, he makes the acquaintance of Josef Viktor Widmann. On the following day, at the opening of the Zurich Music Festival, he directs a performance of the *Triumphlied* (which he has previously conducted at Basle on 9 June). **8 November** First Gesellschaft der Musikfreunde concert of the 1874–75 season. (There will be further concerts on 6 December, 10 January, 28 February, 23 March, and 18 April.) **Late December** Brahms departs for Breslau [Wrocław, Poland], where he performs at concerts on 29 December and 2 January.

1875 **18 April** The final Gesellschaft der Musikfreunde concert of the season is also the last to be conducted by Brahms as artistic director of the society, for by mutual agreement his contract has been dissolved effective 1 May. His successor will be Johann von Herbeck. **Late April** Brahms leaves for Germany, stopping first at Munich where he quarrels with Hermann Levi. The incident will permanently affect their relationship. **Beginning of May–mid-September** During the major part of this period Brahms vacations at Ziegelhausen, near Heidelberg. **18 November** At a concert of the Hellmesberger Quartet at the Musikverein at which Brahms takes part in the first public performance of his Piano Quartet op. 60, he is introduced to Cosima Wagner. Quite probably he also meets (and sees for the last time) her husband, who likewise attends the concert.

1876 Second half of January Brahms undertakes a concert tour of Holland. At Utrecht he stays (as he will also on later Dutch tours) with Wilhelm and Emma Engelmann. **February** Brahms appears at a number of concerts in various German cities, usually playing or conducting his own works. **Late March** Brahms performs at two concerts at Breslau. **May** Brahms is informed by G. W. Macfarren, professor of music at the University of Cambridge, that the university wishes to confer an honorary doctorate upon him. (However, since he declines to appear in person, the degree will not be bestowed.) **Mid-June** Brahms arrives at Sassnitz on the island of Rügen, where he will spend several weeks. In July Henschel joins him there for ten days. **August–early September** Brahms spends most of this period in Hamburg. **September–October** Brahms stays at Baden-Baden/Lichtental, where he puts the finishing touches on his First Symphony, on which he has been working for many years. On 25 September he plays the first and last movements and, on 10 October, plays the entire work for Clara Schumann. **November** Otto Dessoff conducts the first performance of the First Symphony at Karlsruhe on 4 November, in Brahms's presence. Brahms himself conducts it at Mannheim on 7 November, and at Munich on 15 November. During his stay in Munich he meets with Levi, probably for the last time. **17 December** At a Gesellschaft der Musikfreunde concert Brahms conducts the Viennese premiere of the First Symphony.

1877 January Brahms conducts his First Symphony at Leipzig (18 January) and at Breslau (23 January). In Leipzig he stays with the Herzogenbergs. At the end of the month, after much cogitation and considerable correspondence, he declines the position of musical director at Düsseldorf that he was offered the previous autumn. **8 March** Joseph Joachim receives an honorary doctorate at Cambridge University; at a concert of the Cambridge University Musical Society he conducts the first English performance of Brahms's First Symphony. **June–October** Brahms vacations at Pörtschach, in Carinthia, and, from mid-September, at Baden-Baden/Lichtental. **30 December** Hans Richter conducts the first performance of Brahms's Second Symphony at a concert of the Vienna Philharmonic Orchestra in Brahms's presence. Shortly before, Brahms and Ignaz Brüll had presented the work in its arrangement for piano duet to a small group of friends at Friedrich Ehrbar's concert hall.

1878 **January–February** Brahms performs at concerts at Leipzig, Hamburg, and Bremen. On 26 January he begins his second Dutch tour with a concert at Utrecht. The tour, which features in particular the new Second Symphony, finishes at Amsterdam on 8 February. **April–May** Brahms spends most of April in Italy with Theodor Billroth, traveling as far south as Naples. (Karl Goldmark accompanies them as far as Rome.) **Early May–September** On his return journey from Italy, Brahms stops at Pörtschach where, with brief interruptions, he will stay until well into September. **September** Clara Schumann takes up residence at Frankfurt am Main, where she has accepted a teaching post at the Hoch Conservatory. **25–28 September** Brahms attends the golden jubilee of the Hamburg Philharmonic Society. At a concert on 28 September he conducts his Second Symphony. While in Hamburg he is introduced to Richard Fellinger (see November 1881). **Late October** Brahms visits Breslau where, on 22 October, he conducts his Second Symphony and on 24 October plays in a performance of his Piano Quartet op. 26. **December** Dvořák visits Vienna and is warmly welcomed by Brahms. It is possible that they meet here for the first time, rather than in Prague in December 1877, as is often stated.

1879 **January** At Leipzig on 1 January, Joachim gives the first performance of Brahms's Violin Concerto, with Brahms himself conducting. They subsequently travel together to Vienna via Prague, where Joachim gives concerts on 3 and 5 January, while Brahms meets, at his own request, a number of Czech composers, Dvořák presumably among them, on 4 January. He promises to give a concert together with Dvořák in Prague at the beginning of the following season (but this promise will not be fulfilled). Joachim gives further performances of the Violin Concerto in Budapest on 8 January (again with Brahms conducting) and in Vienna on 14 January (Joseph Hellmesberger conducting). **March** The University of Breslau awards Brahms an honorary doctorate. **11 April** Brahms conducts his Requiem at Bremen. **Late May–early September** Brahms vacations again at Pörtschach. There he meets the talented young violinist Marie Soldat, whom he takes under his wing. **September** In the latter half of September Brahms gives concerts with Joachim in Hungary and Transylvania. **December** Brahms pays a brief visit to Budapest where he takes part in a performance of his Piano Quartet op. 60 at a concert of the Krancsevics Quartet on 8 December and, two days later, plays his First Piano Concerto and conducts his Second Symphony at a concert of the philharmonic orchestra.

1880 January Brahms is active as pianist (notably in his First Concerto) and conductor (especially of the Requiem and the Second Symphony) at concerts in Frankfurt, Cologne, Krefeld, Bonn, and Hanover. At Krefeld he strikes up a friendship with Rudolf von der Leyen, at whose house he stays on this and later visits to the town. **February** Brahms gives concerts with Joachim in Krakow, Lemberg (Lviv), and Prague. **April** At concerts at Schwerin and Königsberg, Brahms plays his First Piano Concerto and conducts his Second Symphony. **2 May** Brahms attends the unveiling of Adolf von Donnhof's monument at Schumann's grave in Bonn. At the festival concert that evening he conducts his Violin Concerto (in which Joachim is once again soloist), as well as Schumann's Third Symphony and *Requiem für Mignon*. **Late May–September** Brahms stays at Ischl. **4 December** Brahms is present at a performance of his Requiem by the students of the Musikhochschule in Berlin, of which Joachim is director. He stays with the Joachims, whose marriage is by this time seriously troubled, since Joachim suspects his wife of infidelity. At the end of the month he will sue for separation, and, after years of legal wrangling, the couple will be divorced in December 1884. Long before then the situation will have resulted in an estrangement between Joachim and Brahms, who firmly believes in Amalie's innocence and does not hesitate to tell Joachim so, and furthermore declares his belief in Amalie's moral integrity in a letter to her that she uses publicly in her legal defense. Although deeply hurt by Brahms's attitude, Joachim never loses his fervent admiration for Brahms's music, which he continues to perform even during the years when they do not meet. (They engage, moreover, in occasional correspondence on musical matters.) It is the Double Concerto that will finally bring them together again (see September 1887). **9 December** Brahms declines an invitation from the Royal Philharmonic Society to conduct three of its concerts during the next season in London.

1881 January Brahms plays and conducts at concerts at Breslau, Leipzig, Münster, and Krefeld. In Breslau on 4 January he directs the first performance of the *Academic Festival Overture*. At Krefeld, on 25 January, he is so delighted with Richard Barth's performance of his Violin Concerto that he arranges for Barth to play the work under his own direction at Amsterdam (31 January) and Haarlem (5 February). **February** While in Vienna, Bülow, who was appointed music director at Meiningen a year earlier, places his orchestra at Brahms's disposal should he ever wish to rehearse a new composition privately. (See October.) **25 March–7 May** Brahms undertakes another trip to Italy, in the company of Billroth, Adolf Exner, and Gustav Nottebohm (who goes no further than Venice). Brahms, Exner, and Billroth travel as far as Sicily; on the return journey Billroth and Exner leave Italy ahead of Brahms, who spends the last two weeks on his own in Rome, Florence, and

Pisa. **22 May** Brahms takes up his summer quarters at Pressbaum, near Vienna. There he works on his Second Piano Concerto. **October** Brahms moves back to Vienna at the beginning of the month and, probably on the 12th, he presents, with Ignaz Brüll's assistance, the two-piano version of his new concerto to a group of friends at Ehrbar's concert hall. Later that month he travels to Meiningen to try out the work with the court orchestra (see February). He also plays on several occasions at the Meiningen court, and generally establishes a personal relationship with Duke Georg II of Sachsen-Meiningen and his wife, Baroness Heldburg, which will become progressively friendlier in future years. **2 November** At the house of mutual friends, Brahms meets Richard and Maria Fellinger, who have recently moved to Vienna (see 25–28 September 1878). They will be among his closest friends during the last years of his life. **9 November** At Budapest, at a concert directed by Alexander Erkel, Brahms gives the first public performance of his Second Piano Concerto. He also conducts the first local performances of the *Academic Festival Overture* and the First Symphony. **November–December** Between 22 November and 26 December, Brahms plays the new concerto in Stuttgart, Meiningen, Zurich, Basle, Strasbourg, Breslau, and Vienna.

1882 January–February Brahms plays the new concerto in Leipzig, Hamburg, Berlin, Kiel, Utrecht, The Hague, Rotterdam, Amsterdam, Frankfurt, and Dresden. On 2 February he is present at an all-Brahms recital given by Bülow in Vienna, which is also attended by Liszt. On the same occasion he makes the acquaintance of Eugen d'Albert (see 14 November 1886). **Mid-May–end of August** Brahms vacations at Ischl. On 25 August, at a "Brahms Matinée" arranged at László Wagner de Zólyom's villa in nearby Altaussee, the Piano Trio op. 87 (with Brahms himself on piano) and the String Quintet op. 88 receive semipublic premieres. Ignaz Brüll opens the program with the Rhapsody op. 79/1. **September** Brahms undertakes a further journey to Italy with Billroth. **19 October** Private Viennese premieres at Billroth's of the Piano Trio op. 87 (with Brahms again as pianist) and the String Quintet op. 88. **December** Brahms conducts performances of *Gesang der Parzen* (composed in Ischl that summer) at Basle, Zurich, and Strasbourg. On **29 December** he gives the public premiere of the Piano Trio op. 87 at Frankfurt with Hugo Heermann and Valentin Müller; at the same concert, the String Quintet op. 88 also receives its first public performance.

1883 Mid-January Brahms embarks on another concert tour, mainly designed to make his Second Piano Concerto known in Germany. In the space of some three weeks he plays it at Bonn, Krefeld, Koblenz, Cologne, Hanover, and Schwerin. **6 April** Brahms plays the Second Piano Concerto and the Rhapsodies op. 79 and conducts *Gesang der Parzen* and the *Academic Festival*

Overture at an all-Brahms concert of the Cäcilien-Verein in Hamburg. **Mid-May–end of September** Brahms vacations at Wiesbaden. During his stay he is in almost daily contact with Rudolf and Laura von Beckerath. **16 July** At a music festival at Koblenz, Hermine Spies sings in a performance of the *Alto Rhapsody* conducted by Brahms. **2 December** At a concert of the Vienna Philharmonic Orchestra, Hans Richter conducts the premiere of Brahms's Third Symphony; the program also includes the earliest Viennese performance of Dvořák's Violin Concerto, played by František Ondříček. Both composers are present.

1884 Mid-January–beginning of April Brahms undertakes an extensive concert tour, in the course of which he presents the Third Symphony at Wiesbaden, Berlin, Meiningen, Leipzig, Cologne, Düsseldorf, Barmen, Amsterdam, Dresden, Frankfurt, and Budapest. **May** Brahms travels with Rudolf von der Leyen to northern Italy, where he spends three weeks. During a large part of that period he is the guest of Duke Georg II and his wife at the Villa Carlotta, their mansion on the shore of Lake Como, near Tremezzo. During his stay there, he entertains his hosts with the two-piano version of the Third Symphony, played by him and Rudolf von der Leyen. **2–3 June** At the Lower Rhine Music Festival at Düsseldorf, Brahms conducts the Third Symphony and *Gesang der Parzen*. **Summer** Brahms vacations at Mürzzuschlag in Styria. During his stay he composes the first two movements of his Fourth Symphony. (A small museum established in 1991 in the house where he lived now commemorates his temporary residence in the town in 1884–85.) **November–December** Brahms joins the Meiningen court orchestra for four concerts of its autumn tour under Bülow: at three of them (in Budapest on 24 November, Graz on 28 November, and Vienna on 2 December) he plays his Second Piano Concerto, and at the fourth (in Vienna on 25 November) he conducts his Third Symphony and the First Piano Concerto, in which Bülow is soloist. Shortly after the second Viennese concert Brahms travels to Germany where, at an all-Brahms concert of the Hamburg Cäcilien-Verein on 9 December, he conducts the Third Symphony, among other compositions. He furthermore plays the Second Piano Concerto at Bremen on 16 December and again at Oldenburg on 19 December (where he also conducts the Third Symphony). Hermine Spies takes part in the last two concerts.

1885 27–30 January Brahms appears as conductor and pianist at three concerts at Krefeld, where he again stays with Rudolf von der Leyen. **Mid-May–end of September** Brahms vacations at Mürzzuschlag. There he completes the Fourth Symphony. **17–26 October** Brahms stays at Meiningen. On 18 October he makes the acquaintance of Richard Strauss, with whom he has already had some correspondence. Later that day he attends a concert at which Strauss, recently appointed the orchestra's assistant music director, plays Mozart's C Minor Piano Concerto (K. 491) and conducts his Symphony in F Minor (op. 12). On 25 October Brahms conducts the premiere of his own Fourth Symphony. On the morning of 26 October he conducts his *Haydn Variations* and *Academic Festival Overture*; for the latter work Bülow handles the cymbals and Strauss beats the big drum. In the afternoon Brahms, Bülow and his wife, Strauss, and some others travel to Weimar. **26–28 October** At Weimar, Strauss is much in Brahms's company. On 28 October Brahms leaves Weimar for Frankfurt, where he stays with Clara Schumann. **1 November** Bülow conducts a further performance of the Fourth Symphony at Meiningen. **3–25 November** Brahms takes part in some of the concerts of the Meiningen orchestra's autumn tour, conducting his Fourth Symphony at Frankfurt, Essen, Elberfeld, Utrecht, Amsterdam, The Hague, Krefeld, Cologne, and Wiesbaden. During the tour, Bülow takes offence at a letter from Brahms and thereupon leaves his post at Meiningen on 1 December. They will not be reconciled until January 1887 (see 1887).

1886 **February–April** Brahms makes several trips from Vienna to Germany, during which he conducts the Fourth Symphony at Cologne, Mannheim, Leipzig, Frankfurt, Dresden, Breslau, Meiningen, Hamburg, and Hanover. While in Leipzig, in February, he makes the acquaintance of Max Klinger. **Late May–early October** Brahms vacations at Hofstetten, near Thun, in Switzerland. There he composes the Cello Sonata op. 99, the Violin Sonata op. 100, and the Piano Trio op. 101. **5 November** Brahms's brother Fritz dies in Hamburg. **14 November** Eugen d'Albert plays Brahms's Second Piano Concerto at a concert of the Vienna Philharmonic Orchestra conducted by Hans Richter. Brahms, who is delighted with his performance, will come to regard d'Albert as an ideal interpreter of his piano concertos. **24 November** Together with Robert Hausmann, Brahms gives the first performance of the Cello Sonata op. 99 in Vienna. **22 December** At a chamber music concert in Budapest, Brahms, Jenö Hubay, and David Popper give the first performance of the Piano Trio op. 101.

1887 Brahms and Clara Schumann return their past letters to each other and subsequently destroy many of them, which largely accounts for the gaps in their published correspondence. Celestine Truxa, the widow of journalist Robert Truxa, becomes Brahms's landlady at 4 Karlsgasse in Vienna. **January** Brahms is awarded the Prussian "Ordre pour le mérite." Bülow, in Vienna for concerts, is reconciled with him. **Late April–mid-May** Brahms undertakes a journey through northern Italy with Fritz Simrock and Theodor Kirchner. **Mid-May** Brahms arrives at Thun, where he will spend the late spring and summer, except for a short break to attend a music festival at Cologne in late

June. While at Thun, he composes the Double Concerto for Violin and Cello. **23 September** At Baden-Baden, with the help of the local orchestra, Brahms conducts a private performance of the Double Concerto, with Joachim and Hausmann as soloists. (According to Gustav Manz's "Brahms-Erinnerungen," the work was played twice.) The renewal of closer relations between Brahms and Joachim dates from this time. **October–November** Brahms, Joachim, and Hausmann give the first public performance of the Double Concerto at Cologne on 18 October. This will be followed by further performances of the concerto by them at Wiesbaden (17 November), Frankfurt (18 November), and Basle (20 November). **December** During a brief visit to Budapest, Brahms takes part in a concert of the Hubay-Popper Quartet on 21 December, playing the Violin Sonata op. 100 with Hubay and the Piano Trio op. 101 with Hubay and Popper (the String Quintet op. 88 is also on the program). Almost immediately after returning to Vienna he leaves for Meiningen, where at a concert on 25 December he conducts the *Haydn Variations*, the Third Symphony, and the Second Piano Concerto (soloist: Eugen d'Albert). At the end of the month Brahms arrives at Leipzig.

1888 January On New Year's Day Brahms conducts a performance of his Double Concerto at the Gewandhaus, once again with Joachim and Hausmann as soloists. On the next day he performs his Piano Trio op. 101 with Adolph Brodsky and Julius Klengel. During his short stay at Leipzig, he makes the acquaintance of Tchaikovsky and of the young Gustav Jenner; he also meets Grieg (whom he knows already). **May** Brahms spends three weeks in Italy with Josef Viktor Widmann. **End of May–mid-September** Brahms stays once more at Thun, in Switzerland. **21 December** In Budapest, Brahms and Hubay give the first performance of the Violin Sonata op. 108.

1889 January–February At a concert at Meiningen on 3 January Brahms conducts his First Piano Concerto (soloist: d'Albert) and the Double Concerto (soloists: Joachim and Hausmann). On 11 January he performs his Violin Sonata op. 108 with Hugo Heermann in Frankfurt; on 13 February he and Joachim give the first performance of the sonata in Vienna. **March** On 1 March Brahms is present at a concert at the Berlin Musikhochschule celebrating the 50th anniversary of Joachim's first concert appearance (in Budapest on 17 March 1839). The following week he takes part in concerts of the Berlin Philharmonic Orchestra. While in Berlin, he attends a banquet given in Ibsen's honor. From Berlin Brahms travels to Hamburg, where he conducts his Fourth Symphony and the *Academic Festival Overture* at a concert of the New Philharmonic Orchestra on 9 March. It is also in March that Alice Barbi, previously unknown to local music lovers, gives three highly acclaimed recitals in Vienna (see notably Hanslick's articles in the *Neue freie*

Presse on 14 and 23 March). At the final concert she sings Brahms's songs "Liebestreu" (op. 3/1) and "Vergebliches Ständchen" (op. 84/4). According to Kalbeck, she is introduced to Brahms by his former pupil Marie Grün. He will later regard Barbi, who regularly returns to Vienna in subsequent years, as a supreme interpreter of his songs; at the same time, he remains by no means insensitive to her beauty. **Mid-May–early September** Brahms vacations at Ischl. During his stay he prepares a new version of the Piano Trio op. 8. **23 May** The mayor of Hamburg, Carl Friedrich Petersen, informs Brahms by letter that the City of Hamburg has awarded him honorary citizenship. Brahms expresses his gratitude and appreciation for the award, first by telegram, and subsequently in a letter dated 30 May. (See also September.) **June** Brahms is awarded the Commander's Cross of the Order of Leopold by Emperor Franz Joseph. **September** Brahms is present in Hamburg on 9 September at the first performance, by Julius Spengel and the enlarged Cäcilien-Verein, of the *Fest-und Gedenksprüche* (which will be published in 1890 with a dedication to Carl Friedrich Petersen). On 14 September he is presented with the certificate of honorary citizenship (see 23 May). It will subsequently be exhibited at the Kunsthalle in Hamburg for several weeks before being transported to Vienna and handed to Brahms by painter Paul Duyffcke in late October. From Hamburg Brahms returns to Vienna via Baden-Baden where he visits Clara Schumann and meets with Josef Viktor Widmann. **30 October** In Hamburg Joachim and Spengel give an all-Brahms recital, which includes the three Violin Sonatas.

1890 January–March Brahms plays in the first performance of the new version of the Piano Trio op. 8 in Budapest (with Hubay and Popper) on 10 January, as well as in further performances in Vienna (at a concert of the Rosé Quartet) on 22 February, in Cologne on 13 March, and in Frankfurt on 23 March. **April** Brahms spends some two weeks in northern Italy with Josef Viktor Widmann. **Mid-May–beginning of October** Brahms vacations at Ischl where he completes the String Quintet op. 11, which he began in Vienna earlier in the year. **16 December** Brahms attends a performance of Mozart's *Don Giovanni* at the Budapest Opera House and is tremendously impressed by the conductor, Gustav Mahler. **17 December** At a concert of the Budapest Philharmonic Orchestra, Brahms conducts the *Academic Festival Overture* and his Second Piano Concerto (soloist: d'Albert).

1891 19 January In Budapest (during what will be his last visit there), Brahms takes part in a concert of the Hubay-Popper Quartet, playing in his Horn Trio op. 40; also on the program: the String Quartet op. 67 and String Quintet op. 111. **13–20 March** Brahms stays as guest of Duke Georg II and his wife at Meiningen, where he attends the premiere of Widmann's play

Oenone, which is given in the author's presence. At concerts at court, according to Widmann's later recollections, Brahms conducts his *Haydn Variations* and First and Fourth Symphonies, and also takes part in a performance of his revised Piano Trio op. 8; Ludwig Wüllner sings the *Magelone-Lieder*. Brahms hears the clarinetist Richard Mühlfeld, whose playing makes a profound impression on him. **20–27 March** Brahms stops at Frankfurt on his return journey to Vienna to see Clara Schumann; his visit is marred by a quarrel. **Mid-May–end of September** Brahms vacations at Ischl, where he composes the Clarinet Trio op. 114 and Clarinet Quintet op. 115. **May** At Ischl, Brahms writes down his will in a letter to Fritz Simrock (usually now referred to as the Ischl Testament). (See also April 1896.) **21–28 November** Brahms has, at his request, been invited to Meiningen where, following rehearsals, his Clarinet Trio and Clarinet Quintet are performed at a private concert at court. Mühlfeld and Hausmann, as well as Joachim, take part. **12 December** The Trio and Quintet receive their first public performances at a concert of the Joachim Quartet in Berlin. (The Trio is again played by Brahms, Mühlfeld, and Hausmann.) **17 December** Brahms, Adalbert Syrinek, and Ferdinand Hellmesberger give the first Viennese performance of the Clarinet Trio.

1892 January There are further performances in Vienna of the Clarinet Trio (by Brahms, Mühlfeld, and Hausmann at a concert of the Joachim Quartet on 21 January) and of the Clarinet Quintet (by the Rosé Quartet and Franz Steiner on 5 January, and by the Joachim Quartet and Mühlfeld on 19 January). (Mühlfeld will be clarinettist in the earliest performances of the two works in England, on 2 April and 28 March, respectively, both at the St. James's Hall in London.) **March** Brahms is made an honorary member of the Hamburg Tonkünstlerverein. **Mid-May–mid-September** Brahms stays at Ischl. **11 June** Death of Brahms's sister Elise. **5 October** At an all-Brahms concert in Berlin, Brahms plays his Violin Sonata op. 108 with Joachim; also on the program: the Clarinet Quintet (performed by the Joachim Quartet and Mühlfeld) and the String Sextet op. 18. This is one of three events arranged by Hermann Wolff to mark the inauguration of the Bechstein Saal (the others feature recitals by Bülow and Anton Rubinstein). **November** Brahms declines an invitation from Cambridge University to visit Cambridge to receive an honorary degree during the next year's golden jubilee celebrations of the Cambridge University Musical Society.

1893 January–February On the way to what will be his last stay in Hamburg, Brahms stops over at Meiningen (where, at a concert on 30 January, he plays in his Clarinet Trio and the Cello Sonata op. 99) and at Frankfurt (where he spends a few pleasant days with Clara Schumann). Sifting through his late sister Elise's belongings in Hamburg, he discovers a considerable number of long, gossipy letters he once sent to her and to his parents, and promptly destroys them. **Mid-April** Brahms sets out on his eighth and final trip to Italy, which he undertakes in the company of Widmann, Friedrich Hegar, and Robert Freund. The journey, which lasts some four weeks, takes them as far as Sicily. **Mid-May–end of September** Brahms vacations at Ischl. **Late 1893** Alice Barbi, who last sang in Vienna in March of this year, returns for a final series of recitals prior to her marriage to Count Wolff-Stomersee in January 1894, after which she will give up her professional career and perform only for charitable purposes. At her last concert on 21 December, she is accompanied on piano by Brahms himself.

1894 6 February Theodor Billroth dies at Abbazia (Opatija, Croatia). **12 February** Hans von Bülow dies in Cairo. **April** Julius von Bernuth having resigned, the position of artistic director of the Hamburg Philharmonic Concerts is offered to Brahms. He declines, declaring that the offer has come "too late" for him. **Mid-May–late September** Brahms vacations at Ischl where he composes the two Sonatas for Clarinet (or Viola) op. 120. In mid-September he meets Mühlfeld at Berchtesgaden where they try out the sonatas at the villas of Anna Franz and Princess Marie. **November** Brahms spends several days at Frankfurt, where he stays at Clara Schumann's and further rehearses the clarinet sonatas with Mühlfeld. He also attends an all-Brahms concert at which Joachim plays his Violin Concerto (9 November), and a concert of the Joachim Quartet, at which his String Quartet op. 67 is performed (11 November). From Frankfurt he travels with Mühlfeld to Schloss Altenstein, near Bad Liebenstein, where they play the sonatas before Duke Georg II and his wife. On 19 November, at the end of his five-day stay, Brahms returns to Vienna via Meiningen.

1895 January–February In Vienna Brahms presents his Clarinet Sonatas, together with Mühlfeld, first to Viennese fellow musicians and music lovers, and then at public concerts: on 7 January, at the Tonkünstlerverein, he and Mühlfeld perform both sonatas; on 8 January, at a concert of the Rosé Quartet, they play the Sonata op. 120/2; and on 11 January, at another concert by the same quartet, they play the Sonata op. 120/1. (The program of the first concert also includes the String Quintet op. 111, that of the last includes the Clarinet Quintet, again with Mühlfeld.) On 27 January Brahms and Mühlfeld play the sonatas in Leipzig, on 15 February in Frankfurt, on 21 February at Merseburg, and on 25 February at Meiningen. While in Leipzig, Brahms also conducts the *Academic Festival Overture* and the two Piano Concertos, both played by Eugen d'Albert, at a Gewandhaus concert on 31 January. **18 March** At a concert of the Gesellschaft der Musikfreunde Conservatory, given in celebration of the 25th anniversary of the opening of the new Musikverein building, Brahms directs a performance by a student orchestra of his *Academic Festival Overture*. It is the last time that he conducts at a concert in Vienna. **3 April** Brahms makes the acquaintance of Felix Weingartner. That evening he hears Weingartner conduct the Berlin Philharmonic Orchestra in a performance of his Second Symphony; in a letter to Fritz Simrock, he describes the performance as "quite wonderful." **Mid-May–mid-September** Brahms stays at Ischl. **25 September** Brahms arrives at Meiningen to attend the music festival (27–29 September) that features compositions by Bach, Beethoven, and himself (*Triumphlied*, First Symphony, Double Concerto for Violin and Cello, *Handel Variations*, Clarinet Sonata op. 120/1, Clarinet Quintet, String Quintet op. 111, and some vocal quartets). This final visit to Meiningen turns into a great personal triumph for Brahms. Before traveling to Frankfurt on 3 October, Brahms spends two days at the duke's residence at Schloss Altenstein. **3–4 October** Brahms pays a brief visit to Frankfurt to see Clara Schumann. It will be their last meeting. **20 October** The festivities on the occasion of the inauguration of the new Tonhalle in Zurich open with a performance of Brahms's *Triumphlied*, which he conducts himself.

1896 **10 January** In Berlin, Eugen d'Albert repeats the tour de force of playing both of Brahms's piano concertos at the same concert (see 31 January 1895); Brahms again conducts. **16 January** Brahms attends a Gewandhaus concert in Leipzig, at which Arthur Nikisch conducts his Fourth Symphony; he is delighted with the performance. **29 January** Bronislaw Hubermann makes a profound impression in Vienna with his performance of Brahms's Violin Concerto. Brahms himself is deeply moved by it and reportedly undertakes to write a *Fantasia* for the 13-year-old boy—a promise he will, however, not keep. Hubermann will play the concerto again at his concert of 11 February. **April** Brahms asks Fritz Simrock to return the letter he sent him in 1891 (the so-called Ischl Testament—see May 1891), and he subsequently makes some changes in it. It will be found in his desk after his death but will eventually, due to its unorthodox nature, not be recognized as his will. (See also February 1897). **Mid-May** Brahms moves into his summer quarters at Ischl. **20 May** Clara Schumann dies in Frankfurt. **24 May** Brahms attends Clara Schumann's funeral in Bonn. He then spends a few days as the guest of Walther and Emmy Weyermann at their villa "Hagerhof" at Bad Honeff. On this occasion he sings (or rather, declaims) his newly composed *4 ernste Gesänge*. From Honeff he returns to Ischl, where he will stay until the end of August. **Summer** Brahms is looking increasingly ill and losing weight. He is examined by several doctors, first at Ischl and, after his return to the capital, in Vienna. **September** Brahms takes the cure at Karlsbad (Karlovy Vary). **14 October** Brahms attends Anton Bruckner's funeral at the Karlskirche. **Winter 1896–97** Joseph Joachim has his final meetings with Brahms on the occasion of one of the Joachim Quartet's visits to Vienna.

1897 February Richard Fellinger draws up a testament for Brahms, which, since Brahms never signs it, will be regarded as invalid after his death. (See May 1891 and April 1896.) **7 March** Brahms is present at a concert of the Vienna Philharmonic Orchestra, at which Hans Richter conducts his Fourth Symphony. It is the last time he attends a public concert. At the same concert, Dvořák's Cello Concerto receives its first Viennese performance (soloist: Hugo Becker). **13 March** Brahms attends the premiere of Johann Strauss's operetta *Die Göttin der Vernunft* at the Theater an der Wien, but feels too ill to remain until the end. It is his last appearance in public. **25 March** Brahms dines for the last time at the house of Viktor and Olga von Miller zu Aichholz. **26 March** Brahms takes to his bed, which he will not leave again. **3 April** Brahms dies of cancer of the liver.

Some Later Dates of Interest

6 April 1897 Brahms's funeral. He is interred in a temporary grave at the Central Cemetery.

11 April 1897 Richard von Perger conducts Brahms's Requiem at a memorial concert of the Gesellschaft der Musikfreunde.

14 June 1897 Brahms's remains are moved to a grave of honor at the Central Cemetery.

7 October 1899 Adolf von Hildebrand's Brahms monument is unveiled at Meiningen. The principal speaker is Joachim. The ceremony is preceded by a performance of Brahms's Requiem and followed by a performance of the *Triumphlied*, both at the Stadtkirche.

25 October 1899 Richard von Perger conducts Brahms's Requiem at a memorial concert for Johann Strauss.

14 April 1902 Brahms's stepmother, Karoline Louise Brahms, dies at Pinneberg in Holstein.

1904 The first part of Max Kalbeck's biography of Brahms is published.

7 May 1908 Rudolf von Weyr's Brahms monument is unveiled in Vienna.

7 May 1909 Max Klinger's statue of Brahms is unveiled at the Musikhalle in Hamburg.

3 July 1910 A bust of Brahms by Maria Fellinger is unveiled in the garden of the Hotel Alte Post at Mürzzuschlag. It is now at the town's Brahms Museum.

The Dictionary

– A –

ABRAHAM, MAX (b. Danzig [Gdańsk, Poland], 3 July 1831; d. Leipzig, 8 December 1900). A lawyer by training, in 1863 he became joint owner and manager of the publishing house C. F. Peters, which had been acquired three years earlier by the Berlin book and music seller Julius Friedländer. The firm's business and its reputation flourished under Abraham's direction, especially as a result of the success of the "Edition Peters," which he launched in 1867 and which offered music lovers excellent and affordable editions of both well-known and new compositions. Upon Friedländer's retirement in 1880, he became sole proprietor of the firm. In 1894 his nephew Henri Hinrichsen (1868–1942) was made a partner, and after Abraham's death he, in turn, became the sole owner. (For the later history of the firm, see H.-M. Plesske's article in *Die Musik in Geschichte und Gegenwart* [see Blume 1949–86], and for a more detailed account, Lindlar's *C. F. Peters Musikverlag . . .*)

Brahms's first contacts with Abraham date from early 1874, when he returned to Leipzig after an absence of some 13 years. Shortly before setting out from Vienna, he had been informed by **Clara Schumann** that Abraham was very eager to publish some of his compositions (Litzmann 1902, vol. 2, 41); Clara added that she was herself greatly indebted to Abraham—no doubt a reference to his publication of several of **Robert Schumann**'s works. The first result of Brahms's contact with Abraham was the appearance in the autumn of 1874 of the *4 Duets* op. 28 in the "Edition Peters"; they had originally been published in 1863 by **C. A. Spina**, who now agreed to their reissue in this series. In early October 1874, Brahms sent Abraham the nine songs of op. 63 and the vocal quartets op. 64, of which Peters released the first editions in November. The link was thus firmly established, but despite Brahms's high regard for Abraham and the latter's repeated requests for further compositions, the association was to yield only three further first editions: *Nänie* in December 1881, and the vocal quartets op. 112 and the canons for women's voices op. 113 in November 1891. (Brahms considered Peters as a possible publisher for the Second Piano Concerto, but finally settled on **Fritz Simrock** and offered Abraham *Nänie* instead.) In

1881 Peters also published Brahms's revised edition of his piano accompaniment to six vocal duets by **Handel** (M. McCorkle 1984, Anhang Ia/11). (Brahms 1974/14; Lindlar 1967; Ollendorff 1931)

ALBERT, EUGEN [EUGÈNE] (FRANCIS CHARLES) D' (b. Glasgow, 10 April 1864; d. Riga, 3 March 1932). Composer and pianist. While he received some musical instruction from his father Charles (a pianist, dancer, and composer of Italian descent), d'Albert was in fact largely self-taught until he entered the New Music School, London, then directed by Arthur Sullivan, in 1874. There, from 1876, he studied piano with Ernst Pauer, a grandson of the musical instrument makers Johann Andreas and Maria Anna [Nanette] **Streicher**, who had been among **Beethoven**'s intimate friends in Vienna.

D'Albert's exceptional gifts soon attracted attention. In March 1881 he played for **Clara Schumann**, who was then giving concerts in London and who was so impressed by his performance of her husband's *Symphonische Etüden* that she wrote in her diary, "I believe he will become a great pianist" (Litzmann 1902, vol. 3, 417). When only 17, he played the **Schumann** Piano Concerto at a concert at the Crystal Palace. Soon afterward he moved to Germany, which became his spiritual home for the rest of his life; although his mother was English, he never considered himself an Englishman. In May 1882 he joined **Liszt**'s master classes at Weimar, where his virtuosity soon made him a favorite of Liszt, who called him "Albertus Magnus" and regarded him as the equal of **Carl Tausig**. His debut recital at Weimar on 29 September 1882 included, in addition to Beethoven's Sonata op. 90, several pieces by **Chopin** and Liszt, as well as some of Tausig's bravura arrangements of music by **Wagner** and Moniuszko. Some three weeks later he dazzled his audience with his performance of Liszt's First Piano Concerto at a concert in honor of the composer's 71st birthday. During the next 20 years, d'Albert enjoyed a brilliant international career, which would no doubt have been much longer had he not chosen to devote himself increasingly to composition. **Hans von Bülow** considered him the preeminent pianist of the younger generation; in a letter to Brahms on 8 January 1891, he referred to him as a *Prachtkerl*, a "splendid fellow" (Hinrichsen 1994, 79). Of d'Albert's numerous compositions, it was the opera *Tiefland* (first performed in Prague on 15 November 1903) that achieved the most lasting success.

D'Albert was introduced to Brahms by **Hans Richter** on the occasion of an all-Brahms recital given by Bülow in Vienna on 2 February 1882. On 13 March he called on Brahms and played for him. Brahms was greatly impressed, and eventually he came to regard d'Albert as the ideal interpreter of his two piano concertos. However, Siegfried Kross's (1997) statement in his Brahms biography that d'Albert appears to have been, after **Julius Röntgen**, the first pianist other than Brahms himself to have played the Second Piano Concerto in public is incorrect (862). Röntgen was by no means the first, nor therefore could d'Albert have been the second (*see* RÖNTGEN, JULIUS.) In any case, d'Albert's performance at Meiningen, which Kross cites in this connection, did not take place on 25 February 1887, as he states, but on 25 December of that year; nor was it d'Albert's earliest performance of that work, for he had already played it at a philharmonic concert in Vienna under Hans Richter's baton on 14 November 1886 (not 4 November, as indicated by Richter's biographer C. Fifield). That performance so greatly moved and delighted Brahms that, according to **Richard Heuberger** (1976), at a dinner that evening he kept stroking d'Albert's hand and calling him a "most excellent young man" (32). Heuberger believes furthermore that a discussion that Brahms had with d'Albert on that occasion about certain aspects of pianistic technique may have been partly responsible for his decision to publish the *51 Exercises* (WoO 6) that **Simrock** issued in 1893 (but on this point see M. McCorkle 1984, 518).

The aforesaid performance of the concerto at Meiningen on 25 December 1887 was conducted by Brahms himself. On 3 January 1889, also at Meiningen and also under Brahms's direction, d'Albert was soloist in the First Piano Concerto. In a letter on 25 November 1888, Brahms had assured **Baroness Helene Heldburg** (*see* GEORG II, DUKE OF SACHSEN-MEININGEN) that the prospect of performing the D Minor Concerto with d'Albert gave him particular pleasure (Brahms 1991, 92). (**Kalbeck** mistakenly believed—and Kross echoes the error—that because Brahms was unable to spend Christmas 1888 at Meiningen, the performance scheduled to take place during the Christmas period was abandoned; in fact, it was only postponed and formed part of the program of the concert of 3 January 1889, which also included the Double Concerto, with **Joseph Joachim** and **Robert Hausmann** as soloists.)

On 17 December 1890, Brahms and d'Albert presented a highly acclaimed performance of the B-flat Concerto in Budapest, but even this success was outshone by the triumph they scored at Leipzig on 31 January 1895, when d'Albert performed both concertos. He was to repeat that tour de force in Berlin on 10 January 1896, again with Brahms conducting. Shortly afterward Heuberger asked Brahms whether he had himself played the piano during his stay in Berlin, and he replied that he did not play any more, since he now had his "court pianist." Brahms had good reason to admire the virtuosity and outstanding musicianship of the "Little Giant" (as he was affectionately known), for d'Albert helped to establish his two piano concertos as part of the standard repertory. It was only fitting, therefore, that he should have been chosen to play the Second Piano Concerto at Meiningen on 7 October 1899, during the festivities accompanying the unveiling of the Brahms monument. For his part, d'Albert expressed his admiration for Brahms by dedicating his String Quartet op. 11 to him. (H. Ehrlich 1893a; Kross 1997; Raupp 1930)

ALEXIS, WILLIBALD [pseudonym of (Georg) Wilhelm (Heinrich) Häring] (b. Breslau [Wrocław, Poland], 29 June 1798; d. Arnstadt, Thuringia, 16 December 1871). Novelist, poet, and journalist, known especially for his novels on historical subjects. Brahms set two of his poems in "Walpurgisnacht" (op. 75/4) and "Entführung" (op. 97/3). (Haberland 1988)

ALLGEYER, JULIUS (b. Haslach, Kinzigtal [Baden-Württemberg], 29 March 1829; d. Munich, 6 September 1900). Etcher and photographer. He made Brahms's acquaintance in 1854 at Düsseldorf, where he was studying engraving with Josef Keller, and he was to remain Brahms's firm friend and admirer ever after. During a lengthy stay in Rome (1856–60) he met **Anselm Feuerbach**, who was to be a key figure in his personal as well as his professional life. Not only did Allgeyer apply himself devotedly to making Feuerbach's paintings and drawings better known through many excellent reproductions (which delighted Brahms, whom Allgeyer had introduced to the artist in 1865); he also sought to promote Feuerbach's reputation by means of a number of articles—the first of which appeared in the *Österreichische Wochenschrift für Wissenschaft und Kunst* in November 1872—and especially through the biography he published in 1894.

While Brahms and Allgeyer maintained some contact in the years immediately following their initial meeting at Düsseldorf, it was not until Brahms became a regular visitor to Baden-Baden and Karlsruhe from 1864 onward that they formed a closer relationship, which extended also to their mutual friend **Hermann Levi**. (The three appear together in a well-known photograph.) Allgeyer was then running a photographic business with his brother Ludwig at Karlsruhe, and in 1866 Brahms stayed with him for several weeks. It was at that time that they began to address each other with the intimate "Du." Speaking to **Sir George Henschel** in 1876, Brahms remembered this visit with great pleasure, not least because during it he had composed the D minor section of the Requiem, as well as the song "Die Mainacht" (op. 43/2); he also spoke with genuine affection of his host, calling him a "fine human being" (Henschel 1978, 48). **Clara Schumann** described Allgeyer in her diary in September 1866 as "a pleasant, highly cultured man whose every word bears witness to a fine intelligence and a profound sensitivity" (Litzmann 1902, vol. 3, 195); and Hermann Levi wrote to Clara three months later: "He is a dear old fellow, true as gold; after spending an evening with him I always feel as if I had taken a refreshing bath" (Litzmann 1902, vol. 3, 197).

In 1872 Allgeyer moved to Munich, where, except for a short break, he worked for the court photographer Josef Albert during the next eight years. In Munich he maintained close personal contact with Levi, who became Bavarian Hofkapellmeister that same year. Furthermore, he remained in correspondence with Brahms, whom he also met occasionally (for instance, in 1873 in Vienna, where he and Levi had gone to visit the international exhibition). Their letters show that, like various other friends of Brahms, he had become involved in the latter's search for a suitable opera libretto. Already in 1869 he had, at Brahms's request, read Calderón's *El secreto a voces* and had even prepared a libretto based on Carlo Gozzi's Italian version of the play, *Il pubblico secreto* (first produced at Modena on 20 May 1769); but in the end Brahms would not be tempted, anymore than he was by any of the various other subjects he considered. He nonetheless kept Allgeyer's text, for he retained his interest in Gozzi. In fact, in 1888 he told **Josef Viktor Widmann** that if he had not adopted the rule "no opera and no marriage," he would at once set *Das laute Geheimnis* (i.e., *Il pubblico secreto*), as well as *König Hirsch* (Brahms 1974/8, 72; *König Hirsch* [*Il re cervo*] is also by Gozzi). Brahms knew Gozzi's plays very well, for his personal library contained F. A. C. Werthes's German translation *Theatralische Werke von Carlo Gozzi* (5 vols., Berne, 1777–79).

In 1875 Brahms dedicated the *Balladen und Romanzen* (op. 75) to Allgeyer, a clear indication of their close relationship at that time. It was, moreover, a particularly appropriate gesture, since it was Allgeyer who had originally brought **Johann Gottfried Herder**'s collections of folk songs to the attention of Brahms, who took the text of "Edward" (op. 75/1) from one of them.

While working for Albert, and also later, Allgeyer devoted much effort and time to the invention of a photoengraving press, but he was unable to produce a marketable model. As a result, he fell on hard times and in 1884 he appealed for a loan to Brahms, with whom he had then been out of touch for some five years; the reasons for their estrangement are not known, beyond the mention in Allgeyer's letter of a "piece of paper" that had driven them apart, but which would have lost its force if only they had been able to discuss its contents in person (Orel 1964, 119–20). Perhaps Brahms had reacted adversely to some written remarks made by Allgeyer in his known efforts to prevent the breakup of Brahms's friendship with Levi. In any case, Brahms now promptly responded to Allgeyer's request for financial assistance, but there is no indication that they ever resumed their earlier close contacts. This explains no doubt why Brahms was quite unaware that Allgeyer was working on a biography of Feuerbach, and was surprised and pleased when he unexpectedly came across it in a Frankfurt bookstore in November 1894. He was especially gratified when he found an inscribed copy waiting for him on his return to Vienna, and he at once wrote to Allgeyer to thank him and congratulate him on what he genuinely regarded as an excellent piece of work. Allgeyer replied that Brahms's kind letter had moved him to tears and declared that whatever success the book might bring him would never mean as much to him as the awareness that Brahms regarded him "still, or once more" as the friend he had known in the past (Orel 1964, 123–24).

In October 1895 Allgeyer traveled to Zurich, mainly perhaps for the purpose of once more meeting Brahms, who played a central part in the music festival arranged there on the occasion of the inauguration of the new concert hall. It may be assumed that the two old friends found some opportunities to converse, but it is perhaps an indication of the rather peripheral position that Allgeyer then occupied in Brahms's circle that he was unaware when Brahms was due to depart. "I have just come from Hegar's [Brahms had stayed with **Friedrich Hegar**], where I learned with very great regret that you have already left Zurich," Allgeyer wrote in what may well have been his last letter to Brahms. It is, at any rate, the final item printed by Alfred Orel in his edition of their correspondence (Orel 1964, 128).

After Clara Schumann's death, Allgeyer was asked by her daughter Marie to write her mother's biography. By the time he died he had completed seven chapters, covering most of her life before her marriage. His text was never published as such, but it was to some extent incorporated by Berthold Litzmann in his own account of Clara's life.

Eventually Allgeyer prepared a completely revised version of his Feuerbach biography on the basis of various letters and written statements by Feuerbach that had previously been unavailable to him. Allgeyer having died in 1900, the new edition was published in 1904 by Carl Neumann, whose main contribution consisted in a reexamination of Allgeyer's list of Feuerbach's works. (Allgeyer 1872, 1904; Brahms 1974/8; Henschel 1978; Litzmann 1902; Lukoschik 1993; Orel 1964)

ALLMERS, HERMANN (b. Rechtenfleth, near Bremen, 11 February 1821; d. Rechtenfleth, 9 March 1902). Poet and writer; one of the founders of the so-called Heimatbewegung that placed emphasis on one's regional, especially rural, background as an important source of inspiration. Brahms set two of his poems in the song "Feldeinsamkeit" (op. 86/2) and the quartet "Spätherbst" (op. 92/2). (J. Schilling 1988)

ANNA (MARIA FRIEDERIKE), born Princess of Prussia, from 1853 was Princess of Hessen, and from 1867 was Landgravine of Hessen (b. Berlin, 17 May 1836; d. Frankfurt, 12 June 1918). Daughter of Prince Carl of Prussia (1801–83) and Marie of Sachsen-Weimar-Eisenach (1808–77), and niece of King Friedrich Wilhelm IV and of King/Emperor Wilhelm I. On 26 May 1853 she married Prince Friedrich Wilhelm of Hessen (1820–84), who was heir apparent to the elector and landgrave Friedrich Wilhelm I of Hessen-Kassel (but by the time of the latter's death in 1875 the electorate had been annexed by Prussia). During the early years of their marriage, the couple, who had three sons and three daughters, resided mainly at Copenhagen, where Princess Anna's salon was much frequented by visiting musicians as well as by the leading Danish composers; but they also traveled, together or separately. In 1857, while she was in Paris, Winterhalter painted a celebrated portrait of her that can now be seen at Schloss Fasanerie, near Fulda. She also stayed occasionally at Baden-Baden. From 1867 the couple lived at various residences in Germany—at Schloss Panker in Holstein, Schloss Philippsruhe near Hanau, Schloss Fasanerie, and at Baden-Baden, Wiesbaden, and Frankfurt. After her husband's death, Anna divided her time mostly between Frankfurt and Schloss Fasanerie. On 10 October 1901 she converted to Catholicism, a decision that greatly displeased the Prussian royal family.

Anna was highly musical and an excellent pianist, having studied with Theodor Kullak in Berlin. Throughout her life she was in contact with many leading composers and piano virtuosos, among them **Liszt**, whom she had first met at Weimar when she was still a child. She enjoyed a particularly close friendship with **Clara Schumann**, and it was through Clara that she became acquainted with Brahms at Baden-Baden in 1864. There, and later in some of her various other residences, she used to play duets with him. It was at Baden-Baden in 1864 that Brahms and Clara played the two-piano version of his Piano Quintet for her. The princess presumably expressed great admiration for the work, for Brahms dedicated the quintet to her in 1865, and also its arrangement for two pianos in 1871; in addition, he gave her an autograph of the latter version, which is preserved at Schloss Fasanerie. The princess responded with a generous gift, which must have delighted Brahms: the autograph of Mozart's G Minor Symphony. Brahms remained in contact with her until his final years. In 1876 he told **Sir George Henschel** that he particularly "admired her for her simple and modest, yet extremely cordial and affable, manners" (Henschel 1978, 24). He also had other reasons to appreciate her interest in him and his music, for she did her best to make his compositions known in Frankfurt. In particular, she has been credited with having created opportunities for him to conduct performances of his orchestral works there on five occasions between 1876 and 1887, and to appear as pianist in his chamber works on seven occasions between 1875 and 1895. Incidentally, Brahms was only one of several composers who dedicated works to her.

Anna's son Alexander Friedrich (1863–1945), though blind, was a noted musician who had studied violin with **Joseph Joachim**, organ with Louis Vierne and Charles-Marie Widor, and composition with Felix Draeseke and **Joachim Raff**; he was also a competent pianist. On 23 October 1885, in Princess's Marie's rooms at Meiningen and in Brahms's presence, he played Brahms's String Quartet op. 67 with three members of the Meiningen Orchestra, not just once but twice. Alexander dedicated his *Fantasiestück* for piano (op. 2) to Brahms. (Henschel 1978; Pessenlehner 1943, 1958)

ARNIM, ACHIM (LUDWIG) VON (b. Berlin, 26 January 1781; d. Berlin, 21 January 1831). Poet and novelist, but probably best known for the collection of folk songs that he published together with Clemens Brentano under the title *Des Knaben Wunderhorn* (3 vols., 1805–8) and that is considered one of the most important documents of the German Romantic movement. In 1811 he married Bettina Brentano (*see* ARNIM, ELISABETH [BETTINA] VON).

Brahms set one of Arnim's poems in "O süsser Mai," for mixed four-voice choir (op. 93a). He furthermore used poems from *Des Knaben Wunderhorn* in the following vocal compositions: "Der Überläufer" (op. 48/2), "Liebesklage des Mädchens" (op. 48/3), "Wiegenlied" (op. 49/4), "Rosmarin" (op. 62/1), "Von alten Liebesliedern" (op. 62/2), "Hüt du dich!" (op. 66/5), and "Guter Rat" (op. 75/2). The text of the song "Das Lied vom Herrn von Falkenstein" (op. 43/4) appears to have been compiled from various sources, including *Des Knaben Wunderhorn*. (On Achim von Arnim, *see also* ARNIM, ELISABETH [BETTINA] VON.) (Sternberg 1988)

ARNIM, ELISABETH [BETTINA] VON (b. Frankfurt am Main, 4 April 1785; d. Berlin, 20 January 1859). Writer, poet, composer, and sculptor; wife of poet **Achim von Arnim** (whom she outlived by almost 30 years), and sister of poet and novelist Clemens Brentano (1778–1842). She was a friend of **Johannn Wolfgang von Goethe** and of **Beethoven** and on close terms with many other prominent contemporaries, an early feminist and advocate of social reform, and altogether one of the most celebrated and flamboyant figures of the German Romantic movement.

Brahms met her and her daughter Gisela (1827–89) through **Robert** and **Clara Schumann** at Düsseldorf in October 1853, and he came to know them better the following month while staying at Hanover. (His friend

Joseph Joachim was greatly attracted to Gisela, who was to marry the writer and art historian Herman Grimm in 1859. Bettina, who was then approaching seventy, had clearly not lost her ability to dazzle and fascinate, for not only did Brahms decide to dedicate to her the *6 Gesänge* (op. 3), which appeared in December, but the impression she made remained with him all his life. **Richard Heuberger** relates that, in a discussion about women writers at **Viktor von Miller zu Aichholz**'s house in February 1895, Brahms exclaimed, "Ah yes, Bettina von Arnim, whom I still knew, now there was a woman one had to take seriously! What a brilliant mind she had!" (Heuberger 1976, 76).

In December 1853, perhaps as a Christmas present or in acknowledgment of the dedication, Bettina sent Brahms a volume of poems by the early Romantic writer Novalis (pseudonym of Baron Friedrich von Hardenberg) and a set of her own songs, *7 Gesangstücke* (published in 1843 and dedicated to Spontini). The following September she amazed and delighted him by sending to him the complete editions of her own and Achim's works. According to Brahms, again as reported by Heuberger, she was not very pleased to discover on a later occasion that none of the pages of her husband's writings had been cut by him (Heuberger 1976, 118). However, Brahms must have amply made up for this early neglect afterward, for Kurt Hofmann noted in his examination of Brahms's private library that each volume of the complete edition of Achim's works bore countless indications that he had read it frequently and with close attention. (Böttger 1990; Heuberger 1976; K. Hofmann 1974; Schultz 1988)

ARNOLD, FRIEDRICH WILHELM (b. Sontheim, 10 March 1810; d. Heilbronn, 13 February 1864). Folk-song collector and music publisher living at Elberfeld (now a part of Wuppertal). In March 1854, **Joseph Joachim** wrote to Brahms that Arnold, "a publisher at Elberfeld," had not long ago expressed to him an interest in publishing some of Brahms's compositions. Joachim added that he had told Arnold that he thought Brahms had an arrangement with **Breitkopf & Härtel** (Brahms 1974/5, 33). There is no record of Brahms having commented on this matter in his correspondence with Joachim, but he was in fact in contact with Arnold later that year, at least partly on behalf of **Robert Schumann**, whose piano pieces collectively entitled *5 Gesänge der Frühe* Arnold was then in the process of publishing; they eventually appeared in December 1855 as Schumann's op. 133. At the same time, Brahms's already strong interest in folk songs was further stimulated and enriched by his connection with Arnold, who permitted him to consult the material he had collected (some of which Brahms copied for his own collection) and even placed at his disposal the manuscript of the

Volkslieder aus dem Siebengebirge—folk songs from the Siebengebirge, a group of hills bordering the Rhine—which Arnold had assembled together with Jakob Grimm; Brahms had a copy made for himself, which is now in the archive of the Gesellschaft der Musikfreunde in Vienna.

Brahms offered Arnold at least one of his own works, the arrangement for two pianos of Schumann's Piano Quartet op. 47. However, although this arrangement (M. McCorkle 1984, Anhang Ia/8) very likely dates from 1855, the offer was probably not made until several years later. Arnold accepted the work, but when it was already set up in print (according to K. Hofmann, it was due to appear in March 1860), it was withdrawn, apparently as a result of objections from Gustav Heinze who had published an arrangement for piano duet by **Carl Reinecke** in August 1859. Brahms's arrangement was eventually issued by the Berlin publisher Adolph Fürstner in January 1887, after the copyright of Schumann's works had expired at the end of the preceding month. (Fürstner had acquired Arnold's firm in 1878.) (Brahms 1974/5; K. Hofmann 1975; F. Reinecke 1889)

ASTEN, JULIE VON. Pianist. When Brahms arrived in Vienna in September 1862, she was living with her mother, Frau Schmuttermayer von Asten, and her sisters Marie and Anna at the Gundelhof, a large apartment complex on Bauernmarkt/Brandstätte. **Clara Schumann**, who was a friend of her mother's, sometimes stayed with the family when she was in Vienna for concerts, and she gave Julie some tuition. According to **Max Kalbeck** (1976), Brahms first met Julie on 15 September 1862, through **Carl Grädener**, and he was soon giving Julie lessons himself (vol. 3, 12). She must, however, already have been quite a competent pianist, for on 31 October 1859 she had performed **Beethoven**'s First Piano Concerto at a concert of the newly founded Orchesterverein of the Gesellschaft der Musikfreunde. (These concerts were distinct from the regular Gesellschaftskonzerte and not open to the public.) After he once remarked that he missed his Hamburg women's choir, Julie and her sister Anna persuaded some members of the Singverein to form a small choral group, which met at their Gundelhof flat to sing under Brahms's direction. Among them were Karoline Bettelheim, Ottilie Hauer (*see* EBNER, OTTILIE), Marie Geissler (who later, according to Kalbeck, also took piano lessons with him), and Anna Franz (*see* WITTGENSTEIN FAMILY). Furthermore, it was apparently through Julie that Brahms made the acquaintance of **Marie Wilt**.

He did his best to further Julie's career. Thus he conducted six of his choruses for female voices at a concert she gave on 10 April 1863; at a charity concert at **Bösendorfer**'s music salon on 18 December of the same year, he partnered with her in **Schumann**'s *Variations for Two Pianos*; and at another of her concerts on 10 April 1864, they played his own *Variations on a Theme by Robert Schumann for Piano Duet* (op. 23). Clara Schumann may herself have performed with Julie in Prague in 1865 (see Litzmann 1970, vol. 1, 497).

In the late 1860s Julie moved to Berlin, where she was later joined by her sister Anna (1848–1903), a singer who had studied with **Pauline Viardot** and became a teacher at the Berlin Hochschule für Musik. (She married a university professor by the name of Schultzen in 1871.) On 19 March 1870, at a Hochschule concert conducted by **Ernst Rudorff**, Anna sang an aria from *Le nozze di Figaro* and took part in the first performance of the orchestrated version of nine of Brahms's *Liebeslieder-Walzer* from opp. 52 and 65. At another concert on 18 February 1875, she sang the duet "Vor der Tür" (op. 28/2) with **Julius Stockhausen**.

Clara Schumann kept in touch with Julie after she had moved to Berlin. On 27 December 1875 they performed Brahms's *Haydn Variations* together at a concert there; and on 9 February 1883 Clara wrote enthusiastically in her diary about a performance of the Mendelssohn Violin Concerto at the house of some friends, in which **Marie Soldat** was accompanied on piano by Julie. A posthumous link between Brahms and Julie von Asten is also worthy of mention: she served on the Ladies' Committee constituted for the purpose of collecting contributions to the Brahms Monument Fund (*see* HORNBOSTEL, [OTTO] ERICH VON). (Litzmann 1970)

ASTOR, EDMUND: *see* RIETER-BIEDERMANN, JAKOB MELCHIOR.

AUER, LEOPOLD (b. Veszprém, Hungary, 7 June 1845; d. Loschwitz, near Dresden, 15 July 1930). Violinist and teacher. He studied with Ridley Kohne in Budapest (1852–55) and with Jacob Dont in Vienna (1856–58), subsequently toured in Hungary, Austria, Holland, and Germany, and eventually received further instruction from **Joseph Joachim** at Hanover (1861–63). In 1864 he was appointed Konzertmeister at Düsseldorf. Subsequently he was active as a violinist at Hamburg and elsewhere, playing especially in chamber music and becoming leader of the Müller String Quartet. From 1868 until 1917 he served on the faculty of the St. Petersburg conservatory. After he left Russia he gave concerts and continued his teaching in America.

When Auer gave a concert in Hamburg on 18 March 1862, Brahms, who had met him at Joachim's, agreed to take part; they played **Beethoven**'s "Kreutzer" Sonata, and Brahms performed **Robert Schumann**'s *Symphonische Etüden.* Six years later, on 16 February 1868, also in Hamburg, he played his own *Handel Variations* at a matinee given by a quartet led by

Auer. In his memoirs Auer gratefully recalled Brahms's generosity in consenting to play with him at the concert in 1862 when he was a largely unknown boy of 16. (Auer 1923)

AVÉ-LALLEMANT, (JOHANN) THEODOR (FRIEDRICH) (b. Magdeburg, 2 February 1806; d. Hamburg, 9 November 1890). Piano teacher, active in Hamburg 1828–74. Member of a highly musical family: his father Jakob (1776–1852) was a harpist and oboist, and was later employed as a music teacher at Lübeck, as were Jakob's brothers Friedrich (1773–1853) and Ludwig (1780–1823). Before moving from Lübeck to Hamburg in 1828, Theodor had for several years played horn at concerts and operatic performances. He was to assume a prominent role in the musical life of Hamburg, especially through his close association with the Philharmonic Society, on whose board of directors he served from 1838 to 1890. Apart from his close contacts with local musicians, he enjoyed friendly relations with many who resided outside Hamburg, notably **Robert** and **Clara Schumann**, **Joseph Joachim**, and **Julius Stockhausen** (later also with **Tchaikovsky**, who dedicated the German score of his Fifth Symphony to him). In 1878, to mark the 50th anniversary of the foundation of the Philharmonic Society, he wrote a survey of its history under the title *Rückerinnerungen eines alten Musikanten* [*Recollections of an Old Musician*].

Brahms made Avé's acquaintance in 1854 and, during the next few years, was a frequent visitor to Avé's home whenever he stayed in Hamburg. One particular attraction for him was Avé's collection of early music. At Christmas 1854 Avé presented him, to his delight, with an 18th century Italian edition of the score of **Christoph Willibald Gluck**'s *Alceste*, and in 1858 Avé gave him Carl von Winterfeld's *Johannes Gabrieli und sein Zeitalter*. The friendship blossomed to such a point that in 1859 Avé paid Brahms a visit at Detmold. The turning point in their relations occurred in November 1862 when the board of directors decided to invite Stockhausen to succeed the ageing **Grund** as conductor of both the Philharmonic Orchestra and the Singakademie. Brahms, who was in Vienna at the time, was informed of the board's decision by Avé (whose letter was dispatched before a firm offer had been made to Stockhausen, let alone accepted by him). On 18 November Brahms sent Avé's communication, which does not appear to have survived, to Clara Schumann in Hamburg, where she was due to give some concerts, together with a letter in which he expressed his profound disappointment at being passed over for this prestigious post by his native city; he was particularly distressed and bitterly resentful because he felt that before his departure for Vienna he had been encouraged to believe that it might be offered to him (Litzmann 1970, vol. 1, 413). When

Clara expressed her indignation to Avé at what she termed a "disgraceful" action, Avé gave her various reasons for the board's decision and indicated that there might be an opening for Brahms at a later stage (see Litzmann 1970, vol. 1, 414–15). To Stockhausen, however, he explained that personality had been an important factor, Brahms being regarded as difficult, while Stockhausen was known to be extremely amiable. (*See also* STOCKHAUSEN, JULIUS [FRANZ CHRISTIAN].)

It seems fairly clear from this that Avé, for what he no doubt genuinely considered to be telling reasons, bore much of the responsibility for the board's preference for Stockhausen. This appears to have been Clara's view and, more importantly, it was manifestly Brahms's own; he felt himself betrayed by someone who had always appeared to be particularly well disposed toward him. In the above-mentioned letter to Clara on 18 November he wrote, "You will moreover be amused by the honey-sweet way in which my friendly enemy hands me the poisoned drink, on the one hand speaking of the bright future in store for me and, on the other, quickly forgetting this, looking forward with pleasure to a future without me" (Litzmann 1970, vol. 1, 413–14). In April 1863 he wrote in a similarly bitter vein to Joachim, comparing his own fate somewhat grandiloquently to that of King Otho of Greece who, while absent from Athens during a tour of the Peloponnesus, was deposed in October 1862 by a hastily constituted provisional government: "I am foolish enough to regret that I have suffered the same fate as the king of Greece and that our pious friend, who was forever murmuring that I was for him the most important person in Hamburg, shut the door behind me as soon as I turned my back to go on a short trip [i.e., to Vienna]" (Brahms 1974/6, vol. 2, 8).

Brahms never resumed his earlier warm relations with Avé, although he did correspond with him occasionally, if only in connection with his arrangements for transferring money to his father. The latter remained in fairly regular contact with Avé and occasionally reported to Brahms on conversations he had had with him or transmitted messages from him. Thus, shortly prior to Brahms's arrival in Hamburg in January 1868, **Johann Jakob Brahms** wrote to say that Avé was hugely looking forward to seeing him, sent him many greetings, and wished him to know that his feelings toward him had not changed. It was Avé who informed him by telegram that his father was dying. Later, he used to send complimentary tickets for certain concerts or rehearsals to Jakob's widow, who mentioned his generosity in her correspondence with Brahms. But Brahms continued to nurse his grievance, as may be deduced from Clara Schumann's remark in a letter to him on 24 October 1877 that "Avé was very unhappy about your last letter, but I told him very frankly what I thought without mincing my words" (Litzmann 1970, vol. 2, 127). Further proof that Brahms never forgot is supplied by **Laura von Beckerath**, who reported in her diary entry for 24 June 1883 (at a time when she frequently saw Brahms, who was then staying at Wiesbaden) his rancorous remarks about "Herr Avé-Lallemant . . . and other Hamburg citizens, who always made important promises to him about a position in Hamburg, but who, when the time came, never gave him a thought" (Stephenson 1979, 30). Today it is easier to consider the matter more objectively (see, among other discussions, K. Hofmann's (1986) *Johannes Brahms und Hamburg: Neue Erkenntnisse zu einem alten Thema*).

Avé-Lallemant's niece Elisabeth Avé-Lallemant (1843–1925), a singer and teacher, was soprano soloist in the first Hamburg performance of Brahms's Requiem, which was given by the Singakademie, conducted by **Julius von Bernuth**, on 23 March 1869. (Avé-Lallemant 1878; Avins and Eisinger 2002; Brahms 1974/6; Hübbe 1902; K. Hofmann 1986; Stephenson 1979)

– B –

BACH, CARL PHILIPP EMANUEL (b. Weimar, 8 March 1714; d. Hamburg, 14 December 1788). Composer and keyboard player; son of **Johann Sebastian Bach** and his first wife, Maria Barbara.

In 1862 **August Cranz** published, under the title *Concerte für das Pianoforte*, Brahms's (anonymous) edition of Nos. 1, 4, and 5 of Bach's *VI Concerti per il cembalo* (Wotquenne 43/1, 43/4–5; Helm 471, 474–75). Two years later **Jakob Melcior Rieter-Biedermann** issued Brahms's (also anonymous) edition of Bach's Violin Sonatas in B Minor and C Minor (Wotquenne 76, 78; Helm 512, 514).

Brahms had long been interested in C. P. E. Bach's music, as he was in that of **Wilhelm Friedemann Bach** (see, for instance, Kalbeck 1976, vol. 1, 259, and Brahms's letters to Rieter-Biedermann of 5 February and 2 April 1859). When trying to persuade Rieter to publish the two violin sonatas, Brahms mentioned, in a letter in December 1863, that he had recently performed the one in C minor with **Joseph Hellmesberger** in Vienna at a concert of the Hellmesberger Quartet (on 6 December) and that the work had been much applauded. (Brahms 1974/14)

BACH, JOHANN SEBASTIAN (b. Eisenach, 21 March 1685; d. Leipzig, 28 July 1750). Composer. The veneration Brahms felt for Bach is amply documented. He came to know many of Bach's compositions through his lessons with **Otto Friedrich Willibald Cossel** and **Eduard Marxsen**, and continued to study his music throughout the remainder of his life. Moreover, he frequently performed it in public and in private (notably the *Goldberg Variations* and the Chromatic Fantasia and Fugue) and acquired the reputation of being an outstanding Bach player. Furthermore, he arranged some of Bach's compositions for the piano (see M. McCorkle 1984, Anhang Ia/1/3–5, Anhang Ia/9, and Anhang IIb/1); and he conducted many of Bach's works with his choir at Detmold, with the Vienna Singakademie, and at concerts of the Gesellschaft der Musikfreunde (in this connection, see M. McCorkle 1984, Anhang Ib/2–9). Lastly, he was an enthusiastic subscriber to the Leipzig Bach Edition: "Each volume is a new world for me" (Helms 1971, 17).

In short, from his youth until his final years, Brahms derived intense pleasure and drew profound consolation from Bach's music. In 1861 he wrote to **Clara Schumann** from Hamburg: "But you missed the most marvelous thing of all, a cantata by Bach, at the very first note of which one felt oneself being transported to high Heaven" (Litzmann 1970, vol. 1, 361). After he had learnt of his mother's death, he was discovered by **Josef Gänsbacher** playing the *Goldberg Variations* with tears streaming down his face. "This is like balm," he told Gänsbacher (Helms 1971, 35). When, many years later, he was himself close to death, he confided to **Anton Sistermans** that, while he could no longer listen to music, he still derived some enjoyment from looking through a Bach score. In fact, Sistermans saw just such a score on his piano, and Dr. **Robert Breuer**, who attended Brahms during the last night of his life, reported seeing the opened score of a Bach Motet on the piano (Kalbeck 1976, vol. 4, 484, 515). For a comprehensive study of Brahms's attitude to Bach's music, see S. Helm's study [1971] "Johannes Brahms und Johann Sebastian Bach." (Helms 1971; Kendall 1941; Litzmann 1970)

BACH, WILHELM FRIEDEMANN (b. Weimar, 22 November 1710; d. Berlin, 1 July 1784). Composer; son of **Johann Sebastian Bach** and his first wife, Maria Barbara. In 1864 **Jakob Melchior Rieter-Biedermann** published Brahms's (anonymous) edition of his *Concerto a duoi cembali concertanti* (Falck 10) under the title *Sonate für zwei Claviere*. (*See also* BACH, CARL PHILIPP EMANUEL.)

BAGGE, SELMAR (b. Coburg, 30 June 1823; d. Basle, 16 July 1896). Composer, critic, and teacher. After studying cello and piano in Prague, he was engaged as principal cellist at the municipal theater at Lemberg (Lviv, Ukraine). From 1842 to 1862 he lived in Vienna, where he received tuition in musical theory from **Simon Sechter** and later taught the subject at the conservatory (1851–55); in 1853 he also became organist of the Protestant church. In 1862 he moved to Leipzig, which he left in 1868 to take up the post of director of the newly founded conservatory at Basle where, in addition, he taught musical history and theory; from 1876 he also lectured at the university. His compositions include symphonies, chamber music, Masses, and songs. In addition, he was the editor of the following music journals, to which he also contributed: *Deutsche Musik-Zeitung* in Vienna (1860–62), the new series of the *Allgemeine musikalische Zeitung*, published by **Breitkopf & Härtel** in Leipzig (1863–65), and lastly the *Leipziger allgemeine musikalische Zeitung* published by **Jakob Melchior Rieter-Biedermann** (1866–68).

After meeting him in Vienna, **Clara Schumann** described him, in a letter to Brahms on 3 March 1860, as a highly cultured man who sought what was best and took a firm stand against the "Music of the Future" (to which, according to his biographer G. Eglinger, he remained hostile all his life). On the strength of Clara's letter, Brahms suggested to **Joseph Joachim** that Bagge should be invited to sign their "Declaration" against the new movement, but he added that, as editor of a journal, Bagge might prefer not to become publicly associated with the manifesto. It is not known whether he was in fact contacted; his name, in any case, did not appear on the document, which was prematurely published by the Berlin journal *Echo* on 6 May. When Brahms made Bagge's acquaintance later that year in Hamburg, he judged him to be a pleasant though not particularly brilliant man. "He was very [taken] with some of my pieces which I played to him," Brahms told Clara (Litzmann 1970, vol. 1, 334). Bagge thus showed an early appreciation for Brahms's compositions, and he was justified in later claiming that the *Deutsche Musik-Zeitung*, under his editorship, had been a champion of Brahms's music. This is not to say, however, that all of Brahms's compositions were to his taste. Thus, in reviewing the works performed at Brahms's first concert appearances in Vienna in November 1862, he expressed his admiration for the A Major Piano Quartet, but his dissatisfaction with the G minor one. In general, he discussed Brahms's compositions with discernment and understanding, and he would continue to do so after assuming responsibility for the *Allgemeine musikalische Zeitung* (but see below regarding his opinion of op. 36).

In response to a request for a contribution, Brahms sent Bagge his Fugue WoO 8, which duly appeared as a supplement to the *Allgemeine musikalische Zeitung* on 20 July 1864, even though he had not yielded to Bagge's plea to transpose the piece into an easier key, no doubt for the sake of the less proficient pianists among the journal's readers. The incident seems, however, to have left Brahms with some lingering irritation, for when, in

October of the same year, Breitkopf & Härtel declined to publish the *9 Lieder und Gesänge* (op. 32) and the *Magelone-Lieder*—partly on account of the fee he demanded, but mainly because of the difficulty of the piano accompaniment—he remarked caustically in a letter to Clara: "I should like to ask them which of the songs Bagge was unable to sight-read" (Litzmann 1970, vol. 1, 472). Bagge was indeed among the musicians routinely consulted by Breitkopf & Härtel on compositions submitted to them and the person whose opinion they most respected. This fact was to assume particular importance in the case of the String Sextet op. 36. In mid-September 1865 Brahms informed Breitkopf & Härtel that he had composed a new sextet and asked if they were interested in publishing it. They immediately accepted the offer without having seen the music, whereupon Brahms dispatched the manuscript to Leipzig. Some 10 days later he was mortified to receive a further communication asking him to release the firm from its commitment, in view of an adverse opinion expressed by an (unnamed) person. **Hermann Levi**, apprised of what had happened, attributed the volte-face to the influence of Bagge and **Carl Reinecke** (letter to Brahms of 7 October, Brahms 1974/7, 25–26). However, Clara Schumann eventually learned that Bagge alone bore the responsibility for it. On 22 December 1866 she wrote to Brahms: "I also know now who the ass was who told the Härtels that your second sextet 'was altogether too crazy for him.' After that, they sent it back to you. . . . I don't need to name him for you" (Litzmann 1970, vol. 1, 546). But evidently Brahms wanted clarification, for on 11 January 1867 she explained: "The ass is Bagge—!" (Litzmann 1970, vol. 1, 552). Some four years later, after speaking with Hermann Härtel, she was able to fill in the rest: "Härtel said that if Reinecke or Schleinitz had advised against publication that time, it would not have influenced their decision; but it was someone who holds you in high esteem, who always wrote in your support, etc. etc. That perplexed them. The ass was—Selmar Bagge!!!" (Litzmann 1970, vol. 1, 645–46).

The sextet was published by the firm N. Simrock in 1866 (*see* SIMROCK, PETER JOSEPH). Brahms never again offered a new composition to Breitkopf & Härtel. (Brahms 1974/7; Eglinger 1897; Litzmann 1910, 1970)

BARBI, ALICE (b. Modena, 1 June 1862; d. Rome, 4 November 1948). Mezzo-soprano, taught by L. Zamboni and A. Busi in Bologna and L. Vannuccini in Florence. She first made her mark at a concert in Milan on 2 April 1882, when she sang arias by **Handel**, **Haydn**, Jommelli, and Rossini. She was also an excellent violinist and a competent pianist, and generally very well educated, with a command of several languages. Eschewing the operatic stage, she became one of the outstanding concert singers of her time, with a special interest in early Italian music and a particular affinity with the German Lied. Her career took her to Russia, England, and Germany, as well as to Austria, where she created a sensation when she gave three concerts there in early 1889. Max Graf (1945) relates in *Legend of a Musical City* that, being quite unknown to the Viennese, she attracted no more than 80 persons to her initial concert, most of those benefitting from free tickets, but that her second and third concerts were sold out. According to Graf, "the combination of Italian sense of melody, southern beauty, true musical form and deep expression flowing from the soul was never more perfect than in this singer" (164). In addition to these qualities, she was said to possess a perfect technique, great vocal agility, evenness of tone, and a clear enunciation. In the *Neue freie Presse* (14 and 23 March 1889), **Eduard Hanslick** hailed her as a singer of outstanding merit and expressed the hope that she would soon return to Vienna; and she did, in fact, become a regular and an always welcome performer there. **Richard Heuberger** noted in his diary on 14 February 1890 that she had "once again caused a great sensation in Vienna" (Heuberger 1976, 44); and **Max Kalbeck** recalls that her concerts were invariably sold out several weeks in advance.

In March 1889, at the final one of that first series of Viennese concerts Barbi sang Brahms's "Liebestreu" (op. 3/10) and "Vergebliches Ständchen" (op. 84/4). In later years she was to become closely associated with his music. She once remarked to the pianist Emil Hess: "The more I sing him, the more I love him; he really is a very special world all by himself" (Hess 1962, 120). According to Kalbeck (1976), she was taken by Brahms's former pupil Marie Grün (née Geissler) to call on him during her stay in Vienna in March 1889, but did not then make a great impression on him, and it was not until Brahms heard her perform some of his own songs at a concert on 5 April 1892 that he came to recognize her superb artistry. "I never knew how beautiful my songs are," he told her afterward, adding, "If I were still young, I would now write love songs." And to a group of his friends he reported, in great excitement: "To-day, just now, I have heard my songs being sung for the first time" (vol. 4, 325–26). However, while he may not previously have properly appreciated her as an interpreter of his own compositions, there is clear evidence that he had become aware of her exceptional qualities well before then. In 1890 he told Heuberger: "We can all learn from someone like Barbi. [She] sings above all with uncommon control, strictly in time, and she strives above all to gain full awareness of the whole structure of the song she is performing" (Heuberger 1976, 44). He was so moved by her singing that he advised **Clara Schumann** to invite Barbi to her house in Frankfurt if she ever had the opportunity, and ask her to sing "some of her beautiful Italian things and also German Lieder" (Litzmann 1970, vol. 2, 406; Clara duly made her acquaintance in late 1890.)

Brahms was, moreover, far from insensitive to Barbi's striking physical appearance. Graf (1949) describes her as "a dark Italian beauty" with "dreamy black eyes" and "luxurious dark hair" (163). There is no doubt that Brahms felt attracted to her, and they were seen together in public on several occasions. A well-known snapshot, taken by an unknown photographer on 18 April 1892, shows them walking on the Ringstrasse just opposite the Imperial Hotel. It must be said that Barbi does not appear particularly beautiful in it, and she looks considerably older than her 30 years; but Kalbeck (1976) states categorically that the photograph entirely failed to do her justice (vol. 4, 328, n. 1). What Brahms really felt for her will, of course, never be known. But Marie Brüll (**Ignaz Brüll**'s widow) told Robert H. Schauffler that Brahms had confided to her that Barbi was the only woman he had ever really wanted to marry after he had reached "middle age"; also, according to Schauffler, Marie Brüll believed that Brahms actually proposed marriage to Barbi, but that she turned him down because he was old and she wanted children.

Instead, she was married at Menton on 30 January 1894 to Baron Boris Wolff-Stomersee (1850–1917), a Russian-born nobleman who, from 1879 to 1892, had been the secretary of Queen Olga of Württemberg, a daughter of Tsar Nicolas I. The marriage led Barbi to give up singing in public, except for charitable causes, but first she went to Vienna in December 1893 for three farewell concerts. (She had last sung there in March of that year.) At the final concert on 21 December, the audience was amazed and thrilled to see Brahms follow her onto the platform as her accompanist. **Ludwig Bösendorfer**, the owner of the concert hall, had arranged for the event to be recorded in a heliogravure (the artist's name is not known). But Graf, in recalling the memorable event, is mistaken in stating that this was an all-Brahms recital: the program announced compositions by **Georges Bizet**, Bononcini, Handel, Pergolesi, **Schubert**, and **Schumann**, in addition to Brahms's "An die Nachtigall" (op. 46/4), "Der Tod, das ist die kühle Nacht" (op. 96/1), "Ich muss hinaus" (op. 3/3), and "Meine Liebe ist grün" (op. 63/5).

After her wedding Barbi resided mostly in Russia and on the Italian Riviera. Nothing is known about later contacts between her and Brahms, other than that he appears to have met her on the occasion of a charity concert at which she sang in Vienna on 14 May 1895 (and at which some of his songs were again on the program). According to some writers (Franken 1991; Swafford 1997, 2001), she attended Brahms's funeral on 6 April 1897; indeed, according to Swafford, she was even the first of the mourners to throw a handful of dust into his grave. However, her presence is not mentioned by Kalbeck, nor is there any reference to her in the detailed account of the funeral, which appeared in the *Neue freie Presse* the next day. The following year Barbi gave two all-Brahms recitals in Vienna, on 30 March and 1 April 1898; the purpose of the first one was to collect funds for the proposed Brahms monument. She made some further appearances at charity concerts in Vienna in 1902, 1903, and 1905. In 1920, three years after her first husband's death, she married the Italian diplomat and statesman Marchese Pietro della Torretta (1873–1962).

Albert J. Gutmann, Barbi's Viennese concert agent, wrote of her in his memoirs: "There was a harmoniousness in her soul, in her heart, in her physical appearance, in her artistic performances. And this harmoniousness, which emanated from her like a magical charm, communicated itself in the concert hall also to the listener, to the entire audience" (Gutmann 1914, 100).

In 1932 a daughter from Barbi's first marriage, Alessandra (d. 1982), became the wife of Pietro della Torretta's nephew Giuseppe Tomasi di Lampedusa (1896–1957), who was to attain posthumous international fame through his novel *Il gattopardo*. (Franken 1991; Gutmann 1914; Graf 1945, 1949; Hess 1962; Heuberger 1976; Litzmann 1970; Schauffler 1972; Swafford 1997; Zapperi 1960)

BARGHEER, ADOLPH (CARL) (b. Bückeburg, 21 October 1840; d. 10 March 1901). Violinist; brother of **Carl Louis Bargheer**. On his musical studies, *see* BARGHEER, CARL LOUIS. He became, in turn, a member of the Detmold court Kapelle (1859–61), Konzertmeister at Münster (1861–66), and Konzertmeister at Basle, and was a professor at the conservatory there (1866–1901).

On 8 June 1874 he took part, with Brahms, **Friedrich Hegar**, and Moritz Kahnt, in a performance of Brahms's Piano Quartet op. 26 at a concert celebrating the golden jubilee of the Basle Gesangverein. (**Max Kalbeck** [1976], and more recently R. and K. Hofmann [1983], mistakenly state that it was Carl Bargheer who played on that occasion. That it was indeed Adolph—as would, in any case, seem logical—is confirmed by an account of the concert published in the *Basler Nachrichten* on 13 June.)

BARGHEER, CARL LOUIS (b. Bückeburg, 31 December 1831; d. Hamburg, 19 April 1902). Violinist, whose teachers included Spohr and **Ferdinand David**. He was also believed to have received instruction from **Joseph Joachim**, but according to Dieter Boeck, it was his brother **Adolph**

Bargheer who studied with Joachim, and not Carl himself. He was, in any case, on close terms with Joachim.

In 1850 Carl Bargheer joined the court Kapelle at Detmold. Five years later he received the title Kammermusicus, in 1860 he became Konzertmeister of the orchestra, and in 1862, following **August Kiel**'s dismissal, he advanced to the position of conductor. In 1864, finally, he was formally appointed court Kapellmeister. A great favorite of the music-loving **Prince Leopold III**, he also regularly played chamber music with **Princess Friederike**. While fulfilling his duties at Detmold to everyone's satisfaction, he gradually built up an international reputation and not only performed in major music centers in Germany, but also visited Holland, Belgium, England, and Russia. Following the abrupt dissolution of the orchestra by Leopold's successor, Prince Woldemar, at the beginning of 1876, he became Konzertmeister of the Hamburg Philharmonic Orchestra and also joined the faculty of the Hamburg conservatory; he occupied both positions until his death.

Brahms probably first met Bargheer at the Düsseldorf Music Festival in 1855. When he settled in Detmold in the autumn of 1857, Bargheer quickly became an intimate friend. Bargheer later recalled that Brahms, whose room at the hotel Stadt Frankfurt was only a few steps away from his own living quarters on the Marktplatz, would call on him every morning and that they would meet once more for lunch at the Stadt Frankfurt, after which they regularly went for a walk. In addition, they frequently played chamber music together. (Bargheer's manuscript "Erinnerungen an Johannes Brahms in Detmold 1857–1859," a rich source of information on Brahms's activities there, remains unpublished, but it has been thoroughly consulted by biographers, and especially by Willi Schramm (1983), who quotes extensively from it in his *Johannes Brahms in Detmold*.) Brahms maintained contact with Bargheer even after he had declined to renew his contract with Detmold in 1860, and when he visited the town in December 1865 he stayed with Bargheer. They were also to meet on various occasions elsewhere.

In 1861 Bargheer married Bertha Wagner, a friend of **Agathe von Siebold**. After her death (1876) he married Fanny Wöhler, another intimate friend of Agathe. (Boeck 1998; Müller-Dombois 1972; Schramm 1983)

BARGIEL, WOLDEMAR (b. Berlin, 3 October 1828; d. Berlin, 23 February 1897). Composer and teacher. Half brother of **Clara Schumann**, being the son of her mother Marianne (1797–1872) by the latter's second husband, music teacher August Adolf Bargiel (1783–1841). He received his musical instruction principally at the Leipzig conservatory, where he studied under Ignaz Moscheles, **Moritz Hauptmann**, **Julius Rietz**, and **Niels Gade**. After making a name for himself as a music teacher in Berlin, in 1859 he was invited to join the faculty of the Cologne conservatory. In 1865 he succeeded **Johannes Verhulst** as Kapellmeister and director of the Rotterdam branch of the Maatschappij tot Bevordering van Toonkunst [Association for the Promotion of Music]. Finally, from 1874 until his death he taught at the Hochschule für Musik in Berlin. He was, on the whole, more successful as a teacher than as a composer, although his works, which were greatly influenced by **Robert Schumann**, were quite widely performed in his lifetime. His output included compositions for the piano and chamber music (notably three piano trios), as well as some orchestral and choral works. Furthermore, he collaborated in the comprehensive **Chopin** and Schumann editions published by **Breitkopf & Härtel**.

Brahms met Bargiel quite early in his career; they appear to have taken to one another from the outset. In June 1854 Brahms asked **Joseph Joachim** to give his greetings to Bargiel "whom I long to see again" (Brahms 1974/5, vol. 1, 47); in his reply Joachim wrote that "Bargiel . . . greets you as warmly as he admires you" (Brahms 1974/5, vol. 1, 50). According to **Max Kalbeck** (1976), Bargiel was Brahms's constant companion on the latter's visits to art galleries during his stay in Berlin in the spring of 1858. Moreover, Bargiel dedicated one of his *Fantasias* for the piano (op. 19) to Brahms. They were to meet repeatedly during later years, usually in Clara Schumann's presence. (Brahms 1974/5; Sietz 1960a)

BARTH, (KARL) HEINRICH (b. Pillau, near Königsberg [Kaliningrad], 12 July 1847; d. Berlin, 23 December 1922). Pianist. His teachers included **Hans von Bülow**, **Hans Bronsart von Schellendorf**, and **Carl Tausig**. He taught in Berlin at the Stern Conservatory (from 1868), and at the Hochschule für Musik (1874–1921). In addition to concertizing as a solo pianist, he formed a highly regarded trio with Heinrich de Ahna and **Robert Hausmann**. At the latest, Barth met Brahms in November 1882 at the Fellingers' in Vienna (see **Richard Fellinger**'s [1997] *Klänge um Brahms*). Later he visited him at Ischl (where Brahms apparently showed him his new Intermezzi and Fantasies opp. 116–17 in 1892) and in Vienna (where, in January 1895, Barth played several of the items from opp. 117–19 at a concert). But Barth is of still greater interest to Brahmsians as one of the first pianists, and quite likely even the very first, after Brahms himself, to have played the Second Piano Concerto in public in Germany, at a concert of the Berlin Singakademie on 3 November 1882 (see the *Allgemeine deutsche Musik-Zeitung* of 10 November 1882; *see also* RÖNTGEN, JULIUS). (H. Ehrlich 1893a; R. Fellinger 1997)

BARTH, RICHARD (b. Gross-Wanzleben, near Magdeburg, 5 June 1850; d. Marburg, 25 December 1923). Violinist, conductor, teacher, and composer. An infant prodigy, he was obliged, before he was four years old, following an accident that severed several tendons in his left hand, to retrain with a view to transferring bowing to that hand and fingering to the right; he soon mastered the new technique. Between the ages of six and 10 he was taught by Franz Beck in Magdeburg, and it was in that town that he made his first public appearance when he was seven, playing a concerto by Charles-Auguste de Bériot. In 1863 he went to Hanover to study with **Joseph Joachim**, on whose recommendation he was, four years later, appointed Konzertmeister at Münster by the municipal music director, Joachim's friend **Julius Otto Grimm**. He held a similar post at Krefeld from 1881 until 1887, but before the end of that period chronic tendonitis had put an end to his flourishing career as a soloist, forcing him to confine himself to orchestral playing and chamber music. He subsequently served as university music director at Marburg (1887–94) before settling in Hamburg where he directed the philharmonic concerts (1894–1904), the Singakademie (from 1895), and the Teachers' Choral Society (1896–1913); in 1908 he was also placed in charge of the conservatory. He finally left Hamburg in 1922, by then a widower, to spend his remaining days with his daughter and son-in-law, Frida and Edmund Stengel, in Marburg (not in Magdeburg, as stated in Sadie 2001). Frida later put together an account of his life (published in *Lebensbilder aus Kurhessen und Waldeck, 1830–1930*), which summarizes, and slightly supplements with a few remarks about the final period of his life, the far more detailed autobiography he himself wrote out for his children and that forms the basis of K. Hofmann's (1979) *Johannes Brahms in den Erinnerungen von Richard Barth*.

Barth first caught sight of Brahms in Joachim's rooms at Hanover in July 1864, but it was some time later that he was actually introduced to him (perhaps at Bremen in April 1868, on the occasion of the performance of the Requiem, which he attended in Grimm's company). Several more years were to pass before he formed a closer relationship with Brahms. According to Barth's own statements, Brahms behaved most affably when he appeared at a concert at Münster in February 1876, but the real turning point occurred in Hamburg during the local Philharmonic Society's golden jubilee in September 1878, when they had several lengthy conversations. A further opportunity for greater intimacy was provided by Brahms's visit to Bremen six months later for another performance of his Requiem (11 April 1879), and it was on that occasion that, at **Karl Reinthaler**'s house, Brahms played for Barth on piano extracts from his recently composed

Violin Concerto, the work that was to firmly cement their association. When Brahms next visited Münster on 6 January 1880, they played it together at Grimm's house, and Brahms was so delighted with Barth's interpretation and his cadenza that shortly afterward he warmly recommended him to **Alwin von Beckerath** who was looking for a suitable soloist for a performance of the work at Krefeld. This eventually took place on 25 January 1881, and afterward Brahms reportedly said to **Rudolf von der Leyen**: "I cannot imagine a more beautiful performance of the violin concerto than Barth's—he really was born with a violin" (K. Hofmann 1979b, 28). On the following day Barth took part in performances of the String Sextet op. 18 and (together with Brahms) of the Piano Quintet at a chamber music concert. Brahms then arranged for Barth to perform the Violin Concerto under his direction in Amsterdam on 31 January and at Haarlem on 5 February.

There is thus no doubt about Brahms's genuine enthusiasm for Barth's violin playing. Further proof of his admiration is furnished by his recommendation of Barth in May 1881 for the position of Konzertmeister at Cologne, in succession to Otto von Königslöw. "I cannot think of anyone more eligible as musician, man, and virtuoso in this case," he assured **Ferdinand Hiller** (Sietz 1958–70, vol. 4, 162). In the event, the post was offered to Gustav Hollaender, but Brahms's support later helped Barth to secure the post of Konzertmeister at Krefeld and the more prestigious appointments in Marburg and Hamburg. Among the highlights of their musical association were the long sessions of chamber music at **Laura von Beckerath**'s house at Rüdesheim in September 1889, when, in the course of three days, no fewer than 16 works were performed, among them the newly revised version of Brahms's Piano Trio op. 8, which was played by Brahms, Barth, and **Wilhelm Engelmann**. As he took his leave, Brahms said to Barth: "My dear Barth, I just want to tell you that you have played more beautifully than anyone else in the world" (K. Hofmann 1979b, 44). In 1892 he presented Barth with the manuscript of the opening movement of his A Major Violin Sonata.

In Marburg (where, on 2 February 1894, he conducted the Requiem) and especially in Hamburg, where he had far superior musicians and singers at his disposal, Barth devoted himself to making Brahms's music better known. In the course of his 10 seasons as director of the Philharmonic Orchestra, he performed the major orchestral and, with the help of the Singakademie, the most important choral works, all of them at least once (the First and Fourth Symphonies he conducted three times each). Barth met Brahms for the last time, and for their final joint music making, at the **Weyermanns** in May 1896, following the funeral of **Clara Schumann**. In a letter to Brahms on 27 March 1897 he expressed the hope that they might see each other during a visit he was planning to make to Vienna that May. He does not appear to have attended the funeral on 6 April, but two days later, in Hamburg, he conducted a memorial concert arranged by the Verein Hamburgischer Musikfreunde [the Society of Hamburg Music Lovers], which had been founded on his initiative; the program comprised the *Tragic Overture*, *Schicksalslied*, two of the *4 ernste Gesänge* sung by E. C. Newman, as well as the final chorus from **Bach**'s *St. Matthew Passion* and **Beethoven**'s "Eroica" Symphony. The first philharmonic concert of the following season (22 October 1897) was also dedicated to Brahms's memory and featured the Requiem and the First Symphony. Barth's penultimate appearance as director of the Philharmonic Orchestra (4 March 1904) was likewise entirely devoted to Brahms (the Fourth Symphony, *4 ernste Gesänge*, the two minuets from the Serenade op. 11, some songs and vocal duets and the *Academic Festival Overture*); and Barth presented yet another all-Brahms concert, this time with the Singakademie, on the evening of 7 May 1909 to celebrate the unveiling of **Max Klinger**'s Brahms statue earlier that day (on the program: a chorus from the Requiem, the *Haydn Variations*, *Schicksalslied*, and the First Symphony). Barth last conducted the Requiem on 21 November 1917, also in Hamburg. In 1904 he published some lectures he had given on Brahms ("Johannes Brahms und seine Musik"), and in 1912 Brahms's correspondence with **Julius Otto Grimm**. His own published compositions ran to 27 opus numbers. They include, notably, a number of songs and some chamber music. (Barth 1904; K. Hofmann 1979b; Sietz 1958–70; Stengel 1958)

BAUER, JULIUS (b. Raab-Sziget, 15/22 October 1853; d. Vienna, 11 June 1941). Writer, journalist, and librettist. He began his journalistic career as a contributor to the satirical *Neuer Kikeriki*, subsequently worked on several other periodicals, and eventually became a highly influential theater critic on the *Illustriertes Wiener Extrablatt*. Together with Hugo Widmann he wrote the librettos for Carl Millöcker's operettas *Der arme Jonathan* (premiere; Theater an der Wien, 4 January 1890) and *Das Sonntagskind* (Theater an der Wien, 16 January 1892), and for **Johann Strauss**'s *Fürstin Ninetta* (Theater an der Wien, 10 January 1893).

A witty conversationalist, he was regularly seen in Brahms's company at Ischl. According to **Max Kalbeck** (1976), they enjoyed a very special relationship, each delighting in teasing the other. On one occasion Bauer addressed Brahms as "the greatest Schimpfoniker in the world" (a play on words, "Symphoniker" meaning "symphonist" and "schimpfen" meaning "to grumble, bitch, curse"). Bauer also wrote an amusing poem describing a concert that, among other works, had featured Brahms's Fourth Symphony. The poem has been published by Kurt and Renate Hofmann (1997) in *Über Brahms: Von Musikern, Dichtern und Liebhabern. Eine Anthologie*. (Czeike 1992–97; Hofmann and Hofmann 1997)

BAUMANN, ALEXANDER (MORITZ) (b. Vienna, 7 February 1814; d. Graz, 25 December 1857). Playwright, librettist, poet, and songwriter. His comedies and Singspiele and poems in dialect enjoyed considerable success; six of the plays were produced at the Burgtheater. As for his songs, for most of which he invented both the words and the music and which he liked to perform at private gatherings, accompanying himself on the zither, they were so highly appreciated that between 1842 and 1856 he published nine sets of six songs each, under the overall title *Gebirgsbleameln* [a dialect term signifying "Mountain Flowers"]. Since he was apparently incapable of writing down the music on paper himself, his friend the composer, conductor, and singer Benedikt Randhartinger had jotted down the melodies while listening to him and had also arranged the accompaniments. (The texts of these 54 songs were reprinted in 1857, together with 12 other poems, under the title *Aus der Heimath*).

For the piano accompaniment of his celebrated "Wiegenlied" (op. 49/4), which Brahms offered to **Bertha Faber** upon the birth of her son Hans in 1868, he drew significantly on the Ländler, which formed the accompaniment to Baumann's song "S'is anderscht" [It's otherwise than you think]. He had heard Bertha sing it when she was staying in Hamburg in 1859, and it had remained in his memory, for, as is evident from the letter that he sent together with the song, he did not possess a copy of it; in fact, he now asked Bertha to supply him with the music and the text. According to Baumann's biographer Walther Jaffé, the melody of "S'is anderscht" was probably not an original one but had been taken by Baumann from an actual folk song. (Jaffé 1913; Kahler 1985; Bottge 2005)

BAUMAYER, MARIE (b. Cilli [Celje, Slovenia], 12 July 1851; d. Vienna, 23 January 1931). Pianist and teacher. A pupil of **Julius Epstein** and **Clara Schumann**, she was generally considered an excellent pianist and was reportedly one of the few women pianists whom Brahms regarded with favor. She performed both his piano concertos with great success. On one occasion, in the course of a discussion about female pianists, Brahms observed to **Richard Heuberger**: "Baumayer is far too musical to be a good woman pianist" (Heuberger 1976, 21). The remark was evidently meant as a compliment.

Brahms knew her well, for she frequently participated in music making at the **Fellingers**' and **Wittgensteins**', and he also met her in more formal musical settings. On 24 November 1886, for instance, he and **Robert Hausmann** gave the first public performance of his Cello Sonata op. 99 at one of her concerts. She frequently played, both in private and in public, with her close friend **Marie Soldat**.

Marie Baumayer has been widely credited with making Brahms's compositions better known and appreciated in Vienna. Pianist and critic Heinrich Ehrlich (1893a) wrote of her: "Her artistic realm is Vienna, her special domain Brahms" (16). (Ehrlich 1893a; Heuberger 1976)

BAYROS, FRANZ WILHELM, MARQUIS DE (b. Agram [Zagreb, Croatia], 28 May 1866; d. Vienna, 2 April 1924). Painter, graphic artist, and illustrator; his style was influenced by Aubrey Beardsley and Alfons Mucha. Among the major works he illustrated were *The Thousand and One Nights* and Boccaccio's *Il decamerone*; he was also known for his portraits of fashionable women.

In 1894 Bayros painted the celebrated *Ein Abend bei Johann Strauss*, which Adèle Strauss presented to her husband on the occasion of the 50th anniversary of his first appearance at Dommayer's Casino on 15 October 1844. The painting depicts a gathering of **Johann Strauss**'s friends and relatives at his house at 4 Igelgasse. (The site of the house, which was destroyed during an air raid in World War II, corresponded to the present 4 Johann-Strauss-Gasse). The painting includes a remarkably good likeness of Brahms. Among other persons depicted are **Karl Goldmark**, the pianist Alfred Grünfeld, **Max Kalbeck**, and **Victor Tilgner**. Bayros also portrayed himself among the guests, but when his marriage to Adèle's daughter Alice broke down (*see* STRAUSS, JOHANN), Adèle was reportedly so angry that she had his face painted over with somebody else's.

The painting is currently exhibited at the Johann Strauss memorial site at 54 Praterstrasse in Vienna, on loan from its owner, Bank Austria. The museum has been established in the flat that, except for a brief interruption in 1871, served Strauss as a place of residence between 1867 and 1874. (Catalog of the "Johann Strauss-Gedenkstätte," Vienna; Czeike 1992–97)

BECHSTEIN. Firm of piano makers founded in Berlin in 1853 by Friedrich Wilhelm Carl Bechstein (b. Gotha, 1 June 1826; d. Berlin, 6 March 1900). In 1856 he produced his first grand, which was inaugurated by **Hans von Bülow**. His reputation grew steadily during the next decades, as did his annual output of instruments, which rose from 300 in the 1860s to 3,000 in the 1890s.

Brahms is known to have played on a Bechstein grand in Berlin in 1868, and pianos made by the Berlin firm were among those on which he performed most frequently at concerts outside Austria during the 1870s and

1880s. His high opinion of Bechstein grands is particularly well documented for the period during which he brought his Second Piano Concerto before the public. After Brahms had tried it out on a Bechstein at Meiningen in October 1881, Bülow, who had conducted, reported to the manufacturer that Brahms had been very pleased with the instrument. In mid-November Brahms wrote to **Julius Otto Grimm**, in preparation for a performance of the concerto at Münster (not Stuttgart, as stated by G. S. Bozarth and S. H. Brady [2000] in their article "Johannes Brahms and his Pianos"): "Would you be so good as to enquire in Cologne or elsewhere whether one could not send us a Bechstein or a **Steinway**? I shall gladly pay for the transportation costs. But I will not play again on some undependable or unreliable instrument" (Brahms 1974/4, 144; the last remark is evidently not a denigration of the Bösendorfer grand on which he had played the concerto for the first time in Budapest a week earlier; it was probably aimed at some of the pianos with which he had been provided at earlier concerts in Germany.) In a similar vein, he inquired hopefully soon afterward (30 December) in a letter to **Julius von Bernuth**, with whom he was due to perform the concerto in Hamburg, whether he might expect to find "a very good and *powerful* Bechstein (or American Steinway)" waiting for him (Avins 1997, 586). And some two years later (11 December 1883) he asked **Franz Wüllner** to find him a "most excellent" Bechstein for their forthcoming performance of the D Minor Concerto in Berlin, and for another one planned for Dresden (Brahms 1974/15, 114).

Incidentally, the Bechstein Saal, for the opening of which Brahms traveled to Berlin in October 1892, was not built by F. W. C. Bechstein as may be thought, but by the well-known concert agent **Hermann Wolff**, who decided to name it after the piano maker with whom he was on very friendly terms. On 4 October the first recital in the new hall was given by Bülow; the second, on the following day, by Brahms and the Joachim Quartet; the third, on 6 October, by **Anton Rubinstein**. (On the other hand, the Bechstein Hall that opened in London in 1901 really did owe its existence to the piano firm, which occupied adjoining premises; it was renamed the Wigmore Hall in 1917.) (Avins 1997; Bozarth and Brady 2000; Brahms 1974/4, 1974/15)

BECKER, CLARA (MARIA JACOBINA), née Winne (bapt. Erfurt, 24 June 1802; d. Baden-Baden, 30 January 1881). In 1853, by which time she was a widow (her late husband, Wolfgang Becker, had been a lawyer), she bought a house at Lichtental, Baden-Baden (Unterbeuern 14, now 8 Hauptstrasse), which she sold in October 1862 to **Clara Schumann**. Subsequently, she acquired the so-called Haus am Hügel [House on the Hill, now

85 Maximilianstrasse] in which she lived until her death. It was there that Brahms, who visited Baden-Baden briefly in 1862 and 1863 and spent three months there in 1864, was to rent rooms from May to November 1865.

Brahms enjoyed the quiet and attractive location of Clara Becker's house, was extremely pleased with the accommodations, and delighted in the splendid views that his rooms commanded of the beautiful surrounding countryside. In short, he found the conditions ideal for composition, and during the six months he spent there in 1865 he wrote, notably, the Horn Trio op. 40 and completed the String Sextet op. 36 and the Cello Sonata op. 38. It is therefore not surprising that he returned to Frau Becker's house repeatedly during his later stays at Baden-Baden—namely, in 1866, 1869, 1871–73, and 1876—and that he usually took rooms for lengthy periods. Among the major compositions on which he worked there are the *Alto Rhapsody*, the Requiem, *Schicksalslied*, *Triumphlied*, the *Liebeslieder-Walzer*, and the First Symphony. Naturally, Clara Schumann's presence at Baden-Baden was also, especially during the earlier years, a major reason for his visits to this area.

The fact that Brahms, during a short stay in 1875 and a longer one in 1877, stayed in a hotel in the town need not be interpreted as reflecting strained relations with Clara Becker; most probably her rooms had been let by the time he decided, at a rather late stage, to head for Baden-Baden. Everything suggests that he was always on good terms with her and she, in turn, had fond feelings for her famous lodger. In June 1878 **Felix Otto Dessoff** wrote from the "Villa Becker" to Brahms, who had that year chosen Pörtschach for his summer quarters: "I get on splendidly with Mother Becker. She is well, sends you her greetings . . . and is looking forward with tremendous pleasure to your arrival. Yesterday she confided to me that she would have wept if you weren't coming" (Brahms 1974/16, 178). Brahms replied: "First of all, I must send greetings to the Villa Becker. I have spent many a happy hour and written much fine music there, both sad and merry" (Brahms 1974/16, 181). He appears to have been planning at the time to take up residence at the "Villa Becker" himself that autumn, but in the end he did not visit Baden-Baden that year; and, in fact, he never stayed at Clara Becker's house again. He did return to Baden-Baden after her death, though, but only briefly, in 1883, 1887, and 1889, putting up at a hotel each time. (Clara Schumann sold her house in 1879, but afterward returned to Baden-Baden several more times.)

Clara Becker's heiress Luise Müller eventually sold the house to a family in whose possession it remained for many years. In 1963, by which time it was in a generally run-down state, there was talk of demolishing it. The news was greeted with dismay and indignation by many Brahms lovers, and in December 1966 the Brahms Gesellschaft Baden-Baden was formed for the purpose of preserving the house. With the help of donations and proceeds from concerts, the society managed to purchase it in June 1967, and after renovation the "Brahmshaus," as it was now called, was opened to the public the following June. The visitor can see not only the rooms that Brahms occupied, but also a number of documents and objects associated with him. (Brahms 1974/16; Heermann 1935)

BECKER, HUGO (JEAN OTTO ERIC) (b. Strasbourg, 13 February 1863; d. Geiselgasteig, near Munich, 30 July 1941). German cellist and teacher; son of **Jean Becker**. His teachers included, apart from his father, Alfredo Piatti and Jules de Swert. When he was only 15 he joined the orchestra of the Mannheim National Theatre, and subsequently he became solo cellist at the Frankfurt Opera (1884–86). Later he had an outstanding career as a soloist as well as in chamber music (in this connection, *see also* BECKER, JEAN); from 1890 to 1896 he was a member of the Heermann Quartet. On 7 March 1897 he gave the first Viennese performance of **Antonín Dvořák**'s Cello Concerto. From 1887 he taught at the Hoch Conservatory in Frankfurt, where he was a colleague of **Clara Schumann**; in 1909 he was appointed to the faculty of the Hochschule für Musik in Berlin. Among his pupils were Beatrice Harrison, Enrico Mainardi, and Rudolf Metzmacher.

Brahms is known to have played together with Hugo Becker both in private and in public. On 25 June 1887 they performed the Cello Sonata op. 99 and, with **Hugo Heermann**, the Piano Trio op. 101 before a small number of invited guests at Clara Schumann's house in Frankfurt. Later that year, Hugo Becker was among the people Brahms invited to the run-through of his Double Concerto at the Kurhaus at Baden-Baden (23 September 1887). In 1890, Brahms rehearsed his recently revised Trio op. 8 with Becker and Heermann at Clara Schumann's (on 18 March) and subsequently performed it with them at a museum concert on 23 March. Incidentally, the earliest known performances of the first three of the Fantasien op. 116 and of the second of the Intermezzi op. 117 are those given by **Ignaz Brüll** at Hugo Becker's concert in Vienna on 30 January 1893. It is a measure of Brahms's admiration for Becker that, as Heermann relates in his autobiography, Brahms advised him to play his Double Concerto only with Becker.

BECKER, JEAN (b. Mannheim, 11 May 1833; d. Mannheim, 10 October 1884). Violinist. He received instruction from his father Karl who ran his own dance band, from Hugo Hildebrandt, and from the Konzertmeister at the Mannheim National Theatre Aloys Kettenus, whose position he later occupied (1855–65). During that time Becker began touring as a virtuoso violinist, and eventually he would concertize throughout Europe. He also turned increasingly to chamber music. The Quartetto Fiorentino, which he founded in 1865 with Enrico Masi, Luigi Chiostri, and Friedrich Hilpert (who, in 1875, would be replaced by Louis Spitzer-Hegyesi), became one of the most celebrated groups of that period; it was disbanded in 1880. Subsequently, Becker performed for a time with a quartet consisting of himself and his three children, Jeanne, Hans, and **Hugo**.

Becker's interest in Brahms's music goes back at least as far as 1863; on 10 June of that year he played the A Major Piano Quartet with **Clara Schumann**, J. Naret-Koning, and cellist Léon Jacquard at her new house at Baden-Baden. According to **Max Kalbeck** (1976), Brahms himself played with the Quartetto Fiorentino at Baden-Baden in 1866, and on 10 June 1869 he performed his Piano Quartet op. 26 with Becker and members of his quartet at Clara Schumann's house. In a letter to **Fritz Simrock** written shortly afterward, he tried to persuade the publisher to visit Baden-Baden later that summer because "at that time the Becker (Florentine) Quartet will be here and will perhaps play for you new items for your publishing house" (Brahms 1974/9, vol. 1, 75; apparently a reference to the op. 51 quartets). Kalbeck states in a note to his edition of the Brahms-Simrock correspondence that it was the private performance of these works by the Florentine Quartet that convinced Brahms that they were not yet ready for publication. In 1870 the quartet visited Vienna; Brahms was among the invited guests when it played at **Theodor Billroth**'s shortly before Christmas. (Brahms 1974/9)

BECKERATH, VON, FAMILY. Memmonite family that settled at Krefeld in the late 17th century and engaged in the linen trade, and later the silk trade, as well as in banking. The following are of special interest to biographers of Brahms:

(FRANZ) RUDOLF VON BECKERATH (1833–88). Vintner, residing at Rüdesheim and Wiesbaden. His grandfather Leonhard von Beckerath (1759–1847), after working for the **Von der Leyens**, set up as an independent wine merchant; his father Wilhelm von Beckerath (1800–65), a vintner and also a keen amateur musician, married Amalie Wolff (1802–63), a daughter of Krefeld's first music director Johann Nikolaus Wolff. Rudolf was himself an excellent violinist and even owned a Stradivarius; his wife **LAURA**, née Deus (1840–1921), was a very good pianist.

It was probably through **Fritz Simrock** that Brahms made Rudolf's acquaintance, at the Lower Rhine Music Festival of May 1874 at the latest, after which he stayed as a guest at the couple's estate at Rüdesheim. Two months later, by which time he had taken up his summer quarters at Rüschlikon, he joined Rudolf and Simrock in a week's excursion to the Swiss Alps. He subsequently remained in contact with Rudolf and his wife, mostly by correspondence, but there were also personal meetings, as when Rudolf traveled to Mannheim in November 1876 to hear Brahms conduct his new First Symphony. Moreover, it was Rudolf who conveyed the invitation from the Krefeld music society to Brahms in 1879; at the concert on 20 January 1880 he played among the violins. The summer of 1883 brought them still closer when Brahms decided to spend several months at Wiesbaden. During that time he visited the Von Beckeraths almost daily at their flat in the town and occasionally stayed with them at Rüdesheim; there was much private music making. (Laura's diary, from which K. Stephenson [1979] quotes in his memoir *Johannes Brahms und die Familie von Beckerath*, provides a most interesting record of those days.) Brahms renewed his contact with the couple when he returned to Wiesbaden in January 1884, mainly for a performance of the Third Symphony, which he had composed there the previous year. After Rudolf's death, Brahms continued to correspond with Laura, and he was her guest at Rüdesheim in February 1895. He last saw her at Whitsun 1896, when both were staying with the **Weyermanns** near Bonn. He had always loved Rhine wines, and the Von Beckeraths had occasionally sent him some from their vineyard at Rüdesheim; Laura did so once more at Christmas that year.

Rudolf and Laura's younger son, **WILLY VON BECKERATH** (1868–1938), a painter and, from 1907, a professor at the Hamburg Academy, has endeared himself to Brahms enthusiasts by the sketches and drawings he made on different occasions of Brahms conducting or playing the piano. He also painted two portraits of Brahms, in 1911 and 1928, and, furthermore, enhanced **Gustav Ophüls**'s edition of the texts set to music by Brahms, most notably by the striking Brahms medallion that served as the frontispiece of the second edition (1908). Willy had several excellent opportunities to observe Brahms, for the last time at the Weyermanns' at Whitsun 1896.

Rudolf's brother **ALWIN VON BECKERATH** (1849–1930), an uncle of **Rudolf von der Leyen** (and, through his marriage to the latter's sister Hedwig Marie, also his brother-in-law), likewise enjoyed very cordial relations with Brahms. A highly competent violinist and violist, he took a very active part in the musical life at Krefeld; his wife was an excellent pianist. He had the distinction of participating in the world premiere of one of Brahms's compositions, namely *2 Gesänge* for contralto, viola, and piano (op. 91) at Krefeld on 30 January 1885; the pianist was Brahms himself, the contralto Auguste Hohenschild. (*See also* WOLFF, LEONHARD regarding Alwin's association with the Horn Trio op. 40.) Alwin met Brahms repeatedly, and not only at Krefeld—for instance, in Cologne in 1890, in Berlin in October 1892 (where he attended the opening concerts at the new Bechstein Saal), and finally at the Weyermanns' in May 1896.

In his "Erinnerungen an Johannes Brahms," Alwin's son **HEINRICH [HEINZ] VON BECKERATH** (1876–1940) drew extensively on the detailed notes made by his father on his contacts with Brahms. Of particular interest is Alwin's description of that memorable final meeting with Brahms at the Weyermanns' house at Bad Honeff; it forms a valuable complement to the account given by Ophüls. Further fascinating recollections of those days at the Hagerhof can be found in a letter written by Alwin to **Eugenie Schumann** in 1826, from which Heinz von Beckerath also quotes at length. His article is illustrated with several photographs taken by himself on that occasion showing Brahms either alone or with other people; it also contains the text of a number of letters addressed by Brahms to Alwin. (Beck 1979; Beckerath 1958; Fusner 1983; E. Ophüls 1992; Stephenson 1979)

BEETHOVEN, LUDWIG VAN (b. Bonn, baptized 17 December 1770; d. Vienna, 26 March 1827). Composer. In her *Werkverzeichnis*, M. L. McCorkle (1984) cites, among works by other composers edited by Brahms (Anhang VI/4), the edition of Beethoven's Piano Sonata in A-flat (op. 110), which appeared in Series XVI, vol. 3, of the collected works published by **Breitkopf & Härtel** in 1862–65. A similar statement had been made by K. Hofmann (1975) in the section "Revisions and Editions of Works by other Composers" (no. 196) of *Die Erstdrucke der Werke von Johannes Brahms*, except that here Brahms is said to have undertaken the revision "together with **Carl Reinecke**."

Both McCorkle and Hofmann refer in this connection to Letters 60 and 61 of the published correspondence between Brahms and Breitkopf & Härtel (Brahms 1974/14). In fact, though, these letters do not bear out the assertion that Brahms edited the sonata or collaborated in its edition. The first letter, probably written on 5 April 1862, accompanied the dispatch by Brahms of a copy of the sonata that appeared to bear corrections in Beethoven's own hand and might therefore prove useful in the preparation of the new edition. In their reply on 8 April, the publishers thanked Brahms warmly for "having thought of us with regard to our edition of Beethoven's works," expressed their conviction that the corrections on the copy had been made by Beethoven himself, and added: "It will certainly be of interest for comparison. We are handing it over for this purpose to Kapellmeister **Reinecke**" (Brahms 1974/14, 67). There is thus no indication in the correspondence that Brahms did more with regard to the edition than make the copy available to the publishers. It was returned to him in due course and was still in his possession at the time of his death. It is now preserved in the archive of the Gesellschaft der Musikfreunde in Vienna. (Brahms 1974/14)

BEHRENS, ADOLPH (b. Manchester, 24 June 1833; d. Richmond, Surrey, 16 March 1896). Wealthy music lover and patron; grandson of Levi Fuld Behrens (1744–1834) of Hamburg, and son of Solomon Levi Behrens (1788–1873), who settled in Manchester in 1814 and there founded the textile business S. L. Behrens & Co. Adolph's death certificate records his occupation as stockholder.

In April 1896 **Joseph Joachim** informed Brahms that a certain Adolph Behrens, who had recently died in England, had bequeathed to Brahms the sum of 1,000 pounds (10,000 gulden) as a token of his "gratitude and sincere admiration"; he had made similar bequests to Joachim himself and to **Woldemar Bargiel**, who had once taught him music in Cologne. Behrens, Joachim wrote, had been a "noble and splendid person," a man entirely devoted to the arts and sciences. Having made Behrens's acquaintance at Pau 30 years ago, he had been in the habit of visiting Behrens whenever he was himself in London, as he held him in high esteem as "the perfect model of a gentleman" ["als vollendetes Muster eines Gentleman"]. Behrens, a bachelor, had been confined to his room by illness for the last 20 years of his life. The Behrens family, Joachim added, had resided in England for the past generation and was extremely rich (Brahms 1974/6, 301–2).

Behrens's gesture delighted Brahms. "That a man I don't know and who moreover has never, as far as I am aware, even addressed a letter to me, should honor me in this fashion moves me most profoundly and sincerely," he wrote to Joachim (Brahms 1974/6, 303). But Brahms's memory was at fault: Behrens had, in fact, contacted him 23 years earlier. On 3 April 1873 Brahms informed Joachim that a "Herr Ad. Behrens of London" had recently sent him a very cordial letter and, with it, "a rare book"; since the letter bore no address, he was unable to acknowledge the gift himself, and he accordingly requested Joachim (who was in London at the time) to convey his thanks to Behrens.

There is a further, and no less significant, reference to Behrens in the Brahms-Joachim correspondence, which Brahms had evidently likewise forgotten. It concerns the earliest English performances of the Clarinet Trio (on 2 and 4 April 1892) and the Clarinet Quintet (on 28 March, 2 April, and 4 April 1892). Joachim reported on these performances to Brahms on 5

April, explaining that **Richard Mühlfeld**'s participation had been made possible by the "splendid Adolph Behrens," who had assumed the expenses (meaning presumably Mühlfeld's traveling costs and fee). Joachim added that he was the same, unfortunately physically seriously disabled, admirer of Brahms "who many years ago offered to have your *Deutsches Requiem* copied and performed at his expense, which now sounds rather bizarre!" (Brahms 1974/6, 276). Confirmation that such an offer was indeed made is provided by a letter **Clara Schumann** wrote to Brahms from London on 26 February 1867. In it she expressed regret that Brahms appeared to have given up all serious efforts to arrange for a performance of the Requiem in Vienna or Berlin, and she added that Joachim, who was also in London at the time, had asked her to inform Brahms that "a great music lover, an Englishman" whom he had met in France had enquired whether Brahms would accept a contribution of 1,000 francs toward the cost of a performance. The donor, though not named, was clearly Adolph Behrens. Clara added that she found "nothing at all wounding" in the offer (Litzmann 1970, vol. 1, 554–55). Brahms's response is not known, but there is no evidence that he ever took the money, nor is there any indication that Behrens ever subsidized the first English performances of the Requiem. For the record, the earliest such performance was a private one conducted by **Julius Stockhausen** (who also sang in it) on 10 July 1871 in Lady Thompson's London drawing room at 35 Wimpole Street, on which occasion the accompaniment, in the arrangement for piano duet, was played by Cipriani Potter and the hostess—who, prior to her marriage to the surgeon Henry (later Sir Henry) Thompson, had been a successful professional pianist under her maiden name Kate Loder. On 1 April 1873 a public rehearsal of the first, second, and fifth movements by students of the Royal Academy of Music was conducted by John Pyke Hullah at the Hanover Square Rooms. It was followed the next day by a performance of the whole work by the Philharmonic Society under William George Cusins at St. James's Hall.

To return to the legacy bequeathed to Brahms in 1896: In May Adolph's brother Edward (1836–1905) wrote to inform Brahms that he and his brother Frank (1839–1902) were holding the sum at his disposal, which Adolph had wished him to regard as "a slight token of gratitude and admiration of your art" (the letter is now in the archive of the Gesellschaft der Musikfreunde in Vienna). Brahms used the money for various donations, the most important being a gift of 6,000 gulden to the Gesellschaft der Musikfreunde.

Adolph Behrens was related to Jacob Behrens (1806–89), who founded a textile firm at Leeds and later another at Bradford; Jacob was knighted in 1882. An obituary in the *Bradford Observer* on 23 April 1889 described him as a "warm-hearted philanthropist." His son Gustav (1846–1936), who became a prosperous Manchester businessman, played a highly significant role in the history of the Hallé Orchestra. (Biba 1987; Brahms 1974/6; Jenkins 2004; Litzmann 1970. Information supplied by several members of the Behrens family is also gratefully acknowledged.)

BERLIOZ, (LOUIS) HECTOR (b. La Côte-St.-André, Isère, 11 December 1803; d. Paris, 8 March 1869). Composer. Brahms made his acquaintance and first heard several of his works when Berlioz, at **Joseph Joachim**'s invitation, gave two concerts at Hanover on 8 and 15 November 1853. They met again at Leipzig the following month. On 4 December, at a reception offered by **Karl Franz Brendel**, Berlioz heard Brahms play some of his compositions. "Brams [sic] is having a great success here," he wrote to Joachim a few days later. "He impressed me very much the other day at Brindel's [sic], with his Scherzo [op. 4] and his Adagio [the Andante from either op. 1 or op. 5]. I thank you for introducing me to this bold and yet very shy young man, who has taken it into his head to write new music. He will suffer much" (Berlioz 1972, 418). Brahms, for his part, reported to Joachim that Berlioz had expressed such admiration for his music that the other persons present could do no more than express similar enthusiasm. He added that Berlioz had been equally friendly at Moscheles' two days later. Arnold Schloenbach, in an account of the reception at Brendel's published in the *Neue Zeitschrift für Musik* on 9 December, relates that Berlioz was so greatly moved that he threw his arms around Brahms "and pressed him to his heart" (Schloenbach 1853). On 10 December Brahms attended one of Berlioz's concerts in Leipzig.

Richard Heuberger (1976) states in his diary that during a conversation on 25 November 1888 Brahms told him that when he and Joachim were preparing their manifesto against **Liszt** and the New German Music (in 1860), Berlioz wrote to indicate his support (38). While no documentary evidence appears to exist to bear this out, it is well known that while Berlioz enjoyed excellent personal relations with Liszt, he did not think very highly of Liszt's compositions; he objected, moreover, to being labeled a representative of the "Music of the Future,'" as he had been by Brendel.

Understandably, Brahms retained a pleasant memory of his contacts with Berlioz in 1853 (in 1879 he still spoke warmly about them to Heuberger), and he probably met him again later, for instance, at Baden-Baden when both spent some time there in August 1863, or in Vienna where Berlioz presented *La Damnation de Faust* at a concert on 16 December 1866. The following evening a banquet was given for him, and on the 18th he was invited to a performance of *Harold en Italie* conducted by **Joseph Hellmesberger** at the conservatory. Brahms is known to have been in Vienna at the time.

While Brahms felt drawn toward Berlioz as a person, he seems in general to have been little attracted by his music. One of the exceptions was "La Fuite en Egypte" (the second part of *L'enfance du Christ*), which, he informed **Clara Schumann** in November 1855, was then his favorite among Berlioz's works; he contrasted its "simplicity" with the composer's usual tendency to "assault one's ears" (Litzmann 1970, vol. 1, 145). Speaking to Heuberger in April 1888, he conceded that Berlioz deserved a measure of respect as a composer and that he had some clever ideas, such as the Queen Mab scherzo (in the dramatic symphony *Roméo et Juliette*) and the *Harold en Italie* symphony (which Brahms had conducted at a Gesellschaft der Musikfreunde concert on 8 November 1874); but for the most part, Berlioz's music was "clumsy, dry, leathery" (Heuberger 1976, 159). On another occasion, in 1895, Brahms dismissed the overture to *Roméo et Juliette* as being "very boring," with only two beautiful passages (see **Ferdinand Schumann**'s [1915] "Erinnerungen an Johannes Brahms"). The most damning pronouncement dates from Brahms's final weeks when, after a performance of the *Symphonie fantastique* at a philharmonic concert on 21 February 1897, which he had not attended, he remarked to Heuberger: "Everyone tells me that it was horrible. Now I'm certainly the last person to prompt people to disparage Berlioz—after all, his skill in orchestration is quite remarkable! And all that long before **Wagner** and Liszt! Nevertheless, his corpses can never be resuscitated" (Heuberger 1976, 122). (Berlioz 1972; Heuberger 1976; Litzmann 1970; Schloenbach 1853; F. Schumann 1915)

BERNAYS, MICHAEL (b. Hamburg, 27 November 1834; d. Karlsruhe, 25 February 1897). Literary historian; also a celebrated lecturer, highly appreciated throughout Germany. The son of a rabbi, he converted to Protestantism at the age of 22 under the influence of **Henriette Feuerbach**. After studying law, classical languages, and literature at Bonn and Heidelberg, he earned his living as a private tutor and lecturer. In 1873 he was appointed professor of modern languages and literatures at the University of Munich, a post he held with distinction until 1890.

He reportedly first met Brahms at Göttingen in 1858, but their closer relations date only from 1860, when both were staying at Bonn. Many years later, in a letter to his friend Erich Schmidt, Bernays recalled the striking impression the young Brahms had made on him, both by his character and his intellect. It was thanks to Brahms, Bernays stated, that he had gained a deep understanding of **Schubert**'s Lieder, and he fondly remembered the "sunny afternoon hours" at Bonn during which Brahms had revealed to him "the lyrical and dramatic life of the 'young nun'[D.828]"; and Bernays added, "I belong to those who, convinced of his talent, declared their admiration for him at a time when the general public dismissed him with scorn and only a small select band was inclined to believe in him." (The relevant passage from Bernays's letter is printed in Uhde-Bernays 1907, 206–7, and Brahms 1974/7, 138–39.)

After Bernays settled at Munich, where his circle included **Hermann Levi** and **Paul Heyse**, he repeatedly met Brahms again when the latter visited the city for concerts. Thus, Brahms was able to report to **Clara Schumann**, after one such occasion in March 1874, "The performances were very good, the audience very friendly, and all of us, beside the musicians, especially Heyse and Bernays, frequently met for merry get-togethers" (Litzmann 1970, vol. 2, 46). (Brahms 1974/7; Litzmann 1970; Uhde-Bernays 1907; Witkowski 1926)

BERNUTH, JULIUS VON (b. Rees, Rhine Province, 8 August 1830; d. Hamburg, 24 December 1902). Conductor and teacher. Originally trained for the legal profession, he switched to music and studied at the Leipzig conservatory (1854–57). Until 1867 he lived mainly in Leipzig, and during his stay there he conducted the choral society "Euterpe" and also the Singakademie. Following a trial concert on 15 March 1867 he was appointed conductor of the Hamburg Philharmonic Society's concerts, in succession to **Julius Stockhausen**; in addition, he assumed responsibility for the Hamburg Singakademie, at first provisionally, and then officially from 1868. He resigned from both positions in 1894 but retained the directorship of the conservatory that he had established in 1873.

Bernuth has been credited with significantly enhancing the quality and range of musical performance in Hamburg. In addition to founding the conservatory, he organized joint concerts by the Singakademie and the Philharmonic Society. Furthermore, he arranged for important structural alterations to be made to the Conventgarten concert hall and for the subsequent installation of a concert organ, thereby enabling the choral societies to present their concerts in better conditions than those existing in some of the churches that had hitherto been their sole possible venue. During his tenure of the Hamburg posts, Bernuth conducted nearly all of Brahms's important orchestral and choral works. Thus, he directed the first local performance of the Requiem at a concert of the Singakademie on 23 March 1869; and at philharmonic concerts he performed all four symphonies, the Violin Concerto (with **Joseph Joachim** as soloist), the *Haydn Variations*, the first

Serenade, *Schicksalslied*, *Triumphlied*, *Alto Rhapsody*, *Tragic Overture*, and again the Requiem (in 1890).

The choice of the largely unknown Bernuth to replace Julius Stockhausen as conductor of the Philharmonic concerts and the Singakademie in 1867 no doubt caused considerable disappointment to Brahms, who was hoping to be offered the position for which he had been passed over a few years earlier. It was therefore rather ironic that, in 1894, he should have been invited to succeed Bernuth at a time when, as he declared in declining the offer, it had come "too late" for him (see Brahms's letter to the Hamburg senator Scheumann, quoted in Kalbeck 1976, vol. 4, 345–46). The position was eventually taken up by **Richard Barth**. (Sittard 1971; Stephenson 1928)

BIBL, RUDOLF (b. Vienna, 6 January 1832; d. Vienna, 2 August 1902). Organist, composer, and teacher. Taught by his father, the cathedral organist Andreas Bibl (1797–1878) and **Simon Sechter**, he was appointed organist at St. Peter's Church in 1850 and at St. Stephen's Cathedral in 1859. In 1863 he became court organist, and in 1897 court Kapellmeister. Among his compositions were works for organ, a number of Masses, and some string quartets. From 1891 he taught organ, harmonium, oboe, and composition at the teachers' training college and at the Horak Music School.

Bibl played the organ at various choral performances directed by Brahms. Thus, at the latter's first concert as conductor of the Singakademie on 15 November 1863, Bibl played the continuo for **Bach**'s cantata "Ich hatte viel Bekümmernis"; on 10 November 1872, at Brahms's first concert as artistic director of the Gesellschaft der Musikfreunde, he provided the continuo for Handel's "Dettingen" Te Deum. (Flotzinger 2002)

BILLROTH, THEODOR (b. Bergen, on the North German island of Rügen, 26 April 1829; d. Abbazia [Opatija, Croatia], 6 February 1894). Surgeon. Son of a pastor, Karl Theodor Billroth (1800–34). He studied medicine at the universities of Greifswald, Göttingen, and Berlin, and qualified as a doctor in 1852 and as a surgeon in 1856. From 1853 until 1860 he was employed as an assistant at the Berlin University clinic directed by the surgeon Bernhard von Langenbeck. In 1860 he became professor of surgery and head of the university surgical unit in Zurich, and in 1867 he took up similar appointments in Vienna. An outstanding physician, blessed with exceptional mental and physical energy as well as with inspiring human qualities, he was greatly admired by his colleagues and venerated by his students. His pioneering work in laryngectomy and, especially, in abdominal surgery (gastric resection) earned him international renown. He was accorded many honors; in 1887 he became a member of the upper chamber [Herrenhaus] of the Austrian parliament.

Billroth was a highly cultured man, with a profound interest in music. In fact, at first he had intended to take it up professionally but was persuaded by his family to turn to medicine instead. He was an excellent pianist and a good violinist, and while residing in Zurich he took lessons on the viola from Jean Eschmann; later he played the viola in a string quartet whose other members were **Theodor Kirchner**, Eschmann, and **Friedrich Hegar**. From his young days he enjoyed friendly relations with many well-known musicians, such as **Arnold Wehner**, the director of music at Göttingen. In Vienna he was well acquainted with all the leading figures in the city's musical circles, and most intimately with **Eduard Hanslick** and Brahms.

It is generally believed that Billroth made Brahms's acquaintance in Zurich in November 1865. However, his son-in-law Otto Gottlieb-Billroth, the editor of their correspondence, thought that they might already have met earlier that year at Basle, where Brahms was a specially invited guest at a performance of **Bach**'s *St. Matthew Passion* on 16 June, and the following day took part in a chamber music concert at which his Piano Quartets opp. 25 and 26 were performed (with Brahms playing the piano part in the former and Kirchner in the latter). Five months later Brahms went to Zurich, where he was to appear at three public concerts, on 21, 25, and 28 November; but as he explained to **Clara Schumann** after the first one,

> some music lovers (notably Dr **Lübke**, Prof. Billroth, and [Otto] Wesendonck) arranged a private concert for the Sunday morning, so that they could also hear my Concerto [op. 15] and the A Major Serenade [op. 16]. They hired the orchestra, sent telegrams in all directions to make sure that the orchestral parts etc. would arrive in time, and anyone interested was quite at liberty to attend. The musicians were very eager to please me, so that the whole affair was most agreeable. (Litzmann 1970, vol. 1, 518)

Brahms directed the performance of the Serenade and was soloist in his First Piano Concerto, which was conducted by Kirchner.

While Billroth's admiration for Brahms was no doubt greatly stimulated by the music he heard at these private and public performances in November 1865, by then he had already formed a high opinion of Brahms's compositions. Gottlieb-Billroth plausibly surmises that the "B" who contributed reports on musical life in Zurich to the Leipzig *Allgemeine musikalische Zeitung* on 30 March and 18 May 1864 was none other than Billroth; regarding a recent performance of the Piano Quartet op. 26, the writer comments that Brahms appears to attain a higher level with each new work. On the other hand, Billroth was not, as Gottlieb-Billroth also supposed, the author of the largely very favorable discussion of the Serenade op. 11, which appeared in the *Neue Zürcher Zeitung* on 18 November 1863 following its performance at a subscription concert on 10 November; that review has since been identified as the work of the Zurich high school teacher Gerold Eberhard. (Billroth did, however, publish some musical criticism in the *Neue Zürcher Zeitung*.)

Billroth met Brahms repeatedly in 1866 when the latter spent more than two months near Zurich, and their closer relations may be said to date from that period. During the first years after his move to Vienna, he saw Brahms on several further occasions. "I like Brahms better and better, the more often we are together," he wrote to Lübke in December 1867 (Fischer 1897, 91). Once Brahms had himself permanently settled in Vienna on becoming artistic director of the Gesellschaft der Musikfreunde, their contacts became regular and frequent, and in 1873 they adopted the informal "Du" address. That same year Brahms dedicated his two String Quartets op. 51 to Billroth. Apart from the genuine respect they evidently felt for one another, each clearly found the other a congenial and stimulating companion, for on no fewer than three occasions they traveled to Italy together (in 1878, 1881, and 1882). Brahms was, moreover, to acknowledge later how much Billroth's admiration and support for his music had meant to him, especially at a time when his reputation had not yet been firmly established. He had so high a regard for Billroth's musical judgment that he eagerly sought his observations on new works still in manuscript, and Billroth furnished such comments with acumen and remarkable speed. Typical is the case of the Second Piano Concerto—or, as Brahms chose to designate it in his accompanying letter, "a few little pieces for the piano"—which Billroth received in July 1881 and studied with such extraordinary concentration and diligence that he was able, just a day later, to provide Brahms with several pages of detailed remarks. Furthermore, Billroth's regular musical soirees offered Brahms invaluable opportunities for hearing some of his latest compositions performed by professional musicians before a small group of sympathetic and discriminating listeners—who, in addition to the cultural entertainment, were always offered an excellent supper. Between 1875 and 1890, these soirees were held in the spacious and beautifully decorated music room of Billroth's house at 20 Alserstrasse. The room was first used for a rehearsal of Brahms's Piano Quartet op. 60, prior to that work's initial public performance by Brahms and members of the Hellmesberger Quartet on 18 November 1875. (Billroth was delighted to discover that **Beethoven** had frequently performed at the house when it was owned by the celebrated physician Peter Frank; the house was demolished in 1906.)

Billroth also attended rehearsals and presentations of Brahms's new compositions elsewhere, when his countless engagements permitted it. Thus, he was present on 8 October 1885 at **Friedrich Konrad Ehrbar**'s concert hall when Brahms and **Ignaz Brüll** played a two-piano version of the new Fourth Symphony before a select group of friends, shortly before the world premiere of the work at Meiningen; indeed, Billroth was not just present, but he and Hanslick even turned the pages for the two pianists. He also attended the final rehearsal of the String Quintet op. 111 on 5 November 1890, a week before it received its first public performance at a chamber music concert of the Rosé Quartet on 11 November (which he likewise attended). After first hearing this work, he wrote to Brahms:

> I have slaved away at all kinds of trivial professional tasks this afternoon—or rather, yesterday afternoon [he was writing at one o'clock on the morning of 6 November]—but I can't settle down to rest before telling you, my dear old friend, what a happy hour you have once again granted me to-day. And if I ever try to recollect at what hours of my life, which has surely been of a richness known to only few mortals, I have felt most profoundly elated, you invariably occupy the largest space. (Gottlieb-Billroth 1935, 458)

Yet their relations had by then become rather strained at times. In 1887 Billroth had a severe attack of bronchitis that left him weakened for several months, although he eventually appeared to regain his earlier energy for a time; but his heart may have been permanently affected. His health grew more fragile during the final years of his life and, perhaps as a result of this, he found it more difficult to tolerate the insensitive and abrasive manner that Brahms sometimes adopted at his soirees toward fellow guests and even toward Billroth himself. Billroth was particularly aggrieved by an incident that occurred in November 1892, by which time he was living at 6 Kolingasse. He had invited Brahms, together with Hanslick, **Max Kalbeck**, and **Adolf Exner**, who had all been promised by their host that Brahms would perform some of his recently composed piano pieces (opp. 116–17) for them. At first Brahms refused to play at all, but after a lengthy supper he was finally persuaded to sit down at the piano. Kalbeck (1976), recalling the incident in his Brahms biography, states that he played "beautifully," first an unknown piece by Bach, then some of his new compositions, and lastly the Rhapsody op. 79 (vol. 4, 272–73). Billroth, on the other hand, gave a very different account in a letter he wrote to his daughter Else that very same evening. Brahms, he reported, arrived late, was excessively merry (and "as insufferably childish as he was 30 years ago when I made his acquaintance in Zurich"), repeatedly made "churlish jokes," and when he started playing his own compositions, he was unable to finish any of them—"he said his fingers were too heavy, he could not play after drinking wine (in fact, he had not drunk much)." After a time he began again, "plunked away rather aimlessly, and finally managed to finish a piece, all of it with bad grace." Billroth added that it was, moreover, not the first time that Brahms had behaved in such a way: "He is always the same, and it really is very difficult to put up with him in such situations. . . . He does make it very hard for one to go on loving him" (Nagel, Schober, and Weiss 1994, 246–47). It was the last time that Billroth invited Brahms to such a party at his house. Some time later, after attending a performance of the Horn Trio (op. 40), with Brahms at the piano, he wrote to Else: "I was hardly able to say anything to him about it. We are increasingly becoming strangers. Pity!" (Nagel, Schober, and Weiss 1994, 247).

After Billroth's death, Brahms told **Josef Viktor Widmann** that he had lost his friend already several years earlier, for his serious illness in 1887 had left him an "old man," a mere shadow of the man formerly so full of vigor and zest for life (Brahms 1974/8, 135). Furthermore, Brahms alleged that even Billroth's musical taste had been adversely affected, otherwise he would never have acclaimed Massenet, whom Brahms himself dismissed as a "French pastrycook." (The operas *Manon* and *Werther* had been performed with great success at the Vienna court opera, *Manon* for the first time on 19 November 1890, and *Werther* at its world premiere on 16 February 1892; on Brahms's and Billroth's divergent opinions concerning Massenet, see Kalbeck 1976, vol. 4, 270–72.) On a more personal level, he attributed to Billroth's failing health and impaired judgment two critical remarks, which he learned Billroth had made about him and which clearly still rankled him years later. On one occasion Billroth had reportedly accused him of harboring a superiority complex after he had refused to write more than his name in the album of a highly placed person to whom Billroth had promised a longer entry. The other and potentially more wounding remark Brahms found in a letter addressed by Billroth to Hanslick, who had passed it on to Brahms because it contained interesting observations on his music; not until it was too late did Hanslick remember that Billroth had, in the same letter, deplored the fact that Brahms, like Beethoven before him, often treated his friends with an insensitive and wounding brusqueness, and that Billroth had concluded that in both cases the behavior was the result of their "wretched upbringing." While Brahms apparently never spoke about these remarks to Billroth, who thus remained unaware that he knew about them, Brahms's indignation, especially about the reproach aimed at his beloved parents, may have accounted for some of the ill humor he displayed soon afterward at the above-mentioned soiree in November 1892.

During the last years of his life, Billroth became engaged in an attempt to define "musicality": on the one hand, why a certain melody is beautiful or not, rich in substance or devoid of it, tedious or interesting; and on the other, who is "musical"? He discussed the subject with Hanslick (who encouraged his efforts) and with Brahms (who was rather skeptical about the usefulness of his approach, which relied largely on physiological considerations, and who moreover disagreed with some of his views). Billroth completed about half of his study, entitled "Wer ist musikalisch?" while the latter part was still in sketchy form at his death. Hanslick published the finished chapters in the *Deutsche Rundschau* in October 1894, and the same chapters together with the uncompleted remainder the following year as a monograph; two further editions followed in 1896 and 1898 (a reprint was issued in 1985). In thanking Billroth's widow Christine for sending him the little book in October 1895, Brahms did not hide his reservations regarding some of the methods used by Billroth, and added that he was almost glad that Billroth had not had the time to present certain affirmations he had been planning to make: "Your husband intended to assert and prove all kinds of things which, while quite astutely and intelligently conceived or thought out, are nevertheless clearly contrary to the facts and to better informed knowledge. I was restrained—and pretty embarrassed—in discussing them with him, and am now glad that I need not contradict him any further" (Gottlieb-Billroth 1935, 493–94). (Billroth 1894–95; Brahms 1974/8; Gottlieb-Billroth 1935; Fischer 1897; Huber 1924; Kahler 1981; Litzmann 1970; Nagel, Schober, and Weiss 1994; Roses 1986, 1987; Wyklicky 1993; Zimmermann 1983)

BISMARCK, OTTO, PRINCE (b. Schönhausen, near Stendal, 1 April 1815; d. Friedrichsruh, near Hamburg, 30 July 1898). Statesman. Brahms's veneration for Bismarck is amply documented. **Rudolf von der Leyen** (1905) recalled that Brahms regularly took with him a volume of Bismarck's speeches or letters on his travels, which he consulted whenever he felt uncertain about any political matter. "What *he* tells me is sufficient for me," he would say, "*that* I believe" (30). According to **Eduard Hanslick**, Brahms complained to **Arthur Faber** three weeks before his death that his mind was no longer able to retain what he read, but he added: "I only want to read about Bismarck; please send me Busch's book *Bismarck und seine Leute* [W. Busch, *Bismarck und seine Leute während des Krieges mit Frankreich*, Leipzig, 1878]" (Hanslick 1897b, *Neue freie Presse*, 6 July 1897, 1). He had been delighted when **Fritz Simrock**'s wife Clara had sent him a "Bismarck Calendar" in December 1896 and looked forward to reading the great man's pronouncements each day (Brahms 1974/12, 207); and

Max Kalbeck (1976) reports that only a few days before he died Brahms stood by his bed in order to read in the calendar what "Bismarck had to say to him" (vol. 4, 488). Simrock himself venerated Bismarck and owned a full-length portrait by Franz von Lenbach.

Yet Brahms had not always been such an ardent admirer of Bismarck. In particular, he had disapproved of the policy followed by Bismarck over Schleswig-Holstein and profoundly regretted that it should have resulted in a war between Prussia and Austria in 1866. While he was and would always remain a fervent German patriot, he felt increasing sympathy for the Austrians and was distressed by the outbreak of hostilities between two German-speaking states. Accordingly he offered his *Männerchöre* op. 41 to **Jakob Melchior Rieter-Biedermann** in 1867, preferring that they should be published in Switzerland rather than be "made Prussian or Austrian" by appearing in either of those countries.

It was the Franco-Prussian war of 1870 and the subsequent establishment of the German Empire that made Bismarck the hero of the German people and inspired in Brahms the intense admiration that he retained for the rest of his life. Although Brahms's *Triumphlied*, which celebrates the German victory over the French, is dedicated to Wilhelm I, there is no doubt that in it Brahms was simultaneously paying homage to Bismarck. In fact, in a letter to Simrock in September 1871, he called the composition his "Bismarck-Gesang." In a later letter to Simrock, in April 1885, Brahms wrote, in reference to the festivities recently held in Berlin to commemorate the 50th anniversary of Bismarck's entry into the Prussian state service and also to mark his 70th birthday: "Truly, we are witnessing and seeing personalities, conditions, and men such as history has never seen before" (Brahms 1974/11, 94). Years later, Brahms reportedly became honorary president of the Viennese branch of the "Club zum Ausspannen der Pferde" [Club for the Unharnessing of the Horses] set up in 1894 by a group of fanatical admirers of the then dismissed chancellor who was about to return to Berlin. (The name of the club reflected their intention to unhitch the horses of Bismarck's carriage and pull it through the streets; the plan was thwarted by the police.)

Brahms treasured a bronze relief of Bismarck, which had been given to him by **Duke Georg II of Sachsen-Meiningen** and which hung in his music room in the Karlsgasse. (Brahms 1974/11, 1974/12; Leyen 1905)

BITTER, KARL HERMANN (b. Schwedt an der Oder, 27 February 1813; d. Berlin, 12 September 1885). Lawyer, Prussian civil servant (1833–82). Among the senior posts he held was that of Regierungspräsident [head of administration] at Düsseldorf in 1876–77 (Düsseldorf being part of Prussia at the time) and Prussian minister of finance (1879–82). He also made a name for himself as a musicologist, particularly through his books on **Johann Sebastian Bach** and his sons.

It was Bitter, supported by Dr. Steinmetz, the legal adviser to the local administration, who conducted negotiations with Brahms throughout the autumn of 1876 and the early weeks of 1877, with a view to persuading him to accept the position of municipal director of music at Düsseldorf. According to **Clara Schumann**'s diary, on 7 October 1876 Brahms received a formal invitation while staying at Lichtental (Litzmann 1902, vol. 3, 340), but the first approaches had been made earlier, for **Max Kalbeck** reproduces a long letter from Brahms to Steinmetz dated September 1876, concerning the offer (Kalbeck 1976, vol. 3, 123–25). Bitter even came to Lichtental to see Brahms, much to the latter's dismay, for, as Brahms told **Joseph Joachim**, "I prefer to negotiate by letter, I do not like to debate and argue" (Brahms 1974/6, 131). Bitter soon believed that they had reached an agreement, and on 22 October he confidently reported back to Düsseldorf that his recent discussions with Brahms would lead to the conclusion of a contract appointing Brahms Musikdirektor.

Under the terms of the proposed arrangement, which was to extend over three years, with the possibility of further yearly renewals, Brahms was to conduct the subscription concerts of the Düsseldorf municipal orchestra, as well as those of the local choral society. From the outset, though, he had felt some misgivings at losing his newly acquired independence (he had, after all, given up the artistic directorship of the Gesellschaft der Musikfreunde only the previous year). His hesitation was increased by two matters relating to the Düsseldorf appointment that threatened to disturb the tranquility of his life there and which he was to cite ultimately as the principal reasons for declining the invitation: the position of **Julius Tausch**, whom he was to replace as music director but who still appeared to command considerable support in the town, and the prospect of probably having to preside over a local conservatory that was likely to be established in the near future. His Düsseldorf sponsors had in fact thought that the establishment of a conservatory would be an added inducement for Brahms to accept the post; but when they discovered that he was dismayed at the prospect of having to expend time and energy on such an institute, he was assured that it would not be created for several years. Nonetheless, the matter continued to trouble him. At the same time, the vote in the municipal council on 19 December, which, while strongly favoring the replacement of Tausch by a more eminent musician, nevertheless still revealed the existence of a substantial minority in his favor (*see* TAUSCH, JULIUS), only served to reinforce Brahms's reluctance to commit himself. In the end, Bitter lost patience with his vacillation and demanded a prompt decision, whereupon Brahms wrote to him in late January 1877 from Vienna formally declining the invitation (Kalbeck 1976, vol. 3, 128–29). Bitter apprised the council of the news on 27 January.

Later that same year, Bitter left Düsseldorf to take up an appointment as assistant secretary of state in the Prussian Ministry of the Interior in Berlin. (Blume 1986; Brahms 1974/6; Litzmann 1902; Romeyk 1994)

BIZET, GEORGES (b. Paris, 25 October 1838; d. Bougival, near Paris, 3 June 1875). Composer. The high regard in which Brahms held Bizet and especially his opera *Carmen* is well documented. The work, which had its premiere at the Opéra Comique in Paris on 3 March 1875, was first produced at the Vienna Opera on 23 October of that year, still with spoken dialogue, although at later performances that dialogue was replaced by the recitatives composed by Bizet's friend Ernest Guiraud.

According to a note inserted by **Max Kalbeck** in his edition of Brahms's correspondence with **Heinrich** and **Elisabeth von Herzogenberg**, Brahms initially disliked *Carmen*, largely because it mixed tragic opera and lighthearted operetta (Brahms 1974/2, 15, no. 1). But he soon changed his opinion and, captivated especially by its wealth of melody, he conceived a profound, even passionate, admiration for the work. In a letter to Elisabeth von Herzogenberg in December 1883, he called it "a very special favorite of mine." (Brahms 1974/2, 15). The previous year he had asked **Fritz Simrock** to obtain the full score ("not the piano reduction") for him from Bizet's Paris publishers (Brahms 1974/10, 213), but it was not until May 1892 that Simrock was able to do so (see Brahms 1974/12, 69). Brahms was also delighted with *Djamileh*—"in which," he remarked to **Richard Heuberger**, Bizet "was clearly already striving for everything he later achieved with such mastery in *Carmen*" (Heuberger 1976, 54). He greatly enjoyed a performance of *Djamileh*, conducted by **Felix Weingartner**, which he attended in Berlin in October of that year. On the other hand, he found *La Jolie Fille de Perth* "totally uninteresting" (Gottlieb-Billroth 1935, 348), and his correspondence also contains some caustic remarks about Bizet's orchestration. Yet he never again wavered in his profound attachment to *Carmen*. Mina Curtiss states in her book *Bizet and His World* that he attended no fewer than 20 performances of that opera and that he declared that he would have been ready to go to the ends of the earth to meet the composer. (She cites no source for the statement, but is clearly drawing on an article by Andrew de Ternant (1924)—*see* DEBUSSY, [ACHILLE] CLAUDE.) For the record, *Carmen* was performed 175 times at the Vienna Opera prior to Brahms's death; *Das Mädchen von Perth* was first given there on 5 May 1883, but achieved only three further performances; and *Djamileh* was not produced there until 1898. (Brahms 1974/2, 1974/10, 1974/12; Curtiss 1959; Gottlieb-Billroth 1935; Heuberger 1976)

BODENSTEDT, FRIEDRICH MARTIN VON (b. Peine, 22 April 1819; d. Wiesbaden, 18 April 1892). Poet, author of travel books, and translator (of Lermontov, Pushkin, **Turgenev**, and Shakespeare). Brahms set one of his poems in "Lied" (op. 3/4). (Goldmann 1989; Stemplinger 1955)

BÖHLER, OTTO (b. Frankfurt am Main, 11 November 1847; d. Vienna, 5 April 1913). Chemist; silhouettist. Younger brother of Albert Böhler (1845–99) and Emil Böhler (1843–82), who, in 1870, moved from Frankfurt to Vienna where they founded the firm Gebrüder Böhler & Co. Initially working as agents for the Gussstahlfabrik Kapfenberg (manufacturers of cast steel at Kapfenberg, in Styria), they later went into steel production by themselves. Their company achieved considerable success.

Otto Böhler's interests lay rather in the artistic field, and he became a pupil of the Viennese painter Wenzel Ottokar Noltsch. He is, however, remembered today not for any paintings he may have executed, but for his extraordinarily clever and amusing silhouettes of musicians, among them **Anton Bruckner** and Brahms. One of the most famous silhouettes shows Brahms, accompanied by a red-colored hedgehog, on his daily walk to his favorite restaurant, the Roter Igel [Red Hedgehog], which faced on to the Wildpretmarkt and was located in a building that was also the seat of the Gesellschaft der Musikfreunde until 1870. Another of Böhler's silhouettes portrays him on his walk from the restaurant back to his rooms, followed by the same animal. A further, far more elaborate, and even more ingenious silhouette shows Brahms's arrival in heaven, where he is warmly welcomed by none other than Bruckner, who advances toward him with outstretched arms. Among the other well-known musicians depicted are **Mozart**, **Franz Schubert**, **Beethoven**, **Liszt**, and **Hans von Bülow**, all easily recognizable.

After Emil Böhler's death, Otto reportedly assisted Albert in the management of the firm, as did yet another brother, Friedrich (1849–1914). (Böhler 1941)

BÖHME, FRANZ MAGNUS (b. Willerstedt, near Weimar, 11 March 1827; d. Dresden, 18 October 1898). Teacher, chorus master, and collector and editor of folk songs. After spending a number of years as a schoolmaster and church cantor in different parts of Thuringia (1846–57), he completed his musical studies under **Moritz Hauptmann** and **Julius Rietz** in Leipzig.

Later he was active as a music teacher and choral conductor at Dresden (1859–78) and subsequently taught at the Hoch Conservatory in Frankfurt (1878–85), after which he returned to Dresden. A fierce critic of **Anton Wilhelm Florentin von Zuccalmaglio** and his approach to folk songs, Böhme published in 1877 a collection of German folk songs, *Altdeutsches Liederbuch*, which failed to meet with Brahms's approval. "What could be less authentic and, moreover, less delectable than so much in Böhme," he wrote to **Franz Wüllner** in October 1888 (Brahms 1974/15, 155).

In 1891 Böhme was invited by the Prussian Ministry of Culture to prepare a revised and expanded version of the *Deutscher Liederhort* published by **Ludwig Erk** in 1856; it appeared, in three volumes, in 1893–94. The new edition greatly displeased Brahms who, as he wrote to **Philipp Spitta** in April 1894, found it exasperating and altogether untrustworthy as a reference work on the German folk song. His objections, particularly as expressed in the penciled comments he wrote in his copies of the *Liederbuch* and *Liederhort* (now in the archive of the Gesellschaft der Musikfreunde in Vienna), concerned not only the editors' general approach to the subject but also the manner in which they dealt with individual items: he disagreed with their view of what constitutes a folk song and, in consequence, also with the choice of songs included in their anthologies, and, furthermore, he was often highly critical of their treatment of the music and of the text of the songs they had selected. His objections were thus founded on historical as well as aesthetic grounds.

It is now generally agreed that Brahms's criticism was excessive, but he felt so strongly about the matter that he even began to prepare a "Streitschrift" [polemical tract] attacking the Erk-Böhme *Liederhort*, in which he intended to illustrate his arguments with examples drawn from the numerous folk songs he had collected, mostly many years earlier, and which he considered more suitable both from the generic and the artistic points of view. In the end, however, he decided not to engage in a public dispute but simply to counter the Erk-Böhme anthology with one of his own. This was published by **Fritz Simrock** in June 1894 in seven books, each containing seven folk songs, under the overall title *Deutsche Volkslieder* (WoO 33). The songs were mostly set for single voice, with a piano accompaniment devised by Brahms himself; the great majority of them had appeared in the Kretzschmer-Zuccalmaglio collection. (Brahms 1974/15; I. Fellinger 1988; Wiora 1953)

BÖIE, JOHN (JOHANN PETER CHRISTIAN) (b. Altona, near Hamburg, 8 March 1822; d. Altona, 19 March 1900). Violinist and conductor of choral music; brother of violinist and composer (Johann Hermann) Heinrich Böie

(1825–79). During his long career, John Böie, who had studied with Carl Müller, made an outstanding contribution to musical life in the Hamburg area, as a summary of his major activities demonstrates: cofounder of the Altona Singakademie in 1853 and its first director of music (1853–68), as well as its conductor (1871–85); conductor of the Hamburg Singakademie (1861–64); Konzertmeister of **Georg Dietrich Otten**'s orchestra; Konzertmeister of the Philharmonic Society orchestra (1861–76); leader, after Carl Hafner's death, of his quartet (1861–72); and conductor, after Heinrich Schäffer's death in 1874, of the Hamburg Liedertafel. Böie played the violin solo in the "Benedictus" at the first performance in Hamburg of **Beethoven**'s *Missa solemnis*, at the Michaeliskirche on 8 November 1861.

Brahms's association with Böie dates at least from 1856. On 20 January of that year they, together with **Carl Grädener**, performed Brahms's Piano Trio op. 8 at a concert in Kiel, and on 2 February, Brahms played Beethoven's "Eroica" *Variations* and his own arrangement of **Bach**'s Organ Toccata in F Major at a concert given by Böie at Altona. Three days later he wrote to **Clara Schumann** that he and Böie intended to play a violin sonata by **Carl Philipp Emanuel Bach** for Otten on his birthday on 8 February. Boïe also took part in the first Hamburg performance of Brahms's Sextet op. 16 on 7 March 1861; and, most memorably of all, he gave, together with Clara Schumann, F. Breyther, and Louis Lee, the first performance anywhere of the Piano Quartet op. 25 on 16 November 1861. (At the same concert, Brahms played **Mozart**'s Sonata for two pianos [K. 448] with Clara and conducted the Hamburg Frauenchor in six of his songs.)

Böie was twice married: in 1849 to Eliza Krumbhaar (1818–62), and in 1873 to **Marie Völckers**, who knew Brahms well, having been a member of his Hamburg Frauenchor. Boïe and his second wife maintained friendly relations with Brahms's family, and in a letter to Clara Schumann following the death of his sister Elise (*see* BRAHMS [LATER: GRUND], ELISABETH [ELISE] WILHELMINE LOUISE) on 11 June 1892, Brahms paid a heartfelt tribute "to the staunch friendship with which they have supported me in everything" (Litzmann 1970, vol. 2, 473). (Litzmann 1970; Sittard 1971)

BÖSENDORFER, LUDWIG (b. Vienna, 10 April 1835; d. Vienna, 9 May 1919). Piano manufacturer. On the death of his father Ignaz (1796–1859) he assumed control of the firm, which the latter had founded in 1828. He became a prominent figure in Viennese musical life, was made an honorary member of the Gesellschaft der Musikfreunde in 1870, and joined its board of directors in 1878. In 1889 he established the Bösendorfer Piano Competition, which is now held every two years.

Brahms played on Bösendorfer grand pianos at his first two public appearances in Vienna (16 and 29 November 1862) but performed almost exclusively on **Streicher** pianos between 1865 and 1875. Subsequently, though, he preferred instruments made by Bösendorfer. (For an interesting discussion of certain technical features of these, as well as of other types of pianos used by Brahms, see G. S. Bozarth and S. H. Brady [2000], "Johannes Brahms and his Pianos.")

In 1872 Bösendorfer opened a new recital hall in the Palais Liechtenstein (on the site now occupied by the Hochhaus [skyscraper] at 6-8 Herrengasse). Its superb acoustics and its size (it seated just under 600 persons) made it an ideal venue for piano and song recitals, as well as for chamber music concerts, and many distinguished artists performed there during the next 40 years. It opened on 19 November 1872 with a recital by **Hans von Bülow**; the last chamber music concert was given there by the Rosé Quartet on 9 November 1913. The building was demolished soon afterward.

Brahms knew Bösendorfer very well, not least because Bösendorfer, like himself, took a lively interest in the Wiener Tonkünstlerverein. Brahms was also very familiar with the recital hall. To cite just three memorable events, it was there, on 5 April 1892, that he was enchanted by **Alice Barbi**'s rendition of his songs; it was also there that he accompanied her at her farewell concert on 21 December 1893 (in March 1898 she would sing a number of his songs there for the benefit of the Brahms Monument Fund); and it was at the Bösendorfer-Saal that he had one of his rare meetings with **Liszt**, on the occasion of Bülow's all-Brahms recital on 2 February 1882. According to **Max Kalbeck** (1976), Brahms often listened to concerts at the Bösendorfer-Saal from a seat placed for him in an attic, which he could reach and leave without being observed. (Antonicek 1988; Bozarth and Brady 2000)

BRAHMS, CHRISTIANE (JOHANNA HENRICA), née Nissen (b. Hamburg, 4 June 1789; d. Hamburg, 2 February 1865). Brahms's mother, married to **Johann Jakob Brahms** on 9 June 1830. Brought up in modest circumstances, she worked hard all her life. By her own account, she was sent out to earn money as a seamstress when only 13, and often continued to sew at home until midnight; from the age of 19 she was employed as a maid in a private household for some 10 years, after which she resumed work as a seamstress. After her sister Christina Friderika (1792–1874) married Johann Diederich Philipp Detmering in 1827, Christiane lived with the couple and looked after the lodgers, as well as helping out in the small shop in which the sisters sold sewing goods; at the same time, she earned some extra money with sewing whenever she could.

In 1829 Johann Jakob Brahms became a lodger, and, according to Christiane, a week later declared his desire to marry her. The precipitous proposal surprised the prospective bride, not least because, at 41, she was 17 years older than her suitor. She was, moreover, lame and rather plain; on the other hand, she was later described as being a modest, kind-hearted, and by no means unintelligent woman, with an interest in literature. She was also usually of a cheerful disposition, at any rate until the final period of her life. **Clara Schumann**, who greatly appreciated her uncomplicated and unassuming character, took a particular liking to her. Furthermore, she thought that Christiane, unlike her husband, had at least an inkling of Johannes's genius (see Litzmann 1902, vol. 2, 372). Certainly, a particularly strong bond linked Christiane and Johannes. "I never forget you when I pray in the evening, and when I get up in the morning, at 6 o'clock, my first thought is of you," she wrote to him in September 1853 (Stephenson 1973, 47–48). The following year he confided to Clara: "How marvelous it is to be staying with my parents! I wish I could take my mother everywhere with me" (Litzmann 1970, vol. 1, 27). And when he saw her after her death: "She was quite unchanged and looked as sweet and gentle as in life" (Litzmann 1970, vol. 1, 490).

Her marriage, during which she bore her husband three children (**Elisabeth [Elise]**, Johannes, and **Friedrich [Fritz]**), became increasingly unhappy (in this connection, *see also* BRAHMS, JOHANN JAKOB). In the week preceding her death, which she doubtless anticipated, she put together a long letter to Johannes, "so that I can die in peace, knowing that my child has no false ideas about me." A detailed account of the numerous grievances she had against her husband, it was prompted by her suspicion that he had maligned her in speaking or writing to Johannes; it may even have been provoked by some injudicious remark made by the latter. It is a distressing document in which Christiane accuses her husband of meanness toward her and her children, and of having generally made her life unnecessarily hard throughout their marriage by frittering away money in a variety of ways—for instance, by repeated and irresponsible moves from one flat to another, by expensive purchases for his own comfort and pleasure, by impracticable schemes such as the raising of rabbits and chickens, and by putting aside cash for the day when he would leave his family, as she suspected him of having planned to do for some time before they actually separated in 1864. (The whole letter is printed in K. Hofmann 1986, 18–24.)

Although Brahms, in speaking to **Richard Heuberger**, later denied the fairly widely held idea that his Requiem had been inspired by his mother's death (Heuberger 1976, 105), it is plausible to assume that the memory of her was present in his mind during its composition. In this connection, **Florence May** reports a statement made to her by **Hermann Deiters**, according to which Brahms himself had told him at Bonn in the summer of 1868 that he had thought of his mother when he recently wrote the fifth movement ("Ihr habt nun Traurigkeit," for soprano solo and chorus), which contains the text "I will comfort you, as a mother comforts her child" from Isaiah (66:13). It has further been suggested that the Adagio mesto movement of the Horn Trio op. 40, written a few months after her death, was inspired by it, and a similar claim has been tentatively advanced with respect to the slow movement of the Violin Sonata op. 78, even though it was not composed until the late 1870s (but, in this connection, *see also* the remarks concerning **Felix Schumann** in SCHUMANN FAMILY). (Heuberger 1976; K. Hofmann 1986; Litzmann 1902, 1970; May 1948; Stephenson 1973)

BRAHMS [LATER: GRUND], ELISABETH [ELISE] WILHELMINE LOUISE (b. Hamburg, 11 February 1831; d. Hamburg, 11 June 1892). Brahms's sister. Of a sickly constitution (all her life she was plagued by severe headaches), for many years she led a somewhat humdrum existence, helping with various household tasks; later she earned some money as a seamstress, and she was listed as a dressmaker in the Hamburg directory for 1866. She was of a cheerful disposition, and **Clara Schumann**, for one, was extremely fond of her. In the summer of 1856, following **Robert Schumann**'s death, she joined Brahms and Clara and two of the latter's children on a trip to Switzerland. When her parents separated in 1864, she firmly took her mother's side and thereafter remained implacably hostile toward her father; but after his death she enjoyed friendly relations with her stepmother and with **Fritz Schnack**.

Although Elise was devoid of any musical talent, she showed an eager interest in Johannes's activities and took great pride in his growing reputation. Her deep affection is reflected in her numerous letters to him, more than 200 of which have survived. "Elise . . . is overjoyed that you intend to come here after Christmas," Clara wrote to Brahms from Hamburg in November 1867 (Litzmann 1970, vol. 1, 568); and Elise herself appealed to Brahms in July 1874: "If only my very dearest wish, to see you among us, could one day be fulfilled! It is now already two-and-half years since we saw you last. Isn't that really a little too long?" (Stephenson 1973, 216). At that time Elise had a special reason for wanting Brahms to visit her. The previous year Clara had written to him: "She longs very much to see you and wishes with all her heart that you could see how happy she is" (Litzmann 1970, vol. 2, 29–30). For at the age of 40, on 5 October 1871, Elise had married. Her husband. Johann Christian Georg Grund (1817–88), a widower with six children, was a clockmaker. When Brahms learned of her intention to marry, he tried to dissuade her, for he feared that it would bring her grief, and he even offered to buy her a place in one the former convents in the city that had been turned into residences for unmarried or widowed women. But Elise was not to be deflected from her plans, and, in fact, the marriage turned out extremely well.

As soon as he could spare the money, Brahms provided financial help for Elise; he continued to do so during her marriage and also after her husband had died. The last months of her life were troubled by an illness that kept her confined to her bed. (Litzmann 1970; Stephenson 1973)

BRAHMS, FRIEDRICH [FRITZ] (b. Hamburg, 26 March 1835; d. Hamburg, 5 November 1886). Piano teacher; Brahms's brother. Like Johannes, he received instruction from **Otto Cossel** and **Eduard Marxsen**. He also took violin lessons with Leopold Lindenau, the Konzertmeister of the Hamburg Philharmonic Orchestra from 1832 to 1859, but he subsequently gave up playing that instrument and sold his violin in 1856.

The relations between Brahms and his younger sibling are known to have been strained, but it is not clear when and in what circumstances tensions first arose. Styra Avins (1997), in *Johannes Brahms: Life and Letters*, speculates that the falling out between them stemmed from the period in 1864 when the financial burden of assisting their newly separated parents fell far more heavily on Johannes than on Fritz. That situation may well have had an impact on their relationship; but it should be noted that they had not always been on the best of terms even before then. This is evident from a letter **Christiane Brahms** wrote to Johannes in April 1854, in which she observed regretfully: "Oh, how much Fritz could have learned from you, if you two brothers had got on well together" (Stephenson 1973, 55). Nonetheless, Brahms took advantage of the contacts he made at Leipzig in late 1853 to secure for Fritz an engagement as music teacher to the children of Count and **Countess Hohenthal** at nearby Dölkau Castle. By early January 1854 Fritz had taken up his position and was told by the countess that his brother must love him very much to recommend him so warmly. Fritz was grateful and he was at first very pleased with his duties, but when he was asked to undertake also certain secretarial tasks his pride was hurt and he promptly took his leave, apparently on Brahms's advice. However, he soon regretted his willful action, for which he blamed his brother's bad counsel (see his letter to Johannes of 13 July 1854 [Stephenson 1973, 57]), and with Marxsen's help he managed to patch things up with the Hohenthals, in whose service he then remained for several more months. Once Brahms had left the parental home, he only saw his brother on his occasional visits to Hamburg, except for a trip they took together along the Rhine in the summer of 1860.

Fritz gradually established himself as a competent music teacher in Hamburg; he also taught for some years at a boarding school for young ladies at nearby Hamm. In addition, he sometimes performed in public. On one such occasion, in October 1863, he gave, together with the English pianist Sidney Smith, the first public performance of his brother's *Schumann Variations*, and on 9 January 1864 he played one of Brahms's piano sonatas and his *Handel Variations* at his own concert. However, he seems to have soon realized that he was not equipped for a career as a professional pianist. When he had played the *Handel Variations* for **Clara Schumann** in private a few months earlier, she concluded that he was not able to do them justice (letter to Brahms of 25 November 1863); on the whole, though, she considered that he possessed quite a good technique, "only I find his playing so very dull" (Litzmann 1970, vol. 1, 433). From 1866 until 1870 Fritz was active as a piano teacher at Caracas in Venezuela, and after his return, he soon resumed his activities in Hamburg.

His relations with his brother did not improve over the years, as is evident from Brahms's letters to his father and, after the latter's death, to his stepmother **Karoline**. Thus he explained to **Johann Jakob** in March 1871 that he would not be staying with him during his forthcoming visit to Hamburg because of Fritz (who occupied a room in their father's flat): "There is no need for me to wish to conceal from you the fact that the reason is Fritz. . . . I have told Fritz how I feel. . . . If he has nothing to say to me, nothing by way of explanation, I really don't see why I should see him" (Stephenson 1973, 181). Four years later he confided to Karoline: "Some things draw me toward Hamburg, but others keep me well away. Notably my relationship with Fritz" (Stephenson 1973, 219).

In the summer of 1876 a reconciliation took place while Brahms was spending several weeks in Hamburg after holidaying on the island of Rügen. Thereafter, during the remaining 10 years of Fritz's life, which were increasingly marked by ill health, Brahms repeatedly and, in the final period, regularly provided him with financial assistance. At the same time, his attempts to establish a more intimate relationship with his younger brother were frustrated by Fritz's failure to respond to them or even to acknowledge receipt of the payments, which, in the end, had to be sent to him through their stepmother, since Brahms did not know his address. In fact, Fritz lived alone in lodgings during this whole period; in the end, his deteriorating health forced him to abandon teaching. Finally, on 17 September 1886, Karoline informed Brahms that Fritz had been diagnosed as suffering from a brain tumor and had been taken to hospital; there, seven weeks later, he died. It was then discovered that, far from being impoverished, he had in fact managed to put by the not insignificant sum of 20,000 marks, presumably for his old age. The money went to Johannes and **Elise**, but Brahms immediately gave his portion to his stepmother. (Avins 1997; Litzmann 1970; Stephenson 1973)

BRAHMS, JOHANN JAKOB (b. Heide, Holstein, 1 June 1806; d. Hamburg, 11 February 1872). Brahms's father. He decided at an early age on a musical career and, having learned to play several instruments (violin, viola, cello, flute, flügelhorn), he made his way to Hamburg in 1826. Initially, he earned a meager income from playing at various places of entertainment and as a street musician. In 1830, a few days after being granted Hamburg citizenship, he joined the Bürgerwehr [Civil Militia], and for 30 years (1837–67) he played the flügelhorn in one of its bands. At the same time, realizing that there was a demand for double-bass players, he largely concentrated on that instrument, which he subsequently played for many years in a sextet performing at the popular Alster Pavilion, as well as in the orchestras of the Stadttheater (from 1853) and the Philharmonic Society concerts (from 1864). Modern research has shown that, contrary to statements made by **Max Kalbeck** and later Brahms biographers, his earnings, though modest, placed him and his family well above the poverty line. Far from being indicative of impoverished circumstances, the frequency with which he changed accommodations (no fewer than eight or possibly even nine times between 1830 and 1864) was, in fact, usually prompted by a desire for larger and more expensive apartments; but his wife considered the repeated moves rather irresponsible (*see* BRAHMS, CHRISTIANE [JOHANNA HENRICA]).

He proposed to Christiane Nissen a few days after becoming her and her sister's lodger in 1829; they were married on 9 June 1830. The considerable differences in their temperaments and in their ages—she was 17 years his senior—must have seemed of relatively small consequence at first, but they weighed more heavily as time passed. When he was still a robust man in his early 50s and leading a fairly active professional life, she had already become an old lady; one of his colleagues, according to **Florence May**, later described her as having faded into a "little old withered mother who busied herself unobtrusively with her own affairs, and was not known outside her dwelling" (May 1948, 53). For her part, as is evident from her last letter to Johannes, written a few days before her death, she felt increasingly exasperated by various aspects of his character that, as she saw it, made her life, both before and after they separated in 1864, much harder than it need have been (on this point, *see also* BRAHMS, CHRISTIANE (JOHANNA HENRICA).

The growing mutual resentment experienced by his parents saddened Brahms, who initially sought to bring about a reconciliation, but ultimately accepted a separation as the best, indeed the inevitable, solution. Even then he tried, though unsuccessfully, to ensure that the break was not total by urging his father to visit his mother occasionally and make use of the room that she and Elise set aside for him in their new flat. As far as one can tell, Brahms did not take sides in the dispute and recognized that it had unhappy consequences for both his parents. Certainly, there is no indication that he ever laid the blame for it squarely on his father, as his sister and brother did. "Believe me that no son can love his father more deeply than I do and that no one can feel the sadness of our position more keenly and sincerely than, unhappily, I now do," he assured his father in October 1864 (Stephenson 1973, 104), after the latter had accused him of acting insensitively in seeking out the agreeable company of friends elsewhere rather than involving himself more directly in the "unpleasant situation" at home. Though devoted to his mother and anxious to help her financially in her predicament, he clearly also felt sympathy for his father, as is evident from a letter he wrote to **Clara Schumann** after his mother's death, in which he expressed the hope that his father could now look forward to "a fairly serene and pleasant old age" (Litzmann 1970, vol. 1, 495). This explains his pleasure at the news that his father had found a new companion and his warm feelings for his stepmother who brought Johann Jakob such happiness in his last years. Johann Jakob married Karoline Pomplun (*see* BRAHMS, KAROLINE LOUISE) on 22 March 1866.

His father had originally expected Johannes to follow in his footsteps by playing in an orchestra, and Brahms's attitude toward his father was always strongly affected by the desire to prove to him that he had indeed made a success in the more hazardous career he had chosen. In her aforesaid last letter to him, his mother recalled that he had wept when told (probably in 1852) that his father was unwilling to provide for him anymore and thought that it was time that Johannes made his own way in the world. In 1855, after a visit to Hamburg, Clara Schumann wrote in her diary: "How sorry I am to see that Johannes is understood least of all by his own family! His mother and sister have just an inkling of his exceptional gifts, his father and brother not even that" (Litzmann 1902, vol. 2, 372). By the time Johann Jakob died, Brahms, who was then approaching 40, had no doubt attained a certain reputation, but he had as yet composed very few of the works that were to assure him lasting renown. As late as 1889 he confided to Clara Schumann, shortly after he had become an honorary citizen of Hamburg, "My first thought in such a case is for my father and the wish that he had lived to see it; but fortunately he was even so not dissatisfied with me when he passed away" (Litzmann 1970, vol. 2, 385). (K. Hofmann 1986; Litzmann 1902, 1970; May 1948; Stephenson 1973)

BRAHMS, KAROLINE LOUISE, née Paasch (b. Neustadt, Holstein, 25 October 1824; d. Pinneberg, Holstein, 14 April 1902). Brahms's stepmother. She was married and widowed three times: in 1846 she married Claus Hinrich Schnack (d. 1854), a carpenter, by whom she had a son (*see* SCHNACK, FRIEDRICH [FRITZ] WILHELM); after his death she married Christian Hermann Pomplun (d. 1865), a blacksmith; and in 1866 she married **Johann Jakob Brahms**. Her roots, like those of Johann Jakob, lay in Holstein, and this common background was doubtless a factor that drew them together.

Brahms's attitude to his stepmother was above all influenced by the gratitude he felt on seeing his beloved father made so happy. She was an extremely kind-hearted, cheerful, and capable woman, experienced in running a household efficiently, and altogether a more congenial partner for Johann Jakob than the far older and increasingly ailing **Christiane** (17 years his senior, while Karoline was 18 years younger than he was). Brahms quickly came to appreciate her qualities, and he conceived a deep affection for her. "I can't attempt . . . to try to console you," he wrote to her shortly after his father's death. "I know all too well what we have lost and how lonely your life has become. But I hope that you are profoundly and doubly conscious of the love which others have for you—the love of your son [Friedrich Schnack], of your admirable sister and her children, and lastly my own love which belongs to you fully and entirely" (Stephenson 1973, 193–94).

For the rest of his life Brahms was to urge Karoline persistently to let him know if she ever needed any money. "I don't need to repeat that you may have as much as you like, at any time and as frequently as you wish," he assured her in August 1878. "You know that it gives me pleasure and doesn't inconvenience me" (Stephenson 1973, 235–36). She was, however, reluctant to ask him for money, and, moreover, managed for several years to derive a modest income from taking lodgers. Nonetheless, Brahms sent her sums from time to time, both while she was still living in Hamburg and after she had moved away in October 1883 to join her son at Pinneberg. Later, he gave her the money that his brother had bequeathed to him. He saw her whenever he went to Hamburg; on the last such occasion, in February 1893, he visited her—not for the first time—at Pinneberg. In his will, he left her a life annuity of 5,000 marks. (K. Hofmann 1981b; Stephenson 1973)

BRANDT, AUGUSTE (b. Hamburg, 13 May 1822; d. Hamburg, 2 September 1887). Daughter of a wealthy Hamburg merchant; married to Carl August Brandt (1804–74). When her husband's first business venture in maritime trading collapsed after his ships were lost with their cargoes in storms, he became an insurance broker, and Auguste improved the family's financial situation by taking in lodgers. Among the latter were, at different times, Bertha Porubszky (*see* FABER, ARTHUR [LUDWIG]) and her two sisters, as well as their brother Emil (who was later to lodge with Brahms's parents). In a letter sent by Brahms to Bertha from Detmold in November 1859, as well as in the diary kept by Franziska Meyer (later Lentz), a member of Brahms's Hamburg Frauenchor, Auguste Brandt is referred to as Bertha's aunt. Like Bertha, Auguste was also a member of the choir, and her house was occasionally used for the group's choir practices. But according to Auguste's granddaughter Gertrud Reye (whose written recollections were later published by her daughter Irmgard Schumann-Reye), what really drew Brahms to the house was the presence of the charming Bertha. He became a regular visitor, often stayed for dinner, and entertained his hostess and her family by "playing his own compositions, improvising on the piano, or tirelessly practicing **Beethoven**'s last sonatas, for hours on end" (Schumann-Reye 1990, 63).

In 1862, when Brahms left Hamburg for Vienna, he gave Auguste a two-volume set of Beethoven sonatas, in which he had inscribed his name and marked some fingering, as well as two volumes of folk songs (perhaps the **Kretzschmer-Zuccalmaglio** collection). He also presented her with a photograph of himself, and with an autograph of the soprano part of three pieces from the repertoire of the Frauenchor, the "Ave Maria" (op. 12), "O bone Jesu," and "Adoramus" (op. 37/1–2). In the introduction to her 1990 edition of Gertrud Reye's memoir, her daughter Irmgard Schumann-Reye states that the sonatas and folk songs were lost in World War II, but that the autograph still remained in the possession of her family.

Gertrud Reye did not know whether Brahms ever saw her grandmother again during his later stays in Hamburg. Her own mother, Auguste's youngest child Clara (1848–1919), who had studied the piano with **Otto Friedrich Willibald Cossel** and singing with **Julius Stockhausen** and who, in 1866 or 1867, had married Dr. Daniel Wilhelm Reye, reintroduced herself to Brahms when he visited Hamburg in September 1889. Gertrud Reye, evidently citing family lore, states that he was absolutely delighted to see Clara again. "Ach, das kleine Clärchen!," he reportedly exclaimed, adding: "I must tell Frau [**Bertha**] **Faber** about this" (Schumann-Reye 1990, 69). (Schumann-Reye 1990)

BREITKOPF & HÄRTEL. Music publishers at Leipzig. At the same time as he prepared to propel Brahms into the public spotlight with his article "Neue Bahnen" (*Neue Zeitschrift für Musik*, 23 October 1853), **Robert**

Schumann brought the young "genius" to the personal attention of Raymund Härtel (1810–88) and Hermann Härtel (1803–75), who were then running the firm. In a letter on 8 October 1853, a week after meeting Brahms, he wrote about a "young man" (but without naming him) "who has moved us most profoundly with his marvellous music and who, I am certain, will arouse tremendous excitement in the world of music" (Kalbeck 1976, vol. 1, 123). In a further letter on 15 October he mentioned Brahms by name, referred to his own forthcoming article about him, and identified the types of compositions Brahms had ready for publication. Finally, on 3 November, he cited the specific works that Brahms wished to publish, with their proposed opus numbers, and indicated what payments Brahms expected for them. (The list and order subsequently underwent some modification.)

The firm responded promptly, indicating its willingness to publish the works in question, though without immediately committing itself to the amounts demanded; Brahms was invited to send the scores to Leipzig. Schumann forwarded the letter to **Joseph Joachim** in Hanover, where Brahms was then staying, and in an accompanying note to Joachim he stressed the desirability of Brahms going to Leipzig as soon as possible, "otherwise his works will be mutilated: he must present them there himself" (Johannes Joachim and Moser 1911–13, vol. 1, 103). On 8 November Brahms sent a number of manuscripts to Breitkopf & Härtel, and on 17 November he left for Leipzig. There **Heinrich von Sahr** took him to meet the Härtels, who, as Brahms reported to **Albert Dietrich**, "received me with immense friendliness" (Dietrich 1898, 9). To Joachim he wrote: "I am now acquainted with Messrs Härtel 1 and 2. . . . Yesterday evening I was at the Härtels' and played my C Major Sonata and the E-flat Minor Scherzo; a lady sang some of the songs" (Brahms 1974/5, 18). The negotiations with the firm went extremely well and publication followed quickly: the Piano Sonata op. 1 and a set of six songs (op. 3) appeared in December, the Piano Sonata op. 2 and another set of six songs (op. 4) in February 1854.

In November of that year Breitkopf & Härtel issued the 6 Songs (op. 7), the Piano Trio op. 8 (first version), and the *Schumann Variations*; but the firm turned down the arrangement for piano duet (M. McCorkle 1984, Anhang IIb/5) of Schumann's Piano Quintet op. 44, which Brahms offered early in 1855, on the grounds that it presented "insurmountable" technical problems. (They later published **Clara Schumann**'s arrangement, likewise for four hands.) The publishers were more enthusiastic about the 4 Ballades (op. 10), which appeared in February 1856. The correspondence then lapsed for more than four years, and its resumption in 1860 carried the seeds of future disagreements: When Brahms offered the firm the Serenade in D Major, "Ave Maria," *Begräbnisgesang*, a set of songs, and the First Piano Concerto (i.e., opp. 11–15), only the Serenade was accepted. "I regret that you have so little faith in my concerto. . . . The other works I sent you do not dignify with a single word," he wrote in some vexation on 13 August (Brahms 1974/14, 43). That same day he proposed the four rejected items to **Jakob Melchior Rieter-Biedermann**, who immediately accepted all of them. The serenade was published by Breitkopf & Härtel in December 1860, and it was followed by the *Handel Variations* in July 1862, and by 2 Motets (op. 29), *Geistliches Lied* (op. 30), and the Quartets op. 31, all in July 1864. In addition, the Fugue for Organ (WoO 8) appeared as a supplement to the firm's journal *Allgemeine Musikalische Zeitung*, also in July 1864.

As it turned out, these were the last of Brahms's compositions to bear the firm's imprint (except for a separate reissue in 1883 of WoO 8). In October 1864 the firm rejected his settings of poems by **August von Platen** and **Georg Friedrich Daumer** (op. 32) as well as his *Magelone-Lieder*, because it considered that the difficult accompaniment would make their publication a commercially unviable proposition. Greater simplicity was desirable: "It is moreover our view that it is not only possible, but indeed proper, that in the case of songs and romances like these the composer ought to make such, assuredly not unjustified, concessions to his public" (Brahms 1974/14, 109). (On the rejection of these songs, *see also* BAGGE, SELMAR.) The criticism so irked Brahms that he did not reply for almost a year, deeming it hurtful to an artist "because you do not trust him to be willing or able to consider and take account of all essential aspects" (Brahms 1974/14, 117). He was to be even more deeply offended by the publishers' action in 1865 when, having unreservedly accepted, unseen, the new String Sextet (op. 36), they sent a further letter after receiving the manuscript, in which they asked "on the explicitly expressed advice of a third party" (Brahms 1974/14, 120) to be released from their commitment. Eventually he was to learn from Clara Schumann that the "third party" had been **Selmar Bagge** (for further details, *see* BAGGE, SELMAR).

Brahms never submitted another composition to Breitkopf & Härtel. He did, however, collaborate in the firm's editions of the collected works of **Chopin**, **Mozart**, **Schubert**, and Schumann. (In this connection, *see also* BEETHOVEN, LUDWIG VAN.) In 1888 Breitkopf & Härtel sold their rights to the Brahms works they had published to **Fritz Simrock**, whose stated ambition it was—as he informed Brahms on 29 March of that year—"to bring all your published works together under my flag" (Stephenson 1961, 209). Brahms was astonished by Simrock's action: "I am supposed to congratulate you!?!? . . . I find it beyond all measure foolish that you should buy works from the Härtels—for, I can't imagine, what high a price—which cost them about 100 L[ouis]dors, and which very soon won't be worth a shot of gunpowder. . . . Very well, I congratulate you, but I wash my hands in carbolic acid and Heavens knows what else!" (Brahms 1974/11, 181). (Brahms 1974/5, 1974/11, 1974/14; Dietrich 1898; Johannes Joachim and Moser 1911–13; Stephenson 1961)

BRENDEL, KARL FRANZ (b. Stolberg, 26 November 1811; d. Leipzig, 25 November 1868). Music historian and critic. After studying philosophy at Leipzig, Berlin, and Freiberg (Saxony), he turned increasingly to music (while at Leipzig he had taken piano lessons from Friedrich Wieck and met **Robert Schumann**). He gave a series of lectures on music at Freiberg and Dresden and, in 1845 in Leipzig, where he had settled the previous year and where he assumed the editorship of the *Neue Zeitschrift für Musik*, the journal founded by Schumann in 1834 (under the name *Neue Leipziger Zeitschrift für Musik*). Under his guidance—he remained its editor until his death—the *Neue Zeitschrift für Musik* became the champion of the "New German School," with **Liszt** figuring prominently among the writers, in addition to Brendel himself.

Brahms made Brendel's acquaintance at Leipzig in late 1853. On 4 December he went to Brendel's customary Sunday afternoon reception, which proved an enjoyable experience, especially as **Hector Berlioz**, who was also present, showered him with praise (*see* BERLIOZ, [LOUIS] HECTOR). Moreover, Brahms's performance at **Ferdinand David**'s concert on 17 December, when he played his Piano Sonata op. 1 and the Scherzo op. 4, evoked favorable comment in the journal. But he doubtless derived less pleasure from the first extensive articles to be devoted to him there in 1855 (*see* POHL, RICHARD). Eventually, the distaste Brahms increasingly felt for the compositions of Liszt and his followers, which he came to regard as offensive to the intrinsic nature of music, drove him in 1860 to prepare, with the help of **Joseph Joachim** and some other friends, a public declaration attacking the "New German School," as well as the periodical that they considered its principal mouthpiece: "The undersigned have long viewed with regret the activities of a certain faction, whose organ is Brendel's *Zeitschrift für Musik*. . . . The undersigned do not recognize the principles proclaimed by Brendel's journal" (Kalbeck 1976, vol. 1, 404–5). The Declaration was prematurely leaked to the *Berliner Musik-Zeitung Echo*, which published it on 6 May 1860 over the names of only four signatories (Brahms, Joachim, **Julius Otto Grimm**, and **Bernhard Scholz**), thereby destroying any effectiveness it might otherwise have had. Moreover, the text had evidently been leaked also to Brendel, since he published a riposte in the form of a parody on 4 May, even before the *Echo* had printed the actual document.

That very same year, the *Neue Zeitschrift für Musik* printed the first of a series of articles on Schumann and his followers by **Adolf Schubring**, an avowed admirer of the composer. The longest item in the series, which was published in several installments in 1862 (*see* SCHUBRING, ADOLF), was a highly sympathetic and generally laudatory, if not entirely uncritical, essay on the music of Brahms. In a later article in the series (4 December 1863), Schubring explained why he had originally decided to submit these articles on Schumann and his school to Brendel: in the absence of a music journal representing the "Schumann line, that is to say the musical centre," he had reasoned that the one most likely to make a place for "Schumannianis," if only out of gratitude toward its founder, was the *Neue Zeitung für Musik*, in spite of its being the mouthpiece of the "Extreme Left." In a comment on this passage, the "editor" (i.e., Brendel) stated that while his journal had willingly offered space to the extreme left to express its aspirations, it did not represent that movement; instead, it constituted the very center that Schubring claimed was no longer represented anywhere; it was, indeed, still Schumann's journal, just as it had been 20 years earlier, and if he had accepted Schubring's articles, it was not out of gratitude toward Schumann but because they deserved to be published. It is unlikely that Brendel's arguments convinced all his opponents.

In addition to his own numerous contributions to the *Neue Zeitschrift für Musik*, Brendel wrote several books on music and from 1846 lectured at the Leipzig conservatory. Furthermore, he edited (1856–61, from 1857 jointly with Richard Pohl) the journal *Anregungen für Kunst, Leben und Wissenschaft*, and was also a cofounder and the first president of the Allgemeiner deutscher Musikverein.

BRENTANO, CLEMENS (b. Ehrenbreitstein, 9 September 1778; d. Aschaffenburg, 28 July 1842). Poet, novelist, and dramatist; brother of **Elisabeth [Bettina] von Arnim**. Together with his close friend **Achim von Arnim** he published the famous collection of German folk songs *Des Knaben Wunderhorn*. In these Brahms set two of his poems: one for single voice in "O kühler Wald" (op. 72/3), and the other for a six-voice choir in "Abendständchen" (op. 42/1). (Frühwald 1989)

BREUER, JOSEF (b. Vienna, 15 January 1842; d. Vienna, 20 June 1925). Internist. He qualified in 1867 and subsequently worked as an assistant at the Vienna University clinic under Johann von Oppolzer. After the latter's death in 1871, he went into private practice and also devoted some of his time to scientific research; in addition, he taught at the university (1875–85). Together with the physiologist Ewald Hering he discovered the mechanism by which the vagus nerves tend to inhibit inspiration. Furthermore, his "cathartic" method for treating hysteria, based on his discovery that unresolved psychological conflicts can lead to mental illness, influenced Sigmund Freud and laid the basis for what was later called psychoanalysis. Together, he and Freud published *Studien über Hysterie* in 1895; but Breuer subsequently distanced himself from certain aspects of Freud's psychoanalytical methods.

Breuer, who was the family doctor of Brahms's friend **Ignaz Brüll**, attended Brahms during his final illness. According to his own later statement, Brahms had probably first consulted him on 1 February 1897. Breuer at once recognized the hopelessness of Brahms's condition, which he attributed to an advanced cancer of the liver, and he accordingly devoted his efforts to alleviating his patient's physical suffering and providing moral support. He did his best to keep Brahms in ignorance of the true nature of his illness, to the extent of telling him that the great weakness that he would be experiencing before long (and which Brahms did, in fact, feel shortly before his death) was a necessary stage in the transition to his ultimate recovery. Brahms, who had a high regard for Breuer—in a letter to **Wilhelm Engelmann** on 23 February 1897 he described him as an "excellent doctor" (Brahms 1974/13, 175)—seemed to believe him, and seemingly remained optimistic about his chances of recuperation until the very end. After Brahms's death, however, Breuer expressed the opinion that, deep down, Brahms could hardly have been unaware of the gravity of his illness, but that he was eager to shield himself, as far as possible, from that knowledge.

It was, however, not Dr. Josef Breuer, but his son **ROBERT** (b. 1 July 1869; d. 9 February 1936), likewise a physician (and incidentally Brüll's son-in-law), who was in attendance during the last night of Brahms's life. At the time, he was employed as an assistant to Dr. **Hermann Nothnagel**; later he was to hold a senior position at a hospital in Linz. Many years afterward (on 19 July 1912), he wrote down a detailed description of what happened that night for **Max Kalbeck**'s benefit (see Kalbeck 1976, vol. 4, 514–16). When Brahms admitted to being in some pain around midnight, Breuer administered a morphine injection. At about four o'clock he gave Brahms a glass of Rhine wine for his thirst. Brahms drank the wine slowly, with evident pleasure, and said afterward, "Ah, that tastes good." Those were the last words Breuer heard Brahms speak. In the morning he had to leave shortly after seven o'clock in order to return to his clinic, and therefore, he was not present when Brahms died around 8:30 a.m. Certain biographers of Brahms (e.g., M. Macdonald and J. Swafford) have attributed the offer of the glass of wine to **Arthur Faber**, who supposedly came by in the early morning hours and, while at Brahms's bedside, handed it to him; but Breuer makes no mention of any visit by Faber. Breuer himself also told R. H. Schauffler about the incident and about Brahms's reaction. (Brahms 1974/13; Schauffler 1972)

BRODSKY, ADOLPH (b. Taganrog, Russia, 21 March 1851; d. Manchester, 22 January 1929). Violinist. He studied with **Joseph Hellmesberger** at the Vienna conservatory (1863–67) and then played in the Vienna Philharmonic Orchestra (1868–70) before returning to Russia. There, during the following years, he made his reputation as an exceptionally gifted violinist; he also taught at the Moscow conservatory. In 1881 he went back to Vienna, where, on 4 December, he gave the world premiere of **Tchaikovsky**'s Violin Concerto. The conductor was **Hans Richter**, and it was also under his baton that Brodsky introduced the work to London audiences on 8 May 1882.

Another concerto with which Brodsky became closely associated was that of Brahms, which he performed, for instance, at the music festival of the Allgemeiner deutscher Musikverein at Leipzig in May 1883 (the year in which he was appointed to the faculty of the Leipzig conservatory, in succession of Henry Schradiek). He played the concerto more than once under the composer's own direction—at Meiningen on 25 October 1885 (at a concert that included the world premiere of Brahms's Fourth Symphony), at Leipzig on 18 February 1886 and in Berlin on 7 March 1889—or at any rate in his presence (in Cologne in June 1887, and in Hamburg in September 1889). Brodsky's interpretation of the work was widely regarded as equaling **Joseph Joachim**'s.

He had originally made Brahms's acquaintance in Vienna, in what circumstances it is not known. When he founded his own quartet in Leipzig, Brahms, who was due to conduct his Third Symphony there on 7 February 1884, agreed to appear at its opening concert the previous day; he and Brodsky performed the Violin Sonata op. 78, and Brahms was reportedly highly appreciative of his partner's playing. Four years later, on 2 January 1888, Brahms, with Brodsky and Julius Spengel, gave the first performance in Leipzig of the Piano Trio op. 101. It was at Brodsky's flat, the previous day, that Brahms had first met Tchaikovsky. A detailed account of the occasion can be found in Anna Brodsky's (1904) memoir *Recollections of a Russian Home* (*see also* GRIEG, EDVARD [HAGERUP]).

In the autumn of 1891 Brodsky went to New York where for the next three years he was leader of the symphony orchestra conducted by Walter Damrosch. It proved a disappointing experience, and although he derived a certain satisfaction from his appearances as a soloist and from his work with the quartet he founded, he was glad to return to Europe and settle in Berlin. However, in 1895 he accepted an invitation from **Sir Charles Hallé** to become leader of his orchestra in Manchester and a senior violin professor at the Royal Manchester College of Music, which had been established in 1893 and of which Hallé was principal. In his letter to Brodsky offering those appointments, Hallé mentioned having heard him play the Brahms Concerto in London in 1883, so that performance had evidently made a very favorable impression on him. As matters turned out, Brodsky only once played under Hallé's baton, at the opening concert of the Liverpool Philharmonic season on 22 October 1895, for Hallé died three days later. The following year Brodsky gave up his position with the orchestra to become the next principal of the college. He nevertheless continued to perform as a soloist, and he also made a further major contribution to the musical life of the city with the Brodsky Quartet, which also performed elsewhere. In 1914 Richter wrote to his son-in-law Sydney Loeb: "Brodsky plays everything superbly, but if you want a special treat, hear him and his quartet playing **Schubert**, in that he is unique; his warmth, his feeling, his fire resulted in a great success in Vienna" (Fifield 1993, 447).

Brodsky saw Brahms probably for the last time in 1896. **Richard Heuberger** records in his diary that he and **Eusebius Mandyczewski** dined with Brahms, Brodsky, and some others at the Goldene Kugel restaurant shortly before Brahms's departure for Karlsbad. For his part, **Max Kalbeck** (1976) states that Brahms, immediately after his return to Vienna, asked Mandyczewski to arrange for some of their friends to meet him at the Roter Igel on 3 October and at the Goldene Kugel on 4 October (vol. 4, 478). Brodsky was invited so that the convivial evening might give him a good idea of Viennese *Gemütlichkeit*. (Avins and Eisinger 2002; Brodsky 1904; Fifield 1993; Heuberger 1976; Kennedy 1971)

BRONSART VON SCHELLENDORF, HANS (AUGUST ALEXANDER) [Hans von Bronsart] (b. Berlin, 11 February 1830; d. Munich, 3 November 1913). Composer, pianist, and conductor. He studied with Siegfried Dehn and Theodor Kullak in Berlin (1849–52) and with **Liszt** at Weimar (1853–57). Devoted to Liszt and intimately associated with **Hans von Bülow**, he closely allied himself with the "New German School." In his turn, Liszt held Bronsart in high regard, both as a man and as a musician, and dedicated to Bronsart his own Second Piano Concerto, of which Bronsart gave the first public performance.

Bronsart came to Hamburg to attend the philharmonic concert on 24 March 1859, at which Brahms (with **Joachim** conducting) first played his Piano Concerto in D minor. (However, they may already have met in 1853 at Weimar or perhaps at Leipzig—see H. R. Jung in Blume 1949–86). Brahms was greatly attracted by Bronsart's personality: "A pleasant man," he reported to **Clara Schumann**. "I only regret that I cannot bring myself to care for his compositions" (Litzmann 1970, vol. 1, 250). Shortly afterward, when Clara was spending some time in Berlin, he wrote, "Have you met Bronsart? You will like him, he is so friendly and modest" (Litzmann 1970, vol. 1, 257). When Bronsart was Intendant at Hanover (1867–86), Brahms occasionally took part in performances of his own music there, and they also exchanged letters. Thus, when Bülow resigned as court Kapellmeister in November 1779, Bronsart sought Brahms's views on **Ernst Frank**'s suitability to succeed him, and Brahms's no doubt positive reply was likely to have been an important factor in Frank's appointment; and in the autumn of 1882 Bronsart sounded Brahms out about his willingness to become artistic director of a conservatory that was to be established in Hanover. (Brahms was not overly enthusiastic.) From 1887 to 1895 Bronsart was Intendant at Weimar; he also served as president of the Allgemeiner Deutscher Musikverein (1888–98). (H. Ehrlich 1893a; Litzmann 1970)

BRUCH, AMALIA [AMÉLIE] JOHANNA HENRIKA FRANZISKA, née Vehoffer (b. Torony, Hungary, around 1821; d. Vienna, 28 May 1871); married Captain Heinrich Bruch (1822–93) in 1851. Brahms probably made her acquaintance in Vienna sometime between autumn 1862 and spring 1863. She studied piano with him and became a good friend who deeply admired his music and liked him greatly as a person. In his turn, Brahms felt respect and affection for her. To his father, who met her during his visit to Austria in 1867 and afterward corresponded with her, Brahms announced her death with genuine sorrow: "A good friend of mine, Frau Bruch, has died in Vienna. She had so many excellent qualities that her death affects me profoundly" (Stephenson 1973, 183). And to **Arthur Faber** he wrote that "anyone who knew her really well is certain to have regarded her as worthy of respect and will have held her dear" (Kalbeck 1976, vol. 4, 476). She was passionately fond of music and enriched her knowledge of it by studying books and scores in the library and archive of the Gesellschaft der Musikfreunde; moreover, her interest in music led her to address several letters to **Friedrich Chrysander**. She also gave piano lessons.

In her will made out on 4 February 1871, she specified that the sum of 12,000 florins, which her uncle had at the time of her wedding deposited in government bonds as "marriage security," should after her death become the property of her husband, but with the proviso—formulated, she added, with her husband's agreement—that, since their union had been childless, her husband should administer that sum in such a manner as to make possible the celebration, after his own death, of a "unique, serene, and happy" relationship that they had jointly enjoyed: "This relationship is with our kind and dear friend, the composer Johannes Brahms. He is herewith designated by us as the subsequent heir of the aforesaid small capital of 12,000 florins" (R. Hofmann 2002, 61). However, Heinrich Bruch remarried in 1873 and at his death in 1893 left not only a wife but also a daughter, so the proviso presumably lost its validity. (**Max Kalbeck** [1976], in his Brahms biography, and **Eduard Hanslick** [1899], in his book *Am Ende des Jahrhunderts*, give erroneous accounts of this whole matter, on which fresh light has now been shed by Renate Hofmann.) In addition, Amalia bequeathed to Brahms what seems to have been a quantity of printed music, including editions of some of his works, with the request that he distribute part of it to her pupils. In fact, he also presented some of it to friends like Hanslick and **Elisabeth von Herzogenberg**. (R. Hofmann 2002)

BRUCH, MAX (KARL AUGUST) (b. Cologne, 6 January 1838; d. Friedenau, near Berlin, 20 October 1920). Composer. Brahms was in contact with him at the latest by March 1860, when Brahms informed **Joseph Joachim** that he was willing to sign their manifesto against the "New German School" (*see* BRENDEL, KARL FRANZ and LISZT, FRANZ). If they met at all during the immediately following years, it could only have been on rare occasions, for in September 1864 Bruch, in the earliest of his letters to Brahms printed by Altmann (as mentioned below), referred to his long-standing desire to become better acquainted with him. That opportunity occurred the following year when he saw something of Brahms first in Vienna and later at Cologne. Thereafter they met occasionally at musical events and in more social circumstances.

However, the partial edition of their correspondence (six letters from Brahms; nine from Bruch) that was published by Wilhelm Altmann in 1912 points to no more than a superficially cordial relationship. In fact, Bruch never took to Brahms, whom he considered an arrogant and disagreeable man, liable to react to any overtures of friendship in a sarcastic fashion. At the same time, his antagonistic feelings toward Brahms were probably also due to some extent to professional jealousy, for he was known to have a prickly and vain character. Though successful and popular enough as a composer, he never enjoyed the great admiration increasingly expected for Brahms. According to his biographer Christopher Fifield, he broke with **Rudolf** and **Laura von Beckerath** because he believed that they were attending Brahms's concerts in preference to his own. After **Clara Schumann** had met him, she told Brahms that he was not nearly as agreeable as his letters. It is therefore not altogether surprising that when Brahms was consulted confidentially in 1882 regarding Bruch's suitability for a post at Breslau [Wrocław, Poland], he should, after praising Bruch's considerable talent and accomplishments, have discreetly suggested that it might be advisable for the Breslau committee to meet him in person before making the appointment. (Bruch was in due course offered the position.)

Despite his unenthusiastic attitude toward Brahms as a person, Bruch appears all his life to have felt a genuinely high esteem for many of his compositions, especially for the Requiem, *Alto Rhapsody*, and certain works for the piano. In the above-mentioned letter of September 1864, he claimed to know several of Brahms's compositions very well, and some of them even by heart. In 1868 he traveled from Sondershausen, where he was court Kapellmeister, to Bremen to attend the first performance of the Requiem, and later that year he dedicated his First Symphony (op. 28) to Brahms. In 1873, at Bremen, at a large party following a performance of his *Odysseus*, he entertained the company with impromptu performances of several pieces by Brahms, including the *Handel Variations*, and subsequently toasted their absent composer as the outstanding contemporary musician. He was, however, less impressed later by the symphonies. In a letter to his former teacher **Ferdinand Hiller** in March 1884, he sarcastically dismissed the claims made for them by some of Brahms's admirers: "I have not so far managed to raise myself to such cultural heights and am for the time being dull-witted enough to find a quite extraordinarily great difference between Brahms's symphonies and those of Beethoven" (Sietz 1958–70, vol. 5, 67). And later that year he wrote to the same correspondent, after conducting Brahms's Third Symphony at Breslau: "It contains much that is beautiful, but also much that lacks originality. As for the orchestration, all I can say is that the rest of us would deserve to be hanged if we orchestrated so wretchedly" (Sietz 1958–70, vol. 5, 109). Presumably he did not feel any more enthusiastic about the Fourth Symphony, for when Brahms arrived in Breslau to conduct it at a concert on 30 March 1886, he reportedly found it inadequately prepared. According to **Max Kalbeck** (1976), this even led to a "heated exchange" between the two men (vol. 4, 2, n. 2).

Little is known about Brahms's opinion of Bruch the composer, but there is evidence that he was considerably impressed with at least one of the earlier works, the *Gesang der heiligen drei Könige*; he warmly recommended it to **Joseph Joachim**, calling it "a beautiful piece of music" (Brahms 1974/6, 37), which, if well performed, should be very effective. Some years later he devoted his final concert as artistic director of the Gesellschaft der Musikfreunde on 18 April 1875 entirely to a—probably somewhat incomplete—performance of *Odysseus*. (He had originally planned to present the work during the preceding season.) In one of his letters, he complimented Bruch, perhaps with his tongue in his cheek, on being such an industrious and productive composer, a fact he noted "with great pleasure (and some envy)" (Brahms 1974/3, 98). He felt little of either emotion, however, when confronted with the oratorio *Moses*, which, he wrote to Clara Schumann in 1895, filled one with great gratitude toward God "for having preserved one from the sin, vice, or bad habit of simply putting notes on paper" (Litzmann 1970, vol. 2, 587–88). (Bozarth 1995; Brahms 1974/3, 1974/6; Fifield 1988; Litzmann 1970; Sietz 1958–70)

BRÜCKE, THEODOR AND EMILIE [MILLY]: *see* WITTGENSTEIN FAMILY.

BRUCKNER, (JOSEPH) ANTON (b. Ansfelden, near Linz, 4 September 1824; d. Vienna, 11 October 1896). Composer, organist, and teacher. By his national and family background (Austrian peasant stock), religious tendencies (extremely pious Catholicism), education (at St. Florian's Monastery), cultural interests (essentially restricted to music), and musical aspirations (substantially influenced by **Richard Wagner**'s operas), Bruckner was the very antithesis of Brahms. It is therefore not surprising that they failed to appreciate each other's compositions or established more than very superficial and uneasy personal relations.

When Bruckner left the provincial life of Linz in the autumn of 1868 to settle in cosmopolitan Vienna, where he joined the faculty of the conservatory and took up a provisional organ post at the imperial chapel, he was as yet little known as a composer there, although his D Minor Mass had been performed by **Johann von Herbeck** with the court Musikkapelle on 10 February 1867. Brahms, on the other hand, while nine years younger, already occupied a prominent position in the city's musical life and as a composer was enjoying a steadily increasing reputation in Austria and Germany (the performance of the Requiem at Bremen Cathedral in April 1868 had attracted considerable attention). Four years later he was offered one of the most important positions in Viennese music making, the artistic directorship of the Gesellschaft der Musikfreunde, whereas Bruckner was frustrated in his greatest ambition, that of becoming court Kapellmeister. Furthermore, he had to struggle for many years to get his symphonies played and, starting with the ill-fated first performance, on 16 December 1877, of the Third Symphony (which he dedicated to Wagner), had to face unrelenting denigration from Vienna's most influential critic, Brahms's fervent admirer **Eduard Hanslick**, who had originally welcomed his appointment at the conservatory.

Thus, as far as professional success and public recognition were concerned, Bruckner never caught up with Brahms. He did, nonetheless, eventually achieve a career of some distinction, for apart from teaching at the conservatory, he managed to secure an appointment as a lecturer at the university in 1875, and in 1878 was accorded the official title of court organist with full salary. Moreover, his music gradually found wider acceptance, but it is a measure of his discouragement and lack of self-confidence that he should have allowed himself to be persuaded to revise some of it, and, even more strikingly, to let others (Herbeck, Franz Schalk) do so, with the object of making it more palatable to audiences. It seems inconceivable that Brahms would ever have taken such a step.

Brahms had little taste for Bruckner's compositions, and he did not present any of them during his three-year tenure as artistic director of the Gesellschaft der Musikfreunde. However, Bruckner, who was famous for his improvisations on the organ, was invited to improvise at the special concert held on 15 November 1872 to celebrate the installation of the society's new organ built by Friedrich Ladegast. At the same concert, Brahms conducted the Singverein in a capella choruses by Eccard and Isaak. But it was only after Herbeck had once again assumed the artistic directorship that a composition by Bruckner was performed at one of the society's concerts: on 20 January 1876 Bruckner himself conducted his Second Symphony, in Herbeck's revised version. Following the world premiere under Arthur Nikisch of Bruckner's Seventh Symphony at Leipzig on 30 December 1884, Brahms wrote to **Elisabeth von Herzogenberg**, who had asked for his views on Bruckner's music: "Everything has its limits. Bruckner lies beyond them, one can't speak of the good or bad points of his music, it's not possible to discuss it at all. Any more than the man himself. He is a poor deranged man, whom the worthy monks of St. Florian have on their conscience" (Kalbeck 1976, vol. 3, 408, n. 1; Kalbeck had omitted this passage in his edition of the Brahms-Herzogenberg correspondence [Brahms 1974/1–2]). On another occasion he averred that the very suggestion that Bruckner's compositions might become "immortal," or that they were even symphonies, "makes one laugh," and he called them "symphonische Riesenschlangen" [giant symphonic serpents] (Kalbeck 1976, vol. 3, 409, n. 1).

Gradually though, even while his opinion of Bruckner's music hardly changed, he came to recognize certain qualities in the man himself. Thus, in 1894, he insisted on improving the tone of a formal letter that the Tonkünstlerverein intended to present to Bruckner (presumably on his 70th birthday), and he said to **Richard Heuberger** in this connection, "I made several corrections in the text myself. I mentioned the students, Bruckner's popularity, etc. I certainly don't see eye to eye with Bruckner in many matters, but he is nevertheless a fellow who is damned serious about what he does and that deserves some respect" (Heuberger 1976, 72). The following year he urged **Richard von Perger**, the newly appointed artistic director of the Gesellschaft der Musikfreunde, to call on Bruckner and, furthermore, to perform one of his choral works at a concert of the society. As a result, Perger conducted Bruckner's *Te Deum* at his second concert on 12 January 1896, which also included four of Brahms's choruses; both composers were present. A year later, on 17 January 1897, Perger gave the first concert performance of Bruckner's D Minor Mass, and that concert also featured some choruses by Brahms, who was again present. Three months earlier, on 13 October 1896, Brahms had attended Bruckner's funeral at the Karlskirche. In his memoirs, Bernhard Paumgartner reports catching sight of him standing apart from the rest of the mourners, in the shadow of a pillar, "with tears coursing down his cheeks." Perhaps Brahms, already a sick man, was weeping for himself as much as for Bruckner. (Biba 1985; Brahms 1974/1–2; Floros 1974, 1980, 1983; Grasberger and Partsch 1991; Gruber 1995; Heuberger 1976; Huschke 1939; Paumgartner 1959)

BRÜLL, IGNAZ (b. Prossnitz [Prostějov, Czech Republic], 7 November 1846; d. Vienna, 17 September 1907). Pianist, teacher, and composer. The son of a prosperous Jewish merchant who, in 1850, moved with his family from Moravia to Vienna, he grew up in a home in which music played a prominent part: his mother was a competent pianist, his father a good amateur singer, and his sister Hermine would become a fine contralto. He himself studied piano with **Julius Epstein**, and was taught composition by Rufinatscha and, later, by **Felix Otto Dessoff**. When he was 14, **Anton Rubinstein** predicted a great musical future for him.

Brüll developed into an outstanding pianist who possessed a splendid technique, but eschewed the display of empty virtuosity in favor of profound and deeply musical readings; in particular, he gained an international reputation as one of the foremost interpreters of **Robert Schumann**, of the late **Beethoven** sonatas, and of the piano works of Brahms. He carried out various successful concert tours, which took him as far as England, and his international career would no doubt have lasted much longer if he had not concentrated more and more on composition and, moreover, had felt increasingly reluctant to be separated from his wife and children—his marriage to Marie Schosberg on 5 November 1882 produced two daughters (one of whom became the wife of the physician Dr. **Robert Breuer** who had attended Brahms during the final night of his life).

Brüll began to compose at an early age and, at 13, played his sonata for violin and piano with **Joseph Hellmesberger** in public; two years later he wrote a piano concerto, of which Epstein gave a well-received performance. His output includes works for solo piano, chamber music, songs, and several operas, of which the most successful was *Das goldene Kreuz*, to a libretto by **Salomon Hermann von Mosenthal**, which was first produced in Berlin on 22 December 1875 (with Lili Lehmann in the leading role of Christine) and was subsequently widely performed throughout Europe (at the Vienna Opera for the first time on 4 October 1876 and in London by the Carl Rosa Opera Company on 2 March 1878). In 1871 Brüll turned down an invitation to join the faculty of the Stern Conservatory in Berlin but the following year began to teach at the Horak Piano Academy in Vienna, a well-regarded school of which he was appointed joint artistic director in 1881.

Brüll was a man of great modesty and of an exceptionally sweet nature, who seems to have been loved by all who came into contact with him; one of his closest friends was **Karl Goldmark**. There was much music making at the Brülls'—in his parents' home and later at his own house—and among the regular visitors who most enjoyed participating in the music was Brahms. In addition to performing some of his own piano compositions, he liked to accompany Brüll's sister Hermine Schwarz in his own songs as well as those written by her brother. Above all, he had the highest regard for Brüll's pianistic skills and for his musical sensitivity, and valued him as an inspired interpreter of his music. In *Ignaz Brüll und sein Freundeskreis*, Hermine (1922) describes an occasion at the Brüll home when Ignaz's performance of the *Handel Variations* so moved Brahms that he went up to Ignaz's mother, kissed her hand, and said "I thank you for your son" (48). His admiration was echoed by many others: **Anton Door** described him as "one of the greatest interpreters of Brahmsian art" (Door 1903, 217) and **Max Kalbeck** (1976) called him "the Brahms pianist *par excellence*" (H. Schwarz 1922, 107). He was also an exceptionally accomplished score and sight reader. Brahms made use of his gifts on more than one occasion when he wished to present new orchestral works to his friends in two-piano versions prior to their first performance. Thus he and Brüll introduced both the Second and the Third Symphony to a select circle of fellow musicians in the music room of the piano manufacturer **Friedrich Ehrbar** a few days before they were first heard in public.

Brüll's family used to spend the summer at Ischl, and in 1880 Brahms asked Brüll to find him suitable rooms there. He was to occupy the same accommodations (Salzburgerstrasse 51) in 1882, and again from 1889 until 1896. During these holidays he naturally saw a good deal of Brüll, either at Ischl or at Unterach on the Attersee, where most of the Brüll clan moved after the death of Brüll's father in 1889. In 1882 Brüll accompanied Brahms on his excursion to Alt-Aussee (*see* WAGNER DE ZÓLYOM,

LÁSZLÓ). At the matinee on 25 August, at which Brahms presented his new Piano Trio op. 87 and the String Quintet op. 88, Brüll opened the concert with a performance of the Rhapsody op. 79/1.

Brüll is credited with having given the first public performances of the Fantasien op. 116/1–3 and the Intermezzo op. 117/2 on 30 January 1893. In September 1896 he gave further evidence of his personal attachment to Brahms when he traveled to Karlsbad to spend a few days with him. At the Brahms memorial concert arranged by the Wiener Tonkünstlerverein on 13 April 1897, he performed the Piano Sonata op. 2; on 3 April 1898, at a further concert in Brahms's memory arranged by the same association, he played the Intermezzo op. 118/6 and the second book of the *Paganini Variations*. He was also a member of the Vienna Brahms monument committee but died before the monument was unveiled on 7 May 1908 (*see* WEYR, RUDOLF VON). (Biba 2001; Door 1903; H. Ehrlich 1893a; H. Schwarz 1922; Wecker 1988)

BÜLOW, HANS (GUIDO) VON (b. Dresden, 8 January 1830; d. Cairo, 12 February 1894). Conductor and pianist. Son of the translator and short story writer Eduard von Bülow (1803–53) and his wife Franziska (1800–88), who were divorced in 1849. He studied musical theory with Max Eberwein and **Moritz Hauptmann**, and piano with Friedrich Wieck, Louis Plaidy, and finally, from 1851, with **Liszt** in Weimar. **Richard Wagner**'s music made a profound impact on him during his formative years—he attended the premiere of *Rienzi* at Dresden on 19 October 1842 and that of *Lohengrin* at Weimar on 28 August 1850—and it was a significant factor in his ultimate decision to make music his career (he also read law in Leipzig and Berlin). He made the acquaintance of Wagner himself in 1846, and four years later Wagner enabled him to gain valuable experience as a conductor in Switzerland.

In March 1853 Bülow began his career as a professional pianist with two recitals in Vienna. He soon established an international reputation as an outstanding performer, both technically and intellectually; but he also had some detractors, among them **Clara Schumann**, who considered his interpretations to be altogether too cerebral: "He really is the most boring player, without a trace of sparkle or enthusiasm, everything is calculated," she wrote to Brahms after hearing him give two recitals in Russia in 1864 (Litzmann 1970, vol. 1, 450). Bülow also made a name for himself as a teacher; from 1855 to 1864 he was on the faculty of the Berliner Hochschule (renamed the Stern Conservatory in 1857). Later he was to enjoy no less renown as a conductor as he did as a pianist; he was particularly acclaimed for his interpretations of the music of **Beethoven**. He held important appointments at Munich (1865–69), where he conducted the world premieres of *Tristan und Isolde* (10 June 1865) and *Die Meistersinger* (21 June 1868) and headed the new conservatory; at Hanover (1877–79), which he left after a quarrel with the tenor Anton Schott; and at Meiningen (1880–85), where he transformed an already quite competent band into one of the finest orchestras in all of Germany. Subsequently he toured widely, regularly conducted the Hamburg and Berlin Philharmonic Orchestras, and taught at the Raff Conservatory at Frankfurt and at Klindworth's conservatory in Berlin. He was an extremely brilliant and energetic man, as this brief summary of his career indicates, with a wide culture and a penetrating mind; he was also highly strung, easily offended, irascible and cantankerous, with a penchant for sarcasm. "When one is on friendly terms with Bülow, one lives through some wonderful moments, but also through years of grief," **Carl Petersen**'s daughter Toni, who was extremely fond of him, once confided to a correspondent (Stargardt-Wolff 1954, 71). He married twice: first, on 18 August 1857, Liszt's daughter Cosima (1837–1930), from whom he was divorced in 1869 after she had left him for Wagner; and secondly, on 29 July 1882, the actress Marie Schanzer (1857–1941), who after his death wrote his biography and also published an important collection of his letters.

When Bülow first met Brahms in January 1854 at Hanover through **Joseph Joachim**, with whom he had become friendly at Weimar, he was greatly impressed by Brahms's musical talent, as well as by his character. On 1 March of that year, at a concert given in Hamburg by the singer Adele Peroni-Glassbrenner, he became the first pianist other than Brahms himself to play one of the latter's compositions in public, namely the opening movement of the First Piano Sonata. Brahms was not present at the concert, but he still remembered the event with gratitude 34 years later. (He had presumably played the sonata for Bülow at Hanover in January; in any case, Bülow had already heard about it from Liszt, who praised it in a letter from Leipzig on 16 December 1853.)

There was little, if any, contact between Brahms and Bülow in the following years. Bülow's relations with Joachim appear to have cooled during that period, and they were to turn decidedly chilly after Joachim broke with Liszt's music and signed the manifesto against the "New German School" with Brahms, **Julius Otto Grimm**, and **Bernhard Scholz** in 1860, for Bülow was among the most ardent supporters of Liszt's and Wagner's music. Not until November 1866 was he reconciled with Joachim, when he went to meet him at Muhlhouse, where Joachim was giving a concert with Brahms. Presumably Bülow also saw Brahms on that occasion. He had, however, little liking for his music at that time. Thus he informed Joachim Raff in a letter on 22 November 1866 that, after once examining all of Brahms's compositions "with a really open mind" during an entire week, he had come to the conclusion that Brahms's music was not to his taste. Nonetheless, he occasionally performed one of Brahms's works, as when he played the Horn Trio op. 40 with Louis Abel and **Hans Richter** at Basle on 26 March 1867. However, it was not until he undertook an examination of his musical preferences during a lengthy stay in Italy in 1869–72 (in the course of which he rejected Liszt and warmed to **Robert Schumann**) that he drew somewhat closer to Brahms. He even had some personal contact with him at Baden-Baden in the autumn of 1872 and later that year visited him in Vienna, where he gave a recital on 2 November. Yet during his first American tour in 1875–76, when he performed at no fewer than 139 concerts, he reportedly played only one composition by Brahms, the *Handel Variations.*

Bülow's first important public contact with Brahms's orchestral music occurred at Hanover on 20 October 1877 when he conducted the First Symphony—which, in a letter to Brahms at the beginning of that month, he had referred to as the "Tenth" [i.e., Beethoven's Tenth Symphony], a bon mot he repeated shortly afterward in *Signale für die musikalische Welt* and which has become famous. Not long afterward he conducted the same work at a concert of the Glasgow Choral Union, no doubt the first time it was heard in Scotland (Joachim had directed its first English performance at Cambridge on 8 March 1877). But Bülow later declared that his wholehearted devotion to Brahms's music dated from the day on which he had first heard the Adagio of the Second Symphony, an experience he likened to St. Paul's conversion on the road to Damascus (letter to Brahms of 23 December 1889); he conducted that symphony himself at Hanover on 26 April 1879.

On 10 February 1880, a few months after resigning as principal court Kapellmeister at Hanover, Bülow was appointed Intendant [director of music] of the Meiningen court orchestra, a post he took up in the autumn of that year and held for some five years. It was during this period that he forged close personal and artistic links with Brahms, who benefited enormously from this association. In February 1881, while in Vienna for some concerts, Bülow placed the orchestra at Brahms's disposal, should he ever wish to rehearse a new composition privately at Meiningen. Brahms first took advantage of this offer in October of that year, when he spent several days at Meiningen for the purpose of trying out his Second Piano Concerto, which he subsequently first played in public in Budapest on 9 November. This first visit to Meiningen was also significant in that it provided Brahms with an opportunity to meet **Duke Georg II of Sachsen-Meiningen** and his wife, with whom he was to enjoy a friendly and very fruitful relationship. Brahms returned to Meiningen for a concert on 27 November that was entirely devoted to his works, including the new concerto; between his two visits Bülow had conducted a performance of part of his Requiem on 20 November. As a further result of Brahms's newly formed links with Bülow and Meiningen, his music was featured prominently at several concerts of the tour that the orchestra undertook in January 1882. At the first of two all-Brahms concerts in Berlin (8 January) Brahms played the Second Piano Concerto, with Bülow conducting, while they switched roles for the performance of the First Concerto the following day. It was apparently after the first of these concerts, which took place on Bülow's birthday, that Brahms proposed that they use the familiar "Du" in addressing each other. A month later (2 February) Bülow gave a piano recital in Vienna that he devoted entirely to Brahms's music. In a letter to Georg II on 17 October 1881, he had described Meiningen's association Brahms as its "most important moral and aesthetic achievement." To his future wife Marie Schanzer, he wrote on 23 May 1882, "You know my opinion of Brahms: after Bach and Beethoven the greatest, the most prestigious of all composers" (M. von Bülow 1895–1908, vol. 6, 176).

Under Bülow, tours became an integral part of the Meiningen orchestra's activities (over the years he conducted some 50 concerts at Meiningen, and some 160 on tour). None of these tours show more strikingly their importance in spreading Brahms's fame than the one that followed the world premiere, under Brahms's baton, of the Fourth Symphony at Meiningen on 25 October 1885 (and a further performance there under Bülow on 1 November). In the course of this tour, which comprised 23 concerts in 23 days, starting at Frankfurt on 3 November and concluding at Wiesbaden on 25 November, Brahms conducted the new symphony at Frankfurt, Essen, Elberfeld, Utrecht, Amsterdam, The Hague, Krefeld, Cologne, and Wiesbaden, and Bülow at Rotterdam. Another performance, to be directed by Bülow, had been scheduled for the orchestra's second visit to Frankfurt, on 24 November. However, Bülow eventually substituted Beethoven's Seventh Symphony after receiving a letter in which Brahms, while leaving him free to conduct the Fourth as planned, expressed regret at not having acceded to a request that he should himself conduct it (in what would have been its second performance at Frankfurt) at a concert of the local Museum society on 5 March 1886. Bülow felt seriously slighted and hurt by the remark, as Brahms was to discover when he met him at Krefeld on 21 November. Two days later Bülow submitted his resignation to the duke, and he quit his post on 1 December. (Regarding his successors at Meiningen, *see* STRAUSS, RICHARD [GEORG] and STEINBACH, FRITZ).

Brahms's attempts to assuage Bülow's hurt feelings at first proved unavailing; but Bülow's resistance finally crumbled when, soon after arriving in Vienna for some concerts in January 1887, he received Brahms's visiting card, simply inscribed with the bars of music that, in *Die Zauberflöte*, accompany Pamina's plaintive question "Soll ich dich, Teurer, nicht mehr seh'n?" [Am I to see you no more, my dearest?]. A few hours later he visited Brahms. "I went to see him in the afternoon and spent an enchanting hour chatting with the great man" he reported to his wife (M. von Bülow 1895–1908, vol. 8, 73). They saw each other daily during the remainder of Bülow's stay, and Bülow even took part in a performance of Brahms's Piano Quintet at the Tonkünstlerverein on 2 February.

Bülow, who after leaving Meiningen had settled in Hamburg, continued to champion Brahms's music for the rest of his life, and Brahms publicly expressed his gratitude for his friendship and support by dedicating his Third Violin Sonata to him when it was published in April 1889. Furthermore, Bülow is credited with having suggested that the city of Hamburg should award honorary citizenship to Brahms, an idea subsequently brought to fruition through the efforts of Carl Petersen. Bülow met Brahms repeatedly when he came to Hamburg in September 1889 to accept the award. The following January, Brahms presented Bülow, for his 60th birthday, with a portrait of Beethoven and with the autograph of his own Third Symphony, inscribed "To his dearly loved Hans von Bülow in faithful friendship."

Bülow's last years were marred by bouts of ill health that incapacitated him more and more frequently; in particular, he was plagued by excruciating headaches. He gave his last public piano recital on 4 October 1892 at the opening of the Bechstein Saal in Berlin (*see* WOLFF, HERMANN). Although Brahms was himself in the audience, they do not appear to have met that day. Bülow was not well enough to attend the second concert on 5 October (given by Brahms and the Joachim Quartet) or the third on 6 October (a recital by **Anton Rubinstein**), and he was too ill to see visitors when Brahms called on him. The latter had to be content with a conversation with Bülow's wife, and it was also through her that he subsequently received news about the final period of his friend's life. After Bülow's death in Cairo, where he had gone in the vain hope of finding relief for his increasingly debilitating condition, it was found that he had suffered from a chronic kidney disease as well as from advanced hardening of the arteries; his headaches had apparently been caused by a tumor that affected the nerves in his neck. His body was brought back to Hamburg where it was cremated on 29 March 1894. (On the music performed on that occasion, *see* STRAUSS, RICHARD [GEORG].)

Finally, since **Max Kalbeck**'s (1976) biography continues to color present-day perceptions of many aspects of Brahms's life, it should be mentioned that Marie von Bülow, in articles in the Vienna *Neue freie Presse* (7

July 1912) and *Vossische Zeitung* (28 June 1914, subsequently reprinted in *Musikpädagogische Blätter* later the same year), severely criticized as biased the description given by Kalbeck of her husband's relationship and association with Brahms. In her view, Kalbeck's account constituted "an unmerited slight on Bülow's memory." (Albrecht 1933; H. von Bülow 1894; M. von Bülow 1895–1908, 1912, 1914, 1925; Erck, Kertscher, and Schaefer 1983; Erck, Müller, and Schneider 1987; Hinrichsen 1994; Huschke 1939; Kern and Müller 1999; Scheman 1955; Schuh and Trenner 1954; Stargardt-Wolff 1954)

BUSONI, FERRUCCIO (DANTE MICHELANGIOLO BENVENUTO) (b. Empoli, near Florence, 1 April 1866; d. Berlin, 27 July 1924). Composer and pianist. Busoni, who made his concert debut at Trieste on 24 November 1873, at the age of seven, went to Vienna with his father in 1875 and made his first appearance at a public concert there on 8 February 1876, prompting a highly favorable review from **Eduard Hanslick** in the *Neue freie Presse* (on 13 February); he was to return to Vienna on numerous occasions throughout his career. It is not certain when exactly Busoni met Brahms, who told **Richard Heuberger** in January 1885 that he had at first taken quite an interest in him and had even sent him to **Gustav Nottebohm** for instruction. (Nottebohm died in October 1882.) However, Busoni had found Nottebohm's tuition so unpalatable that he did not remain his pupil for long, whereupon, Brahms said, he had largely ceased contact with Busoni, since he did not care for children who considered themselves infant prodigies (Heuberger 1976, 27). From late 1879 until April 1881 Busoni took lessons with Wilhelm Mayer in Graz.

Busoni wrote later that he visited Brahms repeatedly, on at least one occasion in order to show him certain compositions that, with Brahms's permission, he intended to dedicate to him. He does not record Brahms's reactions, but it was perhaps after looking at these or other youthful compositions by Busoni that Brahms advised him to study composition and counterpoint with Nottebohm. (Busoni began composing at an early age; thus, at the above-mentioned concert in Vienna in February 1876, when he was not yet 10 years old, he played several of his own pieces.) Altogether, Busoni was to dedicate the following works to Brahms: *Six Études* for piano, probably published in 1883 (BV 203 [op. 16]); *Étude in Form of Variations* for piano (BV 206 [op. 17]), published in 1884; and an arrangement for two pianos (BV B 109), published by **Breitkopf & Härtel** in 1888, of **Robert Schumann**'s *Introduction and Allegro* for piano and orchestra op. 134. In addition, he arranged for solo piano Nos. 4, 5, and 8–11 of Brahms's 11 *Choral Preludes* for organ op. 122; these arrangements (BV B 50) appeared in 1902, the same year as the posthumous edition of the organ pieces themselves. Finally, in 1913, Busoni wrote a cadenza (BV B 5) for Brahms's Violin Concerto—a work that only three years earlier he had, in a letter to his wife, described as second rate and, moreover, stolen from Beethoven. (In the same letter, he had compared Brahms's compositional gifts to those of Louis Spohr.) However, as a pianist, he evidently had a particular regard for the Piano Sonata op. 5, the First Piano Concerto, and the *Handel* and *Paganini Variations*, all of which figured prominently in his concert repertory for many years. When, in the autumn of 1898, he gave a series of four concerts in Berlin, at which he presented 14 piano concertos by composers ranging from **Bach** to his own contemporaries, he included Brahms's op. 15. As for Brahms's possible influence on Busoni's early works, Dent states that only the *Variations and Fugue on Chopin's C Minor Prelude op. 28, no. 10* (BV 213 [op. 22]) show that indebtedness directly, while other writers, such as Roggenkamp, claim to have discerned it elsewhere as well.

Notwithstanding the aforementioned somewhat less than enthusiastic view that Brahms expressed to Heuberger about Busoni in January 1885, he reportedly furnished him with a letter of introduction to **Carl Reinecke** when Busoni departed for Leipzig the following month. One may nevertheless wonder whether Brahms really ever felt—then, or earlier or later—the great admiration for Busoni's compositions attributed to him by Friedrich Schnapp, who, in his 1935 edition of Busoni's letters to his wife Gerda, cites a declaration allegedly made by Brahms that he "would do for Busoni what Schumann did for me" (392).

On 6 April 1897, the day of Brahms's funeral, Busoni was the soloist in a performance of his First Piano Concerto, which the Berlin Philharmonic Orchestra, conducted by **Felix Weingartner**, gave at the Musikverein. Earlier that day he had walked in the funeral procession. He also happened to be in Vienna when **Rudolf von Weyr**'s statue of Brahms was unveiled there on 7 May 1908 and duly attended the ceremony. (Busoni 1929; Dent 1974; Heuberger 1976; Kindermann 1980; Roggenkamp 1999; Schnapp 1935; Stuckenschmidt 1970)

BUTHS, JULIUS (EMIL MARTIN) (b. Wiesbaden, 7 May 1851; d. Düsseldorf, 12 March 1920). Conductor, pianist, and composer. He received his first piano lessons from his father Carl Buths (1823–1901), oboist at the Wiesbaden Court Theatre, and later studied piano and composition with **Ferdinand Hiller** and **Friedrich Gernsheim** at the Cologne conservatory (1869–72). In 1876 he took up residence at Breslau [Wrocław, Poland], where he was in contact with **Bernhard Scholz**, directed a choral society and appeared as a pianist. In 1880 he succeeded Hermann Schorstein as director of the Gesangverein and conductor of the Concert Gesellschaft at Elberfeld. Finally, in 1890, he was appointed music director at Düsseldorf; he was also, solely or jointly, responsible for the five Lower Rhine Festivals held in that city between 1890 and 1905. In addition, he founded the Düsseldorf conservatory with Otto Neitzel in 1902 and taught there until his death.

Buths came to Brahms's attention when, substituting for the indisposed Scholz, he prepared the Breslau orchestra for the performance of the First Symphony, which Brahms conducted on 23 January 1877. "I have found out in Breslau that it is a very good thing if someone else conducts the early rehearsals," Brahms afterward wrote to **Heinrich** and **Elisabeth von Herzogenberg**. "This was done quite splendidly by the young and very talented Buths. So all I had to do was to continue rehearsing, and the result was excellent" (Brahms 1974/1, 16). He added that Buths was also a very good pianist and had written a concerto that **Carl Reinecke** might be interested to present at the Gewandhaus. It was reportedly Brahms who later recommended Buths for the post at Elberfeld. On 23 February 1884, evidently at Buth's invitation, he appeared at a concert there, playing his Second Piano Concerto and conducting the *Gesang der Parzen*, the *Alto Rhapsody*, and the *Academic Festival Overture.*

Buths is of particular interest to English music lovers, for among the numerous contemporary works he performed was Elgar's *The Dream of Gerontius*, which he presented, in his own translation of Cardinal Newman's text, at the Lower Rhine Festival in Düsseldorf on 20 May 1902, in the composer's presence. Elgar dedicated his *Skizze* for piano to him the following year. (Alf 1952; Brahms 1974/1; Thoene 1960)

– C –

CANDIDUS, CARL AUGUST (b. Bischweiler [Bischwiller], Alsace, 14 April 1817; d. Feodosiya, Crimea, 16 July 1871). Poet. Brahms set poems by Candidus in the following songs: "Schwermut" (op. 58/5), "Tambourliedchen" (op. 69/5), "Lerchengesang" (op. 70/2), "Geheimnis" (op. 71/3), "Alte Liebe" (op. 72/1), and "Sommerfäden" (op. 72/2). He also used a text by Candidus in the duet "Jägerlied" (op. 66/4). (Krafft 1957)

CHAMISSO, ADELBERT VON (b. Boncourt Castle, Champagne, 30 January 1781; d. Berlin, 21 August 1838). Poet and prose writer, best known for the cycle *Frauen-Liebe und -Leben*, which was set to music by **Robert Schumann**, and for the story *Peter Schlemihls wundersame Geschichte*.

Brahms set one of his poems in "Die Müllerin" (op. 44/5). For another setting by Brahms of the same text, see M. McCorkle 1984, Anhang III/13.

CHLEDOWSKA, LEONTINE, BARONESS (b. Oberwerth, near Koblenz, 13 March 1854; d. Wiesbaden, 15 February 1955). Daughter of Ritter Jakob Ludwig von Chledowski (b. Lemberg [Lviv, Ukraine], 25 July 1820; d. Oberwerth, 29 May 1897) and his wife Ida, née Cramer von Pfaffenhofen (b. Grinzing, near Vienna, 25 February 1818; d. Oberwerth, 20 November 1906). Ida was the adopted daughter of Count Franz Pfaffenhofen, and she inherited the island of Oberwerth on her father's death on 8 April 1840; she married Chledowski in Paris on 17 December 1846.

Ludwig Kaufmann, who was director of the Wiesbaden Opera from 1948 until 1952, recalled some time before his death in 1980 that "in about 1956" [obviously an error, presumably for 1952 or early 1953] he had visited a "Baroness Chledowka," then in her 98th year, whose room was filled with memories of Brahms—photographs showing them together, piously preserved gifts she had received from him, and, in a glass cabinet, a bundle of letters tied with a silk ribbon. She told Kaufmann that she and Brahms had wished to become engaged, but that her father, "Regierungspräsident at Koblenz," had forbidden it, declaring that he would never allow her to become the wife of a musician. She had never married. Kaufmann added that he and a colleague had, at her request, played Brahms's E Minor Cello Sonata for her on her 99th birthday, and that he had later visited her on several further occasions. (Kaufmann's recollections concerning the baroness are contained in a typescript preserved at the Hessische Landesbibliothek, Wiesbaden, and were partly quoted by Bärbel Schwitzgebel [1997] in her article "Johannes Brahms in Wiesbaden.")

There appears to be no mention of the baroness in any biography of Brahms, who is most likely to have met her during the summer of 1883, which he spent at Wiesbaden. At that time he was 50 years old, a fact that would fit in with her reported remark to Kaufmann that he was then "bereits in reiferen Jahren" [already at a mature age]; she herself would have been 29 years old. According to an article in the *Wiesbadener Kurier* on 17 February 1955, she did not take up permanent residence at Wiesbaden until 1903. The same article makes reference to her special interest in music.

It has not been possible to ascertain any further information about Brahms's supposed relationship with the baroness. There is, incidentally, no mention in Horst Romeyk's (1994) authoritative book on the senior officials of the Prussian Rhine Province during the period 1816–1945 of her father having ever been a "Regierungspräsident" [chief administrator] at Koblenz. (Romeyk 1994; Schwitzgebel 1997)

CHOPIN, FRYDERYK FRANCISZEK [Frédéric François] (b. Žlazowa Wola, near Warsaw, ?1 March 1810; d. Paris, 17 October 1849). Composer. In his recollections of Brahms, **Ernst Rudorff** states that he had, on the whole, little liking for Chopin's music. When **Joachim Raff**, after hearing **Liszt** sight read Brahms's Scherzo op. 4 at Weimar in 1853, remarked that certain parts of it reminded him of Chopin's B-flat Minor Scherzo, Brahms, according to **William Mason**, said that he had never seen or heard any of Chopin's compositions; and **Max Kalbeck** (1976) states that, as far as he knows, Brahms only once played a piece by Chopin in public, namely a Nocturne in Vienna on 18 December 1863. In fact, Brahms performed compositions by Chopin on more than one occasion, for the first time at Celle (the Polonaise op. 40/1) on 2 May 1853, just a few weeks before his arrival at Weimar.

When **Breitkopf & Härtel** invited Brahms in 1877 to participate in a complete edition of Chopin's compositions, he readily agreed to assume the task in overall collaboration with Rudorff and **Woldemar Bargiel** (with whom he also shared responsibility for some of the volumes in which he was involved). Such misgivings as he voiced related to the difficulty of establishing authentic versions and not to any stated distaste for the music itself. (In this connection, see Brahms's correspondence with Rudorff [Brahms 1974/3] and Breitkopf & Härtel [Brahms 1974/14].) Among the works he edited were the Barcarolle (op. 60), Fantasie (op. 49), some of the Mazurkas (in which he expressed particular interest), and two of the sonatas (for a complete list, see M. McCorkle 1984, 750). (Brahms 1974/3, 1974/14; Mason 1901; H. Müller 1997; Rudorff 1957)

CHROBAK, RUDOLF (b. Troppau, Silesia [Opava, Czech Republic], 8 July 1843; d. Vienna, 1 October 1910). Prominent gynecologist and teacher in Vienna; director of a women's clinic (1889–1908). Brahms met him quite frequently during the last 10 years of his life, either at Chrobak's house (on one occasion Brahms took part in a performance of his Horn Trio there) or at that of Chrobak's colleague and friend **Theodor Billroth** (where, for instance, Chrobak and his wife were among the guests at a private performance of Brahms's recently composed *Zigeunerlieder* in March or April 1888).

Brahms is likely to have made Chrobak's acquaintance either through Billroth or through Chrobak's wife, the former Helene [Nelly] Lumpe (1847–1900), who had studied singing with **Josef Gänsbacher** and whom he had met, presumably through Gänsbacher, in his early years in Vienna. According to **Max Kalbeck** (1976), Nelly Chrobak remembered Brahms showing her a newly written song—then apparently called "Ewig," later retitled "Von ewiger Liebe" (op. 43/1)—in the spring of 1864. Furthermore, Kalbeck quotes several mock-flirtatious references to the attractive Nelly in Brahms's letters to Gänsbacher from Baden-Baden in 1865–66, as well as from a letter addressed by Brahms to Nelly herself in the summer of 1866. In August 1867 Brahms and his father stayed briefly at her family's holiday villa at Aussee (her father, Hofrat E. Lumpe, was, like her future husband, a successful gynecologist). Earlier that year, at Brahms's concert in Vienna on 7 April 1867, Nelly had taken the alto part in the first documented public performance of the vocal quartet "An die Heimat" (op. 64/1).

Kalbeck also hints at a link between Nelly and her sister Rosa and the vocal duet "Die Schwestern" (op. 61/1), which is based on a poem by Eduard Mörike. Otto Gottlieb-Billroth (1935), in his edition of the Brahms-Billroth correspondence, turns the hint into the assertion that Brahms had the sisters in mind when he composed the duet "during his first stay in Vienna." However, this assumption is contradicted by the fact that the duet already appears in the list that Brahms himself drew up in 1860 of his then still unpublished works. Its composition accordingly predates his arrival in Vienna in September 1862. (G. S. Bozarth speculates that it could perhaps be assigned to the autumn of 1858; the first setting later underwent revision—according to Bozarth, in the early 1870s—and the duet was published, as part of op. 61, in 1874.)

Nelly married Rudolf Chrobak in 1868. (Bozarth 1983a; Gottlieb-Billroth 1935; *ÖBL* 1957–; Peham 1903)

CHRYSANDER, (KARL FRANZ) FRIEDRICH (b. Lübtheen, Mecklenburg, 8 July 1826; d. Bergedorf, near Hamburg, 3 September 1901). Musicologist. His research and his writings concerned a vast number of composers but focused primarily on **Handel**. As a cofounder of the Deutsche Händel-Gesellschaft in 1856, he was responsible for virtually all of the close to 100 volumes of the collected edition of Handel's works that appeared under the society's auspices between 1858 and 1894. Moreover, he not only edited the music but also took on the task of engraving and printing most of those volumes at his home at Bergedorf, where he settled in 1866. He was able to finance this vast project partly through assistance he received from **King Georg V of Hanover** and later, after the annexation of Hanover by Prussia, from the Prussian state; partly with income obtained from editing journals, notably the *Allgemeine musikalische Zeitung* (1868–71, 1875–82); and partly from the sale of produce and flowers from his market garden. In addition to editing Handel's compositions, he worked on a biography of the composer, which, however, he never completed. The first volume was published in 1858, the second in 1860, and a part of the third in 1867.

Chrysander was highly respected as a scholar and widely admired for the single-mindedness with which he pursued his difficult projects. Among those who greatly appreciated both his erudition and his character was Brahms, who, as Karl Geiringer has pointed out, shared with him the "homely, upright, rugged, unassuming nature" typical of a North German, as well as a certain reticence and an aversion to intimacy. They met occasionally, for instance, when Chrysander attended a concert given by Brahms and **Joseph Joachim** in Vienna on 9 November 1867; they also corresponded. In the *Monthly Musical Record*, in 1937–38, Geiringer printed the partial or complete text of 16 letters addressed by Chrysander to Brahms, the first dating from 26 July 1869, the last from 16 December 1880; in 1956 Gustav Fock published nine letters and four postcards written by Brahms to Chrysander.

Chrysander was no stranger to London, where his married daughter was living and where he conducted an important part of his research on Handel. He was, in consequence, in contact with various leading English musicians, and in several of the above-mentioned letters he attempted, though unsuccessfully, to persuade Brahms to accept their invitations to conduct concerts in London. Some other of Chrysander's letters were occasioned by Brahms's readiness to write continuo parts for a number of duets and trios by Handel, which subsequently appeared in volume 32 (first in 1870 and in augmented form in 1880) of the collected edition (see also M. McCorkle 1984, Anhang Ia/10–11). When C. F. Peters, at Brahms's suggestion, published separately the six additional duets included in the 1880 edition, Brahms insisted on sharing his fee of 1,000 marks with Chrysander, who had translated the text from the original Italian into German. In response to the view expressed by **Max Abraham**, the proprietor of C. F. Peters, that one-fifth of the fee would constitute an adequate payment for the translation, Brahms stressed the debt he felt was owed to Chrysander in this matter, and his remarks at the same time reflect the profound regard that he felt for him altogether: "These Duets have cost me as much or more time and effort than any of my own compositions. Yet I consider my contribution to them to be slight, whereas it is clear that Chrysander has, quite simply, presented them to the world. I must confess that it is only because of what he did that the idea of our undertaking came to me at all. To that capable and hardworking man we owe a great deal" (Kalbeck 1976, vol. 3, 268). Apart from his contribution to the Handel edition, Brahms was also involved in the edition of books 1 and 2 of **François Couperin**'s *Pièces de clavecin* that Chrysander published. (For details, *see* COUPERIN, FRANÇOIS).

One of the letters printed by Geiringer suggests that Brahms may in 1878 have made a financial contribution toward the costs of Chrysander's Handel project. What is quite certain is that he was at least partly responsible for **Hans von Bülow**'s decision to offer to Chrysander, as an aid toward the financing of the Handel project, the 10,000 marks that his friends had handed to him on his 60th birthday, with the request that he should donate the sum to a worthy musical cause. Writing to Chrysander on 8 January 1891, Bülow stated that his choice Chrysander as the recipient of this donation had been taken in consultation with "our mutual friend, the eminent composer Dr Johannes Brahms" (M. von Bülow 1895–1908, vol. 8, 321–22). After some hesitation Chrysander accepted the gift, and in a note published in the *Hamburger Nachrichten* on 20 February 1891, he announced his intention to use 2,500 marks for the production of a facsimile of Handel's autograph of *Messiah* and the remaining 7,500 marks for the purchase of early musical instruments for the Kunst-und Gewerbemuseum [Museum of Art and Trade] in Hamburg. (Brahms 1974/14; Fock 1956; Geiringer 1937–38a; M. von Bülow 1895–1908; Rackwitz 1999; Schardig 1986)

CONRAT, HUGO. Son of the Breslau [Wrocław, Poland] merchant Isaak Cohn; brother of the well-known botanist Ferdinand Julius Cohn (1828–98), of the writer Oscar Justinus (1839–93), and of the legal historian Max Conrat (1848–1911). Hugo settled in Vienna, where he became a wealthy merchant. He and his wife Ida were very musical, and also generous and popular hosts; at their flat at 12 Walfischgasse, they entertained their numerous friends with dinners and suppers, and held chamber music sessions. They both attended the concerts of the Tonkünstlerverein.

According to Conrat's own account, he entered into closer contact with Brahms in 1887. He had published his German version of 25 gypsy songs in Budapest, with a piano accompaniment provided by Zoltán Nagy. (His text was based on a German translation prepared by a Hungarian nursemaid in his employment.) He brought these songs to the attention of Brahms, who found them highly attractive and promptly set 11 of them for four voices, with his own piano accompaniment (op. 103). Private performances at **Theodor Billroth**'s in Vienna in March or April 1888 and at **Julius Stockhausen**'s at Frankfurt on 15 October 1888 were followed by the first public performance in Berlin on 31 October 1888 (among the singers was **Amalie Joachim**). That same month the songs were published by **Fritz Simrock**. In addition, Brahms arranged eight of the songs for single voice; this version appeared the following year. Some time later Brahms turned four more songs from the Conrat-Nagy collection into vocal quartets, again with piano accompaniment, and these were to form part of the *6 Quartets* (op. 112) that C. F. Peters brought out in 1891.

Brahms was very pleased when Conrat, having witnessed his anger at the news that one of his letters to his father was to be sold at public auction in Berlin, secretly purchased it and sent it to Brahms, still in the envelope sealed by the auctioneer as proof that he had not himself been so indiscreet as to read it. Thereafter, he and Brahms saw one another regularly, in Conrat's flat that Brahms frequently visited, in Brahms's own rooms, at the house of mutual friends, and at the Tonkünstlerverein. Conrat also often joined Brahms on his Sunday walks in the country, and he also went to see him at Ischl. Their last meeting took place on 25 March 1897, when Conrat visited Brahms in his flat in Karlsgasse. (Conrat 1903, 1904; Lienau 1934)

CONRAT, ILSE, married name: Twartowska [?Twavdorska] (b. Vienna, 20 January 1880). Daughter of **Hugo Conrat**. Sculptress. She studied with Josef Breitner in Vienna and Ch. Vanderstappen in Brussels. In 1928 she settled in Munich, where she had already lived at different times prior to 1924. She had known Brahms well as a child.

Her sculptures, which bore the influence of the Jugendstil, were shown at numerous exhibitions of the Vienna Secession. Her best-known work is the monument she created for Brahms's tomb at the Vienna central cemetery. It incorporates a bust of the composer, which shows him consulting a musical score. It was unveiled on 7 May 1903, the 70th anniversary of his birth. In 1906 Conrad made a marble copy of the bust for Helene Magnus-Hornbostel (*see* HORNBOSTEL, (OTTO) ERICH VON), who presented it to **Julius Stockhausen** on his 80th birthday in July of that year (Wirth 1927, 445). (Czeike 1992–97; Wirth 1927)

CORNELIUS, (CARL AUGUST) PETER (b. Mainz, 24 December 1824; d. Mainz, 26 October 1874). Composer and poet. The son of two actors, he was himself trained for the stage and, in addition, received instruction in music from violinist Joseph Panny and later from conductor and composer Heinrich Esser; by 1840 he played violin in the orchestra at the Mainz Theatre. After his father's death in 1843, he settled in Berlin, where he pursued his music studies with Siegfried Dehn. In March 1852, during a visit to Weimar, he introduced himself to **Liszt**, and immediately fell under his spell; following several further stays at Weimar, in November 1853 he was finally invited to take up permanent residence at the Altburg, where he profited as a composer from Liszt's encouragement. From that time on his musical gods were Liszt, **Richard Wagner**, and **Hector Berlioz**. He spent the years 1859–64 in Vienna and then took up residence in Munich where King Ludwig II, at Wagner's suggestion, provided him with a generous salary; in 1866 he joined the faculty of the Royal Bavarian Musikschule. Nearly all of his numerous compositions were written for voice, in the form of choral music, duets, or songs; he also completed two operas, *DerBarbier von Bagdad* and *Der Cid.*

While he is known to have been at Weimar earlier in 1853, he does not appear to have been there when Brahms visited the town in June. Their meeting at Düsseldorf in October of that year may therefore have been their first. On 28 October **Robert Schumann** recorded in his personal journal, "H[er]r Cornelius" (Nauhaus 1982, 640). Brahms met Cornelius once more at Leipzig at the beginning of December, after which there is no record of any further contact between them until Brahms went to Vienna some nine years later. There he soon saw a good deal of Cornelius and of **Carl Tausig**, who were then sharing accommodations. According to the American pianist **William Mason**, who had known him at Weimar, Cornelius was a delightful and intensely musical man. Brahms evidently shared this view, for at the end of December 1862 he wrote to **Joseph Joachim**: "I am mostly in the company of Cornelius and Tausig—who vehemently deny being or ever having been 'Lisztians' and who, moreover, doubtless accomplish more with their little finger than all the other musicians with their whole head and all their fingers" (Brahms 1974/5, 332). Brahms complimented Cornelius on *Der Barbier von Bagdad*; but when the opera was eventually produced in Vienna, on 4 October 1890, he told **Richard Heuberger** that in his opinion it hardly merited all the excitement it was then generating (Heuberger 1976, 45). Cornelius, for his part, quickly recognized Brahms's outstanding talent and later readily acknowledged his superiority; a certain lack of confidence in his own accomplishments was, in any case, a characteristic trait of his.

Brahms continued his contacts with Cornelius during the winter of 1863–64. Cornelius and Tausig may have helped to arrange his visit to Richard Wagner's house at Penzing on 6 February 1864 (on this event, *see* STANDTHARTNER, JOSEPH and WAGNER, [WILHELM] RICHARD), and in May the three of them spent several days together at Bratislava, where Tausig's future bride Seraphine Vrabély was living. Both Brahms and Cornelius attended their wedding that November. But there are signs that the friendship between Brahms and Cornelius was cooling off. Thus, Cornelius, in a letter to his sister Susanne in March 1864, refers to Brahms as "the famous young composer who once in a while finds his way to my lodgings" (Cornelius 1904–5, vol. 1, 757); this does not suggest frequent contacts. Furthermore, when Cornelius bade Brahms a warm farewell prior to the latter's departure for Hamburg that June, he was disconcerted by Brahms's cold manner, which, he confided to his diary, made him regret having kissed Brahms; yet, later that same day he went to Brahms's lodgings to leave for him, as a farewell gift, the first edition of the score of *Tannhäuser* (which he had reportedly been given by Liszt).

The pronounced difference in their temperaments is likely to have been one of the principal factors that drove them apart, for Cornelius's effusiveness and his tendency to go into raptures over matters that pleased him were alien to Brahms's nature and may well have grated on him (many years later he told Richard Heuberger that Cornelius's "schwärmerisches Wesen" was partly affectation, but that he really was "one of those persons for whom unnaturalness had become their very nature" (Heuberger 1976, 43). It is not known, however, by what word or action Brahms, never the most tactful of men, so deeply offended Cornelius that he wrote in his diary in December 1864 that he was completely finished with "Herr Johannes Brahms," who was a profoundly egotistical man who had a very lofty opinion of himself (Cornelius 1904–5, vol. 1, 794). Shortly afterward, Cornelius moved to Munich.

This was nevertheless not the end of their contacts. Several months later Cornelius was, to his great embarrassment, drawn into a dispute between Wagner (and Cosima) and Brahms, as a result of which he was obliged to write to Brahms in August 1865 (*see* WAGNER, [WILHELM] RICHARD). There was also at least one further meeting between them, namely in the spring of 1873, when Brahms, who was vacationing at Tutzing and repeatedly traveled to Munich, called on Cornelius one day. The latter mentioned the visit in a letter to his sister Elise but offered no details. In the same letter, he contrasted his own labored compositional process and modest output with the facility and fecundity of such "great" contemporaries as **Max Bruch**, Brahms, **Joachim Raff**, and **Anton Rubinstein**, and singled out Brahms's Requiem as the finest work written by any of them.

Brahms seems to have retained pleasant memories of his contacts with Cornelius, as well as considerable respect for his musicianship. In 1890 he remarked to Heuberger, "Even though I didn't like everything about Tausig and Cornelius, the two of them would nevertheless be my favorite companions to-day. Each of them is surely worth more than all the present Viennese musicians taken together" (Heuberger 1976, 44). (Brahms 1974/5; Cornelius 1904–5, 1925; Heuberger 1976; Huschke 1939; Lederer 1977; Nauhaus 1982)

CORNET-KIEL, FRANZISKA (b. Kassel, 23 January 1808; d. Braunschweig, 7 August 1870). Soprano; sister of **August Kiel**. In 1825 she married Julius Cornet (1793–1860) who had a successful career as a tenor and theater manager (director of the Stadttheater, Hamburg, 1841–47; the Kärntnertor-Theater, Vienna, 1853–58; and the Viktoriatheater, Berlin, 1858–60). Her principal engagements were at Hamburg (1825–32), Braunschweig (1832–41), and again Hamburg (1841–47). Among her leading roles were the Countess in *Le nozze di Figaro*, Leonore in *Fidelio*, and Romeo in Bellini's *I Capuleti e i Montecchi*. In 1848, together with her husband, she played a significant role in the establishment of the Hamburg conservatory, at which she herself became an instructor. Some time after her husband's death, she retired to Braunschweig. Both she and her daughter **Adele Passy-Cornet** took part in Brahms's first two public concerts at Hamburg on 21 September 1848 and 14 April 1849. (Kutsch and Riemens 1987–94)

COSSEL, OTTO FRIEDRICH WILLIBALD (b. 1813; d. Hamburg, 28 August 1865). Piano teacher active in Hamburg; a pupil of **Eduard Marxsen**. He began to give Brahms lessons in the winter of 1840–41 and continued to do so until at least 1843, by which time their relationship had become a very close one, as is evident from the letter he received from the then eight-year-old boy at New Year in 1842, in which the latter addressed him as "Geliebter Lehrer" [Beloved teacher]. If, as seems reasonable, one assumes that the text of this letter was concocted with the help of his parents, it clearly shows how much they appreciated the interest Cossel took in their son's progress and welfare. It was reportedly Cossel who dissuaded **Johann Jakob Brahms** from accepting an impresario's offer to send the exceptionally talented child on a concert tour to America, and it was also Cossel who was instrumental in persuading the rather reluctant Marxsen to take him on as a student. At Marxsen's request, Cossel still continued his own lessons for a while, but before long the instruction was left entirely in Marxsen's hands. (Cossel also taught Brahms's brother **Fritz**.)

It is clear that Brahms greatly benefited from Cossel's tuition, and for the rest of his life he was to preserve a profound admiration for Cossel as a teacher and a deep affection for him as a person. "He was a quite special and exceptional human being and teacher," he told **Klaus Groth** in 1887 (Lohmeier 1997, 114); and in a conversation with **Richard Heuberger** in 1896, he asserted that an instruction as thorough as the one he had received from Cossel was then no longer available anywhere (Heuberger 1976, 108). Also, in 1896 he wrote to Cossel's daughter Marie (1849–1935), with whom he had kept in touch over the years, about her "dear, unforgettable father, whose memory is one of the most sacred and precious of my life" (part of a fragment preserved at the Brahms-Institut, Lübeck; for an English translation of the entire fragment, see Avins 1997, 740–41). Brahms was a godfather of her younger sister Christine Luise Johanna (b. 1853).

Cossel's remark, reported by **Julius Spengel**, that the young Brahms could become an excellent pianist if he would only refrain from constantly wanting to compose, has greatly amused Brahmsians; yet, it was surely not an altogether unreasonable one at the time. (Heuberger 1976; Lohmeier 1997; J. Spengel 1898)

COUPERIN, FRANÇOIS (b. Paris, 10 November 1668; d. Paris, 11 September 1733). Composer, harpsichordist, and organist. Brahms's interest in Couperin's compositions is most strikingly exemplified by his involvement in **Friedrich Chrysander**'s publication, in his Denkmäler der Tonkunst series, of books I and II of the *Pièces de clavecin*. Chrysander secured his offer of collaboration during a visit to Vienna in the autumn of 1867. Book I appeared in 1869 and was reissued two years later together with book II, with Brahms being identified each time as the sole editor. However, as E. Kelly has convincingly demonstrated, Chrysander sought Brahms's participation mainly for the prestige his name would bring to the whole project, and it was in fact Chrysander himself who undertook most of the editorial work, while Brahms's contribution was essentially confined to assistance with the correction of the proofs. Indeed, when the London music publisher Augener reissued the two books in 1888, Brahms and Chrysander were cited as their joint editors; Chrysander alone took responsibility for the edition of books III and IV, which appeared with them.

At the same time, there is no doubt as to Brahms's genuine interest in Couperin's music. His copy of Augener's edition of books III and IV, now in the Archive of the Gesellschaft der Musikfreunde in Vienna, bears a number of annotations in his hand, some of them, according to Kelly, of an "editorial type," others "highlighting form and motivic content" (Kelly 2004, 593). Moreover, he played a piece by Couperin at more than one of his concerts—for instance, in Vienna on 20 February 1869 and at The Hague on 19 January 1876. (However, to claim, as Kelly does, that Couperin's harpsichord pieces "featured prominently" in his piano repertory is surely an overstatement.) Finally, Kelly judges that the *style brisé*, which is so characteristic an aspect of Couperin's music, left significant traces in Brahms's later piano compositions. Thus, she considers that *style brisé* textures "predominate" in the Intermezzo op. 117/2 and that the central section of the Intermezzo op. 117/3 "is awash with the rich harmonic colours that arise from the sonorities of the *style brisé*; its "ethereal and enigmatic spirit," she concludes, "is perhaps best captured in the Intermezzo in B Minor op. 119, no.1" (Kelly 2004, 600). (Kelly 2004; Rackwitz 1999)

CRANZ, AUGUST. Firm of publishers founded by August Cranz (1789–1870) in Hamburg in 1814, and, from 1857, directed by his son Alwin (1834–1923). In 1876 Alwin also acquired the Viennese firm **C. A. Spina**. Alwin's son Oskar became a partner in 1896, and the following year he moved the firm to Leipzig.

Brahms entered into contact with the Cranz family while still in his teens. **Max Kalbeck** (1976) refers to Alwin as "his pupil and friend" (vol. 1, 38–39), and Brahms made arrangements of various operatic numbers and national songs for piano solo or duet for August Cranz, which were published under the pseudonym "G. W. Marks" (but the same name was apparently also used by the firm for other arrangers). Brahms was probably responsible for preparing the six fantasies on Russian and gypsy airs that Cranz issued some time before 1852 under the collective title *Souvenir de la Russie* (see M. McCorkle 1984, Anhang IV/6).

Brahms later told Max Kalbeck that Cranz had also offered to buy any original compositions he might have been willing to sell to him, but that, conscious of their shortcomings, he had not allowed himself to be "seduced," as much as he needed the money. He described the same situation, again mentioning Cranz's name, in a letter to **Clara Schumann** in August 1894 (Litzmann 1970, vol. 2, 562–63). In fact, the only original compositions by Brahms that the firm would ever publish were the *3 Gesänge* op. 42 in 1868 or 1869, and those it obtained only after they had been rejected by **Fritz Simrock**, **Breitkopf & Härtel**, and **Jakob Melchior Rieter-Biedermann**. The firm also published Brahms's editions of three of **C. P. E. Bach**'s *6 Concerti per il cembalo* in 1862, but with no indication as to the editor's identity (M. McCorkle 1984, Anhang VI/1). (Litzmann 1970)

– D –

DALWIGK ZU LICHTENFELS, REINHARD LUDWIG KARL GUSTAV, BARON (b. Kassel, 21 January 1818; d. Wehlheiden, near Kassel, 3 June 1897). Senior official at the court of Grand Duke Nikolaus Friedrich Peter of Oldenburg (reigned 1853–1900); son of Alexander Felix von Dalwigk (1776–1839), court marshal to the Elector of Hessen. After studying law at the universities of Heidelberg and Marburg, he entered the service of Grand Duke Paul Friedrich August of Oldenberg in 1847, and in 1850 became chamberlain of his son Nikolaus Friedrich Peter. A highly cultured man, Dalwigk was placed in charge of the court Kapelle in 1854, and he also served as codirector of the theater from 1865. In addition, he became a member of the board of directors of the Art Society in 1856, and later its president (1873–93). In 1873 he was appointed court marshal, and in 1877 accorded the title "Exzellenz." He resigned all his offices in 1893, on reaching the age of 75.

He was naturally in close contact with **Albert Dietrich**, who held the post of court Kapellmeister at Oldenburg from 1861 until 1890, and it was presumably through him that Dalwigk met Brahms in 1862. At a concert on 14 March of that year Brahms was the soloist in **Beethoven**'s Fourth Piano Concerto; the program also featured his own Serenade op. 11. The following year Brahms dedicated his Piano Quartet op. 25 to Dalwigk. Shortly before its publication he wrote to **Fritz Simrock**:

> I have just learned from Dietrich that he has sent you the title 'Chamberlain' and other details. No doubt he has explained to you more clearly than to me just how necessary it is to insert the title on my title sheet. However, I think that if the information arrives too late or causes too much bother, it will not be impolite to omit it. As I know him, the man is sufficiently broad-minded not to miss the titles (which, in any case, don't sound all that grand) any more than I do, and to accept a friendly gesture readily in the spirit in which it is offered. (Brahms 1974/9, 43–44).

In the event, the dedication simply read "to Baron Reinhard von Dalwigk." (Brahms 1974/9; Friedl 1992)

DAUMER, GEORG FRIEDRICH (b. Nuremberg, 5 March 1800; d. Würzburg, 13 December 1875). Writer on religion; poet. Raised as a protestant, he later lost his Christian faith but he eventually recovered it, becoming a Catholic. His views on religion provoked criticism, as did his poetry, which was condemned by some as an overt celebration of the pleasures of the flesh, especially in his portrayal of women in *Frauenbilder und Huldigungen*. Similar offence was caused in certain quarters by many of his translations of foreign verse, which he published notably in *Hafis*, a collection of poems based mainly on the work of the 14th-century bard **Hafiz**, and in *Polydora*, an anthology of poems drawn from many languages.

Brahms, who owned copies of the three above-mentioned books (as well as a copy of Daumer's *Mahomed und sein Werk*, "a collection of oriental poems"), was clearly greatly attracted by many of his original poems and translations, as he set altogether 35 of them to music: op. 32/2; five from *Frauenbilder und Huldigungen* (op. 57/1, 4–6, 8); six from *Hafis* (op. 32/7–9; op. 47/1–2; op. 57/2); and 23 from *Polydora* (op. 46/1–2; op. 52/1–18; op. 57/3, 7; op. 59/6). Particularly striking is the fact that all 18 texts of the *Liebeslieder-Walzer* are taken from the last-named collection; they are of Russian, Polish, and Hungarian origin.

On 29 April 1872, in the course of a journey from Nuremberg to Karlsruhe, Brahms called on Daumer at Würzburg. He soon realized, as he later told **Max Kalbeck**, that the "little wizened old man" knew absolutely nothing about him, nor had he any knowledge of the settings Brahms had made of his texts. Brahms, who had apparently brought some of these settings with him, subsequently arranged for his publishers to send Daumer others. This was the only time that Brahms met the poet to whom he owed so much. In September 1875, when he stopped at Würzburg on his return journey from Ziegelhausen to Vienna, he was unable to see Daumer, who was already mortally ill. (Kluncker 1984; Otto 1980)

DAVID, FERDINAND (b. Hamburg, 19 January 1810; d. Klosters, Switzerland, 18 [?19] July 1873). Violinist, composer, and teacher. After studying the violin with Louis Spohr and theory with **Moritz Hauptmann** at Kassel (1823–25), he toured with his sister Louise (1811–50), a pianist who later became well known in England under the name of Louise Dulcken. From 1826 to 1829 he played in the orchestra of the Königstädtisches Theater in Berlin, and from 1829 to 1835 he was the leader of a private quartet maintained by Landrat Karl von Liphardt at Dorpal (Tartu, Estonia). On 1 March 1836 he became Konzertmeister of the Leipzig Gewandhaus Orchestra, thanks to the support of its recently appointed conductor Felix Mendelssohn, with whom David had been linked in a close friendship and fruitful artistic collaboration during his earlier stay in Berlin. (He would give the first performance of Mendelssohn's Violin Concerto in Leipzig on 13 March 1845.) David also led the orchestra at the Leipzig Stadttheater and presented regular quartet sessions. Moreover, he taught at the conservatory from its foundation in 1843; among his students were **Joseph Joachim**, **Wilhelm Joseph von Wasielewski**, and August Wilhelmj. He was, in addition, a prolific composer, especially of works involving the violin.

David's contribution to the musical life of Leipzig was thus an outstanding one, and the role he played in it became even more prominent at about the time Brahms arrived there in the late autumn of 1853. In the years immediately following Mendelssohn's death in 1847, the Gewandhaus Orchestra had been conducted by **Niels Wilhelm Gade** (1847–48) and **Julius Rietz** (1848–52). The 1852–53 season had been entrusted jointly to David and Gade, each conducting 10 concerts; but during the 1853–54 season, David was solely responsible for all the concerts.

Given David's influential position, it was fortunate that he was from the outset well disposed toward Brahms and eager to promote his career. Soon after arriving in Leipzig, Brahms called on David, who promptly returned the visit and, moreover, paid Brahms the compliment of playing with him the Violin Sonata that he had brought with him (evidently the one in A minor that was subsequently lost). Furthermore, David, as well as some of Brahms's other new acquaintances, urged him to introduce himself to the local public by taking part in one of the chamber music concerts. Brahms did so on 17 December 1853, when he performed his First Piano Sonata and the Scherzo op. 4 at a concert given by David.

Brahms remained in contact with David during the following years, and he had again reason to appreciate David's support when his performance of his First Piano Concerto received a generally frosty reception in Leipzig in 1859. No one, he reported to Joachim, said a word about it to him except David "who was very friendly and showed great interest in it" (Brahms 1974/5, 233). Two years later (on 8 March 1861) Brahms played **Beethoven**'s Triple Concerto with David and Karl Davidoff at a Philharmonic Society concert in Hamburg.

Brahms was later also on friendly terms with David's son Paul (b. Leipzig, 4 August 1840; d. Oxford, 21 January 1932), who was Konzertmeister of the Karlsruhe Orchestra from 1862 to 1865. In the latter year he was appointed music master at Uppingham School in England, but he apparently still kept in touch with Brahms, for, according to **Max Kalbeck**, he visited him at Tutzing in July 1873. Upon his retirement from the school in 1908, Paul David moved to Oxford; that same year he was awarded the honorary degree of master of music by Cambridge University. (Brahms 1974/5; Forner 1972, 1981; and information kindly supplied by Mr. Jim Peschek, director of music at Uppingham School, England.)

DAVIES, FANNY (b. Guernsey, 27 June 1861; d. London, 1 September 1934). Pianist. After studying with **Carl Reinecke** and Oskar Paul at the Leipzig conservatory (1882–83) and with **Clara Schumann** at Frankfurt (1883–85), she first appeared in public at the Crystal Palace in London on 9 September 1885, playing the first movement of **Beethoven**'s Third Piano Concerto and Mendelssohn's Scherzo Capriccio in F-sharp Minor. She enjoyed a highly successful career, both in England and on the continent. In addition to concertizing as a solo pianist, she also made a name for herself in chamber music, collaborating with such well-known performers as Casals, **Joseph Joachim**, **Richard Mühlfeld**, Piatti, and the Bohemian String Quartet.

Her acquaintance with Brahms probably dates from September 1887, when she was present at the informal performances that he gave at Baden-Baden of the Piano Trio op. 101 (with Joachim and **Robert Hausmann**) and the Cello Sonata op. 99 (with Hausmann). Many years later she was to give a detailed account of this performance of the Trio, and especially of the manner in which Brahms played the piano part, in her article "Some

Personal Recollections of Brahms as Pianist and Interpreter" (printed below Donald Tovey's comprehensive study of Brahms's chamber music in *Cobbett's Cyclopedic Survey of Chamber Music*). Davies met Brahms on several further occasions, notably in Vienna at the houses of **Anna Franz** (*see* WITTGENSTEIN FAMILY) and **Richard and Maria Fellinger**; according to **Max Kalbeck**, they repeatedly played duets together at the Fellingers'. She probably last saw Brahms during her stay in Vienna in 1895–96. On 26 November 1895 she played in a performance of his Piano Quartet op. 25 at a concert of the Rosé Quartet. Four days later she and Brahms were among the guests at lunch at **Hans Richter**'s house; she also visited him in his rooms in Karlsgasse.

Fanny Davies gained the reputation of being a particularly fine interpreter of the works of Beethoven, **Robert Schumann**, and Brahms. She was the first to play some of Brahms's Fantasien op. 116 and Intermezzi op. 117 in England (30 January 1893), and she also took part in the first English performances of the Violin Sonata op. 108 (with **Ludwig Straus**, on 7 May 1889), the Clarinet Trio op. 114 (with Mühlfeld and Piatti, on 2 April 1892), and the Clarinet Sonatas op. 120 (with Mühlfeld, on 24 June 1895). (Anon 1905; Davies 1963; H. Ehrlich 1893a; Pascall 2001)

DEBROIS VAN BRUYCK, KARL (b. Brünn [Brno], 14 March 1828; d. Waidhofen an der Ybbs, 5 August 1902). Composer and writer on music. A fervent admirer of the music of **Robert Schumann**, with whom, moreover, he was in correspondence in the early 1850s, he was one of the first of the Viennese critics to take an interest in the young Hamburg composer whom Schumann praised so enthusiastically. When **Clara Schumann** introduced Viennese audiences to a Gavotte and Saravande by Brahms (from WoO 3 and 5) in her recital of 20 January 1856, and to the Andante and Scherzo from his Piano Sonata op. 1 on 12 February 1856, Debrois commented favorably on the pieces in the *Wiener Zeitung*, saying that they confirmed the high opinion he had already formed of the composer's rare talent. On 25 September 1857 Debrois, who had little liking for the "Music of the Future," published in the same newspaper an essay reviewing the work of various outstanding contemporary composers, among whom he placed Brahms. Of the compositions opp. 1–10, he singled out the *Schumann Variations* for particular praise, though not without some reservations; next to them, his preference was for the songs. Altogether, he predicted a rosy future for the young composer, especially if he were able to control a certain tendency toward excessive refinement and an apparent predilection for the demonic and the fantastic.

Debrois sent a copy of this essay to Clara Schumann, who read it with mixed feelings. While she agreed with much of it, she was riled by certain remarks about Brahms, as well as by Debrois's rather low opinion of **Joseph Joachim**'s compositions. (Joachim had already expressed his hostility toward Debrois in a letter to Brahms in March 1855, accusing him of ignorance and arrogance [Brahms 1974/5, 107].) Clara Schumann's diary records that she expressed her reactions in a frank letter to Debrois (Litzmann 1902, vol. 3, 24, n. 1). At the same time, she sent the essay to Brahms, who was then at Detmold, together with a (now lost) letter, in which she evidently criticized it. Brahms, however, largely disagreed with her objections, at any rate as far as Debrois's remarks concerning himself were concerned (those regarding Joachim he dismissed as "rubbish"): "What he writes about me. . . . I found sensible beyond all expectations, except for a few downright inanities" (Litzmann 1970, vol. 1, 207).

In 1860 Brahms and Joachim sent their anti-Liszt manifesto to Vienna for Debrois to sign, but he did not do so. However, Brahms established contact with him after moving to Vienna some two years later, as is apparent from Clara Schumann's letter of 3 November 1862: "Concerning your question about Debrois: you seem to have forgotten that we broke off all relations a long time ago, because of yourself and Joachim. . . . It is strange how things often turn out: it was because of you that we broke off our relations, and now you are on friendly terms with him" (Litzmann 1970, vol. 1, 411). Nothing seems to be known about any later contacts between Brahms and Debrois. (Brahms 1974/5; Litzmann 1902, 1970; *ÖBL* 1957–)

DEBUSSY, (ACHILLE) CLAUDE (b. St. Germain-en-Laye, 22 August 1862; d. Paris, 25 March 1918). Composer. In 1924 the following three articles appeared in the English journal *The Musical Times* over the name "Andrew de Ternant": "Debussy and Brahms" (July), "Debussy and Some Italian Musicians" (September), and "Debussy and Some Others on Sullivan" (December). These articles offer details reportedly confided to Ternant by his friend Debussy concerning certain trips the latter undertook to Italy, Austria, and England, and the conversations he had there with various prominent musicians. When Debussy finally left the Villa Medici in Rome (in February 1887), Ternant (1924) writes, "he made up his mind to become personally acquainted with as many eminent foreign composers as possible, and his 'greatest capture' was Johannes Brahms" (608).

The article on Debussy and Brahms contains a detailed account of Debussy's supposed meetings with Brahms in Vienna and of Brahms's remarks on a variety of subjects, including his high regard for Bizet's *Carmen*. He is even said to have invited Debussy to a performance of it, telling him that it would be the 21st time he had seen the opera; he also greatly regretted never having had an opportunity to meet Bizet ("he would have gone to the end of the earth to embrace the composer of *Carmen*" (Ternant

1924, 609), who had, moreover, expressed a desire to see Brahms. It appears, though, that Ternant's article on Debussy and Brahms, like the other two of the series, is pure fiction—see "The Hoaxes of André de Ternant" in Edward Lockspeiser's (1962–65) *Debussy: His Life and Mind* (Lockspeiser gives the author's first name as "André," but, as indicated above, the articles are actually signed "Andrew de Ternant"). Incidentally, Debussy had visited Vienna in 1882, at the age of 20, as a member of Nadezha von Meck's entourage. (Lockspeiser 1962–65; Ternant 1924)

DEICHMANN, WILHELM LUDWIG (b. Rodenberg, Hesse, 3 August 1798; d. Mehlem, 23 November 1876). Banker residing at Cologne; married in 1830 to Elisabeth (Lilla) Jacobine Eleonore Schaaffhausen (b. Cologne, 12 May 1811; d. Bonn, 7 July 1888). From 1818 he worked for the bank that his future father-in-law, Abraham Schaaffhausen (1756–1824), had established in Cologne and of which he would himself assume sole control in 1830. After it became the first private joint-stock bank in Germany in 1848 under the name A. Schaaffhausen Bankverein, Deichmann was appointed one of the directors of the new concern. In 1858 he left to found his own bank, Deichmann & Co., together with Adolph vom Rath. Deichmann and his wife entertained generously, both at their house in Cologne and at the villa they acquired at Mehlem in 1836. Their regular visitors at Mehlem included several prominent citizens from nearby Bonn, and since the couple were great music lovers, a number of musicians.

Brahms arrived at Mehlem on 2 September 1853 at the end of a week's walking tour along the Rhine, carrying a letter of introduction to the Deichmanns from **Arnold Wehner**. His fears that he might be in for a formal reception were quickly dispelled, and by the following morning he felt so much at ease that, as he was to inform **Joachim** a few days later, he had dropped all thoughts of leaving promptly. His hosts were "the most splendid persons" and the children "utterly delightful." He reported further that he had met again, among the other visitors, several people he already knew, and that he had also made the acquaintance of "those delightful gentlemen" **(Wilhelm von) Wasielewski** and (Christian) **Reimers**, who both frequently came to the villa (Brahms 1974/5, 5–6). The Deichmanns must have liked Brahms as much as he liked them, for they arranged for him to take their three sons on a trip along the Rhine.

It was from Mehlem that Brahms set out for Düsseldorf at the end of September 1853 to call on **Robert Schumann**. He himself, in another letter to Joachim written from there in October, stated that it was only since his departure from Hamburg, "and especially during his stay at Mehlem," that he had come to know Schumann's compositions and appreciate their greatness (Litzmann 1970, vol. 1, 12). Commentators on this letter have attributed this new insight into Schumann's music on Brahms's part to his study of the many scores he found at the Deichmanns' house, and it is, of course, quite likely that his hosts possessed an extensive music library. But it is also more than probable that he benefited from discussions he had at their house with musicians closely associated with Schumann, such as Wasielewski and Reimers, and furthermore from performances of Schumann's music, which he heard at Mehlem. In a speech at the Cologne conservatory on 2 May 1897, **Franz Wüllner** recalled, "I lived [in the summer of 1853] for some months at Honnef in close contact with the Bonn musicians Wasielewski and Reimers and with the hospitable family Deichmann at Mehlem, where we frequently met to make music" (Brahms 1974/15, 186; Brill 1957).

As it turned out, therefore, Brahms's first stay with the Deichmanns was of considerable importance in his musical education. Nothing specific is known about his further relations with the family, but he is likely to have met some of its members on later occasions—for instance, in February 1878, when he stopped off at Cologne on his way back to Vienna from Holland, while **Clara Schumann** was concertizing there. As she and **Marie Fillunger** were staying with the Deichmanns (Wilhelm Ludwig had died over a year earlier, but his widow was still alive), it would be strange if Brahms did not take the opportunity to renew his acquaintance with the family. (Brahms 1974/5, 1974/15; Brill 1957; R. Hofmann 1997; Kleinpass 1975)

DEITERS, HERMANN (CLEMENS OTTO) (b. Bonn, 27 June 1833; d. Koblenz, 11 May 1907). Schoolteacher, philologist, and writer on music. The son of a professor of law at Bonn University, he himself qualified as a lawyer in 1854, but he subsequently undertook the study of classical philology, culminating in a dissertation in Latin on Hesiod's description of Heracles' shield, which he presented in 1858. That same year he began his teaching career at Bonn. From 1869 he taught at Düren, and subsequently was appointed director of the Gymnasiums at Konitz (1874), Posen [Poznan, Poland] (1877), and Bonn (1883). From 1885 until 1903 he served as Provinzialschulrat [provincial inspector of schools] at Koblenz.

Essentially self-taught in musical matters, he was a prolific contributor on musical subjects to various periodical publications, notably the *Deutsche Musik-Zeitung* in Vienna (1861–62), **Breitkopf & Härtel**'s *Allgemeine musikalische Zeitung* (1863–65), **Jakob Melchior Rieter-Biedermann**'s *Leipziger allgemeine musikalische Zeitung/Allgemeine musikalische Zeitung* (1866–82), *Ergänzungsblätter zur Kenntnis der*

Gegenwart (1868–71), and Breitkopf & Härtel's *Vierteljahrschrift für Musikwissenschaft* (1888–93). He was particularly interested in the music of **Beethoven**, **Robert Schumann**, Brahms, **Max Bruch**, **Theodor Kirchner**, and **Woldemar Bargiel**, while showing little sympathy for **Richard Wagner** and for the "New German School." He regarded Brahms as the outstanding contemporary composer and devoted several articles and an entire book to him. His *Johannes Brahms*, published in 1880, offers some interesting observations on Brahms's music, but it also demonstrates how little accurate information was then available about his life. Admittedly, Brahms had done very little to assist Deiters's efforts to obtain reliable data, professing himself unable to supply him with more than the correct date of his birth. A French translation of the book by **Henriette Fritsch-Estrangin** appeared in Leipzig and Brussels in 1884, and an English version by Rose Newmarch in London in 1888.

According to Wilhelm Altmann, who edited a number of letters from Brahms to Deiters, they originally met at Bonn in 1855 or 1856. Moreover, Brahms is known to have been in contact with Deiters while staying at Bonn in the summer of 1868; otherwise, there is no firm evidence of later meetings, but there may well have been some. Thus Brahms mentioned in a letter to **Bernhard Scholz** in December 1880 that Deiters was planning to come from Posen to Breslau [Wrocław] to attend the concert he was giving there on 4 January 1881.

Deiters is best known today for his involvement in publications on **Mozart** and Beethoven. He was responsible for the third (1889–91) and fourth (1905–7) editions of **Otto Jahn**'s *W. A. Mozart* (originally published in 1856–59, followed by a revised version, prepared by Jahn himself, in 1867). It was also to Deiters that Alexander Wheelock Thayer turned over in 1865 the English text of his biography of Beethoven, and it was thus Deiters who prepared and published the first three volumes of the original German edition of *Ludwig van Beethovens Leben*: vol. 1 in 1866 (with a revised edition in 1901), vol. 2 in 1872, vol. 3 in 1879. After Thayer's death in 1897 Deiters took on the task of completing the remainder, but he died before the fourth volume was ready for publication. (It then fell to Hugo Riemann to bring out vol. 4 in 1907, and vol. 5 in 1908.) Deiters's interest in both classical civilization and music also led him to publish an edition of Aristides Quintilianus's treatise *On Music*.

Styra Avins (1997) mistakenly states in her *Johannes Brahms: Life and Letters* that Deiters was "organist at the Evangelical church in Vienna" and at one time editor of the *Allgemeine musikalische Zeitung* (778). She appears to have confused him with **Selmar Bagge**. (Avins 1997; Brahms 1974/3; Deiters 1880; Herttrich 1997; Kahl 1933, 1960)

DE LARA [TILBURY], (LOTTIE) ADELINA (b. Carlisle, 23 January 1872; d. Woking, 25 November 1961). English pianist. A child prodigy, she studied with **Fanny Davies**, and from 1886 with **Clara Schumann** in Frankfurt. At the latter's house she met Brahms, and in her memoirs entitled *Finale,* she states that he coached her in some of his piano compositions and recalls the instructions he gave her in that connection. Apart from some other memories of Brahms, De Lara's book contains interesting recollections of her lessons with Clara Schumann. (De Lara 1955)

DEPPE, LUDWIG (b. Alverdissen, Lippe, 7 November 1828; d. Bad Pyrmont, 5 September 1890). Pianist, teacher, conductor, and composer. He studied piano with Brahms's teacher **Eduard Marxsen** in Hamburg (1849), and later composition with Johann Christian Lobe in Leipzig. He returned to Hamburg around 1857 and subsequently founded a musical society there, whose concerts he himself conducted. These concentrated particularly on **Handel**'s oratorios, and among the well-known singers participating in the performances were **Julius Stockhausen** and **Amalie Joachim**. Deppe was clearly well regarded in Hamburg, for Brahms wrote to **Clara Schumann** in December 1862 that only Deppe and he had been thought to be in the running for a senior position with the Singverein. (In the event, the authorities chose Stockhausen at the same time they appointed him conductor of the Philharmonic Orchestra.) Deppe relinquished his position as conductor of his society's concerts at the end of 1866; they continued for about another year under the direction of Carl von Holten. From 1874 until 1886 Deppe was Kapellmeister of the Royal Opera in Berlin and also conducted concerts there.

However, it was especially as a piano teacher that Deppe made his mark, first in Hamburg and then in Berlin. In particular, his teaching method that placed emphasis on the desirability of "muscular synergy," by which the hand is freed of the restricting weight of the arm, influenced contemporary pedagogy, and some of his ideas were taken up by such prominent theoreticians as Theodor Leschetitzky, Rudolf Breithaupt, and Donald Tovey. His theories were presented to a specialized public in technical treatises written by some of his students, and to a much wider range of readers in America by Amy Fay, whose account of her experiences as a piano student under various German teachers, entitled *Music-Study in Germany in the Nineteenth Century*, was published in 1881 and had gone through some 20 editions by 1912. Deppe's most famous pupil was **Emil von Sauer**.

It may be assumed that Brahms was personally acquainted with Deppe since his early days in Hamburg, although almost nothing is known about their contacts; however, there is later evidence that he and Brahms were on intimate "Du" terms. In December 1867 Brahms spent some time with Deppe when the latter visited Vienna; in a letter to his father, he mentioned having been with Deppe in a tavern on Christmas Eve and having gone with him, **Gustav Nottebohm**, and others to Schönbrunn the next day. (Fay 1965; Sittard 1971, Stephenson 1973)

DESSOFF, FELIX OTTO (b. Leipzig, 14 January 1835; d. Frankfurt am Main, 28 October 1892). Conductor, pianist, and composer. Encouraged by **Liszt**, he decided on a musical career and enrolled in 1851 at the Leipzig conservatory, where he studied piano with Ignaz Moscheles and L. Plaidy, composition with **Moritz Hauptmann**, and conducting with **Julius Rietz**. For some years after leaving the conservatory in 1854, he gained useful experience as a Kapellmeister at Altenburg, Chemnitz, Düsseldorf, Aachen, Magdeburg, and Kassel. As a result of a highly successful appearance as guest conductor in Vienna on 7 September 1859, when he conducted Rossini's *Guillaume Tell* without a score, he was offered a contract as Kapellmeister at the court opera from 1 January 1860. He also took over the direction of the philharmonic concerts later that year (first concert on 4 November 1860), and the following year was entrusted with the composition class at the conservatory of the Gesellschaft der Musikfreunde. For the next 15 years he was thus one of the most important figures in the musical life of Vienna. His students at the conservatory included **Robert Fuchs**, Joseph Hellmesberger Jr., **Heinrich von Herzogenberg**, **Richard Heuberger**, Felix Mottl, **Arthur Nikisch**, and Ernst von Schuch. He left Vienna in 1875 to become court Kapellmeister at Karlsruhe; from late 1880 until his death, he was principal Kapellmeister at the Frankfurt theater.

Dessoff enjoyed friendly relations with Brahms over a period of 30 years, dating from Brahms's arrival in Vienna in 1862 (according to **Max Kalbeck**, they had first met in Leipzig in 1853). Their relations were both on an artistic and a personal level (Brahms was regularly invited to lunch by Dessoff and his wife Friederike [1841–1907], a former actress whom Dessoff had married in 1861). To cite some of their artistic contacts: on 3 March 1863 Brahms conducted his Serenade op. 16 at a philharmonic concert; on 25 March 1863 he played **Beethoven**'s Fourth Piano Concerto, as well as piano music by **Franz Schubert** and **Robert Schumann**, at a concert in aid of a Viennese hospital, which was conducted by Dessoff at the court opera house; on 12 December 1869 he conducted his Serenade op. 11 at another philharmonic concert (Dessoff had been so incensed when, at one of his own rehearsals of this work, some members of the orchestra had refused to play it that he had resigned, but he eventually withdrew his resignation and the work was duly rehearsed, though presented at a later concert than had been planned); on 22 January 1871 Brahms was the soloist in the first Viennese performance of his First Piano Concerto, at a philharmonic concert; on 2 November 1873, also at a philharmonic concert, he conducted the first-ever performance of his *Haydn Variations*; and on 14 November 1874 he and Dessoff played the piano parts at a performance of 10 of the *Liebeslieder-Waltzer* at an artists' soiree of the Gesellschaft der Musikfreunde.

In her article on Dessoff in the encyclopedia *Die Musik in Geschichte und Gegenwart*, Imogen Fellinger calls him "one of the outstanding conductors of his time," and adds that his performances were regarded as "exemplary" by his contemporaries. The fact that he was consistently reelected by the members of the philharmonic orchestra to direct their concerts also indicates that his stock among professional musicians stood high. Indeed, Kalbeck goes so far as to claim that the Viennese philharmonic concerts owed their international reputation above all to Dessoff's "dynamic and purposeful direction" (Kalbeck 1976, vol. 2, 20–21). Yet further proof of the high regard he enjoyed can be seen in the fact that prior to his departure in 1875 a special concert was arranged in his honor by a committee composed of **Johann von Herbeck**, **Joseph Hellmesberger**, **Louise Dustmann-Meyer**, and Amalie Materna.

Therefore, it is very puzzling that Brahms should have expressed such a very low opinion of Dessoff in replying in April 1869 to **Hermann Levi**'s inquiry about the "competition" he would have to face if he were to accept the position of Kapellmeister in Vienna. Dessoff, Brahms averred, was "most definitely and in no respect" the right person to conduct the philharmonic concerts; and he added that the standard of the orchestra had declined under him. ("There are special reasons why he is still beating time," Brahms remarked enigmatically.) In short, Brahms wrote, if Levi were to come to Vienna, he could count on being entrusted with the direction of the concerts the following year (Brahms 1974/7, 46). However, Levi decided to remain in Munich.

Dessoff was no doubt unaware of the unfavorable view taken by Brahms of his qualities as a conductor, and their friendship remained intact as evidenced by his aforesaid vehement quarrel with the orchestra over the merits of the Serenade op. 11 later that same year. After he moved to Karlsruhe, Brahms was among his earliest visitors. The 1874–75 season of subscription concerts was already over when Dessoff assumed his position there in April 1875, but he promptly arranged a special concert for 8 May, the program of which included the first performance anywhere of the *Neue Liebeslieder-Walzer*, with Dessoff and Brahms accompanying the singers on piano. That summer Dessoff visited Brahms at Ziegelhausen; subsequently, they were to remain in regular correspondence during Dessoff's stay at Karlsruhe, and by far the greatest number of their published letters date from the years 1875–79. That there are only a few from Dessoff's years in Vienna is understandable since, living in the same city, they had no need to correspond. On the other hand, it may seem surprising that the collection contains only one letter from the 12-year period Dessoff spent in Frankfurt. The main reason is no doubt that, except during the final year there, Dessoff had practically no opportunity to conduct orchestral concerts, which were the preserve of the Museum society. Accordingly, Dessoff was not involved in any discussions relating to Brahms's visits to Frankfurt during that period.

The highlight of Dessoff's Karlsruhe years for Brahmsians is, of course, his conducting the first performance of the First Symphony there on 4 November 1876. "It has always been my secret, fond wish to hear the work for the first time in a small town which has a good friend, a good conductor, and a good orchestra," Brahms had written to Dessoff shortly before (Brahms 1974/16, 144). Evidently his opinion of Dessoff's capabilities had greatly improved by then, and he must, moreover, have been pleased with the actual performance, for from that time onward they addressed each other with the familiar "Du." On that occasion Brahms stayed with the Dessoffs. Many years later, after Dessoff had died in Frankfurt, Brahms wrote to **Clara Schumann**: "In Dessoff you have lost much—I am certain of it, for we had the same experience when he left here. . . . He was a splendid person and a vibrantly sensitive, highly accomplished musician" (Litzmann 1970, vol. 2, 486).

Dessoff composed a quartet and a quintet, some piano music, and a number of Lieder. The quartet he sent to Brahms for his comments, and Brahms encouraged him to publish it and even accepted its dedication, though in terms that fall markedly short of outright enthusiasm: "You give me the greatest pleasure by writing my name on the title page of the quartet—in that way we shall share the blows if people should consider it too puerile" (Brahms 1974/16, 182).

Dessoff's daughter Margarete (b. Vienna, 11 June 1874; d. Locarno, 19 November 1944) had a very successful career as conductor of various choirs in Germany and New York. At its first public appearance, at the Brahms Festival at Wiesbaden in 1912, her Dessoffscher Frauenchor [Women's Choir] performed the *Gesänge* op. 17 and the *Lieder und Romanzen* op. 44. (Brahms 1974/7, 1974/16; Draheim 1983, 2001a, 2001b; Draheim and Jahn 2001; Hellsberg 2001; Höft 2001; A. Jahn 2001; Litzmann 1970)

DETMERING, (JOHANN) CHRISTIAN (b. Hamburg, 22 January 1830; d. Hamburg, 22 September 1892). Brahms's cousin; son of Johann

Diederich Philipp Detmering (1793–1841) and Christina Friderika Detmering, née Nissen (1792–1874), a sister of Brahms's mother. He was given music lessons by **Johann Jakob Brahms**, and in June 1857 opened a musical instruments shop, which his wife Sophie Johanna Philippine, whom he had married in 1866, ran after his death until their son Fritz took it over in 1895.

Brahms seems to have been in regular contact with Christian, especially during the final period of his sister Elisabeth's life. Uneasy about her spending habits, he arranged for his frequent contributions to her living expenses to be sent to Christian, who, at his request, then acted as a kind of administrator of the funds in question. Similarly, in the original testamentary instructions he conveyed to **Fritz Simrock** in May 1891, he specified that Elisabeth should receive a yearly sum of 5,000 marks "through Christian Detmering in Hamburg" (Kalbeck 1976, vol. 4, 228). It was Christian who telegraphed the news of her death to Brahms.

DETMOLD: *see* FRIEDERIKE, PRINCESS ZUR LIPPE and LEOPOLD III, PRINCE ZUR LIPPE.

DIETRICH, ALBERT (HERMANN) (b. Forsthaus Golk, near Meissen, 28 August 1829; d. Berlin, 20 November 1908). Conductor, pianist, and composer. While attending high school at Dresden (1842–47), he studied piano and composition with Julius Otto and subsequently received instruction from Ignaz Moscheles, **Julius Rietz**, and **Moritz Hauptmann** at the Leipzig conservatory. In 1851 he settled at Düsseldorf, where he was in close contact with **Robert** and **Clara Schumann**. After serving as music director at Bonn (1855–60), he was, on **Joseph Joachim**'s recommendation, appointed court Kapellmeister at Oldenburg, a position he held with considerable success for 30 years (with the exception of the 1863–64 season, during which, having suffered a nervous breakdown, he was replaced by **Heinrich von Sahr**). In addition to conducting the regular orchestral concerts, he directed the local Singverein and furthermore appeared as solo pianist and accompanist. He conducted his final concert on 28 March 1890, and last performed as a pianist at a concert given by the soprano Fanny Moran-Olden and her then husband, the tenor Carl Moran, on 17 October 1891; apart from acting as accompanist, he played one of **Chopin**'s Ballades and the Andante from Brahms's Piano Sonata op. 5. It is appropriate that he should have concluded his public appearances at Oldenburg with a piece by Brahms, for Brahms was one of the three composers he championed most devotedly throughout his years there, the others being **Bach** and Schumann. After his retirement he lived first in Leipzig and then in Berlin.

Dietrich immediately succumbed to the impact of Brahms's personality when he met him at Düsseldorf in the autumn of 1853. "Brahms is a delightful, splendid fellow," he informed his friend **Ernst Naumann**. "Genius is written all over his face and shines out of his bright blue eyes" (Dietrich 1898, 6). They spent much time together, and in a celebrated episode collaborated with Schumann in the composition of the F–A–E violin sonata as a greeting for the visiting Joseph Joachim. After Brahms eventually left for Hanover, Dietrich wrote to Joachim: "I miss Brahms very much and would have wished for my sake that he had remained here, but I am delighted for you" (Johannes Joachim and Moser 1911–13, vol. 1, 102).

He and Brahms saw one another frequently over the next few years, and later met on various occasions—in Bonn, Oldenburg, and elsewhere (in June 1862 they even shared accommodations near Münster am Stein, where Clara Schumann was vacationing). They also corresponded. In his *Erinnerungen an Johannes Brahms* (1898) Dietrich published a number of the letters he had received from Brahms, but by his own admission he excluded those which had meant most to him, namely the ones dating from the most painful periods of his life and which had most strikingly reflected the depth and sincerity of Brahms's feelings for him. Dietrich remained all his life under the spell of Brahms's personality and music. Their friendship seems to have been unclouded. Brahms was godfather of Dietrich's first child Max, an honor he shared with Joachim and Sahr.

Dietrich's admiration for Brahms's compositions not only helped to make them known to Oldenburg music lovers, but he was also in no small measure responsible for the first performance of the Requiem in Bremen in April 1868. When Brahms sent him the manuscript in 1867, he was so greatly moved by the work that he promptly went to Bremen to show it to **Karl Reinthaler**, who decided that it should be performed there on Good Friday the following year. It was subsequently performed at Oldenburg in 1870, 1877, and 1886. Brahms himself appeared at concerts in Oldenburg on several occasions, the first time in March 1862, when he played **Beethoven**'s Fourth Piano Concerto and Bach's *Chromatic Fantasia and Fugue* (the Serenade op. 11 was also on the program), and the last time in December 1884, when he conducted his *Tragic Overture* and Third Symphony, played the solo part in his Second Piano Concerto, and, with Dietrich, the accompaniment to the *Liebeslieder-Walzer*; **Hermine Spies** also sang four of his songs.

As a composer, Dietrich enjoyed a certain reputation in his day. He wrote pieces for the piano, as well as chamber music, orchestral works, songs, and two operas, *Robin Hood* (premiered at Frankfurt on 16 March 1879, with Brahms in the audience) and *Das Sonntagskind* (produced in Bremen on 21 March 1886). Brahms does not appear to have been greatly impressed by Dietrich's compositions, at any rate the earlier ones. In a letter to Clara Schumann in October 1868, he warned her that she would be hearing a symphony by Dietrich during her forthcoming visit to Oldenburg and cautioned her to be diplomatic rather than frank in her reaction. (Dietrich later dedicated this work, his Second Symphony in D Minor, to Brahms.)

Brahms did not entirely lose contact with Dietrich during his final years. Writing to Clara Schumann from Leipzig in January 1894, he mentioned having called on Dietrich and his wife there. (Dietrich 1898; Herttrich 1997; Linnemann 1956; Sietz 1960b)

DOBJANSKY, ANNA DE. Russian pianist and composer. She probably grew up in St. Petersburg and later studied with **Joachim Raff**. Brahms met her at Baden-Baden in the summer of 1869 and clearly took to her. In a letter to **Fritz Simrock** on 29 August he described her as quite talented, and he tried to interest Simrock in publishing some nocturnes and other piano pieces she had composed. Simrock agreed, and in fact considered them "very pretty." Their attractiveness may have owed something to the fact that Brahms had made certain improvements in the original versions. Before he left for Vienna in October, Brahms asked Simrock to send the proofs to him in Vienna. In due course, having looked through them, he sent them to Anna with a note in which he informed her that he had deliberately left several errors uncorrected, so that the public would be in no doubt that "this beautiful music" was "the product of a feminine pen." He fondly recalled the "wonderful" summer they had spent at Baden-Baden and assured her that he was with her "with all my soul." (A translation of Brahms's letter was included by Nicolas Slonimsky [1954] in his article "Musical Oddities" [4].)

Anna was evidently charming; but to judge by her letter of 21 August 1869 to **Ferdinand Hiller**, she was also somewhat naive. After reporting that she had managed to complete the first three movements of a piano sonata, but was having difficulty with the finale, she mentioned that **Clara Schumann**, **Jacob Rosenhain**, and Brahms all thought that she had a talent for composition, but that Brahms was of the opinion that while she had good ideas, she failed to develop them with sufficient care. She then went on: "He told me that if I wanted to sell him my compositions for a good price, he would work them up in his fashion while keeping my ideas, and would afterward have them printed under his name. You must admit the proposition is flattering" (Sietz 1958–70, vol. 2, 136). Brahms would no doubt have been delighted, had he known that his suggestion was being taken seriously.

Anna dedicated her *Capriccietto et Nocturne* op. 2, which Simrock published in 1870, to Brahms. (Sietz 1958–70; Slonimsky 1954)

DÖMPKE [DOEMPKE], GUSTAV (1853–1923). Music critic. A native of Barten, near Rastenburg, he studied philology at Königsberg [Kaliningrad]. In the 1870s he began to write music criticism for the *Königsberger allgemeine Zeitung*; in November 1883 he went to Vienna, where, on **Eduard Hanslick**'s recommendation, he became music critic on the *Wiener allgemeine Zeitung* in succession to **Max Kalbeck**. He returned to Königsberg in 1887 and the following year was appointed music critic of the *Königsberger allgemeine Zeitung.* In 1897 he switched to the *Hartungsche Zeitung* (likewise published at Königsberg), for which he wrote until his death.

Dömpke was a staunch champion of Brahms's music—**Hans von Bülow**, after visiting Königsberg in January 1890, called him in a letter to Brahms a "splendid apostle." To cite two examples of his profound admiration for Brahms, in 1883 he published a comprehensive and highly sympathetic (though not entirely uncritical) study of opp. 84–89 in the periodical *Die Gegenwart*; and on the occasion of the first performance of the Third Symphony he hailed Brahms as "one of the supreme masters since **Beethoven** and by far the greatest since **Schumann**" *(Wiener allgemeine Zeitung,* 5 December 1883, 1).

Dömpke made Brahms's acquaintance when the latter came to Königsberg to conduct his Second Symphony and perform his First Piano Concerto at a concert on 13 April 1880. During his later stay in Vienna they met frequently, and Dömpke was among the handful of persons whom Brahms invited to the run-through of the two-piano version of the Fourth Symphony at **Friedrich Konrad Ehrbar**'s music room on 8 October 1885. They remained in contact even after Dömpke had moved back to Königsberg; in 1888 he visited Brahms at Thun. In June 1894 Brahms asked **Fritz Simrock** to send Dömpke a copy of the newly published *Deutsche Volkslieder* (WoO 33): "You would give the good fellow a great deal of pleasure, and I think he deserves it for what he has done for both of us" (Brahms 1974/12, 144–45). In July 1896 Brahms similarly asked Simrock to send Dömpke a copy of the *4 ernste Gesänge*. (Brahms 1974/12; Dömpke 1883a, 1883b; Hinrichsen 1994; Kroll 1966)

DOOR [REALLY: DOCTOR], ANTON (b. Vienna, 20 June 1833; d. Vienna, 7 November 1919). Pianist and teacher. He studied piano with Carl Czerny and theory with **Simon Sechter**. In the 1850s he undertook concert tours in Germany and Italy. After spending some time in Stockholm, where he was appointed a court pianist, and a longer period in Moscow, where he taught at the conservatory, he served on the faculty of the Vienna conservatory from 1869 until 1901.

He first caught sight of Brahms (but apparently without exchanging any words with him) when he called on **Joseph Joachim** at Danzig [Gdańsk] in November 1855. (Joachim, Brahms, and **Clara Schumann** were appearing together at concerts there on 14 and 16 November.) He did not become personally acquainted with Brahms until some 15 years later, when, having once more settled in Vienna, he met him at the house of the singer **Helene Magnus** (*see* HORNBOSTEL, [OTTO] ERICH VON). During the early 1770s their contacts grew more frequent and intimate, largely due to the fact that Door arranged a series of chamber music concerts, mainly together with violinist Heckmann (from Cologne) and cellist Krumpholz (from Stuttgart), at which he presented, among other compositions, certain works by Brahms. Asked for his advice regarding tempo and interpretation, Brahms took to attending the rehearsals of his works. In March 1873 Door was the soloist in what was the first Viennese performance of Brahms's First Piano Concerto by a pianist other than Brahms himself (who had played it at a philharmonic concert on 22 January 1871). Furthermore, it was at a concert given by Door's students on 10 February 1874 that the two-piano version of the *Haydn Variations* received its first public performance (by Malwine von Benfeld and Gabriele Brauner). These various events help to explain why, within a few years of their first meeting, Door was on close terms with Brahms and had become a regular member of his dining circle as well as of his Sunday morning walking group.

Their friendship continued throughout the rest of Brahms's life. On 6 May 1887 Door wrote to a correspondent: "I am on very intimate terms with him, see him almost daily, and he often visits us" (Brahms Exhibition 1983, 67). Frequent opportunities for additional contacts also occurred at the evenings of the Wiener Tonkünstlerverein, which both regularly attended. (At the meeting on 23 November 1885, at which the Verein was formally established, Door was appointed second vice president; Brahms was elected its honorary president on 14 December 1886). It was largely on Door's initiative that the Tonkünstlerverein eventually presented some musical soirees that were open to the public. At one of these, on 3 April 1889, the complete set of Brahms's *5 Gesänge* (op. 104) was first performed, under the direction of **Eusebius Mandyczewski**.

During Brahms's final illness, Door's wife Ernestine (Tini) frequently visited him. She saw him for the last time on 24 March. (Brahms Exhibition 1983; Door 1903; H. Ehrlich 1893a)

DUNKL, JOHANN [JÁNOS] NEPOMUK (b. Vienna, 6 August 1832; d. Budapest, 29 January 1910). Hungarian pianist and music publisher. It is difficult to establish the precise chronology of his activities, since even his own brief memoirs, *Aus den Erinnerungen eines Musikers*, offer a rather confused account of them, but the main events appear to be as set out below.

After early musical studies in Pest [Budapest] he returned in the middle or later 1840s to Vienna where his most important teachers were **Anton Rubinstein** and **Liszt** (who spent some time there in 1846). Dunkl remained in Vienna, with various interruptions, until 1852, in which year he went back to Hungary for further studies. However, he was soon back in Vienna, which was to be his principal place of residence until 1866; during the last two years of his stay, he ran a music shop on the Kohlmarkt. While in Vienna, he renewed his acquaintance with Rubinstein and Liszt; among other musicians with whom he enjoyed close contact were, according to his memoirs, **Karl Goldmark** and Brahms. He also performed at various concerts, but neither in Austria nor in Hungary does he ever seem to have been particularly highly regarded as a solo pianist.

In 1866 he was persuaded by his brother-in-law Norbert Grinzweil (1823–90) to close down his Viennese shop and become a partner in Grinzweil's music publishing business Rózsavölgyi és Tarsa [Rózsavölgyi & Co.] in Budapest. (According to Á. Gádor and W. Ebert [see below], Dunkl's shop in Vienna was in fact a branch of that Budapest firm, but in his own memoirs Dunkl presents it as an independent venture.) Rózsavölgyi és Tarsa had been jointly founded in 1850 by Grinzweil and Gyula Rózsavölgyi, a son of violin virtuoso Márk Rózsavölgyi. Gyula Rózsavöglyi died in 1861, but the firm retained its original name. It had done well from the outset and continued to prosper; by the end of the century it would be Hungary's leading music publisher. In addition to its publishing interests, it undertook the promotion of concerts, and it was this aspect of its activities that enabled Dunkl to maintain his contacts with Brahms.

In 1993 Ágnes Gádor and Wolfgang Ebert published 21 letters from Brahms to Dunkl, written between 1867 and 1879; the majority of them discuss either arrangements for forthcoming concerts or possible dates for future ones. However, the collection almost certainly does not contain all the letters addressed by Brahms to Dunkl during this period, and it is very likely that Dunkl was also involved in preparations for other concerts not covered in the published series. The earliest letters relate to Brahms's very first visit to Budapest, in the spring of 1867, when he gave two concerts, on 22 and 26 April. Also, Dunkl is shown to have been responsible for organizing Brahms's next concert appearances: on 7 and 10 December 1867 he was partnered by **Joseph Joachim**, while on 9 December he performed with the Grün Quartet.

Little is known about Dunkl's pianistic activities after his return to Budapest in 1866. On at least two occasions he played in public together with Liszt: on 12 January 1873 they performed, together with Ödön Mihalovich, **Bach**'s D Minor Concerto for three pianos at a concert at the Hotel Hungaria, and on 31 March of the same year he and Liszt played the latter's two-piano arrangement of the Rákózy March at a charity concert. Dunkl also sometimes acted as accompanist for his wife Josefa, who was an accomplished singer. (Dunkel 1933; Dunkl 1876; Frank and Altmann 1983; Gádor and Ebert 1993; Gárdonyi 1963)

DUSTMANN-MEYER, LOUISE, née Meyer (b. Aachen [Aix-la-Chapelle], 22 August 1831; d. Berlin, 2 March 1899). She married the Viennese bookseller Adalbert Dustmann in 1858. Soprano. She first appeared on the Viennese stage (at the Theater in der Josefstadt) in 1848, and subsequently sang at Breslau [Wrocław] and later at Kassel (1850–51), Dresden (1852–54), and Prague (1854–56). On 12 July 1855 she made a guest appearance at the Vienna Opera as Valentine in Meyerbeer's *Les Huguenots*, and from 1857 until 1875 she was a permanent, and leading, member of the company.

Among her greatest roles in Vienna were Leonore in *Fidelio* (her singing in that role greatly moved Brahms), Donna Anna in *Don Giovanni* (a role she also interpreted at the opening of the new opera house on 25 May 1869), the title roles in Bellini's *Norma* and **Robert Schumann**'s *Genoveva*, and four great **Richard Wagner** roles: Senta (*Der fliegende Holländer*), Eva (*Die Meistersinger*), Elsa (*Lohengrin*), and Elisabeth (*Tannhäuser*). She sang the last two parts at the Viennese premieres of those operas, on 19 August 1858 and 19 November 1859, respectively. On the other hand, she was not, as Styra Avins (1997) states in *Johannes Brahms: Life and Letters*, the first Viennese Isolde. It is true that Wagner wanted her to sing Isolde in what would have been not only the Viennese, but, in fact, the world premiere of that opera. (He had been obliged to give up an earlier plan to stage the premiere with Dustmann-Meyer or Jenny Ney in Paris in the summer of 1860, since neither singer was then available.) But the rehearsals in Vienna were doomed to failure—initially because of the vocal inadequacy of the intended Tristan, Alois Ander, and later when Dustmann-Meyer turned against Wagner after he arrived in Vienna in November 1862 in the company of her sister Friederike Meyer, a minor actress at the Frankfurt theater with whom he was believed to have formed a liaison. Dustmann-Meyer reportedly felt that her own position in

Vienna was compromised by her sister's presence. In the circumstances, the planned Viennese production of *Tristan und Isolde* had to be shelved. The first performance of the opera there did not take place until 4 October 1883, when the principal roles were taken by Hermann Winkelmann and Amalie Materna. (At the actual world premiere, in Munich on 10 June 1865, the part of Isolde was sung by Malvina Schnorr von Carolsfeld, while the part of Tristan was sung by Malvina's husband Ludwig.)

Brahms made Dustmann-Meyer's acquaintance at the Lower Rhine Music Festival at Cologne in June 1862. He was immediately attracted by her personality, and **Max Kalbeck** speculates that her glowing description of life in Vienna may have confirmed his intention of going there. Once in Vienna, he remained in regular and perhaps even intimate contact with her. Its precise nature cannot be determined, but it may be more than coincidence that she was at Tutzing at the same time as Brahms in the summer of 1873, and at Pörtschach when he was there in 1879. She is said to have been the only person ever to address him in a letter as "Hansi." (One letter in which she uses that more intimate form of his name, which is believed to have been written around 1866, is preserved at the Brahms-Institut at Lübeck; it is signed "Fidelio.") Brahms also associated with her in a professional capacity. To cite some examples, she was one of the soloists in a partial performance of the *Liebeslieder-Walzer* on 5 December 1869, and again at the first performance of the complete set on 5 January 1870 (at which the singers were accompanied by **Clara Schumann** and Brahms); she was also a soloist at a performance of **Bach**'s *St. Matthew Passion* that he conducted on 23 March 1875; and at a concert he arranged at Pörtschach on 12 August 1879, mainly for the benefit of **Marie Soldat**, he accompanied Dustmann-Meyer in some of his own songs. (In 1873 he informed **Johann Nepomuk Dunkl** that she would very much like to sing at a concert he contemplated giving in Budapest in the near future, but the plans for that concert fell through.)

In addition, Dustmann-Meyer is credited in M. L. McCorkle's (1984) *Werkverzeichnis* with having given the first public performances of the following songs: "Wie bist du, meine Königin" (op. 32/9), "Der Gang zum Liebchen" (op. 48/1), "Gold überwiegt die Liebe" (op. 48/4), "Am Sonntag Morgen" (op. 49/1), and "Wiegenlied" (op. 49/4), on 22 December 1869; "Botschaft" (op. 47/1), on 6 January 1871; "Blinde Kuh" (op. 58/1) and "Während des Regens" (op. 58//2), on 27 January 1872; "Serenade" (op. 58/8), on 14 March 1874; and "Es liebt sich so lieblich im Lenze!" (op. 71/1), "An den Mond" (op. 71/2), and perhaps also "Tambourliedchen" (op. 69/5), on 8 April 1878.

At the end of 1875, by which time her vocal powers were on the decline, Dustmann-Meyer ceased to be a full-time member of the Vienna Opera company. She intended, however, to continue to sing at concerts. Thanks to Brahms, she was engaged by **Bernhard Scholz** to appear at two concerts of the Orchester-Verein in Breslau in April 1876. (Shortly before, on 20 March, she had made a much acclaimed appearance in *Fidelio* in Vienna.) But when she went to Breslau to give a concert of her own in 1877, the event turned into such a personal disaster for her that Louise Scholz appealed to Brahms to persuade her to sing only in private in future (Brahms 1974/3, 214). She taught at the Vienna Conservatory until 1880, when she moved to Berlin. There she lived in modest circumstances, and in March 1896 Brahms arranged a collection for her benefit in Vienna, which, to his delight, yielded the sum of 2,000 gulden within a few days. (Avins 1997; Brahms 1974/3; Kapp 1932; R. Wagner 1976)

DÜYFFCKE, PAUL (b. Hamburg, 17 December 1847; d. Hamburg, January 1910). Painter and sculptor, best known for his wall decorations in the Hamburg Rathaus. In late October 1889, at the request of the mayor of Hamburg, **Carl Friedrich Petersen**, he delivered to Brahms in Vienna the certificate of honorary citizenship that had been presented to Brahms at a ceremony in Hamburg on 14 September and had subsequently been exhibited at the Kunsthalle there. The sumptuous presentation box contained, in addition to the certificate, a gouache painted by Düyffcke that has usually been thought to depict the crowning of Music by Harmonia, but this interpretation has recently been challenged. As part of the Brahms-Nachlass, these various items are preserved in the archive of the Gesellschaft der Musikfreunde in Vienna.

Düffcke was among the artists whose designs for a Brahms monument in Hamburg were exhibited at the Kunsthalle in May 1901 (in this connection, *see* KLINGER, MAX and also FELDERHOFF, REINHOLD).

DVOŘÁK, ANTONÍN (LEOPOLD) (b. Nelahozeves, near Kralupy, 8 September 1841; d. Prague, 1 May 1904). Composer. Brahms's attitude toward Dvořák is an outstanding example of the generosity that he was capable of displaying toward younger composers he regarded as particularly gifted and whose music especially appealed to him. He first became aware of Dvořák's outstanding talent through being a member of a committee, chaired by **Eduard Hanslick**, which was responsible for recommending young, poor, and gifted composers for state stipends. Dvořák was awarded a stipend for each of the five years 1875–79. In informing him on 30 November 1877 of his award for the coming year, Hanslick mentioned that

Brahms had been greatly impressed with his Czech vocal duets and intended to show them to his publisher (**Fritz Simrock**). Hanslick advised Dvořák to write directly to Brahms and maybe also send him some of his other compositions (Clapham 1971, 242). On 3 December Dvořák wrote to Brahms (Šourek 1984, 38). Brahms replied promptly, stressing the desirability of having the texts translated into German (Šourek 1984, 39). He also wrote to Simrock, explaining that he had for several years enjoyed reviewing Dvořák's submissions to the committee and recommending the duets as highly attractive and very suitable for publication (Brahms 1974/10, 60–61; although undated, and left without a date in **Max Kalbeck**'s edition of Brahms's letters to Simrock, it is clear from internal evidence that this letter was written on 7 December.) Simrock did indeed publish the duets, as in due course he would publish a considerable number of other compositions by Dvořák.

Thus began a relationship that would prove of crucial importance for Dvořák, whose career had until then been a relatively modest one, confined to his native country. His association with German publishers—above all, thanks to Brahms, with Simrock—made his name known not only in Germany, but also in other countries, and Brahms's championship of his music opened many doors for him and helped to find an increasingly frequent place for his compositions in the concert repertory. In short, without Brahms's generous support, he might never have attained the international renown he was to enjoy, and he would almost certainly not have achieved it in such a relatively short time (in 1891 he received an honorary doctorate at Cambridge University). He never forgot what he owed to Brahms (to whom he dedicated his String Quartet op. 34/B35). In a letter to Hanslick on 28 June 1889, he referred to Brahms as "that great man and artist, whom . . . I have to thank for all my present good fortune" (Kuna 1987–89, vol. 2, 372). Five years later (28 December 1894) he wrote to Brahms himself: "Thank you, thank you from the bottom of my heart, for all your kindness to me and for all you have done on my behalf" (Kuna 1987–89, vol. 3, 340). He had at that time renewed cause to appreciate Brahms's generosity, for the latter had willingly assumed the task of proofreading Dvořák's compositions prior to publication during a part of his absence in America. "I can hardly believe there is another musician of his standing who would do this," Dvořák had written to Simrock on 5 February 1894 (Kuna 1987–89, vol. 3, 249).

As for Brahms, the association with Dvořák brought him a great deal of pleasure, for Dvořák's music delighted him by its gracefulness, freshness, wealth of invention, and sonorous beauty, and moreover, he thoroughly enjoyed the younger man's company. Siegfried Kross, in his Brahms biography, states that the two men first met in December 1877, when Brahms returned to Vienna from Budapest (where he had appeared at a concert on 28 November) via Prague, for the express purpose of making Dvořák's acquaintance. This assumption is probably incorrect (see, for instance, Dvořák's letters to Brahms of 3 and 19 December 1877 and 23 January 1878, and Brahms's statement "I don't know Dvořák" in his letter to Simrock of 25 June 1878 [Brahms 1974/10, 77]). Their first meeting is more likely to have taken place in Vienna in December 1878, on which occasion, according to the Czech music journal *Dalibor*, Dvořák received a warm welcome from Brahms. (On the chronology of their early relationship, both by letter and in person, see especially Beveridge 1993.) They met again in January 1879 when Brahms and **Joseph Joachim** traveled to Prague from Leipzig, where they had given the world premiere of Brahms's Violin Concerto. Joachim had concert engagements in Prague on 3 and 5 January, while Brahms, on 4 January, met at his request a number of Czech composers, to whom he promised to give an orchestral concert there, together with Dvořák, at the beginning of the next concert season. (However, such a concert never took place.)

Brahms and Dvořák were to see one another repeatedly thereafter. Beveridge lists no fewer than nine known occasions on which they met between November 1879 and December 1889, some extending over several days. Thus, Dvořák reported to Simrock in November 1880 that during his recent visit to Vienna, which had lasted almost a week, he had spent many enjoyable hours in Brahms's company; in November 1883, after another stay in Vienna, he mentioned having lunched and dined each day with Brahms, and furthermore, as evidence of their growing intimacy, that Brahms, usually so reserved where his own compositions were concerned, had readily played for him parts of his new (Third) symphony; and on 6 December 1887 he wrote to Simrock that he had spent several "wonderful hours" with Brahms (Kuna 1987–89, vol. 2, 288). Moreover, according to W. Ebert's *Johannes Brahms and Budapest*, Brahms accompanied Dvořák to Budapest when he conducted his Seventh Symphony there in December 1883, and again in 1887 when Dvořák's Violin Concerto was first performed there.

Brahms more than once, in his correspondence with Simrock, expressed the fondness he felt for Dvořák as a person. He was particularly pleased to meet Dvořák once more in late 1895, after a break of six years (for a part of that period Dvořák had been in America): the visit of Dvořák and his wife, he wrote to Simrock, "has been a great joy for me" (Brahms 1974/12, 185). He even tried to induce Dvořák to move to Vienna, as he thought it would benefit his career, and he offered to place his private fortune at

Dvořák's disposal to enable him to do so, and also undertook to obtain a teaching position for him at the conservatory; but Dvořák would not be persuaded. He saw Brahms for the last time in March 1897; shortly afterward he returned to Vienna to attend his funeral.

As already mentioned, Brahms greatly admired many of Dvořák's compositions, and he did not stint with praise in speaking about them to his friends. The *Slavonic Rhapsody* (op. 45/B86, no. 1) he described as intensely "musical" (Heuberger 1976, 149), the String Sextet (op. 48/B80) as "infinitely beautiful" (Heuberger 1976, 99), the E Minor Symphony (op. 95/B178) as "so indescribably talented, so refreshing, that one must rejoice in it" (Heuberger 1976, 93); and regarding the String Quartets op. 80/B57 and op. 34/B75 he was moved to declare: "The best qualities a musician needs, Dvořák has them all, and they are also in these compositions" (Brahms 1974/10, 71). Brahms's admiration for Dvořák's Cello Concerto is of particular interest. Writing to Simrock in January 1896 while correcting the proofs, he declared that cellists had cause to be grateful to the composer for giving them "such a great and accomplished work," which he considered "better and also more practical" than Dvořák's Piano and Violin Concertos (Brahms 1974/12, 189). **Florence May** relates in her biography of Brahms that when **Robert Hausmann** was in Vienna as a member of the Joachim Quartet in December 1896–January 1897, Brahms asked him to come to his flat to play the concerto. Brahms, who accompanied on the piano, expressed his delight at the end of each movement, and afterward exclaimed that if he had known that such a concerto could be composed for the cello, he would have tried to write one himself. Although May had no doubt heard all this directly from Hausmann, with whom, as she indicates, she was in contact during the preparation of her book, Styra Avins (1997, in *Johannes Brahms: Life and Letters*) dismisses the story as apocryphal, on the grounds that Brahms's above-mentioned letter to Simrock shows that he had already been familiar with the work a year earlier, "at a time when he was in perfect health and in full command of his faculties"; accordingly, if he did not subsequently (i.e., during the year 1896) compose a cello concerto himself, it was clearly "not for lack of knowing the instrument's capabilities" (that is to say, because he did not yet know Dvořák's work). He could not therefore, Avins argues, have "in early 1897" made the statement to Hausmann that May attributed to him, and she adds that this "just goes to show how difficult it is even for the most conscientious biographer to arrive at the truth" (730).

However, the truth may very well be that Florence May's account is perfectly correct, for it is possible to see Brahms's situation at that time in quite a different light. In the first place, it is worth pointing out that during the period of almost two years following the completion of the Clarinet Sonatas in the summer of 1894, Brahms wrote no new pieces at all, nor did he ever resume composition after working on the *4 ernste Gesänge* and the *Choral Preludes* in May–June 1896. What is more, he had told **Clara Schumann** in October 1895 that he no longer composed for the public, only a few pieces for himself, adding that one's capacity for composition normally declined after the age of 50, and that the fact that he had himself still written some music later did not impair the general truth of his statement (see **Ferdinand Schumann**'s [1915] "Erinnerungen an Johannes Brahms"). It is accordingly highly questionable whether he would have felt capable of attempting a large-scale work such a cello concerto in the months following his letter to Simrock of January 1896. Moreover, when Hausmann played the concerto for him in December 1896 or January 1897, it was almost certainly the first time that Brahms was actually *hearing* the cello part; and while he had undoubtedly been capable previously of deriving a fairly clear and correct impression of the work from looking at the printed score, the impact of the sound of the instrument during the "live" performance in his rooms is nonetheless likely to have been an extremely powerful one, further intensifying his admiration for the work and, quite conceivably, prompting the celebrated remark—which thus signifies, not that this was his first encounter with the work, but that if he had heard it years earlier (meaning also, well before 1896), he would have felt eager to try his hand at a similar composition. Incidentally, as Avins acknowledges, Hausmann told a largely similar story to Donald Tovey (1935–39), who was to relate it in his discussion of the concerto in *Essays in Musical Analysis*. In describing the incident to May and Tovey, Hausmann was recalling an event that had occurred only a few years earlier, so his memory is likely to have been fairly reliable.

Some three months after Hausmann's visit, on 7 March 1897, Brahms, by then a very sick man, attended a philharmonic concert that featured his own Fourth Symphony—and the first Viennese performance of Dvořák's Cello Concerto, conducted by **Hans Richter** and with **Hugo Becker** as the soloist. (Dvořák had conducted the world premiere of the work in London on 19 March 1896, with Leo Stern as soloist.) Meeting **Josef Gänsbacher** before the concert, Brahms assured him that he would find it an inspiring experience.

The Brahms-Dvořák association may have been significant for yet another reason. It is generally accepted that Brahms's music exercised an influence on some of the chamber music and orchestral works that Dvořák composed in the years immediately following his first contacts with Brahms. But it has also been suggested, if more cautiously, that Brahms may himself have been indebted to Dvořák in certain compositions—the String Quintet op. 88, the Third Symphony, and perhaps in the *4 ernste Gesänge*, in which, it has been speculated, Brahms could conceivably have taken the idea of setting biblical texts as songs with piano accompaniment from Dvořák's biblical songs.

Finally, by way of a postscript: On 8 June 1897 Simrock asked Dvořák if he would make orchestral arrangements of three of the *Klavierstücke* from opp. 118–19; Brahms had agreed to do so, but had been prevented by his illness from carrying out the project. Dvořák did not comply with the request. (Altmann 1929; Avins 1997; Brahms 1974/10, 1974/12; Beckermann 1986, 1993; Beveridge 1993; Clapham 1958; Döge 1991; Kross 1997; Kuna 1987–89, 1992; Petersen 1984; F. Schumann 1915; Šourek 1984)

– E –

EBER, PAUL (b. Kitzingen, 8 November 1511; d. Wittenberg, 10 December 1569). Teacher, scholar, pastor, poet; a close collaborator of Philipp Melanchthon. Brahms set one of his texts in the motet "Wenn wir in höchsten Nöten sein" (op. 110/3). (Scheible 1989)

EBNER, OTTILIE, née Hauer (b. Oed, near Waldegg, southwest of Vienna, 3 December 1836; d. Elefánt, Hungary, 8 July 1920). Pianist and singer. She was initially taught by her father Joseph Hauer (1802–76), the local doctor, who was a great music lover and played several instruments. He had been a boy chorister and a boarder at the Stadtkonvikt. A close friend of **Franz Schubert**, he took part in the first run-through of the "Death and the Maiden" String Quartet on 29 January 1826. Styra Avins (1997), in *Johannes Brahms: Life and Letters*, writes that he had been "one of Franz Schubert's comrades at the school of the Wiener Sängerknaben" (779). This is incorrect. In a letter to Heinrich Kreissle, who printed it in his Schubert biography, Hauer stated explicitly that he did not become personally acquainted with Schubert until 1825; according to Kreissle, he had been placed in the Stadtkonvikt in 1816, that is, three years after Schubert had left it. (Avins also mistakenly situates Oed northwest, instead of southwest, of Vienna.) Hauer was in contact with a number of musicians and musicologists, including, apart from Kreissle, **Josef Gänsbacher**, **Otto Jahn**, Ludwig Köchel, and **Gustav Nottebohm**; he was also a close friend of the dramatist Ferdinand Raimund.

Ottilie began giving music lessons while still in her teens, at Waldegg. She made her own concert debut on 30 January 1858 at Frankfurt am Main, when she was asked at very short notice to replace her uncle Karl Baumann, a tenor at the opera, with whom she was then staying. At this concert, which took place at the Hôtel de Russie, her performance of songs by Mendelssohn, **Robert Schumann**, and Georg Goltmann was enthusiastically received; indeed, one critic reported that it had "electrified" the audience. Her success that day led to several further concert appearances in Frankfurt, at one of which, on 26 February, she sang Pamina's aria "Ach, ich fühls" from *Die Zauberflöte* and duets together with her uncle. On that occasion she made the acquaintance of **Joseph Joachim**, who was performing **Beethoven**'s Violin Concerto at the same event. In the autumn of 1858 she moved to Vienna, where she lodged with friends and earned her living by giving piano and singing lessons (among her pupils was the young **Marie Fillunger**). At the same time she improved her own musical skills through studies with Mathilde Marchesi and Anna Falconi, and she soon became known to Viennese music lovers; on 29 March 1860, at an all-**Mozart** concert of the recently established Orchesterverein of the Gesellschaft der Musikfreunde, she sang the aria *Misera! Dove son . . . Ah non so io che parlo* (K. 369). She also joined the Singakademie.

She made Brahms's acquaintance soon after his arrival in Vienna in 1862, when she became a member of the small choral group formed by **Julie** and Anna **von Asten**, which met at their flat to sing under Brahms's direction. Thus began a friendship that was to last until Brahms's death, and which might at one time have led to an even closer relationship. In her memoir *Die Brahmsfreundin Ottilie Ebner und ihr Kreis*, Ottilie's daughter Ottilie von Balassa states that Brahms and her mother saw each other almost daily during a two-year period, that Brahms gave her piano lessons, and that she sang for him his newest and still unpublished songs, which, moreover, he readily revised at her suggestion. What is certain is that they undoubtedly met frequently during this initial period, which was, in fact, considerably shorter than two years, for Brahms arrived in Vienna in September 1862 and Ottilie moved to Budapest shortly after her marriage in March 1864 (in addition, Brahms was absent for several months during the spring and summer of 1863). He clearly formed a very high regard for her singing and was also greatly attracted to her as a person, and she was evidently far from indifferent to him, for many of her friends and relatives thought that she might marry him; but when Edward Ebner, a friend of long standing, proposed to her on Christmas Day 1863, she accepted. According to one of her nieces, Brahms "came on the afternoon of the same day with the same intention, but he came too late" (Balassa 1933, 46). While there is no confirmation of this story, it is not implausible, for he confided to **Clara Schumann** some months later that he would probably have "made a fool of himself" over a certain pretty girl, "if someone else had not, fortunately, snapped her up at Christmas" (Litzmann 1970, vol. 1, 446).

Ebner came from Budapest, and it was there that the couple spent the first five years of their married life. Thereafter, they lived in Vienna (1870–80) and Wiener Neustadt (1880–85), before returning to Hungary. They also regularly stayed at Oed, where they had acquired a property. Brahms remained in contact with them until his death, both in person and by correspondence, and Ottilie von Balassa prints many of the letters he and her mother exchanged, all of which bear witness to an exceptionally warm relationship. In 1870 he reminded his father that, during the latter's visit to Austria in 1867, they had stayed at Oed with "Herr Dr. Ebner and his wife," adding, "I'm delighted to say that they are now living in Vienna" (Stephenson 1973, 180); and when Ottilie was prostrated with grief over the death of her five-year-old son, Brahms would call every day and play for her, anxious to console her and at the same time draw her back to music, which she was inclined to shun in her anguish. (*See also* STEINWAY.) In January 1877, when she was staying at Gorizia where her daughter was recuperating from an illness, he assured her that "not as a soprano or as a listener or as a friend can you be spared or replaced" (Balassa 1933, 90). While their musical association occurred largely in private houses (as mentioned below), it was not confined to those occasions. In 1863–64 Ottilie even took part in the first performances, accompanied by Brahms on the piano, of two of his vocal quartets: "Wechsellied zum Tanze" (op. 31/1), at the **Bösendorfer** Salon on 18 December 1863, and "Neckereien" (op. 31/2), at an evening entertainment presented by the Singakademie on 11 January 1864 (she also sang in another performance of "Wechsellied"). In 1867, when Brahms was planning his first visit to Budapest, he enquired of his concert agent (*see* DUNKL, JOHANN [JÁNOS] NEPOMUK) whether Ottilie Ebner might be willing to appear with him, and he was delighted when informed that she was prepared to do so. At the first concert (22 April) he accompanied her in songs by Mendelssohn, Beethoven, Schubert, and Schumann, at the second (26 April) in songs by Schubert, Schumann, and **RobertVolkmann**. The critic of the *Pester Lloyd* described her as a "highly accomplished amateur" and warmly praised her performances. (Furthermore, at Brahms's request, she sang at Clara Schumann's concert in Budapest on 1 December 1868. Clara Schumann stayed with the Ebners on that occasion, as she would also do later in Vienna.)

After she moved back from Budapest to Vienna in 1870, Ottilie Ebner resumed her close contact with Brahms. Ottilie von Balassa, who was born in 1874, writes about having been present on countless occasions when her mother and Brahms made music together at her house, performing songs and playing piano duets. Ottilie Ebner also performed at her own as well as at friends' musical soirees. "You would give us great pleasure if you were to delight us with some songs by Brahms tomorrow evening," **Theodor Billroth** wrote to her on 3 November 1877 (Balassa 1933, 92). Likewise at Billroth's, on 29 January 1878, she sang the duet "Weg der Liebe" (op. 20/1) with **Rosa Girzick**. She also formed her own choir, which she conducted herself. "My wife and I invite you and your husband most cordially for next Monday evening," Billroth wrote on another occasion. "We request everything, *Liebeslieder* (complete), the three Quartets op. 31" (Balassa 1933, 91). When she was living at Wiener Neustadt, she arranged various concerts, in some of which, according to her daughter, she sang herself; and after the Ebners moved back to Budapest in 1885, their house quickly became a center for music making that attracted many prominent musicians. It was there that Brahms held some of the rehearsals for his own concerts. Ottilie Ebner last saw him in 1897, when she and her daughter stopped in Vienna on their way to Italy. They attended the concert on 7 March, at which his Fourth Symphony was performed in his presence, and visited him in Karlsgasse. The news of his death reached them in Italy.

Ottilie Ebner owned a number of Brahms autographs (for details, see M. L. McCorkle's [1984] *Werkverzeichnis*). After her death these passed into the possession of her daughter, who sold them in 1924 to Jerome Stonborough, the husband of Margarethe **Wittgenstein**. Most of them, like other autographs in Stonborough's collection, were acquired by the Library of Congress, Washington, D.C., in the 1940s. (Avins 1997; Balassa 1933; Dunkl 1876; Litzmann 1970; Stephenson 1973)

EHLERT, LOUIS (b. Königsberg, 1825; d. Wiesbaden, 4 January 1884). Pianist, teacher, and writer on music. He studied under Mendelssohn and **Robert Schumann** at the Leipzig conservatory and further pursued his musical education in Vienna and later in Berlin, where he lived until 1876, except for the years 1863–65, which he spent in Florence; during his stay there he conducted the choral ensemble "Società Cherubini." In 1876 he settled at Wiesbaden. Ehlert contributed essays on music to a number of journals (including *Grenzboten*, *Allgemeine musikalische Zeitung*, and *Deutsche Rundschau*), and wrote various piano and vocal compositions, as well as some instrumental ones. He published a number of his articles in 1877 under the title *Aus der Tonwelt*; a further series appeared under the same title in 1884. He taught for a time at **Tausig**'s music academy in Berlin.

Brahms was most favorably impressed by Ehlert's essay "Robert Schumann und his Schule," which appeared in the *Deutsche Rundschau* in December 1876. "It seemed to me that one couldn't draw a more beautiful portrait of an artist," he wrote to **Fritz Simrock**, whom he asked to send Ehlert the score of his recently published String Quartet op. 67 and also to invite him to the performance of the First Symphony that Brahms was due to conduct in Leipzig on 18 January 1877 (Brahms 1974/10, 19–20).

The June 1880 issue of the *Deutsche Rundschau* carried a long and very interesting study by Ehlert (subsequently reprinted in Ehlert 1884, 215–48) of Brahms's compositions up to Violin Sonata op. 78, which Simrock had published in November of the preceding year and which Ehlert regarded as one of Brahms's finest musical achievements ("The first movement, entirely lyrical and totally devoid of pathos, is one of the purest and most entrancing works of art ever created for two such disparate instruments" (Ehlert 1884, 241). Ehlert's approach to Brahms's music in this study is nonetheless, as he himself acknowledges, a critical and not a blindly eulogistic one. Thus, while expressing great admiration for the choral works (in particular, the *Schicksalslied* and the Requiem), for the Serenades, the first Sextet, the Piano Quintet, the *Variations* for orchestra and the piano (especially those on a theme by **Handel**), and certain compositions for single and several voices, he does not shrink from voicing some reservations, for instance, about certain aspects of the symphonies in C minor and D major or about the Violin Concerto ("It is to be regretted that the hope of placing a third master work by the side of the two great ones of the violin literature [i.e., the concertos of **Beethoven** and Mendelssohn] has gone unfulfilled this time" [Ehlert 1884, 241]). Overall, though, Ehlert's study is a most sympathetic one, and **Max Kalbeck** is quite justified in his remark that the article expressed warm appreciation for Brahms's music.

Ehlert's essay appears to have had no adverse effect on his relations with Brahms, who must have read a large part of it, at least, with satisfaction. Kalbeck relates that during Brahms's lengthy stay at Wiesbaden in 1883 he called on Ehlert almost daily after lunch to drink a black coffee and converse with him; indeed, according to Kalbeck, Brahms grew increasingly fond of Ehlert as their contacts became more intimate. They also met elsewhere. Thus **Hermine Spies** mentions in her diary on 4 September 1883 a musical evening at the **Beckerath**s' devoted to Brahms's music, at which both Ehlert and Brahms were present. A few months later, Ehlert collapsed while attending a concert. (Brahms 1974/10; Ehlert 1884; Spies 1894)

EHRBAR, FRIEDRICH KONRAD (b. Hildesheim, Germany, 26 April 1827; d. Hart, near Gloggnitz, Lower Austria, 23 February 1905 [see note at end]). Piano manufacturer. After training at Friederici's firm at Gera (1841–48), he worked for Eduard Seuffert in Vienna. After the latter's death in 1855, he married Seuffert's widow Rosa and took over the firm in his own name. His business prospered, and in 1876–77 he built himself a house at 28 Mühlbachgasse (now Mühlgasse, in the Fourth District), which contained a sizeable concert hall. This house, together with the adjoining one at 30 Mühlbachgasse built by his son Friedrich Benedikt in 1911, is now the seat of the Konservatorium für Musik und dramatische Kunst. Ehrbar also made a name for himself as a patron of the arts. In 1898 he handed the firm over to his above-mentioned son.

Starting in 1877, Brahms fell into the habit of presenting major compositions, prior to their first public performances, to a small number of invited friends at Ehrbar's, where he would present the new work, with **Ignaz Brüll**'s assistance, in an arrangement for two pianos. He is known to have done so in the case of the Second Symphony (before its world premiere in Vienna on 30 December 1877), the Second Piano Concerto (probably on 12 October 1881, before he left to try it out with the Meiningen Orchestra and subsequently first played it in public in Budapest on 9 November), the Third Symphony (9 November 1883, prior to its world premiere in Vienna on 2 December), and the Fourth Symphony (on 8 October 1885, before first conducting it in public at Meiningen on 25 October). Following the first Viennese performance of the Fourth Symphony, on 17 January 1886, **Theodor Billroth** invited about a dozen persons, including Ehrbar, to Sacher's restaurant. (It was, incidentally, at Ehrbar's concert hall that **Adolf Wallnöfer** presented his all-Brahms concert on 24 April 1880.) (Bozarth and Brady 2000. The date of death is erroneously given in Hopfner [1999] and Flotzinger [2002] as 25 February, which is in fact the date of Ehrbar's funeral; the correct date appears in Czeike [1992–97], Frank [1983], and *ÖBL* 1957– .)

EIBENSCHÜTZ, ILONA (b. Budapest, 8 May 1873; d. London, 21 May 1967). Pianist. She reportedly first played in public at the age of six. In 1882 she enrolled at the Vienna conservatory, where her teacher was Hans Schmitt. On leaving the conservatory she spent four years (probably starting in 1885) at Frankfurt am Main as a student of **Clara Schumann**, who held her in high regard as a pianist and grew extremely fond of her as a person. After making her debut as a mature artist at a Gürzenich concert at Cologne in 1890, she performed in Leipzig and Vienna, and on 12 January 1891 made her first appearance in England, playing **Robert Schumann**'s *Études symphoniques* and, with Alfredo Piatti, **Beethoven**'s Cello Sonata op. 69 at a Monday Popular Concert in London.

Over the next 10 years she enjoyed a very successful career, but she gave up concertizing almost completely following her marriage in 1902 to Carl Derenburg, a wealthy stockbroker of German origin who had settled in

London; nor did she resume her career after he died in 1927. Only very rarely did she play at a public concert after 1902; one such occasion occurred when she took part, on 13 April 1910, in the first of three Schumann Centenary Concerts presented by the Classical Concert Society at the Bechstein Hall. She apparently performed occasionally at private functions; at any rate, **Adelina de Lara**, who had studied under Clara Schumann at the same time as Eibenschütz, mentions in her memoirs, published in 1955, that they had "recently" given a two-piano recital at a private house. In 1953 Eibenschütz broadcast a talk, with piano illustrations, on the BBC and also performed Brahms's Piano Quintet op. 34 with the Amadeus Quartet.

On 1 July 1926 she published an article entitled "My Recollections of Brahms" in the *Musical Times* (598–600). In it she recalled that she had made Brahms's acquaintance when he stayed at Clara Schumann's house a few months after her own arrival at Frankfurt. She came to know him better when she played at a musical evening of the Vienna Tonkünstlerverein, probably in 1891 (?1892). After she had played Schumann's *Études symphoniques* and some smaller pieces by Scarlatti and by Brahms himself, he came up to her and asked her to play Beethoven's Sonata op. 111. "I did so, and I believe that henceforth Brahms was my friend. At supper, after the concert, I had to sit next to him. He wished to know all my plans." Over the following years, she saw him frequently, in Vienna and especially at Ischl, where her family often spent the summer months. He clearly derived great pleasure both from hearing her play, especially his own compositions, and from her company; **Max Kalbeck** called her Brahms's "favorite woman pianist" (Kalbeck 1976, vol. 4, 440). She seems to have felt a special affinity with his works and was to become a great champion of his music. She was also a very attractive girl—Adelina de Lara described her as "beautiful: slight, with lovely Eastern eyes and long thick lashes" (De Lara 1955, 42). **Ludwig Karpath**, who knew her well and met Brahms through her, attributed the latter's warm feelings for her to a variety of reasons: he felt close to her because of her association with Clara Schumann (who, as already mentioned, liked her a good deal); he considered her an excellent interpreter of his works; he was attracted by her charming personality; and, last but not least, her mother made a delicious goulash (Karpath 1934, 325). (Regarding the final point, there is an amusing and touching story of Brahms, already gravely ill, saying to the doctor who advised him to avoid all spicy dishes, including goulash, "I shall pretend that I did not consult you until to-morrow and then I can eat goulash at the Eibenschütz' today—for they make it specially for me" [Kalbeck 1976, vol. 4, 464].)

There was a lot of music making at Ischl, which was the preferred summer resort of so many prominent musicians. In her aforementioned article,

Eibenschütz mentions two performances of Brahms's compositions in which she took part there, and at which he was present. One such occasion was Alice Strauss's engagement party, at which she and members of the Kneisel Quartet played the Piano Quartet op. 25 (since Alice, Adèle's daughter by her first husband, married the painter **Franz de Bayros** on 27 February 1896, the party was presumably held during the summer of 1895). Another time she played the three violin sonatas with **Franz Kneisel** ("We had fixed the day, and asked only **Nikisch**, **Koessler**, **Wendt**, and Professor **Grün**, to come and listen. But I told Brahms he might come if he liked, and, to our great pleasure, he came" [Eibenschütz 1926, 599]). On yet another occasion, after banishing her sister and Gustav Wendt from the room, he invited her to listen to "a few exercises which I have just composed"—in fact, the *Klavierstücke* opp. 118–19. (Eibenschütz mistakenly describes this incident as having taken place in the summer of 1892 instead of the following year.) On 2 September 1893 Clara Schumann wrote to Brahms: "Ilona has written that she has heard the new pieces—she was enchanted by them and by your kindness toward her. She is a dear girl and deserves it" (Litzmann 1970, vol. 2, 528). She was to give the first public performances of some pieces from each set at a Monday Popular Concert in London on 22 January 1894, and of the two complete sets at another concert there on 7 March. She had previously given the first performance of no. 6 of the *7 Fantasien* op. 116, also in London, on 15 March 1893. She presumably last saw Brahms in late 1896, when she took part in two chamber music concerts in Vienna. At the first, on 3 November, she played Brahms's Piano Trio op. 101 with A. Kolakowski and **David Popper**; at the second, on 18 November, she played the Ballade op. 118/3, the Intermezzo op. 119/3, and the Rhapsody op. 119/4.

Ilona's older brother Siegmund (1856–1922) was a conductor and pianist who had studied with **Liszt**, **Robert Volkmann**, and Ferenc Erkel. He reportedly toured with his sister throughout Europe before settling in Vienna. There he worked as a coach for several singing teachers, including **Louise Dustmann-Meyer**. In 1907 he became joint director of the Carl Theater, and subsequently its sole director (1908–22). Another brother, Albert (1857–1930), was a highly regarded pianist and teacher, as well as a composer. (De Lara 1955; H. Ehrlich 1893a; Eibenschütz 1926; Karpath 1934; Litzmann 1970; Pascall 2001; Rountree 1994)

EICHENDORFF, JOSEPH, BARON VON (b. Lubowitz Castle, neat Ratibor, Upper Silesia, 10 March 1788; d. Neisse, Silesia, 26 November 1857). Poet, author of narrative works, as well as of a number of books on the history of German literature. Brahms set poems by Eichendorff in the following songs: "In der Fremde" (op. 3/5), "Lied" (op. 3/6), "Parole" (op. 7/2),

"Anklänge" (op. 7/3), "Der Gärtner" (op. 17/3), "Vom Strande" (op. 69/6), and "Mondnacht" (WoO 21). He also used texts by Eichendorff in the duet "Die Nonne und der Ritter" (op. 28/1), in the quartet for women's voices "Der Bräutigam" (op. 44/1), in "Tafellied" for six mixed voices (op. 93b), and in the canons for women's voices op. 113/7–8. (Purver 1989)

ELDERING, BRAM (b. Groningen, 8 July 1865; d. Cologne, June 1943). Violinist. He studied first with Poortmann at Groningen, and subsequently with **Jenö Hubay** in Brussels. When Hubay moved to Budapest in 1886 he took Eldering with him; Eldering did some teaching at the conservatory and became the violist of the newly founded Hubay Quartet. During his stay in Budapest he became very friendly with Edward and **Ottilie Ebner**.

As a member of the Hubay Quartet he played in various performances of Brahms's chamber music works, in some of which Brahms himself took part (*see* HUBAY [HUBER], JENÖ [EUGEN]). In 1888 he went to study with **Joseph Joachim** in Berlin, and from 1891 to 1894 he served as Konzertmeister of the Berlin Philharmonic. In the latter year he was appointed, probably on Joachim's recommendation, to a similar position in the court orchestra at Meiningen, where he remained until November 1899. At Meiningen he was able to renew his personal and professional contacts with Brahms (*see also* PIENING, KARL THEODOR). His last meeting—and music making—with Brahms took place at the Hagerhof, near Bad Honnef, in May 1896, following **Clara Schumann**'s funeral.

After leaving Meiningen, Eldering joined the faculty of the Amsterdam conservatory, and, finally, in 1903, he settled at Cologne. There he became Konzertmeister of the Gürzenich Concerts, led the Gürzenich Quartet, and taught at the conservatory (among his students was Adolf Busch). (Anon 1935; Enthoven 1954)

ENDERES, KARL VON (b. Teschen [Český Těšin, Czech Republic], 6 January 1788; d. Kremsmünster, 6 October 1860). Senior civil servant in the Austrian ministry of finance, with the title "Hofrat"; amateur botanist. A close friend of Joseph von Spaun, he was a popular figure in **Franz Schubert**'s circle during the last years of the composer's life; he hosted several Schubertiads and was present at others.

His connection with Brahms is an indirect, but not uninteresting, one. He owned an autograph by Schubert that contained the famous song "Der Wanderer" (D489), as well as the song "Der Hirt" (D490). After Enderes's death it passed into the possession of his son Karl Sebastian, and was eventually (perhaps in 1865) acquired by Brahms. It is possible that other Schubert manuscripts owned by Brahms came from the same source. (In her *Johannes Brahms: Life and Letters*, Styra Avins [1997] mistakenly states that Brahms acquired Schubert manuscripts directly from Hofrat Enderes; he died before Brahms first arrived in Vienna.) (Lorenz 2000)

ENGELMANN, (THEODOR) WILHELM (b. Leipzig, 14 November 1843; d. Berlin, 20 May 1909). Physiologist; son of the Leipzig publisher Wilhelm Friedrich Engelmann (1808–78) and brother of the astronomer Rudolf Engelmann (1841–88). He studied at Jena, Heidelberg, Göttingen, and finally at Leipzig. His doctoral dissertation (1867) on the cornea of the eye brought him to the attention of the well-known Dutch ophthalmologist Frans Cornelis Donders, who offered him a position as his associate at Utrecht University. Engelmann served with distinction on the faculty of that university for some 30 years (as associate professor of general physiology and histology and, after Donders retired in 1888, as professor of physiology). In 1897 he succeeded the celebrated physiologist Emil Heinrich Du Bois-Reymond (who had died in December 1896) as professor of physiology at the University of Berlin. Engelmann was the author of some 250 scientific publications, his principal areas of research being microbiology and muscle physiology; he was particularly interested in studying the effect of light on microorganisms.

In 1869 Engelmann married Professor Donders's daughter Marie, who died the following year after giving birth to twins. In 1874 he married **EMMA** Brandes (b. 1854), a brilliant young pianist who thereupon renounced what promised to be a splendid career. She had been presented to **Clara Schumann** by her teacher, the Schwerin Hofkapellmeister **Georg Aloys Schmitt**, in August 1969. Clara Schumann was greatly impressed by her talent and her excellent technique but was, for various reasons, unable to accept her immediately as a pupil (Litzmann 1902, vol. 3, 231). It is, however, very likely that she did so in the course of the following months. In July 1870 she recorded in her diary that Emma had recently spent a week at her house at Baden-Baden. Clara Schumann was deeply affected by Emma's playing and also liked her very much as a person:

> She gave me great joy, and with each passing day I grew fonder of her. It was a very exciting time for me, I relived my earliest youth through her; and yet, in the midst of the joy I felt at actually seeing at last a talent develop in the way I wished, and above all also an interpreter for **Robert**'s compositions, I was struck by the melancholy thought that there would soon be no further need now for me to be there—this girl will take my place! . . . With every piece she played for me, she astonished and delighted me anew. (Litzmann 1902, vol. 3, 241)

On 22 November 1870, after Emma had played Mendelssohn's First Piano Concerto at a Gürzenich concert at Cologne, Clara Schumann wrote to **Ferdinand Hiller**: "I am sure that Emma Brandes will have given you much pleasure! Hers is a talent which truly delights one, she plays so splendidly and is so seriously engaged in her music. I have already grown very fond of her and consider that she excels by far all the talented young pianists who have appeared in the past twenty years" (Sietz 1958–70, vol. 3, 46). Emma's burgeoning career even took her to London, where, on 24 April 1871, she played Mendelssohn's First Piano Concerto at a Philharmonic Society concert. **Dame Ethel Smyth**, who visited the Engelmanns at Utrecht in 1878, later recalled, "Off the music stool my hostess was a pleasant, childlike, not very interesting little person, who seemed to spend most of her time laughing at nothing in particular; at the piano the whole woman changed, and you were in the presence of a grave, inspired, passion-wrought pythoness" (Smyth 1919, vol. 2, 255).

Emma seems to have been greatly loved by all who came into contact with her. **Elisabeth von Herzogenberg**, a close friend, wrote to Brahms on 19 January 1878: "Give my regards to the charming lady who is able to do so much: play the piano with her little white paws in such an inimitable fashion, laugh like a little pigeon, enchant all hearts—and bring little children into the world, which is no doubt the quintessential and loveliest function that a little wife can fulfil on earth" (Brahms 1974/1, 46–47; altogether, Emma was to bear her husband four children, whereas Elisabeth, to her lasting regret, had none.)

The Engelmanns' house at Utrecht became a center for music making, for Emma continued to play in private and her husband was a fine cellist. (In September 1889, at **Laura von Beckerath**'s at Rüdesheim, he played several trios, including Brahms's revised op. 8, with Brahms and **Richard Barth**, apparently to the complete satisfaction of his partners.) Among the Engelmanns' visitors were Brahms, **Joseph Joachim**, **Anton Rubinstein**, **Edvard Grieg**, and Clara Schumann. Brahms had made Engelmann's acquaintance at the Schumann Festival in Bonn in 1873; according to **Julius Röntgen**, he had met Emma at Clara Schumann's house in Baden-Baden in 1869.

Engelmann played, moreover, an important part in Dutch musical life in a wider sense, for he was in contact with all the prominent music lovers and concert organizers in Holland. At a meeting in October 1875, attended by the persons responsible for organizing concerts in the five major musical centers (Amsterdam, Arnheim, The Hague, Rotterdam, and Utrecht), and at which Engelmann was present, it was unanimously decided to invite Brahms to visit Holland during the coming winter and to take part in concerts in those towns. It was Engelmann who conveyed this invitation to Brahms and who was subsequently responsible for corresponding with him concerning the programs. This first Dutch tour by Brahms was followed by several more over the next 10 years. He stayed with the Engelmanns at

Utrecht several times during these tours, and he also met one or both of them on various occasions outside Holland (for instance, in Leipzig in January 1877 and January 1879, at Schwerin in April 1880, and at Wiesbaden in the summer of 1883). He last saw Wilhelm Engelmann in September 1896 at Karlsbad [Karlovy Vary], where Engelmann, claiming to be on a business trip, had in fact gone specially in order to form his own opinion of his friend's condition. He was left in little doubt as to the nature of the mortal illness that had stricken Brahms but nonetheless kept up until the very end the pretence that a cure might still be possible. He last wrote to Brahms four days before his death.

The published correspondence between Brahms and the Engelmanns, in Julius Röntgen's edition, covers the period from December 1874 to March 1897. It contains Brahms's letters to Wilhelm and Emma, and Wilhelm's letters to Brahms. Emma's letters are, however, not included, which is particularly regrettable since, according to Röntgen, they "are surely the most delightful and uninhibited ones he ever received" (Brahms 1974/13, 7).

In 1876 Brahms dedicated his String Quartet op. 67 to Engelmann. His wife is said to have hoped that he would dedicate the Second Piano Concerto to her, and to have been disappointed when he did not do so. (Brahms 1974/1, 1974/13; Kamen 1986; Litzmann 1902; Sietz 1958–70; Smyth 1919)

EPSTEIN, JULIUS (b. Agram [Zagreb], 7 August 1832; d. Vienna, 2 March 1926). Pianist and teacher. He received his early musical instruction from Ignaz Lichtenegger, the choirmaster at Agram cathedral. In 1850 he moved to Vienna, where he studied piano with Anton Halm and composition with Johann Rufinatscha. He became an extremely successful pianist, particularly admired as an interpreter of the music of **Mozart** and **Franz Schubert**. In addition, he taught, both privately and at the conservatory (1867–1901); among his pupils were **Ignaz Brüll**, the young Baroness Elisabeth Stockhausen (*see* HERZOGENBERG, ELISABETH VON), and **Gustav Mahler** (and perhaps also **Bertha Porubszky** [*see* FABER, ARTHUR (LUDWIG)]). His wife Amalie (1838–1915) was likewise a highly regarded pianist.

Brahms made Epstein's acquaintance soon after his arrival in Vienna in 1862. According to **Max Kalbeck**, Epstein had been introduced to Brahms's music by Bertha Porubszky, and it was also she who now suggested that Brahms should call on Epstein, who was then living in the house in which Mozart had composed *Le nozze di Figaro* (5 Domgasse/8 Schulerstrasse). During his visit Brahms played for Epstein, who later remarked that Brahms's playing had made a more profound impression on him than that of any other pianist before or afterward. Hearing that Brahms had composed two (as yet unperformed) piano quartets, he arranged for the Hellmesberger Quartet to come to his own rooms for an impromptu performance, in which Brahms presumably took the piano part (*see also* HELLMESBERGER, JOSEPH). As a result, **Hellmesberger** offered to put the Piano Quartet in op. 25 on the program of his concert of 16 November, and he also joined, with two other members of his quartet and Brahms, in performing the Piano Quartet op. 26 at Brahms's own concert on 29 November. Whether, as Kalbeck (1976) states, Epstein's generosity extended to hiring the Musikverein concert hall for Brahms "behind his back" for the latter concert (vol. 2, 25) cannot be confirmed either from the records of the Gesellschaft der Musikfreunde or from other sources.

Over the next quarter of a century Brahms and Epstein maintained a friendly relationship, frequently meeting for meals at the Roter Igel restaurant, on Sunday walks, at musical events, at the Tonkünstlerverein (of which Epstein was a cofounder), at the houses of mutual acquaintances such as **Viktor von Miller zu Aichholz**, and even during their vacations in the country. In addition, Epstein played in various performances of Brahms's works. Thus, he performed the Violin Sonata op. 78 with Joseph Hellmesberger at **Adolf Wallnöfer**'s all-Brahms concert on 16 April 1880; at the concert on 23 February 1883, at which **Gustav Walter**, accompanied by Brahms himself, gave the first known public performances of the songs "Waldeseinsamkeit" (op. 85/6) and "Feldeinsamkeit" (op. 86/2), Epstein played the *Variations on a Theme by Schumann* (op. 23) with **Anton Door**; and at a concert of the Rosé Quartet on 5 March 1883, he took part in a performance of the Horn Trio (op. 40). At Brahms's first appearance as artistic director of the Gesellschaft der Musikfreunde, on 10 November 1872, Epstein accompanied **Marie Wilt** in Mozart's concert aria *Ch'io mi scordi di te?* (K. 505). (Menczigar 1957)

ÉRARD. French firm of piano and harp makers and music publishers, founded by Sébastien Érard (b. Strasbourg, 5 April 1772; d. La Muette, near Passy, 5 August 1831) who went into partnership with his brother Jean-Baptiste (d. 1826) in 1780; later the firm was successfully managed by Sébastien's nephew Pierre Érard (1796–1855). Its leading position among manufacturers and its popularity in the second quarter of the 19th century with concert artists such as **Liszt** and Mendelssohn owed much to Sébastien Érard's invention of the "double-escapement" action, which improved repetition and the pianist's overall control. The firm's impact on the market declined somewhat in the later 19th century; in 1960 it was amalgamated with Gaveau.

During her first London season in 1856, **Clara Schumann** played on Érard pianos, and at the end of it she was presented with a splendid concert grand by the manufacturers, who maintained a factory in London from the late 18th century until 1890. The piano was delivered to the Schumanns' house at Düsseldorf; in 1862, while in Paris for a series of concerts, Clara was invited by the firm to select a second Érard piano. According to **Florence May**, Érard pianos were Clara Schumann's favorite pianos until she used a Broadwood in her concerts in England in 1867—on which occasion she was promptly given a concert grand by the English firm. When May became her pupil at Baden-Baden in 1871, she found a Broadwood in the drawing room of her house and an Érard in the dining room. She adds that Clara Schumann and Brahms used to play duets on the Broadwood after afternoon coffee, and that Brahms one evening played several numbers of the still unpublished 3rd and 4th books of Hungarian Dances on the Érard, "his eyes flashing fire the while" (May 1948, vol. 1, 208). In their article "Johannes Brahms and his Pianos," G. S. Bozarth and S. H. Brady (2000) argue that this indicates that Brahms regarded the Érard as a more suitable instrument for his purpose, which could well have been the case. On the other hand, their statement that "in 1858, Brahms declined to premiere his First Piano Concerto in Hamburg because an Érard grand could not be secured for the performance" (Bozarth and Brady 2000, 430), with its implication that he was on principle unwilling to accept any other make, reads perhaps more into the letter he addressed to Clara Schumann on that occasion than is warranted. "[**August**] **Cranz** will not let me have me his Érard," he wrote. "I cannot get hold of a grand piano anywhere else" (letter of 28 February 1858, Litzmann 1970, vol. 1, 218). To **Joseph Joachim** he wrote on the following day: "I am not allowed to use the only decent piano there is here, which is owned by Herr Cranz" (Brahms 1974/5, 202). It sounds as if he would have been willing to accept a grand of another make, provided that it was a "decent" one.

In December 1865, in another letter to Clara Schumann, he commented favorably on the Érard he had played in Zurich and Winterthur the previous month (Litzmann 1970, vol. 1, 518). (Bozarth and Brady 2000; Brahms 1974/5; Good 2001; Litzmann 1970; May 1948)

ERK, LUDWIG (CHRISTIAN) (b. Wetzlar, 6 January 1807; d. Berlin, 25 November 1883). Editor of folk songs, teacher, chorus master, and composer. In 1835 he settled in Berlin, where he taught music at the municipal teachers' training institute until 1877. During that period he also founded two important choral societies in that city, one for men (1845) and another for mixed voices (in 1852), with which he gave concerts of folk songs. Furthermore, he published a large number of editions of folk songs, as well as of school songs. The most celebrated of his publications is the collection of folk songs entitled *Deutscher Liederhort* [*Treasury of German Songs*] that appeared in Berlin in 1856; 10 years after his death, **Franz Magnus Böhme** brought out a revised and augmented edition of this collection. (For Brahms's views on these collections, *see* BÖHME, FRANZ MAGNUS and ZUCCALMAGLIO, ANTON WILHELM FLORENTIN VON.) (Bolt 1937; H. Walter 1960)

ERKEL, SÁNDOR (b. Pest [Budapest], 2 January 1846; d. Békéscsaba, 14 October 1900). Conductor and composer; son of the far more celebrated composer and conductor Ferenc Erkel (1810–93). He became musical director of the National Theatre in 1876, in succession to **Hans Richter**, under whom he had served as first conductor (1874–76). In addition, he directed the Budapest Philharmonic Society concerts from 1875 to 1890.

At one of the society's concerts, on 9 November 1881, he conducted (from the manuscript) the premiere of Brahms's Second Piano Concerto, with the composer as soloist. The program also included Cherubini's overture to *Medea* (conducted by Erkel), and Brahms's *Academic Festival Overture* and First Symphony (both conducted by Brahms).

ETTLINGER, ANNA (b. Karlsruhe, 1841; d. Karlsruhe, 17 February 1934). Daughter of Veit Ettlinger (around 1796–1877), a prominent and widely respected lawyer, who was for almost 30 years (1844–72) a member of the Supreme Council, the highest Jewish religious authority in the Grand Duchy of Baden; moreover, he was the first Jew to serve on the Karlsruhe City Council (1848–70). The family took an active part in the cultural life of the town, and among the musicians who visited their house at 44 Zähringerstrasse (the building no longer exists) were Brahms and **Hermann Levi**, who frequently played duets there. Anna sang in local choirs and thus took part, with some of her sisters, in the performance of the Requiem conducted by Brahms on 12 May 1869 (and probably also in its first Karlsruhe performance, which Levi had directed on 6 March of that year). She also sang at the very first performance of *Schicksalslied*, conducted by Brahms at Karlsruhe on 18 October 1871, and possibly at the first complete performance of the *Triumphlied*, conducted by Levi at Karlsruhe on 5 June 1872. In 1871, at Levi's suggestion, she wrote *Melusine*, an opera libretto in verse, which Levi sent to Brahms without at first revealing the author's name. It failed to impress Brahms, let alone inspire him, and Anna later described it as a youthful and very amateurish piece of work.

After Levi moved to Munich, Anna still met Brahms and Levi occasionally during her visits to her older sister Emilie, who had settled in

Munich in 1862 with her banker husband Hermann Kaula. Emilie, who had a fine contralto voice, had studied with **Pauline Viardot** in Paris; after her husband's death she became a well-known teacher, and she formed her own vocal quartet and later a small choral society with which, among other works, she performed compositions by Brahms. On one occasion they performed the *Liebeslieder-Walzer* in Levi's rooms, with Levi and Brahms accompanying. But when Brahms eventually broke with Levi, he also ceased all contact with Levi's friends, including Anna and her family.

Anna's article "Erinnerungen an Brahms und Levi" and especially her memoirs, *Lebenserinnerungen*, are of considerable interest. She also knew **Julius Allgeyer** well, and a curious memento of her association with the three men is a little manuscript book containing amusing portraits and poems that she and her sisters Rudolfine and Emma (they humorously called themselves "Die Ettlingerei") sent to Brahms at Christmas 1873. It is preserved in the Sibley Library of the Eastman School of Music in Rochester. (Draheim et al. 1983; Ettlinger 1913, 1920; Geiringer 1988)

EWER & CO. London firm of music importers, sellers, and publishers, founded around 1823 by John Jeremiah Ewer, who not long afterward went into partnership with Julius Johanning, after which the business was carried on under the name "Ewer & Johanning" until around 1829; Johanning having withdrawn, it was then continued as "J. J. Ewer & Co." until 1867. In that year the firm was acquired by Novello & Co.; the new firm was known as "Novello, Ewer & Co." until 1898, when the name "Ewer" was dropped.

Ewer & Co. was the English distributor for the first editions of the following compositions by Brahms published by **Jakob Melchior Rieter-Biedermann**: the *Variations on a Theme by Schumann* for piano duet (April 1863); the arrangement for piano duet of the First Piano Concerto (April/May 1864); the arrangement for mixed choir of *Marienlieder* (October 1864); the Piano Quintet (December 1865); the *Paganini Variations* (January 1866); and the arrangement for piano duet of the *Waltzes* op. 39 (September 1866).

EXNER, ADOLF (b. Prague, 5 February 1841; d. Kufstein, Austria, 10 September 1894). Jurist; academic. Son of the philosopher Franz Exner (1802–53) and brother of the physiologist Sigmund Exner (1846–1926) and the physicist Franz Exner (1849–1926). Adolf Exner taught at Zurich University (1868–72) and from 1872 at the University of Vienna, where he became dean (1883–84) and rector (1891–92). Brahms met him socially in Vienna (*see* BILLROTH, THEODOR), and he was also one of Brahms's companions on his trip to Sicily in 1881.

– F –

FABER, ARTHUR (LUDWIG) (b. Penzing, near Vienna, 25 May 1839; d. Vienna, 11 January 1907) and **(LOUISE MARIE) BERTHA** (b. Vienna, 4 December 1841; d. Vienna, 9 November 1910). The Fabers were among Brahms's closest friends in Vienna. Bertha, a daughter of Pastor Gustav Porubszky (d. 17 July 1876), made Brahms's acquaintance through her singing teacher **Carl Grädener** in Hamburg in 1859 and became a member of his women's choir. He took pleasure in hearing her sing Austrian folk songs and was altogether greatly attracted by her personality. In fact, **Max Kalbeck** goes so far as to suggest that his acquaintance with this "incarnation of Viennese charm" confirmed him in his already strong desire to visit Vienna. He corresponded with Bertha after once more taking up his appointment in Detmold in the autumn of 1859, and in his last letter, written in January 1860 shortly before his return to Hamburg, he indicated that he expected to see her again there; but nothing is known about any further meetings at that time (*see also* BRANDT, AUGUSTE).

When Brahms arrived in Vienna in 1862 he met Bertha again (*see also* EPSTEIN, JULIUS) and learned that she was engaged to Arthur Faber; they were married on 10 February 1863. For the rest of his life Brahms was on intimate terms with the couple (he addressed the husband with the familiar "Du"), and he frequently enjoyed their hospitality (on his return to Vienna in late November 1866, after an absence of some 18 months, he even stayed with them for a few weeks until he found a new apartment); and for a number of years he regularly spent Christmas Eve with them. Arthur Faber, a prosperous businessman, assisted Brahms in various financial transactions. The "Wiegenlied" [Cradle Song] (op. 49/4) that Brahms composed in July 1868 was inspired by the birth of the Fabers' son Hans on 7(?) June of that year (in the register of births at the Protestant Church in Vienna the figure "3" has been penciled in above the "7," but the latter figure has not been crossed out). The child was baptized on 21 June; Brahms was not in Vienna on that day. (Regarding the "Wiegenlied," *see also* BAUMANN, ALEXANDER [MORITZ].)

Bertha later organized a small women's choir that met at her house and was conducted by **Eusebius Mandyczewski**. Naturally Brahms's compositions figured prominently among the music rehearsed. The choir was occasionally augmented with male voices. **Eduard Hanslick**, writing in the *Neue freie Presse* on 23 March 1889, praised its excellent recent rendition of Brahms's *5 Gesänge* for mixed choir (op. 104). This performance, which was given at a private soiree, was followed by another, on 3 April, at the Tonkünstlerverein.

The Fabers were closely involved in the plan to erect a Brahms statue in Vienna. Arthur became president of the executive committee after Nikolaus Dumba's death in 1900 (his place was later taken by **Viktor von Miller zu Aichholz**), while Bertha presided over the ladies' committee that was formed in 1898.

FANTIN-LATOUR, HENRI (b. Grenoble, 14 January 1836; d. Buré [Orne], 25 August 1904). Painter and lithographer. Two of his lithographs were inspired by Brahms's death. One of these, which was exhibited at Kiel in 1983 and in Hamburg in 1997, shows Music weeping over his death, while another female figure, Fama, representing glory, proclaims his eternal renown.

FARMER, JOHN (b. Nottingham, 16 August 1835; d. Oxford, 17 July 1901). Composer and teacher. The son of a lace manufacturer and proficient amateur cellist, he studied for three years at the Leipzig conservatory with Ignaz Moscheles, Louis Plaidy, **Moritz Hauptmann**, and Ernst Friedrich Richter, and at Coburg with Andreas Spaeth. Later, he was active as a music teacher at Zurich (1857–61), and after his return to England he taught with great success at Harrow School from 1864 until 1885, when he was appointed organist at Balliol College, Oxford. As a composer, he became best known for his school songs; his other works included the fairy opera *Cinderella.*

Farmer was a great admirer of Brahms, whom he first met and heard play when he visited Hamburg in 1861 or 1862, armed with a letter of introduction from **Jakob Melchior Rieter-Biedermann**. In April 1868 he traveled to Bremen to attend the performance of the Requiem at the Minster. Later he recalled in a letter to Brahms (now in the archive of the Gesellschaft der Musikfreunde in Vienna) that when he asked Brahms's father after the performance if he felt proud of his son's success, his only reply was "Es hat sich ganz gut gemacht" [It has turned out quite well]. Farmer commented, "He took it for granted that his son would triumph."

Farmer is generally credited with having helped to establish Brahms's reputation in England. Thus, **Florence May**, referring to his position at Harrow School, claims that his "influence, authoritatively exercised in an important educational centre, was sufficiently stimulating to create, during the late sixties, a local interest in Brahms's art that became operative in the course of the seventies in various parts of the United Kingdom" (May 1948, vol. 2, 450). (May 1948; Walker and Jones 2004)

FELDERHOFF, REINHOLD (b. Elbing, 25 January1865; d. Berlin, 18 December 1919). Sculptor; a pupil of Reinhold Begas. When, in late

December 1900, he traveled to Hamburg to deliver in person his model—a standing figure—for the proposed Brahms monument, he was already well known as the creator of such major works as the statues of Margrave Johann II and Wilhelm Röntgen in Berlin; he had also participated in the construction there of the monument of Emperor Wilhelm I. Moreover, he was, as he had previously informed **Julius Spengel**, able to draw on "not insignificant personal memories" of Brahms (K. Hofmann 2002, 119); he had presumably met Brahms in Berlin. However, when the designs submitted by 13 artists for the Brahms monument were exhibited at the Hamburg Kunsthalle in May 1901, Felderhoff's was reportedly not among them. The commission was eventually offered to **Max Klinger**.

Felderhoff's had, in fact, wished to submit two different designs, but he was unable to finish the second one, showing Brahms seated, in time. Later he managed to complete the second design, which was then to be used for a Brahms monument due to be erected at Ischl in 1914, but the project was abandoned after the outbreak of the First World War. A model, which is now at the Brahms Institute in Lübeck, was shown at the Brahms Exhibition in Hamburg in 1997.

It was Felderhoff who made the tombstone for **Richard Mühlfeld**'s grave at Meiningen cemetery. (Brahms Exhibition 1997b; Turner 1996; K. Hofmann 2002)

FELLINGER, RICHARD ALBERT (b. Elberfeld [now part of Wuppertal], 11 March 1848; d. Vienna, 13 October 1903) and **MARIA REGINA**, née Köstlin (b. Tübingen, 14 March 1849; d. Berlin, 12 April 1925). Probably Brahms's closest friends in Vienna during the final years of his life. Richard came from a family of merchants and manufacturers (his father Gustav Rudolph [1810–65] owned a chemical plant), while Maria's ancestors were drawn to music and literature. Her great-grandmother Sabine Hitzelberger, née Renk (b. 1755; d. after 1807), was a well-known coloratura soprano and singing teacher at Würzburg; her grandmother Regina Hitzelberger, later Lang (1786–1827), a pupil of Carl Cannabich and the Abbé Vogler, was a much admired member of the Munich court opera; and her mother Josephine Caroline Köstlin (1815–80) was an accomplished singer and pianist, as well as a gifted composer of songs. She was married to Christian Reinhold Köstlin (1813–56), a law professor at Tübingen University who, under the pseudonym "C. Reinhold," published poems, novellas, and plays. (Four of his poems were set to music by Brahms—*see* REINHOLD, C.)

Richard Fellinger studied chemistry at Tübingen University, and subsequently served in the Franco-Prussian war of 1870–71. On 15 June 1871, at Tübingen, he married Maria Köstlin. The young couple settled at Elberfeld, where Richard first worked at a local chemical plant before founding, together with his older brother, a factory for the production of aniline and alizarin dyes. The business failed to prosper and was forced to close down a few years later. Richard thereupon studied electrical engineering, and in 1877 the Fellingers moved to Berlin, where Richard worked for the firm Siemens & Halske, which specialized in the manufacture of telegraphic equipment. In the spring of 1881 he took up the position of manager of the firm's branch in Vienna, with responsibility for Austria and Hungary; he joined its board of directors in 1897. The Fellingers had two sons: Richard Joseph (1872–1952) and Robert Felix (1873–1955). In 1933 the former published *Klänge um Brahms*, a valuable account of his family's contacts with Brahms; the book was reissued in 1997, in a new edition prepared by his granddaughter Imogen Fellinger.

The Fellingers were great music lovers; Richard played piano, and Maria had a good, though untrained, soprano voice. They counted many musicians among their friends, including **Clara Schumann**, whom they knew from their days at Elberfeld and frequently met while living in Berlin. (Clara, who became godmother of their younger son Robert, had been in contact with Maria's mother since 1852.) It was Clara Schumann who introduced Richard Fellinger to Brahms at the 50th jubilee of the Hamburg Philharmonic Society in September 1878. When the couple moved to Vienna three years later, she provided them with a letter of introduction to her former pupil **Anna Franz** (*see* WITTGENSTEIN FAMILY), with whom Maria formed a close friendship. The two women regularly got together for music sessions, in which Brahms's songs figured prominently; Maria's son Richard states that his mother knew all of Brahms's songs well and sang most of them. It was at the house of Emil and Anna Franz, on 2 November 1881, that the Fellingers met Brahms for the first time in Vienna. Two days later they called on him in his rooms in Karlsgasse and afterward dined with him at the Roter Igel restaurant; he returned their visit shortly afterward. Thus began a friendship that was to grow increasingly close over the years and which assumed a particularly important role in Brahms's life in the 1890s. (However, the relationship never became entirely intimate; until the end, Brahms addressed the Fellingers as "Herr Doktor" and "Frau Doktor," and they no doubt observed a similar formality.)

According to *Klänge um Brahms*, he first dined at the Fellingers' flat on 12 November 1882 (the Fellingers were then living at the "Bretanohaus," Erdbergstrasse 19), and he dined with them for the first time more intimately, as their sole guest, on 6 January 1884, by which time they had moved to Geusaugasse 7. (From May 1884 they were to live at Apostelgasse 12, and from September 1893 at the Arenberg Palais on Landstrasse-Hauptstrasse [see below]. All these streets are located in Vienna's third district.) Brahms would be their guest on countless occasions. Indeed, in later years he regularly dined with them on Sundays (and occasionally also during the week) when in Vienna, usually by invitation, sometimes inviting himself, always warmly welcomed. He was considerably upset if Maria's chronically fragile health ever forced a break in this routine. Returning after several weeks' absence in April 1895, he confided, "It is like a dream for me to be at your house once more" (R. Fellinger 1997, 108). From 1892 he regularly spent Christmas Eve with the Fellingers, and in 1896 he even returned on the following two days. He took a lively interest in Richard's prospering career, felt affection and respect for Maria—to **Eduard Hanslick**, in a letter in 1884, he described her as "an extremely charming and talented lady" (R. Fellinger 1997, 26)—and he was very fond of the two boys. (Richard Jr. later named his first child, born in 1899, after him.) As for the Fellingers, they loved and worshipped Brahms. In June 1885 Maria wrote to him:

> My husband once said: 'As long as there are men with a child-like heart and a heroic character like Brahms I shall have no fear for mankind.' To which I said: 'Right, and Amen.' And when he added 'When I entertain good, noble, and profound thoughts, Brahms's melodies always accompany me,' then I was even more and doubly conscious of how great, how infinitely great is the gratitude we owe you. (Brahms 1974/7, 242)

In October 1886 Richard wrote to **Robert Hausmann**: "Brahms, who returned from Switzerland two days ago and has dined with us alone here today, has just left. We have fallen in love with Brahms the man all over again" (R. Fellinger 1997, 51). At the same time, knowing Brahms's often prickly character, the Fellingers were careful not to irritate or embarrass him with excessive demonstrations of their feelings. As a result, he felt very comfortable in their house, enjoying their unwavering, but discreet, affection and appreciating the happy family atmosphere that reigned there, for the Fellingers were devoted to each other. "Tell your parents, they need only whistle and I'll come," he once told the boys (R. Fellinger 1997, 64). Richard Fellinger earned Brahms's particular gratitude when he surprised him one day by secretly having electrical lighting installed in his rooms while he was dining at their house.

Of course, Brahms was also responsible for much of the music making at the Fellingers'. On one memorable occasion, on 21 October 1886, he partnered the violinist **Marie Soldat** and the cellist Robert Hausmann (both close friends of the Fellingers) in his recently composed Cello Sonata op. 99, Violin Sonata op. 100, and Piano Trio op. 101 before a number of guests, prior to the first public performances of those works. Among others closely associated with Brahms who performed at the Fellingers' were **Hermine Spies**, **Richard Mühlfeld**, and the Joachim Quartet.

It is a measure of the reliance Brahms had come to place on the Fellingers' advice in certain matters that he should have discussed with them at great length, on 7 February 1897, the terms of a new will he wished to make; at the same time he asked Richard Fellinger to act as executor of his estate. Fellinger subsequently drew up the will in accordance with Brahms's wishes and delivered it to him the following morning, explaining that if Brahms were to write it out himself and date and sign it, it would be recognized as valid under Austrian law. However, Brahms never did this, and only Fellinger's draft was found in his rooms after his death. (This account of what happened is taken from **Florence May**'s Brahms biography and differs somewhat from that given in *Klänge um Brahms*; but May states that she obtained her information directly from Maria Fellinger.) In the absence of a valid new will, Fellinger, who was duly appointed curator of the estate on 5 April, became embroiled in legal disputes that continued for years after his own death in 1903 and were not finally settled until 1915. (On this subject, see O. Biba's [1987] article "New Light on the Brahms *Nachlass*"; *see also* SIMROCK, FRIEDRICH [FRITZ] [AUGUST].)

In one way or another, the Fellingers offered Brahms what comfort they could during his fatal illness. They even apparently considered the possibility of having him moved to their apartment if he became bedridden. In the event, the deterioration in his condition happened too rapidly to make such a plan practicable. On the evening of 2 April 1897, which turned out to have been the last day of Brahms's life, Richard Fellinger spent a long time at his bedside. His son relates in *Klänge um Brahms* that the dying man looked at him with great affection and was loath to see him leave. The Fellingers cherished Brahms's memory. After visiting them in 1898, **Julius Röntgen** reported to his wife, "Everything there breathes 'Brahms'" (Röntgen 1934, 82–83).

In fact, nobody did more to keep his memory alive than Maria Fellinger. A extremely gifted artist, she had studied painting with Karl Gussow in Berlin and later in Vienna with Heinrich von Angeli and Karl Fröschl (whose brother Rudolf, incidentally, became the doctor of the Fellinger family and, on their recommendation, of Brahms). She made a number of excellent drawings and portraits, and after she had taken up sculpture as well, of busts of Brahms. One of the earliest, if not the first, of the portraits in oils dates from 1885 and copies a photograph taken of him in 1852, which he had given her; the others show him as he appeared in his later years. While he never actually sat for her, she clearly had countless opportunities to observe him and she was always able to achieve a remarkable likeness. A portrait that she executed in the summer of 1885, when she was in daily contact with him at Mürzzuschlag, was publicly exhibited at the Österreichischer Kunst-Verein in Vienna the following winter. The first bust, a small one, was created in 1898, and that same year she also modeled a far larger one. She later gave a bronze cast of the latter to Toni Schruf, the proprietor of the Hotel Post at Mürzzuschlag, who placed it in the hotel garden, where this particular Brahms monument was unveiled on 3 July 1910. Later, the bust came into the possession of the Wintersport- und Heimatmuseum [Winter Sports and Local History Museum] of that town; now, on permanent loan from that museum, it is exhibited in the music room of the local Brahms Museum (which also displays, at its entrance, a plaster copy of it). Lastly, since the 1950s, a cast of this bust can be seen in the local Dietrichpark, where it stands on the plinth that originally formed part of the Hotel Post monument. Clearly, Mürzzuschlag has not forgotten its distinguished visitor.

In 1899 Maria Fellinger depicted Brahms in a highly successful relief; furthermore, she made an amusing statuette showing him holding a cigar, which was based on a photograph she had once taken. This was merely one of a large number of informal photographs she took of Brahms, showing him either by himself or together with other guests of the Fellingers at the so-called Arenberg Palais (96 Landstrasse-Hauptstrasse), where they occupied a flat from September 1893 (at first on the ground floor, and then from 1896 upstairs) and where they also had a large garden at their disposal. It is evident from the photographs that Brahms felt very much at ease there; a particularly charming one shows him with Marie Soldat. (The Palais was demolished in 1958 and replaced by a modern building.)

However, it was at the Fellingers' flat at 12 Apostelgasse that the only known sound recording of Brahms playing the piano was made on 2 December 1889 by Thomas Edison's agent Theo Wangemann. Brahms had reportedly practiced his Rhapsody op. 79/2 for the session, but irritated by the lengthy preparations, he changed his mind and instead played a shortened version of the Hungarian Dance WoO 1/1 and his own paraphrase of Joseph Strauss's polka mazurka *Die Libelle* (op. 204). The Fellingers' **Streicher** grand piano, on which Brahms played on this occasion, has recently been carefully restored by Gert Hecher and is now at the Brahms Museum in Mürzzuschlag. The recording itself has been issued, in a restored version, by the Verlag der Österreichische Akademie der Wissenschaften

(*Tondokumente aus dem Phonogrammarchiv: Historische Stimmen aus Wien*, 5: "Brahms spielt Klavier" [OEAW PHA CD5], 1997). On its history, see especially the leaflet accompanying the recording, as well as the article published jointly by H. Kowar, F. Lechleitner, and D. Schüller (1984) in the *Phonographic Bulletin*, which dealt with an earlier rerecording.

Copies of some of Maria Fellinger's busts of Brahms were placed on sale, with the proceeds going to the Viennese Brahms Monument Fund. She also published collections of her photographs of Brahms in Vienna in 1900, and in a second, enlarged edition at Leipzig in 1911. (Brahms 1974/7; M. Fellinger 1911; R. Fellinger 1997; Kowar, Lechleitner, and Schüller 1984; May 1948)

FERRAND, EDUARD [pseudonym of Eduard Schulz] (1813–42). Poet. Brahms set a text by Ferrand in the song "Treue Liebe" (op. 7/1).

FEUERBACH, ANSELM (b. Speyer, 12 September 1829; d. Venice, 4 January 1880). Painter and draughtsman; member of an exceptionally gifted family: his grandfather Johann Paul Anselm (1775–1833) was a celebrated jurist, his father Anselm (1798–1851) became professor of classical philology and archaeology at the University of Freiburg im Breisgau, and his uncle Ludwig (1804–72) was a well-known philosopher. Anselm's mother Amalie (née Keerl) died in 1829 shortly after his birth, and his father married Henriette Heydenreich (1812–92) in 1834. Henriette became utterly devoted to her stepson, whose career she supported in every possible way, and he amply returned her love (*see* FEUERBACH, HENRIETTE).

Anselm Jr. studied with Wilhelm von Schadow, Carl Sohn, and Wilhelm Schirmer at Düsseldorf, and with Karl Rahl in Munich, Gustav Wappers at Antwerp, and Thomas Couture in Paris. In 1855 he was able to travel to Italy thanks to a stipend granted to him by Prince Regent Friedrich (later Grand Duke Friedrich I) of Baden. After spending some time in Venice and Florence, in 1856 he moved to Rome, which was to be his principal place of residence for most of the rest of his life. From 1873 he taught at the Akademie der bildenden Künste in Vienna, but he resigned his professorship in 1876, mainly because of ill health; however, his decision was also motivated by certain other reasons, not least among them the hostile reaction that his paintings evoked among the Viennese critics, whom he held in ever-increasing contempt.

Feuerbach created a number of landscapes, but his principal interest lay in the idealistic depiction of predominantly classical scenes, in a style greatly influenced by the painters of the Italian Renaissance, notably Titian and Paolo Veronese. While he had numerous detractors, he was not without admirers, and the offer to join the faculty of the Viennese Academy clearly testifies to the standing he enjoyed in certain circles. Among his admirers, none was more devoted to him than his friend and future biographer **Julius Allgeyer**. It was he who introduced Brahms to Feuerbach at Baden-Baden in 1865. During the following years he repeatedly stimulated Brahms's interest in Feuerbach by his own writings and also through the photographs of Feuerbach's art that he sent Brahms on several occasions. In a letter written in January 1872 (which **Max Kalbeck** wrongly ascribed to 1875), Brahms asked **Hermann Levi** to tell Allgeyer that the latter had given him very great pleasure "with the Feuerbachs," which Allgeyer had sent as a Christmas present (Brahms 1974/7, 92). At the same time he wrote to Allgeyer himself in order to thank him and ask for further copies for friends to whom he had shown the photographs (Orel 1964, 73). Brahms's enthusiasm for Feuerbach's paintings is thus well documented. Moreover, he is believed to have been instrumental in arranging in 1872 for the publication of an article by Allgeyer on Feuerbach in the *Österreichische Wochenschrift für Wissenschaft und Kunst*, with whose guiding spirits, the influential art historians Rudolf von Eitelberger and Bruno Adalbert Bucher, Brahms was well acquainted.

Feuerbach counted on making his mark in Vienna with two monumental recent paintings, *Plato's Symposium* (second version) and *The Battle of the Amazons*. Brahms, who was familiar with the tastes of the Viennese, cautioned him not to set his expectations too high, but his well-meant, though perhaps somewhat clumsily expressed, advice offended Feuerbach. One result of the incident was that Feuerbach, who had started on a portrait of Brahms, put the canvas to one side and, although relations were by no means broken off between the two men, he never resumed work on it. (Apparently the only time Feuerbach portrayed Brahms was in a drawing he once made of a group of acquaintances, including Brahms, with whom he was dining at Gause's restaurant in Johannesgasse. **Richard Heuberger** saw the drawing in Brahms's rooms, but it has since been lost. When *Plato's Symposium* and *The Battle of the Amazons* were exhibited in Vienna early in 1874, they met with the hostile reception predicted by Brahms. The setback did not shake Feuerbach's conviction that he was a genius but merely confirmed him in his already well-developed view that he was a gravely misunderstood one. The following extracts from his correspondence with his stepmother are characteristic of his attitude:

> Today the scales fell, as it were, from my eyes as to what I am capable of still accomplishing. . . . My paintings are quite magnificent. . . . The *Symposium* is now completed and has turned into a splendid painting. . . . If there were at least a reason [for the criticism] I would keep silent, but that one can dare to

drag what is best and noblest through the mire with impunity, that can only happen in an uncultured nation. (Allgeyer 1904, vol. 2, 222, 227, 235)

While Brahms continued to hold Feuerbach's paintings in high regard (although he confessed to Levi that he did not understand *The Battle of the Amazons*), his contacts with the artist grew rarer. In fact, he felt increasingly out of sympathy with Feuerbach's behavior. In March 1876, shortly before Feuerbach left Vienna, Brahms wrote to Allgeyer: "I have been ready to forgive much to Feuerbach, whose art, which has been misunderstood for so long and so widely, I esteem most highly. But I find his utter indifference toward all and sundry . . . quite intolerable. I see him almost daily, and regretfully, content myself with greeting him" (Orel 1964, 110).

The news of Feuerbach's death four years later profoundly affected Brahms and led him to set Schiller's poem *Nänie* in memory of his former friend, and to dedicate it to Anselm's stepmother (*see* FEUERBACH, HENRIETTE); the work was published by C. F. Peters in December 1881. Soon afterward there appeared a very different kind of memorial to the artist, a small book entitled *Ein Vermächtnis von Anselm Feuerbach* [*Anselm Feuerbach's Legacy*], for which Henriette Feuerbach was responsible. It offered the reader Anselm's own account of the creation of certain of his works and of his battle against what he regarded as uninformed and ill-disposed critics, together with a number of aphorisms about life and art and various passages from his letters to his stepmother. The volume appears to have met with some success, since it went through several editions. Incidentally, not all modern commentators have been impressed by Feuerbach's allegations of having been cruelly misunderstood by the Philistines; one modern writer, the (unidentified) author of the entry on Feuerbach in the *Oxford Companion to Art*, has even been moved to assert that "it is this element of self-pity which makes his book *Ein Vermächtnis* . . . one of the most pathetic and repellent autobiographies ever written" (Osborne 1970, 406). What Brahms thought of it is not documented, other than that Henriette Feuerbach wrote in a letter to him in February 1882 that "your opinion about the *Vermächtnis* has greatly reassured me" (Uhde-Bernays 1913, 403). On the other hand, there is clear evidence that Brahms greatly admired Allgeyer's biography of Feuerbach; indeed, he enjoyed it so much that he resumed his friendly relations with its author, after a lapse of some 10 years (*See* ALLGEYER, JULIUS).

Brahms never wavered in his admiration for Feuerbach's works. **Richard Heuberger** records an occasion in 1888 when Brahms showed him his extensive collection of copies of the artist's sketches and photographs of his paintings and drawings. Heuberger adds, "Brahms war ebenso wie ich Feuer und Flamme" [Brahms, like myself, was full of enthusiasm] (Heuberger

1976, 37). His friends were evidently well aware of the pleasure Brahms derived from Feuerbach's works, for on his 62nd birthday in 1895 he received Feuerbach's oil painting *Diana Stepping from Her Bath* from **Viktor von Miller zu Aichholz**, and a photograph of one of the artist's self-portraits from **Felix Hecht**, in whose house in Frankfurt he had previously admired the original.

One positive result of Feuerbach's in many respects disappointing stay in Vienna was a commission to provide the decoration for part of the ceiling of the main hall of the new Akademie der bildenden Künste, then under construction. His contribution was a large oval area in the center of the ceiling, depicting the *Fall of the Titans*. He continued to work on it after leaving Vienna, and it was installed some years after his death. (Allgeyer 1872, 1904; Brahms 1974/7; Brinkmann 1999; H. Ebert 1907; Feuerbach 1902; Heuberger 1976; Huschke 1931, 1939; Orel 1964; Osborne 1970; Uhde-Bernays 1912, 1913)

FEUERBACH, HENRIETTE, née Heydenreich (b. Ermetzhofen, near Steinach, Franconia, 13 August 1812; d. Ansbach, 5 August 1892). By her marriage in 1834 to Anselm Feuerbach (1798–1851), then on the staff of the Speyer Gymnasium and later professor at the University of Freiburg im Breisgau, she became the stepmother of future painter **Anselm Feuerbach**. She was a highly intelligent and well-educated woman who studied, among other subjects, philosophy, astronomy, and music, and learned Greek, English, and Spanish; she contributed to various journals and published a study of poets Johann Peter Uz and Johann Friedrich von Cronegk. Above all, she devoted much of her life to sustaining her stepson Anselm's efforts to make a name for himself as an artist, and, after his death, to establishing his reputation on a firm and permanent basis.

Brahms made her acquaintance, at the same time as Anselm's, at Baden-Baden in 1865, and thereafter remained in intermittent contact with her throughout the rest of her life. She highly admired his compositions and, in particular, regarded his Requiem as the greatest contemporary musical work. She also liked Brahms as a person, without being blind to certain disconcerting aspects of his nature. "He really is, essentially, quite uncomplicated and happy-go-lucky, but he can also be haughty and arrogant, and extremely inconsiderate," she wrote to **Julius Allgeyer** in 1869 (Uhde-Bernays 1913, 275). A scenario entitled *Fortunat*, which she may have sketched out as the basis for an opera libretto for Brahms, was found among his papers after his death (it was later published in Hermann Uhde-Bernaÿs's *Henriette Feuerbach: Ihr Leben in ihren Briefen*).

In August 1881 Brahms asked Henriette Feuerbach's permission to dedicate to her his recent setting of **Friedrich von Schiller**'s poem *Nänie*, as a tangible expression of the fact that he had composed it in Anselm's memory. He felt somewhat uncertain how she would react, for, characteristically, he had not written to her after Anselm's death ("yet there will have been few persons who thought of you more sincerely" (H. Ebert 1907, 310). She was, in fact, greatly moved by his letter and assured him in her reply that she had not for a moment misinterpreted his silence. As for Anselm, she wrote, "he loved you as a person and placed you above all other artists, without ever allowing himself to be led astray by different gods" (Uhde-Bernays 1913, 389). When the score was issued by C. F. Peters in December 1881, it duly bore a dedication to "Frau Hofrath Henriette Feuerbach." She was unable to attend the first performance of the work, which Brahms conducted in Zurich on 6 December; but soon afterward, on 5 February 1882, while she was spending a few days at Leipzig, a private performance was arranged for her at Professor Wach's house by **Heinrich and Elisabeth von Herzogenberg**, in which members of the Bach-Verein sang to a piano accompaniment. The work made a deep impression on Henriette Feuerbach: "I will not forget the experience in my own last hour," she wrote to Brahms afterward (Uhde-Bernays 1913, 403). She reportedly met him for the last time at Leipzig in February 1886, but they were still corresponding in 1888. Brahms retained his high opinion of her to the end. In a letter to Allgeyer written shortly after the publication of the latter's biography of Feuerbach, he referred to mother and son as "this splendid woman and her illustrious son" (Orel 1964, 126). (Feuerbach 1902; Orel 1964; Uhde-Bernays 1912, 1913)

FILLUNGER, MARIE (b. Vienna, 27 January 1850; d. Interlaken, 23 December 1930). Soprano. She owed her acquaintance with Brahms to **Ottilie Ebner** and began her long association with his music while still a student at the Vienna conservatory, where her teacher was Mathilde Marchesi (1869–73). At her concert on 27 November 1872, she gave the earliest documented performance of "Von waldbekränzter Höhe" (op. 57/1); and on 23 March 1873, at a concert of the Gesellschaft der Musikfreunde, she sang the solo part in the first known performance, directed by Brahms himself, of his arrangement for soprano, women's chorus, and wind instruments (M. McCorkle 1984, Anhang Ia/17) of **Franz Schubert**'s song "Ellens Zweiter Gesang" D838. Subsequently, she continued her studies, reportedly on Brahms's advice, at the Musikhochschule in Berlin. While there, she made several public appearances, mainly in oratorio, in northern Germany, Switzerland, and Holland. At Leipzig, on 1 December 1874, she gave the first known public performance of "An die Nachtigall" (op. 46/4).

During her stay in Berlin she came to know **Clara Schumann** well and formed a particularly close and loving relationship with her daughter **Eugenie** (*see* SCHUMANN FAMILY). When Clara, after a break of some 18 months, gave a concert at Kiel on 18 March 1875, she invited Fillunger to take part, which "Fillu" (as she was called by her intimates) did with considerable success. The following year Fillunger sang an aria by Mendelssohn, songs by Schubert, and Brahms's "Wehe, so willst Du mich wieder" (op. 32/5) at a Museum concert in Frankfurt (18 February 1876), at which Brahms played his First Piano Concerto and conducted the *Haydn Variations*. During those years, Fillunger's relations with Clara Schumann became increasingly close, and when, in 1878, Clara moved with her daughters **Marie** and Eugenie to Frankfurt, Fillunger moved too and went to live with them. She assisted at Clara Schumann's lessons and acted as her secretary, but at the same time, she continued to make a name for herself as a singer, and Brahms's music not infrequently appeared on her programs. On 16 March 1884 she performed the *Liedeslieder-Walzer* with **Julius Stockhausen**, Fides Keller, and Raimund von zur Mühlen in Frankfurt, with Brahms himself and Lazaro Uzielli providing the accompaniment; on 28 January 1885, she sang "Meine Liebe ist grün" (op. 63/5) and took part in the vocal quartets opp. 31/1, 64/1, and 92/1 at Krefeld, again to Brahms's accompaniment; moreover, she sang in what appears to have been the earliest performances in Frankfurt of the *Zigeunerlieder* (op. 103), first at Stockhausen's apartment on 15 October 1888 and subsequently at a concert he gave on 4 November. "No one else here sings them nearly as well [as she does]," Clara reported to Brahms on 23 November (Litzmann 1970, vol. 2, 368).

Shortly afterward Fillunger left the Schumann household as a result of tensions arising between her and Marie over her increasingly intimate friendship with Eugenie, with Clara Schumann taking Marie's side. Before long Fillunger settled in England, where, at her debut, at a Popular Concert at St. James's Hall on 4 February 1889 she greatly pleased the audience with her singing of Schubert songs; on 4 March she took the solo soprano part in a performance of **Beethoven**'s Ninth Symphony conducted by August Manns at the Crystal Palace. Fillunger was to enjoy a highly successful career in England, with numerous appearances in London and various provincial centers. In 1891 she accompanied **Sir Charles Hallé** and his wife, violinist Wilma Neruda, on a concert tour of Australia, and four years later she went with them to South Africa. From 1904 until 1913 she taught at the Royal College of Music in Manchester.

In 1892 Eugenie Schumann joined Fillunger in London, where she was active as a piano teacher. They remained together there until 1912, when

Eugenie went to stay with Marie, who had been living at Interlaken since their mother's death, and Fillunger returned to Vienna. However, two years later she and Eugenie once more set up house together, this time at Matten near Interlaken, and there she spent the rest of her life. Marie (d. 1929), "Fillu" (d. 1930), and Eugenie (d. 1938) share a common grave at Wilderswyl cemetery, near Interlaken. (Kutsch and Riemens 1987–94; Litzmann 1902, 1970; Rieger 2002; E. Schumann 1995)

FLATZ, FRANZ (b. 1824/5; d. Vienna, 22 June 1889) and **IDA**. A Viennese couple friendly with Brahms, who is likely to have met the husband soon after arriving in Vienna in the autumn of 1862. Flatz served on the board of directors of the Vienna Singakademie, and the following year he was, together with **Josef Gänsbacher**, instrumental in bringing about the election of Brahms as conductor of that choral society; he promptly sent a telegram to Hamburg to announce the good news to Brahms. After Brahms took up the position, they naturally remained in regular contact. **Rosa (Neuda) Bernstein**, to whom Brahms gave piano lessons sometime in 1864–65, later recalled having frequently met Flatz in Brahms's rooms at 7 Singerstrasse (Kalbeck 1976, vol. 2, 108). Some time afterward, Flatz, who seems to have shared Brahms's enthusiasm for **Franz Schubert**'s music, compiled a catalog of his works, of which he himself wrote out a copy for Brahms, to the latter's great pleasure. Neither manuscript has survived.

Ida Flatz sang in several of the concerts conducted by Brahms during his tenure as conductor of the Singakademie, including the very first one on 15 November 1863. Moreover, she took part in the first known performances of the duets "Die Nonne und der Ritter" and "Vor der Tür" (op. 28/1–2) at a private musical soiree at the Bösendorfer Salon on 18 December 1863, and in that of the quartet "Wechsellied zum Tanze" (op. 31/1) at the same concert, and that of "Neckereien" (op. 31/2) at a Singakademie concert on 11 January 1864.

When **Clara Schumann** stayed in Vienna for three months (with brief interruptions) in the early part of 1866, she saw, as she reported to Brahms, "a good deal of your friends, especially the Flatzs"; and before she left, she wrote with evident pleasure of the evenings she had spent with them and their intimate friend, the actor **Josef Lewinsky**, either at their house or at her flat (Litzmann 1970, vol. 1, 533, 536). When Brahms returned to Vienna in November of that year, after an absence of 19 months, he quickly resumed his friendly relations with the couple (see Clara Schumann's letter to Brahms of 30 December 1866 in Litzmann 1970, vol. 1, 548). (Biba 1984c; Litzmann 1970)

FLEMMING [FLEMING], PAUL (b. Hartenstein, Vogtland, 5 October 1609; d. Hamburg, 2 April 1640). Poet. Brahms set texts by Flemming in the songs "O liebliche Wangen" (op. 47/4) and "An die Stolze" (op. 107/1), and also in "Geistliches Lied" (op. 30), a composition for a four-voice chorus. (Flemming 1961; Meid 1989)

FRANK, ERNST (b. Munich, 7 February 1847; d. Oberdöbling, near Vienna, 17 August 1889). Conductor, pianist, and composer, whose teachers included **Franz Lachner** for composition and Mortier de Fontaine for the piano. He was appointed a court organist in Munich in 1866 and sometimes conducted the university choir; in due course, he also became a répétiteur at the opera. Subsequently, he held the position of Kapellmeister at the Würzburg Stadttheater during the 1868–69 season, and in October 1869 he became répétiteur and assistant chorus master at the Vienna Opera. In 1870–71 he was in charge of the Singverein of the Gesellschaft der Musikfreunde, and in 1871–72 he conducted the Akademischer Gesangverein, with which he gave the first Viennese performance of Brahms's *Alto Rhapsody* on 19 March 1871 (soloist: Henriette Burenne). On 8 December 1871 he directed the earliest documented performances of "Ich schwing mein Horn ins Jammertal" and "Gebt Acht" (op. 41/1 and 5), as well as a rendition of Brahms's arrangement of **Franz Schubert**'s song "An Schwager Kronos" (M. McCorkle 1984, Anhang Ia/12) and the first known performance of Brahms's arrangement of Schubert's "Gruppe aus dem Tartarus" (M. McCorkle 1984, Anhang Ia/14).

In December 1872 Frank became court Kapellmeister at Mannheim in succession to **Vincenz Lachner**. He resigned in November 1877, mainly, it appears, in reaction to the growing opposition from certain local Wagnerians (even though he had never shown any hostility for **Richard Wagner**'s operas, several of which he had, in fact, given good performances), and partly because he was subjected to anti-Semitic attacks, for he was Jewish. (Styra Avins [1997] is in error in writing of his "dismissal" and stating that he "lost his job" [514, n. 1, and 782]. In fact, in the spring of 1877 he was offered a five-year extension of his contract, but the proposed salary was below the 8,000 marks he demanded.)

From September 1878 until February 1879 Frank was employed at the Stadttheater in Frankfurt am Main, in which town he was subsequently active as a piano teacher. Finally, he served as court Kapellmeister at Hanover in succession to **Hans von Bülow** from December 1879 until 1887, when a nervous collapse led to his being confined to a mental asylum at Ilten, near Hanover. The following year he was transferred to a similar institution at Oberdöbling, on the outskirts of Vienna, and there he remained until his death. He had been married since 1876 to Cornelia [Nelly] von Hornbostel (1849–1911), a sister of **Erich von Hornbostel**.

Frank very likely made Brahms's acquaintance soon after the latter returned to Vienna in the autumn of 1869, and they maintained regular contact after Frank moved back to Germany three years later. An edition of their correspondence, extending from July 1870 to December 1886, was published by Robert Münster in 1995; it is probably fairly complete as far as Brahms's letters and cards are concerned, clearly less so in the case of the letters sent by Frank (the former amount to 62 items, the latter to 21). A significant proportion of the correspondence relates to actual or proposed concert appearances by Brahms at Mannheim and Hanover, for Frank, apart from presenting compositions by Brahms at his own concerts, repeatedly invited him to perform some of them himself (for instance, on 7 November 1876, three days after the C Minor Symphony was first conducted by **Felix Otto Dessoff** at Karlsruhe, Brahms conducted it himself at Mannheim). In addition, they met on various occasions over the years in Vienna, which Frank visited from time to time, as well as during Brahms's summer vacations at Tutzing, Ziegelhausen, and Ischl. (*See also* GOETZ [GÖTZ], HERMANN [GUSTAV].)

They enjoyed particularly close relations in 1875 when Brahms was staying at Ziegelhausen, near Heidelberg, which is only some 20 kilometers from Mannheim. "Brahms has been staying near Heidelberg for the past four weeks and often comes to visit me here," Frank reported to **Hermann Goetz** on 14 June. "He is really a nice person and I like him [more] every day, and my regard for his way of thinking increases constantly" (Kalbeck 1976, vol. 3, 61). By the following year they were addressing each other with the familiar "Du." Yet, notwithstanding this seemingly greater intimacy, they must always have been aware of the distance that separated them, not merely in age (some 14 years), but also in fame and genius. Frank, at any rate, was certainly very conscious of his "inferiority." On 10 January 1877 he wrote to Brahms:

> When I think what a marvellous stimulus your compositions and your very character have offered me in recent years. . . . I thank you, thank you with all my heart—and ask you to look also in future with kindliness on someone completely devoted to you and who, even if himself incapable of taking flight, nonetheless admires with joy and gratitude those whom Providence has endowed not only with the urge, but also with the power to soar into the brilliant sunshine, like the lark or like the eagle. (Münster 1995, 102)

In another letter, on 28 November of the same year, Frank stated his view that composers fall into two categories: "Some give to the world what God has granted to them. They accomplish the highest deed of which man is capable. The others listen to them and utter their own chirping sounds" (Münster 1995, 118–19). Frank, as a matter of fact, "chirped" a good deal: operas, church music, instrumental works, and, especially, songs and vocal duets, of which he wrote more than two hundred; but his greatest strength probably lay in his conducting.

It is likely that Brahms and Frank met for the last time in April 1886, when Brahms broke his journey from Hamburg to Vienna at Hanover. On 14 April, at Brahms's request, Frank arranged a performance of his opera *Hero* (first produced in Berlin on 26 November 1884). The following day, at one of the regular local subscription concerts, Brahms conducted his Fourth Symphony, *Nänie*, and the *Academic Festival Overture*. Although Frank spent the final 17 months of his life at an asylum near Vienna, there seems to be no evidence that Brahms ever visited him there. (*Akad Gesangverein* 1908; Avins 1997; Münster 1974, 1995)

FRANZ, ANNA: *see* WITTGENSTEIN FAMILY.

FRANZ, ROBERT [original name: Knauth, officially changed to Franz in 1847] (b. Halle, 28 June 1815; d. Halle, 24 October 1892). Choirmaster; composer of choral music and especially of songs, of which he wrote some 350 (about a quarter of them settings of poems by **Heinrich Heine**). He was held in high regard by many of his contemporaries, not least by the champions of the "New German School," and one of his greatest admirers was **Liszt**, who even published a book on him in 1872. For his part, Franz, while not a fervent partisan of the "New German School," greatly valued Liszt's support, so that when **Joseph Joachim** contacted him in 1860 in connection with the planned anti-Liszt manifesto (*see* LISZT, FRANZ), he was reluctant to sign (see Johannes Joachim and Moser 1911–13, vol. 2, 79–83). In his later years when deafness had forced him to relinquish his official appointments, he particularly appreciated Liszt's generous efforts to ease his financial distress: "Without him I might have starved," he told August Göllerich in 1885 (Göllerich 1908, 112).

On 19 December 1853 Brahms called on Franz at Halle and played for him his Sonata op. 1, of which he had just given the first public performance at Leipzig. The next day Franz sent a devastating critique of it to Theodor Twietmeyer, in which he expressed his firm conviction that Brahms, though talented, was already beyond help and doomed to fail. More than likely, Franz had made Brahms well aware of his strong disapproval, for he had a reputation for voicing his opinions forcefully and even rudely. (His close friend Baron Arnold Senfft von Pilsach once assured him that he would win the hearts of many if he were to show "just a little benevolence and friendliness toward others, and some appreciation instead of scorn" (Golther 1907, 53). If Brahms had indeed been roughly treated by Franz on that occasion, it might account for his statement in a letter to **Albert Dietrich** in 1862 that he would have been interested in Franz's observations on a trio by Ludwig Meinardus but could not bring himself to contact the man, as he found him too repulsive. (The letter is preserved at the university of Hamburg; the relevant sentence was omitted by Dietrich in his *Erinnerungen an Johannes Brahms.*) As for Franz, it is evident from his correspondence with Senfft von Pilsach that he never ceased to be revolted by Brahms's music. Thus he writes scathingly about "this maestro's musical abstractions" (January 1874), condemns his "exorbitant sensuality" (September 1877), and refers dismissively to "Brahmsian bombast" (July 1885) (Golther 1907, 187, 272, 337).

Apart from his original compositions, Franz was known for the numerous editions he published of works by **Handel** and **Bach**. His activity in this regard drew criticism from certain musicologists who condemned as often anachronistic the arrangements he made and, especially, the accompaniment he devised. The controversy produced, notably, a debate in the *Musikalisches Wochenblatt* and the *Allgemeine musikalische Zeitung* in the 1870s between **Philipp Spitta**, who opposed Franz's method, and Julius Schaeffer, who defended it. Brahms was firmly on the side of the purists but did not join in the public discussion. (Dietrich 1898; I. Fellinger 1984; Göllerich 1908; Golther 1907; Heuberger 1976; Johannes Joachim and Moser 1911–13; Liszt 1872; Pfordten 1923)

FREGE, LIVIA, née Gerhardt (b. Gera, 13 June 1818; d. Leipzig, 22 August 1891). Soprano. She studied with Christian August Pohlenz and made her debut at a concert she gave jointly with Clara Wieck (the future **Clara Schumann**) at the Leipzig Gewandhaus in July 1832, when she was merely 14 and Clara only 12 years old. She became a lifelong friend of Clara's, was greatly appreciated as a singer by **Robert Schumann** (on 4 December 1843 she sang Peri at the first performance of *Das Paradies und die Peri*), and was also a close friend of Mendelssohn. She enjoyed a successful if very brief career in opera, making her first appearance in the title role of Louis Spohr's *Jessonda* at Leipzig in 1833 and accepting an engagement in Berlin in 1835; but she retired from the stage the following year upon her marriage to the jurist Richard Woldemar Frege (1811–90). They lived at Leipzig, where their house became an important center for music making.

Livia Frege seems to have been rather slow to warm to Brahms's music. "From the reaction of Livia, who, after all, has a poetic nature and is more than willing to immerse herself in something new, I realize once again how difficult it may be for Johannes's compositions to find a sympathetic reception," Clara Schumann wrote in her diary in 1855, after trying to interest her friend in the Ballades op. 10; she had to play them several times before Livia "at last responded quite warmly to them" (Litzmann 1902, vol. 2, 385). Eventually, under Clara's influence, Livia became a firm admirer of Brahms's music, and she was enraged by the hostile reaction that his First Piano Concerto provoked in Leipzig on 27 January 1859. "As for myself, it interested me greatly," she wrote to Clara. She had particularly liked the first two movements, the third somewhat less; but the work as a whole had, in her view, "demonstrated so clearly what a wealth of talent and poetry B[rahms] possesses that I was most profoundly moved"; and she had strongly defended the work against several detractors (Litzmann 1902, vol. 3, 53). Three days after his ill-fated concert at the Gewandhaus, Brahms played the piano part in a performance of Schumann's *Szenen aus Goethes "Faust"* at the Freges'. On a later occasion, in 1861, Livia Frege expressed her delight with the *Handel Variations*, and some time after the rather mediocre performance of the Requiem at the Gewandhaus under **Carl Reinecke** on 18 February 1869 she arranged a performance of the work at her house. Although not given under the most favorable conditions (with a reduced choir, and a piano and double string quartet replacing the orchestra), it was, according to Hermann Kretzschmar, "more successful than the one at the Gewandhaus" (Forner 1984, 7). (Forner 1984; Litzmann 1902, 1970)

FREUND, ROBERT (b. Budapest, 7 April 1852; d. Budapest, 8 April 1936). Pianist and teacher. He studied with Ignaz Moscheles in Leipzig (1865–68), **Carl Tausig** in Berlin, and **Liszt** in Budapest (1871–72). For most of his professional life he lived in Zurich, where he settled in 1875 and, with two brief interruptions, remained until 1912; in 1876 he joined the faculty of the new Musikschule there. In addition to his teaching activities, he frequently appeared at concerts as soloist and in chamber music.

According to Freund's memoirs, he made Brahms's acquaintance in Vienna in 1874. They met repeatedly thereafter: in November 1881 in Budapest, when they spent many hours together during the week Brahms stayed there; in December 1882 in Zurich, where Freund was again much in Brahms's company; in the spring of 1884 in Vienna and in Budapest, where Brahms conducted his Third Symphony and asked Freund to accompany him on a visit to Liszt, who, however, was not at home (Freund mistakenly placed this visit to Budapest in the year 1895); in February 1886 at Mannheim, where Freund had gone to hear Brahms's still unpublished Fourth Symphony; in May 1887 in Berne, where, at **Josef Victor Widmann**'s house, Freund was present when Brahms, with **Friedrich** and

Julius **Hegar**, played the recently published Cello Sonata op. 99, Violin Sonata op. 100, and Piano Trio op. 101; and in November 1887 at Basle, where Freund attended a performance of the Double Concerto op. 102 by **Joseph Joachim** and **Robert Hausmann** under Brahms's direction.

Brahms evidently liked Freund, since he readily accepted a suggestion from Friedrich Hegar and Widmann in the spring of 1893 that the four of them should travel to Sicily together. In the event, he found himself alone with Freund on the return journey, for Widmann had broken a leg in Naples and traveled back directly from there to Switzerland with Hegar, while Brahms and Freund spent some time in Venice. Brahms afterward wrote to **Clara Schumann** that Freund was "a most agreeable and cultured young man" (Litzmann 1970, vol. 2, 508). Later that year Brahms asked Freund to visit him at Ischl, where he played most of the newly composed *Klavierstücke* opp. 118–19 for him and invited him, as an experienced pedagogue, to comment on the *Übungen* WoO 6.

Freund was to meet Brahms at least once more, at the inauguration of the new Tonhalle in Zurich in 1895. On 20 October Brahms conducted his *Triumphlied*, but, according to Freund, he did not wish to take part in a concert that was to be given by the Joachim Quartet two days later and proposed that Freund should play in his place. Accordingly, Freund played the piano part in Brahms's Piano Quintet.

In 1915 Freund wrote down some recollections of his musical education and career, which were intended only for a small circle of friends and acquaintances, to whom they were distributed in typescript; but in 1951 they were published by the Allgemeine Musikgesellschaft Zurich under the title *Memoiren eines Pianisten*. They are particularly valuable for Freund's account of his contact with Brahms. (Freund 1951; Litzmann 1970)

FREY, ADOLF (b. Aarau, 18 February 1855; d. Zurich, 12 February 1920). Novelist, dramatist, and poet. Brahms set a text by Frey in the song "Meine Lieder" (op. 106/4). (Linsmayer 1989)

FRIEDERIKE, PRINCESS ZUR LIPPE (b. 1 December 1825; d. 12 March 1897). Daughter of Prince Leopold II (1796–1851) and Princess Emilie, née Princess of Schwarzburg-Sondershausen (1800–67); sister of **Leopold III**. Pupil of **Clara Schumann** and Brahms. Berthold Litzmann states that among those attending the Lower Rhine Music Festival held at Düsseldorf from 27 to 29 May 1855 were "three young princesses of Lippe from Detmold"—evidently Luise (1822–87), Friederike, and Pauline (1834–1906)—and that Clara Schumann was invited by them to come to Detmold for the purpose of teaching Friederike (Litzmann 1902, vol. 2,

378–79). Accordingly, she spent the latter half of June 1855 at Detmold, where she was gratified to discover that Friederike was an accomplished pianist, indeed "an amateur of a high quality rarely found among princesses" (vol. 2, 379).

Friederike arrived in Düsseldorf in September of the same year for several weeks' further study with Clara Schumann, and it was on that occasion, according to **Max Kalbeck**, that she made Brahms's acquaintance. (It is not impossible, however, that he had already met her in May, since he was then living at the Schumanns' house and had also attended the Lower Rhine Music Festival.) When, in due course, he in his turn accepted an invitation to spend the last three months of 1857 at Detmold, one of his principal duties was to give tuition to the princess (*see also* LEOPOLD III, PRINCE ZUR LIPPE), and he continued to do so during his further stays at Detmold in 1858 and 1859. In October 1858 he wrote to **Julius Otto Grimm**: "My noble pupil gives me very great joy. She has really made remarkable progress" (Brahms 1974/4, 69). (Brahms 1974/4; Litzmann 1902; Schramm 1983)

FRIEDLAENDER [FRIEDLÄNDER], MAX (b. Brieg [Brzeg, Poland], 12 October 1852; d. Berlin, 2 May 1934). Musicologist. A successful singer (baritone) who had been taught by Manuel García and **Julius Stockhausen**, he studied musicology and obtained his doctorate at Rostock University in 1887 with a dissertation on **Franz Schubert**. He became a professor and director of music at the University of Berlin.

Friedlaender, who focused his later research primarily on German folk songs and Lieder, greatly admired the folk-song collections of **Ludwig Erk** and **Franz Magnus Böhme**, which Brahms disliked, and was critical of Kretzschmer's and **Anton Wilhelm von Zuccalmaglio**'s *Deutsche Volkslieder mit ihren Originalweisen*, which Brahms treasured, but which, in Friedlaender's judgment, contained a host of unauthentic items. According to **Richard Heuberger**, Brahms "fell out" with Friedlaender as a result of their opposing views. (It would be tempting to assume that the quarrel was prompted or, at any rate, came to a head because Friedlaender had expressed reservations about the folk songs published by Brahms in 1894 [WoO 33]; in fact, though, Heuberger's remark occurs in a diary entry dating from 1889.)

In 1902 Friedlaender published in the *Jahrbuch der Musikbibliothek Peters* an examination of the folk songs included in Brahms's edition, most of which Brahms took from Kretzschmer's and Zuccalmaglio's collection. Friedlaender alleged that the majority of these were unauthentic, having been composed either by Zuccalmaglio or by Johann Friedrich Reichardt. The latter, he believed, had written several of them for

Christoph Friedrich Nicolai's *Eyn feiner, kleyner Almanach vol schönerr echterr liblicherr Volckslieder* (1778–79), where they were found by Kretzschmer and Zuccalmaglio who mistook them for the genuine article. However, it has since been established that many items in Kretzschmer's and Zuccalmaglio's collection (and Brahms's edition) that Friedlaender dismissed as forgeries were authentic examples of the German folk song (see W. Wiora [1953], *Die rheinisch-bergischen Melodien bei Zuccalmaglio und Brahms*).

The "falling-out" mentioned by Heuberger in his diary in 1889 was evidently not permanent, for Friedlaender did not hesitate to call on Brahms when he happened to be in Vienna in late January 1897; moreover, he must have been cordially received, for he went back a second time, at Brahms's request. The account Friedlaender gave to **Gustav Ophüls** of these meetings (and which Ophüls reproduced in his *Erinnerungen an Johannes Brahms*) is a moving document concerning Brahms's state of mind some two months before his death and provides yet one more indication that he must have been well aware of the fatal nature of his illness. On the first occasion Friedlaender was deeply shocked by the extremely sickly appearance of Brahms who, even though his room was "as hot as a furnace," was shivering with cold. When Friedlaender suggested that Brahms might be more comfortable in the warmer climate of Italy, where he had seen him in such a happy mood not long before (this must, in fact, have been several years earlier, since Brahms most recent visit to Italy had taken place in 1893), Brahms replied, "No, I leave such short journeys to you, young man—I shall in the near future be leaving on a long, long journey, of which you will be hearing soon" (Ophüls 1983b, 43). When Friedlaender returned two days later, he found Brahms lying on the sofa with tears in his eyes.

Later Friedlaender served on the board of directors of the Deutsche Brahms-Gesellschaft, which was founded on 7 March 1906. In 1922 he published a study of Brahms's songs and duets (*Brahms' Lieder . . .*); an English translation by C. S. Leese appeared in London in 1934. (Friedlaender 1902, 1918, 1922, 1923; Heuberger 1976; G. Ophüls 1983b)

FRITSCH-ESTRANGIN, HENRIETTE (b. Marseilles, 18 August 1852; d. January 1943). French friend of Brahms and a great admirer of his music. Her family was linked by marriage to the wealthy Pastré family, which played a key role in the commercial development of Marseilles in the 19th century (her grandfather Jean Alexis Estrangin had married Amélie Pastré in 1821). Her father Henri Estrangin, a prominent merchant, donated a fountain to the city in 1890, which promptly changed the name of the square where the fountain was installed from Place Paradis to Place Estrangin-Pastré, which it bears to this day.

In 1870 Henriette married Emil [Émile] Fritsch (1843–1915), a young businessman born in Frankfurt and then living at Marseilles, who adopted the name Fritsch-Estrangin and was to play an increasingly important part in his father-in-law's business activities. Henriette and her husband used to spend some time each summer in Frankfurt, where they may have owned a house. It was there, according to his memoirs, that **Hugo Heermann** introduced Brahms to Henriette at a concert at which he first played his D Minor Piano Concerto (i.e., on 18 February 1876; see Heermann 1935, 33). Brahms met Henriette and her husband on various occasions thereafter. On 5 May 1879 **Clara Schumann**, who had given Henriette some lessons, wrote to Brahms: "You will probably be seeing Frau Fritsch soon—she was a diligent pupil and has, I believe, benefited from the tuition" (Litzmann 1970, vol. 2, 172). The following year, when Brahms began to plan the trip he was to make with **Theodor Billroth** to Italy in 1881, he toyed, however briefly, with the idea of returning through France, with stops in Paris and Marseilles, but he eventually dropped that idea. Nevertheless, he did meet Henriette in 1881, for she traveled to Stuttgart for the express purpose of attending the concert at which he played his new Second Piano Concerto on 22 November ("Frau Fritsch is looking forward tremendously to Stuttgart—I wish I could come with her," Clara Schumann had written to him a week earlier (Litzmann 1970, vol. 2, 245); presumably Henriette had then once more been staying in Frankfurt. And two years later, on 2 December 1883, Henriette was present at the first performance of the Third Symphony in Vienna; afterward, she was a guest at the banquet offered by **Arthur and Bertha Faber**. In 1884 the admiration she felt for Brahms and his music found an even more striking expression: her French translation of **Hermann Deiters**'s (1880) book *Johannes Brahms* ("traduit de l'allemand par Mme. H. F.") was published in Leipzig and Brussels.

In the summer of 1888 the Fritsch-Estrangins visited Brahms at Thun, in Switzerland, where they also made the acquaintance of **Klaus Groth**. In his recollections of Brahms (published by Dieter Lohmeier [1997] as a supplement to his edition of the Brahms-Groth correspondence), Groth describes the encounter in some detail (but he mistakenly places it in the year 1889). In particular, he praises Henriette's piano playing, calling her one of the most competent amateur women pianists he had ever heard. He was especially impressed by her rendition of Brahms's compositions that "she performed like a true virtuoso, from memory," and he adds that she was quite capable of assuming the solo parts in his piano concertos (Lohmeier 1997, 196). Though not a professional musician, Henriette did perform in public on at least one occasion—at a concert of the Cercle artistique in Marseilles, she performed **Beethoven**'s "Emperor" Concerto "d'une façon magistrale" (Roux 1892, 353). She had reportedly impressed both **Hans von Bülow** and **Liszt** with her playing in her youth.

Later Henriette and her husband also visited Brahms at Ischl. Moreover, they endeared themselves to him by sending him from time to time packets of excellent mocha beans, with which he loved to brew the coffee he so much enjoyed. They also corresponded with him; Heermann states that when **Max Kalbeck** was preparing his biography of Brahms, Henriette made available to him 75 letters she had received from Brahms. The Fritsch-Estrangins cherished Brahms's memory. Among the contributions to the Viennese Brahms Monument Fund (*see* WEYR, RUDOLF VON) were one of 1,000 kronen from "Fritsch-Estrangin E., Herr und Frau" and another one, for the same amount, from "Fritsch-Estrangin Henriette" (according to the list published in the brochure *Zur Enthüllung des Brahms-Denkmal in Wien, 7. Mai 1908* [Vienna, 1908]).

Henriette's portrait can be seen at the Château Pastré, the Pastré family's former palatial residence (157 Avenue de Montredon), which is now owned by the City of Marseilles and houses its Musée de la faïence. Not far from it, also on the Campagne Pastré (as the Pastrés' estate, situated some 7 kilometers south of the city center, was called), stands the splendid Château Estrangin, of which Henriette became the proprietor. Lastly, a portrait of Émile Fritsch-Estrangin is on view at the Villa provençale, yet another mansion on the estate. (Blès 1989; Brahms Monument 1908; Caty et al. 2001; Heermann 1935; Litzmann 1970; Lohmeier 1997; Roux 1892)

FRITZSCH, ERNST WILHELM (b. Lützen, 24 August 1840; d. Leipzig, 14 August 1902). Music publisher at Leipzig. He attended the Leipzig conservatory (1857–62), and in 1866 founded his own publishing business after acquiring the Bromnitz music shop. His list of composers included **Peter Cornelius**, **Edvard Grieg**, **Heinrich von Herzogenberg**, Rheinberger, and **Richard Wagner**. Being a keen Wagnerite did not, however, prevent him from also admiring Brahms's music. From 1870 he published a weekly periodical, *Musikalisches Wochenblatt*, to which Brahms subscribed for many years. In 1887 Brahms described it, in a letter to **Elisabeth von Herzogenberg**, as "the most useful, the least aggravating, I would almost say the best" of all then existing music journals; as for Fritzsch himself, he was "a pleasant, well-intentioned man" (Brahms 1974/2, 152–53).

Brahms's first contact with Fritzsch occurred in 1871, when, in response to a request for a musical autograph (to form part of a series of such documents that the *Musikalisches Wochenblatt* was then presenting), he sent the canon "Töne, lindernder Klang" (WoO 28, second version). The facsimile of the canon and of Brahms's signature appeared in the journal on 19 January 1872. (Its resolution by Ferdinand Böhme was printed on 14 July 1876.) From this time on, Brahms remained in correspondence with Fritzsch until the end of his life. It was, however, not until he stayed at Leipzig in late January/early February 1874 that he actually made his personal acquaintance; later they met on several further occasions. The first meeting took place under particularly auspicious circumstances, for it was in January 1874 that the *Musikalisches Wochenblatt* began publication of **Hermann Kretzschmar**'s very favorable study of Brahms's recent works.

When Fritzsch founded *Blätter für Hausmusik*, a periodic publication designed to make suitable music available for performance at home, Brahms sent him the song "Abendregen" for inclusion in the initial number (1 October 1875); two years later it was published as the last of the *Vier Gesänge* (op. 70) by **Fritz Simrock**. In 1876 Brahms sent Fritzsch **Franz Schubert**'s song "Der Strom" (D565), of which he owned the autograph, likewise for insertion in *Blätter für Hausmusik.* However, it was not printed in that journal but issued separately by Fritzsch in 1877.

In February 1881 Brahms sent another of his canons, "Mir lächelt kein Frühling" (WoO 25), to Elisabeth von Herzogenberg, with the suggestion that she might like to offer it to Fritzsch, which she duly did. It appeared in the *Musikalisches Wochenblatt* on 28 April 1881, simply attributed, as Brahms had stipulated, to "J. B." A resolution, again by Ferdinand Böhme, was printed on 4 August of the same year, but although Brahms, in a note to Fritzsch, pronounced it "correct and acceptable," it did not correspond with his own. He therefore asked Fritzsch to publish the latter also, in a future number, but Fritzsch did not oblige. Whether for that reason or another, Brahms did not provide Fritzsch with any more canons, as he had proposed. By then he had, however, already offered Fritzsch a somewhat more substantial work, the *Choral Prelude and Fugue* WoO 7, and this eventually appeared as a supplement to the *Musikalisches Wochenblatt* in July 1882. It marked the end of their professional association, but they still corresponded and saw each other occasionally. When they met at Leipzig in January 1895, it was very probably for the last time.

After Fritzsch's death the firm was owned by C. F. W. Siegel, who continued to publish the *Musikalisches Wochenblatt* until 1910 (during the last four years it was combined with the *Neue Zeitschrift für Musik*). (Brahms 1974/2, 1974/14)

FRÖSCHL, RUDOLF (d. ?1926). Physician. He was the family doctor and a personal friend of **Richard and Maria Fellinger**, and Brahms no doubt knew him socially before becoming his patient. There are several references to him in **Richard Heuberger**'s diary that show that he had begun to treat Brahms in the latter half of 1896 at the latest. On 16 October Richard Fellinger told Heuberger that Fröschl, who previously had feared that Brahms might die before March 1897, now felt somewhat more hopeful; he was giving Brahms massages. On 22 October Brahms mentioned to Heuberger that he was drinking half a bottle of champagne every evening, which Fröschl had prescribed to make him sleep better. Another entry in Heuberger's diary, on 12 November, records that Fröschl had that day massaged Brahms at the Kaiserbad. After that there is no further mention of him in Heuberger's diary. He seems to have been replaced by Dr. **Josef Breuer** in the new year. (Heuberger 1976)

FUCHS, ROBERT (b. Frauenthal, Styria, 15 February 1847; d. Vienna, 19 February 1927). Composer, teacher, organist, and conductor. The youngest of the 13 children of a village schoolmaster and organist, he studied violin, piano, organ, and flute, as well as thoroughbass, with his brother-in-law Martin Bischof while still a boy, and later was taught composition by **Felix Otto Dessoff** at the Vienna conservatory (1865–69). In 1866 he was appointed organist at the Piaristenkirche, and with his salary and the money he earned from teaching, he managed to make a modest living. In 1875 he became the conductor of the Orchesterverein of the Gesellschaft der Musikfreunde and also joined the faculty of the conservatory, on which he served until 1912, teaching harmony, theory, and counterpoint; among his students were **Hugo Wolf**, **Gustav Mahler**, Franz Schreker, Sibelius, and **Alexander Zemlinsky**. In 1894 he was named "prospective" [Exspektant] court organist, and from 1902 to 1905 he held the full title.

He started composing early but did not make a name for himself with the Viennese public until his first Serenade for strings was performed at a Philharmonic Society concert on 15 November 1874. His output was considerable and included several symphonies and serenades (in fact, he became known as "Serenaden-Fuchs"), a large amount of chamber and piano music, songs, choral music, Masses, and two operas. He enjoyed a considerable reputation as a composer in his lifetime, and among his admirers was Brahms, whose acquaintance he made in the late 1870s and who did his best to further his career. Thus, Brahms warmly recommended a cello sonata written by Fuchs to **Fritz Simrock** in May 1881, describing it as "his best and most spirited work to date" and Fuchs himself as the possessor of "probably the brightest talent" in Vienna and altogether a charming person (Brahms 1974/10, 173–74). Simrock did not take the bait that time (the sonata [op. 29] was subsequently accepted by the Leipzig firm Kistner that had already published many of Fuchs's earlier compositions); but when, three years later, Brahms brought Fuchs's Symphony in C Major (op. 37) to Simrock's attention—"how lively and spirited, how delightfully musical" (Brahms 1974/11, 78–79)—Simrock took it at once, and he was also to publish Fuchs's opp. 38–47, which included his Second Symphony in E-flat Major and his first opera, *Die Königsbraut*.

Fuchs was among the friends who accompanied Brahms on some of his Sunday walks, and according to Fuchs's biographer Anton Mayr, Brahms was generally the first person with whom Fuchs played his new piano duets, such as the series *In der Dämmerstunde* (op. 38), the *Wiener Walzer* (op. 42), and *Traumbilder* (op. 48). Brahms recommended the last-named work in late April 1890 to **Max Abraham**, the proprietor of the publishing house C. F. Peters, in the following manner: "I have a special favorite among my colleagues whom I have long wished to see associated with you. . . . He is Robert Fuchs, with some of whose orchestral music and piano pieces you are no doubt familiar, so there is no need for me to dwell at length on his genuine musical talent and on the beautiful and natural simplicity, gracefulness, and charm which characterize his compositions" (Brahms 1984/14, 384–85). Another publisher whom Brahms successfully tried to interest in Fuchs's works was E. R. **Lienau**. Fuchs dedicated his Piano Trio op. 22 to Brahms. Furthermore, he arranged Brahms's songs "Vergebliches Ständchen" (op. 84/4) and "Dort in den Weiden" and "Trennung" (op. 97/4, 6) for male chorus. These arrangements, like the songs themselves, were published by Simrock.

Brahms also thought highly of Fuchs's older brother Johann Nepomuk (1842–99), who taught at the Vienna conservatory from 1888, became its director in 1893, and was appointed assistant court Kapellmeister in 1894. (Brahms 1974/10, 1974/11, 1974/14; Mayr 1934; Pascall 1988b)

– G –

GADE, NIELS (WILHELM) (b. Copenhagen, 22 February 1817; d. Copenhagen, 21 December 1890). Composer, conductor, violinist, organist, and teacher. From 1844 until 1848 he lived in Leipzig, where he taught at the conservatory and served as assistant conductor, and finally chief conductor, of the Gewandhaus Orchestra; during this time he became very friendly with Mendelssohn and **Robert Schumann**. He returned to Copenhagen in 1848 and for the rest of his life played a leading role in its musical life.

Brahms met Gade on various occasions, at music festivals in Germany and, in March 1868, in Copenhagen, where Brahms was giving some concerts with **Julius Stockhausen**. In fact, it was at a party given by Gade that Brahms made his famous tactless remark regretting that the Thorvaldsen Museum was located in Copenhagen and not Berlin, which so aroused public anger among patriotic Danes that he thought it wise to leave the town sooner than he had planned.

Gade himself does not appear to have nursed a grudge; indeed, he liked Brahms as a person and admired him as a composer. In September 1878, while attending the golden jubilee of the Hamburg Philharmonic Orchestra, he wrote enthusiastically to his family about Brahms's Second Symphony, as well as about Brahms himself: "He is very amiable and I like him a good deal; he is also the most talented of the younger Germans" (Gade 1894, 209).

(The "Gade," who with Brahms and a cellist named D'Arien performed a piano trio by "Karl Würth" [a pseudonym of Brahms] at a private concert that took place in Hamburg on 5 July 1851 in celebration of the silver wedding anniversary of the piano manufacturer Christian Heinrich Schröder, was the Hamburg musician Johann Gade [1817–98].) (Gade 1894; Forner 1981)

GÄNSBACHER, JOSEF (b. Vienna, 6 October 1829; d. Vienna, 5 June 1911). Cellist, pianist, singer, composer, and teacher. Son of the composer and conductor Johann Gänsbacher (1778–1844). He trained as a lawyer but was also taught music from an early age and became a highly successful singing teacher; from 1875 until 1904 he taught at the conservatory of the Gesellschaft der Musik.

Brahms became well acquainted with him soon after arriving in Vienna in September 1862; he was among the musicians invited by **Julius Epstein** to private performances at his flat of Brahms's Piano Quartets opp. 25–26. The following year Gänsbacher, who was a member of the board of directors of the Singakademie, was largely responsible (together with **Franz Flatz**) for Brahms being offered the position of choirmaster. Brahms was soon on "Du" terms with Gänsbacher, and he was to enjoy friendly relations with him for the rest of his life. In August 1867 Gänsbacher accompanied Brahms and his father on a part of their trip and walking tour outside of Vienna (**Max Kalbeck** quotes Gänsbacher's amusing account of his ascent, together with Brahms, of the Hochschwab); he occasionally joined Brahms in his Sunday excursions and on several occasions visited him in his summer vacation quarters; and during the last decade of Brahms's life, they also saw each other regularly at the Wiener Tonkünstlerverein. Gänsbacher had been one of the moving spirits behind its foundation in 1885, and at its first general meeting on 23 November of that year he was appointed the society's treasurer.

Altogether, Brahms is said to have had a high opinion of Gänsbacher's musicianship, even though he was reportedly rather critical of his singing and cello playing at times. When Gänsbacher once complained that Brahms's loud playing was making it difficult to hear the cello, Brahms is said to have retorted "You should be glad" (Gottlieb-Billroth 1935, 346, n. 1). (Gottlieb-Billroth 1935)

GASTEIGER, BERTHA VON (b. Graz, 20 October 1860; d. Graz, 3 March 1940). Pianist who made a significant contribution to the musical life in Graz. She had studied with **Clara Schumann** in Frankfurt and Max Pauer in Stuttgart, and was a close friend of **Marie Soldat** and **Marie Baumayer**. She was also on friendly terms with **Richard and Maria Fellinger**, at whose house she repeatedly met Brahms. In consequence, she appears in some of the well-known photographs that Maria Fellinger took of Brahms surrounded by some of her other guests. In his memoirs *Klänge um Brahms*, Maria's son Richard cites some passages from his mother's letters to Bertha Gasteiger relating to Brahms. (R. Fellinger 1997; Suppan 1962–66)

GEIBEL, (FRANZ) EMANUEL (AUGUST) VON (b. Lübeck, 17 October 1815; d. Lübeck, 6 April 1884). Poet and dramatist. Together with **Paul Heyse** he published the *Spanisches Liederbuch* in 1852, from which **Hugo Wolf** was to set more than 20 poems. As for Brahms, he set texts by Geibel in the songs "Frühlingslied" (op. 85/5), "Geistliches Wiegenlied" (op. 91/2, after Lope de Vega, from the *Spanisches Liederbuch*), and "Mein Herz ist schwer" (op. 94/3). (See also M. McCorkle 1984, Anhang IIa/25.) (Frevel 1989)

GEORG II, DUKE OF SACHSEN-MEININGEN (b. Meiningen, 2 April 1826; d. Bad Wildungen, 25 June 1914); he succeeded his father, Duke Bernhard Erich Freund (1800–82), in September 1866. Georg married three times: in 1850, Princess Charlotte of Prussia (1831–55); in 1858, Princess Feodore of Hohenlohe-Langenburg (1839–72); and, in 1873 the actress Helene [Ellen] Franz (b. Naumburg, 30 May 1839; d. Meiningen, 24 March 1923), on whom Georg II bestowed the title of "Baroness **Heldburg**." In 1845 her father, Hermann Franz (1803–70), had been appointed director of the Königliche Handelsschule [Commercial College] in Berlin. There Ellen had studied the piano with Theodor Kullak and **Hans von Bülow**, but in the end gave up earlier thoughts of becoming a concert pianist in favor of a career in the theater. She made her debut at Gotha in 1860 as Jane Eyre in Charlotte Birch-Pfeiffer's *Die Waise von Lowood*, and subsequently appeared at Coburg, Stettin, Mannheim, and Oldenburg (where she rejected a proposal of marriage from **Julius Stockhausen**). Eventually she was offered a permanent engagement at Meiningen. Her first role there, on 20 October 1867, was Shakespeare's Juliet, and over the next five and a half years she was to interpret some 140 different roles, last appearing as Lady Macbeth on 9 March 1873. Nine days later she became the morganatic wife of the duke.

Georg, who in his youth had studied law, history, and art, was a man of wide culture, with a passionate interest in the theater and music; he was also a gifted artist. Under his guidance and close supervision, the Meiningen theater company and the Meiningen orchestra, for both of which he assumed personal and financial responsibility in 1873, reached a standard of excellence that was recognized far beyond the confines of the small duchy. The theatrical productions reflected the importance the duke attached to ensemble acting, to the realistic staging of crowd scenes, and to the historical accuracy of the decor and costumes, some of which he designed himself. In addition to its performances at Meiningen, the company, under the direction of Ludwig Chronegk, between 1774 and 1790 presented close to 2,900 performances in 36 other cities (among them Vienna, St. Petersburg, Copenhagen, and London) in nine different countries. Its productions greatly influenced both André Antoine and Konstantin Stanislavsky.

As for the Hofkapelle, it owed its renown in the first place to Hans von Bülow, who, in the five years during which he served as its music director (1880–85), succeeded in moulding what was already a very competent band into a superb orchestra. Its reputation continued to flourish under **Fritz Steinbach** (1886–1903) and, though to a somewhat lesser extent, under Wilhelm Berger (1903–11) and **Max Reger** (1911–14). Between 1880 and 1914 the orchestra performed regularly and with considerable success in many other German cities, and on a few occasions it even ventured abroad, to Austria, Switzerland, Hungary, Czechoslovakia, Belgium, Holland, Denmark, and, in 1902, England (*see* STEINBACH, FRITZ). It also supplied, for several years, the bulk of the Bayreuth Festival orchestra.

Brahms's career as a composer benefited enormously from his association with Meiningen (for some details, *see* BÜLOW, HANS [GUIDO] VON). His early visits in 1881 marked the first stages of what was to be an intermittent, but extremely useful, contact with the Hofkapelle; at the same time, they laid the basis for a friendly relationship with the duke and his wife that continued until Brahms's death. Already on the occasion of his second visit to the town, in November 1881, he stayed as a guest at the palace, and he was to do so regularly thereafter. He was, moreover, repeatedly and warmly invited during the following years to visit the couple not only in Meiningen but also at Schloss Altenstein (their property near Bad Liebenstein, in Thuringia) and at the Villa Carlotta, their beautiful mansion in Italy. (It was named after Georg's first wife Charlotte, having been presented to the couple on their marriage in 1850 by the bride's mother, Princess Marianne. It stands near Tremezzo, on the shore of Lake Como—and not, as stated by S. Avins [1997] in *Johannes Brahms: Life and Letters*, on an island in the lake.) Brahms declined most of these invitations, explaining more than once to the baroness, who was his usual correspondent at court, that he needed quiet and solitude for his work. He did, nevertheless, stay at Schloss Altenstein in November 1894 (*see* MÜHLFELD, RICHARD [BERNHARD HERMANN] and WÜLLNER, LUDWIG) and again in the following autumn, and he visited the Villa Carlotta on at least three occasions, though on two of these, in September 1882 and April 1890, only briefly in the owners' absence; but, in May 1884 he spent two weeks there, and during this visit he and his friend **Rudolf von der Leyen** entertained their hosts with a rendition of the two-piano arrangement of his Third Symphony, with the duke turning the pages for one of them and the baroness for the other.

The purpose of Brahms's visits to Meiningen was to give, or to hear, performances of certain of his own compositions, especially recent ones. His music was, of course, also played in his absence, for under Bülow and, later, Steinbach, a veritable Brahms cult flourished in the small Thuringian town. Still, his active participation in the performances constituted red-letter days in the orchestra's—and the court's—calendar. To mention some of these occasions: On 2 April 1883 he conducted part of a "Brahms Concert" that included the *Gesang der Parzen* (a composition he had dedicated to the duke); at a concert on 3 February 1884, he conducted his new Third Symphony—not once, but twice; on 25 December 1887, at another "Brahms Concert," he directed performances of, among others, the Third Symphony and the Second Piano Concerto (with **Eugen d'Albert** as the soloist); and on 3 January 1889 d'Albert played the First Piano Concerto, and **Joseph Joachim** and **Robert Hausmann** the Double Concerto, under his direction. But the highlight of his musical activity at Meiningen undoubtedly occurred on 25 October 1885 when the orchestra, under his baton, gave the world premiere of the Fourth Symphony. Two musicians present at this concert—pianist Frederic Lamond and violinist **Adolph Brodsky** (who played Brahms's Violin Concerto on that occasion) later recalled that, after the general public had left, the whole symphony was repeated at the duke's request. (According to a contemporary newspaper report, only the first and third movements were played again.) Shortly after this concert Brahms joined Bülow and the orchestra in a three-week tour (3–25 November), in the course of which he conducted his new symphony no fewer than nine times. Finally, yet another reason why Brahms had good cause to appreciate the Meiningen connection was that it brought him into close contact with the orchestra's principal clarinettist **Richard Mühlfeld**.

It is clear from Baroness Heldburg's numerous letters to Brahms, and from the duke's much rarer ones, that both felt not only great admiration but also considerable affection for him. "We once again feel a great longing to see you," she assured him on 23 November 1886, urging him, unsuccessfully, to spend Christmas with them (Brahms 1991, 67). "You are an angel!" she wired him on 23 December 1887 (Brahms 1991, 77), after he had unexpectedly announced his intention of arriving at Meiningen two days later. And on 11 April 1891 she wrote, "But I think you must know how much we love you and how greatly we venerate you, in a word, what you mean to us" (Brahms 1991, 109). They sent him Christmas presents, and when he was ill the baroness sent him slipper socks that had been knitted by children from the orphanage she sponsored. On 12 April 1897, a few days after his death, the baroness wrote to her friend **Richard Voss**: "Ah, Brahms! How we loved him, and how we shall go on loving him, as long as we are capable of love! . . . Dear, dear Master!" (Heldburg 1926, 48).

At least two of Duke Georg's children were very musical. Princess Marie (1853–1923) was a competent pianist, having studied with **Theodor Kirchner**, Bülow, and Steinbach, and she is known to have played duets with Brahms and Steinbach, and to have accompanied Mühlfeld; she was also a composer. Her brother Prince Bernhard (1851–1928), the heir to the dukedom (later Bernhard III), wrote incidental music for Aeschylus's drama *The Persians*.

The duchy of Sachsen-Meiningen did not long survive Georg II's death in 1914. On 5 November 1918 it was proclaimed a free state, and five days later Bernhard III, the then reigning duke, abdicated. In 1920 the state became a part of the Land of Thuringia. (Brahms 1991; Erck and Schneider 1997; Heldburg 1926; Hofmann and Hofmann 2003; Lamond 1949; Lindau 1916–17; J. Widmann 1897a)

GEORG V, KING OF HANOVER (b. Berlin, 27 May 1819; d. Paris, 12 June 1878, interred on 24 June in St. George's Chapel at Windsor, England). Son of King Ernst August (1771–1851), whom he succeeded on 18 November 1851), and grandson of King George III of Hanover and of Great Britain and Ireland; he was married to Princess Marie of Sachsen-Altenburg (1818–1907). Two days after their victory over the Prussians at Langensalza, in Thuringia, on 27 June 1866, the Hanoverians were forced to capitulate there and the king went into exile. The annexation of the kingdom of Hanover was approved in the Prussian Landtag on 20 September, and formally decreed on 3 October. From August 1866 the king lived in Vienna and, starting in 1868, spent his summers at Gmunden, in the Salzkammergut. In the mid-1870s he moved for health reasons to Paris; but in 1877 he stayed—as it turned out, for the last time—at Gmunden.

Despite being totally blind from the age of 14, Georg V was a fine pianist and a prolific composer. Under his guidance Hanover experienced a period of high-level musical activity, not least as a result of the appointment of **Joseph Joachim** as Konzertmeister, following the death of Georg Hellmesberger in November 1852. When Eduard **Reményi** (*see* REMENYI, EDE [EDUARD]) visited Hanover with the 20-year-old Brahms in the spring of 1853, they were granted an opportunity to play at court. In an interview Reményi gave many years later in New York, which was published in the *New York Herald* on 18 January 1879 (and later reprinted in Kelley and Upton 1906), he stated that Joachim—whom he had known at the Vienna conservatory—had obtained an audience with the king for him, who inquired whom he wanted for an accompanist, to which he replied "Your Majesty, I want none, because I have one with me whom I regard as a great musical genius" (Kelley and Upton 1906, 860). When Brahms, at the concert that evening, was asked to perform some of his own compositions, he played the Scherzo op. 4, as well as some other pieces. He failed to impress; according to Heinrich Ehrlich, who was court pianist at the time, "the violinist pleased a great deal, the pianist less so" (Kalbeck 1976, vol. 1, 74). In the aforementioned interview, Reményi recalled that the king had said to him afterward: "I believe you are carried away by your enthusiasm; your musical genius has no genius at all" (Kelley and Upton 1906, 86). It is therefore not surprising that when the post of court pianist fell vacant in 1855, following Ehrlich's departure, it was not offered to Brahms, as he had apparently hoped. Later the king's opinion of Brahms's talents rose considerably, and Reményi stated in the interview that when he met the king in Paris in 1874, the latter acknowledged that he had been wrong in his initial judgment.

It is uncertain whether Brahms ever had any contact with the king when the latter was staying in Vienna, although he may well have done so, since the king frequently attended concerts (**Theodor Billroth**, writing to **Wilhelm Lübke** on 29 March 1873 about one conducted by Brahms six days earlier, mentioned that "the old king of Hanover was almost delirious in his musical intoxication" [halb toll vor musikalischem Rausch] (Fischer 1897, 160). Later, Brahms was received by Queen Marie on at least one occasion: on 5 September 1893 he partnered Joachim in an informal recital at her villa at Gmunden. (H. Ehrlich 1888; Fischer 1897; Gottlieb-Billroth 1935; Kelley and Upton 1906; Rosendahl 1928)

GERNSHEIM, FRIEDRICH (b. Worms, 17 July 1839; d. Berlin, 10/11 September 1916). Composer, pianist, choral conductor, and teacher. An infant prodigy, he was admitted at the age of 13 to the Leipzig conservatory, where his teachers were Ignaz Moscheles for piano, **Ferdinand David** for violin, and **Moritz Hauptmann** for theory. During a lengthy stay in Paris (1855–61) he studied piano with Antoine François Marmontel. On his return to Germany he took up an appointment as director of two choral societies and of an instrumental ensemble at Saarbrücken, and in 1865 he was engaged by **Ferdinand Hiller** as professor for piano and composition at the Cologne conservatory; in addition, he conducted several local choirs. Among the composers whose choral works he introduced to Cologne audiences was Brahms, whose acquaintance he had made at the Cologne music festival in 1862 (unless, as A. L. Ringer believes, he had already met him at Leipzig in 1853). Gernsheim had an opportunity to develop closer contacts with Brahms when the latter spent the summer of 1868 at Bonn.

In Cologne, Gernsheim was responsible for the first local performances of the *Alto Rhapsody* and of the complete Requiem. The latter work was first heard on 10 November 1870, and was repeated on 16 March and 7 April 1871. All three performances were intended to commemorate the Germans killed in the Franco-Prussian War, as well as to yield financial aid for the bereaved, the wounded, and returning soldiers in need. After the initial performance, Brahms, who had been unable to attend, wrote to Gernsheim to express his appreciation for having been associated with such a worthy cause. When he learned shortly afterward that Gersheim was coming to Vienna to play his C Minor Piano Concerto at a Philharmonic Society concert on 26 December 1870, he offered to make the necessary hotel arrangements and order a suitable piano, and also proposed his services as a "fairly knowledgeable guide" (Brahms 1974/7, 209).

Little is known about their later contacts. In 1874 Gernsheim was appointed music director in Rotterdam, so Brahms must have met him on the occasion of his concert appearances in that city on 20 January 1876 and 26 January 1882; two letters from him to Gernsheim relating to the second concert have been published. Gernsheim continued to champion Brahms's music while he was in Rotterdam, and there also he gave the earliest local performance of the *Alto Rhapsody* and the Requiem. In 1890 he became conductor of the Sternscher Gesangverein in Berlin and also joined the faculty of the Stern Conservatory; he relinquished the latter position in 1897 and the former in 1904. In 1893 he traveled to Vienna to present his hymn *Phoebus Apollon* as part of the golden jubilee celebrations of the Wiener Männergesangverein. (Brahms 1974/7; Holl 1928; Kahl 1964; Ringer 1980/81)

GIESEMANN, ADOLPH HEINRICH (b. Hajen, near Hameln, about 1809; buried Winsen-an-der-Luhe, 20 April 1865) and his wife Caroline Friederike, née Sülter (b. 1811; d. after 1889), lived at Winsen-an-der-Luhe (a small town some 35 kilometers southeast of Hamburg), where he owned a paper mill. In 1847, in the course of his regular business trips to Hamburg, he made the acquaintance, at the Alster Pavilion, of Brahms's father, who played double bass in a six-man band there. At "Uncle" and "Aunt" Giesemann's invitation, the young Brahms stayed with them at Winsen during the spring or summer of 1847, 1848, and 1851, and all his life he was to look back with great pleasure to these visits and to retain extremely fond memories of his hosts: "I think of few persons so often and with such affection," he assured their daughter Elisabeth [Elise, Lieschen] in 1880 (Kohlweyer 2002, 91); and, in 1889, after she had sent him a photograph of a double portrait of her parents, he wrote, "You may be sure that I have not forgotten them and never shall" (Kohlweyer 2002, 95).

While at Winsen, Brahms frequently gave piano lessons to Elise, and he also conducted the local men's choral society, for which he also wrote some compositions. Among these, according to **Florence May**, was a setting of **August Heinrich Hoffmann von Fallersleben**'s "Des Postillions Morgenlied" (M. McCorkle 1984, Anhang IIa/23). Many years later he asked for the return of the manuscripts, which he had given the Giesemanns, and they were handed back to him in April 1868 at Bremen where he had gone for the performance of his Requiem; he subsequently destroyed them, for, as he explained to Elise, "One doesn't like to preserve the visible signs of one's youthful pranks (and early compositions are part of them)" (Kohlweyer 2002, 89).

In 1856 Elise (1834–1910) married Anton Bernhard Denninghoff (b. 1823; d. probably 1912), with whom she went to live at Wilhelmshaven, where he ran a hotel. It appears from the letter she addressed to Brahms on 16 October 1880 that he had visited them there once (perhaps in 1871?), after which there had been no further contact between them. The purpose of her letter was to enlist his help in securing a stipend for her daughter Agnes, who was then studying singing with Anna Schultzen von Asten (*see* ASTEN, JULIE VON) at the Hochschule für Musik in Berlin, of which **Joseph Joachim** was the director. Brahms immediately wrote to Joachim about the matter, and on being told that there were then no funds available for such a stipend, he arranged to pay for her tuition himself. (He briefly met Agnes and heard her sing during his visit to Berlin in December of that year.) He also sent an affectionate reply to Elise, recalling with gratitude and pleasure the happy days he had spent at Winsen; she only learned of his generosity later. A few more communications were to pass between them, the last in 1890. Their correspondence, as published by Gerhard Kohlweyer in *Brahms-Studien*, runs to nine items.

As for Agnes (1860–1945), who, after her studies in Berlin (1879–82), received further tuition from Johanna Wagner-Jachmann in Munich (1884–86), she was to enjoy a highly successful career—initially under the name "Agnes Denis," and later under her married name—at Weimar (where she was a member of the Hoftheater ensemble from 1886 to 1898) and elsewhere. She made some guest appearances at the Vienna Opera in August 1889 (as Agathe in *Der Freischütz*, Elsa in *Lohengrin*, and Micaela in *Carmen*), and the following year sang at two concerts that her husband, the pianist and conductor Bernhard Stavenhagen whom she had married a few months before, gave in Vienna on 28 November and 5 December 1890. It is not known whether she met Brahms during either of those visits to Austria. (Brahms 1900; Brahms 1974/6; Kohlweyer 2002; May 1948)

GIRZICK, ROSA [married name: Bromeissl] (b. Vienna, ?1850; d. Vienna, 23 January 1915). Singer (contralto) and teacher. Nothing is known about her family or early childhood, except that she studied at the conservatory of the Gesellschaft der Musikfreunde in 1861–62. **Max Kalbeck** implies that she first met Brahms in 1868, at Bad Neuenahr in Germany. He does not mention her studies at the conservatory but states that she was a member of the Singakademie in 1862; that in 1863, at the age of 13, she traveled to Hamburg "on her own initiative and without any means of subsistence," with the intention of "devoting herself to music"; that in Hamburg she worked in a music hall ("Singspielhalle') until she was rescued from there by the Brahms family, who looked after her and found some kind sponsors ready to help her develop her talent for singing; and that, having heard **Julius Stockhausen** sing in **Robert Schumann**'s *Szenen aus Goethes "Faust,"* she wanted above all to study with him, which she did in due course (Kalbeck 1976, vol. 2, 272).

It is possible that Kalbeck obtained these bare details from Girzick herself, for it is evident that he was in contact with her while preparing his Brahms biography (he even reproduces a long letter addressed to her by Brahms, and quotes part of another one). However, his account may not tell the full story. In particular, it does not provide answers to two obvious questions: why did Girzick choose Hamburg as her destination in 1863, and how did she come into contact with Brahms's family there? The most plausible explanation may well be that she had met Brahms prior to her departure from Vienna, that he spoke to her about Stockhausen and thereby gave her the idea of going to Hamburg, where Stockhausen had assumed the conductorship of the philharmonic orchestra and the Singakademie in March 1863, and that he provided her with an introduction to his parents. (Kalbeck does not specify when in 1863 she left for Hamburg. If she was still in Vienna in the autumn of that year and still a member of the Vienna Singakademie, she would have had plenty of opportunities to make Brahms's acquaintance, since he took charge of the Singakademie at that time; his first concert as its conductor took place on 15 November.) As for her hearing Stockhausen sing in Schumann's *Szenen aus Goethes "Faust"* in Hamburg, she could have done so at his very first concert as conductor of the Hamburg Singakademie on 12 January 1864, when the program included the third part of that work. The impression that his singing made on her on that occasion may well have confirmed her in her intention to become his pupil. (*Szenen* had been first performed under **Ferdinand Hiller**'s direction in Cologne on 13 January 1862, with Stockhausen as the soloist.)

During the summer of 1868, Stockhausen stayed at Bad Neuenahr, where he was joined by some of his pupils, including Girzick. Among his visitors was Brahms, who, discovering that Girzick was short of funds, encouraged her to give a concert, in which he promised to participate together with Stockhausen. At this concert, which she gave at Bad Neuenahr jointly with August Keller, a court opera singer at Hanover, on 25 July 1868, she performed a song by **Franz Schubert** and the aria *Ah, rendimi quel core* (believed by François-Joseph Fétis to be part of an opera by Francesco Rossi supposedly called *Mitrane*, a statement repeated by Kalbeck but now thought to be part of some late 18th-century opera that included a character named Mitrane, such as Francesco Bianchi's *La vendetta di Nino*—see Sadie 2001). In addition, Girzick sang Brahms's Duets op. 28 with Stockhausen, and the latter sang an aria from Boieldieu's *Le Chaperon rouge* and also took part in a trio from Mozart's *La clemenza di Tito*. Brahms played several piano pieces and Viennese waltzes, as well as some waltzes from his op. 39; in addition, he accompanied the vocal numbers.

Brahms must have been pleased by Girzick's singing on that occasion, for she was invited to perform at concerts that he and Stockhausen gave in Hamburg on 11 and 15 November of the same year; at the first she sang the Duets op. 28/1–2, at the second op. 28/3, with Stockhausen. Subsequently, Brahms informed **Karl Reinthaler**, to whom he recommended her, that "she sang quite excellently at our two concerts here and has been engaged for *Elias*" (Brahms 1974/3, 26; Mendelssohn's *Elijah* was performed in Hamburg on 3 February 1869). After his return to Vienna in November 1868, he tried to persuade Baron Franz Dingelstedt, the director of the opera, and Heinrich Esser, the Kapellmeister at the opera, to offer Girzick an engagement. In January 1869, while the matter was still unsettled and after she had written to him for guidance (and sent him her portrait), he advised her to approach **Julius Stern** in Berlin, if there should be no opening for her in Vienna; Stern could coach her in various roles and later help her find engagements. (Brahms even offered to cover a part of her expenses in Berlin.) But she must have arrived back in Vienna not long afterward, for at a Brahms-Stockhausen concert on 5 March she sang, with Stockhausen, in the earliest known Viennese performances of Brahms's duets "Es rauchet das Wasser" and "Der Jäger und sein Liebchen" (op. 28/3, 4).

Her association with Brahms continued both on a professional and on a personal basis; Kalbeck quotes from a letter Brahms wrote to her from Baden-Baden in August 1871. In particular, she also sang (according to M. L. McCorkle's [1984] *Werkverzeichnis*) in the first public performances of the following compositions: the *Liebeslieder Walzer* (op. 52), together with **Louise Dustmann-Meyer**, **Gustav Walter**, and **Emil Krauss**, accompanied by **Clara Schumann** and Brahms, on 5 January 1870; the songs "Nicht mehr zu dir zu gehen" and "Ich schleich umher betrübt und stumm" (op. 32/2, 3), on 11 March 1872; and the songs op. 57/2–8, on 18 December 1872. At a musical soiree at **Theodor Billroth**'s, on 29 January 1878, she took part, together with **Ottilie Ebner**, in the earliest known performance of "Guter Rat" (op. 75/2). Finally, it may be of interest that at the first concert conducted by Brahms as artistic director of the Gesellschaft der Musikfreunde, on 10 November 1872, she was a soloist in **Handel**'s "Dettingen" *Te Deum*.

Girzick became a well-known singing teacher; among her pupils were the two daughters of Theodor Billroth. (Brahms 1974/3)

GLUCK, CHRISTOPH WILLIBALD (b. Erasbach, near Berching, Palatinate, 2 July 1714; d. Vienna, 15 November 1787). Brahms's admiration for his music is especially well documented in the case of the opera *Alceste*. When **Theodor Avé-Lallemant** presented him with an 18th-century edition of the Italian version at Christmas 1854, Brahms described it as a "marvellous treasure" in a letter to **Clara Schumann** (Litzmann 1970, vol. 1, 50); in 1864 he received a copy of the Paris version from her. (The two scores were still in his library at the time of his death, together with those of several other Gluck operas.) On 8 December 1872 he put an aria from *Alceste* on the program of one the earliest concerts he conducted as artistic director of the Gesellschaft der Musikfreunde; it was sung by **Amalie Joachim** (in this connection, see M. McCorkle 1984, Anhang Ib/22). Years later, in 1885, **Sir Charles Villiers Stanford** sat with him through a rehearsal of *Alceste* at the Vienna Opera "over which he waxed enthusiastic" (Stanford 1908, 113). The rehearsal was for a new production of the work, the first there since 1810.

At a concert in Hamburg on 11 November 1868, Brahms played a piano arrangement he had recently made of the Gavotte in A Major from the second act of *Iphigénie en Aulide* (M. McCorkle 1984, Anhang Ia/2). The arrangement was published in Leipzig by **Bartolf Wilhelm Senff** in late 1871 or early 1872, with a dedication to Clara Schumann. When she performed it in London in February 1872, the audience, so she reported to Brahms, "was beyond itself with delight" (Litzmann 1970, vol. 2, 6). (Litzmann 1970; Stanford 1908)

GOETHE, JOHANN WOLFGANG VON (b. Frankfurt am Main, 28 August 1749; d. Weimar, 22 March 1832). Writer and poet. Brahms set texts by Goethe in the songs "Die Liebende schreibt" (op. 47/5), "Trost in Tränen" (op. 48/5), "Dämmrung senkte sich von oben" (op. 59/1), "Serenade" (op. 70/3), and "Unüberwindlich" (op. 72/5); in the duets "Es rauschet das Wasser" (op. 28/3) and "Phänomen" (op. 61/3); in the vocal quartets "Wechsellied zum Tanze" (op. 31/1), "Nun ihr Musen, genug!" (op. 65/15), and "Warum" (op. 92/4); in "Beherzigung" (op. 93a/6) for mixed chorus; in the canons for women's voices op. 113/1–2, and WoO posthum 24; in the cantata *Rinaldo* (op. 50; see also M. McCorkle 1984, Anhang IIa/18); in the *Alto Rhapsody* (op. 53); and in *Gesang der Parzen* (op. 89). (See also M. McCorkle 1984, Anhang III/7.)

GOETZ [GÖTZ], HERMANN (GUSTAV) (b. Königsberg [Kaliningrad], 7 December 1840; d. Hottingen, near Zurich, 3 December 1876). Composer. He studied the piano and harmony with Louis Köhler at Königsberg and in 1860 enrolled at the Stern Conservatory in Berlin, where his teachers were **Julius Stern**, Hugo Ulrich, and **Hans von Bülow**. In 1863 he succeeded **Theodor Kirchner** as organist at Winterthur; he also founded a choral society there and was active as a teacher. In 1870 he took up residence at Hottingen, near Zurich, but he retained his post at Winterthur until 1872, when ill health (he was suffering from tuberculosis) forced him to restrict his activities. He composed a number of songs and choral pieces (of which the most impressive was *Nenie*, based on **Schiller**'s poem), as well as orchestral and chamber music and some works for solo piano; but such renown as he achieved in his lifetime resulted primarily from his comic opera *Der Widerspenstigen Zähmung*, for which **Josef Viktor Widmann** had provided a libretto based on Shakespeare's *The Taming of the Shrew*. The opera received its first performance at Mannheim on 11 October 1874 under **Ernst Frank**, who was to become a close friend. A second opera, *Francesca von Rimini*, remained uncompleted at Goetz's death (as mentioned below).

Brahms made Goetz's acquaintance on the occasion of a concert Brahms gave with **Friedrich Hegar** at Winterthur on 29 November 1865; he met Goetz once more the following year on the occasion of another concert appearance there (29 October 1866). In July 1874, when Brahms attended the Zurich music festival, at which he conducted his *Triumphlied*, Goetz invited him to lunch, together with Hegar and Widmann. On arrival at the Goetz residence in Hottingen, they were told by his wife that he was too ill to join his guests but wished them to stay and proposed to listen to their conversation from a darkened adjoining room. Brahms and Goetz thus had only very limited personal contact, and given their very different characters, it is in any case unlikely that they would ever have become intimate friends; but they felt considerable respect for each other. In a letter to **Eduard Hanslick** written some time after Goetz's death, Brahms calls him a "splendid man" and a "most estimable musician" (Hanslick 1897b, *Neue freie Presse*, 1 July, 1). As for Goetz, he gave striking proof of the high regard he had for Brahms both as a man and a composer. He dedicated his Piano Quartet in E major, published in 1870, to Brahms, and when he knew himself to be close to death and realized that he would be unable to complete *Francesca von Rimini*, he expressed the wish that Frank should compose the missing third act on the basis of an already existing sketch and that Brahms should thereafter undertake the final revision. In the event, Brahms was reluctant to play an active part in the composition of the music, perhaps because he genuinely considered Frank to be better qualified for the task by his practical experience of theatrical productions and his greater familiarity with Goetz's style. He did, however, discuss Frank's score with him during a brief visit Frank paid to Vienna for that purpose in April 1877. Frank conducted the premiere of the opera at Mannheim on 30 September of that year, with Brahms (as well as Goetz's widow, Widmann, and **Clara Schumann**) in the audience.

True to his usual behavior where the work of other musicians was concerned, Brahms seems to have been reluctant to express a firm opinion about Goetz's compositions. Probably at Frank's request, he brought Goetz's Piano Concerto in B-flat Major to **Fritz Simrock**'s attention, though without great enthusiasm: "Unfortunately I never got very far in my reading of the score, so I cannot really say anything about it. For the rest, I know, as you no doubt do, some attractive things he has composed, and he has made quite a name for himself with *Widerspenstige* [*Der Widerspenstigen Zähmung*]" (letter of 21 September 1875 [Brahms 1974/9, 204–5]). Simrock did not publish the concerto. But the following year Brahms asked Frank to play it at the concert at which he himself presented his First Symphony to a Mannheim audience on 7 November 1776 (three days after its first performance at Karlsruhe). The concerto was eventually published in 1880. Lastly, it was probably Goetz's *Nenie* (composed and published in 1874) that first brought Schiller's poem to Brahms's attention. In a letter in June 1875, Frank told Goetz that Brahms was "itching" to set the text himself, but did not think it right to do just then—meaning, presumably, so soon after Goetz's death (Kalbeck 1976, vol. 3, 62). It was in fact not until more than four years after Goetz's death that Brahms composed his *Nänie*.

There may be a further link between Goetz and Brahms: **Max Kalbeck** suggests that Brahms composed the motet op. 74/2 at Pörtschach in 1877 in memory of Goetz, who had died the previous December. (**Heinrich von Herzogenberg**, on the other hand, believed that it had been inspired by Franz von Holstein's death on 22 May 1878.) (Brahms 1974/9; Hanslick 1897b; Kruse 1920; Münster 1995; Ninck 1959; Weigl 1907; Zimmermann 1983)

GOLDMARK, KARL (b. Keszthely, Hungary, 18 May 1830; d. Vienna, 2 January 1915). Composer. At the age of 14 he was sent by his father to Vienna, where, with some interruptions in the earlier years, he was to live for the remainder of his life. He studied violin with L. Jansa and Joseph Böhm, played for a time in the orchestras of the Josefstädter Theater and the Carltheater, and gave private piano lessons. As a composer, he first made his mark when his String Quartet op. 8 was performed by the Hellmesberger Quartet in 1860. He continued to compose throughout his life: pieces for piano, chamber music, orchestral music (of which the Overture *Sakuntala* and the symphonic poem *Die ländliche Hochzeit* [The Rustic Wedding] are probably best remembered today), songs and choral works, and several operas, of which his first and most famous, *Die Königin von Saba*, was very well received by the public, if not the critics, when produced at the Vienna Opera on 10 March 1875.

In his memoirs *Erinnerungen aus meinem Leben*, Goldmark was unable to state precisely when and where in Vienna he had made Brahms's acquaintance, but he thought that it had probably happened not later than 1860–61 at the Café Čech at the Trattnerhof on the Graben, which, he added, was their favorite meeting place for some time afterward. Of course, Brahms did not arrive in Vienna until September 1862; he is likely to have met Goldmark soon afterward. He soon had, in any case, good reason to feel well disposed toward Goldmark, who published a mostly very appreciative review of his concert of 29 November in the *Constitutionelle Österreichische Zeitung* on 5 December, in which he warmly praised his *Handel Variations* and also, if a little less enthusiastically, his Piano Quartet op. 26, and above all paid tribute to his excellence as a pianist. Goldmark, who played viola in an amateur quartet, also took part in a private performance, in Brahms's presence, of the latter's recently composed String Quintet (which would eventually become the Piano Quintet op. 34).

These early contacts led to a lasting and generally friendly relationship between Brahms and Goldmark, who possessed, in fact, an exceptionally pleasing personality that captivated all who knew him. "One is bound to like the man very much," **Elisabeth von Herzogenberg** wrote to Brahms in January 1877 (Brahms 1974/1, 4). Later that same year, in a letter to Elisabeth, Brahms expressed regret at Goldmark's frequent absences from Vienna: "I wish he would stay here. He is a most delightful fellow" (Brahms 1974/1, 32).

Over the years, Goldmark and Brahms were to meet innumerable times, in public as well as in private—over dinner or coffee at restaurants and cafés, at friends' houses, at concerts and banquets, on walking excursions, and during the summer holidays in the Salzkammergut. On one occasion, they even traveled to Italy, together with **Theodor Billroth**.

In his memoirs Goldmark staunchly affirms that Brahms "was as great a man as he was an artist" (Goldmark 1922, 86). Yet, as time passed, he felt increasingly inhibited in Brahms's presence and came to the conclusion that Brahms did not really like him. He seems to have accepted fairly philosophically the fact that Brahms did not care for much of his music, and that he made no secret of his opinions (Brahms did, though, express admiration for the *Rustic Wedding* symphony and for the opera *Merlin*). It was more Brahms's personal manner toward him that Goldmark found disconcerting, at times warm and friendly, at others cold and reserved. Also, Brahms frequently took pleasure in teasing him, which must occasionally have grated on him. But there was also an extraordinary incident that hurt Goldmark profoundly: at a dinner at **Ignaz Brüll**'s on 3 December 1893, following the successful performance, at a concert of the Gesellschaft der Musikfreunde, of Goldmark's choral setting of Martin Luther's "Wer sich die Musik erkiest" [He who chooses music]. Brahms, in Goldmark's presence, aggressively expressed his objection to a Jew presuming to set any text by Luther. Goldmark was so affected by Brahms's outburst that he broke off relations with him. (In his memoirs Goldmark attributes Brahms's offensive behavior to his annoyance at having missed a text he would have liked to set himself.) Eventually, there was a reconciliation, also at Brüll's house, and the contacts resumed. Goldmark states that he last saw Brahms a few weeks before his death when they were both guests at a dinner hosted by **Julius Epstein**.

Goldmark dedicated his *Frühlingshymne op.* 23 to Brahms. (Brahms 1974/1; Goldmark 1922)

GOTTHARD, J. P. [original name: Bohumil Pazdírek] (b. Drahanowitz [Drahanovice, near Olomouc, Czech Republic], 18 January 1839; d. Vöslau, near Vienna, 17 May 1919). Publisher, composer, and teacher. In 1854 or 1855 he moved to Vienna, where he completed his education; little is known about his studies, other than that his teachers included **Simon Sechter**. He became a private tutor, and later was employed as an assistant by the music publishers Ludwig Doblinger and Gustav Lewy; subsequently, he either worked for **C. A. Spina**, or at any rate had some connection with him. At some stage he adopted the name "J. P. Gotthard"; an official document issued in March 1869 confirms his right to continue to use it. (The death certificate of 26 March 1919 gives his Christian names as "Josef Paul," while in some reference works they appear as "Johann Peter." On the other hand, Alexander Weinmann believed that the initials "J. P." probably stood for "Josef Pazdírek.")

In 1868 or 1869 he established a music shop and publishing business under his new name. In addition to a number of his own compositions, his list included works by **Ignaz Brüll**, **Ernst Frank**, **Karl Goldmark**, **Heinrich von Herzogenberg**, **Mozart**, **Franz Schubert**, and **Julius Stockhausen**. Although the firm went bankrupt in 1873, he continued to trade, first under the name "H. Jägermann" (he had married Bertha Anna Josefa Jägermann in 1870), and later as "Jägermann & Germ," but in 1879 a second bankruptcy put an end to his publishing activities. He subsequently taught music at the Theresian Academy (1882–1909) and was also active as a journalist. Among his own compositions were five operas, orchestral music, string quartets, songs, and sacred works.

In connection with a choral festival Gotthard was planning for August 1862—he had recently founded a men's choral society, the "Wiener kaufmännischer Verein" [Viennese Merchants' Society]—he wrote in the spring of that year to Brahms, with whose already published choral compositions (opp. 12, 13, 17) he was evidently familiar. In response to his request for a composition suitable for his male choir, Brahms sent him, from Hamburg, a manuscript copy of "Geleit" (which would later be published as op. 41/3). However, according to **Max Kalbeck**, the piece failed to please the members of Gotthard's choir, who refused to perform it, whereupon he resigned as its director.

Brahms is sure to have heard about this incident after he arrived in Vienna in September 1862. Not long afterward, Gotthard further endeared himself to Brahms by arranging for Spina to publish his setting of Psalm 13 (op. 27) and the four duets op. 28. Gotthard was also among the group of Brahms's friends who regularly joined him for meals at Vater's restaurant during the remainder of the 1860s. In fact, there is every indication that they were in frequent contact for many years—sometimes at friends' houses, for Gotthard, who played the violin and viola, frequently took part in private chamber music performances, including those at **Theodor Billroth**'s. Brahms even asked some of his correspondents to send mail, and especially parcels, intended for him to Gotthard's music business.

One important link between the two men was their great admiration for Schubert's music, of which Gotthard issued numerous first editions. In 1869 he published versions for two and four hands of each of 20 Ländler (D366/1–16 and D814/1–4); some of these versions had been made by Schubert himself, while others were prepared by Brahms (see M. McCorkle 1984, Anhang Ia/6). Furthermore, in 1873 Brahms arranged for the publication by Gotthard of Mozart's offertory "Venite populi" (K260/248a—see M. McCorkle 1984, Anhang Ib/29), which he had performed at a Gesellschaft der Musikfreunde concert on 8 December 1872.

Gotthard dedicated his *10 Stücke in Tanzform* for piano (op. 58) to Brahms. (Biba 1984c; Clive 1997; Weinmann 1979, 1981)

GRÄDENER, CARL (GEORG PETER) (b. Rostock, 14 January 1812; d. Hamburg, 10 June 1883). Composer, conductor, cellist, and teacher. He studied law at Halle and Göttingen (1832–33), but before long decided to switch to a career in music, which he began as a cellist and quartet player in Helsinki (1835–38). In 1838 he was appointed director of music at Kiel University, a position he left 10 years later to earn his living as a private teacher in Hamburg; there he also founded a concert and singing academy in 1851. On 14 September 1958, at the Katharinen-Kirche, he conducted the first Hamburg performance of **Bach**'s *St. Matthew Passion*. In 1862 he moved with his family to Vienna, where he taught privately as well as at the conservatory of the Gesellschaft der Musikfreunde. (In a recent article in the *American Brahms Society Newsletter*, Styra Avins [2003] states that his hopes of being appointed to the conservatory remained unfulfilled, but that he eventually "taught students through the Conservatory" [no. 2, 5]. In actual fact, he appears in the faculty list in the conservatory's annual reports for 1861–62, 1862–63, and 1863–64, initially as a teacher of singing, and later as an instructor in harmony.) He also became organist at the Protestant church. Yet he seems to have found it difficult to make a comfortable living and, moreover, failed to make his mark as a composer. His first concert, on 20 November 1862, at which he presented a selection of his own works, with the help of **Julius Epstein**, the bass Emil Förchtgott, and the Hellmesberger Quartet, was badly received by the audience and by the critics. Above all, unlike Brahms, he disliked the Viennese and their way of life. In 1865 he returned to Hamburg, where he spent the rest of his life. In 1867 he was a cofounder of the Hamburg Tonkünstlerverein, of which he became the first president, and from 1873 he taught at the newly established conservatory. He was greatly respected as a teacher and also enjoyed a certain reputation as a composer, particularly for his piano and chamber music.

Brahms made Grädener's acquaintance, through **Theodor Avé-Lallemant**, in the autumn of 1854. Grädener was very friendly toward him, and Brahms, in his turn, felt attracted to the older man. They were henceforth to meet repeatedly, and Brahms clearly enjoyed his company. "You are sure to like Grädener, he is a highly gifted man," he wrote in early November 1854 to **Clara Schumann**, who was about to come to Hamburg. "He has a most attractive nature, extremely lively and animated. After hearing music until 1 o'clock, he sits in a bar until gone 3 o'clock, and grows steadily more jovial" (Litzmann 1970, vol. 1, 32). Brahms also thought highly of Grädener's compositions: "I will show you an interesting piano sonata," he promised Clara in the same letter, and went on to praise Grädener's latest string quartet. He even attempted, though unsuccessfully, to interest the Leipzig music publisher **Bartolf Wilhelm Senff** in some of Grädener's piano compositions. Grädener dedicated his Piano Trio op. 35 to him.

Over the next few years, whenever he was in Hamburg, Brahms saw a good deal of Grädener (for further details, see especially the Brahms–Joachim correspondence (Brahms 1974/5–6); and, notwithstanding the age gap, they were soon on "Du" terms. Grädener was, moreover, highly supportive of Brahms's efforts to make a name for himself as a composer, and following Brahms's performance of the First Piano Concerto in Hamburg on 24 March 1859, two months after its disastrous premiere at Leipzig, Grädener published a report in the *Neue Berliner Musikzeitung* (on 29 June), in which he stressed the great quality of the new work and firmly rejected the very negative assessment [by Ernst Berndorf] that had appeared in *Signale für die musikalische Welt* on 3 February. Furthermore, he referred favorably to the first performance of the Serenade op. 11 (in its version for small orchestra), of which **Joseph Joachim** had conducted the first performance in Hamburg on 28 March. Brahms and Grädener also performed together, in private and occasionally even in public—for instance, at Kiel on 20 January 1856 when Brahms played his Piano Trio op. 8 with Grädener and **John Böie**. At one of Grädener's Hamburg concerts, on 2 May 1860, Brahms conducted his women's choir in the first performances of his *Ave Maria* (op. 12) and *Begräbnisgesang* (op. 13), at another one on 2 May 1860 in three of the *4 Gesänge* (op. 17); at Grädener's concert of 25 October 1861, he played **Robert Schumann**'s *Andante and Variations* for two pianos (op. 46) with

Clara Schumann; and, according to **Max Kalbeck**, he had a week earlier played at Altona in a new piano quartet by Grädener.

After Brahms and Grädener moved to Vienna, where Brahms's career prospered while Grädener's faltered, their relations became less close. Brahms adapted comparatively easily and, indeed, with some relish to the Viennese way of life, enjoyed agreeable social contacts and soon scored some musical successes, whereas Grädener, a middle-aged man with a family to support, struggled to create a new existence for himself and felt himself largely ignored by a society with which he had little in common and in which he found much to criticize. Almost inevitably, their relations became less cordial and quite often even acrimonious, for Grädener had come to the conclusion that Brahms's smooth progress must be due to a willingness to compromise, if not his artistic conscience, at any rate certain ethical ideals such as frankness, guilelessness, and truthfulness. "I don't understand him," he wrote somewhat censoriously to Avé-Lallemant in January 1863, adding that Brahms might well be aware of his thoughts; for while Brahms was not deliberately avoiding him, he was making no particular effort to meet him (Avins 2003, no. 2, 6). The following year Grädener contributed a caustic review of Brahms's second concert with the Singakademie on 6 January 1864 to the Viennese journal *Recensionen und Mittheilungen über Theater und Musik* (issue of 9 January); but a week later he published in the same periodical a favorable study of the Sextet op. 18.

Once Grädener had returned to Hamburg, they appear to have met occasionally when Brahms visited his native city—for the last time when Brahms went there to conduct the concert that **Julius Spengel**'s Cäcilien Verein devoted to his music on 6 April 1883. The news of Grädener's death two months later profoundly moved him. In a letter to Grädener's older son, he recalled the important place his father had occupied in his youth and referred to him as that "good and excellent man, friend, and colleague" (Kalbeck 1976, vol. 3, 379, n. 2). Brahms also greatly admired Grädener's wife Maria Wilhelmine Henriette (1816–88): "Such an intelligent and highly cultured woman is very rare. I have known only two or three women like that," he told **Richard Heuberger** when he heard of her death (Heuberger 1976, 37). He was, on the other hand, rather less fond of the Grädeners' son Hermann (1844–1929), whom he had known as a child in Hamburg and was to meet on various later occasions in Vienna, where Hermann, after attending the conservatory (1862–65), had a successful career as violinist, conductor, composer, and teacher. (Avins 2003; Avins and Eisinger 2002; Brahms 1974/5–6; Graedener 1920; Heuberger 1976; Litzmann 1970)

GRAF, CONRAD (b. Riedlingen, Württemberg, 11 November 1782; d. Vienna, 17 March 1851.) Piano manufacturer in Vienna. When **Clara** Wieck married **Robert Schumann** on 12 September 1840, Graf presented a grand piano to her. It may have been on this piano that Brahms played his compositions to the Schumanns on his memorable visit to Düsseldorf in the autumn of 1853. After Robert's death, Clara gave the piano to Brahms, who had it transported to Hamburg, where it was to lead a rather peripatetic existence. For several years it stood in the family's flat, but when Brahms rented a room from Dr. **Elisabeth Rösing** at Hamm (now a part of Hamburg) in July 1861, he had it taken there; and he left it with her when he went to Vienna in the autumn of 1862. However, when Dr. Rösing moved to Hanover in 1868, he was obliged to find a new location for the piano, and he then put it into storage with the Hamburg firm Baumgardten & Heins. Its last location in Hamburg was the flat on the Anscharplatz into which his father moved with his second wife in 1871 (and which she continued to occupy for several years after **Johann Jakob Brahms**'s death in 1872). Finally, in 1873 Brahms arranged for the piano to be sent to Vienna, where it was shown at the World Exhibition that year. Afterward, Brahms presented it to the Gesellschaft der Musikfreunde, whose artistic director he then was.

A meticulous description of the technical features of the piano, which is now on loan to the Kunsthistorisches Museum in Vienna, can be found in Deborah Whyte's (1984) article "The Pianos of Conrad Graf." Some of its aspects are also discussed by G. S. Bozarth and S. H. Brady (2000) in their article "Johannes Brahms and his Pianos," which, moreover, offers a detailed account of the instrument's peregrinations. As its authors furthermore point out, it was during the period in which Brahms had use of the Graf piano that he composed the *Handel Variations*, the Piano Quartets opp. 25 and 26, the Piano Quintet, some of the *Magelone-Lieder*, and a part of the Cello Sonata op. 38.

The Schumanns' Graf piano was not the only piano by that manufacturer that Brahms had at his disposal over a prolonged period. During his three stays at Detmold in 1857–59 he had in his room at the Hotel Stadt Frankfurt a Graf piano lent to him by the Court Marshal's wife **Meta Sophie Luise von Meysenbug** (who also possessed a Streicher grand that had been played by **Liszt** and Clara Schumann). The Graf piano, though no longer in prime condition, was still sufficiently good to be used by Brahms at many musical evenings with **Carl Louis Bargheer** and other new acquaintances. Among the compositions he worked on at Detmold were the Serenades opp. 11 and 16, *Begräbnisgesang* (op. 13), and various songs. (Bozarth and Brady 2000; Geiser 1976; Pollens 2006; Whyte 1984)

GRASSL VON RECHTEN, JOHANNA (b. 1841/42; d. Vienna, 2 December 1932). Daughter of Ignaz Grassl von Rechten (1795–1889), professor of jurisprudence at Vienna University (ennobled 1868). She became Brahms's pupil in 1862. In his Brahms biography, **Max Kalbeck** (1976) quotes her account of her contacts with Brahms at this time, but it is not clear whether the lessons resumed after Brahms's return to Vienna the following year. He remained, at any rate, in contact with her at least through the rest of the 1860s, for Kalbeck also refers to a letter addressed by Brahms to Johanna in the summer of 1865, as well as to his meeting, in his father's company, with "the Nawratil family and Frl. Hania Grassl" by the Mondsee, near Salzburg, in August 1867 (vol. 2, 232). The following year he spent Christmas Eve at the Grassls'. (*See also* NAWRATIL, KARL.) (*ÖBL* 1957–)

GRIEG, EDVARD (HAGERUP) (b. Bergen, 15 June 1843; d. Bergen, 4 September 1907). Norwegian composer. It seems difficult to determine when he first met Brahms, except that it was not later than 1887, for Anna Brodsky (the wife of the violinist **Adolph Brodsky**), who gives a detailed and fascinating account in her memoir *Recollections of a Russian Home* of a dinner at their flat in Leipzig on 1 January 1888, at which Brahms, **Tchaikovsky**, and Grieg and his wife were all present, mentions that the Griegs already knew Brahms then. In fact, the first meeting is likely to have taken place some years earlier, if **Julius Röntgen** (1930) is correct in stating in his book on Grieg that the latter made Brahms's acquaintance at the Leipzig home of **Heinrich** and **Elisabeth von Herzogenberg** (who lived there from 1872 to 1885). Röntgen adds that on that occasion Grieg performed one of his *Folkelivsbilleder* (op. 19/2), while Brahms played his G Minor Rhapsody (op. 79/2), but "I had the impression that neither enjoyed the other's composition . . . only much later, in Vienna, did [their] relationship become a friendly one" (J. Röntgen 1930, 25).

Grieg was, however, already a great admirer of Brahms's Requiem. "For me it is beyond comparison the most beautiful work B[rahms] has composed," he wrote to Röntgen in February 1885 (J. Röntgen 1930, 23); and in 1896 he told **Richard Heuberger** that the Requiem exemplified "the Brahms he loved" (Heuberger 1976, 99). He was also profoundly impressed by many of Brahms's songs and by some of his chamber music; thus, in another letter to Röntgen, he called the G Minor Piano Quartet (op. 25) "a work of genius" (Röntgen 1930, 26). Later he was to reprove his future biographer Henry T. Finck for failing to recognize Brahms's greatness: "That you, with your great, wide horizon, have failed to discover the real Brahms, is really quite extraordinary. . . . For me there is no doubt concerning

Brahms. A landscape, torn by mists and clouds, in which I can see ruins of old churches, as well as of Greek temples—that is Brahms" (Finck 1971, xvii). For his part Brahms, according to Röntgen, once greatly praised Grieg's Ballade in G Minor (op. 24). Moreover, Heuberger (1976) reports that he regarded Grieg as a superb pianist (99).

Brahms met Grieg several times in Vienna during the final period of his life. Grieg was there in March 1896 (on the 24th of that month he conducted a concert of his own works), and at a banquet arranged in his own honor he delivered a eulogy of Brahms that apparently greatly moved its subject. During the winter of 1896–97, Grieg spent several weeks in Vienna. On 16 December he took part in a chamber music concert, and on 19 December he conducted the Vienna Philharmonic Orchestra in a program featuring his overture *In Autumn*, the *Holberg Suite*, the piano concerto, in which Ferruccio Busoni was soloist, and several songs interpreted by **Anton Sistermans**. (By a curious coincidence, when the concerto was first performed by V. von Stepanoff at a Philharmonic Society concert in Vienna on 26 March 1882, the other major work on the program was Brahms's First Symphony; neither composition elicited much enthusiasm then.) On 2 January 1897 Grieg attended a concert by the Joachim Quartet, at which Brahms's String Quintet op. 111 was played. His account, in a letter to Röntgen the next day, of the extraordinary ovation accorded to Brahms on that occasion complements that given by **Max Kalbeck**. (Finck 1971; Hauch 1922; Heuberger 1976; A. Röntgen 1934; J. Röntgen 1930)

GRIMM, JULIUS OTTO (b. Pernau, Livonia [Pärnu, Estonia], 6 March 1827; d. Münster, Westphalia, 7 December 1903). Composer, conductor, pianist, and teacher. He studied philosophy and philology at the university in Dorpat [Tartu, Estonia] and, while there, made the acquaintance of **Robert** and **Clara Schumann**, who stopped briefly in that town on their journey to Russia in 1844. From an early age he had taken a passionate interest in music and, after being employed as a private tutor at St. Petersburg (1848–51), he enrolled at the Leipzig conservatory in April 1851; his teachers included **Ferdinand David**, **Moritz Hauptmann**, **Julius Rietz**, and Ignaz Moscheles. After leaving the conservatory in October 1852, he remained at Leipzig, and it was there, in November 1853, that he first met Brahms and began a friendship that, except for a period of strain following the breakup of the latter's relationship with **Agathe von Siebold**, lasted until Brahms's death. They were in particularly close contact throughout most of the year 1854, a large part of which Grimm, like Brahms, spent at Düsseldorf with the object of making himself useful to the Schumanns in their tragic circumstances (Grimm had renewed his acquaintance with them in

Leipzig in 1852). In a letter to Gisela von Arnim on 20 October 1854, **Joseph Joachim** referred to Grimm as "Brahms's best friend" (Johannes Joachim 1911, 64).

After a relatively short stay at Hanover, where he saw a good deal of Joachim and tried, none too successfully, to set up as a piano teacher, Grimm moved to Göttingen in April 1855. There he soon acquired a satisfactory number of music students, among them Agathe von Siebold and Philippine Ritmüller (1835–96, a daughter of piano manufacturer Wilhelm Ritmüller), whom he married on 8 May 1856; Philippine (called "Pine Gur" by her husband and friends) was an excellent pianist. In addition to his teaching, Grimm was active as conductor of a local choir, as well as of an orchestra that, though largely made up of amateurs, he managed to weld into quite a competent ensemble; but he failed to obtain the post of university music director to which he aspired (it was offered to Eduard Hille). On 1 November 1860 he became municipal music director at Münster, and there he spent the rest of his life.

The Grimm-Brahms correspondence published by **Richard Barth** (Brahms 1974/4), which clearly does not contain all the letters exchanged by them, testifies to the warm feelings the two men had for one another, even though their contacts appear to have been rather spasmodic at certain periods. (Regarding Grimm's role in precipitating the crucial crisis in Brahms's relations with Agathe von Siebold, *see* SIEBOLD, [SOPHIE LUISE BERTHA] AGATHE VON.) Brahms visited Münster several times during Grimm's stay there, when he usually performed at concerts—for the first time on 19 January 1862, on which occasion he played Schumann's Piano Concerto and, with Joachim, **Beethoven**'s "Kreutzer" Sonata. On later visits (as in 1876, 1881, 1882) he mainly performed his own compositions. Grimm did his best to bring Brahms's works to the attention of the local music lovers. Thus, he informed Brahms on 19 March 1869 that the Requiem had received "a wonderfully successful performance" the previous day, and that "in two or three weeks we shall be performing your Requiem once more" (Brahms 1974/4, 115–16); in 1870 he reported impressive performances of the *Alto Rhapsody* and the *Liebeslieder-Walzer*; and by March 1890 he was able to assure Brahms that "in almost every programme of our Musikverein concerts there is a composition by you" (Brahms 1974/4, 151). Their final meeting may have occurred that same month when Grimm and his wife enthusiastically accepted Brahms's suggestion to attend a concert at Cologne on 13 March, in which Brahms was to take part: "We, my wife and myself, thank you warmly and we shall of course come and are looking forward to it as if we were over 30 years younger," Grimm wrote (Brahms 1974/4, 150–51). The last item in the published correspondence is the following telegram from Brahms congratulating Grimm on his birthday on 6 March 1897: "To his dear and deeply loved friend all best wishes on his birthday from his devoted and faithful old Johannes Brahms" (Brahms 1974/4, 158).

Grimm started to compose in his youth and continued into his later years, although the time he could devote to such work was limited; even in old age he was still obliged to allot many hours each day to teaching to make ends meet. His published compositions attained only 28 opus numbers. Most of them were songs, and a number were written for the piano. Only a few were for string or full orchestra; one of the latter, the Suite II in form of a canon (op. 16), he dedicated in 1870 to Brahms, who had himself dedicated his 4 Ballades for piano (op. 10) to him in 1855. (Brahms 1974/4; Grimm 1900/1; Johannes Joachim 1911; Ludwig 1925)

GROHE, MELCHIOR (1829–1906). Poet. Brahms set one of Grohe's texts in the song "O komme, holde Sommernacht" (op. 58/4).

GROTH, KLAUS (JOHANN) (b. Heide, Holstein, 24 April 1819; d. Kiel, 1 June 1899). Poet, best known for *Quickborn*, a collection of poems in Plattdeutsch [Low German] that he first published in 1852 (actually, the book bears the date 1853) and that subsequently went through several augmented editions. Among its admirers was Brahms, who remained all his life deeply conscious of his North German roots.

Groth was to write later that he had made Brahms's acquaintance at the Lower Rhine Music Festival in 1856, a statement repeated by **Max Kalbeck** in his Brahms biography and more recently by Styra Avins (1997) in *Johannes Brahms: Life and Letters* (where, incidentally, the festival is incorrectly said to have taken place at Cologne instead of at Düsseldorf). However, as Dieter Lohmeier points out in his edition of the Brahms-Groth correspondence, they had already met prior to the festival, which took place on 11–13 May—probably at Bonn in April. Moreover, Groth had inscribed a copy of *Hundert Blätter* (another volume of poetry, this time in High German) for Brahms at Düsseldorf on 2 May 1856. The festival would therefore have provided an opportunity for renewing these first contacts; they met again soon afterward at Bonn, from where, on 8 June, Groth, **Albert Dietrich**, and **Otto Jahn** accompanied Brahms to Endenich, although only Brahms actually saw **Robert Schumann**. At that period Groth still knew very little of Brahms's music, and even later it took him some time to fully appreciate certain works; but, increasingly convinced of Brahms's genius, he persisted in his efforts to understand them and ultimately came to regard Brahms as the greatest contemporary composer. He thus described his experience in the case of the *Magelone-Lieder*: "At first one enters a jungle, one distinguishes nothing, then one recognizes that it is a footpath, and finally one realizes with amazement that it is in fact a large new avenue leading to the distant land of poetry" (Lohmeier 1997, 173).

Nothing definite is known about any meetings between Groth and Brahms during the period 1857–67. The earliest item in the published correspondence (*Briefe der Freundschaft*), which also includes letters from Groth's wife Doris, dates from February 1868 and refers to Brahms's and **Julius Stockhausen**'s forthcoming concert at Kiel on 13 March; the last item dates from December 1896. From the time they met during the golden jubilee celebrations of the Hamburg Philharmonic Society in September 1878, they addressed each other with the familiar "Du." As a source of information about Groth's relations with Brahms during this period, the correspondence is amply supplemented by his "Erinnerungen an Johannes Brahms" [Memories of Johannes Brahms], which appeared in the periodical *Die Gegenwart* in November 1897 (and are reprinted in *Briefe der Freundschaft* [Lohmeier 1997]). It was at Thun, where Groth visited Brahms in the summer of 1888, that Christian Wilhelm Allers made the well-known amusing drawing of the two men, seen from the back while out walking. Groth last saw Brahms in December 1891, in Hamburg. (Also in *Die Gegenwart*, in November 1897, Groth published "Musikalische Erlebnisse" [Musical Experiences], where he describes his youth at Heide and his contacts with the Brahms family there.)

Brahms set texts by Groth in the songs "Regenlied" (op. 59/3; the melody later played a significant thematic role in the Violin Sonata op. 78), "Nachklang" (op. 59/4; see also WoO posthum 23), "Mein wundes Herz" (op. 59/7), "Dein blaues Auge" (op. 59/8), "Heimweh I," "Heimweh II," and "Heimweh III" (op. 63/7–9), "Komm bald" (op. 97/5), and "Wie Melodien zieht es mir" (op. 105/1); in the duets "Klänge I" and "Klänge II" (op. 66/1–2); and in "Im Herbst" (op.104/5) for mixed choir. It may seem odd that Brahms, who was so fond of Plattdeutsch (*see also* KUPFER, [THEODOR] WILHELM), and, in particular, of Groth's poems in that dialect, should not have set any of the texts in *Quickborn*. In fact, he once told Groth that he had tried, but failed, because he responded to Plattdeutsch at a very profound level and it meant more to him than simply a language. Numerous other composers set poems in Low and High German by Groth; they include **Karl Goldmark**, **Carl Grädener**, **Julius Otto Grimm**, **Moritz Hauptmann**, Otto Jahn, and **Carl Reinecke**. (Langner 1990; Lohmeier 1997; Miesner 1933; Selig 1924)

GRÜN, ANASTASIUS [pseudonym of Count Anton Alexander Auersperg] (b. Laibach [Ljubljana, Slovenia], 11 April 1808; d. Graz, 12 September 1876). Poet. Brahms set Grün's translation of a Slovenian folk song in "Fragen" (op. 44/4). (W. Bauer 1989)

GRÜN, JAKOB MORITZ (b. Pest [Budapest], 13 March 1837; d. Baden, near Vienna, 1 October 1916). After studying with Joseph Böhm in Vienna and **Moritz Hauptmann** in Leipzig, he became Konzertmeister of the court Kapelle at Weimar (1858–61) and subsequently of the one at Hanover, where he was engaged on **Joseph Joachim**'s recommendation. After **King Georg V of Hanover** had refused to appoint him Kammermusikus (a title that carried with it full membership in the orchestra and pension rights), he accepted in 1868 the post of Konzertmeister of the court opera orchestra in Vienna. He also taught at the conservatory (1877–1909), where **Franz Kneisel** was among his students.

Brahms had become professionally associated with Grün even before he took up the position in Vienna. On 26 April 1867 they played **Beethoven**'s "Kreutzer" Sonata in Budapest, and on 9 December 1867, also in Budapest, Brahms joined members of the Grün-Moldner-Sabatiel-Udél Quartet in a performance of his own Piano Quartet op. 25. Grün maintained his interest in Brahms's music after settling in Vienna. Thus, on 19 January 1879, he performed Brahms's Horn Trio op. 40 with **Clara Schumann** and Wilhelm Kleinecke, and later that year Brahms himself took part in a performance of his Piano Quartet op. 25 at one of Grün's chamber music concerts. (Fischer 1903)

GRUND, FRIEDRICH WILHELM (b. Hamburg, 7 October 1791; d. Hamburg, 24 November 1874). Conductor and teacher. He came from a musical family, and several of his 10 siblings performed in public (his brother Eduard became Konzertmeister of the Meiningen orchestra). Obliged to abandon his hopes of a career as a virtuoso cellist on account of a nervous complaint, he devoted his life and considerable energy to the enrichment of Hamburg's musical activities by founding some competent choral and orchestral societies and conducting their concerts for many years; he was also a fine pianist and a composer of a large variety of works, including two operas.

He established the Gesangverein in 1819 together with Jacob St. Steinfeld, and they directed it jointly until 1833, after which Grund remained in sole charge (it was renamed "Sing-Akademie" in 1868); and in 1828 he was among the founders of the Philharmonic Society, which he served as its first musical director. He remained responsible for both societies until

1863, when he retired and was succeeded by **Julius Stockhausen**. His achievements were widely admired and after his death were commemorated in a special concert given jointly by the Sing-Akademie and the Philharmonic Society on 27 April 1875; the program included the Introduction, Chorale, and Chorus from Grund's oratorio *Die Himmelfahrt und Auferstehung Christi* and **Mozart**'s Requiem. Yet the quality of his performances had declined toward the end, and the hold he retained into old age over the most prestigious musical appointments in the city was resented by some of the younger musicians, all of which may account for the remarkable attack made on him by Brahms in a letter to **Clara Schumann** in November 1854. After a scathing criticism of a rehearsal of **Beethoven**'s Ninth Symphony conducted by Grund, he wrote, "And because of this old, dried-up philistine who has been killing all musical life in Hamburg for over 20 years, bright young men like **Georg Dietrich Otten** and **Carl Grädener** can do nothing and must spend their time giving lessons, and can in no way make their mark in public" (Litzmann 1970, vol. 1, 41).

However, Brahms could not complain, over the next few years, that he was being totally neglected by Grund, for he was more than once invited to take part in concerts of the Philharmonic Society, both as pianist and composer. On 22 November 1856, at a concert in **Robert Schumann**'s memory, he played Schumann's Piano Concerto, as well as, with **Joseph Joachim**, two of the *Phantasiestücke* (op. 73); on 24 March 1859 he performed his own First Piano Concerto, with Joseph Joachim conducting (it was played again by Clara Schumann on 3 December 1861, Brahms conducting); on 10 February 1860 he again played Schumann's concerto and conducted his own Serenade op. 16; and on 8 March 1861 he played Beethoven's Triple Concerto with **Ferdinand David** and Karl Davidoff. (Litzmann 1970; Sittard 1971; Stephenson 1928)

GRUPPE, OTTO FRIEDRICH (b. Danzig [Gdansk], 15 April 1804; d. Berlin, 7 January 1876). Brahms set a poem by Gruppe in the song "Das Mädchen spricht" (op. 107/3). (Kempski 1966)

GRÜTERS, AUGUST (b. Uerdingen, near Krefeld, 7 December 1841; d. Frankfurt am Main, 28 January 1911). Chorus master and orchestral conductor. Son of Uerdingen organist and music teacher Matthäus Grüters (1808–90) and brother of Hugo Grüters (1851–1928), music director at Duisburg (1884–99) and Bonn (1899–1922). He studied violin at the Cologne conservatory and later, in Paris, violin with Delphin Alard and piano with Antoine François Marmontel; he also received some instruction from Ambroise Thomas. In 1859 he was engaged as a conductor at Troyes, which he left in 1867 to become chorus master of the Liedertafel (a male choir) at Krefeld; in addition, in late 1870, he succeeded **Hermann Wolff** as conductor of the town's Singverein (a mixed choir). He conducted both choirs until 1893, as well as the symphony concerts of the local Konzertgesellschaft. In 1893 he moved to Frankfurt, where he took charge of the Cäcilienverein, a well-known choral society founded in 1818; he held this position until 1909.

The powerful and influential position that Grüters, a great admirer of Brahms, occupied in the cultural life of Krefeld enabled him to promote the performance of Brahms's compositions and to foster understanding for them at Krefeld. In the spring of 1871, during his first year at the helm of the Singverein, he presented a performance of the Requiem that proved considerably more successful than that conducted by Wolff in April 1870. Most importantly, he was instrumental in bringing Brahms to Krefeld (according to **Rudolf von der Leyen**, it was **Rudolf von Beckerath** who actually transmitted the invitation to Brahms). At the concert on 20 January 1880 Brahms conducted his Second Symphony (which Grüters had already performed in 1878), the *Alto Rhapsody* (in which Adele Assmann was the soloist), and the *Triumphlied*, and in addition gave the first performances of the two Rhapsodies op. 79.

In Krefeld, Brahms found a competent orchestra, a very good choir, an excellent music director who had prepared his works to his satisfaction, and a congenial circle of enthusiastic musical amateurs with whom he established lasting friendly relationships. Therefore, it is not surprising that he returned to Krefeld on several more occasions. On 25 January 1881 he conducted the *Academic Festival Overture*, the *Schicksalslied*, and the Violin Concerto (in which the soloist was **Richard Barth**, who was appointed Konzertmeister of the Krefeld orchestra that year and was to hold that position until 1887); in addition, Jenny Hahn sang three Lieder by Brahms, and Grüters directed performances of **Beethoven**'s "Egmont" Overture and of the *Sanctus* from **Bach**'s Mass in B Minor. On 23 January 1883 Brahms was soloist in his Second Piano Concerto (with Grüters conducting), and he conducted *Gesang der Parzen* and the fifth movement of the Requiem (in which **Antonia Kufferath** was one of the soloists and also sang "Liebestreu" [op. 3/1]). Heinrich Melsbach's (1925) article "Crefelder Brahmserinnerungen," which essentially reproduces notes left by Grüters and augmented by his widow, states that at the final rehearsals of *Gesang der Parzen* Brahms was so delighted with the quality of the choral singing that he declared that nowhere, except perhaps in Vienna, had he ever heard a chorus sing so beautifully. At the concert, the work was encored (according to Melsbach's "Crefelder Brahmserinnerungen," Grüters, seated in the first row, applauded so long and enthusiastically that Brahms finally agreed to repeat the work). Some time after the concert Brahms sent Grüters the autograph of the score, with a dedication reading "To my friends in Crefeld in sincere gratitude" (it is now preserved in the town's archives). Furthermore, Brahms sent autographs of the vocal duets "Die Schwestern" and "Klosterfräulein" (op. 61/1–2) to Grüters's wife. (Quite apart from the circumstantial account that it gives of Brahms's various visits to Krefeld, Melsbach's article is of great interest, since it prints the text of several letters addressed by Brahms to Grüters that do not appear to have been published elsewhere.)

Brahms's next appearance at a Krefeld concert took place on 27 January 1885, when he conducted his Third Symphony, the first chorus of the *Triumphlied*, and the first five of the Lieder und Romanzen op. 93a, and accompanied **Sir George Henschel** in several of his songs. When, in response to the audience's warm applause, Henschel proposed that they perform one of the *Magelone-Lieder* as an encore, Brahms reportedly laughed and said that he could not play the accompaniment from memory but that Grüters would no doubt be able to do so, which was indeed the case. The following day, at a concert commemorating the golden jubilee of the Krefeld Singverein, Brahms conducted three of the Lieder und Romanzen of op. 93a, accompanied the quartets "An die Heimat" (op. 64/1), "O schöne Nacht" (op. 92/1), and "Wechsellied zum Tanze" (op. 31/1), and played a capriccio by **Robert Schumann** and a march by **Franz Schubert**; among the singers was **Marie Fillunger**, who also performed Schumann's "Rastlose Liebe" and Brahms's "Meine Liebe ist grün" (op. 63, no. 5). At the same concert Grüters conducted the chorus "Am Himmelfahrtstage" by Mendelssohn.

One further musical collaboration between Brahms and Grüters is documented in Melsbach's article but incorrectly assigned there to the year 1886. Prior to the concert on 21 November 1885, at which Brahms was to introduce his new Fourth Symphony to a Krefeld audience, he and Grüters twice played the two-piano version at Grüters's house before a small number of persons.

Grüters enjoyed a high reputation. When **Clara Schumann** learned of his forthcoming move to Frankfurt, she wrote from there to Brahms: "I am sure that you know about Grueters's appointment. I am very pleased about it—he's a good musician, don't you agree?" (Litzmann 1970, vol. 2, 514). Brahms is likely to have met Grüters more than once in Frankfurt. **Max Kalbeck** mentions one occasion, a musical soiree at the house of Louis Sommerhoff and his wife, the former Elise Schumann, on 11 November 1894, when the musical entertainment included performances by Brahms and **Richard Mühlfeld** of Brahms's two clarinet sonatas; Grüters is said to have been among the invited guests (Kalbeck 1976, vol. 4, 371). On 3 April 1898 he took part in a Brahms memorial concert in Frankfurt, arranged by **Julius Stockhausen**'s school of singing. (Klusen, Stoffels, and Zart 1979–80; Leyen 1905; Litzmann 1970; Melsbach 1925)

GUTMANN, ALBERT J. (b. Fürth, Bavaria, 20 June 1851; d. Vienna, 7 March 1915). Publisher, concert agent, and owner of a Viennese music shop. Established in 1873, the business flourished, and Gutmann soon had numerous performers, individuals as well as ensembles, on his books, both from inside Austria and from other countries; by 1910 he had offices in Paris, London, and Berlin. Furthermore, he brought certain celebrated foreign orchestras to Vienna—during Brahms's lifetime, notably the Meiningen court Kapelle in 1884 and the Berlin Philharmonic Orchestra in 1895 (on which occasion **Felix Weingartner** conducted a performance of Brahms's Second Symphony, which delighted Brahms). When the latter orchestra was again engaged for a series of concerts in April 1897, Gutmann regularly discussed the proposed programs with Brahms, several of whose works were due to be performed. In fact, Gutmann later stated that he had in that connection called on Brahms every day for several weeks and that Brahms's landlady had subsequently told him that the very last lines Brahms ever wrote were in a note addressed to him a few hours before his death. In the event, the first concert by the Berlin Philharmonic Orchestra, conducted by Weingartner on 5 April, was, at Gutmann's suggestion, turned into a memorial concert, which included the *Tragic Overture*, two of the *4 ernste Gesänge* sung by **Anton Sistermans**, and **Beethoven**'s "Eroica" Symphony (see the announcement in the *Neue freie Presse* that day).

In his memoirs *Aus dem Wiener Musikleben* Gutmann relates that he often visited Brahms, sometimes lunched with him at the Roter Igel restaurant or took coffee with him at the café in the Stadtpark where Brahms liked to stop on his way home from the restaurant; he adds that Brahms was also in the habit of calling at his shop, which was located in the same building as the opera, in order to study the scores of *Die Meistersinger*, *Tristan und Isolde*, or *Götterdämmerung* in his private office. Gutmann was a fervent admirer of **Richard Wagner**'s operas, as well as of the music of **Liszt** and, later, of **Anton Bruckner** (some of whose compositions he published). He would also have liked to publish Brahms's Third Symphony. In fact, on 5 December 1883, three days after its first performance under **Hans Richter**, the Viennese daily *Die Presse* printed a letter from him to Brahms, in which he offered 10,000 gulden for it. However, Brahms remained faithful to **Fritz Simrock**, to whom he entrusted practically all his major works during the last 30 years of his life. But he took care to bring Gutmann's letter to the attention of Simrock, who could not afford to pay such a sum.

Brahms no doubt appreciated Gutmann's efforts to bring so many talented performers to Vienna, especially since **Alice Barbi** was among them. As for his view of Gutmann's personality, a clue is perhaps provided by a story he once told **Richard Heuberger**. It described a scene that had taken place in Gutmann's shop, in which Gutmann, "unctuous and stupid as always," approached **Hans von Bülow** and so exasperated him with a foolish and pompous remark that Bülow rushed out of the shop shouting, "I'll have nothing to do with such a crazy man" (Heuberger 1976, 26). In any case, notwithstanding the reported frequency of their meetings (Gutmann was also a member of the Tonkünstlerverein), it is unlikely that Brahms's relations with Gutmann were ever at all intimate. (Gutmann 1914; Heuberger 1976)

– H –

HAFIZ [really: Shams-ud-din Mohammed] (b. Shiraz, ca. 1300 AD; d. Shiraz, 1388 AD). Persian poet. Brahms set poems by Hafiz in the following vocal compositions: in the songs "Bitteres zu sagen denkst du," "So stehn wir, ich und meine Weide," "Wie bist du, meine Königin" (op. 32/7–9), "Botschaft," "Liebesglut" (op. 47/1–2), and "Wenn du nur zuweilen lächelst" (op. 57/2), using German translations by **Georg Friedrich Daumer**; in the quartet "Finstere Schatten der Nacht" (op. 65/2), based on a German version by an unidentified translator; and in the canon "Einförmig ist der Liebe Gram" (op. 113/13), in a translation by **Friedrich Rückert**.

HALLÉ, SIR CHARLES (b. Hagen, Westphalia, 11 April 1819; d. Manchester, 25 October 1895). Pianist and conductor. He knew Brahms quite well. On 9 October 1880 he wrote to one of his daughters from Vienna: "Brahms is the most delightful and good-natured creature imaginable, and what a musician!" (Hallé 1896, 303). He added that they dined together every day at the Roter Igel Restaurant and met again for several hours in the evening.

According to R. Pascall, Hallé was involved in the first English performances of the following works by Brahms: the Serenade op. 16 in Manchester on 6 March 1873; Piano Quartet op. 25 in London on 26 January 1874; *Haydn Variations* for two pianos op. 56b (with **Hans von Bülow**) in Manchester on 12 February 1874; Piano Quartet op. 60 in London on 20

November 1876; and Piano Trio op. 87 in London on 22 January 1883. In addition, he took part in many early English performances of other works.

In his memoirs, **Edward Speyer** (1937) states that Brahms once told him that he nearly went to England on one occasion. He had met Hallé at one of the Lower Rhine Music Festivals, and Hallé had invited him to come to Manchester and conduct the Hallé Orchestra in a concert of his own works. After returning to England, Hallé wrote fixing the date of the concert, but the fee offered was, Brahms alleged, lower than he was receiving in some of the smallest German towns. "Had I been asked to go merely for the honour, I might have accepted, but it was the meanness of the offer after all his big talk, which made me refuse it with indignation" (Speyer 1937, 87). Speyer adds that long afterward he mentioned the matter to Hallé, who "tried to show that Brahms was under a misapprehension, but his arguments left me unconvinced." It may well be, of course, that Brahms was only too glad to find a pretext for backing out of an engagement that would have entailed a journey to England. (Hallé 1896; Kennedy 1960, 1971; Pascall 2001; Speyer 1937)

HALLIER FAMILY. Hamburg family, headed by the prosperous merchant Johann Gottfried Hallier (1804–82). Brahms was well acquainted with the Halliers in his youth and often attended their regular Wednesday evening receptions. **Clara Schumann** occasionally stayed with them when in Hamburg for concerts, as in January and October 1861, and she took part in musical soirees there on 17 and 30 January 1861, as did Brahms.

In addition to a flat in the town, Hallier possessed a country house at Eppendorf (now part of Hamburg), which the family occupied in the summer. It stood in a large garden, in which Brahms was fond of holding practice sessions of his Frauenchor; Hallier's daughters Marie (1838–96) and Julie (1834–1907) were members of the choir. In 1860 Brahms studied Latin with their brother Emil (who in 1862 married **Carl Grädener**'s daughter Emma). (Hübbe 1902)

HALM, FRIEDRICH [pseudonym of Baron Eligius Franz Joseph Münch von Bellinghausen] (b. Krakow, 2 April 1806; d. Vienna, 22 May 1871). Austrian civil servant (in 1867 he was appointed director of the court library as well as general manager of the two court theaters); dramatist and poet. Brahms set poems by him in the following songs: "Steig auf, geliebter Schatten" (op. 94/2), "Kein Haus, keine Heimat" (op. 94/5), "Bei dir sind meine Gedanken," "Beim Abschied," and "Der Jäger" (op. 95/2–4). He also set Halm's poem "Winternacht" but discarded the song (M. McCorkle 1984, Anhang IIa/28) after **Elisabeth von Herzogenberg**

had expressed the opinion that the text "does not merit being set to music by you" (Brahms 1974/2, 65). (Brahms 1974/2; Eke 1989)

HANDEL, GEORGE FRIDERIC [Händel, Georg Friedrich] (b. Halle, 23 February 1685; d. London, 14 April 1759). Composer. Brahms may have attained his thorough acquaintance with Handel's works somewhat later than his profound knowledge of **Bach**'s, yet he eventually formed an equally great admiration for them. "In any proper choral concert there ought without question to be a composition by Bach or Handel," he once remarked to **Prince Reuss-Kostritz, Heinrich XXIV** (Kalbeck 1976, vol. 4, 89, n. 1). It is characteristic of his high regard for Handel that he should have opened his very first concert as artistic director of the Gesellschaft der Musikfreunde, on 10 November 1872, with the "Dettingen" *Te Deum*. In addition, during his first two seasons as the orchestra's conductor, he offered Viennese music lovers Handel's organ concerto op. 7/4 (8 December 1872) and three of his oratorios, *Saul* (28 February 1873, the first Viennese performance of that work), *Alexander's Feast* (9 November 1873), and *Solomon* (31 March 1874), with a chorus from the last-named work being repeated at another concert on 19 April 1874. To **Robert Kahn** he once expressed his very great admiration for *Israel in Egypt*, and on learning that Kahn did not know the work, he promptly sent him the score the following morning (Kahn 1994, 644).

In 1861 he had taken the theme for his *Handel Variations* (op. 24) from Vol. 2 of *Suites de pièces pour le clavecin* (London, J. Walsh, 1733), and he was still deriving enjoyment from that collection at the end of his life, for when **Max Kalbeck** called on him on 13 February 1897, he found him playing some of the items. Furthermore, he took a keen interest in the progress of **Friedrich Chrysander**'s collected edition of Handel's works, to which he subscribed from the outset, and he even contributed to it, devising the basso continuo for seven duets and two trios (M. McCorkle 1984, Anhang Ia/10), which appeared in Vol. 32 in 1870, and for six more duets (Anhang Ia/11) included in the second edition in 1880.

The extent to which Handel's music may have influenced Brahms's own compositions, especially the choral ones, has been examined by several writers, with varying conclusions. It has also been noted that on more than one occasion a major work by Brahms was juxtaposed at a concert with one by Handel, presumably with his approval. Thus, at Cologne, on 24 May 1874, the *Triumphlied* (which he conducted himself) was preceded by *Samson* (conducted by **Ferdinand Hiller**), and in Vienna, on 2 November 1879, the Requiem (conducted by himself) was preceded by the Overture to *Athalia*. At the world premiere at Bremen on 10 April 1868 of the Requiem (less the as yet unwritten fifth movement), the concert concluded with the aria "Ich weiss, dass mein Erlöser lebt" (sung by **Amalie Joachim**) and the Hallelujah Chorus, both from *Messiah*. (I. Fellinger 1989; Kahn 1994; Siegmund-Schultze 1983)

HANSLICK, EDUARD (b. Prague, 11 September 1825; d. Baden, near Vienna, 6 August 1904). Music critic, aesthetician, musicologist, and Austrian civil servant. He received his first musical instruction from his father Joseph-Adolph (1786–1859), and from 1843 studied piano, theory, and composition with Václav Jan Křtitel Tomášek. In 1844 he embarked on legal studies, which he later completed in Vienna, where he had settled in 1846. After qualifying in 1849, he entered the civil service; from 1850 to 1852 he was employed as a treasury official at Klagenfurt and, following his return to Vienna, worked first at the Ministry of Finance, and subsequently at the Ministry of Education and Cultural Affairs.

He also quickly made a name for himself as a music critic, writing in turn for the *Wiener Musikzeitung* (from 1846), *Wiener Zeitung* (from 1848/49), *Presse* (1855–64), and ultimately for the *Neue freie Presse* (which he joined upon its foundation in 1864). In addition, he attracted considerable attention with a short treatise on aesthetic aspects of music, *Vom Musikalisch-Schönen*, which appeared in 1854 and went through 10 editions before the end of the century, as well as being translated into several foreign languages. Brahms initially considered the treatise to contain so many "silly" statements that he put it down without finishing it (see his letter to **Clara Schumann** of 15 January 1856 [Litzmann 1970, vol. 1, 168]), but many years afterward, on the occasion of a later edition, he sent a flattering note about it to the author.) The University of Vienna, where Hanslick had been studying musicology, accepted the treatise as his "Habilitationsschrift," thereby authorizing him to give lectures there, which he started to do in October 1856. In 1861 he was appointed to the salaried position of a university lecturer "in the history and aesthetics of music" and retired from the civil service, but he maintained his links with the Ministry of Education, which consulted him on various musical matters. When a commission was established in 1863 charged with making recommendations for the award of scholarships to promising young poets, artists, and composers, he was named chairman of the music section (*see* DVOŘÁK, ANTONÍN [LEOPOLD]). In addition to his university lectures, which continued for more than three decades until 1894, in the early years of his academic career, he also presented three popular series of public lectures at other locations in Vienna, of which the first one, in 1858, discussed "The History of Music from Its Beginnings to **Beethoven**," the second

"The History of Music from Beethoven to Modern Times," and the third "The History of Opera." The opening talk of the second series, on 21 February 1863, was devoted to Beethoven, with Brahms providing the illustrations—in *Aus meinem Leben* Hanslick states that Brahms played the *32 Variations in C Minor* on that occasion, whereas, according to **Max Kalbeck**, he performed the Piano Sonata op. 111).

Hanslick had briefly met Brahms at the 33rd Lower Rhine Music Festival at Düsseldorf in 1855; in his autobiography *Aus meinem Leben* he was to recall that "with his long blond hair, his forget-me-not eyes, and a complexion like milk and blood" the young Brahms "resembled one of the ideal youths portrayed by Jean Paul" (Hanslick 1894, vol. 1, 261). They quickly established friendly relations after Brahms arrived in Vienna in 1862 and by the following year were on "Du" terms. Hanslick soon became a great, though not blindly uncritical, supporter of Brahms's music, and the generally warm approbation he expressed in his various articles in the daily newspaper *Die Presse* undoubtedly helped to smooth Brahms's path in Vienna in those early days. Thus, in his review (3 December 1862) of Brahms's concert of 29 November, he particularly praised the *Handel Variations* and expressed admiration for Brahms's pianistic skills; on 10 December, writing about the performance of the Serenade op. 16 by **Johann von Herbeck** (on 7 December), he singled out the first minuet as "the jewel of the entire work, and perhaps the most attractive piece of music Brahms has so far composed"; on 8 January 1863 he placed the Andante of the Piano Sonata op. 5, which Brahms had played at his concert of 6 January, "among the most deeply-felt pieces existing in modern piano music," and in the same article he also expressed the hope that "Brahms is not yet thinking of bidding farewell to Vienna, where, as an artist and a man, he has made so many and such good friends"; and on 29 December 1863 he praised the Sextet op. 18, performed at **Joseph Hellmesberger**'s concert two days before, as not only one of the best of Brahms's compositions but also as "one of the most beautiful produced by recent chamber music." (Kalbeck mistakenly describes this last concert as having taken place on 27 December 1862.) When Brahms became conductor of the Singakademie, Hanslick hailed the appointment enthusiastically. Brahms later dedicated to him the Waltzes op. 39, both the version for piano duet (1866) and the one for solo piano (1867).

Hanslick remained Brahms's champion throughout his life, even though he did not feel equally enthusiastic about all his works, a fact of which Brahms was well aware and which he accepted with good grace (Hanslick notably had no great admiration for the First and Third Symphonies, the Piano Trio op. 8, and the Piano Quintet). Overall, though, Hanslick considered

Brahms to be not merely the outstanding contemporary composer, but also one of the greatest composers of all time—"Ought the blond Johannes not to be counted among the benefactors of mankind?" he asked in one of his articles (*Neue freie Presse*, 5 December 1883). It should be added that, unlike Brahms, he derived very limited enjoyment from pre-Mozartian music. "I would gladly give the whole of **Handel** (and **Gluck** on top of it) for Brahms's symphonies—and even more readily for Brahms's chamber music, which I prefer to the symphonies," he wrote to **Hans von Bülow** in 1891 (M. von Bülow 1895, vol. 8, 329). To **Theodor Billroth** he once remarked: "I would sooner see the whole of Heinrich Schütz go up in flames than the 'German Requiem,' sooner the works of Palestrina that those of Mendelssohn, and sooner all the concertos and sonatas of **Bach** than the quartets of **Robert Schumann** and Brahms"; and later in the same conversation (as he himself reported in *Aus meinem Leben*), he told Billroth: "From a historical point of view, our modern music begins for me with Bach and Handel. In my heart, it begins only with **Mozart**, and reaches its peak in Beethoven, Schumann, and Brahms" (Hanslick 1894, 304, 307). Hanslick disliked **Liszt**'s compositions, cared little for **Anton Bruckner**'s, and, though in his youth he had written an enthusiastic article about *Tannhäuser* (in the *Wiener allgemeine Musik-Zeitung* in November-December 1846), he detested most of **Richard Wagner**'s later music.

Brahms was personally very fond of Hanslick. In 1887 they even planned to travel to Italy together but eventually made different arrangements. Writing to **Baroness Helene Heldburg** (*see* GEORG II, DUKE OF SACHSEN-MEININGEN) in January 1895 concerning a possible visit by him and Hanslick to Meiningen that autumn, he praised his friend's good and amiable character and his still vigorous enthusiasm for all things attractive and beautiful, and he assured the baroness that she would like him very much indeed (Brahms 1991, 135; in the end, however, ill health prevented Hanslick from accompanying Brahms on the trip). To Clara Schumann Brahms wrote that August, in connection with Hanslick's approaching 70th birthday, "I know few persons for whom I feel as deep affection as I do for him. To be so naturally good, well-intentioned, honest, truly modest, and everything else I know him to be, seems to me very fine and very rare" (Litzmann 1970, vol. 2, 596). Brahms had a further opportunity to proclaim his warm feelings for Hanslick at a birthday luncheon at **Viktor von Miller zu Aichholz**'s house at Gmunden on 11 September of the same year. Greatly moved, he paid tribute, in a short speech, to Hanslick's fine personal and intellectual qualities, and declared that while they by no means saw eye to eye on all matters and their interests diverged considerably, he had rarely known a more discerning or excellent man. According to **Richard Heuberger** (1976), who was among the guests, "the two men wept as they kissed each other" (86).

Hanslick's numerous publications, in newspapers and in book form, provide an invaluable record of the musical life of the period, particularly in Vienna. (Adler 1906; Brahms 1991; Floros 1988; Gay 1978; Hanslick 1869, 1886, 1894, 1897, 1897, 1899, 1900; Heuberger 1976; Karnes 2004; Khittl 1992; Litzmann 1970; Rienäcker 1997)

HARTMANN, MATHILDE (b. Düsseldorf, 13 June 1817; d. Düsseldorf, 3 November 1902). Soprano; friend of the Schumanns, godmother of their son Felix. On 27 August 1854, Brahms wrote from Düsseldorf to **Clara Schumann**, who was then staying at Ostend: "I have called on Fräulein Hartmann twice. The second time she sang for me some Lieder by [Julius] Schäffer and myself. . . . She sang my songs very beautifully, with warmth and great expression, I was quite surprised" (Litzmann 1970, vol. 1, 19). Hartmann would, in fact, be one of the first singers to perform his songs in public—for instance, at a concert at Elberfeld on 18 October 1855, at which Clara Schumann and **Joseph Joachim** played **Beethoven**'s Violin Sonata in A Major (op. 47)—and she herself sang Lieder by Clara and **Robert Schumann**, as well as by Brahms. (Litzmann 1970)

HAUPTMANN, MORITZ (b. Dresden, 13 October 1792; d. Leipzig, 3 January 1868). Composer, violinist, theorist, and teacher. He was appointed Kantor at the Thomasschule in Leipzig in 1842 and the following year became professor of theory at the newly established conservatory in that city. In 1850 he was a cofounder of the Bach Gesellschaft, and he subsequently edited three volumes of the edition of **Bach**'s works issued by that society. His study of Bach's use of the fugue (*Erläuterungen zu Bachs Kunst der Fuge*), first published at Leipzig in 1841, became an essential textbook for anyone interested in the fugue, as Brahms was, and it is therefore not surprising that a copy of it was found in his personal library. Hauptmann's other theoretical writings also gained very wide respect.

It is not known whether Brahms met Hauptmann during his two visits to Leipzig in late 1853. However, he had probably already made Hauptmann's acquaintance earlier that year at Göttingen. In his *Personal Recollections of Johannes Brahms*, **Sir George Henschel** (1978) reproduces a diary entry he made on 13 July 1876, while staying with Brahms on the island of Rügen. In the course of a conversation about a recently published edition of Hauptmann's letters to Louis Spohr and others (i.e., Hiller 1876), which Henschel had brought with him, Brahms pointed to one describing Hauptmann's encounter with a rather haughty young composer whose name was replaced in the edition by asterisks. He himself, Brahms told Henschel, was the person in question; for as a young man he had played his Sonata in C (op. 1) for Hauptmann at Göttingen. Hauptmann had expressed considerable criticism of the composition, which, Brahms said, he had out of modesty listened to in total silence; but afterward he had heard that his silence had been interpreted as arrogance by Hauptmann. (Henschel 1978, 40; Brahms appears to be referring to a passage in Hauptmann's letter to Spohr of 27 March 1855.) The meeting at Göttingen had presumably taken place while Brahms was staying there with **Joseph Joachim** from July–August 1853.

Early in 1859 Brahms, whose interest in choral works, particularly Bach's, had been greatly stimulated by his musical activities at Detmold, wrote to ask Hauptmann's advice on certain aspects of the performance of Bach's cantatas and oratorios. In his reply, dated 15 February 1859, Hauptmann set out his views in great detail in a very long and interesting letter (which was published by Erwin R. Jacobi [1969] in the *Bach-Jahrbuch* of 1969). (Forner 1972; G. Henschel 1978; Hiller 1876; Jacobi 1969)

HAUSMANN, ROBERT (b. Rottleberode, Lower Harz, 13 August 1852; d. Vienna, 18 January 1909). Cellist. He studied with Theodor Müller (a member of the original Müller Quartet) in Braunschweig and, from 1869, with Theodor's nephew Wilhelm Müller at the Hochschule für Musik in Berlin; in 1871 he went to London to receive instruction from Alfredo Piatti, and subsequently returned to Berlin to pursue his studies there. From 1872 to 1876 he was a member of a quartet that performed for three months each year at Count Hochberg's estate in Silesia. In 1879 he succeeded Wilhelm Müller as cellist of the Joachim Quartet, and he retained that position until **Joseph Joachim**'s death in 1907. He was also on the faculty of the Hochschule für Musik in Berlin.

Hausmann had a distinguished career, both as a soloist and in chamber music. Moreover, he was blessed with a winning personality that made him many friends—he was, for instance, on very cordial terms with the **Herzogenberg**s and had particularly close relations with **Richard and Maria Fellinger**, whom he no doubt knew in Berlin before meeting them again in Vienna, where he repeatedly stayed with them. **Max Kalbeck** (1976) wrote of him in his Brahms biography: "Whoever saw him was bound to trust him unconditionally, and whoever heard him play fell completely under his spell." (vol. 4, 32).

Today Hausmann is remembered primarily for his association with Brahms. When first introduced to Brahms in 1872, his reaction was somewhat mixed: "I greatly prefer the music to the man," he reported to his mother (Hausmann 1987, 23). But in the 1880s he came to know and presumably like Brahms much better, while his admiration for Brahms's compositions only increased with the years. He became one of the foremost interpreters of Brahms's music, and they performed together on various occasions; more importantly, Hausmann's playing inspired Brahms to compose at least two major works, the Cello Sonata op. 99 and the Double Concerto. It would be pointless to trace in full detail the story of their meetings and musical association, but a few events may be mentioned here. **Hermine Spies** describes in her diary a musical evening at **Rudolf von Beckerath**'s at Wiesbaden on 4 September 1883 at which Brahms and Hausmann were present. Among the works performed, she records, was "Brahms's Trio"—probably the Piano Trio in B Minor (op. 8, then still in its original version). The following year Hausmann visited Brahms at Mürzzuschlag, where, according to Kalbeck, he asked Brahms to write a new work for the cello. It was at that time that Brahms wrote to **Eduard Hanslick**: "If Herr Robert Hausmann from Berlin should pay you a visit in the near future, do receive him. You will derive pleasure from the young man in every respect, even without his excellent cello [playing]" (Hanslick 1897b, *Neue freie Presse*, 1 July 1897, 4).

Brahms did not immediately act upon Hausmann's request, and at his Viennese debut on 7 March 1885 Hausmann played, with considerable success, the cello sonata Brahms had written in 1862–65 (op. 38). But during his holiday at Thun in 1886 Brahms did write a new sonata for the cello (op. 99), and on 24 November of that year he and Hausmann gave its first performance at the Kleiner Musikvereinssaal in Vienna; from Brahms's correspondence with **Theodor Billroth**, it seems likely that they had already played it at the latter's musical soiree the previous day. Furthermore, while again staying at Thun the following year, Brahms composed the Double Concerto for violin and cello, with Joachim and Hausmann in mind; and following rehearsals at Baden-Baden in September, he conducted the first public performance of the work, with those two soloists, at Cologne on 18 October. The three of them were to collaborate in several further performances of the Double Concerto, at Wiesbaden (17 November 1887), Frankfurt (18 November 1887), Basle (20 November 1887), Leipzig (1 January 1888), and Meiningen (3 January 1889). Finally, mention must be made of Hausmann's participation in the first performances, at a concert by the Joachim Quartet in Berlin on 12 December 1891, of the Clarinet Trio and the Clarinet Quintet. For the latter work **Richard Mühlfeld** joined the Joachim Quartet, while the trio was played by Mühlfeld, Brahms, and Hausmann, and they were to play the work again in Vienna on 21 January. Kalbeck (1976) suggests, incidentally, that certain songs Brahms composed in those years likewise testified to the impact that Hausmann's cello playing made on his imagination; writing about Brahms's setting of **Hermann von Lingg**'s "Immer leiser wird mein Schlummer" (op. 105/2), he comments, "Here also one sometimes seems to hear a cello in the bass" (vol. 4, 137).

Hausmann had various opportunities to meet Brahms during the annual appearances of the Joachim Quartet in Vienna from 1892 onward. The last of these in Brahms's lifetime took place in December 1896–January 1897. On that occasion Hausmann paid him a visit that was to acquire a special significance in Brahms literature (*see* DVOŘÁK, ANTONÍN [LEOPOLD]). (R. Fellinger 1997; Gottlieb-Billroth 1935; Hausmann 1987; Spies 1894)

HAYDN, (FRANZ) JOSEPH (b. Rohrau, Lower Austria, 31 March 1732; d. Vienna, 31 May 1809). Composer. Brahms's well-known admiration for Haydn's music found its most celebrated expression in the *Variations on a Theme by Haydn*, which he composed in the summer of 1873 in versions for two pianos (op. 56a) and for orchestra (op. 56b). The theme is the so-called *St. Anthony Chorale* that formed a part of Haydn's *Divertimento* (Hob. II:46); whether Haydn actually invented it, as Brahms believed, or simply orchestrated it, is uncertain. Brahms had discovered it in 1870 among the music that his friend **Carl Ferdinand Pohl** had assembled while preparing his Haydn biography. Brahms liked it so much that he promptly copied it, and at more or less the same time he also copied the Andante from Haydn's Symphony in B-flat Major (Hob. I:16).

The intense pleasure Brahms derived from Haydn's music was, however, abundantly attested long before 1870. His enthusiasm was shared, and indeed probably partially stimulated, by **Joseph Joachim**, who delighted in performing Haydn's chamber music. (On one occasion, at a private house, Joachim led performances of no fewer than five of the quartets, which was too much even for Brahms's musical stamina.) Brahms's letters to **Clara Schumann** show that he and Joachim explored many of these compositions together at Düsseldorf in June 1855. In one letter he reports their playing some of the piano trios "with huge delight," without the cello part—which, as he explains in another letter, one can readily omit, since it constantly echoes the bass of the piano part (Litzmann 1970, vol. 1, 112, 110). Another time he writes, "Do you remember a trio with a Hungarian Rondo in G? It always drives us quite wild" (evidently a reference to the Gypsy Rondo [all'ongarese] of the Trio Hob. XV:25); and, on yet another occasion, "How wonderfully beautiful and masterly these quartets are, a wealth of beautiful and original ideas, especially in the marvellous Adagios, which defies comprehension" (Litzmann 1970, vol. 1, 111, 118). Ten years later, for Christmas 1865, Joachim presented Brahms with an edition of the quartets; and some 20 years later still, Brahms bought the autograph of six quartets for his private collection. (At one public concert at least, in Danzig on 14 November 1855, Brahms and Joachim played a violin sonata by Haydn.)

Brahms's admiration for Haydn's genius never waned. In February 1896, a little over a year before his death, he extolled it to **Richard Heuberger**: "That we are living at a time when, exactly a hundred years ago, Haydn created our whole music, when he composed one symphony after another, no one ever thinks of that. . . . What a man! How puny we are compared to him!" (Heuberger 1976, 94). Brahms would no doubt have been delighted to know that a room devoted to his memory was established in 1980 in the house in which Haydn lived during the last 12 years of his life. The house (now 19 Haydngasse) also contains Vienna's Haydn Museum. (Brahms 1974/5–6; Heuberger 1976; Litzmann 1970)

HEBBEL, (CHRISTIAN) FRIEDRICH (b. Wesselburen, 18 March 1813; d. Vienna, 13 December 1863). Dramatist, short-story writer, and poet. Brahms visited Hebbel in 1862 or 1863 and came away with an autograph bearing a distich. Some years later he set texts by Hebbel in the songs "In der Gasse" and "Vorüber" (op. 58/6–7) and in the quartet "Abendlied" (op. 92/3). (Bozarth 2001; Keller 1990; Huschke 1939; Langner 1990)

HECHT, FELIX (b. Friedberg, Hessen, 27 November 1847; d. Weimar, 18 October 1909). Banker residing at Mannheim. He studied jurisprudence and political science at the universities of Giessen, Heidelberg, and Göttingen, and qualified as a university teacher in 1869, but was obliged to give up lecturing after becoming president of the newly founded Rheinische Hypothekenbank (a bank specializing in mortgages) at Mannheim in 1871. In 1886 he also assumed the position of president of the Pfälzische Hypothekenbank. He relinquished these appointments in 1901 in order to work on various legislative projects intended to regulate banking. He also wrote extensively on the latter subject.

Brahms probably made Hecht's acquaintance through **Ernst Frank**, perhaps during his visits to Mannheim in the summer of 1875. For the past two years Hecht had been sharing accommodations with Frank (according to Leopold Schmidt, the editor of Brahms's letters to Hecht). Later that year Hecht married Helene Bamberger (1854–1940), and thereafter Brahms used to stay with them whenever he came to Mannheim. In 1891 Hecht was in Vienna, and two years later the couple visited Brahms during a journey to Asia Minor and Greece. Their description of the trip, which includes an account of their meeting with Brahms, was subsequently printed under Helene's name. Twenty, mainly short, letters dating from the years 1884–97, addressed by Brahms to either the husband or the wife, were published in 1910. Their tone is pleasant, but their content is of no particular interest to Brahms biographers.

Hecht died suddenly while on a journey to Berlin; his wife died at the age of 86, while being transported to a concentration camp at Gurs, near Pau. (Brahms 1974/7)

HEERMANN, HUGO (b. Heilbronn, 3 March 1844; d. Merano, 6 November 1935). Violinist and teacher. He studied at the Brussels Conservatory under J. Meerts and lived for a time in Paris. Later he made the acquaintance of **Clara Schumann**, with whom he played much chamber music at Baden-Baden and through whom he met Brahms in 1863. He was appointed Konzertmeister of the Museum Concerts Orchestra in Frankfurt am Main in 1865, and he also succeeded **Ludwig Straus** (who had moved to England in 1864) as leader of the Frankfurt String Quartet, which became known as the Heermann Quartet and from 1870 performed under the auspices of the Museum Society. In 1878 he was appointed a professor at the new Hoch Conservatory, where he was Clara Schumann's colleague; he remained on its faculty until 1904, when he established his own violin school. It was also in 1904 that he first concertized in America, where he was to settle for several years (first in Chicago, and then in Cincinnati) after leaving Frankfurt in 1907. On his return to Europe, he lived briefly in Berlin before taking up permanent residence in Geneva in 1911; he retired from concertizing in 1922.

The chamber music concerts given by Heermann and his quartet offered the Frankfurt public numerous performances (some of them Frankfurt premieres) of Brahms's chamber music, occasionally with the participation of Brahms himself. Thus, between 1873 and 1885 the concerts featured performances of the Piano Trio op. 87, Piano Quartets opp. 25–26 and 60, Piano Quintet op. 34, Horn Trio op. 40, String Quartets opp. 51/1–2 and 67, String Quintet op. 88, String Sextets opp. 18 and 36, Violin Sonata op. 78 (played by Clara Schumann and **Joseph Joachim** on 20 December 1880), and Cello Sonata op. 38. (At a concert on 16 March 1884, Brahms played in the Piano Quartet op. 60 and also, with Lazaro Uzielli, accompanied **Marie Fillunger**, Fides Keller, Raimund von Zur Mühlen, and **Julius Stockhausen** in the *Liebeslieder-Walzer* op. 52). At later concerts of Heermann's Quartet, Clara Schumann played the Piano Trio op. 101 with Heermann and Valentin Müller in October 1887, and the Violin Sonata op. 100 with Heermann in April 1888, whilst Brahms played the Violin Sonata op. 108 with Heermann on 11 January 1889, and on 23 March 1890 took part in a performance with Heermann and **Hugo Becker** of the revised Piano Trio op. 8 (at the same concert, he accompanied the *Zigeunerlieder* op. 103 sung by Fillunger, Keller, Robert Kaufmann, and Stockhausen). (*See also* SPEYER, EDWARD.)

Brahms had good reason therefore to be grateful for Heermann's support for his music. Moreover, Heermann occasionally performed Brahms's compositions with his quartet also outside Frankfurt. Thus the quartet (or, at any rate, Heermann and two other members) traveled to Wiesbaden in February 1876 to perform the Piano Quartet op. 60 with Brahms at the house of the princess of Hessen-Barchfeld; and on 14 February 1895 the quartet played the Clarinet Quintet with **Richard Mühlfeld**, in Brahms's presence, at Mannheim.

Heermann also frequently joined Clara Schumann in music making at her house in Frankfurt. "He always readily accepts when I invite him to come and play, is never too tired or weary, and always willing to rehearse," she wrote appreciatively in her diary on 18 May 1888 (Litzmann 1902, vol. 3, 502). In a letter to **Hermann Levi** in April 1879 she mentions having played Brahms's Violin Concerto with Heermann several times (Litzmann 1902, vol. 3, 400); Brahms had sent her a manuscript copy of the piano reduction of the orchestral score. It was Joachim who gave the first public performance of the concerto in Frankfurt on 5 December 1879 (and another one there on 19 October 1883); but later Heermann also played it at Museum concerts, for the first time on 20 February 1885. He also played it in Vienna, for the first time at a philharmonic concert on 12 March 1882, then later at a Gesellschaft der Musikfreunde concert on 9 February 1896, and again with the Berlin Philharmonic Orchestra under **Arthur Nikisch** on 8 April 1897, a few days after Brahms's death. Furthermore, he states with evident pride in his memoirs (*Lebenserinnerungen*) that he was the first violinist to perform the concerto in Paris and in Holland, and he also played it with different American orchestras.

It is evident from his memoirs that he had the greatest admiration for Brahms, both as a musician and as a person. On at least one occasion, in February 1876, Brahms stayed with the Heermanns while in Frankfurt. It was also apparently Heermann who found Brahms rooms at **Clara Becker**'s house at Baden-Baden, and it was he who introduced him to **Henriette Fritsch-Estrangin** in Frankfurt.

Brahms no doubt knew Heermann's sister Helene (b. 1845), who was a harpist. She performed at a concert at Baden-Baden on 29 August 1872, at which Brahms played **Robert Schumann**'s Piano Concerto and conducted his Serenade op. 16. (Bary 1937; Baser 1973; Heermann 1935; Litzmann 1970)

HEGAR, EMIL (b. Basle, 3 January 1843; d. Basle, 13 June 1921). Cellist; brother of **Friedrich Hegar**. After studying at the Leipzig conservatory, he was active as a cellist, including as a member of a string quartet, in Hamburg (1863–66), and subsequently became principal cellist of the Gewandhaus Orchestra at Leipzig (1866–75). When a hand ailment forced him to give up his career as a cellist, he took singing lessons with **Julius Stockhausen** and from 1876 lived at Basle, where he sang at concerts and taught at the conservatory. His daughter Valerie (1873–1953) and son Peter (1882–1946) also became singers.

He gave the first public performance, with **Carl Reinecke**, of Brahms's Cello Sonata op. 38 at Leipzig on 14 January 1871. (*See also* HEGAR, FRIEDRICH.)

HEGAR, FRIEDRICH (b. Basle, 11 October 1841; d. Zurich, 2 June 1927). Violinist, conductor, and composer; member of a family of musicians. Son of Ernst Friedrich Hegar (1816–88), a music teacher, engraver, and owner of a music shop at Basle; brother of **Emil Hegar**. Friedrich studied with **Moritz Hauptmann**, **Julius Rietz**, and **Ferdinand David** at the Leipzig conservatory. In 1860 he accepted the position of Konzertmeister in Warsaw, and the following year a similar one under **Julius Stockhausen** at Gebweiler in Alsace. From 1863 he was active in Zurich where, over the next 50 years, he was to occupy various important posts and exercise a dominant influence on local musical life. He served as Konzertmeister of the Zurich orchestra (1862–65); conductor of the mixed choir (1865–1901), of the symphony concerts of the Allgemeine Musikgesellschaft (1865–1906), and of the male choir "Harmonie" (1875–78); and director of the conservatory (1876–1914). He also led a string quartet for many years. His compositions include a violin concerto, a cello concerto, some chamber music, and numerous works for male, female, and mixed choirs. His oratorio *Manasse* (text by **Joseph Viktor Widmann**) was frequently performed in his lifetime.

In his book *Johannes Brahms und Zürich*, Hans Erismann (1974) states that Hegar first met Brahms at **Jakob Melchior Rieter-Biedermann**'s house at Winterthur in 1864, but as Brahms is not otherwise known to have visited Switzerland that year, this information may be incorrect. On the other hand, Hegar certainly made Brahms's acquaintance not later than 1865, for on 17 June of that year he took part at Basle with his brother Emil and Louis Abel in a performance of the Piano Quartet op. 25, with Brahms himself playing the piano part, on his first concert appearance in Switzerland. At the same concert **Theodor Furchtegott Kirchner**, Friedrich Hegar, Emil Hegar, and Abel performed the Adagio from Brahms's Piano

Quartet op. 26. Later that same year Friedrich Hegar renewed his musical association with Brahms at Zurich, where Brahms took part in another performance of the Piano Quartet op. 25 (on 25 November), as well as in the first performance anywhere of the Horn Trio op. 40 on 28 November.

The next year, 1866, was of crucial importance to the budding friendship between Brahms and Friedrich Hegar, for during the several months that Brahms spent in Switzerland, first at Winterthur and then, from early June, at Fluntern just outside Zurich, he saw a good deal of Hegar. From Fluntern he came into the town most days, and there was regular music making at Theodor Kirchner's in the afternoons and at **Theodor Billroth**'s in the evenings. Often, reluctant to set out on his lengthy walk to his room on the Zurichberg late at night, Brahms would sleep on a sofa in Hegar's flat. Still further opportunities to meet and make music with Hegar occurred that autumn when Brahms undertook a concert tour of Switzerland with **Joseph Joachim**. The friendship cemented that year endured until the end of Brahms's life; he even became the godfather of Hegar's son Johannes (1874–1929), who was to have a successful career as a cellist and teacher. Hegar's wife Albertine (née Volkart) was a singer; with Ida Suter-Weber she gave the first documented public performance of the duet "Die Boten der Liebe" (op. 61/4) at Zurich on 19 December 1876; she also was the first to sing the song "Erinnerung" (op. 63, no. 2) in public, at Zurich on 6 May 1877.

The following are a few highlights of Brahms's later personal and professional association with Hegar: on 17 September 1868, at the request of Brahms who was visiting Zurich with his father, Hegar arranged and conducted a private performance of the fifth movement of the Requiem, composed earlier that year; during the summer of 1886, which he spent near Thun, Brahms, while visiting Joseph Viktor Widmann at his house at Berne, played his newly composed Violin Sonata op. 100 there with Hegar, and his new Piano Trio op. 101 with Hegar and his brother Julius (1847–1917); in 1893 Hegar invited Brahms to celebrate his 60th birthday with some special musical performances in Zurich, but Brahms, as ever averse to such sentimental suggestions, proposed instead a trip to Sicily, on which, in due course, he set out with Hegar, **Robert Freund**, and Widmann in April (he had originally intended to travel there with Hegar and Widmann in 1891, but the journey had been postponed following the death of Albertine Hegar in February 1891); on the occasion of the inauguration of the new concert hall in Zurich in October 1895, Brahms stayed with Hegar, as did Widmann (this was the last meeting between Brahms and his two closest Swiss friends). Lastly, Hegar published his own arrangements for three women's voices of the song "Trennung" (op. 97/6) and of 12 folk songs from WoO 33, as well as arrangements for a capella male chorus of 24 items from the latter set.

At a Brahms memorial concert at the Tonhalle in Zurich on 13 June 1897, Hegar conducted the Requiem. Later he served on the international committee promoting the construction of a Brahms statue in Vienna. In recognition of his devotion to Brahms, a group of his Zurich admirers presented him on his 60th birthday in 1901 with the autograph score of the Fourth Symphony. It is now in the possession of the Allgemeine Musikgesellschaft, Zurich. (Brahms 1958; Erismann 1974; K. Hofmann 1999; Steiner 1928; Zimmermann 1983)

HEIMSOETH, FRIEDRICH (b. Cologne, 11 February 1814; d. Bonn, 16 October 1877). Academic; chorus master. A professor of classical philology at Bonn University, for over 30 years he played an active and influential role in the musical life of the town; among other activities, he founded a choir in the 1840s with which he performed ecclesiastical music, initially only during Holy Week, later also at evening services in certain Bonn churches. He served on the organizing committee of the **Beethoven** Festival in 1845, on which occasion he engaged in a public polemic about the proposed program against its president Heinrich Karl Breidenstein, who was director of music at the university and thus his colleague. Given his prominence in musical and academic circles (in 1869–70 he was rector of the university), it is not surprising that he was invited to serve on the committee that was set up in 1872 to prepare the Schumann Festival planned to take place on 17–19 August of the following year for the purpose of raising funds for a memorial at **Robert Schumann**'s grave; the musical direction of the festival was entrusted jointly to **Wilhelm von Wasielewski**, the director of music and conductor of the Gesangverein at Bonn, and to **Joseph Joachim**.

While Brahms was not consulted regarding the music chosen for the festival, it appears to have been assumed from the outset that his name would figure on the opening day's program; the question debated by the committee, and even discussed by Heimsoeth with **Clara Schumann** when they met at Cologne in October 1872, was whether Brahms should be represented by his Requiem or perhaps by a new work specially composed for the occasion; Heimsoeth strongly favored the second option, and Clara Schumann was quite willing to accept it. The discussion dragged on rather haphazardly for several months and was to produce some strain in Brahms's relations with Clara Schumann and Joachim, partly as a result of the course pursued by the committee, which failed to treat him with proper honesty and tactfulness, but also partly because of his own somewhat sibylline pronouncements that sowed uncertainty in his correspondents' minds about his true feelings in the matter; it may even be that his own attitude shifted uneasily in the process. He was first told of the committee's preference for a new composition by Clara Schumann when she was in Vienna for concerts in late 1872 (he had previously been given to understand by Joachim that the intention was to perform the Requiem). On 10 December Clara informed Heimsoeth that Brahms might be prepared to comply with the request, provided a suitable text could be found, and she suggested that Heimsoeth ought now to contact Brahms directly, which he did shortly afterward. After a certain delay, Brahms replied early in 1873, declining the invitation, mainly on the grounds that he knew of no adequate text and did not expect to discover one, but at the same time leaving it unclear whether he would really be willing to compose such a work if a suitable text could, after all, be found, or even if he considered it at all appropriate for any music other than Schumann's to be performed at the festival. He heard no more from Heimsoeth (or from any other member of the committee), which aggrieved him; but the correspondence with Joachim during the next few months contained various references by both to the forthcoming performance of the Requiem (Joachim was planning to conduct it, as well as Schumann's Second Symphony, on the first day of the festival). In June, however, Brahms read in a newspaper to his surprise that the Requiem was no longer on the program. When challenged, Joachim explained that the decision had been his own, his explicitly stated reason being that he deemed the time allotted to him for rehearsals insufficient to guarantee a satisfactory performance of the work; but he conceded that there had been a further reason, namely that certain remarks made by Brahms had left him in some doubt as to whether he really cared to have the Requiem performed on this occasion and, more specifically, whether he really wanted it to be conducted by Joachim. In the event, the opening concert, like the subsequent ones, featured an all-Schumann program (the Fourth Symphony, conducted by Joachim, and *Das Paradies und die Peri*, conducted by Wasielewski). Brahms duly attended the Festival; by then the strains that had recently affected his friendship with Joachim and Clara Schumann had been smoothed over.

This is the only known instance of any contacts by Brahms with Heimsoeth, and the letters mentioned above are the only ones known to have been exchanged by them. It is accordingly uncertain whether, for instance, he had seen anything of Heimsoeth during his lengthy stay at Bonn in the summer of 1868; nor are there any pointers as to when Heimsoeth may have presented him with the photograph of his wife and himself that was found among Brahms's belongings after his death, and which has been reproduced in *Johannes Brahms und Bonn* (see Gutiérrez-Denhoff 1997a).

Finally, to describe Heimsoeth as **Hermann Deiters**'s father-in-law, as Styra Avins (1997) does in her *Johannes Brahms: Life and Letters*, is somewhat misleading: in fact, it was not until 1886, nine years after Heimsoeth's death, that Deiters took Heimsoeth's daughter Sibylle for his second wife, his first having died in 1884. (Brahms 1974/3, 1974/5–6; Gutiérrez-Denhoff 1997a; Kahl 1960b)

HEINE, HEINRICH [Harry] (b. Düsseldorf, 13 December 1797; d. Paris, 17 February 1856). Poet and journalist. Brahms set Heine poems in the following songs: "Es liebt sich so lieblich im Lenze!" (op. 71/1), "Sommerabend" and "Mondenschein" (op. 85/1–2), "Der Tod, das ist die kühle Nacht," "Es schauen die Blumen," and "Meerfahrt" (op. 96/1, 3–4). Brahms also set another poem by Heine, "Wie der Mond sich leuchtend dränget," but appears to have discarded the song (M. McCorkle 1984, Anhang IIa/27) when it failed to please **Elisabeth von Herzogenberg**. (Brahms 1974/2)

HELDBURG, HELENE, BARONESS: *see* GEORG II, DUKE OF SACHSEN-MEININGEN.

HELLMESBERGER, JOSEPH (b. Vienna, 3 November 1828; d. Vienna, 24 October 1893). Violinist, conductor, and teacher. Son of violin virtuoso and conductor Georg Hellmesberger (1800–73), who was a professor at the Vienna Conservatory, Konzertmeister at the court opera, and a cofounder and conductor of the concerts of the Gesellschaft der Musikfreunde. Joseph's brother Georg (1830–52) was **Joseph Joachim**'s predecessor in the post of Konzertmeister at the Hanoverian court (in his rather short life, he composed some 100 musical works, including eight operas).

Joseph Hellmesberger had an even more brilliant career than his father. He was conductor of the Gesellschaft der Musikfreunde concerts, professor and director of the conservatory, Konzertmeister at the court opera from 1860, and court Kapellmeister from 1877; but perhaps his greatest achievement was the formation of the Hellmesberger String Quartet, which he founded in 1849 and led until 1891. The other original members were violinist Matthias Durst, the violist Karl Heissler, and cellist Karl Schlesinger; by 1870 the second violin desk was occupied by Hellmesberger's second son, likewise called Joseph (1855–1907). For over 40 years, the quartet made a major contribution to Viennese musical life. In particular, it was instrumental in fostering recognition of the excellence of **Beethoven**'s late quartets and in familiarizing Viennese music lovers with **Franz Schubert**'s chamber music, several compositions receiving their first public performances. Hellmesberger was much admired as a violinist. **Max Kalbeck** (1976) wrote of him, "His playing had the hot breath and the agitated pulse of human passion, his violin the ethereal tone of an angel's voice" (vol. 2, 19).

The importance of the support that Hellmesberger gave Brahms, at the very outset of his stay in Vienna, cannot be exaggerated. Having taken part, together with Brahms himself, in private performances of the two Piano Quartets opp. 25–26 at **Julius Epstein**'s in October 1862, he was so delighted with the music that he hailed the 29-year-old composer as "Beethoven's heir" (Kalbeck 1976, vol. 2, 19; in later years, according to Kalbeck, when his enthusiasm for Brahms had somewhat waned, he attributed his very enthusiastic reaction on that occasion to an excessive consumption of Epstein's Croatian wine.) The profound impression that the two compositions made on him led him to place the Quartet op. 25 on the program of the quartet's opening concert of the 1862–63 season on 16 November, when the executants, in addition to Brahms and Hellmesberger, were violist Franz Dobyhal and cellist Heinrich Röver; the same people played the Quartet op. 26 at Brahms's own first Viennese concert on 29 November, in what is the earliest known public performance of that work. Furthermore, Brahms and Hellmesberger performed together at a concert given by **Adele Passy-Cornet** on 20 December, playing **Bach**'s Violin Sonata in E Major (BWV 1016)—wrongly identified in the printed program as "Beethoven's Sonata in E Major" (Beethoven never, in fact, wrote a violin sonata in that key).

Altogether, between 1862 and 1880 Brahms appeared as pianist at nine subscription concerts of the Hellmesberger Quartet, which also presented some of his other chamber music, such as the String Sextet op. 18 at its concert of 27 December 1863. Apart from the already mentioned rendition of the Piano Quartet op. 26 on 29 November 1862, Hellmesberger was involved in the first public performances of the following works by Brahms: the String Quartet op. 51/1 on 11 December 1873; the Piano Quartet op. 60 on 18 November 1875; and the Violin Sonata op. 100 on 2 September 1886. In the two last-named performances Brahms was himself at the piano.

Thus, Brahms had every reason to feel well disposed toward Hellmesberger. Yet their relations never became really intimate, if only because the temperamental differences between the typically Viennese Hellmesberger and the characteristically North German Brahms made close association difficult. Moreover, once Brahms began to establish a certain reputation, Hellmesberger felt at times jealous of his contacts with any other chamber music ensemble, such as that of **Ferdinand Laub**. Lastly,

Brahms never really trusted Hellmesberger, but this did not affect his very great admiration for his playing. In 1892 he said to **Richard Heuberger**, "Hellmesberger is always telling lies, except when he makes music; then he cannot lie" (Heuberger 1976, 52).

On 17 December 1891, five days after presenting the very first public performance of his Clarinet Trio (op. 114) with **Richard Mühlfeld** and **Robert Hausmann** in Berlin, Brahms took part in its first Viennese performance, together with the clarinettist Adalbert Syrinek and Hellmesberger's son Ferdinand (1863–1940). (Clive 1997; Heuberger 1976; Prosl 1947)

HENSCHEL, SIR (ISIDOR) GEORGE [Georg] (b. Breslau [Wrocław], 18 February 1850; d. Aviemore, Scotland, 10 September 1934). Singer (baritone), conductor, pianist, composer, and teacher. He studied at Leipzig (1867–70) with Ignaz Moscheles (piano), **Carl Reinecke** and Ernst Friedrich Richter (theory), and Franz Goetze (singing), and later in Berlin with Adolf Schulze (singing) and Friedrich Kiel (composition). He soon made a name for himself as a singer in Germany (in May 1874 he was chosen to sing the part of Harapha in **Handel**'s *Samson* at the Lower Rhine Music Festival at Cologne); and on 19 February 1877 he made his debut in England, singing Handel and **Franz Schubert** at a Monday Popular Concert in London. On 8 March he made his first appearance at a concert of the London Philharmonic Society, singing an aria by Handel and in a duet from Méhul's *Joseph*. From 1881 until 1884 he conducted the newly founded Boston Symphony Orchestra. Subsequently he settled in Britain, eventually taking British nationality in 1890; he was knighted in 1914. He was highly popular as a singer (often accompanying himself), as well as a teacher (including, from 1886 to 1888, at the Royal College of Music); in addition, in 1886 he established the London Symphony Concerts, which he conducted for some 11 years. (His orchestra, known as the London Symphony Orchestra, should not be confused with the current orchestra bearing that name, which was not founded until 1904).

When Brahms met Henschel at the Lower Rhine Festival in May 1874, he not only appreciated his musicianship, but he was also greatly attracted by his personality. Henschel must indeed have been a delightful young man. Edith Hipkins, a witness to his considerable and instant success in London, was to recall later that he "swept all before him" and that "he burst upon us all like a great wind, with his glorious voice, his flashing eyes and his splendid vitality" (H. Henschel 1944, 14). He would retain much of his vocal excellence and his robust energy into old age: in 1931, 81 years old, he returned to Boston to conduct the opening concert of the Boston Symphony Orchestra's 50th anniversary season; and on his 84th birthday, just a few months before his death, he sang on the radio.)

Not long after hearing him perform at the 1874 festival, Brahms invited Henschel to take part in the last two concerts he was to conduct as artistic director of the Gesellschaft der Musikfreunde in Vienna: on 23 March 1875 Henschel sang the part of Christ in **Bach**'s *St. Matthew Passion*, and on 18 April 1875 he sang the title role in **Max Bruch**'s oratorio *Odysseus*. During his lengthy stay in Vienna, he regularly met Brahms, and everything points to the fact that a remarkable intimacy sprung up between the two men, notwithstanding the significant difference in their ages. In his *Recollections of Brahms*, Henschel (1978) writes about their daily walks in the Prater, and he singles out for special mention the hours they spent on 26 March, the anniversary of **Beethoven**'s death, in the very room in which he had died at the Schwarzspanierhaus, which then formed part of a flat occupied by mutual friends of theirs. The year 1876 brought several further instances of musical collaboration, as well as striking proof of Brahms's enjoyment of the younger musician's company. On 5 February Henschel sang in a performance of the *Triumphlied* that Brahms conducted at Münster, and later that same month they took part in concerts at Koblenz and Wiesbaden, as well as at a matinee at the house of the princess of Hessen-Barchfeld (on which occasion Brahms performed his Piano Quartet op. 60 with members of the Heermann Quartet and accompanied Henschel in one of the *Magelone-Lieder*, "Wie soll ich die Freude, die Wonne denn tragen" [op. 33/6]). On the last night of the short tour they shared a room at a Frankfurt hotel, and while they were there, Brahms proposed that they should spend a week or two of their summer vacation together at some quiet, remote spot. Henschel suggested the island of Rügen, and in July he joined Brahms there for 10 days (Brahms himself remained somewhat longer on the island). Excerpts of the diary Henschel kept during his stay on Rügen were published by **Max Kalbeck** in the Viennese newspaper *Neues Wiener Tagblatt* on 2 and 5 April 1897 under the heading "Neues über Brahms" and appeared in an English translation in the *Century Magazine* in 1901. The diary was later printed in its entirety in Henschel's (1978) *Recollections of Johannes Brahms*, which also contain a series of letters he had received from Brahms. Finally, the text of *Recollections*, including the diaries but omitting the letters, was reproduced in Helen Henschel's (1944) memoir of her father, *When Soft Voices Die*.

The years 1875–76 thus marked the beginning of a friendship that was to endure until Brahms's death, although opportunities for collaboration and meetings grew infrequent. However, when Brahms first presented his C Minor Symphony to a Leipzig audience on 18 January 1877, the program also included seven of his songs, in which he accompanied Henschel. Of their later meetings, Henschel (1978) in his *Recollections* describes at some length a visit he and his wife paid to Vienna in April 1894 "for the sole purpose of spending a few days in Brahms's company" (55). He was to see Brahms only once more after that, at Leipzig in January 1896.

As well as feeling profound affection for the man, Henschel also greatly admired his music, and he did his best to make it better known. Thus, he directed the first English performances of *Triumphlied* in London on 2 December 1879 (at the same concert he also conducted the First Symphony), and of the Double Concerto (with **Joseph Joachim** and **Robert Hausmann** as soloists) in London on 15 February 1888; and while in Boston, he conducted the first American performance of the *Alto Rhapsody* on 11 February 1882 (soloist: Mary H. How). Henschel dedicated his *Serbisches Liederspiel* (op. 32) to Brahms. (Geiringer 1938; G. Henschel 1978; H. Henschel 1944)

HERBECK, JOHANN VON (b. Vienna, 25 December 1831; d. Vienna, 28 October 1877). Conductor and composer. His formal training was essentially confined to the teaching he received as a choirboy at the Cistertian monastery of Heiligenkreuz and to brief periods of instruction in composition from choirmaster and composer Ludwig Rotter in 1845–46. Yet, despite being largely an autodidact in musical matters, he managed to secure, within an astonishingly short time, the most prestigious appointments available to a musician in contemporary Vienna. According to **Max Kalbeck** (1976), "he combined the talents of a field marshal with the ambition of a conqueror" and "took these posts mostly, as one would enemy positions, by storm" (vol. 2, 35). Handsome, highly intelligent, very knowledgeable, and blessed with a dynamic and charismatic personality, he became an inspiring conductor who relished controlling large orchestras and choirs ("Probably no conductor," Kalbeck observes, " has directed so many music festivals so successfully as he has" [vol. 2, 36]). In short, to quote **Carl Ferdinand Pohl** (1883), "no one could resist him" (13).

He began his musical career in 1852 as choirmaster at the Piarists' Church in Vienna. (In 1847 he had enrolled at the University of Vienna to study philosophy and law but never completed his degree.) From 1856 until 1866 he was choirmaster of the Männergesangverein, and in 1858 he was, in addition, appointed director of the Singverein, a newly formed mixed choir of the Gesellschaft der Musikfreunde. Furthermore, he was in charge of the latter society's concerts from 1859 until 1870 and would resume that function from 1875 until 1877. The list of his responsibilities does not end even there. In 1863 he became deputy Kapellmeister of the court Kapelle, and three years later succeeded Benedikt Randhartinger in the post of Kapellmeister. Lastly, he was named codirector of the opera in 1869 and its director the following year. Styra Avins (1997), in her *Johannes Brahms: Life and Letters*, mistakenly writes that he "first associated with the Court Opera in 1863" (thus confusing "Hofkapelle" with "Hofoper"), nor is she quite correct in stating that Herbeck was "dismissed" from his post of director of the opera in 1875 (786). The truth is that he was driven to resign, which he did on 5 April of that year, after disagreements with the general manager of the court theaters, Hofrat von Salzmann, and following a humiliating audience with the court chamberlain, Prince Constantin zu Hohenlohe-Schillingsfürst. (His letter of resignation is preserved in the Austrian state archive.)

Upon his appointment as director of the opera, Herbeck had relinquished his position as artistic director of the Gesellschaft der Musikfreunde; he conducted his last concert on 30 April 1870. The post was subsequently occupied by **Joseph Hellmesberger** (1870–71), by **Anton Rubinstein** (1871–72), and by Brahms (1872–75). The circumstances under which Brahms relinquished the artistic directorship in April 1875 are not altogether easy to disentangle. Asked by **Hermann Levi** for his reasons for giving up the position, he replied, "It can, to be sure, all be told in one word: Herbeck! Nothing has happened, but the prospects are not pleasant and so I prefer to leave. I don't wish either to quarrel with him or wait to be ousted by him" (Brahms 1974/7, 183). Clearly, therefore, Herbeck played a major role in Brahms's decision to seek release from his post, even though the board of directors was in fact close to appointing **Hans Richter** as Brahms's replacement, after the latter had on 3 April signed a document providing for an amicable dissolution of his contract; it was only when Herbeck suddenly became available, following his resignation from the opera on 5 April, that the board's preference swung around in his favor. Very probably, Brahms was in any case only too glad to be freed from many of the activities, notably the administrative ones, which the artistic director was expected to carry out. Significantly, at the board's meeting of 30 March, one director referred to Brahms's reluctance to "identify himself with the society's interests" [according to the minutes of the meeting preserved in the archive of the Gesellschaft der Musikfreunde in Vienna]).

In a conversation with **Richard Heuberger** in 1885, Brahms described Herbeck as an "outstanding conductor" (Heuberger 1976, 30). He had met him soon after his arrival in Vienna in 1862 and must have been gratified when Herbeck opened the concert of the Gesellschaft der Musikfreunde on 7 December with his Serenade op. 11. Five years later Herbeck, at his own suggestion, scheduled a performance of the first three movements of the Requiem (on 1 December 1867), but this earliest public performance of any part of that work, though well-enough received by most of the audience, was apparently a mediocre one. It was at another Gesellschaft der Musikfreunde concert directed by Herbeck, on 17 December 1876, that Brahms conducted the first Viennese performance of his C Minor Symphony. Herbeck had sought his permission to put the new composition on the program of one of his concerts; yet Ludwig von Herbeck revealed in his biography of his father that he was not, on the whole, greatly attracted by Brahms's music and considered the praise bestowed on it by certain critics to be excessive. Among the19th-century composers Herbeck especially admired were **Franz Schubert**, **Robert Schumann**, **Liszt**, **Anton Bruckner**, and **Richard Wagner**. Regarding Brahms's supposed spiritual relationship with Schumann, he once remarked, "With Schumann he has only one thing in common, namely a lack of clarity. Schumann is immeasurably superior to Brahms" (Herbeck 1885, 135).

Brahms told Heuberger that he used to be for a time on very good terms with Herbeck, but that he would often tease him about his compositions (Heuberger 1976, 30). This rather tactless behavior is unlikely to have endeared him to Herbeck, who was known to be mortified that his compositions were not taken very seriously by his contemporaries. He wrote a number of sacred works (including several Masses), as well as four symphonies, and some chamber and piano music. On Herbeck's major contribution to the revival of interest in Schubert's music, *see* SCHUBERT, FRANZ (PETER). (Avins 1997; Biba 1988; Brahms 1974/7; Clive 1997; Herbeck 1885; Heuberger 1976; C. Pohl 1883)

HERDER, JOHANN GOTTFRIED (b. Mohrungen, East Prussia, 25 August 1744; d. Weimar, 18 December 1803). Critic, philosopher, and preacher. His ideas on literature played a significant role in the formation of the "Sturm und Drang" movement. He was greatly influenced by George Hamann's view that "poetry is the original language of the human race" and, as a result, came to attach particular importance to folk songs and to works such as those of Homer and Shakespeare and the Ossian poems, which he considered to be especially close to nature. He translated many foreign folk songs, which he published in a two-volume collection (*Volkslieder*) in 1778–79. It was reissued, edited by Johannes von Müller, as *Stimmen der Völker in Liedern* in 1807, and this title was retained in subsequent editions. The collection was reprinted in the complete edition of Herder's works published by J. G. Cotta in 1827–30, which Brahms bought in 1856 and kept in his personal library until his death. The numerous blue and black pencil marks bear witness to the great interest and care with which he read *Stimmen der Völker.*

Brahms turned to Herder's collection of folk songs for the text of the following vocal pieces: "Vom verwundeten Knaben," "Murrays Ermordung," "Ein Sonett" (op. 14/2–4), "Gesang aus Fingal" (op. 17/4), "Weg der Liebe" (op. 20/1–2), "Darthulas Grabesgesang" (op. 42/1), "Das Lied vom Herrn von Falkenstein" (op. 43/4), and "Edward" (op. 75/1). In addition, he used a quotation (as translated by Herder) from the song "Lady Anne Bothwell's Lament" as the "motto" for the first of the three *Intermezzi* for piano (op. 117). (*See also* MACPHERSON, JAMES.) (Pross 1990)

HERMANN, FRIEDRICH (b. Frankfurt am Main, 1 February 1828; d. Leipzig, 27 September 1907). Violinist and teacher. He studied at the Leipzig conservatory (1843–46) and in 1848 was appointed a member of its faculty; he also played in the Gewandhaus Orchestra. Brahms most probably made his acquaintance during his first visit to Leipzig in 1853; he had been urged to do so "as soon as possible" by their mutual friend **Joseph Joachim**: "He is a member of the Leipzig Orchestra: violist, violinist, pianist, composer, clarinettist, and a very sound musician . . . he will receive you with open arms if you show him this note" (Brahms 1974/5, 16).

Hermann is of interest to Brahms scholars because he prepared reductions of a considerable number of his compositions, which appeared mainly in the 1870s. Some of the arrangements were for solo piano, but most of them were for piano trio (piano, violin, and cello). The works in question included the two String Sextets, the Piano Quintet, the three Piano Quartets, and the First and Third Symphonies. (The arrangements of the two symphonies, the last to appear, were published in 1897, perhaps after Brahms's death.) Of the *Liebeslieder-Walzer* (op. 52) Hermann made several different arrangements: for piano duet, violin, and cello; piano duet and violin; piano and flute; piano, flute, and violin (or piano and two flutes); two violins; and string quintet or string orchestra. (Brahms 1974/5)

HERZFELD, VIKTOR VON (b. Pressburg [Bratislava], 8 October 1856; d. Budapest, 20 February 1920). Composer and violinist. Following music studies at the Vienna conservatory and later in Berlin, he lived from 1886 mainly in Budapest, where he taught at the Academy of Music and played second violin in the Hubay Quartet. He thus took part in several concerts with Brahms (*see* HUBAY [HUBER], JENÖ [EUGEN]). His interest in Brahms's music is further illustrated by his participation in an all-Brahms chamber music concert in Budapest on 27 November 1893, which featured the Piano Trio op. 8 (new version), the Piano Sonata op. 1, and the Clarinet Quintet op. 115.

Herzfeld was a frequent visitor to Edward and **Ottilie Ebner**'s house in

Budapest, and Brahms is likely to have met him there during some of his later visits to that city. Very probably they also met at Ischl.

HERZOGENBERG, ELISABETH [ELISABET, LISL] VON, Baroness (usually referred to simply as Elisabeth von Herzogenberg), née von Stockhausen (b. Paris, 13 April 1847; d. San Remo, 7 January 1892); youngest child of Bodo Albrecht von Stockhausen (1810–85) and his wife Clothilde Annette, née Countess Baudissin (1818–91). A highly cultured man and a great music lover and fine pianist, Stockhausen had received tuition from Valentin Alkan and **Chopin** (who dedicated his G Minor Ballade to him and the Barcarolle to his wife). He became Hanoverian ambassador in Vienna in 1853; earlier he had held a diplomatic post in Paris.

Elisabeth was blonde and attractive, intensely musical, highly cultivated, and endowed with great charm and a delightful sense of humor. Men as well as women found her irresistible. **Julius Epstein**, who became her piano teacher in 1861, later declared that one could not but fall in love with her. Moreover, he was immensely impressed by her musical talent: "She had the most delicate touch, the most fluent technique, the quickest powers of comprehension, the most extraordinary memory, and the most profound expressiveness in her playing—in short, she was a genius" (Brahms 1974/1, x). **Dame Ethel Smyth**, whom Elisabeth von Herzogenberg took under her wing when the 20-year-old English girl arrived in Leipzig as a music student in 1877, later described her as having been "not really beautiful but better than beautiful, at once dazzling and bewitching" (Smyth 1919, vol. 1, 192). It has been suggested that Brahms also rapidly fell under her spell when he replaced Epstein as her piano teacher soon after arriving in Vienna in 1862, and that it was the reason why, uneasy about the situation into which his feelings might draw him, he insisted on handing his pupil back to Epstein on the pretext that the latter might otherwise be hurt and offended. According to **Max Kalbeck** (Brahms 1974/1, xiii), Brahms had originally been asked to take over the lessons by Elisabeth's father, whose acquaintance he had made at the house of Pastor Gustav Porubszky (*see* FABER, ARTHUR (LUDWIG)). Like Brahms, the Stockhausens were Protestants; yet it was a Catholic, **Heinrich von Herzogenberg**, whom Elisabeth married on 26 November 1868.

It was not until Brahms, in early 1874, went to Leipzig, where the Herzogenbergs had moved two years earlier, that he established a close contact with the couple. Their relationship blossomed into friendship when, at their invitation, he stayed with them on his next visit to Leipzig in January 1877. For the rest of their lives the Herzogenbergs revered Brahms; he, for his part, developed a deep affection for Elisabeth and a sincere respect for her husband. Their correspondence with Brahms, which was later published by Max Kalbeck (Brahms 1974/1–2), was mainly carried on by Elisabeth, who showed herself an altogether delightful letter writer, full of affection, charm, and wit. Moreover, she possessed a striking capacity for musical analysis, which she employed in abundant measure to the numerous compositions that Brahms sent her almost as soon as he had written them—see, for instance, the detailed comments on the Fourth Symphony (Brahms 1974/2, 94–95, 98–103) and on the String Quintet op. 111 (Brahms 1974/2, 239–42, 247–49). He clearly attached considerable weight to her opinions, even if they happened to be critical (*see also* HALM, FRIEDRICH and HEINE, HEINRICH). For although she was full of the highest praise for most of his works ("Your music . . . forms an integral part of our lives, like the air and light and warmth" [Brahms 1974/1, 173–74]), she did not hesitate to express some criticism where she deemed it appropriate, "because I have an unfortunate love of truth" (Brahms 1974/1, 27); or, as she explained regarding her remarks about the songs and choral pieces of opp. 104–7, "I would not dare to say a word about what fills me with enthusiasm in these sets, if I were to remain silent about what fails to move me" (Brahms 1974/2, 201). Her reservations were, however, expressed in a manner and tone that were unlikely to cause offence; nor, it would appear, did they ever do so. The same applies to one occasion when she took Brahms to task for having unthinkingly and unjustifiably slighted her husband "who loves you like a poodle, like a child, as a catholic loves his favourite saints" (Brahms 1974/1, 59).

The Herzogenbergs often expressed great regret at not being able to meet Brahms more frequently, for, as Elisabeth assured him, "I truly believe that there are not many persons who deserve as greatly as we do to be with you more often—at any rate, none who are better able to appreciate it from a musical and human point of view" (Brahms 1974/2, 193–94). In reply, Brahms wrote to her: "You should know and believe that you are among the few persons whom one holds so dear that one cannot tell them so—since your husband is always reading and hearing everything; but he also belongs to the select few" (Brahms 1974/2, 196). Earlier that year he had told her that her photograph stood on his writing desk. Kalbeck, in his edition of the correspondence, comments that it remained there until Brahms's death, but R. H. Schauffler (1972) states in *The Unknown Brahms* that, according to **Celestine Truxa**, that was not the case, but that it had disappeared from the desk one day and that Brahms had given her the frame and suggested that she put her own husband's portrait in it. She had suspected some strain in their friendship. However, apart from an occasion in 1886—that is, two years prior to Brahms's reference to the photograph—when, according to Kalbeck, Elisabeth had broken off the correspondence for nine months on the strength of what later turned out to have been incorrect information conveyed to her by a third party (Brahms 1974/2, 130, n. 2), nothing is known about any serious tensions in their relations. Several other more or less lengthy gaps did indeed occur in their later correspondence, but there seems to be no reason to attach any special significance to them.

There is no doubt that Brahms was profoundly affected by Elisabeth's death (see Brahms 1974/2, 258). As for the letters he had received from her, he confided to Herzogenberg: "I preserve [in them] above all one of the most precious memories of my life, and furthermore a rich treasure of feelings and wit—which, of course, belongs to me alone" (Brahms 1974/2, 261).

Brahms dedicated the Rhapsodies op. 79 to Elisabeth in 1880. She herself published 24 *Volkskinderlieder* [Folk songs for children], and one song she had composed appeared as her husband's op. 44/7. After her death he arranged for the publication of eight pieces she had written for the piano. (Brahms 1974/1–2; W. Frisch 1986; Huschke 1927; Ruhbaum 2002a, 2002b; Schauffler 1972; U. Schilling 1994; Smyth 1919, 1936)

HERZOGENBERG, (LEOPOLD) HEINRICH VON (PICOT DE PECCADUC), Baron (usually referred to simply as Heinrich von Herzogenberg) (b. Graz, 10 June 1843; d. Wiesbaden, 9 October 1900). Descendant of an old French aristocratic family; son of August von Herzogenberg (1815–46), an Austrian court official, and his wife Natalie Wilhelmine Constanze, née Countess Rothkirch und Panthen (1816–63). Heinrich von Herzogenberg made Brahms's acquaintance while studying composition with **Felix Otto Dessoff** at the Viennese conservatory (1862–65), and in March 1864 Brahms recommended him to **Jakob Melchior Rieter-Biedermann**, who thereupon published six songs he had composed (op. 1: settings of poems by **Joseph von Eichendorff**, **Emanuel von Geibel**, **Heinrich Heine**, and Nikolaus Lenau) and the ballad "Der verirrte Jäger" (op. 2, text by Eichendorff). Herzogenberg subsequently found other publishers, but eventually he returned to the firm Rieter-Biedermann, which was to issue his opp. 23–109.

Following his marriage to Elisabeth von Stockhausen (*see* HERZOGENBERG, ELISABETH [ELISABET, LISL] VON) in 1886, he lived at Graz, where he devoted himself mainly to composition. In 1872 they moved to Leipzig. There he was one of the founders (together with, notably, Franz von Holstein, **Philipp Spitta**, and Alfred Volkland) of the Leipzig Bach-

Verein, which was constituted on 31 January 1875. After first serving as its secretary, he became its conductor the following year. Furthermore, it was during his early years at Leipzig that he started to teach; among his first students were **Dame Ethel Smyth** and **Prince Heinrich XXIV Reuss-Köstritz**. In 1885 he joined the faculty of the Hochschule für Musik in Berlin and soon afterward was also appointed a senator of the Academy of Arts. Over the next 15 years he was to teach with considerable success at the Hochschule and the academy, but with lengthy breaks, due in part to his wife's chronic heart ailment that necessitated sojourns in warmer climates and in part to his own frail health, the result of chronic rheumatism.

As a composer, Herzogenberg covered a wide range, from orchestral, chamber, and keyboard music to secular vocal and, especially in his last years, sacred choral works. Much of it has been judged to be derivative, the dominant influence, in the case of the chamber music, being Brahms. To Herzogenberg's chagrin, the latter refused to be drawn into any serious critical assessments of his compositions, arguing, on at least one occasion, that he would be inclined to express such lavish praise that Herzogenberg might suspect his sincerity (Brahms 1974/2, 23). It is unlikely that the Herzogenbergs were deceived. "Of course," Elisabeth wrote on 27 July 1887, "the poor devil would have been pleased if you had been able to say about one or other of the movements: I liked it" (Brahms 1974/2, 162–63). The truth was most probably that, while Brahms respected Herzogenberg's technical craftsmanship and thorough musical knowledge, he felt no great enthusiasm for the compositions themselves. (In recent years Herzogenberg has begun to be rediscovered as a gifted and inventive composer in his own right. Certain of his works for solo piano, piano duet, and two pianos—including the *Variations on a Theme by Brahms* for piano duet [see below]—have been splendidly recorded by the English pianists Anthony Goldstone and Caroline Clemmow.)

Whatever he may have felt about Herzogenberg's compositions, it nevertheless seems curious, given their very friendly relations, that Brahms, who dedicated his Rhapsodies op. 79 to Elisabeth in 1880, should never have dedicated any of his works to her husband. Yet the latter offered him numerous tokens of his profound admiration and great affection. Apart from composing the aforementioned variations on a theme by Brahms (op. 23, published in 1876, the theme being taken from Brahms's song "Mei Mueter mag mi net," op. 7/5) and dedicating to him the three String Quartets op. 42 (in 1884) and the Piano Quartet op. 75 (in 1897), Herzogenberg declared his feelings in more than one letter. On 25 November 1880, at a time when he was already in his late thirties, he wrote to Brahms: "When you were in contact with **Schumann**, you were, I believe, 17 years old [actually 20]. I feel that I shall never be older than that in relation to yourself, or at most 18 years, so you must excuse if such a young stripling writes you a kind of love letter once in a while" (Brahms 1974/1, 128). And four years later he wrote, "The light and warmth which you project throughout the entire world would mean nothing to me if I did not feel that it is also for my sake, for my small private pleasure, that you have ascended to your eminence" (Brahms 1974/2, 22). On 26 March 1897, in his last letter to Brahms, he confessed: "There are two things which I cannot stop myself from doing: to compose, and to ask myself, as I did 34 years ago, 'What will He think of this?' The 'He' is, of course, yourself" (Brahms 1974/2, 276). Four days later he wrote in the same vein to **Joseph Joachim**: "For the past 35 years I have asked myself about every note I have composed: what will Brahms think of it? The thought of him and his opinion has been responsible for whatever I may have made of myself. He has been my perseverance, my ambition, my courage." (Johannes Joachim and Moser 1911–13, vol. 3, 469). When news of Brahms's death reached him, he hurried to Vienna. "I had to experience the incomprehensible with my own eyes," he wrote to Joachim. "It is impossible to assess as yet the full implications [of his death]—as I stood at the open, yawning grave, I had the feeling that it was going to swallow everything we love, all the estimable men still remaining, all the music we carry in our hearts. I only wished that I could end it all and join him down there, to sleep, to dream!" (Johannes Joachim and Moser 1911–13, vol. 3, 469). (Altmann 1903; Brahms 1974/1–2; W. Frisch 1986; Johannes Joachim and Moser 1911–13; Ruhbaum 2002a, 2002b; U. Schilling 1994; Wiechert 1997)

HEUBERGER, RICHARD (FRANZ JOSEPH) (b. Graz, 18 June 1850; d. Vienna, 28 October 1914). Critic, composer, conductor, and teacher. A qualified engineer, in 1876 he decided to make his career in music (he had studied with Wilhelm Mayer-Remy, the director of the Graz Musikverein, and was also a member of the Graz Singverein). He was initially appointed conductor of the Wiener Akademischer Gesangverein, later of the Singakademie, and eventually of the Wiener Männer-Gesangverein. In 1881 he became a music critic on the *Neues Wiener Tagblatt*, and the recognition and respect he earned in that position led to his being engaged as assistant critic to **Eduard Hanslick** on the *Neue freie Presse* (1895–1902); he also wrote for a time for the Munich *Allgemeine Zeitung*. As a composer he was particularly noteworthy for his songs, his choral works (mostly for male chorus), and his operettas. Today, he is known almost exclusively for *Der Opernball* (premiered at the Theater an der Wien on 5 January 1898), and more specifically, at any rate internationally, for a duet from that operetta,

"Geh'n wir in's Chambre séparée" (which has now become even more popular as a vocal solo). It is a matter of some interest that Heuberger was some years later offered the libretto of *Die lustige Witwe*, but he did not warm to its subject and the libretto was then handed to Franz Lehár.

Heuberger has stated that his enthusiasm for Brahms's music dated from the performance of the Requiem that Brahms conducted at the Gesellschaft der Musikfreunde concert of 28 February 1875. He had been presented to Brahms before then (probably in Graz in April 1873), but it was not until 1876, by which time he had become conductor of the Akademischer Gesangverein, that he was able to engage in meaningful contact with him. From then until Brahms's death some 20 years later, they met frequently, and before long Heuberger took to keeping a record of their conversations, which is particularly comprehensive for the period 1885–97. This diary forms the kernel of Heuberger's (1976) *Erinnerungen an Johannes Brahms*, one of the most fascinating documents in all Brahms literature, which was first published by Kurt Hofmann in 1971 (a revised and augmented edition prepared by the same scholar appeared in 1976). Not the least interesting of the diary entries are those citing Brahms's critical observations on certain of Heuberger's early compositions; they bear out the latter's assertion that Brahms possessed great pedagogical talent. Heuberger even believed that Brahms might have let himself be persuaded to do some teaching at the conservatory, perhaps in the form of master classes. (Grunsky 2002; Heuberger 1976)

HEYSE, PAUL (JOHANN LUDWIG) (b. Berlin, 15 March 1830; d. Munich, 2 April 1914). Poet, novelist, short story writer, dramatist, and translator. From 1854 he lived in Munich, where king Maximilian II granted him a pension. He quickly established a reputation as a gifted writer, above all of short stories (he published some 150), while his plays (of which he wrote about 70) proved less successful. His poems, particularly those based on foreign models, have inspired a number of composers, including Brahms, **Peter Cornelius**, and especially **Hugo Wolf**. In 1910 he was awarded the Nobel Prize for literature.

Brahms set 12 of his texts to music. What is interesting about them, apart from their quality, is that the dates of their composition range from 1852 to 1886 and thus span the major part of the period during which Brahms wrote for the voice. He discovered Heyse's writings early in life and retained his admiration for them until the end. "The appearance of a new novella by Heyse is a red-letter day for me," he told **Richard Heuberger** in 1885. "I don't read this kind of work just once, I keep it by my side for several weeks and dip into it again and again" (Heuberger 1976, 27).

Brahms was eager to meet Heyse and presented himself at his house when visiting Munich in 1864, 1869, and 1870, but Heyse was away each time, and it was not until May 1873 that Brahms made his acquaintance; he saw him several more times that summer. Heyse had a wide circle of friends in Munich, which included **Hermann Levi** and **Franz Wüllner**. Brahms was charmed by his personality: "He knew how to animate and liven up the atmosphere in a room—as soon as he entered it, one felt that the sun was suddenly shining into it," he told **Max Kalbeck** many years later (Kalbeck 1976, vol 2, 439, n. 2). One matter he and Heyse discussed in those days was the possibility of collaborating on an opera. Heyse got as far as producing the outline of a libretto entitled *Ritter Bayard*, but the idea of composing an opera about that celebrated medieval French knight, known as the "Chevalier sans peur et sans reproche," evidently failed to attract Brahms. However, he kept the outline among his papers, and it is now in the archive of the Gesellschaft der Musikfreunde.

Brahms had further opportunities to enjoy Heyse's company when he returned to Munich for concert appearances in March 1874 and again in November 1876. On the latter occasion, according to Robert Münster (1984), who states that he is basing himself on an entry in Heyse's diary, the two men "tranken . . . Brüderschaft" [literally: "drank brotherhood" (Münster 1974, 350). This expression normally signifies the adoption of the intimate "Du"; yet in the only surviving letter from Brahms to Heyse, which dates from late March 1885, he addresses Heyse with the formal "Sie" (Münster 1974, 352). In that same letter Brahms recalls the intense pleasure he had over many years derived from Heyse writings, "for since *Jungbrunnen* and *Francesca* I have been your enthusiastic reader." (*Jungbrunnen*, Heyse's first story, was published in 1849, the tragedy *Francesca da Rimini* in 1850.) Heyse, for his part, greatly admired Brahms's music, which is known to have been played at some of the musical soirees that he arranged from time to time at his villa.

Contact between Heyse and Brahms during the last 20 years of the latter's life seems to have been almost entirely by correspondence, either directly or indirectly through mutual friends like Kalbeck. They did, however, meet at least once, but it was an accidental encounter: they happened to run into each other at Genoa railway station in May 1885; Heyse's wife reportedly met Brahms during a visit to Vienna in March 1887. It was Kalbeck who later kept Heyse informed about Brahms's increasingly alarming state of health. After learning of Brahms's death, Heyse wrote a poem in his memory.

Brahms set texts by Heyse in the following compositions: "Spanisches Lied" (op. 6/1), "Am Sonntag Morgen" (op. 49/1), "Mädchenlied" (op.

95/6), and "Mädchenlied" (op. 107/5, with a different text), for single voice; "Nun stehn die Rosen in Blüte," "Die Berge sind spitz," "Am Wildbach die Weiden," and "Und gehst du über den Kirchhof," (op. 44/7–10), for four-voice women's choir; and "Waldesnacht," "Dein Herzlein mild," "Alle meine Herzgedanken," and "Es geht ein Wehen" (op. 62/3–6), for mixed choir. In addition, Brahms made another setting of "Dein Herzlein mild" for four-voice women's choir (WoO posthum 19), and in his abovementioned letter to Heyse in late March 1885, he mentions having also set "Brautlied," but, being dissatisfied with the result, he did not publish it. The composition is lost (see M. McCorkle 1984, Anhang IIa/29). (Häntzschel 1990; Heuberger 1976; Münster 1984)

HILDEBRAND, ADOLF VON (b. Marburg, 6 October 1847; d. Munich, 18 January 1921). Sculptor. He studied in Nuremberg, Munich (with Caspar von Zumbusch), Rome (where he formed close friendships with the art historian Konrad Fiedler and the painter Hans von Marées), and Berlin. In 1872 he settled in Italy, and in 1874 he bought the former monastery San Francesco di Paola near Florence, which was to be his main residence for more than 20 years. From 1891 until the outset of World War I, he divided his time between Florence and Munich, where he built himself a house in 1897.

It was at Meiningen in November 1891 that Hildebrand first met Brahms, who had come to rehearse and perform his new Clarinet Trio (op. 114) and Clarinet Quintet (op. 115), while Hildebrand was working on a bust of **Duke Georg II of Sachsen-Meiningen**. During his career, Hildebrand made numerous portrait busts (among his subjects were **Clara Schumann** and **Elisabeth von Herzogenberg**), as well as several monuments, including those of the Bavarian Prince Regent Luitpold in Munich, **Joseph Joachim** in Berlin, **Friedrich von Schiller** in Nuremberg, **Otto Bismarck** in Bremen, and Brahms at Meiningen. Working from photographs, he completed the model for the bust of Brahms, which was to form the centerpiece of the Brahms monument in the English Garden, in 1898, and the bust itself by the following spring. It was unveiled on 7 October 1899, the principal speaker on that occasion being Joachim. The ceremony was preceded by a performance of the Requiem at the Stadtkirche, conducted by **Fritz Steinbach**, who had been one of the main initiators of the whole project, and it was followed by a performance of the *Triumphlied*, also at the Stadtkirche. (*See also* ALBERT, EUGEN [EUGÈNE] [FRANCIS CHARLES] D'.)

Other celebrated examples of Hildebrand's art are the tombs of Elisabeth von Herzogenberg at San Remo and of her husband **Heinrich von Herzogenberg** at Wiesbaden, of Duke Georg II and Baroness Heldburg (*see*

GEORG II, DUKE OF SACHSEN-MEININGEN) at Meiningen, of **Philipp Spitta** in Berlin, and of **Hans von Bülow** in Hamburg. His other works include two busts of **Joseph Joachim**. One of them formed the centerpiece of the Joachim monument unveiled on 5 June 1913 at the Hochschule für Musik in Berlin, of which Joachim had been the director for many years; the monument was broken up by the National Socialists in 1938. A copy of Hildebrand's first bust, made in Joachim's lifetime, was installed on 18 January 1982 in the same building (which now houses the Berlin University of the Arts). Furthermore, Hildebrand designed several famous fountains, notably the Wittelsbach fountain for Munich and a fountain with the bronze figure of Father Rhine for Strasbourg. (Borchard 2005; Esche-Braunfels 1993)

HILLER, FERDINAND (VON) (b. Frankfurt am Main, 24 October 1811; d. Cologne, 11 May 1885). Composer, conductor, pianist, teacher, and writer on music. He studied with pianist Alois Schmitt in Frankfurt and later (1825–27) with Johann Nepomuk Hummel at Weimar. After spending the years 1828–36 in Paris and most of the period 1837–42 in Italy, he returned to Germany, where he engaged in various musical activities in Leipzig and Dresden before being appointed music director at Düsseldorf in 1847, in succession to **Julius Rietz**. In 1850 he took up a similar position at Cologne, which he occupied until 1884 (except for the period October 1881–October 1882 when he conducted the Italian opera in Paris). He also founded and directed the Cologne conservatory. He was a prolific composer, writing several operas, as well as much choral, orchestral, and chamber music, but he was more deeply and widely admired as a conductor and pianist.

R. Sietz states in his edition of Hiller's correspondence that he made Brahms's acquaintance on 1 April 1855 at **Clara Schumann**'s house at Düsseldorf, on the occasion of a performance of **Beethoven**'s *Missa solemnis* in that town. However, the performance of the Mass did not take place at Düsseldorf but at Cologne, as is evident from the following entry in Clara's diary: "On Sunday, 1 April, I traveled with Johannes to Cologne [from Düsseldorf], to hear that most colossal of all works, Beethoven's *Missa solemnis*" (Litzmann 1902, vol. 2, 370). In any case, if they really did meet that day at Clara's house or elsewhere, it would not have been for the first time, if **Carl Reinecke**'s memory served him well when, in the journal *Dur und Moll* in 1897, he recalled that Brahms had introduced himself to him in Cologne "towards the end of the summer of 1853" and that, before accompanying Brahms to the railway station where Brahms was to take the train to Düsseldorf to visit **Robert Schumann**, he had taken him to see Hiller (Reinecke 1897, 129).

Whatever may be the date of their initial meeting, there is some evidence that it was not until the Lower Rhine Music Festival of 1856 that their relations became closer. Thereafter, they met many times in Cologne and elsewhere, and on several of these occasions they collaborated in musical performances as, for instance, in 1865 in Cologne, when Brahms played Beethoven's "Emperor" Concerto and conducted his Serenade op. 11 at a concert under Hiller's overall direction on 12 December, and played his *Schumann Variations* (op. 23) with Hiller at a chamber music soiree on 19 December. From 1774 they were on "Du" terms; that year Brahms stayed with Hiller during the Lower Rhine Festival (24–26 May), at which he conducted his *Triumphlied.* Hiller was responsible for directing 11 of these festivals, the last one in 1883.

Hiller was sufficiently impressed with Brahms's music and personality by 1858 to propose that he be offered a teaching post at the Cologne conservatory, in succession to the pianist and conductor Eduard Franck, but Brahms declined the offer, preferring to keep his engagement at Detmold, which, among other advantages, left him free for the major part of the year. When Hiller retired in 1884 as director of the Gürzenich concerts and head of the conservatory, Brahms was offered the combined position. "I am today asking you to become my successor," Hiller wrote on 17 April (Sietz 1958–70, vol. 5, 72); but Brahms declined the offer. Thereupon Hiller explained the situation to his former pupil **Max Bruch**: "I am sure you will have found it natural that the position should have been offered to Brahms in the first place; but he is the hero of the day, has no official attachment, no wife, is therefore entirely free, so one cannot hold it against him if he wishes to remain free" (Sietz 1958–70, vol. 5, 74). Hiller now proposed Bruch for the post, but the committee chose **Franz Wüllner**, whom Brahms, among others, had warmly recommended.

Despite his close personal friendship with Brahms and the high respect he so evidently felt for him, Hiller was by no means an unconditional admirer of his music. On 30 March 1884, a few days before he announced his retirement and some three weeks before he contacted Brahms to urge him to become his successor, he had confided to Bruch: "As far as Brahms is concerned, it is certain that he is eminently talented, but the claims his supporters make for him are quite excessive. I cannot consider his symphonies to be equal to those of Mendelssohn, nor to Schumann's or to **Gade**'s best ones . . . let alone Beethoven's!" (Sietz 1958–70. vol. 5, 68). As for Brahms's opinion of Hiller's compositions, he wrote to **Joseph Joachim** in

March 1855: "I have recently looked through Hiller's opera *Traum in der Christnacht*, and the experience has reassured me that we are not doing him any great injustice with our dislike" (Brahms 1974/5, 101). It is not known whether he later changed his views about Hiller's music, but it may be significant that during his three years as artistic director of the Gesellschaft der Musikfreunde, he performed only one work by Hiller, the *Concert Overture* in D Major (on 5 January 1873). (Brahms 1974/5; H. Ehrlich 1888; Litzmann 1902; Reinecke 1897; Sietz 1958–70, 1960c)

HOFFMANN, E(RNST) T(HEODOR) A(MADEUS) [Ernst Theodor Wilhelm] (b. Königsberg [Kaliningrad, Russia], 24 January 1776; d. Berlin, 25 June 1822). Writer, composer (notably of the opera *Undine*, to a libretto by Friedrich de La Motte Fouqué), and critic (inter alia, he wrote articles and reviews for the Leipzig *Allgemeine musikalische Zeitung* from 1809 until 1815). A lawyer by training, and for the major part of his life by profession, he was also a skillful draftsman and painter as well as a gifted musician, but it was above all as a writer of highly imaginative stories and novels, which often treat fantastic and even supernatural subjects, that he achieved wide success.

When he was around 20, Brahms was an enthusiastic reader of Hoffmann; in particular, he identified himself as an artist with the Kapellmeister Johannes Kreisler, a central character in several of Hoffmann's tales, and especially in the unfinished novel *Lebensansichten des Kater Murr* (literally, *The Tom Cat Murr's Views on Life*, usually known in English as *The Life and Opinions of Kater Murr*). Thus, he named his collection of literary quotations "*Des jungen Kreislers Schatzkästlein*" [*The Young Kreisler's Little Treasure Chest*], in reference to an episode in *Kater Murr* where the term "Schatzkästlein" is applied to Kreisler's heart or soul; and he signed the autograph of the Piano Sonata op. 1 "Joh. Kreisler jun." and that of the Piano Sonata op. 5 "Kreisler jun." In the same spirit, his friend **Julius Otto Grimm** repeatedly addressed him as "Kreisler" in his letters in 1853–54 (**Joseph Joachim** also did so on one occasion), and Grimm even referred to Brahms by that name when writing to Joachim. At the same time, as Siegfried Kross has very plausibly argued, Brahms's identification with Kreisler was probably, as far as *Kater Murr* is concerned, prompted less by Kreisler's adventures in that novel than by various statements about the nature of the romantic artist and his function in society.

The fact that in the autograph of the *Schumann Variations* (op. 9) the double bars at the end of certain variations are extended to form the letter "K" (for "Kreisler"), while those at the end of other variations form a "B" (for "Brahms"), may indicate that by June 1854, when this composition was written, Brahms had become more confident in his personal identity as an artist and was beginning to dissociate himself from his erstwhile literary model. Yet that same month he was still proposing to entitle a number of piano pieces "Leaves from a Musician's Diary, edited by the Young Kreisler" (Brahms 1974/5, 46), but Joachim strongly advised against this type of "mystification," which, in his view, had lost its attractiveness through being used by too many budding young poets (Brahms 1974/5, 50–51). In the end, Brahms decided not publish that set of compositions. He appears to have generally ceased to identify with Kreisler after 1854, but S. Kross argues persuasively that the inscription "Benedictus qui venit in nomine Domini," which Brahms wrote above the Adagio in an autograph of the First Piano Concerto, may be a significant allusion to the appearance of the same words on the portal of the Abbey Kanzheim, where, in the novel, Johannes Kreisler finally found peace of mind. (It is, of course, a quotation from the 128th Psalm.) (Brahms 1974/5; Ehinger 1954; Kross 1981a; Neumann 1990)

HOFFMANN VON FALLERSLEBEN, AUGUST HEINRICH (b. Fallersleben, 2 April 1798; d. Corvey, 19 January 1874). Poet. Brahms set texts by Hoffmann von Fallersleben in the songs "Liebe und Frühling I" and "Liebe und Frühling II" (op. 3/2–3), "Wie die Wolke nach der Sonne" and "Nachtigallen schwingen lustig" (op. 6/5–6), and "Von ewiger Liebe" (op. 43, no. 1); in the duet "Der Jäger und sein Liebchen" (op. 28/4); and in the canons op. 113, no. 6 (for women's voices) and WoO posthum 27. (See also M. McCorkle 1984, Anhang IIa/23.)

Brahms made Hoffmann von Fallersleben's acquaintance at **Arnold Wehner**'s house at Göttingen in July 1853. At the end of August Brahms called on him at his home at Neuwied, on the Rhine, and the next day they made a joint excursion to the village of Brohl and Rheineck Castle. In his memoirs, Hoffmann von Fallersleben recalled his meeting with Brahms and added, "He had set many of my poems to music, but I do not know if he has published any of them" (Hoffmann von Fallersleben 1868, vol. 5, 224). In fact, of the above-mentioned compositions, only the first four had been written when Brahms visited Hoffmann von Fallersleben at Neuwied; they appeared in print later that year. (The duet was published in 1863, the song of op. 43 in December 1868.) (Hoffmann von Fallersleben 1868; R. Hofmann 1997; Schmitz 1990)

HOHENTHAL, IDA, COUNTESS, née Countess Seherr-Thoss (b. 15 March 1814; d. Leipzig, 4 July 1890). Married since 9 November 1833 to Count Karl Peter Emil Hohenthal (b. 8 October 1808; d. 19 January 1879).

The couple, who had seven children (three boys and four girls), lived at Castle Dölkau, near Leipzig. Brahms made their acquaintance while staying at Leipzig in late 1853. According to **Florence May**, he was presented to the countess by **Julius Otto Grimm**, while **Max Kalbeck** believed that he was probably introduced to the family by **Heinrich von Sahr**.

Brahms dedicated the Piano Sonata op. 5, which **Bartolf Wilhelm Senff** published in February 1854, to the countess. (Her maiden name was misspelt as "Scherr-Thoss" on the title page.) Max Kalbeck suggested that the dedication had been prompted by gratitude for the hospitality offered to him, but it seems at least as likely that it was a mark of appreciation for the Hohenthals' decision to engage his brother Fritz as music teacher to their children. (On Fritz's relations with the Hohenthals, *see* BRAHMS, FRIEDRICH [FRITZ]) (May 1948)

HOL, RIJK [RICHARD] (b. Amsterdam, 23 July 1825; d. Utrecht, 14 May 1904). Conductor, pianist, composer, and teacher. He was active as a teacher, choirmaster, and conductor in Amsterdam before moving in 1862 to Utrecht where, over the next four decades, he occupied various leading positions as conductor, organist, and director of the local conservatory. In addition, he held appointments as conductor of the concerts of the Cecilia male choir and the Diligentia Society at The Hague.

Brahms had a high opinion of Hol, whom he presumably first met during his Dutch tour of 1876. He is not likely to have been unaware of the fact that Hol had written favorably about some of Brahms's compositions in the Dutch journal *Caecilia*; he had been particularly enthusiastic about the *Magelone-Lieder*, declaring that Brahms was a composer "by the grace of God" (Zwart 2001, 200). In 1871 he had been responsible for the first Dutch performance of the Requiem, at Utrecht, and on that occasion had published a long and very complimentary study of that work in *Caecilia*, calling it "one of the greatest compositions of recent times" (Zwart 2001, 201). He conducted further performances of it in 1872, 1882, and 1892, and was also responsible for performances of the *Liebeslieder-Walzer* (in 1877), *Nänie* (1885), and *Gesang der Parzen* (1887). After Brahms conducted his First Symphony at Utrecht on 26 January 1878, he reported to **Clara Schumann** that the orchestra had been rather mediocre, but that Hol had rehearsed the work so superbly that the performance had been very enjoyable (Litzmann 1970, vol. 2, 133). Four years later, on 21 January 1882, also at Utrecht, Hol conducted the first performance in Holland of the Second Piano Concerto, with Brahms as soloist.

Yet further evidence of Brahms's regard for Hol comes from a letter he wrote to **Eduard Hanslick** (1897b) in 1880, which states that "Hol . . . is without a doubt the most competent young conductor and musician in The Hague" (*Neue freie Presse*, 1 July 1897, 3). The choice of the adjective "young" is a curious one, for Hol was then 55 years old, and moreover eight years older than Brahms. (Hanslick 1897b; Litzmann 1970; Zwart 2001)

HÖLDERLIN, (JOHANN CHRISTIAN) FRIEDRICH (b. Lauffen am Neckar, 20 March 1770; d. Tübingen, 7 June 1843). Poet, dramatist, and novelist. Brahms's *Schicksalslied* was inspired by a poem contained in book 2 of Hölderlin's novel *Hyperion, oder der Eremit aus Griechenland*. (On Brahms's "discovery" of the text, see Dietrich 1898 and also Kreutziger-Herr 1999.) (Dietrich 1898; Kreutziger-Herr 1999; Kurz 1990; Nolthenius 1904)

HÖLTY, LUDWIG CHRISTOPH HEINRICH (b. Mariensee, near Hanover, 21 December 1748; d. Hanover, 1 September 1776). Poet. Brahms set texts by Hölty in the following songs: "Der Kuss" (op. 19/1), "Die Mainacht" (op. 43/2), "Die Schale der Vergessenheit" and "An die Nachtigall" (op. 46/3–4), "An ein Veilchen" (op. 49/2), and "Minnelied" (op. 71/5). (Kranefuss 1990)

HORNBOSTEL, (OTTO) ERICH VON (b. Vienna, 24 October 1846; d. Vienna, 7 March 1910). Lawyer, son of industrialist Theodor Friedrich von Hornbostel (1815–88), and father of Erich M(oritz) von Hornbostel (1877–1935), an internationally famous scholar active in the fields of experimental psychology and musicology. In 1876 Erich von Hornbostel Sr. married the singer Helene Magnus (b. Hamburg, 1840; d. Vienna, 18 October 1914) who had studied with **Julius Stockhausen** in Hamburg and was to enjoy a warm friendship with him until his death in 1906. (For his 80th birthday, she presented him with a marble bust of Brahms that had been specially made for her by **Ilse Conrat**, who based it on the head she had modeled for the monument at Brahms's grave.)

Helene Magnus made her Viennese debut at a concert given by **Julius Epstein** on 17 February 1867, when she sang Lieder by **Franz Schubert** and **Robert Schumann**. On 1 December of the same year she sang the Romance from Schubert's *Rosamunde* at the Gesellschaft der Musikfreunde concert, at which **Johann von Herbeck** conducted the very first performance of the three opening movements of Brahms's Requiem. Since Brahms attended the concert and was quite likely present at some of the rehearsals, he may well have made Magnus's acquaintance at this time, if he had not already met her. Later, she became directly associated with his music.

Thus, at a concert in Vienna on 9 April 1869, she joined Stockhausen, **Gustav Walter**, and **Rosa Girzick** in performances of the quartets "An die Heimat" (op. 64/1) and "Wechsellied zum Tanze" (op. 31/1), accompanied by Brahms himself; on 30 December 1871 she gave what is believed to be the first public performance of "Volkslied" (op. 7/4); and on 22 February 1874 she sang three of the *Magelone-Lieder* (op. 33) at a concert she presented together with Epstein.

After her marriage she more or less gave up public appearances, but she had a successful career as a teacher. At the same time, the Hornbostels were prominent in Viennese musical circles, and their activities did not fail to reflect their great interest in Brahms's compositions. In a letter to **Max Abraham** on 31 October 1891 (Brahms 1974/14, 402), Brahms mentioned that **Eusebius Mandyczewski** had been rehearsing the canons op. 113 with "a women's choir," which, in M. L. McCorkle's (1984) *Werkverzeichnis*, is identified as the "Hornbostel'scher Damenchor." Five years later, **Anton Sistermans** gave a private performance of the *4 ernste Gesänge* at the Hornbostels', which, according to him, made "an indescribable impression" in that intimate setting (Kalbeck 1976, vol. 4, 484). Brahms was not present on that occasion, but he was reportedly a frequent visitor to the Hornbostels' house (*see also* CONRAT, ILSE).

Erich von Hornbostel was later to play an important role in the disposal of Brahms's estate. The rather sad story of the protracted litigation to which it gave rise—the legal process took no fewer than 18 years—has been told by Otto Biba in "New Light on the Brahms *Nachlass*" (Biba 1987). One of the major points at issue in the dispute between the Gesellschaft der Musikfreunde and the legally recognized heirs (who were represented by Dr. Josef Reitzes) concerned the fate of the large number of letters addressed to Brahms that were found among his possessions after his death. On 26 May 1903 the courts instructed the two parties to nominate a person whose task it would be to examine each letter for the purpose of determining whether it ought to be destroyed (should its personal or confidential nature make this desirable), or returned to its writer or the latter's nominee, or deposited with the Gesellschaft (if the first course was deemed unnecessary and the second found to be impossible or inadvisable). The person appointed to undertake this task was Erich von Hornbostel (not the then 26-year-old son, as has been suggested, but evidently his father, who was particularly well qualified for this delicate task by his legal expertise and his long friendship with Brahms). No record exists of what was then destroyed and what was handed over. Under a final decision taken by the courts on 14 December 1915, any letters then already held by the Gesellschaft were to remain in its possession. According to Biba, its archive now contains fewer than 1,500 letters from 167 correspondents, out of the approximately 4,000 letters from close to 400 correspondents that were originally found among Brahms's belongings.

Hornbostel was a member of the seven-men committee that was responsible for the foundation of the Vienna "Brahms-Gesellschaft" in April 1904. The others were **Arthur Faber**, **Max Kalbeck**, Hofrat Adolf Koch von Langentreu (then the president of the Gesellschaft der Musikfreunde and a brother of the composer Josef Koch von Langentreu), Eusebius Mandyczewski, Generalkonsul Gotthelf Meyer, and **Viktor von Miller zu Aichholz**. (Brahms 1974/14; Biba 1987; *ÖBL* 1957–)

HUBAY [HUBER], JENÖ [EUGEN] (b. Pest [Budapest], 15 September 1858; d. Budapest, 12 March 1937). Violinist and composer. His first teacher was his father Karl Hubay [Huber] who was on the faculty of the Budapest Conservatory and Kapellmeister of the Hungarian National Opera company. Later Jenö studied for five years under **Joseph Joachim** at the Hochschule für Musik in Berlin. He made his public debut at the age of 11. In 1882 he became principal violin professor at the Brussels conservatory, and in 1886 he took over his father's position at the Budapest conservatory. That same year saw the foundation of the Hubay Quartet, with himself as first violin, **Viktor von Herzfeld** second violin, **Bram Eldering** viola, and **David Popper** cello (the composition of the group was to change later).

The Hubay Quartet gave its first concert in Budapest on 10 November 1886 (not on 24 October, as is sometimes stated). Wolfgang Ebert (1986) mentions in his article "Brahms in Ungarn" that shortly afterward Hubay sent his brother Karl to Vienna to invite Brahms to appear at one of the Quartet's concerts, an engagement Brahms readily accepted; but in an article Hubay had published in the *Pester Lloyd* in 1933, he had described this visit as having been undertaken by himself. The concert that took place in Budapest on 22 December 1886 (not 20, as stated in M. L. McCorkle's [1984] *Werkverzeichnis*) featured three compositions by Brahms: the Piano Trio op. 101 (played by Hubay, Popper, and Brahms), the Cello Sonata op. 99 (performed by Popper and Brahms), and the String Sextet op. 18. On this, as on most subsequent visits, Brahms made a point of bringing one of his recently composed chamber works with him; thus, the Piano Trio, which was played from the manuscript, was receiving its world premiere.

Brahms must have found the experience rewarding, for he returned to Budapest for further concerts with Hubay and his colleagues during each of the following four winters. On 21 December 1887, the program consisted of the Violin Sonata op. 100, the Quintet op. 88, and again the Piano Trio op. 101; the concert of 21 December 1888 offered the first public performance of the Violin Sonata op. 108 (by Hubay and Brahms), as well as renditions of the Sextet op. 36, and of six recent songs (among them "Ständchen" and "Auf dem See," op. 106/1–2), sung by **Gustav Walter** to Brahms's accompaniment; the concert on 10 January 1890 featured the String Quartet op. 67, the Sextet op. 18, and the Piano Trio op. 8 in its revised version (another first performance); and on 19 January 1891, Brahms's final appearance with the Hubay Quartet, there were performances of the String Quartet op. 67, the Quintet op. 11, and the Horn Trio op. 40 (in which Brahms played the piano part).

Apart from their various meetings in Budapest, Brahms and Hubay also saw each other in Vienna, which Hubay visited on several occasions. In the above-mentioned article in the *Pester Lloyd*, he particularly mentioned calling on Brahms, at the latter's request, every day for one whole week for the purpose of playing through the D Minor Violin Sonata, so that Brahms could make such changes as he deemed necessary. Finally satisfied, Brahms then arranged a private performance at **Theodor Billroth**'s (on 12 December 1888), in the presence of **Eduard Hanslick**, **Max Kalbeck**, and others—whose response, according to Hubay, was anything but enthusiastic. (Hubay had given a somewhat different account of the event in an interview printed in the *Musical Times* three years earlier.) Nine days after this trial run at Billroth's, Hubay and Brahms gave the aforementioned first public performance of the sonata in Budapest. (W. Ebert 1984, 1986; Gottlieb-Billroth 1935; Hubay 1930, 1933)

HUBERMAN, BRONISLAW (b. Częstochowa, 19 December 1882; d. Corsier-sur-Vevey, 15 June 1947). Violinist. The then 12-year-old Huberman created a sensation with his rendition of the first movement of Mendelssohn's concerto at Adelina Patti's farewell concert in Vienna on 22 January 1895, and in the space of the next few weeks, he gave no fewer than 10 concerts there. He returned the following year, when he made a profound impression with his interpretation of Brahms's concerto at his first concert on 29 January 1896. Brahms himself was present, and deeply moved. **Max Kalbeck** (1976) describes him wiping his eyes during the Adagio, and at the end of the performance "embracing the boy and stroking his cheeks," and he presented Huberman with his photograph, inscribed from "a highly delighted and grateful listener" (vol. 4, 430). Brahms reportedly also promised to compose a Fantasia for him, but he never did. At his third and last concert on 6 March, Huberman again played Brahms's concerto, as well as Mendelssohn's. (Gutmann 1914; Hermann 1932; Huberman 1912)

HUMMER, REINHOLD. Cellist; member of the Vienna Opera orchestra and the Philharmonic Orchestra, and, for a time, of the Rosé Quartet (*see* ROSÉ, ARNOLD). In November 1874, in a letter to **Robert Volkmann**, whose Cello Concerto Hummer was to perform at a Gesellschaft der Musikfreunde concert conducted by Brahms on 28 February 1875, Brahms referred to him as "the young, very talented Herr Hummer" (Volkmann 1912, 8). For unknown reasons, the concerto was eventually omitted from the program.

It was as a member of the Rosé Quartet that Hummer took part in the first performance of Brahms's String Quintet, op. 111, in Vienna on 11 November 1890. Both **Max Kalbeck** and **Richard Heuberger** accuse him of having played in a sullen mood and indifferently on that occasion, and hold him responsible for the work's rather tepid reception. He had reportedly been very dissatisfied during rehearsals with the opening of the first movement, where the cello, which carries the principal theme, has to contend with accompanying music provided by the other four instruments, all instructed by the composer to play *sempre forte*. Although known for his ability to produce a rich, full sound, Hummer believed that he was being drowned by the other strings; according to Kalbeck (1976), he expressed his silent despair at the first rehearsal "by reproachfully gazing at Brahms like a faithful, ill-treated mastiff" (Kalbeck 1976, vol. 4, 208). Brahms remained unsympathetic: "In my view, they are far too much inclined here to accompany every solo *piano*, and so the cellist Hummer also immediately said that he had to have a *piano* above him in this case," he wrote to **Joseph Joachim** on 27 November. "I didn't yield, but they didn't achieve the correct sound either" (Brahms 1974/6, 255–56). Still, notwithstanding his assertion of intransigence, Brahms does appear to have been sufficiently moved by the doleful glances of the anguished cellist, and also by a suggestion made by Sigmund Bachrich, the first violist, to agree to the other strings playing more softly at this point; but the extant first violin part bears his note "only for the Rosé Quartet and at the wish of Herr Hummer" (M. McCorkle 1984, 446).

In their concert in Berlin on 10 December, the Joachim Quartet and **Robert Hausmann**, having been forewarned by Brahms of the problem they might have to face and offered by him some suggestions as to how they might best deal with it, managed to resolve it more or less adequately, at any rate in Joachim's view (Brahms 1974/6, 259). Yet **Elisabeth von Herzogenberg**, who was present at the concert and had moreover had an opportunity to study the score, clearly found the performance less than completely satisfying and blamed the dynamic construction of the opening bars. "Could you not, dear Master," she enquired with admirable tact, "make the passage even more beautiful?" (Brahms 1974/2, 248); in this connection, see also Brahms's letter to **Adolph Brodsky** in Avins and Eisinger 2002).

An earlier performance of Brahms's music in which Hummer had taken part is also worthy of mention. On 22 February 1890 he had played the revised version of the Piano Trio op. 8 with Brahms and **Arnold Rosé** in Vienna, just a few weeks after its first performance in Budapest. (Avins and Eisinger 2002; Brahms 1974/2, 1974/6; Volkmann 1912)

– I –

IBSEN, HENRIK JOHAN (b. Skien, 20 March 1828; d. Christiania [Oslo], 28 May 1906). Norwegian poet and dramatist. According to **Max Kalbeck**, he made Brahms's acquaintance at Meiningen in December 1887, on the occasion of a performance of his play *Ghosts*, but this statement, which is repeated by S. Avins in *Johannes Brahms: His Life and Letters*, is almost certainly incorrect (Kalbeck 1976, vol. 4, 80; Avins 1997, 653, n. 1). When the play was first performed at Meiningen in Ibsen's presence on 21 December 1886, Brahms, though invited, had been unable to attend, since, as he explained in a letter to Baroness Heldburg, he was due to take part in a concert in Budapest on the 22nd (Brahms 1991, 69; on the concert, *see* HUBAY [HUBER], JENÖ [EUGEN]). In fact, Brahms arrived in Budapest on the 20th. In 1887 he stayed at Meiningen from 25 to 29 December, and during his visit he did indeed see a performance of *Ghosts*, as he subsequently informed **Josef Viktor Widmann**, but there is no evidence that Ibsen was present at that time. (In his letter to Widmann, Brahms even misspells the dramatist's name as "Ipsen" [Brahms 1974/8, 73]).

If the poet and playwright **Richard Voss** is correct, the first meeting between Brahms and Ibsen did not take place until April 1891, and then not at Meiningen but in Vienna, where Ibsen had gone to attend a veritable festival of his plays, which included the Austrian premiere of *The Pretenders*, as well as productions of *An Enemy of the People* and *The Wild Duck*. Voss, who was also in Vienna at the time, relates in his memoirs that when, at his suggestion, the well-known Viennese society hostess Baroness Sophie Todesco decided to give a breakfast in Ibsen's honor, to which "only those would be asked whose acquaintance Ibsen wished to make," the only such person Ibsen named was Brahms. Voss transmitted the baroness's invitation to Brahms, who accepted it, but Voss accuses him of behaving very boorishly at the breakfast, treating Ibsen with something close to hostility, while offending his hostess by telling Jewish stories and making remarks alleging the Jews' love of ostentation—and that, Voss writes, in the house of a Jewess who was "the noblest and kindest of her race" (for his account of this incident, see R. Voss 1920, 267–68). Voss gives no hint as to the cause of Brahms's animosity toward Ibsen, but Kalbeck indicates that Brahms cared little for naturalistic drama and was, moreover, not greatly attracted by Ibsen's personality. (This, incidentally, was not Ibsen's first visit to Vienna. He had spent several weeks there in the early summer of 1873, on the occasion of the International Exhibition, at a time when Brahms was vacationing at Tutzing, near Munich.)

There is, however, strong evidence that Brahms had already made Ibsen's acquaintance prior to 1891, for he is known to have been present at a banquet given at the hotel Askanischer Hof in Berlin in early March 1889 in honor of Ibsen, who had come to Berlin to attend performances of *The Lady from the Sea* and *The Wild Duck*. It seems highly improbable that the two men would not been introduced to each other on that occasion (in this connection, see Kalbeck 1976, vol. 4, 146–47). Perhaps Ibsen simply wished, two years later in Vienna, to become *better* acquainted with Brahms. If so, Voss's account of the breakfast at Baroness Todesco's suggests that he may not have enjoyed the experience.

Brahms met Ibsen at least once more, for he was seated next to him at another banquet in Berlin in January 1896. (Brahms 1974/8, 1991; Bryan 1984; Koht 1971; Lindau 1916–17; Meyer 1971; R. Voss 1920)

– J –

JAËLL, ALFRED (b. Trieste, 5 March 1832; d. Paris, 27 February 1882). Pianist; son of the violinist Eduard Jaëll (d. 1849). A pupil of Carl Czerny and Ignaz Moscheles, he had a highly successful career as a virtuoso pianist, during which he toured widely in Europe and was enthusiastically acclaimed in America, where he performed between November 1851 and 1854. In 1856 he became court pianist to **King Georg V of Hanover**, and as a result he came into close contact with **Joseph Joachim** and appeared at various concerts conducted by the latter. (They also played together elsewhere; thus, in 1864, they performed **Schumann**'s Violin Sonata op. 105 in London.)

Jaëll was widely admired as an interpreter of **Chopin**, and he also achieved much popular success with his own drawing-room pieces and brilliant concert transcriptions. His compositions were, however, not to everyone's taste, and no one was less enchanted by them than Brahms and Joachim. In a letter to **Clara Schumann** from Hamburg in December

1855, Brahms wrote about Jaëll's "horrible" paraphrases of **Richard Wagner**'s music, and he continued, "He played some of them for us yesterday, also arrangements of songs by Schumann and **Franz**. It would be difficult to hear anything more wretched and more shallow" (Litzmann 1970, vol. 1, 160–61). Two days later he reported: "At the concert on Saturday he played very well, he plays with a lot of bravura, but trash!" (vol. 1, 162). As for Joachim, he wrote to Brahms from Hanover in March 1858: "Jaëll is here, the same shallow, twitchy fellow as always" (Brahms 1974/5, 205). On 22 December 1863 he reported that Jaëll had, in Hanover a few days earlier, played in Brahms's A-Major Quartet, "quite well on the whole, but without the vigour of a certain greater pianist [i.e., Brahms himself]" (Brahms 1974/6, 20). Jaëll appears, in fact, to have liked Brahms's compositions; in the above-mentioned letter to Clara Schumann in December 1855, Brahms told her that Jaëll went "into raptures" over his music and had played the F-sharp Minor Piano Sonata (op. 2) in public in Frankfurt (Litzmann 1970, vol. 1, 1650). There thus seems indeed to have been some substance to Jaëll's declared admiration for Brahms's music. Hélène Klener even states in her article on Jaëll in the encyclopedia *Die Musik in Geschichte und Gegenwart* that he was responsible for introducing it to Italian audiences and that he had also been among the first to present the piano quartets in London. It is not possible to verify the former claim. The latter statement, however, is not supported by R. Pascall's report on early performances of Brahms's compositions in England, for according to him, Jaëll did not play in any of the first three performances there of the Piano Quartet op. 25, and only in the second one of the Piano Quartet op. 26, on 23 May 1871; he was furthermore the second pianist to play the First Piano Concerto there, on 23 June 1873. (Pascall 2001, 309, 311).

In 1866 Jaëll married Marie Trautmann (1846–1925), who was likewise a brilliant and highly successful pianist, as well as a composer and influential teacher. The couple lived in Paris, from where they undertook various concert tours of Europe. (Brahms 1974/5–6; H. Ehrlich 1893a; Litzmann 1970; Pascall 2001)

JAHN, OTTO (b. Kiel, 16 June 1813; d. Göttingen, 9 September 1869). Philologist, archaeologist, and writer on music. He studied at Kiel, Leipzig, and Berlin, and later taught at the universities of Greifswald, Leipzig, and, from 1855, Bonn. He was regarded as one of the outstanding classical scholars of his time; in musical matters he is best known for his groundbreaking biography of **Mozart** (4 vols., 1856–59).

It is generally assumed that Brahms made Jahn's acquaintance at the Lower Rhine Music Festival at Düsseldorf in May 1855, but W. Kahl speculates that they may have first met at the house of Carl Gottlieb Kyllmann, a wealthy merchant and great music lover who settled at Bonn in 1854–55; Jahn himself moved there around Easter 1855. By then Jahn's name was certainly not unknown to Brahms; in fact, Hedwig Salomon mentioned in her "Fliegendes Blatt aus Düsseldorf" in May 1854 that during a visit to the **Schumann**s she had heard Brahms speak "animatedly" about Jahn (Kalbeck 1976, vol. 1, 169). Perhaps he was discussing an article Jahn had recently published in the journal *Die Grenzboten*, on the occasion of a performance of *Lohengrin* at Leipzig; it had contained some ironical remarks about the self-proclaimed "musicians of the future," whom Jahn detested and among whom he appears at that time to have placed Brahms.

Brahms became better acquainted with Jahn when, at Clara Schumann's request, he went to Bonn in April 1856 to discuss with him and **Albert Dietrich** the treatment that her husband was receiving at the clinic at Endenich. "Recently Brahms spent a few days here," Jahn wrote to Hermann Härtel on 22 April. "Dietrich brought him to see me. At first he was ill at ease and hostile toward me, but I took no notice since the matter seemed too important to me, and in the course of several long conversations I believe I succeeded in gaining his confidence, so that he became really friendly and quite attached to me. . . . I liked Brahms a great deal. There is a competent and energetic quality in his character, and at the same time he is sensitive and nice, and, it seems to me, straightforward and unpretentious" (Michaelis and Petersen 1913, 133–34). On 8 June, Schumann's birthday, they walked over to Endenich, together with Dietrich and **Klaus Groth**, to take Schumann a present, but only Brahms actually went inside to see him.

Next to nothing is known about Brahms's later contacts with Jahn, although they no doubt saw each other on various occasions. In May 1863 they both attended one of Amalie Weiss's (*see* JOACHIM, AMALIE) farewell performances in **Christoph Willibald Gluck**'s *Orfeo* at Hanover, prior to her marriage to **Joseph Joachim**; Clara Schumann was also present. (Herttrich 1997; Kahl 1962; Michaelis and Petersen 1913)

JAPHA-LANGHANS, LOUISE (HERMINE) (b. Hamburg, 2 February 1826; d. Wiesbaden, 13 October 1910). Pianist and composer. Her early teachers were Fritz Wahrendorf, Georg August Gross, and **Friedrich Wilhelm Grund**; later she studied with **Clara Schumann**. **Florence May** states that she became a well-known pianist in Germany and had great success in Paris. (On 24 March 1868 she played in the first Paris performance of Brahms's Piano Quintet at the Salle Érard.) She was, in addition, a gifted composer of songs (one set of five, *Fünf Gesänge*, she dedicated to Princess

Anna of Hessen [*see* ANNA (MARIA FRIEDERIKE)]). In 1858, in Hamburg, she married violinist Friedrich Wilhelm Langhans (1832–92); they were divorced in 1874. She lived in Düsseldorf, Hamburg, from 1871 in Berlin, and from 1874 at Wiesbaden.

According to her own recollections (quoted in Kalbeck 1976, vol. 1, 35–36), she first met Brahms in the showroom of the Hamburg piano manufacturer C. H. Schröder when he was "about eleven or twelve years old" (but A. Pilipczuk suggests that this initial meeting probably took place on the premises of the firm Baumgardten & Heins [Pilipczuk 1990, 28]). On that occasion Brahms, according to Japha, played a sonata of his own composition for her ("as far as I remember, it was in G minor"), which she thought was very good considering his age. Several years later they met again in the showroom of another piano manufacturer (she names Baumgardten & Heins, but Pilpczuk speculates that it may really have been Schröder this time). Japha adds that they became good friends and played much music together on two pianos. When Brahms arrived in Düsseldorf in 1853 he was delighted to find her there. She had gone to Düsseldorf to study composition and the piano with the **Schumanns** (but, by her own account, saw little of Robert). Her sister Minna was also in Düsseldorf then, receiving instruction in painting from Carl Sohn at the local Academy of Art. Brahms appears to have met them frequently, and on one occasion they presented him with an anthology of poetry. He, in his turn, dedicated the *6 Gesänge* (op. 6) to the two sisters when they were published by **Bartolf Wilhelm Senff** in December 1853. (Pilipczuk 1990)

JENNER, GUSTAV (b. Keitum, Isle of Sylt, 3 December 1865; d. Marburg, 29 August 1920). Composer. In 1870 he moved with his family to Kettwig, in 1874 to Mülheim an der Ruhr, and in 1879 to Gleschendorf, near Lübeck; from 1880 he attended the Gymnasium at Kiel. It was at Kiel that he received his early musical instruction from Theodor Gänge, a local music teacher and organist, and from Hermann Stange, a prominent church organist and, from 1878, also director of music at the university. Jenner's desire to become a professional musician came to the notice of **Klaus Groth**. Believing him to be talented, in 1887 Groth sent some songs Jenner had composed to **Fritz Simrock**, who showed them to Brahms at Thun later that year. Brahms considered them promising but immature and lacking in musical competence; he added that if he were to see Jenner he could explain to him what was wrong and show him how it could be corrected. Encouraged by these remarks that Simrock transmitted to him, Groth arranged for Brahms to meet Jenner during his stay at Leipzig in January 1888. In what proved to be a severely chastening experience for the young composer, Brahms pointed out to Jenner the multiple shortcomings of the various songs and stressed that he was in need of much further study. On his return from Leipzig, Jenner wrote to Brahms and appealed to him to make an exception in his own case to his usual rule of not taking pupils. Brahms replied that if Jenner were to come to Vienna, it should be for the purpose of studying counterpoint with **Eusebius Mandyczewski**, but that he himself was also willing to help him. On the strength of that promise Jenner promptly set out for Vienna, with the financial support of some of Groth's friends.

Jenner arrived in Vienna on 13 February 1888 and remained there until 1895 (except for the summers and the period September 1889–September 1890, which he spent in Germany performing his military service). Soon after his arrival in Vienna, he was introduced by Brahms to Mandyczewski, with whom he was to study for several years. He also saw a good deal of Brahms, not only to discuss his compositions but also socially, regularly joining him for meals at the Roter Igel restaurant. It has frequently been stated that Jenner was the only person who could rightly claim to have studied composition with Brahms. However, this statement needs qualifying inasmuch as Brahms does not appear to have ever given Jenner any formal instruction. The "tuition," which took place at irregular intervals, consisted in his offering a critical and brutally frank analysis of whatever composition Jenner had shown him, together with suggestions as to how it could be improved. Between 10 September 1890 and 31 May 1891, for instance, Jenner is known to have called on Brahms for this purpose on at least 10 occasions.

But Jenner owed far more to Brahms than this invaluable practical advice; through Brahms he met a number of prominent Viennese musicians and gained entrance to certain private houses (especially that of **Richard and Maria Fellinger**), where he was afforded splendid opportunities for hearing, and even participating in, much excellent amateur and professional music making. Furthermore, he regularly attended the meetings and concerts of the Tonkünstlerverein, of which Brahms was honorary president and of which he himself became secretary. On 27 December 1892 Jenner's *12 Trios* for women's voices were given their first performance at the Fellingers' by Fanny Tschampa, Bertha von Asztalos, and Rosa Bromeissl (the former **Rosa Girzick**), who sang them again at the Tonkünstlerverein on 23 January 1893. (The same singers performed the Trios once more at a concert given by **Marie Baumayer** on 6 February of that year.) In January 1894 Jenner twice played his Violin Sonata in B-flat Major with **Marie Soldat** at the Fellingers', and they subsequently performed it at the Tonkünstlervererin. He also gained useful musical experience by conducting small and larger choirs. For some time he directed a church choir at Baden near Vienna, and for several years he conducted a women's choir that met at the house of Justine von Hochstetter, the widow of the celebrated geologist Ferdinand von Hochstetter. (Jenner married Justine's daughter Julie in September 1895.)

It was no doubt largely on Brahms's recommendation that Jenner was offered the post of director of music at Marburg University in 1895, in succession to **Richard Barth**. He occupied it with distinction until his death; in 1900 he was accorded the title "Professor," and four years later he was awarded an honorary doctorate. He last saw Brahms in March 1897.

Jenner's compositions include about 200 songs and some vocal duets, trios, and quartets (most of which remained unpublished), as well as works for choirs and a considerable amount of instrumental music. Furthermore, he wrote an interesting account of his contacts with Brahms, "Johannes Brahms als Mensch, Lehrer und Künstler," which appeared in the journal *Musik* in 1903 before being issued in book form in 1905 (his widow published a second, unchanged, edition in 1930). Maria Fellinger took a number of photographs of the young Jenner, for the most part together with Brahms and members of her family. She also painted Jenner's portrait, which is now at Marburg University; it was reproduced in the 1930 edition of his memoir on Brahms. (R. Fellinger 1997; Heussner 1988; Jenner 1930; Lohmeier 1997)

JENSEN, ADOLF (b. Königsberg [Kaliningrad], 12 January 1837; d. Baden-Baden, 23 January 1879). Composer and pianist. While he greatly admired **Liszt** and venerated **Richard Wagner** (every bar of whose music appeared to him "to have been dictated by a god"), he was wary of certain aspects of the so-called Music of the Future, and regarded **Beethoven** and **Robert Schumann** as the "pillars of all music, past, present, and future" (Niggli 1900, 26). In 1862 he dedicated his *Fantasiestücke* for the piano (op. 7) and in 1864 his Piano Sonata op. 25 to Brahms, who is known to have thought highly of the latter work (Kienzl 1909, 600).

After Jensen settled in 1875 at Baden-Baden, where his chronic throat and lung affliction virtually turned him into a permanent invalid (though he continued to compose), Brahms visited him on several occasions. Jensen liked him and enjoyed his company: "He is an honest man who loves children, and with whom one can talk without having to fear an explosion. . . . He is extremely compassionate, unaffected, and affable, though towards strangers he is, admittedly, usually cold, even unfriendly. But if he recognizes a man's worth, one can rely on him" (Niggli 1900, 97). Jensen also admired Brahms's music; he was, Jensen wrote to a friend in 1872, "apart from Wagner, no doubt the most important composer now living" (Niggli 1900, 69).

As for Brahms, he had a high opinion of Jensen's early compositions, although he considered them "somewhat too sugary," but he judged Jensen's last works for the piano to be less successful. His view of the man was also rather critical. Jensen, he told **Richard Heuberger** in 1885, normally had a very high opinion of himself; moreover, his letters showed a good deal of vanity, and he was much given to "philosophizing" in them about his compositions. "I could never do that," Brahms remarked (Heuberger 1976, 29). (Baser 1973; Heuberger 1976; Kienzl 1909; Niggli 1900)

JOACHIM, AMALIE, née Schneeweiss [stage name: Amalie Weiss] (b. Marburg, Styria [Maribor, Slovenia], 10 May 1839; d. Berlin, 3 February 1899). (The year of her death is wrongly given as 1898 in several reference works, as in Styra Avins's [1997] *Johannes Brahms: Life and Letters* [788]). Mezzo-soprano. Her father, Magistratsrat Franz Maximilian Schneeweiss (1801–51), was a competent violinist who played in amateur quartets.

She started her career as a singer in 1853, at the age of 14, at Troppau [Opava, Czech Republic]; in 1854 she appeared at the theater at Hermannstadt [Sibiu, Romania] and that same year was engaged at the Theater am Kärntnertor in Vienna, where she made her debut as Fatima in Weber's *Oberon* on 17 December. She remained with the company for several years, during which she grew increasingly frustrated, as she was assigned only minor roles. Eventually she was engaged by **Bernhard Scholz** for the court theater at Hanover, where she made a highly acclaimed debut on 24 April 1862 as Fidès in Meyerbeer's *Le Prophète.* Her further roles at Hanover included Azucena in *Il Trovatore*, Nancy in Flotow's *Martha*, and Marguerite in Boieldieu's *La Dame blanche.* At her first appearance at a symphony concert, on 13 December 1862, she sang an aria from **Handel**'s oratorio *Theodora* and Leonora's aria "Abscheulicher! Wo eilst du hin?" from *Fidelio*. At the same concert **Joseph Joachim**, whose acquaintance she had made earlier, was the soloist in **Beethoven**'s Violin Concerto. They became engaged on 11 February 1863. Two months later, on 15 April, they participated in the first performance at Hanover of **Christoph Willibald Gluck**'s *Orfeo*, with Amalie taking the title role and Joachim, at Queen Marie's suggestion, conducting. Amalie made her farewell appearance at Hanover in *Fidelio* on 30 May, and on 10 June she married Joachim; they were to have six children (not five, as stated by Avins).

Amalie, who, according to the usual practice and also at Joachim's express wish, retired from the stage after her marriage, was eventually to establish a reputation as an outstanding oratorio and Lieder singer; in particular, she was widely praised as an exceptionally gifted and moving interpreter of the music of **Franz Schubert**, **Robert Schumann**, and Brahms. She possessed a rich and thrilling voice, and a flawless technique. Her association with Brahms, which continued even after the breakup of her marriage (as mentioned below), was a highly rewarding one for both. He was immediately impressed by her at their first meeting in Hanover in May 1863, on which occasion he also heard her in *Orfeo*; to **Albert Dietrich** he wrote that he found her quite "delightful," both as a person and as a singer (Dietrich 1898, 49). Later that year he dedicated the *4 Duette* (op. 28) to her when they were published by **C. A. Spina**.

Beatrix Borchard states that in the course of her career Amalie Joachim sang no fewer than 139 of Brahms's compositions—most frequently "Feldeinsamkeit" (op. 86/2), followed by "Wiegenlied" (op. 49/4), "Vergebliches Ständchen" (op. 74/4), and "Zigeunerlieder" (op. 103) (Borchard 2001, 278). Above all, she came to be regarded as an ideal performer of the *Alto Rhapsody*, in which she was soloist at Bremen on 9 November 1871 and on numerous occasions thereafter. According to M. L. McCorkle's (1984) *Werkverzeichnis*, she furthermore sang in the first public performances of the following compositions: *Liebeslieder-Walzer* (op. 52, version with orchestral accompaniment) at the Hochschule für Musik in Berlin, on 19 March 1870; "Agnes" (op. 59/5) in Hamburg on 2 April 1875; "Klosterfräulein" (op. 61/2) at Merseburg on 21 February 1895; "Des Liebsten Schwur" (op. 69/4) in Berlin on 31 October 1877; "So lass uns wandern!" (op. 75/3) in Berlin on 7 March 1880; "Der Kranz" (op. 84/2) in Berlin on 17 February 1884 (but Borchard records an even earlier public performance of this song by her, namely at Leipzig on the 11th of the preceding month); and *Zigeunerlieder* (op. 103, in the version for vocal quartet) and "Salamander" (op. 107/2), in Berlin on 31 October 1888.

Sometimes Brahms accompanied her on piano, as at Strasbourg on 20 December 1882, when she sang "Der Kranz" and "Vergebliches Ständchen" (op. 84/ 2, 4), or he sometimes conducted works in which she sang (e.g., the *Alto Rhapsody* at Leipzig on 5 February 1874, in Vienna on 10 January 1875, and in Holland in January 1882). She also took part in the concert at which the Requiem (then still in only six movements) received its first performance at Bremen on 10 April 1868 (*see* REINTHALER, KARL [MARTIN]). Later, Brahms invited her to perform at some of the concerts he conducted as artistic director of the Gesellschaft der Musikfreunde in Vienna. Thus she sang the aria "Wo bin ich, unglückliche Alceste" from **Christoph Willibald Gluck**'s *Alceste* at a concert on 8 December 1872, and the aria "O ewiges Feuer" from **Bach**'s *Pfingstkantata* and the solo part in the *Alto Rhapsody* on 10 January 1875. There is thus ample evidence of the admiration Brahms felt for her as an artist. **Max Kalbeck** claims moreover that Amalie's beautiful voice inspired and stimulated the composition of many of Brahms's songs.

No less striking is the proof he gave of his esteem for Amalie as a person, even at the cost of her husband's friendship. By the early 1880s her marriage was in serious trouble, as Joachim suspected her of infidelity; in particular, he accused her of entertaining an illicit relationship with the publisher **Fritz Simrock**. Brahms was utterly certain that she was innocent, and he repeatedly, though unsuccessfully, strove to convince Joachim that his suspicions were groundless. In December 1880, during a brief stay in Berlin, Brahms realized that their relations had reached a critical point, but though he would have wished to, he apparently was unable to discuss the situation with Amalie. However, when she wrote to him about it later, he seized the opportunity to state his attitude at considerable length and with great compassion, assuring her of his absolute trust in her integrity and deploring what he considered her husband's delusional tendencies in such matters. In a further letter he authorized her to communicate his thoughts to anyone she wanted to. (For the full text of these two letters, see Holde 1959, 319–21; for an English version of the first letter, *see* Avins 1979, 572-74). Brahms was nonetheless taken aback when Amalie subsequently produced the first letter in her defense during the divorce proceedings brought against her by Joachim. Despite the fact that he had not anticipated the public disclosure of what was a private communication, Brahms made it clear to Joachim in October 1883 that he did not regret having conveyed to Amalie in writing certain opinions that he had so frequently expressed to him in conversation. Joachim, however, who had previously reacted angrily to Brahms's arguments and admonishments, regarded the written declaration as a betrayal of their long friendship. They were not to resume cordial personal relations until some years later (*see* JOACHIM, JOSEPH). The Joachims were officially divorced in December 1884, responsibility for the collapse of the marriage being placed on the husband (who in a letter to his brother Heinrich, which is now at the Brahms Institut, Lübeck, called the judgment a travesty of human justice).

After the divorce Brahms remained in touch with Amalie, occasionally concertized with her, and did his best to obtain engagements for her. She continued to perform his songs, and occasionally arranged all-Brahms concerts, for instance, at Leipzig on 17 March 1887 when she sang more than a dozen of his songs while pianist **Willy Rehberg** played the Rhapsodies op. 79, with Henri Petri the Violin Sonata op. 100, and together with him and Alwin Schröder the Piano Trio op. 101; the program was subsequently repeated at her concert in Berlin on 14 April. (In his "Brahms-Erinnerungen," Rehberg (1933) states that she had persuaded Fritz Simrock not to publish opp. 99–101 until they had received their earliest performances in Germany at her concerts; they appeared in April 1887.) During the 1890s she was once again much sought after as an oratorio and concert singer; an attempt to revive her operatic career had, however, been less successful. In 1892 she gave a series of recitals in America (the program of her first concert in New York, on 30 March, included Brahms's "Feldeinsamkeit"). At a concert in Berlin on 17 January 1897, she sang his *4 ernste Gesänge*, and on 11 April of that year she gave a recital there in his memory. Moreover, from 1895 she taught at the Klindworth-Scharwenka Conservatory in Berlin, and two years later she opened her own school of singing.

Not long before her death, she and Joachim were reconciled, when he apparently accepted her renewed protestations that she had never been unfaithful to him. (Some letters addressed by Amalie to Joachim subsequent to their divorce are printed in Borchard 2005, 392–401). He saw her during her last illness and was able to grieve genuinely over her death. On the day of her funeral (7 February 1899) he wrote to his nephew Anton Singer: "We were divorced, but never have I felt more vividly how profoundly I loved her and her many glorious qualities than when I twice visited her during the last days before her operation [for gallstones]." He had even, he added, contemplated living with her again "for the sake of the children" (Johannes Joachim and Moser 1911–13, vol. 3, 490). Yet it seems that he could never rid himself entirely of his agonizing doubts. Kalbeck (1976) relates a conversation at Gmunden in 1903, in the course of which Joachim entreated him to say how Brahms had really judged his wife's behavior. "The assurance that Brahms had been firmly convinced of her innocence appeared to give him temporary relief. He sighed profoundly and passed his hand over his eyes" (vol 3, 301, n. 1). (Borchard 2001, 2005; Brahms 1974/5–6; Dietrich 1898; Holde 1959; Johannes Joachim and Moser 1911–13; Plaschke 1899; Rehberg 1933)

JOACHIM, JOSEPH (b. Kitsee [Köpcsény], near Pressburg [Bratislava], 28 June 1831; d. Berlin, 15 August 1907). Violinist, composer, conductor, and teacher. One of the most admired and best-loved musicians of his time, particularly popular in England, which he regularly visited over many years. Brahms first heard him play when he performed the **Beethoven** Violin Concerto with the Hamburg Philharmonic Orchestra on 11 March 1848. By the time Brahms called on him at Hanover in April 1853 in the company of Eduard Reményi (*see* REMÉNYI, EDE [EDUARD]), Joachim, though still only 21 years old, had established a solid reputation as an outstandingly gifted performer and had recently taken up the position of Konzertmeister at the court of **King Georg V of Hanover**.

At the unveiling of the Brahms monument at Meiningen in 1899, Joachim recalled the stunning effect that the compositions of the "delicate, dreamy-looking Johannes" and his piano playing had made on him that day at Hanover (Joseph Joachim 1899, 623). The two young men were to see a good deal of each other during the months following this first meeting, for, after parting from Reményi at Weimar, Brahms spent the summer with Joachim at Göttingen (where Joachim was attending lectures at the university) and the autumn and the early part of the following year with him at Hanover. These early contacts laid the basis for an artistic association, which, as far as Joachim's championship of Brahms's music was concerned, extended to the very end of his public concertizing. They exchanged contrapuntal exercises for a time, and Brahms was to seek Joachim's advice during the composition of some of his most important works, notably the First Piano Concerto and the Violin Concerto. Moreover, Joachim played a key role in presenting some of Brahms's newest works to the public. In the case of the Violin Concerto, the numerous early performances he gave, beginning with the premiere at Leipzig on 1 January 1879, were particularly useful to Brahms inasmuch as they led him, partly at Joachim's suggestion, to make certain changes in the score before sending it to the printers (in this connection, see their correspondence for 1879 (Brahms 1974/6).

Altogether, Joachim participated in the first performances of the following works, either as conductor, soloist, or leader of the Joachim Quartet, which he had founded in Berlin in 1869 with colleagues from the Berlin Hochschule für Musik, of which he had assumed the directorship the previous year (original members of the quartet: Joachim, Ernst Schiever, Heinrich de Ahna, and Wilhelm Müller): the Serenade op. 11, First Piano Concerto, String Sextet op. 18, String Quartet op. 51/2, String Quartet op. 67, Violin Concerto, Concerto for Violin and Cello, Clarinet Trio, and Clarinet Quintet (for details, see M. L. McCorkle's [1984] *Werkverzeichnis*). He also appeared at the concert at Bremen Cathedral on 10 April 1868, at which Brahms conducted the world premiere of the Requiem, though still without its later fifth movement (*see* REINTHALER, KARL [MARTIN]). In addition, Joachim and Brahms appeared together at numerous other concerts over the years: they undertook a joint concert tour of Switzerland in October–November 1866, and another tour in November–December of the following year, in the course of which they performed in Vienna and other Austrian towns, as well as in Budapest; and in September 1879 they gave concerts in Budapest and in several towns in Transylvania. (Their very first joint concert, according to **Florence May**, had taken place at Göttingen in 1853.) Moreover, they not only enjoyed making music together, but they also shared an identical attitude toward certain contemporary trends in music, notably those represented by **Liszt**. Joachim, who, unlike Brahms, had been close to Liszt—they were on "Du" terms—had by 1855 turned against his music, and in 1857 he informed Liszt in a remarkably frank letter of the hostility it aroused in him. (They were not to meet again for over 20 years.) Joachim's involvement in the preparation of the declaration attacking the "New German School" in 1860 comes therefore as no surprise. (On this subject, *see* BRENDEL, KARL FRANZ and LISZT, FRANZ.)

Yet, despite the long artistic association that proved so rewarding and satisfying to both men, their personal relationship, which had started on such a warm note, was far from untroubled. In fact, as greatly as Joachim usually enjoyed Brahms's company and however intimate their contacts generally were over many years, Joachim never seems to have felt entirely at ease with Brahms, because he had quickly become aware of certain character traits in his new friend that were liable to bring about unwelcome changes in his behavior. Thus, as early as November 1853, he referred to Brahms's "egoism" in a letter to Gisela von Arnim, and almost exactly a year later, he informed the same correspondent that Brahms's latest visit had not been very agreeable, "although I once again recognized all his good and indeed rare qualities." Brahms, he complained, was "the most unmitigated egoist anyone could imagine, and quite unaware of it" (Johannes Joachim 1911, 65). Joachim attributed the lack of consideration, which Brahms displayed at times toward others without even realizing it, to an unsatisfactory upbringing (a similar idea was expressed many years later by **Theodor Billroth**). Significantly, Joachim returned to the subject yet again in January 1856, in a further letter to Gisela von Arnim. There were two sides to Brahms's character, he explained: on the one hand, a guileless brilliance (which was the one mostly in evidence and which, Joachim declared, he loved tremendously), and on the other, a fierce pugnaciousness that, in certain circumstances, could turn into an "obsessive desire to dominate" (Johannes Joachim 1911, 78). Joachim evidently struggled over the years to accept Brahms as he was, "warts and all"; after attending the performance in Vienna on 1 December 1867 of the first three movements of the Requiem, he wrote to his wife that the grandiose, profound, and original work had convinced him that Brahms was a "superior human being," and he himself would never again criticize any minor faults he discerned in him. (The letter is now at the Brahms Institute in Lübeck.)

Nonetheless, Joachim's relations with Brahms were to experience two significant crises. The first occurred on the occasion of the **Schumann** Festival held at Bonn from 16 to 18 August 1873 and was fairly quickly settled (*see* HEIMSOETH, FRIEDRICH); the second, which arose in connection with the breakup of Joachim's marriage and Brahms's firmly expressed sympathy for Amalie, marred their friendship for several years. (On the Joachims' marital problems, *see* JOACHIM, AMALIE.) Styra Avins (1997) is incorrect in stating, in *Johannes Brahms: Life and Letters*, that they separated but did not divorce; their divorce was in fact pronounced in December 1884.

It should, however, be stressed that even during the years of his estrangement from Brahms Joachim did not cease to cherish his music. "Even if I no longer have any claim on your person, I retain my love for the beauty you create" he assured Brahms on one occasion (Brahms 1974/6, 212). In consequence, he eagerly accepted Brahms's offer to make the new Third Symphony available to himself for performance in Berlin, following its Viennese premiere on 2 December 1883, and Joachim conducted the symphony in Berlin on 4 January. Brahms himself conducted two further performances of the work there on 28 and 29 January 1884, but on that occasion he brusquely declined to meet Joachim who, after a few days' absence from Berlin, was due to return there early on the 29th ("Forgive me if I save the attempt to see you until next time. I really need the few hours of this, my only free day here, most urgently for a mass of correspondence" [Brahms 1974/6, 213]). It should be added that Joachim had refused to shake Brahms's proffered hand at the Cologne Festival the previous May.

On 1 February 1886 Joachim conducted the first Berlin performance of the Fourth Symphony, an event that led to a further exchange of correspondence between the two men. But it was another work, the Concerto for Violin and Cello, that finally brought them together again. In July 1887 Brahms, writing from Thun, reported its composition and, encouraged by Joachim, dispatched the manuscript to Berlin, where Joachim examined it with **Robert Hausmann** (whom Brahms had mentioned as the prospective cellist) before sending it back to Brahms with suggestions for a few changes in the violin part. They all met for a run-through of the new concerto at **Clara Schumann**'s house at Baden-Baden on 21 September. She noted in her diary, "This concerto is, as it were, a work of reconciliation. Joachim and Brahms have spoken to each other for the first time in years" (Litzmann 1902, vol 3, 496). A private performance, with the Baden-Baden Kurorchester, took place two days later. Brahms, Joachim, and Hausmann subsequently gave the first public performance of the work at Cologne on 18 October. Thereafter, Brahms and Joachim resumed their former cordial relations, without, however, ever quite recovering their earlier intimacy. Three years later, the String Quintet op. 111 was first performed at a concert of the

Joachim Quartet in Berlin on 10 December 1890, and it was at another concert given by the Quartet in Berlin on 12 December 1891, and in which Brahms took part, that the Clarinet Trio and the Clarinet Quintet received their world premieres.

Joachim had his final meetings with Brahms when the quartet visited Vienna in the winter of 1896–97. In a letter to their mutual friend **Julius Otto Grimm** on 17 December 1896, he mentioned having spent much time during the previous week with Brahms, who most days had sat up with the members of the quartet until late into the night. Brahms appears to have been especially pleased with the performance of the String Quintet op. 111 at the quartet's concert on 2 January 1897. "I had never heard him express his appreciation so warmly before," Joachim recalled in a letter to **Ernst Rudorff** shortly after Brahms's death, adding rather sadly: "On a personal level, I could offer him little these last years" (Johannes Joachim and Moser 1911–13, vol. 3, 471).

Brahms dedicated his very first published work, the Piano Sonata in C Major, to Joachim, who, in his turn, dedicated his "Hungarian" Violin Concerto op. 11 (Leipzig, 1861) to Brahms. The latter did not present any of Joachim's original compositions during his three years as artistic director of the Gesellschaft der Musikfreunde, but he concluded his very first concert, on 10 November 1872, with a performance of Joachim's orchestrated version of **Franz Schubert**'s Sonata in C Major (op. 140 [D812], known as the "Grand Duo"). Later, he also dedicated his Violin Concerto to Joachim. Brahms was a godfather of the Joachims' first child, Johannes, born on 12 September 1864. (Concerning Joachim, *see also* HILDEBRAND, ADOLF VON.) (Borchard 2005; Brahms 1974/5–6; W. Ebert 1991; Fischer 1903; Holde 1959; Johannes Joachim and Moser 1911–13; Joseph Joachim 1899; Litzmann 1902, 1970; May 1948; A. Moser 1908, 1923; Pulver 1925; U. Schilling 1994)

– K –

KAHN, ROBERT (b. Mannheim, 21 July 1865; d. Biddenden, England, 29 May 1951). Composer, pianist, and teacher. Son of the banker Bernhard Kahn (1827–1905). While still at school, Robert was taught the piano by **Ernst Frank** and Emil Paur, and theory by **Vincenz Lachner**, and later he continued his studies with Friedrich Kiel, **Woldemar Bargiel**, and **Ernst Rudorff** at the Musikhochschule in Berlin (during which time he also came to know **Joseph Joachim**) and with Joseph Rheinberger in Munich. From 1890 to 1893 he was employed as assistant conductor at the Stadt theater in Leipzig, and also founded and directed a women's choir in that city; subsequently, he served on the faculty of the Musikhochschule in Berlin (1894–1930). In 1937 he emigrated to England. His numerous compositions range from chamber music to songs and choral works.

Kahn first met Brahms at Mannheim on 13 February 1886, at a reception—probably given by his uncle and aunt Emil and Berta Hirsch, both prominent figures in local society—following a concert at which Brahms had conducted the local premiere of his Fourth Symphony and played his Second Piano Concerto. In 1887 Kahn spent three months (February to April) in Vienna, and during that time he frequently met Brahms, regularly joining him at lunch at the Roter Igel restaurant and in the evening at Gause's bierkeller. Kahn's account of his contacts with Brahms was published by Burkhard Laugwitz in the journal *Das Orchester* in 1986. In it he described the impact that Brahms's personality had made on him as "tremendous" and as the strongest he had ever received from another human being: "I have, to be sure, encountered more stimulating, more intelligent, more communicative men, but none other whose every word, indeed every movement, bore in such high degree the imprint of a truly original character" (Laugwitz 1986, 646). When Kahn mentioned that he intended to take lessons with Theodor Leschetitzky, Brahms, who did not approve of the latter's teaching method, strongly advised against it and even offered to teach Kahn himself. But Kahn states that he was too diffident to accept. It was perhaps for the same reason that he also declined Brahms's invitation to join him and **Theodor Kirchner** and **Fritz Simrock** on a forthcoming trip to Italy. Evidently, Brahms had taken a liking to him.

Kahn met Brahms once more in 1887, at Baden-Baden. While there, he attended the matinee at which Brahms tried out his newly composed Double Concerto with Joachim and **Robert Hausmann** (23 September 1887), and he was also present that afternoon at the private performance at **Clara Schumann**'s house of the recently published Piano Trio op. 101 ("I was permitted to come along—no one else" [Laugwitz 1986, 647]). In later years he met Brahms on several further occasions, particularly in Berlin, but, by his own account, he never again achieved the intimate contact he had so much enjoyed in Vienna.

Robert's younger brother Otto (1867–1934) became a leading American banker, as well as chairman (1911–18) and president (1918–31) of the Metropolitan Opera Company, New York. (Kahn 1994; Laugwitz 1986; Rilling 1975)

KAISERFELD, MORITZ (CLEMENS AUGUST) VON (b. Birkfeld, Styria, 13 August 1839; d. Graz, 9 January 1909). Son of Moriz Judas

Thaddäus von Kaiserfeld (1811–85), a prosperous landowner, who had a distinguished political career, both at the national level (he was president of the House of Representatives of the Reichsrat) and in the province of Styria (of which he was governor from 1870 to 1884).

A professional soldier with the rank of Rittmeister, Moritz von Kaiserfeld quit the service in 1867 after being seriously wounded at the battle of Königgrätz [Hradek Králové, Czech Republic] in July 1866; and devoted the remainder of his life to his great passion for music, hunting, and traveling. He played a prominent part in the musical life of Graz, particularly through his active support of the Musikverein für Steiermark. Furthermore, he contributed articles on music to the *Grazer Tagespost* between 1893 and 1897. He was himself an excellent violinist, and his wife Antonie, née von Franck (1847–1933), was a gifted pianist. The couple made Brahms's acquaintance at Pörtschach in 1877 and later met him occasionally at the house of **Anna Franz** (*see* WITTGENSTEIN FAMILY) in Vienna, where they often spent the winter. They last saw him shortly before his death. In her memoirs Antonie devoted a chapter to Brahms.

Through being in the right place at the right time, Kaiserfeld had the good fortune to be invited to take part in the very first (private) performance of Brahms's String Quintet (op. 88). When Brahms, who was vacationing at Ischl, visited **László Wagner de Zólyom** at Altaussee in August 1882, he brought with him the manuscripts of his new Piano Trio (op. 87) and of his new Quintet, which is scored for two violins, two violas, and a cello. It was reportedly Brahms who, having spotted Kaiserfeld among those present, asked him to join his host's string quartet as second violist, and Kaiserfeld, though not used to playing the viola, agreed. He seems to have acquitted himself well enough, for after the performance Brahms gave him a signed autograph, in which he had written out some bars from the first and second viola parts, and underneath them: "Viola I debatable, Viola II definitely commendable! . . . Greatly obliged to Herr von Kayserfeld for his excellent viola playing" (W. Ebert 1997a, 44). (On the concert as a whole, *see* WAGNER DE ZÓLYOM, LÁSZLÓ.) (W. Ebert 1982, 1997; A. Kaiserfeld 1932; H. Kaiserfeld 1996; M. Kaiserfeld 1898; *ÖBL* 1957–)

KALBECK, MAX (b. Breslau [Wrocław, Poland], 4 January 1850; d. Vienna, 4 May 1921). Author, music critic, and editor. He received his first lessons in music and violin at the age of six, and subsequently sang as a boy chorister under Leopold Damrosch and in his later teens appeared as a singer at church services and concerts. He began legal studies at Breslau University but also attended lectures on various other subjects. In 1870 he published a volume of poetry under the title *Aus Natur und Leben*. The following year he continued his studies in Munich, but before long he decided to switch to music and in 1873 enrolled at the conservatory where he studied composition with Joseph Rheinberger, the violin with Josef Walter, and orchestral playing and choral singing with **Franz Wüllner**. In 1874 he returned to Breslau, and there he worked as a music, art, and drama critic on the *Schlesische Zeitung* and later on the *Breslauer Zeitung*. He first went to Vienna in 1877 to study art. In 1880 he settled permanently there, and with the support of **Eduard Hanslick** he soon established himself as an influential music critic, writing first for the *Wiener allgemeine Zeitung* (1880–83) and then for *Die Presse* (1883–90), *Montags-Revue* (1890–95), and, from 1895, the *Neues Wiener Tagblatt* (on which newspaper he had already served as drama critic since 1886). A fervent partisan of Brahms, he had little sympathy and understanding for the music of **Liszt**, **Richard Wagner**, and **Anton Bruckner**.

In addition to his journalistic activity, Kalbeck published a number of studies (the earliest of which were devoted to Wagner's operas) and he furthermore made a name for himself as a prolific translator and reviser of operatic librettos. He produced new ones for **Mozart**'s *Bastien und Bastienne* and *La finta giardiniera*, and made fresh versions of those of *Don Giovanni* and Gluck's *Orfeo*). He also wrote some original ones—for example, for **Sir George Henschel**'s opera *Nubia* (first given at Dresden in 1889) and, with Gustav Davis, provided the text for **Johann Strauss**'s operetta *Jabuka* (premiered at the Theater an der Wien on 12 October 1894). Moreover, several of his poems were set by contemporary composers, including **Ignaz Brüll**, **Josef Gänsbacher**, **Richard Heuberger**, and Brahms, who used two of them in "Nachtwandler" (op. 86/3) and "Letztes Glück" (op. 104/3).

Kalbeck was introduced to Brahms at Breslau on 29 December 1874 by Adolph Kaufmann, the founder and president of the local Orchesterverein, at a rehearsal for a concert, at which Brahms played his D Minor Piano Concerto and directed performances of three of his Hungarian dances. In his Brahms biography, Kalbeck declares that the impact that Brahms's personality and musicianship made on him then was so powerful that he knew at once that he would henceforth be totally devoted both to the man and the musician. (He had, in fact, already seen Brahms at Tutzing in the summer of the preceding year but without, at the time, realizing who he was.) Once Kalbeck had settled in Vienna and entered into regular contact with Brahms, he proved himself a steadfast admirer and an unwavering friend. "His love for Brahms and his faithfulness to him were exemplary," the music critic Richard Specht (1928), who knew him well, wrote in his own book on the composer. "He loved what [Brahms] loved . . . hated what he hated." Specht describes Kalbeck himself as "a splendid, blond giant" who always remained "a great, good-hearted child," a larger-than-life figure with a strong sense of humor, and as a critic never indifferent but given to violent bouts of praise or scorn (205–6).

While it is obvious that Kalbeck's attitude toward Brahms fell little short of idolatry, there is no clear evidence about the nature of Brahms's feelings for him. He must surely have appreciated his staunch support and faithful friendship; on the other hand, it is less certain that he rated him very highly as a critic. To Richard Heuberger he once observed that Kalbeck did not possess the intellectual humility without which no man could achieve excellence (Heuberger 1976, 162); and Specht recalls hearing Brahms making sarcastic remarks about Kalbeck on several occasions, and moreover, he relates an incident at a private dinner party when Brahms was so exasperated by a tirade of Kalbeck's in which he perorated about Wagner's operas comparing them unfavorably with Cherubini's *Medea*, that he struck the table with his fist and brutally told Kalbeck not to speak of matters he did not understand. The sequel, as reported by Specht, is a charming demonstration of the reverence and awe Kalbeck felt for Brahms. Meeting Specht a few days after this humiliating experience, Kalbeck told him that he had been unwilling to put up with Brahms's insulting behavior and had written him a long letter in which he had not minced his words. When Specht asked how Brahms had reacted, Kalbeck admitted with a rueful laugh that he had not sent the letter (Specht 1928, 207). Of course, Brahms's propensity for rudeness and irritability was well known to his intimates, so much so that they were saddened by the sudden gentleness that characterized his manner at the onset of his fatal illness. Kalbeck's letter to his great friend **Paul Heyse** on 2 November 1896 is revealing in this connection: "We only realised how greatly we loved this marvellous man when it appeared that we might lose him, and we were overjoyed when he recently hurled massively rude remarks at my and dear Brüll's heads, whereas before he overflowed with uncanny sweetness and mildness. Now, thank Heavens, he is cursing once more!" (Münster 1984, 356). After Brahms's death, he wrote to Heyse on 4 May 1897: "When Brahms dies, who dares to live?" (Münster 1984, 357).

Kalbeck's greatest and most lasting achievement is undoubtedly his four-volume study of the life and music of Brahms (1904–14, 2nd ed. 1908–15, 3rd ed. 1912–22). It is by no means factually faultless, and certainly not totally unbiased in the presentation of its subject's relations with the large cast of supporting characters. Marie von Bülow, for one, expressed strong objections to his portrayal of her husband's association with

Brahms (see M. von Bülow 1912, 1914). Nevertheless, the biographical account that forms the essential part of the work remains an invaluable document, of outstanding interest to all modern Brahmsians. It draws its material from countless published and unpublished sources, as well as from the author's own extensive memories of his often close contacts with Brahms. (M. von Bülow 1912, 1914; Floros 2001; Harten 1985; Heuberger 1976; Kalbeck 1898, 1976; Meisner 1977; Münster 1984; Musgrave 1988; Specht 1928)

KAPPER, SIEGFRIED (1821–77). Brahms set texts by Kapper in the songs "Mädchenfluch" (op. 69/9), "Mädchenlied" (op. 85/3), "Ade!" (op. 85/4), "Das Mädchen" and "Vorschneller Schwur" (op. 95/1, 5), and in the compositions for four-voice mixed chorus "Das Mädchen" (op. 93a/2; same text as op. 95/1) and "Der Falke" (op. 93a/5). All the texts were translations of Serbian poems except for "Ade," which was based on a Czech poem.

KARPATH, LUDWIG (b. Pest [Budapest], 27 April 1866; d. Vienna, 8 September 1936). Music critic. Having given up his original plan to become an opera singer, he settled around 1894 in Vienna and subsequently worked for many years as a music critic for the *Neues Wiener Tagblatt*, retiring in 1921; in addition, he edited the journal *Der Merker* (1914–17). Later he acted as consultant to the state theaters. He was acquainted with many prominent musicians, among them **Arthur Nikisch** and **Gustav Mahler**, for whose appointment as director of the Vienna Opera he was to some extent responsible. **Richard Strauss** dedicated the ballet *Schlagobers* to him in 1924.

Karpath's book *Begegnung mit dem Genius* contains a chapter on Brahms, to whom he was introduced at Ischl in the summer of 1894 by **Ilona Eibenschütz**. He makes it clear that he was never on intimate terms with Brahms, although he met him repeatedly. One of the most interesting aspects of the chapter is the information it provides on Brahms's stay at Karlsbad in September 1896. (Karpath 1934)

KÄSSMAYER, MORIZ (b. Vienna, 20 March 1831; d. Vienna, 9 November 1884). Composer and conductor. He attended the Vienna conservatory (1843–47), studying the violin with Georg Hellmesberger and Joseph Böhm, and theory with Gottfried von Preyer. In 1856 he was engaged as a violinist in the Philharmonic Orchestra, and later became conductor of ballet music at the court opera, as well as a member of the court Kapelle. He was a prolific composer whose output covered a variety of genres, from orchestral and chamber music to vocal works, the latter including humorous pieces for male chorus and church music, and he also wrote an opera, *Das Landhaus in Meudon*, which was produced at the opera in 1869. Most widely appreciated of all his compositions were his entertaining arrangements for string quartet of Austrian, Bohemian, and Hungarian folk songs, of which he published numerous volumes. Among their admirers was Brahms who, according to **Max Kalbeck**, used to enjoy listening to them at Kässmayer's house, where the host held regular fortnightly quartet sessions with **Alois Mayer**, Heinrich Zöllner, and **Josef Gänsbacher**. In fact, it was Brahms who recommended these pieces to Emil Robert Lienau (*see* LIENAU), the owner of the Berlin publishing house Schlesinger, which published them.

After Kässmayer's death, Brahms spoke warmly about him to **Richard Heuberger**, describing him as a splendid musician, a good man, and an excellent colleague (Heuberger 1976, 26). (Heuberger 1976; Lienau 1934; *ÖBL* 1957–)

KELLER, GOTTFRIED (Zurich, 19 July 1819; d. Zurich, 15 July 1890). Swiss poet, novelist, and short story writer. Brahms first met him in Switzerland in 1866 and came to know him quite well when he was staying at Rüschlikon, on Lake Zurich, in the summer of 1874. In July of that year Keller went to Vienna to attend the wedding of his friend Sigmund Exner, a brother of **Adolf Exner**, and while there he wrote to Brahms (who was still in Switzerland) to ask him to set a humorous text he had written, as a wedding cantata. Brahms obliged (WoO 16), though with little enthusiasm, since, as he told Keller, he did not consider the words very suitable for setting to music, nor indeed for the occasion. Brahms met Keller repeatedly when he visited Zurich in December 1881.

Brahms greatly admired Keller as a writer and poet, and he set three of his poems in the songs "Salome" (op. 69/8), "Abendregen" (op. 70/4), and "Therese" (op. 86/1), taking the texts from Keller's *Neuere Gedichte* (1851). Brahms also hugely appreciated Keller's epistolary style. When he was given access in the autumn of 1890 to letters Keller had written to Adolf Exner and his sister Marie, and to the Viennese journalist Emil Kuh, he found them so entertaining and interesting that he copied many passages for his personal pleasure and sent eight pages of extracts to **Joseph Viktor Widmann**. Moreover, he spent an entire afternoon reading many of them to **Max Kalbeck**. In a letter to Keller's biographer J. Bächtold in December 1890, he called Keller "your great and wonderful compatriot" (Steiner 1898–99, 32). (Brahms 1974/8; Erismann 1974; H. Frisch 1981; Steiner 1898–99; Zimmermann 1983)

KELLER, ROBERT (b. Harpersdorf [Twardocice, Poland], near Liegnitz [Legnica], 6 January 1828; d. Berlin, 16 June 1891). Music teacher, editor, and arranger. From 1862 he taught the piano at the Stern Conservatory in Berlin, of which he was himself a graduate. He was to work for several music publishers, most notably **Fritz Simrock**, and among the composers on the latter's list it was Brahms who most consistently engaged his attention.

The earliest reference to Keller in Brahms's letters to Simrock (as edited by **Max Kalbeck**) occurs in November 1871 and concerns his proofreading of the *Schicksalslied* (Brahms 1974/9, 107). His assistance with the publication of Brahms's compositions issued by Simrock thus extends roughly from that work to the String Quintet op. 111, which appeared in February 1891, four months before his death. In addition, he made a very considerable number of arrangements of Brahms's works (for details, see Bozarth 1996, appendix F). Brahms repeatedly expressed his appreciation of Keller's careful editing and proofreading, but he thought less highly of Keller's arrangements, which he found pedestrian, and he usually preferred not to see them before they were published; on more than one occasion he urged Simrock to employ **Theodor Kirchner** instead for such tasks. Therefore, he was genuinely surprised when he saw Keller's two-piano transcription of the First Symphony in May 1890; for once, he approved of Keller's work, which, he informed Simrock, had given him "no vexation, but genuine pleasure" (Brahms 1974/12, 23). Kalbeck states that Brahms's commendation relates to an arrangement of the Double Concerto op. 102, but it seems more logical in the light of an earlier letter from Brahms and the letter from Keller mentioned below to connect it, as Bozarth does, with Keller's transcription of the First Symphony.)

The earliest letter from Brahms to Keller in Bozarth's edition was written in September 1877 and relates to the First Symphony, of which Keller was then correcting the galley proofs; the final item in the correspondence is a letter from Keller dated 30 May 1890 in which he expresses his great pleasure at Brahms's praise for his work and adds that he will need a few more weeks to complete the arrangement of the Second Symphony. Furthermore, he recalls a visit Brahms had once paid him while both were vacationing in Switzerland. (It had taken place in early August of 1888 when Brahms traveled from Thun, where he was then staying, to spend a few days with Keller at Weesen, on the Wallensee.)

Keller was also responsible for the preparation of the thematic catalog of Brahms's works, which was published by Simrock in 1887. Brahms had strongly opposed the project, considering it unnecessary and pretentious ("You will not be able to convince anyone that I am not trying to set up a monument to myself," he had complained to Keller [Bozarth 1996, 98]). But, being unable to prevent its realization, he endeavored to exercise at least some control over it and, in particular, managed to foil Simrock's plan to issue the catalog simultaneously with his op. 100, which seemed an especially pompous idea to him. In the event, the catalog covered opp. 1–101 and eight works without opus numbers. In 1897, most probably after Brahms's death, Simrock was to bring out a considerably expanded version of this catalog, which took account of all compositions published in Brahms's lifetime, with or without opus numbers, as well as all arrangements of them made by Brahms himself and most of those so far prepared by other persons. Subsequently, the Simrock Verlag published some further issues of the catalog, which also included information about those published after his death. (For a close discussion of Simrock's *Verzeichniss*, see D. McCorkle 1973.)

In his letter of 30 May 1890, Keller calls himself "an enthusiastic apostle of your gospel" (Bozarth 1996, 148), and it is evident, if only from his willingness and indeed eagerness to devote such a large part of his life to the service of Brahms's music, that he deeply revered him. For his part, Brahms respected and liked Keller (on more than one occasion he refers to him as a "good, dear fellow") and he was genuinely saddened by his death. (Brahms 1974/9, 1974/12; Bozarth 1996; D. McCorkle 1973)

KERNER, JUSTINUS (ANDREAS CHRISTIAN) (b. Ludwigsburg, 18 September 1786; d. Weinsberg, 21 February 1862). Physician, with a strong interest in parapsychology; poet. Brahms set a text by Kerner in the duet "Klosterfräulein" (op. 61/2). (Fröschle 1990)

KIEL, (CLEMENS) AUGUST (b. Wiesbaden, 26 May 1813; d. Detmold, 28 December 1871). Violinist, conductor, and composer. He belonged to a family that was greatly involved with music and the theater: his father, Friedrich Wilhelm Kiel, was a singing teacher, and later administrator of the theater at Sondershausen; one of his sisters, Franziska, was a singer and teacher (*see* CORNET-KIEL, FRANZISKA); another, Amalie, was a singer at the theater at Kassel; a third, Marie, was a member of the company of the Sondershausen theater; and a brother, Adolf, was an opera singer at Schwerin.

Kiel studied the violin and composition with Louis Spohr. In June 1832 he became a member of the orchestra at Detmold (the "Hautboisten-Corps, later renamed "Hofkapelle"). Following the death of Kapellmeister Wilhelm Marburg in August 1836, he assumed the functions of the orchestra's conductor, initially with the title of "Konzertmeister," and from 1845 with that of "Kapellmeister"; he was also made responsible for operatic performances. The performance of *Tannhäuser* that he conducted in 1855 was the first of any **Richard Wagner** opera to be presented at Detmold.

During the three seasons (1857–59) that Brahms spent at Detmold (*see* LEOPOLD III, PRINCE ZUR LIPPE), he appears to have kept his distance from Kiel, who by all accounts viewed his appointment with some unease, seeing in him a possible rival for the favor of the court and even a potential successor. In December 1857 Brahms informed **Joseph Joachim** that he got on with Kiel "somewhat better than not at all" (Brahms 1974/5, 192). Almost certainly Kiel, who must normally have enjoyed considerable prestige as the supreme musical authority in the town, was in some degree pushed out of the limelight by the brilliant young pianist and composer who taught **Princess Friederike zur Lippe** and various members of the local high society, directed a choir that counted the ruling prince and his three sisters among its members, and was on friendly terms with the prominent and influential **Meysenbug** family. Of course, Brahms's official duties were such that his and Kiel's responsibilities did not overlap, except perhaps insofar as the direction of the orchestra, which was normally Kiel's preserve, was assigned to Brahms for rehearsals and concerts of the choral society. But Brahms seems to have been increasingly eager to also conduct it outside those limits, and at any rate did so on those occasions when the princess performed in concertos she had studied with him. In 1860, finally, he made it a condition of any further appointment that he should be placed in sole charge of the court concerts. This demand was refused by the prince on the grounds that during all the years in which Kiel had held his present post, his conduct had never given rise to any complaints. Brahms subsequently cited this refusal as one of his reasons for declining another contract at Detmold.

Kiel, a man then still in the prime of life, was a good violinist and a capable enough conductor; he was also a composer, with a number of songs and a flute concerto to his credit. If he had an obvious failing, it was not an insufficiency of musical skills but an overfondness for alcohol, and it was this weakness that cost him his position in 1862, when he was summarily dismissed by the prince following a drunken brawl, in which he had insulted a young officer and aristocrat. He never recovered from this disgrace and died a broken man. (Brahms 1974/5; Müller-Dombois 1972; Schramm 1983)

KIRCHNER, THEODOR FÜRCHTEGOTT (b. Neukirchen, Saxony, 10 October 1823; d. Hamburg, 18 September 1903). Composer, organist, and pianist. He studied music with A. H. Stahlknecht at Chemnitz, and later piano with Julius Knorr and organ and theory with Carl Ferdinand Becker at Leipzig, where he was also in contact with Mendelssohn and **Robert Schumann**. In 1843 he was, on Mendelssohn's recommendation, appointed organist at Winterthur. In 1862 he settled in Zurich where, initially, he conducted the subscription concerts and a local choir but subsequently was active mainly as organist, pianist, and accompanist (notably to **Julius Stockhausen**); he was also, as already previously at Winterthur, quite successful as a teacher. After a short engagement as court pianist and music teacher to Princess Marie at Meiningen, he became, in 1873, director of the Würzburg conservatory, a position he left after just three years. He then endeavored to earn his living as a composer and teacher, first at Leipzig (from 1876) and then at Dresden (from 1883), but experienced increasing financial difficulties. He was saved by a collection taken up by his publishers Leuckart & Hofmeister, to which many friends, including Brahms, contributed. (Brahms was to support him with several further payments in later years.) Finally, in 1890, Kirchner moved to Hamburg, where, during his last years, when he was partially paralyzed and blind, he was looked after by a former pupil, Mathilde Schlüter. (His wife, the singer Maria Schmidt [1842–1917], whom he had married in 1868, and his two children had stayed behind at Dresden.)

If **Max Kalbeck**'s statement (1976, vol. 1, 273), which has been repeated by many writers, that Brahms first met Kirchner at the Lower Rhine Music Festival at Düsseldorf in May 1856 is correct, it could only have been a glancing encounter, for in February 1858 Brahms asked **Clara Schumann**, who was then on a concert tour of Switzerland, to give his greetings to Kirchner "unbekannterweise," that is, "even though I don't know him personally" (Litzmann 1970, vol. 1, 220). And in May 1864 Kirchner informed a correspondent that he hoped to make Brahms's acquaintance during a forthcoming trip to Hamburg (R. Hofmann 1996, 23). According to the catalog of the 1997 Hamburg Brahms Exhibition, they first met when Kirchner called on Brahms at Baden-Baden in June 1865 in order to invite him to attend a performance of **Bach**'s *St. Matthew Passion* at Basle on the 16th of that month (Brahms Exhibition 1997b, 212). However, even if they really did not meet until 1865, they had certainly been in correspondence long before then; in March 1860 Brahms informed **Joseph Joachim** that Kirchner had agreed to sign their manifesto against the "Music of the Future," and in early May he informed him that Kirchner had done so (Brahms 1974/5, 264, 273).

In any case, whether or not Brahms's previous contact with Kirchner had been by correspondence only, there is no doubt that it was in June 1865, at Basle, that their relations first became close. Kirchner was the organist at the above-mentioned performance of the *St. Matthew Passion*, at which Brahms's friend Julius Stockhausen sang the part of Christ. At a concert next day, Brahms took part in a performance of his Piano Quartet op. 25, while Kirchner assumed the piano part in the Adagio from the Piano Quartet op. 26 and played some of his own *Albumblätter.* In addition, there was music making at the house of the banker **Friedrich Riggenbach-Stehlin**, so Kirchner and Brahms had ample opportunity to become well acquainted.

All this occurred just about a year after Kirchner's friendship with Clara Schumann had broken up. It is not possible to trace fully the history of Clara's contacts with Kirchner because a significant part of their correspondence was subsequently destroyed. Only seven of Clara's letters are still extant, but a further 43 have fortunately been preserved in a handwritten copy; on the other hand, none of Kirchner's letters have survived. (On this whole matter, see Renate Hofmann's 1996 edition of Clara's letters to Kirchner; her introduction also includes a survey of Kirchner's life.) It can nevertheless be stated with some confidence that if, as appears almost certain, their relationship included some sexual intimacy, it did so for only a relatively short period. There seems no basis for the assertions made by Clara's biographer Eva Weissweiler that Clara decided to take Kirchner as her lover in 1857 because he was unassertive in character and would appear only when she needed him, and that the affair then continued uninterruptedly for eight years. Clara's diary does indeed show that in 1857, in Switzerland, she renewed her acquaintance with Kirchner, whom she had presumably not seen for quite a few years, and that she found him congenial company, especially since he revered her late husband. At the same time, however, she considered that he had lacked fiber, both as a man and as an artist, and she was in fact to make several efforts over the next few years to instill some in him; thus, she exhorted him, in July 1862, "Pull yourself together, dear Kirchner, you are still a man in full possession of his mental and physical powers" (R. Hofmann 1996, 80). Later that summer they saw one another at Interlaken and Lucerne, and the renewed and sustained contact must have heightened Kirchner's feelings for Clara, to judge by the reproving tone she adopted in a letter that December: "Where will it lead if you continue to go into such raptures as you do in your letters? You say yourself that you feel you are going beyond the limits of friendship." Most significantly, she firmly rejected the use of the intimate "Du," and she added, "Although you may find it difficult to do so at the moment, you will soon recognise how right I was not to let anything unnatural exist between us; only in that way shall I feel secure in your friendship" (R. Hofmann 1996, 121). All this hardly points to a physical relationship at that time. Yet, the situation must have changed dramatically when Kirchner stayed at Clara's house in Baden-Baden in the summer of 1863, for in a note she sent him on 15 August, when he had temporarily left Baden-Baden, she not only at last uses the intimate "Du," but also calls him "my beloved," and in a much longer letter written during a concert tour the following February, she likewise expresses feelings of profound love for him (R. Hofmann 1996, 183, 186–92). However, all this changed within a year. What exactly happened when Kirchner briefly returned to Baden-Baden in June 1864 is not known, but in a letter the following month Clara reverted to the formal "Sie" and firmly put an end to their relations (R. Hofmann 1996, 193–94). (In a letter to **Elisabeth von Herzogenberg** many years later—also quoted by Renate Hofmann (20–21)—Clara was to link the rupture with Kirchner's addiction to gambling, which had saddled him with perennial debts and had led him, after she had given him substantial amounts of money to clear some of them, to squander away those sums also at the gaming tables; when she had refused further financial aid he had, she alleged, behaved in a despicable manner.

In June 1865 Clara, writing from London, warned Brahms, who was about to return to Baden-Baden from Zurich in Kirchner's company, never to bring him to her house there, for he was "too great a scoundrel" (Litzmann 1970, vol. 1, 513, n. 1). However, whatever she may have told Brahms about her reasons for breaking with Kirchner, it is evident that her hostility toward the latter did not cause Brahms to cease his own contacts with him. On the contrary, their relationship became still closer in 1866 when Brahms spent several weeks at Fluntern, near Zurich, during which time they met constantly. Thereafter, they were to carry on a sporadic correspondence, and Brahms took care that his publishers sent Kirchner copies of his compositions. In the spring of 1887 Kirchner even joined Brahms and **Fritz Simrock** on a trip to northern Italy; they last met in Hamburg in February 1893. As already mentioned, Brahms provided Kirchner with some financial support in his later years.

Kirchner greatly admired Brahms's music, and he had done his best to make Brahms's name known in Zurich already before the latter's visit there in 1865. Thus, he was instrumental in bringing about the performance of the String Sextet op. 18 on 20 January 1863; it was so successful that the work was repeated "by popular request" two weeks later (3 February). He was probably also responsible for the performance of the Serenade op. 11 on 10 November of the same year, and for further performances of Brahms's works in 1864. As a composer, Kirchner wrote a number of songs and some chamber music, but the vast majority of his approximately 1,000 works consisted of relatively short pieces for the piano that were extremely popular in his time. Brahms liked them a good deal and was also highly appreciative of Kirchner's skill at making arrangements of the works of other musicians. In particular, he was delighted with the arrangements that Kirchner prepared of Brahms's own compositions, and he encouraged his publisher Fritz Simrock to induce Kirchner to make new ones (*see* KELLER, ROBERT). Accordingly, Kirchner made arrangements of numerous songs and other vocal works by Brahms, including *Liebeslieder* (op. 52), *Neue Liebeslieder* (op. 65), *Ziegeunerlieder* (op. 103), and even the Requiem; he arranged the two String Sextets for piano trio, and the First Piano Concerto for two pianos, eight hands; and he also made arrangements of the *Variations* on themes by Schumann and **Handel** (opp. 23–4). (Brahms 1974/5; Brahms Exhibition 1997a; H. Ehrlich 1893a; K. Hofmann 1981a; R. Hofmann 1996; Hunziker 1909; Litzmann 1902, 1970; Sietz 1960e, 1971; Weissweiler 1990; Zimmermann 1983)

KLENGEL, JULIUS (b. Leipzig, 24 September 1859; d. Leipzig, 27 October 1933). Cellist and composer; brother of **Paul Klengel**. He belonged to an outstandingly musical family: his grandfather Moritz Gotthold Klengel (1793–1870) led the second violins of the Gewandhaus Orchestra for over 50 years and taught at the conservatory; his father Julius (1818–79) was a composer and singing teacher; and three of his five brothers and sisters were musicians. The younger Julius studied cello with **Emil Hegar** and composition with Samuel Jadassohn. When he was only 15 he joined the Gewandhaus Orchestra, and he was to be its principal cellist for more than 40 years (1881–1924). In addition, he was a member of the Gewandhaus Quartet and a professor at the conservatory (1881–1933); among his many pupils were Emanuel Feuermann, Guilhermina Suggia, and Gregor Piatigorsky. He toured widely in Europe and enjoyed an international reputation, thanks to his splendid technique, great taste, and fine sense of style. His compositions were written primarily for the cello; they included four concertos, and a *Hymnus* for 12 cellos (which was performed at **Arthur Nikisch**'s funeral service).

According to **Max Kalbeck**, Klengel played for Brahms at the latter's request when Brahms visited his house at Leipzig in January 1895. Brahms, who had apparently never heard him play as a solo performer, was enthralled. Kalbeck (1976) reports that when Klengel had finished, Brahms looked at him for awhile without speaking, then slapped him on the shoulder and said, "I have, of course, heard about your phenomenal technique, but I would never have believed it possible that such wonderful things could be produced on your instrument" (vol. 4, 383). Yet Brahms had played his Piano Trio op. 101 with Klengel and **Adolph Brodsky** in Leipzig on 2 January 1888. Julius Klengel must have taken part in many other performances of Brahms's works in the course of his long career as an orchestral and chamber music player. (On 20 June 1888 he partnered **Joseph Joachim** in the Double Concerto at a concert at Stuttgart.)

According to M. L. McCorkle's (1984) *Werkverzeichnis*, he (and not his brother Paul, as might otherwise be assumed) was responsible for the two-piano arrangements of the Piano Quartets opp. 25–26, which **Fritz Simrock** published in 1897.

KLENGEL, PAUL (b. Leipzig, 13 May 1854; d. Leipzig, 24 April 1935). Conductor, violinist, pianist, and composer; brother of **Julius Klengel**. He attended the Leipzig Conservatory (1868–72), studying violin (with **Ferdinand David**) and piano (with **Carl Reinecke**), as well as theory and composition. He joined the Gewandhaus Orchestra as a violinist in 1873, later assumed responsibility for the "Euterpe" concerts (1881–86) and taught at the conservatory (1883–87). He spent the years 1887–91 at Stuttgart (initially as director of music at the Hoftheater, and from 1888, as court Kapellmeister), and subsequently moved back to Leipzig, where he conducted the Singakademie (1892–98) and "Arion" choral society (1893–98). He next directed the "Deutscher Liederkranz" in New York (1898–1902), before finally settling for the rest of his life in Leipzig, where he again conducted the "Arion" society (1903–21) and until 1934 was on the faculty of the conservatory.

Paul Klengel's compositions include songs and instrumental works. He also made numerous arrangements of other composers' works, and it is in this connection that his name deserves to be mentioned in any book dealing with Brahms's music, for he prepared arrangements, mainly for piano duet or two pianos, of a considerable number of Brahms's compositions—and even, in some cases, more than one of the same work (of the intermezzo op. 116/4 he produced arrangements for piano duet, violin and piano, cello and piano, viola or clarinet and piano, and full orchestra). These different versions were published by **Fritz Simrock** between 1892 and 1897. Among the other works Klengel arranged are the Intermezzi op. 117, the Piano Sonatas opp. 1–2, the String Sextet op. 18, the String Quartets opp. 51 and 67, the Piano Quartet op. 60, the Violin Sonata op. 78, the Clarinet Trio op. 114, the Clarinet Quintet op. 115 (four arrangements), the Clarinet Sonatas op. 120, and even the *Variations* for two pianos op. 56b (which Klengel arranged for two pianos and eight hands).

Brahms was particularly pleased with one of Klengel's scores. "I look at the arrangement with great pleasure, it seems to me to be a very good one indeed," he wrote to Simrock in February 1892 about an arrangement of the Clarinet Quintet that Simrock had recently sent him (Brahms 1974/12,

59). Since no fewer than three arrangements of this work, all by Klengel, were published in 1892 (for piano duet, for two pianos, and for violin and piano), it is not clear which is the one so warmly praised by Brahms, but it may well have been the last one, which was singled out by Hugh Butler, the author of the article on Paul Klengel in early editions of *Grove's Dictionary of Music and Musicians*, as "one of the best examples" of the "exceptional skill and tact" that characterized Klengel's arrangements. On the other hand, Brahms wrote to Simrock in some irritation in September 1894: "But do tell me now: do your accursed orchestral arrangements really bring in so much money, and is the utterly inartistic insipidity so absolutely necessary for that reason?" (Brahms 1974/12, 150). The outburst was perhaps provoked by Brahms's lingering displeasure over Simrock's publication the previous year of Klengel's orchestral version of the Intermezzo op. 117/1. (Also in 1893, Simrock had published an orchestral arrangement by Klengel of the Intermezzo op. 116/4.) However, Brahms's protest appears to have been directed essentially against Simrock's eagerness to earn money by turning piano compositions into works for a whole orchestra rather than against the unsatisfactory quality of Klengel's arrangements, which seemed to him almost inevitable in the circumstances, for he continued, "I have at times considered combining several piano pieces and making some kind of large rhapsody out of them. A single piano piece is simply not an orchestral piece and will never become one. If it is absolutely essential for business reasons, at least wait until someone makes one of his own accord—and makes an impression with it!" (Brahms 1974/12)

KLINGER, MAX (b. Leipzig, 18 February 1857; d. Grossjena, near Naumburg, 4 July 1920). Painter, etcher, and sculptor. One of the most original, highly productive, and influential artists of the turn of the 20th century, particularly famous for his cycles of etchings (*Intermezzi*, *Paraphrase on the Discovery of a Glove*, *A Life*, *Dramas*, *Love*, *Of Death*, *Brahms Fantasy*, *The Tent*). Among his admirers was Brahms.

A great music lover and excellent pianist and improviser, Klinger especially revered the compositions of **Beethoven**, **Robert Schumann**, and Brahms; characteristically, he made use of musical terms such as "Capriccio," "Intermezzo," and "Fantasy" for his artistic creations and numbered them by opus numbers. He wished to dedicate his Opus I, a series entitled *Etched Sketches*, to Brahms, but his publisher disapproved of the idea; however, in 1880 he dedicated to him Opus V, his illustrations for Reinhold Jachmann's German translation of the tale of Cupid and Psyche (taken from Apuleius's *Golden Ass*), and he sent Brahms a splendidly bound copy. In an accompanying letter (15 December 1880), he expressed his gratitude for "the happy hours which hearing and remembering the performance of your compositions has afforded me" (Kersten 1993, vol. 2, 164). Brahms liked the illustrations so much that he recommended them to **Fritz Simrock**, and he also asked him to buy a copy and send it to **Clara Schumann**.

Simrock later commissioned Klinger to provide illustrations for two sets of Brahms's songs (op. 96–97). Unfortunately, while Brahms had greatly liked the sketches that Klinger had made for certain of his compositions, above all those for the song "Feldeinsamkeit" (op. 86/2) and the Cello Sonata op. 38, he was less pleased by Klinger's contribution (the outside and inside title pages) to the printed editions of opp. 96–97, and he made his dissatisfaction known both to Simrock and, in gentle but unambiguous terms, to Klinger himself. It was probably to compensate for this failure that Klinger, during the following years, created his *Brahms Fantasy*, an attempt to fashion a synthesis (designated in German by the term "Gesamtkunstwerk") of several different arts, in this case music, language, and image, with particular application to the works of Brahms; published in 1894, it was numbered Opus XII and comprised 41 etchings. Not all refer to specific compositions, but Brahms, who was deeply impressed by the whole work, was particularly delighted with the prints inspired by his *Schicksalslied.*

In February 1885 Brahms wrote to Simrock: "I envy you knowing Max Klinger, for, to judge by his works and imaginative creations, he must be a most interesting man and artist" (Brahms 1974/11, 87). He reportedly made Klinger's acquaintance a year later when he went to Leipzig to conduct his Fourth Symphony and the Violin Concerto in February 1886. They met again in Vienna in the spring of 1894 when Klinger broke his journey to Greece there, and once more early the following year in Leipzig, where Brahms took part in two concerts (27 and 31 January 1895). Nothing definite is known about any other meetings between them. In the autumn of 1895 Klinger was offered, but declined, a professorship in Vienna.

Klinger had dedicated the *Fantasy* to Brahms, and the composer returned the compliment by dedicating the *4 ernste Gesänge* to Klinger in 1896. Klinger's father had died not long before, a fact to which Brahms alluded in a letter in June 1896 when he assured Klinger that he had frequently thought of him while composing them "and of the profound effect the glorious words, so pregnant with meaning, might have on you" (Brahms 1924, 11).

Six letters from Brahms to Klinger, of which the earliest dates from March 1886 and the last from October 1896, were published in Leipzig in 1924, and Ursula Kersten (1993), in her book *Max Klinger und die Musik*, prints nine letters addressed by Klinger to Brahms between December

1880 and late 1896 or early 1897; but it is clear from these 15 letters that they do not constitute the whole correspondence exchanged by the two men. In his last published letter, Klinger mentions the possibility of again stopping over in Vienna during the spring of 1897, in connection with another trip to Greece (where he went primarily for the purpose of procuring marble for his sculptures). Instead, he was to travel there in April 1897 to attend Brahms's funeral. However, his association with Brahms was far from over. In the first place, Klinger was among the artists invited to submit models for the proposed Brahms monument in Vienna, and he participated in the discussions that took place in May–June 1902 in Vienna to choose the most suitable place for the statue. (In April of that year he had opened an exhibition at the Secession, of which his monumental, polychromatic statue of Beethoven was the centerpiece.) Klinger submitted an entry for the Brahms monument (of which a photomontage is preserved at the Museum der bildenden Künste in Leipzig), but he subsequently withdrew from the competition. On the other hand, he signed a contract in 1904 for the creation of a Brahms statue in Hamburg. After being exhibited at Dresden for several weeks, it was unveiled in the foyer of the Musikhalle on 7 May 1909. To mark the occasion, a special Brahms concert was conducted by **Richard Barth** that evening at the Musikhalle, the program consisting of the second movement of the Requiem, the *Haydn Variations*, *Schicksalslied*, and First Symphony.

Klinger also made busts of **Liszt**, **Max Reger**, **Richard Strauss**, and **Richard Wagner**. He furthermore worked for years on a large marble statue of Wagner for Leipzig, which was never completed. Among his earlier sculptures was a *Salome*, which fascinated Brahms. (Bozarth 1986; Brahms 1924, 1974/11; Brinkmann 1999; Gleisberg 1992; Hevesi 1903; Huschke 1933, 1939; Kersten 1993; Mayer-Pasinski 1981; Richter 1973)

KNEBEL, KARL LUDWIG VON (1744–1834). Brahms set a text by Knebel in the canon for four voices "Töne, lindernder Klang" (WoO 28).

KNEISEL, FRANZ (b. Bucharest, 26 January 1865; d. New York, 26 March 1926). Violinist and conductor. The son of a military band conductor, he studied at the Bucharest conservatory and later (1879–82) at the Vienna conservatory, where his teachers were **Jakob Moritz Grün** and **Joseph Hellmesberger**. After playing in the Burgtheater orchestra in Vienna and in Bilse's orchestra in Berlin, he was engaged in 1885, when only 20, as concertmaster of the Boston Symphony Orchestra by its conductor, the Austrian-born Wilhelm Gericke, who had been sent to Europe for the purpose of hiring competent young musicians to strengthen the orchestra. Kneisel began his duties on 17 October 1885 and first appeared as soloist with the orchestra, in **Beethoven**'s Violin Concerto, on the last day of that month.

It had been the aim of the orchestra's founder, Henry Lee Higginson, to form a string quartet from among its best musicians, and his wishes were now quickly realized with the establishment of the Kneisel Quartet, which gave its first concert in Boston on 28 December 1885. It was initially composed of Franz Kneisel (leader), Emanuel Fiedler (second violin), Louis Svečenski (viola), and Fritz Giese (cello), all of them young men still in their 20s; moreover, the first three, who had been recruited by Gericke that summer, had all studied with Jakob Grün. (Giese, a Dutchman who had been trained at The Hague conservatory, had been brought to America by the Mendelssohn Quintet Club in 1879 and had joined the Boston Symphony Orchestra as solo cellist in 1884.) The quartet regularly gave performances in Boston and, from 1888, also in New York; it was disbanded by Kneisel in 1917. Apart from Franz Kneisel, Svečenski remained with the group throughout; the other two positions were refilled more than once. At most of its concerts, the quartet was assisted by one or more other artists, thus enabling it to tackle chamber music compositions outside the range of its four string players.

According to the American music critic Richard Aldrich (1928), Kneisel and his quartet made a profound impact on American musical culture by the exceptionally high standards of their performances: "Such performances as he offered were a new revelation in this country, where quartet playing, before his time, had generally been a by-product, the result of orchestral players' leisure moments. With him it was, even from the first, a chief end" (276). Moreover, the Kneisel Quartet played a key role in making Brahms's chamber music better known in the United States. According to Victor B. Danek (1962), it presented altogether 250 complete performances of 21 of his compositions, including the American premiere of the String Quintet op. 111 at Boston on 6 November 1891 (215, 229). It may be worth mentioning that its final concert in Boston, on 13 March 1917, included Brahms's Piano Quartet op. 26, while its "Farewell Concert" in New York on 3 April 1917 had the String Quartet op. 51/1 on its program. Moreover, of the two earliest American performances of the Violin Concerto, Kneisel gave one in Boston on 6 December and the other in New York on 17 December 1889, both with the Boston Symphony Orchestra conducted by **Arthur Nikisch**.

Danek writes that Kneisel first met Brahms when he was invited to substitute, at the last moment, for his teacher Joseph Hellmesberger ("called to conduct at the Ringtheater that evening") in a private performance of the String Quintet op. 88 at **Theodor Billroth**'s house on 26 April 1882, that composition being then "played for the first time from manuscript" (140).

Danek is evidently basing himself on Dorothy Crowthers's article "Franz Kneisel Recalls Some Yesterdays. . . . An Interview" (*Musical Observer*, July 1924), where Kneisel is quoted as assigning the event to "Billroth's birthday" in the year 1882 (without actually citing the date "26 April," though that was, of course, the date of his birthday). However, Danek's statement is manifestly wrong on two important counts: the Ringtheater had burnt down on 8 December 1881 (and was never rebuilt), and the quintet was not composed until May 1882, at Ischl (see M. L. McCorkle's [1984] *Werkverzeichnis*). It is in any case clear from Billroth's letter to Brahms of 2 July 1882, in which he recorded his first superficial impressions of the quintet, of which Brahms had just sent him the manuscript from Ischl, that it could not have been performed as early as April of that year. As far as is known, it received its first private performance on 25 August at **László Wagner de Zólyom**'s villa at Altaussee. The performance at Billroth's most probably did not take place until October (perhaps on the 19th). It is, of course, possible that on that occasion Kneisel really did replace Hellmesberger. (The quintet received its first public performance at Frankfurt am Main, on 29 December 1882.)

What is certain is that in the 1890s Kneisel met Brahms repeatedly at Ischl, where he and other members of the quartet stayed in the summer. There he had several occasions to play Brahms's chamber music for him, and apparently also with him. Kneisel later recalled some of these experiences in his conversation with Dorothy Crowther, in which he placed his own first visit to the spa in 1893. Further, and in some respects more precise, information about these contacts with Brahms can be found in **Ilona Eibenschütz**'s article "My Recollections of Brahms," published in the *Musical Times* in 1926, although the chronology of the events she describes is not made clear. In the article she mentions playing the Piano Quartet op. 25 with the Kneisel Quartet, and the three Violin Sonatas with Franz Kneisel, each time in Brahms's presence; and she remembers with particular fondness "the most wonderful performance I ever heard" of the Clarinet Quintet (op. 115), given by **Richard Mühlfeld** and the Kneisel Quartet at Kneisel's house, before an audience consisting of Brahms, **Fritz Steinbach** and his wife, Arthur Nikisch and his wife, and her: "Mühlfeld played marvellously on his clarinet, and when they finished playing this heavenly work, we were all so moved that nobody found a word to say. But Nikisch fell on his knee before Brahms, and that exactly expressed our feelings" (Eibenschütz 1926, 599).

In 1903 Kneisel resigned his position with the Boston Symphony Orchestra and moved to New York; from 1905 he taught at the Institute of Musical Art there. (Aldrich 1928; Crowthers 1924; Danek 1962; Eibenschütz 1926; Ewen 1942; Gottlieb-Billroth 1935; Johnson 1979)

KNORR, IWAN (OTTO ARMAND) (b. Mewe, West Prussia, 3 January 1853; d. Frankfurt am Main, 22 January 1916). Composer, teacher, and writer. Between the ages of 4 and 15 he lived in Russia. After the family settled in Leipzig in 1868, he enrolled at the conservatory, where he studied piano with Ignaz Moscheles, theory with Ernst Friedrich Richter, and composition with **Carl Reinecke**. In 1874 he was appointed a professor of music at the Imperial Institute for Ladies of the Aristocracy at Khar'kov, and in 1878 he joined the faculty of the Khar'kov division of the Russian Imperial Musical Society.

From Khar'kov, Knorr sent one of his early compositions, the *Variations on a Ukrainian Folk-song*, to Brahms for his comments and was gratified to receive a reply in which Brahms warmly praised the work and expressed his desire to know more about its composer. (In August 1877, in a letter to **Clara Schumann**, Brahms described the *Variations* as "quite superb" [Litzmann 1970, vol. 2, 121.]) Knorr visited Brahms at Pörtschach in August 1877 and spent some pleasant days with him and **Franz Wüllner**, who was also vacationing there. Later Knorr gave a fairly detailed account of this first contact with Brahms (see Kalbeck 1976, vol. 3, 152–54). In addition to discussing the variations with Knorr, Brahms did his best to find a publisher for them. At the same time, he suggested to Knorr that he should prepare an arrangement of his variations for piano duet, which he then proposed to play himself, together with Clara Schumann, for **Fritz Simrock**. Presumably Knorr did not act upon this suggestion; at any rate, nothing is known about any performance of such an arrangement in Simrock's presence. But in December 1877, Brahms, writing from Vienna, tried to interest Simrock in "some excellent variations for orchestra" written by a young Russian (Brahms 1974/10, 62). In his next letter, Simrock wondered whether the Russian in question might be "Tschaikowski." After this there is no further reference to the matter in the published correspondence between Brahms and Simrock. In the end, the *Variations* were published by **Breitkopf & Härtel**, and that firm also brought out editions of several other compositions by Knorr.

According to Knorr, it was thanks to Brahms that he was appointed to the faculty of the Hoch Conservatory at Frankfurt in 1883. There he taught piano, theory, and music history, and from 1886 also composition; from 1888 he concentrated on theory and composition. Among his students were Cyril Scott, Hans Pfitzner, and Ernst Toch. In 1908 he became director of the conservatory. After he had moved to Frankfurt, he met Brahms on several occasions, especially at Clara Schumann's house, but, he later told **Max Kalbeck**, he was never able to recapture the intimacy he had enjoyed at Pörtschach. (M. Bauer 1916; Brahms 1974/10; Litzmann 1970; Stephenson 1961)

KOESSLER [KÖSSLER], HANS (b. Waldeck, Bavaria, 1 January 1853; d. Ansbach, 23 May 1926). Composer, organist, and teacher. After being employed as an organist at Neumarkt (Upper Palatinate) from 1871 until 1874, he pursued advanced musical studies under Joseph Rheinberger and **Franz Wüllner** at the Musikschule in Munich. He subsequently taught theory and choral singing at the Dresden conservatory from 1877 to 1881 (from 1879 he also conducted the Dresden Liedertafel) and, following a brief spell as conductor at the Staatstheater in Cologne, he joined the faculty of the Budapest Academy of Music in 1882. There he taught organ and choral music before succeeding **Robert Volkmann** in 1883 as a professor of composition, a post he held until his retirement in 1908. In 1920, by which time he had settled at Ansbach, he returned to the Budapest Academy and for the next five years resumed his classes in composition.

Brahms probably made Koessler's acquaintance in December 1883, when the latter called on him in Vienna (see Brahms 1974/15, 115–16). He was to meet him repeatedly thereafter—at Thun in Switzerland, in Vienna, and especially at Ischl, where Koessler stayed several times—and according to **Ilona Eibenschütz** he liked him very much (Eibenschütz 1926, 599). Koessler also visited him at Karlsbad [Karlovy Vary] in 1896 and apparently managed to reassure him with the statement that jaundice was caused by great excitement. Brahms is said to have exclaimed delightedly that that was exactly his own case, and to have promptly ordered some champagne. Koessler last saw him in Vienna a few weeks before his death, and he attended the funeral.

Koessler's compositions include an opera, *Der Münzenfranz*, and a large number of choral works and songs, as well as some instrumental works. In 1889 the Vienna Tonkünstlerverein awarded him a prize for his choral work *Bitte*. It is not known whether Brahms had a hand in this award. However, W. Ebert seems to be in error in stating (in *Brahms und Budapest*), allegedly on **Kalbeck**'s authority, that Brahms conducted a performance of that composition at Cologne in 1890. Kalbeck makes it clear enough that Brahms's role in this concert presented by the Cologne conservatory on 13 March of that year was limited to his participation in a performance of the new version of his Piano Trio op. 8. The remainder of the concert, which included Brahms's opp. 109–110, was evidently conducted by the conservatory's director, Franz Wüllner. Some years after Brahms's death, Koessler composed a set of *Symphonic Variations* for large orchestra, which he dedicated "to the memory of Johannes Brahms"; they were first performed by **Arthur Nikisch** in 1901. (Brahms 1974/15; W. Ebert 1984; Eibenschütz 1926)

KOPISCH, AUGUST (b. Breslau [Wrocław, Poland], 26 May 1799; d. Berlin, 6 February 1853). Painter and art historian; poet and writer. Brahms set a text by Kopisch in "Während des Regens" (op. 58/2) and two of his translations from the Italian in "Blinde Kuh" and "Die Spröde" (op. 58/1, 3). (Jäger 1980; Zenker 1990)

KÖSTLIN, CHRISTIAN REINHOLD: *see* REINHOLD, C.

KRAUS, FELIX VON (b. Vienna, 3 October 1870; d. Munich, 30 October 1937). Bass. He pursued studies in the history of music and in 1894 obtained his doctorate with a dissertation on Antonio Caldara; at the same time, he also received instruction in harmony from **Anton Bruckner** and in musical theory from **Eusebius Mandyczewski** (with whom he would later be on very friendly terms). As a singer he was essentially self-taught, although he did, on Brahms's advice, briefly study with **Julius Stockhausen** in Frankfurt in 1895. When he initially hesitated between an academic career as a historian of music and the career of a professional singer, Brahms strongly encouraged him to follow the latter.

Kraus, who possessed a splendid voice, great artistic sensitivity, and clearly a highly agreeable personality, soon attracted Brahms's attention and benevolent interest. On 7 November 1894, at the Tonkünstlerverein, he gave the earliest documented performances of three of the *49 deutsche Volkslieder* (WoO 33/5, 13, 42), and on 11 October 1895, at Brahms's suggestion, he performed at another meeting of the Tonkünstlerverein, on which occasion he sang **Franz Schubert**'s "Der Taucher" (D 77) and Brahms's "Mit vierzig Jahren" (op. 94/1) and "Verrat" (op. 105/5). (*See also* PROHASKA, KARL.) Kraus would long be regarded as the ideal interpreter of the *4 ernste Gesänge*, which Brahms had indeed, as he told Kraus himself, written with his voice in mind (Kraus 1961, 42). Kraus sang all of them at the Tonkünstlerverein on 30 October 1896, shortly before they received their first complete public performance by **Anton Sistermans** on 9 November; Kraus sang them again at Leipzig, accompanied by **Arthur Nikisch**, on 18 February 1897, and also, with the same accompanist, at a Brahms memorial concert at Leipzig on 7 October of that year. He furthermore sang them at Meiningen on 7 October 1899 on the occasion of the unveiling of the Brahms monument.

Kraus had a distinguished career, both in opera—he regularly sang at Bayreuth (1899–1909)—and on the concert stage. Furthermore, he taught at the Munich conservatory from 1908 until 1929. (Kutsch and Riemens 1987–94)

KRAUSS, EMIL (b. Schässburg [Sighişoara, Romania], 1 June 1840; d. Hamburg, 1 September 1889). Baritone. A qualified physician, he had also trained as a singer, concluding his voice studies in Vienna. He first appeared at the Vienna Opera in 1869 and was under contract there from 1870 until 1873. He was then engaged in Zurich (1873–76), Chemnitz (1876–77), Zurich again (1877–78), Cologne (1778–81), and lastly Hamburg (1881–89). He made guest appearances at various leading opera houses, including the Drury Lane Theatre in London where, in 1882, he sang the roles of Kurwenal and Kothner in the English premieres of *Tristan und Isolde* and *Die Meistersinger.*

Krauss took part in the first complete public performance of the *Liebeslieder-Walzer* in Vienna on 5 January 1870, in which Brahms and **Clara Schumann** played the accompaniment. He was also a soloist at a performance of the Requiem, which Brahms conducted at a Gesellschaft der Musikfreunde concert in Vienna on 5 March 1871 (the first time Brahms conducted the complete work), and furthermore he appeared as soloist in **Handel**'s "Dettingen" *Te Deum* at the first concert Brahms conducted as the society's artistic director on 10 November 1872.

KREISLER, FRITZ (b. Vienna, 2 February 1875; d. New York, 29 January 1962). Violinist and composer. In 1942, speaking to Olin Downes about his early musical experiences, he recalled: "I had the inexpressible good fortune to sit in quartets to whom [Brahms] more than once brought the manuscript of a new chamber composition, for us to run through for him. He would stop us, and change a note or two, or discuss the scoring of a passage. To . . . actually be present at the creation of superb music, was priceless" (Downes 1942).

At one of the meetings of the Tonkünstlerverein, Kreisler happened to be seated at the same table as Brahms and **Joseph Joachim** when they were discussing one of **Robert Schumann**'s last orchestral works, the Fantasia for violin and orchestra op. 131. Joachim, for whom the Fantasia had been written and who frequently performed it, expressed the view that it might be forgotten after his death, for he was obliged to acknowledge that, while often extremely beautiful, it had serious weaknesses due to Schumann's unbalanced state of mind at the time he composed it. Thereupon Brahms, who recognized those shortcomings, urged Joachim to revise it in order to ensure its survival as a concert piece after he was gone. The words Brahms actually used, Kreisler told his biographer Louis P. Lochner (1950), were "Das Werk muss von seinem Gestrüpp befreit werden" [The composition must be stripped of its undergrowth]. Whereupon Kreisler's former teacher

Joseph Hellmesberger, who was sitting at the same table, said to him, "You heard what Meister Brahms said. Don't you ever forget it" (54).

When Kreisler discovered, after Joachim's death, that he had never even begun the proposed revision, he decided to undertake the task himself. He first played the work in its new form in New York during the 1915–16 season, but he continued to refine his revision over the next two decades and eventually presented the final version at a recital in Carnegie Hall on 17 October 1936. (Downes 1942; Lochner 1950)

KRETZSCHMAR, HERMANN (b. Olbernhau, 19 January 1848; d. Berlin, 10 May 1924). Conductor, teacher, and musicologist. The son of a cantor and composer of church music, he studied musicology at Leipzig University (from 1868) and also attended the Leipzig conservatory (1869–70); at both institutions his principal teacher was Oskar Paul. Kretzschmar taught theory, composition, piano, and organ at the conservatory (1871–75); he was also active as a conductor of local choral societies (for a brief time, in 1875, he conducted the Leipzig Bach-Verein). In 1877 he became director of music at Rostock University, and in 1887 he was appointed to a similar post at the University of Leipzig. He later rejoined the faculty of the Leipzig conservatory to teach the history and aesthetics of music (1898–1904). Furthermore, he assumed the direction of the Riedel-Verein after the death in 1888 of its founder, **Carl Riedel**, and he conducted that choral society until 1897. Yet another of his important contributions to the musical life of Leipzig was his foundation in 1890 of a second orchestra in the city, in addition to that of the Gewandhaus. The new orchestra, of which the kernel was supplied by the band of an infantry regiment, presented its Akademische Orchester-Konzerte until 1895. Kretzschmar finally left Leipzig in 1904 to take up a professorship at Berlin University.

Kretzschmar was an early and influential supporter of Brahms's music. In the Leipzig weekly journal *Musikalisches Wochenblatt* (*see* FRITZSCH, ERNST WILHELM), he published a discerning and highly appreciative account of Brahms's recent compositions ("Neue Werke von Johannes Brahms"); it was spread over 11 issues, from January to March 1874, and dealt with, among other works, the *Alto Rhapsody* and *Rinaldo*, which Brahms performed during his concert appearances in Leipzig in early February. Ten years later Kretzschmar published a further but no less enthusiastic study ("Johannes Brahms") in the periodical *Die Grenzboten.* It was subsequently reprinted in his *Gesammelte Aufsätze.*

Kretzschmar also actively promoted the performance of Brahms's works. During his tenure as director of the Riedel-Verein, he conducted the Requiem and the *Fest-und Gedenksprüche*, and with his own orchestra he gave, between 1890 and 1895, performances of the first three symphonies, *Parzengesang*, and the *Academic Festival Overture.* His rendition of the First Symphony, on 10 March 1891, did a lot to wipe out the memory of **Carl Reinecke**'s rather lackluster performance of that work at the Gewandhaus the previous October. At the same concert, Kretzschmar's wife Clara was soloist in the Second Piano Concerto.

As a writer on music, Kretzschmar was best known to the wider public through his *Führer durch den Konzert-Saal* (3 vols., Leipzig, 1888–90). (Abert 1924; Kretzschmar 1874, 1884)

KUFFERATH, ANTONIA (b. Brussels, 28 October 1857; d. Shenley, Hertfordshire, 26 October 1939). Soprano; daughter of (Hubert) Ferdinand Kufferath (1818–96), a composer and pianist of German origin who taught composition at the Brussels conservatory. She studied with **Julius Stockhausen** in Berlin and **Pauline Viardot** in Paris, and subsequently enjoyed a successful, though brief, international career as a concert and oratorio singer, which she gave up upon her marriage to **Edward Speyer** on 2 June 1885 (but she did, many years later, perform again in public in England).

Both Antonia and Brahms participated in the festival that took place at Bonn on the occasion of the unveiling on 2 May 1880 of Donndor's monument at **Robert Schumann**'s grave. At a concert that same day, she sang Schumann's *Requiem für Mignon* and the soprano part in his *Manfred.* Brahms conducted the former work but probably not the latter. According to **Max Kalbeck**, he firmly declined **Joseph Joachim**'s request to do so, since he was already due to conduct Schumann's Third Symphony and his own Violin Concerto (with Joachim as soloist), in addition to *Requiem für Mignon.* Andreas Moser, in his edition of the Brahms-Joachim correspondence, likewise remarks, "Joachim conducted *Manfred*, Brahms the rest" (Brahms 1974/6, 188, n. 1). Yet Antonia Kufferath, in her recollections of Brahms, which her husband inserted into his memoirs (see Speyer 1937), recalled that it was Brahms who conducted *Manfred*, while Joachim "behind the scene directed the men's chorus which sang the Dirge for Manfred." She even added that, the arrangements being somewhat primitive, the men missed their entry because the two conductors were unable to see each other, so that Brahms "was obliged to give them their cue with his husky voice, which sadly marred the effect of this deeply moving moment" (Speyer 1937, 109). Nevertheless, it must be assumed that Antonia Kufferath is in error, perhaps confusing this performance with another one in which she took part, for **Clara Schumann** recorded in her diary entry for 2 May that "*Manfred*, conducted by Joachim and spoken by [Ernst] von

Possart, was too long" (Litzmann 1902, vol. 3, 409). It is not certain whether this was the first time Antonia met Brahms. (Clara Schumann had been on very friendly terms with the Kufferaths since 1861, repeatedly visiting them on her journeys to and from England.)

In the summer of 1882, Antonia and her father, while staying at the Belgian seaside resort of Heyst, made the acquaintance of **Rudolf** and Hedwig **von der Leyen**, who were subsequently their guests in Brussels. They in their turn invited Antonia and her father to attend a concert Brahms was to give at Krefeld early the following year, and eventually Antonia was asked to sing the soprano solo from Brahms's Requiem, as well as some songs, at the concert that took place on 23 January 1883. One of the songs she sang was Brahms's "Liebestreu" (op. 3/1). Of her performance in the Requiem extract that day, Von der Leyen (1905) wrote in his recollections of Brahms (*Johannes Brahms als Mensch und Freund*) that it was "a pearl of the noblest kind and unforgettable for anyone privileged to have heard that marvellous artist," and he adds that Antonia later often sang to Brahms's accompaniment at his house and that no more beautiful performances of his songs could be imagined (Leyen 1905, 27). Antonia mentions "a most delightful gathering" at the Von der Leyens in 1884, when Brahms accompanied her in several songs, among them "Frühlingstrost" (op. 63/1), for which he played the difficult piano part "with a good many grunts" (Speyer 1937, 112–13). On the previous day they had performed the "Heimweh Lieder" (op. 63/7–9) at a concert at Barmen.

According to Speyer (1937), Brahms felt "almost filial veneration" for Antonia's father (72). He was particularly touched when the then seventy-seven-year-old man traveled from Brussels to Meiningen in September 1895, together with his daughter, son-in-law, and son Maurice (later director of the Théâtre de la Monnaie), in order to attend the music festival, which featured compositions by **Bach**, **Beethoven**, and Brahms, in Speyer's words, it was to prove "an apotheosis for Brahms and a crowning of his life's work" (Speyer 1937, 101). They all met again a few evenings later at Clara Schumann's in Frankfurt, when Brahms accompanied Antonia in some Lieder. Ferdinand Kufferath died on 23 June 1896, just a few weeks after the death of Clara Schumann. (Brahms 1974/6; Leyen 1905; Litzmann 1902, 1970; Speyer 1937)

KUGLER, FRANZ (THEODOR) (b. Stettin, 19 January 1808; d. Berlin, 18 March 1858). Art historian; poet, writer, and dramatist. Brahms set three of his poems in the song "Ständchen" (op. 106/1) and the vocal quartets "Sehnsucht" and "Nächtens" (op. 112/1–2). (Berbig 1990)

KUNDMANN, KARL (b. Vienna, 15 June 1838; d. Vienna, 9 June 1919). Sculptor. After studying with Franz Bauer, Josef Cesar, and Ernst Julius Hähnel (the creator of the **Beethoven** statue at Bonn), he spent the years 1865–67 in Rome. Among his best-known monuments in Vienna are those of **Franz Schubert** (1872), Admiral Tegetthoff (1886), and Franz Grillparzer (1889). He also made sculptures for the facades of some of the monumental buildings (Naturhistorisches Museum, Kunsthistorisches Museum, and Burgtheater) on the new Ringstrasse.

In late 1892 he was commissioned by **Anna Franz** (*see* WITTGENSTEIN FAMILY) to make a bust of Brahms. The latter, who had not so long ago been persuaded to sit for **Victor Tilgner**, agreed, though with even less enthusiasm, to do so again for Kundmann. Brahms already knew him: "I myself also like the silent and dreamy-looking Kundmann very much," he had written to **Maria Fellinger** in June 1892 (Brahms 1974/7, 282). According to **Max Kalbeck**, Kundmann had been present at the house of **Richard** and Maria **Fellinger** when the Joachim Quartet and **Richard Mühlfeld** rehearsed the Clarinet Quintet (op. 115) prior to their public performance of it on 19 January of that year.

Brahms sent the plaster copy he received as a present to his friend **Fritz Simrock** in November 1892. In an accompanying letter, he expressed his admiration for Kundmann, who, he declared, had created the best monuments in Vienna; furthermore, he told Simrock that he liked Kundmann as a person, adding, in his usual self-mocking manner, "All the more reprehensible of me, therefore, to have granted him so little time" (Brahms 1974/12, 85–86). This last sentence has been interpreted (e.g., by S. Kross) as implying that Brahms did not like the bust. Moreover, Kalbeck, who had expressed no disapproval of the bust in his biography of Brahms, reserving his criticism for Tilgner's alone, stated in his edition of Brahms's letters to Fritz Simrock that the finished work had displeased "the persons involved" (Brahms 1974/12, 86, n. 1), presumably meaning Anna Franz and Brahms, and possibly Kundmann himself; in fact, Richard Fellinger states in *Klänge um Brahms* that Kundmann later came to regard the bust as "too soft and mild" (R. Fellinger 1997, 138). Yet there is no indication that Brahms was really dissatisfied with Kundmann's representation of himself, for not only did he offer the plaster copy to Simrock, but he even suggested that Simrock might address "a few friendly words" to the sculptor, and also write to Anna Franz in this connection (Brahms 1974/12, 86).

It was Kundmann who, on 3 April 1897, took Brahms's death mask. (Brahms 1974/7, 1974/12; R. Fellinger 1997; Kross 1997)

KUPELWIESER, BERTHA: *see* WITTGENSTEIN FAMILY.

KUPFER, (THEODOR) WILHELM [William] (b. Hamburg, 1840; d. Vienna, 12 December 1914 [**Max Kalbeck** gives Kupfer's date of birth as 1843, but Kupfer himself writes in a brief autobiographical statement—printed in Biba 1997c—that he was born in 1840.] Cellist, composer, and music copyist. He belonged to a very musical family; his grandfather Carl was a musician, as was his father Heinrich who played in the Hamburg Stadttheater orchestra and was a member of the Böie String Quartet; his uncle Wilhelm was for many years a cellist in the Vienna court opera orchestra and also, from 1860 to 1868, in the Vienna Philharmonic Orchestra; and his brother Eduard was solo violist in the orchestra of the Grand Duke of Mecklenburg-Schwerin.

Kupfer received cello lessons from Carl Wiemann in Hamburg and later from F. A. Kummer in Dresden. From the age of 14 he played in orchestras in Hamburg and other towns (Dresden, Ischl, Salzburg, Brno); he appears to have settled in Vienna in 1865, but he also continued to perform elsewhere. Thus, he was engaged as solo cellist for the Italian opera seasons at Tbilisi, Georgia (1865–72). In Vienna he subsequently played in various theater orchestras and also, for a time, in Eduard Strauss's band.

Kupfer had grown up in Hamburg, where his family lived not far from Brahms's childhood home on Dammtorwall, and he had come to know both Brahms and his father. In Vienna, Brahms met him again some time before 1867, for in February of that year he told his father that Kupfer had recently taken part in a performance of "his sextet" (presumably op. 36, which had had its European premiere only three months earlier). Brahms added, "I only see him on these occasions, and then we converse in Plattdeutsch [the informal language of northern Germany]. Of course he asked after you and sends you his greetings" (Stephenson 1973, 127). When **Johann Jakob Brahms** visited Vienna in August 1867, he spent much time with Kupfer's uncle Wilhelm. At a concert given by **Clara Schumann** in Vienna on 28 November 1868, Kupfer (or his uncle Wilhelm—only the pianists are named in the program) took part in a performance of **Robert Schumann**'s *Andante and Variations* in the original version, where the two pianos (on this occasion played by Clara Schumann and Brahms) are accompanied by two cellos and a horn.

By 1881 Kupfer had begun to work as a copyist, and Brahms became his most illustrious client (for a list of the numerous compositions by Brahms that he copied, see M. L. McCorkle's [1984] *Werkverzeichnis*). The two men now came to enjoy closer personal relations. Brahms greatly appreciated Kupfer's profound knowledge of music and his competence and reliability as a copyist (see also Brahms's letter to Guido Adler in Avins and Eisinger 2002). Moreover, the fact that Kupfer was, like himself, born in Hamburg evidently established a firm link between them; with him Brahms was able to discuss current events happening in their native city. Expressing his gratification at regularly receiving news about the musical life in Hamburg through the newspapers that his brother Fritz was then sending him, Brahms wrote to his stepmother in October 1894: "Apart from myself, it is always read by my copyist Herr Kupfer and his wife, who both come from Hamburg" (Stephenson 1973, 283). Kalbeck (1976) states that during the last 10 years of his life Brahms used to invite Kupfer to the final rehearsals of his chamber music, and describes Kupfer's comportment on those occasions as that of a "silent and shy man who stayed modestly in the background and was greatly embarrassed if the Master addressed a word to him" (vol. 4, 549).

In January 1888 Brahms recommended to **Fritz Simrock** some Études Kupfer had written for the cello, and even suggested a suitable fee, adding, "The poor fellow . . . has great need of it" (Brahms 1974/11, 170). Simrock published them as *Akkordstudien für Violoncell*. Brahms was godfather of Kupfer's son Johannes. (Avins and Eisinger 2002; Biba 1997c; Brahms 1974/11; Gottlieb-Billroth 1935; Stephenson 1973)

– L –

LACHNER, FRANZ (PAUL) (b. Rain am Lech, Bavaria, 2 April 1803; d. Munich, 20 January 1890). Composer and conductor; the most celebrated of the four sons of Anton Lachner, municipal organist at Rain, all of whom were remarkable for their musical talent, as well as for their longevity: Franz lived to the age of 86, Theodor to 89, **Ignaz** to 87, and **Vincenz** to 81.

In 1823 Franz Lachner won a competition for the post of organist at the Protestant church in Vienna. During his stay in that city he studied with **Simon Sechter** and the Abbé Stadler, became assistant conductor (1827) and chief conductor (1829) at the Kärntnertor-Theater, enjoyed very friendly relations with **Franz Schubert** and Moritz von Schwind, and knew **Beethoven**. After leaving Vienna in 1834, he was employed as a court conductor at Mannheim before settling two years later at Munich, where he became conductor of the court opera and of the concerts of the Musikalische Akademie; in 1852 he was made Generalmusikdirektor. He was a prolific composer of sacred music and secular works; the latter included several operas, of which the best known was *Catarina Cornaro* (first produced at Munich in 1841).

Brahms's acquaintance with Lachner probably dated from May 1855, when both attended the 33rd Lower Rhine Music Festival at Düsseldorf. Later, Brahms was repeatedly in contact with Lachner, especially when he was staying in or near Munich, as in the summer of 1870 (when he also visited Lachner and his brothers at their summer home at Bernried on Lake Starnberg), in 1873 when he spent several months in the area (mostly at Tutzing), and again during his visit to Munich in March 1874. On the last occasion, when, as he told **Clara Schumann**, Lachner was constantly among the persons with whom he socialized (Litzmann 1970, vol. 2, 46), Brahms had a special reason for feeling friendly toward him, for Lachner had been largely responsible for his being made a Knight of the Bavarian Order of Maximilian for Science and Art the previous December. (Litzmann 1970)

LACHNER, IGNAZ (b. Rain am Lech, Bavaria, 11 September 1807; d. Hanover, 24 February 1895). Composer and conductor. Brother of **Franz Lachner**, whom he succeeded as organist of the Protestant church in Vienna; he also became assistant conductor at the Vienna court opera. In the course of a highly peripatetic career, he subsequently held important posts at Stuttgart (from 1831), Munich (1842), Hamburg (1853), Stockholm (1858), and finally Frankfurt am Main (1861–75). According to **Max Kalbeck**, Brahms first met him at the Lower Rhine Music Festival at Düsseldorf in 1855, and later came to know him quite well in Hamburg. Kalbeck states further that Lachner was among those who early on discerned signs of genius in Brahms and that he never wavered in his conviction that Brahms was destined for a distinguished career.

LACHNER, VINCENZ (b. Rain am Lech, Bavaria, 19 July 1811; d. Karlsruhe, 22 January 1893). Conductor and composer. He succeeded his brother **Franz Lachner** as conductor at the Kärntnertor-Theater in Vienna in 1834, and as Kapellmeister at Mannheim in 1836. From 1872 he lived at Karlsruhe, where he later taught at the local conservatory.

Like his brothers Franz and **Ignaz**, Vincenz Lachner regarded the musical trends set by **Liszt** and especially **Richard Wagner** as aberrations, but he was also puzzled and displeased by certain aspects of Brahms's musical aesthetics, while feeling profound admiration for his artistic integrity and technical mastery. To his former pupil **Hermann Levi** he wrote (in an undated letter),

> I must confess to you that much in his music appears ugly, bizarre, and exaggerated to me, and I cannot comprehend why he, who is such a tremendous harmonist, so frequently and so deliberately offends against tonal beauty. In-

> deed, I consider that in the creation of noble and beautiful thoughts directly impacting on our sensations—which, in my view, is the highest and supreme task for the artist and the very touchstone of genius—he comes off quite poorly.(Walter 1931, 24)

Lachner's difficulty in coming to terms with Brahms's aesthetics was also strikingly expressed in an affectionate letter he addressed to Brahms on the subject of his Second Symphony in August 1879, by which time the two men had long been on very cordial terms. Lachner's remarks focus above all on the opening movement, in which he finds countless features worthy of the deepest admiration ("If I were to touch on all the ingenious aspects, on all the beauty of this first movement, I would fill a whole book"); but he also voices certain objections, particularly against the sudden injection of darker elements into the prevailing ambience of radiant sunshine: "Why do you throw the angry drum roll and the gloomy, lugubrious sounds of the trombones and tubas into the idyllically serene mood created at the beginning of the first movement?" Another criticism concerns what he regards as the displeasing tonal effect at the end of that movement. Lachner's letter drew a remarkably interesting reply from Brahms in which, addressing Lachner as his "very dear friend," he stoutly defended his use of the instruments in question, as well as the other musical solutions he had adopted. Regarding the "contamination" of the sunny atmosphere, he explained that he was a "deeply melancholy person," constantly aware of the "black wings" flapping above the heads of all men; and he added that it was therefore perhaps no accident that the symphony [op. 23] was immediately followed in his compositions by "a brief discourse on the great 'Warum' [Why]"—a reference to the motet "Warum ist das Licht gegeben dem Mühseligen" (op. 74/1), which is a setting of Job's harrowing questioning of the purpose of life. Brahms continued, "If you do not know it [i.e., this motet] I will send it to you. It throws the necessary shadow across the light-hearted symphony and maybe explains those drums and trombones." (For the full text of these two letters and a detailed discussion of their content, see Brinkmann 1989.) (Brinkmann 1989; F. Walter 1931)

LA MARA: *see* LIPSIUS, MARIE.

LANGE, DE, FAMILY. Dutch family of musicians.

SAMUEL DE LANGE (b. Rotterdam, 9 June 1811; d. Rotterdam, 15 May 1884) was employed as organist at several Rotterdam churches (finally, from 1864, at the St. Laurenskerke) and also taught from 1844 at the school of the Maatschappij tot Bevordering der Toonkunst in Rotterdam.

He played **Handel**'s Organ Concerto in D Minor and **Bach**'s Prelude and Fugue in E-flat Major at a special concert of the Gesellschaft der Musikfreunde conducted by Brahms as artistic director of the society, on 8 December 1872. In July 1873 he visited Brahms at Tutzing.

His son **SAMUEL** (b. Rotterdam, 22 February 1840; d. Stuttgart, 7 July 1911), a pianist and organist, taught at the same music school in Rotterdam at which his father taught and was organist at the Waalse Kerk in that city. Between 1874 and 1884 he was active as a teacher, performer, and choral conductor in Basle, Paris, and Cologne, but he returned to Holland in 1884 to become director of the conservatory at The Hague. In 1893 he joined the faculty of the Stuttgart conservatory, of which he eventually became director (1900–1908). Among the composers whose music he championed were **Liszt** and Brahms. In the later 1860s, he took part in performances in Rotterdam of the Piano Quartets opp. 25–26 and the Piano Quintet op. 34; furthermore, he was the soloist in the first Dutch performance of the D Minor Piano Concerto at a concert of the Erudito Musica Konzertverein, also at Rotterdam, in 1871.

Samuel de Lange's second son, **DANIËL** (b. Rotterdam, 11 June 1841; d. Point Loma, California, 31 January 1918), was likewise an organist, but he was even better known as a cellist. He taught that instrument at the Rotterdam conservatory in 1863–64, after which he was employed as organist and chorus master in Paris until 1870. He then went to live in Amsterdam, where he taught at the school of the local Maatschappij tot Bevordering der Toonkunst. Among other musical activities, he conducted the concerts of the Caecilia Orchestra (1886–89) and the Amstels Mannenkoor, and served as director of the Amsterdam conservatory (1895–1913). He also wrote a number of books on music and, from 1876, contributed music criticism to the newspaper *Nieuws van den Dag*. In 1914 he was appointed director of the music department of the Isis Conservatory of Art, Music, and Drama at Point Loma in California.

Shortly before Brahms set out on his first tour of Holland in 1876, his friend **Wilhelm Engelmann** mentioned in a letter (19 December 1875) that Daniël de Lange, "a very competent musician" who was also one of Brahms's warmest admirers in Holland, had recently conducted a performance of *Rinaldo* (Brahms 1974/13, 26). No doubt Brahms met Lange during this and later tours, and he evidently took a liking to him, for in 1880 he recommended to **Eduard Hanslick**, when the latter was about to leave on a journey to the Low Countries, three "very good guides" in Amsterdam: **Jerome Alexander Sillem**, **Julius Röntgen**, and "De Lange . . . one of the best Dutch musicians, a cellist, a prolific composer, and a critic and also a pleasant man—as, after all, happens sometime" (Hanslick 1897b, *Neue freie Presse*, 1 July 1997, 3; the last quip was evidently aimed, affectionately, at Hanslick himself).

The father and both sons were composers, writing in a variety of genres. The younger Samuel de Lange dedicated one of his organ sonatas to Brahms. (Brahms 1974/13; Hanslick 1897b; Zwart 2001)

LAUB, FERDINAND (b. Prague, 19 January 1832; d. Gries, near Bozen [Bolzano], 18 March 1875). Czech violinist and composer. One of the greatest violin virtuosos of his time, he enjoyed an international reputation both as a soloist and as a chamber music player; he attained the peak of his performing career between 1858 and 1865. Both in Berlin (1858–62) and later in Vienna (1862–66) he presented numerous chamber music concerts, in which he focused especially on the quartets of **Beethoven**, including the late ones. Brahms held him in high, if not unqualified, regard. "He really is an excellent violinist," he wrote to **Joseph Joachim** in February 1863. "What is missing in his playing which would make it truly delightful to me he lacks so greatly in his own person that it would be unreasonable to demand or expect it" (Brahms 1974/5, 334).

At a concert given by Laub in Vienna on 22 November 1863, Brahms took part in a performance of his Piano Quartet op. 25; at another of Laub's chamber music concerts, on 3 November 1864, Brahms performed **Robert Schumann**'s Violin Sonata in D Minor with him.

Laub was on the staff of the Stern Conservatory in Berlin from 1855 until 1857, and on the faculty of the Moscow conservatory from 1866 until 1874. (Brahms 1974/5)

LAURENS, JEAN-JOSEPH-BONAVENTURE (b. Carpentras, 14 July 1801; d. Montpellier, 29 June 1890). Portraitist, graphic artist, musician, and writer on art; brother of the painter Jules Laurens (1825–1901) and father of the painter Rosalba Vignée (d. 1886). From 1835 until his retirement in 1867, he was employed as secretary and treasurer of the École de Médecine at the University of Montpellier. Music was his passion; in 1841 he edited a selection of **François Couperin**'s music, and in 1843 he published his own translation of Johann Peter Lyser's novella *Sebastian Bach und seine Söhne*. He and Valentin Alkan were reportedly the first two Frenchmen to join the Bach Gesellschaft founded in Germany in 1850. Laurens was an accomplished performer on piano, organ, violin, and cello, and also composed religious music. Moreover, he was acquainted with many French and German musicians and regularly corresponded with several of them. As he liked to sketch the musicians he met, he gradually assembled an impressive number of portraits. His subjects included **Chopin**, Ernst, Fétis, Stephen Heller, Gounod, **Ferdinand Hiller**, **Joseph Joachim**, Johann Christian Heinrich Rinck, Saint-Saëns, Schnyder von Wartensee, Ambroise Thomas, and Widor. Two years before his death he donated this collection, together with much other material, to the city of Carpentras, where all of it is preserved at the Bibliothèque Inguimbertine. Of his writings on art, the *Essai sur la théorie du Beau pittoresque* (1849) is probably most deserving of mention.

In October 1853, on his return journey from Dresden where he had visited the landscape painter Ludwig Richter, he stopped at Düsseldorf in order to see **Robert Schumann**, with whom he had corresponded for the past five years. They first met on 11 October at the house of the painter Johann Wilhelm Schirmer (on which occasion Brahms may also have been present). During his stay at Düsseldorf, Laurens drew several portraits of Robert and one of **Clara Schumann**, and at Schumann's request he also made some drawings of Brahms. On 16 October Schumann noted in his Haushaltbuch, "Last time Laurens" (Nauhaus 1982, 639).

Laurens's portraits of the 20-year-old Brahms must surely rank among the most delightful and charming ever made of a young musician—or, indeed, of any young man. Three versions are known, all of them in profile. One, done on reddish-brown paper and showing Brahms looking to his left, was kept by the Schumanns; Robert liked it so much that when he was at the clinic at Endenich he asked for it to be sent there. Eventually, Clara presented it to **Marie Völkers**-Böie, and it is now exhibited at the Schumann Haus (182 Sebastianstrasse) at Endenich-Bonn, on permanent loan from the Königslöw family. At bottom right there appears a later note: "Dessiné / à la demande / de R. Schumann / à Düsseldorf, 15 Sept. [sic] 1852 [sic] / fec. Laurent [sic]." This is the portrait by Laurens that has been most frequently reproduced in biographies and exhibition catalogs.

Another version, which likewise depicts the subject in left profile, was retained by Laurens and is now at the Bibliothèque Inguimbertine at Carpentras. Brahms's signature stands under the sketch, and below it Brahms wrote out the first three bars of the Scherzo op. 4. Below the music there is the indication "Düsseldorf Sept [sic] 1853," apparently still in Brahms's writing. On the right, a later note explains, "Célèbre compositeur / contemporain / âgé de 20 ans." This portrait was described in some detail, and also reproduced, by R. Caillet and E. Göpel in their article "Ein Brahmsfund in Südfrankreich" in *Zeitschrift für Musikwissenschaft*; further reproductions can be found in K. Laux's *Der Einsame*, K. Geiringer's *Brahms*, and D. Boeck's *Johannes Brahms*. (In his 1997 biography of Brahms, S. Kross mistakenly states that the sketch passed as part of Brahms's estate into the possession of the Gesellschaft der Musikfreunde in Vienna; he also wrongly identifies the music as the opening of the Piano Sonata op. 5.)

Lastly, the Carpentras library possesses still another sketch of Brahms made by Laurens during his visit to Düsseldorf, this time in right profile. It was reproduced by R. Caillet in his article "Les Portraits des musiciens par Bonaventure Laurens à la Bibliothèque de Carpentras," and, more recently, in Boeck's book. Particulars of this right-profile portrait are given in the abovementioned article by Caillet and Göpel.

As a parting gift, Schumann presented Laurens with an autograph sketch for his Piano Quartet op. 44. As for Brahms, he gave Laurens the autograph of his song "Liebestreu" (op. 3/1); the dedication to Laurens is dated "16 Oct. 53." Both autographs are now at the Bibliothèque Inguimbertine. (Boeck 1998; Caillet 1929; Caillet and Göpel 1933; Kross 1997; Laux 1944; Nauhaus 1982; Tessier 1930)

LEMCKE, KARL (b. Schwerin, 1831; d. Munich, 1913). Poet and literary historian, who reportedly taught at Heidelberg, Munich, Amsterdam, Aix la Chapelle, and Stuttgart. Brahms used poems by Lemcke in the songs "Ùber die See" (op. 69/7), "Im Garten am Seegestade" (op. 70/1), "Willst du, dass ich geh?" (op. 71/4), "Verzagen" (op. 72/4), "In Waldeseinsamkeit" (op. 85/6), "Verrat" (op. 105/5), and "Salamander" (op. 107/ 2), and in the settings for four-voice male choir of the patriotic poems "Freiwillige," "Geleit," "Marschieren," and "Gebt Acht" (op. 41/2–5). Brahms took the texts from Lemcke's *Lieder und Gedichte*, published in Hamburg in 1861.

Nothing appears to be known about any direct contacts Brahms may have had with Lemcke, but he arranged for copies of opp. 69–72 (published in 1877) and op. 105 and op. 107 (both published in 1888) to be sent to Lemcke by **Fritz Simrock** when they appeared. The choruses had been published by **Jakob Melchior Rieter-Biedermann** in 1867. (Brahms 1974/10–11)

LEOPOLD III, PRINCE ZUR LIPPE (b. 1 September 1821; d. 8 December 1875); son of Leopold II (1796–1851) and Emilie, née Princess of Schwarzburg-Sondershausen (1800–67). He succeeded his father as ruler of Lippe-Detmold in 1851, and the following year married Princess Elisabeth von Schwarzburg-Rudolstadt (1833–96). The couple had no children, and upon his death Leopold III was succeeded by his brother Woldemar (1824–95), whose own marriage to Princess Sophie of Bavaria was likewise childless and who was, in consequence, himself followed as ruler of the principality by yet another son of Leopold II, Alexander (1831–1905). Leopold II also had three daughters: Luise (1822–87), **Princess Friederike zur Lippe** (1825–97), and Pauline (1834–1906). (In her book *Johannes Brahms: Life and Letters*, Styra Avins (1997) mistakenly states that Leopold III ruled until 1876, that Brahms's pupil Princess Friederike was his wife, and that his successor was his son [791]). Brahms owed his association with the principality of Lippe-Detmold to his friendship with **Clara**

Schumann. The latter had spent the second half of June 1855 at Detmold for the purpose of giving tuition to Princess Friederike, who was then already an accomplished pianist. During her stay, Clara no doubt spoke highly of the gifted young composer and pianist from Hamburg. That summer Brahms was already giving lessons to Laura **von Meysenbug** at Düsseldorf, and in September he made the acquaintance of Princess Friederike there (if he had not already done so at the Lower Rhine Music Festival a few months earlier). Before the end of that year, he received an invitation to give a concert at Detmold, but it was not until the spring of 1857 that he seized the opportunity to impress the court with the brilliance of his playing. He arrived on 31 May and spent the following week at Detmold, and during his visit he played **Beethoven**'s 4th Piano Concerto, took part in a performance of **Franz Schubert**'s "Trout" Quintet, and repeatedly played privately at court. As a result, the prince was eager to bind him to a long engagement. "**[Carl Louis] Bargheer** hopes very much that Joh. will spend several months at Detmold," **Joseph Joachim** wrote to Clara Schumann on 18 August. "The prince has spoken about it very frequently" (Johannes Joachim and Moser 1911–13, vol. 1, 438). Not long afterward, Brahms accepted a contract that provided for his stay at Detmold from late September until the end of that year, during which time he was to teach Princess Friederike, conduct the small choral society that met at the palace, and furthermore perform at concerts, as well as at musical soirees at court. In addition to receiving a generous fee, he was granted free accommodations at the hotel Stadt Frankfurt, located opposite the main entrance to the palace grounds.

The contract was renewed for the corresponding period in each of the following two years, but when it was again proposed in 1860, Brahms declined the offer, partly on the grounds that he would need the months in question to prepare the publication of certain of his compositions, but mainly because he was not granted his request to be placed in sole charge of the orchestra at court concerts (*see* KIEL, [CLEMENS] AUGUST). He had, however, derived much enjoyment from his stays at Detmold, the surroundings of which are exceptionally beautiful. From a professional point of view, moreover, his contact with the local orchestra and choir provided him with invaluable experience for his future career. Among the compositions on which he worked at Detmold were the Serenades opp. 11 and 16, the *Begräbnisgesang* (op. 13), and various songs.

Brahms returned to Detmold in December 1865, when at court concerts he played the "Emperor" Concerto and, with Bargheer, Beethoven's "Kreutzer" Sonata. His own Serenade op. 16 was also performed. (Avins 1997; Johannes Joachim and Moser 1911–13; Schramm 1983)

LESSING, KARL FRIEDRICH (b. Breslau [Wrocław, Poland], 15 February 1808; d. Karlsruhe, 5 June 1880). Painter; great-nephew of the writer Gotthold Ephraim Lessing. He initially studied architecture in Berlin, but subsequently switched to painting. Among his teachers was Wilhelm von Schadow, and when the latter became director of the Düsseldorf academy in 1826, Lessing followed him there. In Düsseldorf, Lessing became friendly with **Robert** and **Clara Schumann**. In 1858 he moved to Karlsruhe, where he had been appointed director of the portrait gallery and print collection. As an artist, he at first specialized in landscapes, then in historical paintings, and later still in subjects drawn from the religious controversies of the 15th and 16th centuries. His wife Ida (1817–80), a sister-in-law of his friend **Adolf Schroedter**, was a talented painter of flowers and a great music lover.

The Lessings, who occupied a large apartment located in a wing of the art gallery, played an important part in the cultural life of Karlsruhe. Their Wednesday musical evenings attracted many prominent local and visiting musicians, among them Clara Schumann, **Ferdinand Hiller**, **Hermann Levi**, and also Brahms, who had known the couple in Düsseldorf and met them again at Karlsruhe in the summer of 1862. He frequently visited them in later years when he was staying at Karlsruhe or at nearby Baden-Baden. He also used to perform at their musical soirees, sometimes playing his own compositions, at other times improvising together with Hermann Levi or Wilhelm Kalliwoda—on one occasion, on **Johann Strauss**'s "Blue Danube" waltz. (Buchholtz 1909)

LEVI, HERMANN (b. Giessen, 7 November 1839; d. Munich, 13 May 1900). Conductor; son of Rabbi Benedikt Levi (1806–99) and his first wife Henriette (1806–42); brother of **Wilhelm Stephan Lindeck**. **Max Kalbeck**'s statement that Levi traveled from Rotterdam to Hamburg in the summer of 1861 for the express purpose of getting to know Brahms (Kalbeck 1976, vol. 1, 443) is surely wrong, since Levi did not move to Rotterdam, where he had been appointed conductor of the German Opera Company, until the following year. Levi's biographer Frithjof Haas (1995), on the other hand, states that Levi made Brahms's acquaintance in Hamburg "in the summer of 1862," while on his way to take up his appointment at Rotterdam (91). From other statements in Haas's book it would appear that, in that case, the meeting took place in August 1862. What is certain is that they met at the latest in May 1863, when Brahms wrote to **Jakob Melchior Rieter-Biedermann** from Hamburg: "To my delight, Hermann Levi was here for a few days" (Brahms 1974/6, 80).

It was during his tenure of the post of court Kapellmeister at Karlsruhe, which he assumed in August 1864, that Levi became a close personal friend of Brahms. At the same time, both Brahms and Levi formed an intimate association with **Julius Allgeyer**. A frequently reproduced photograph shows the three of them together, looking at a plate that they are said to have presented as a wedding present to **Julie Schumann** (*see* SCHUMANN FAMILY). During this period Brahms saw a good deal of Levi, both at Baden-Baden and at Karlsruhe where he stayed with Levi on several occasions. On 18 April 1866, following one of these visits, Levi wrote to **Clara Schumann**: "You can imagine what a gap his departure has left in my life. What a man! . . . One cannot measure him by any of the standards we are accustomed to apply to persons like ourselves" (Litzmann 1902, vol. 3, 190).

Moreover, the friendship led to a mutually profitable musical association in Karlsruhe. Thus, at a concert of the court orchestra on 3 November 1865, Brahms was soloist in his First Piano Concerto, which was conducted by Levi, who also accompanied two of Brahms's vocal quartets on piano; on 16 April 1866 they appeared together at a concert at court, at which Brahms played his piano version of the second movement of his String Sextet op. 67 and a march by **Franz Schubert**; on 6 March 1869 Levi conducted Brahms's Requiem. (He had urged Brahms to direct the performance himself, but Brahms had declined; however, he did conduct a further performance of the work on 12 May of that year. Levi was to perform the Requiem again on 5 April 1871.) On 6 October 1869, in Brahms's presence, Levi and Clara Schumann accompanied the first public performance of a number of the *Liebeslieder-Walzer* (op. 52); on 19 October 1869 Brahms played his Piano Quintet with members of the court orchestra; and last, but not least, the first performances of the *Schicksalslied* (18 October 1871) and *Triumphlied* (5 June 1872) took place at Karlsruhe, the former conducted by Brahms, the latter by Levi. The concert on 5 June 1872, at which Brahms was present, served as a farewell concert for Levi, who was about to assume the post of court Kapellmeister in Munich; Clara Schumann took part, playing her husband's Piano Concerto and two solos, one of them Brahms's arrangement of the Gavotte from **Christoph Willibald Gluck**'s *Iphigénie en Aulide* (M. McCorkle 1984, Anhang Ia/2).

However, not long after he moved to Munich, Levi's relations with Brahms changed significantly for the worse. The rivalry with the conductor **Franz Wüllner**, into which, to his dismay, he found himself propelled in Munich and which brought to the fore certain aspects of his character that might have irritated Brahms, probably contributed to their estrangement. Thus, when Brahms authorized Wüllner, at the latter's request, to conduct the first Munich performance (on 10 December 1873) of his recently composed *Haydn Variations*, Levi was much aggrieved and expressed his disappointment to Brahms in more than one letter, assuring him at the same time that it was not motivated by vanity but by his conviction that he was better qualified than Wüllner to do justice to a new Brahms composition (as, indeed, he may well have been). Brahms, who had then known Wüllner for some 20 years and clearly respected his talents, and who, moreover, never liked getting involved in other people's quarrels, may not have felt the greatest sympathy for Levi's reaction. But it is at the same time worth pointing out that he was then on terms of far greater intimacy with Levi than with Wüllner. He and Levi had addressed each other with the familiar "Du" for many years (as is evidenced by its use in Levi's letter of 9 November 1864, which opens their published correspondence), whereas it was not until the late autumn of 1876 that this mode of address would be adopted by Brahms and Wüllner. In any case, Brahms did his best to assuage Levi's injured feelings by agreeing to take part in a concert directed by Levi on 13 March 1874, at which Brahms conducted the *Haydn Variations*, among other items, and performed his First Piano Concerto.

An incident that occurred during a visit by Brahms to Munich in late April 1875 was to have more far-reaching consequences. A letter Levi wrote to Brahms shortly afterward indicates that the latter had harshly reproached him for his "Wandlungen" (the word is cited by Levi in quotation marks), that is, for having undergone a change, namely in his musical aesthetics. This accusation appears to have been prompted by Brahms's belief that what he perceived to be an increasing fascination on Levi's part with the operas of **Richard Wagner** was leading him to abandon his former musical ideals, among which Brahms evidently included his own music—a charge that Levi strongly refuted: "Anyone who saw me after the recent performance of *Schicksalslied* would never imagine that anything I have really loved could fade before new impressions," he assured Brahms, who had been so angry that he had cut short his visit to Munich. (For the text of this letter, see Brahms 1974/7, 184–85; it ends with a declaration of profound affection.)

Styra Avins (1997) states firmly that the idea, which "is the obvious conclusion from the contents of Levi's letter" and which has been expressed by many commentators, that the friendship broke up because of Levi's increasing regard for Wagner's music "is not an explanation which stands up to scrutiny," seeing that Wüllner never lost Brahms's friendship, despite the fact that he conducted the premieres of *Die Walküre* (on 22 September 1869) and *Das Rheingold* (on 26 June 1870) and at various other times performed compositions by Wagner as well as by **Anton Bruckner** (474). And it is, of course, quite true that Brahms not only did not hold this against Wüllner, he had even himself attended performances of the two operas, again conducted by Wüllner, in Munich in July 1870. However, to conclude from this that Wagner could not have been a major factor in the crisis that Levi's relations with Brahms underwent in April 1875 is to ignore certain important aspects of the situation and, in particular, Levi's unusual character.

As Peter Gay (1978) has shown in his perceptive study of Levi's personality (in *Freud, Jews and Other Germans*), he had an instinctive need to worship idols, to the point of obsequiousness and even (as in the case of Wagner) to the point of self-abasement. In December 1880 he was to write to **Paul Heyse**: "You have known for a long time that I am completely, body and soul, under the spell of that man"; and he explained that if he had not lately visited Heyse (who evidently did not share his idolatrous attitude) it was because he had been in a state akin to intoxication during Wagner's recent three-weeks' stay in Munich and could not have endured a single derisive or ironic remark about him (216).

There is little doubt that Levi had either reached, or at any rate was close to, that state of adulation by the summer of 1875, when he attended rehearsals of *Siegfried* and *Götterdämmerung* at Bayreuth, which, as he reported to his father, "completely overwhelmed" him (Haas 1995, 190). In fact, his feelings for the music and personality of Wagner had probably already reached a stage of feverish enthusiasm at the time of his crucial meeting with Brahms a few months earlier. In a letter on 21 February of that year, he had informed Brahms that he had been "tremendously impressed" when Wagner had played the whole of *Götterdämmerung* for him two years earlier, and that he was planning to spend several weeks at Bayreuth the following year, in order to attend many rehearsals for the imminent first *Ring* cycle (Brahms 1974/7, 181). It is thus quite likely that Brahms became acutely aware, during his visit to Munich in April 1875, of Levi's growing or already well-established infatuation—"body and soul"—with Wagner the man as well as Wagner the composer, that he was shocked by it, and that it was to this infatuation that he so angrily reacted. (He certainly never found himself in a similar situation with Wüllner.) Rightly or wrongly, Brahms may have felt, moreover, that his friend had essentially transferred to Wagner the fervent admiration and affection he had felt for his own music as well as himself. Avins (1997) contends further that to attribute the breakup to Levi's devotion to Wagner's music "makes even less sense" (475) in the light of the fact that Clara Schumann, who was indeed far more hostile to that music than Brahms, nonetheless continued to maintain cordial relations with Levi. However, as should be clear from the above remarks, her situation in this matter was significantly different from Brahms's: she was never in a position to suspect or accuse Levi of unfaithfulness or betrayal.

To Allgeyer, who subsequently pleaded with him not to turn away from Levi, Brahms replied, on 18 March 1876, that his feelings toward Levi had in no way changed, "only the manner of contact," and he added, "I need not explain to you at length that one may have the best and highest opinion of one's friends, and nonetheless also have cause to avoid any particularly close or intimate contact" (Orel 1964). He did, in fact, meet Levi again when he went to Munich to conduct his First Symphony there on 15 November 1876. The reunion passed pleasantly enough, no reference being apparently made to the acrimonious meeting of the preceding year; and Levi was left with the mistaken impression that, as he reported to Clara Schumann on 22 November, "all is as it used to be, and even much better" (Litzmann 1902, vol. 3, 342). Rather pathetically, he added that from hints that Allgeyer had given him about remarks made by Brahms, he had gained "the conviction (which I didn't dare to entertain even in the days of our closest contacts) that he really does feel some affection for me and that he has not been altogether happy about our estrangement"—a remark characteristic of the subordinate position Levi was wont to adopt in his relations with certain people such as Brahms and, later, Wagner. But any expectations Levi may have had of a further long and agreeable association with Brahms were not realized. The meeting in November 1876 seems to have been their last.

Even their correspondence (at any rate as printed in Leopold Schmidt's edition) petered out in early 1878, after a rather confused exchange about a possible Munich performance of the new Second Symphony, perhaps under Brahms himself, had come to nothing. In one letter Brahms even offered to conduct the premiere in Munich in December, but Levi felt unable to change the program already announced for that particular concert. In the end, it was **Hans Richter** who directed the first performance in Vienna on 30th December. When Levi subsequently proposed that a performance of the new work be conducted in Munich by Brahms during Lent, Brahms declined the invitation; and at that point the correspondence appears to have come to a halt. On 27 March 1878, in place of the hoped for performance of the Second Symphony, Levi conducted another one of the First—which met with an extremely hostile reception, for Munich audiences were generally slow to warm to Brahms's music, especially the symphonies. Nevertheless, Levi did not neglect these altogether, directing performances of the Second (1888), Third (1884), Fourth (1886), and First again (1893); he also presented the *Haydn Variations* (1881, 1890), the Second Piano Concerto (1883, 1886), and the *Tragic* (1881) and *Academic Festival* (1882) Overtures. He retired from his Munich post in 1896. (Avins 1997; Brahms 1974/6, 1974/7; Ettlinger 1913; Gay 1978; Haas 1995; Litzmann 1902; Orel 1964; Possart 1901)

LEWINSKY, JOSEF (b. Vienna, 20 September, 1835; d. Vienna, 27 February 1907). Actor. Following a brief, disastrous engagement at the Theater an der Wien in 1854, he went first to Troppau [Opava] and then to Brünn [Brno], where he scored his first great success as Franz Moor in **Frederich von Schiller**'s *Die Räuber* on 11 February 1858. He was subsequently offered a contract at the Vienna Burgtheater, and he made his debut there in the same role on 4 May of that year. He soon established himself as one of the outstanding members of the company, admired particularly for his superb diction and declamatory powers. Among his most celebrated roles, in addition to Franz Moor, were Hassan in Schiller's *Die Verschwörung des Fiesko zu Genua*, Nathan in Lessing's *Nathan der Weise*, and Shakespeare's Iago and Richard III.

Clara Schumann, who saw him in *Die Räuber* while staying in Vienna in December 1858, was tremendously impressed by his performance ("quite brilliant"—see her letter to Brahms of 9 December, and also that of 3 March 1860, in which she declared that Lewinsky made one fully experience the "power of genius" (Litzmann 1970, vol. 1, 231, 302). She was just as favorably impressed when she met him in private. On 3 November 1862, a few weeks after Brahms's arrival in Vienna, she wrote to him: "I expect you will by now have called on Lewinsky, to whom I spoke at great length about you, and perhaps you have already grown fond of him" (Litzmann 1970, vol. 1, 411). Brahms's reaction to Lewinsky must have been as positive as Clara Schumann's, to judge by her letter of 21 November: "I knew in advance that you would be enchanted with him—didn't I always tell you that he was a genius?" (Litzmann 1970, vol. 1, 417).

Brahms is likely to have seen a good deal of Lewinsky during the following years (they even both performed at a private concert on 18 December 1863), and he very likely met Lewinsky repeatedly at the home of **Franz Flatz**, which Lewinsky frequently visited (see Clara Schumann's letters to Brahms of 15 March 1866 and especially of 30 December 1866; in the latter she refers to an evening spent by Brahms at Flatz's apartment in Lewinsky's company [Litzmann 1970, vol. 1, 533, 548]). In November 1873, at Lewinsky's request, Brahms composed the five *Ophelia* songs (WoO posthum 22) for **Olga Precheisen**, then Lewinsky's fiancée and later his wife. At a Gesellschaft der Musikfreunde concert conducted by Brahms on 2 March 1874, Lewinsky took part in a performance of **Robert Schumann**'s music to *Manfred*, speaking the Prologue and a linking poem by F. Kürnberger. (Haeussermann 1975; Litzmann 1970; *ÖBL* 1957–)

LEYEN, (FRANZ) RUDOLF VON DER (b. Krefeld, 22 November 1851; d. Bonn, 3 January 1910). Merchant and banker; descendant of a

Mennonite family that settled at Krefeld in the second half of the 17th century and later attained a dominant position in the local silk industry. (In 1650 the Mennonites accounted for some 50 percent of the population of Krefeld, in 1816 for 22 percent, in 1812 for 5 percent, and by 1956 for only 0.5 percent.) Rudolf was the son of Franz Heinrich von der Leyen (1825–1914) and his first wife Clara, née von Beckerath (1829–56); he was a nephew of **Rudolf von Beckerath**. In 1876 he married Hedwig von Randow (1858–1924), a daughter of the banker Adolf von Randow.

He was extremely musical and an outstanding pianist. Violinist **Richard Barth**, for several years Konzertmeister of the Krefeld orchestra, described him as "a noble and splendid man, brilliantly gifted musically, [who] played the piano quite beautifully, far surpassing amateur standard" (K. Hofmann 1979b, 30). A long-time admirer of Brahms's music, Von der Leyen readily offered him the hospitality of his house when Brahms first came to Krefeld in January 1880. It was the beginning of a friendship that lasted until Brahms's death. Brahms was again the guest of the Von der Leyens on the occasion of his later concerts at Krefeld (January 1881, January 1883, January 1885, and November 1885 [with the Meiningen orchestra]); in addition, he paid them some private visits (February 1884, March 1890). Rudolf von der Leyen also met Brahms on certain occasions outside Krefeld, for instance, in Cologne in June 1887 and March 1890, in Frankfurt in January 1889, and at Meiningen in November 1891. They even shared a vacation abroad: when Von der Leyen was staying at Trento in May 1884, Brahms joined him there, and they then spent a holiday together in northern Italy, in the course of which they played the two-piano version of Brahms's new Third Symphony for **Duke Georg II** and his wife at their villa near Tremezzo. Afterward, Von der Leyen, who had gone on to Milan, wrote to Brahms, who had remained at the Villa Carlotta: "For someone like myself who from his early days has lived in your music and has derived such happiness from it (and from you), it was a rare pleasure to be permitted to experience such a work with you, and especially the *bellissima terza*!" (Leyen 1905, 56). Eventually they traveled back to Germany together, Brahms to Düsseldorf for the local music festival and Von der Leyen to Krefeld.

Brahms evidently grew very fond of Von der Leyen. When, at one point, they parted company in Italy, "his eyes filled with heavy tears as we said good-bye," Von der Leyen reported, greatly moved, to his wife (Leyen 1905, 50). Further striking proof of the intimate relationship that linked Brahms to the much younger man is provided by an incident at **Clara Schumann**'s funeral in May 1896, as later described by Von der Leyen

(1905): in the funeral chapel Brahms "threw his arms round my neck, sobbing, and holding on to me, he cried for a long time" (97). It was Von der Leyen who after the funeral suggested that Brahms accompany him to the house of his sister and brother-in-law at nearby Bad Honnef, an invitation that Brahms accepted. (On those memorable days at the Hagerhof, *see* BECKERATH, VON, FAMILY; OPHÜLS, GUSTAV; and WEYERMANN, WALTHER.) (Beckerath 1958; Buschbell 1953–54; K. Hofmann 1979b; Kurschat 1933; Leyen 1905)

LIENAU. Music publishers. Emil Robert Lienau (b. Neustadt, Holstein, 28 December 1838; d. Neustadt, 22 July 1920), who had studied piano with Ignaz Moscheles and theory and composition with Ernst Friedrich Richter and **Julius Rietz**, joined the Schlesinger publishing house in Berlin in 1863; the following year he bought the firm, retaining its former name, to which he added his own. In 1875 he considerably expanded the business by acquiring the Viennese firm of "Carl Haslinger quondam Tobias" (so renamed in 1848 by Tobias's son Carl, who had himself died in 1868). After Lienau retired at the end of the century, the two firms were managed by his sons Robert (Heinrich) (b. Neustadt, 27 July 1866; d. Berlin, 8 November 1949) in Berlin and Friedrich Wilhelm (b. Berlin, 6 January 1876; d. Vienna, 15 November 1973) in Vienna. (For the later history of the business, see the articles in Blume 1949–86 and Sadie 2001). According to his son Robert, Emil Robert made Brahms's personal acquaintance in Vienna in the spring of 1876. However, the (incomplete) correspondence between the elder Lienau and Brahms published by Wilhelm Altmann in 1920 shows that the two men had been in contact by early 1875 at the latest, for the first letter printed in that collection, a communication from Lienau dated 19 March 1875, refers to what was evidently a reply by Brahms to an even earlier letter Lienau had sent him. At that time Lienau was trying to interest Brahms in an operatic project, for which his friend, writer Julius Leopold Klein, was proposing to write a libretto based on an episode in Homer's *Iliad*; Brahms's score was to be published by Lienau's firm. However, Brahms responded with only scant enthusiasm, and although Klein, at his suggestion, sent him a scenario of the plot, nothing came of the idea. Lienau met Brahms repeatedly during his numerous later trips to Vienna and established a friendly relationship with him, but his firm never published any of Brahms's compositions.

When his son Robert first visited Vienna in 1890, he was very cordially received by Brahms, and during the more than two years he subsequently spent there (October 1891 to November 1893), they saw each other frequently. He regularly dined with Brahms and his friends at the Roter Igel restaurant, met him at the house of mutual acquaintances such as **Hugo Conrat** and at the musical and social functions of the Tonkünstlerverein, and joined him and his fellow walkers on their Sunday excursions. After he left Vienna in late November 1893, he was to see Brahms again on at least three further occasions: in Berlin during the winter of 1894–95, at Leipzig in January 1895, and, for the last time, in Zurich in October 1895. Later, learning of Brahms's mortal illness, he wanted to visit him once more but was dissuaded from doing so by **Fritz Simrock**, who had been greatly distressed at finding Brahms in such a wretched condition. Lienau did not attend the funeral, but he was present at the unveiling of **Ilse Conrat**'s monument at Brahms's grave in 1903, and also at the unveiling of the Brahms monument at Meiningen (*see* HILDEBRAND, ADOLF VON). His recollections of Brahms, originally written for the benefit of his family but later published under the title *Unvergessliche Jahre mit Johannes Brahms*, contain many interesting anecdotes about Brahms and his circle. (Brahms 1974/14; Lienau 1934)

LILIENCRON, DETLEV VON [really: Baron Adolph Axel Lilienkron] (b. Kiel, 3 June 1844; d. Alt-Rahlstedt, near Hamburg, 22 July 1909). Poet and writer. Brahms set two of his poems in the songs "Auf dem Kirchhofe" (op. 105/4) and "Maienkätzchen" (op. 107/4). (Zenker 1990b)

LIMBURGER, PAUL BERNHARD (b. 1826; d. Leipzig, 10 October 1891). Konsul Limburger was a wealthy wool merchant and, according to **Dame Ethel Smyth** (1919), who enjoyed his friendship and hospitality while she was a student at Leipzig, "the only real man of the world in Leipzig, gay, handsome, well turned out, and without a touch of German heaviness." He was, she recalled, "the moving spirit of the whole place"; he organized the Gewandhaus Balls, started innovations in sport "such as paper-chases on horseback and I think polo," and to crown it all, he had the best cook in the town (vol. 1, 196–97).

From 1868 he served on the board of directors of the Gewandhaus, becoming its president in 1881, in which year he also joined the board of the Leipzig Conservatory. Characteristically, his musical tastes were progressive, unlike that of most of his colleagues; in particular, he was a champion of Brahms, in a city that took some time to warm to his compositions. Their earliest contact went back to the autumn of 1876, when Limburger, having heard of the completion of the C Minor Symphony and eager to secure its first performance for Leipzig, invited Brahms to conduct the work there in the near future. His hopes of having the first performance given by the Gewandthaus Orchestra were, however, to be disappointed, as happened also, with one exception (as mentioned below), in the case of certain other works by Brahms that he sought to "bring out" in Leipzig. His lack of success in this regard was probably due mainly to the fact that the tight schedule of the orchestra's activities allowed only a maximum of two rehearsals for any concert, whereas Brahms was able to obtain more generous conditions for the preparation of his new works elsewhere. The Symphony in C Minor was first performed at Karlsruhe on 4 November 1876 (and subsequently in Mannheim, Munich, and Vienna), but on 18 January 1877 Brahms did conduct it in Leipzig, and during his stay there he made Limburger's personal acquaintance and was entertained at his house. He was to return to Leipzig repeatedly in future years, and no doubt met Limburger on each occasion. On 1 January 1779 Limburger had the great satisfaction of witnessing the very first performance of the Violin Concerto, conducted by Brahms and performed by **Joseph Joachim** and the Gewandhaus Orchestra. (Forner 1984, 1987; Smyth 1919)

LINDECK [REALLY: LEVI], WILHELM STEPHAN (b. Giessen, 24 November 1833; d. Mannheim, 6 March 1911). Singer (bass), later banker; brother of **Hermann Levi**. In 1851 he embarked on legal studies, which, however, he soon abandoned in order to study music and singing, completing his training at the Paris conservatory. For several years, beginning probably in 1858, he performed in opera at theaters at Cologne and later in Nuremberg under the stage name "Lindeck" (which he kept all his life). His marriage to Emma Bieger in 1866 led to his conversion from Judaism to Catholicism, as well as to his retirement from the stage. In 1868 he moved to Mannheim, his mother's native city and there, the following year, he joined the prominent banking house W. H. Ladenburg & Söhne, which had been founded in 1785 by his great-grandfather Wolf Haium Ladenburg (1766–1851). He quickly rose to a senior position and was for many years a director of the bank and subsequently, until his death, of the joint-stock Süddeutsche Diskonto-Gesellschaft, which replaced the bank after it merged with the Berlin-based Diskonto-Gesellschaft in 1905.

At Levi's suggestion, Brahms entrusted the financial handling of much of his money and investment to Lindeck in 1872 (but he also left some of his money in the care of **Arthur Faber** in Vienna). From time to time he asked Lindeck to send certain sums to him or to others, but otherwise seems to have left him a free hand. Lindeck submitted annual statements of account, which Brahms formally approved without, he once admitted, ever looking at them. This situation continued until 1877 when Brahms, though in no way dissatisfied with Lindeck's management of his financial affairs, decided to transfer the principal responsibility for them to his friend and publisher **Fritz Simrock**. It has been suggested that his wish to relieve Lindeck of the responsibility for handling his money was not entirely unconnected with the fact that his relations with Levi had considerably cooled by then. However, whether out of a desire not to offend Lindeck or for some other reason, he still left a portion of his financial holdings in Lindeck's care, and it was not until 1882 that the remaining assets were transferred to Berlin. At that time Brahms warmly thanked Lindeck for his assistance over the past years and, as a token of his gratitude, sent him a signed photograph and an autograph of his song "Die Feldeinsamkeit" (op. 86/2), in a version he had specially made for the bass voice.

Thus ended what had been purely a business relationship. Brahms had in fact met Lindeck and his wife on at least one occasion, during a visit to Mannheim, but their published correspondence reflects no feelings of a personal nature. Brahms did, however, have some social contact with certain members of the Ladenburg family. In his final letter to Lindeck, in April 1882, he mentioned the recent death of Delphine Ladenburg (1809–89), the wife of Wolf Haium Ladenburg's youngest son Leopold Ladenburg, and added, "I have always liked and respected the deceased and her husband" (Martin 1983, 46). Furthermore, Brahms is known to have been present at the house of Leopold's nephew Emil Ladenburg in Frankfurt when the Joachim Quartet rehearsed there on 10 November 1894 prior to a public concert that included a performance of his String Quartet op. 67. After the concert Brahms and the members of the quartet were entertained at lunch by Ladenburg. (Jacob 1971; Martin 1983; Watzinger 1984)

LINGG, HERMANN VON (b. Lindau, 22 January 1820; d. Munich, 18 June 1905). Poet, playwright, and novelist. Brahms set a poem by Lingg in the song "Immer leiser wird mein Schlummer" (op. 105/2), which he composed at Thun in August 1886. (Selbmann 1990)

LIPSIUS, MARIE [pseudonym "La Mara"] (b. Leipzig, 30 December 1837; d. Schmölen, near Wurzen, Saxony, 2 March 1927). Writer on music. She was the author of numerous studies on a wide range of contemporary and earlier composers, and also edited several volumes of **Liszt**'s letters after his death.

Brahms reportedly made her acquaintance during his visit to Leipzig in January–February 1874. In November of that year, she published a long article on Brahms in *Westermanns illustrierte deutsche Monatshefte*, which, apart from some biographical information, offered a generally perceptive and appreciative examination of his music. It was reprinted the following year in her book *Musikalische Studienköpfe aus der Jüngstvergangenheit und Gegenwart* with only some minor changes, which were designed to bring the text up to date. Brahms referred to this article in a letter to **Hermann Deiters** in 1880, in which he declined to supply any biographical data other than his date of birth, even though he knew that Deiters was then preparing a book on him: "I really don't know any of the dates or years concerning my life. . . . I need hardly add that I do not like speaking about myself, and do not enjoy reading anything dealing with my private life. . . . I can see no value in what La Mara and others find to tell about my life, and I do not see why it should repeated again and again" (Brahms 1974/3, 122).

In 1886 Lipsius published *Musikerbriefe aus fünf Jahrhunderten*, a two-volume collection of letters written by musicians, past and present. When she had contacted Brahms the previous year, he had asked her not to print the particular letters written by him that she was proposing to use, but he did give her permission to include his current reply in her book, which she did. In it he had explained why he did not consider any of his letters suitable for reproduction: "I know and recognize that I never write otherwise than reluctantly, hastily, and perfunctorily." He was aware, he added, that there were many persons who enjoyed writing letters and indeed wrote good ones, but "there are also those of my kind, whose letters need . . . to be read and interpreted with indulgence and care." He went on to compare this kind of casual, unpolished, and often very private correspondence to the unpublished drafts, sketches, and compositions left behind by musicians, which, if printed and thereby released to a wide public, might be similarly "misunderstood and misinterpreted." It would be preferable to have those manuscripts copied and for the copies to be placed in major libraries, where they could be consulted by specialists (La Mara 1886, 349). Brahms had already expressed his reservations about the inclusion of such musical material in posthumous "complete editions" of a composer's works in a letter to **Eduard Hanslick** in May 1884 (Hanslick 1897b, *Neue freie Presse*, 27 June 1897, 2–3); but in this connection *see also* SCHUBERT, FRANZ (PETER).) (Brahms 1974/3; Hanslick 1897b; La Mara 1875a, 1886)

LISZT, FRANZ [FERENC], (b. Raiding [Doborján] in Hungary [now in the Austrian province of Burgenland], 22 October 1811; d. Bayreuth, 31 July 1886). Composer, pianist, and teacher. When Brahms and Reményi (*see* REMÉNYI, EDE [EDUARD]) arrived at Bayreuth in June 1853, they were cordially received by Liszt and promptly offered accommodations at the Altenburg. In a letter to **Joseph Joachim** on 23 June, Liszt thanked him for sending the two young men to him and went on to observe, "I like to hope that they will become serious artists" (Johannes Joachim and Moser 1911–13, vol. 1, 63). While Reményi was to become a lifelong friend, Liszt would never be on close terms with Brahms.

Exactly what Brahms did during the two to three weeks he spent at Weimar will no doubt never be known. What would have been the most direct and authoritative source of information, namely the letters he wrote to his family at the time, he destroyed many years later when they came into his possession following the death of his sister **Elisabeth** in 1892. "I had quite forgotten how fully I had written to my parents about all that," he told **Richard Heuberger**, tantalizingly (Heuberger 1976, 60). He had not stayed very long in Weimar, he added, because he soon realized that the musical preferences of Liszt and his circle were not to his taste, nor, one suspects, was the ambience of hero worship prevalent in his host's circle (he probably fell out with Reményi at least partly for that reason).

Brahms's testimony would have been particularly interesting with regard to the most famous incident associated with his visit to Weimar, for which the two principal sources are the generally unreliable and self-serving story told by Reményi in an interview published in the *New York Herald* on 18 January 1879 (reprinted in Kelley and Upton 1906, 79–95—*see* REMÉNYI, EDE [EDUARD]) and the account given in **William Mason**'s (1901) *Memoirs of a Musical Life* (127–31). Mason relates that Brahms professed himself too nervous to play any of his compositions when invited to do so by Liszt, whereupon the latter brilliantly sight-read his E-flat Minor Scherzo (op. 4) and part of his C Major Piano Sonata (op. 1) from the manuscript. When, a little later, Liszt was playing his own recently composed Piano Sonata, he glanced at his listeners at "a very expressive part" of the work and found that Brahms was asleep in his chair. Liszt finished playing the sonata, then got up and walked out of the room—the implication being evidently that he was annoyed and offended by Brahms's behavior. Unfortunately, Mason is not an authoritative witness, for, as he explains, he could not himself see Brahms from where he was seated and heard the story afterward from someone else—"I think it was Reményi." (In the above-mentioned interview, Reményi claims that when he remonstrated with Brahms about his apparent rudeness, Brahms said that he had been "overcome with fatigue.") Mason adds that, reluctant to simply trust his own memory of the event, he had (presumably when writing his memoirs) contacted Karl Klindworth, who had likewise been present on that occasion, and that Klindworth's report of what happened that day at Weimar "corroborated my description in every particular, except that he made no specific reference to the drowsiness of Brahms." Of course, the fact that there is no written support for the statements made by the often unreliable Reményi does not prove that they were untrue. What does seem to be fairly well established, in any case, is that Brahms did not care for what he heard of Liszt's music during this visit to Weimar; he later told Heuberger, "This was the prime time when all that stuff was written, the 'symphonic poems' and suchlike, and I soon found it hideous. . . . I left after a few weeks" (Heuberger 1976, 60–61). Moreover, Liszt was evidently not unaware of his negative reaction, for Brahms added, "Although we treated each other with superficial cordiality whenever we met after that, it was as if a cord had been cut between us."

In fact, there was never an overt break between them. On Brahms's departure, Liszt presented him with a cigar case bearing an autographic inscription (in which his name was misspelled as "Brams"), and Brahms appears to have made an effort to be especially pleasant when they next saw each other, which happened at Leipzig in December of that same year: "He was the first person on whom I called. . . . I was very cordially received," he reported to Joachim on 7 December (Brahms 1974/5, 22); and Liszt, on his side, writing from Leipzig on 16 December to his friend and former student **Hans von Bülow**, who was shortly to make Brahms's acquaintance at Joachim's in Hanover, stated that Brahms ("auquel je m'intéresse sincèrement") had been behaving "avec tact et bon goût" toward him and that he had asked Brahms several times to dinner (Hinrichsen 1994, 11). Furthermore, in his letter to Bülow, Liszt praised Brahms's C Major Piano Sonata, of which he had seen the proofs in Leipzig (it was then being published by **Breitkopf & Härtel**) and which he considered the most successful of Brahms's compositions he had so far come across. He even expressed the hope that Brahms might draw closer to Weimar in the future. Similarly, his correspondence with Joachim gives no indication of ill feelings. Thus, on 28 March 1854, he asked for news of Brahms ("How is he? What is he composing? Give him my cordial greetings"—see Johannes Joachim and Moser 1911–13, vol. 1, 179), and on 21 May Joachim informed Brahms (who was then in Hamburg) that Liszt was shortly coming to Hanover and would very much like to see him there (Brahms 1974/5, 44); but Brahms did not travel to Hanover then. He and Liszt did, however, renew their acquaintance at the Lower Rhine Music Festival at Düsseldorf in May 1855.

Brahms's instinctive antipathy to Liszt's music was doubtless strengthened by the extremely hostile attitude adopted by **Robert** and **Clara Schumann**. When, at Clara's request, Brahms played for her in May 1854 Liszt's Sonata (which was dedicated to Robert) and some other compositions Liszt had just sent her, she noted in her diary on 25 May, "The pieces are dreadful. . . . I felt quite ill" (Litzmann 1902, vol. 2, 317). Robert, in a letter to Joachim on 7 October 1853 in which he had hailed Brahms as the "true apostle" and called Joachim the "apostle Joseph," had referred to Liszt as "Judas Iscariot" (Johannes Joachim and Moser 1911–13, vol. 1, 84). As for Joachim, who had initially been among Liszt's admirers, he eventually joined the opposition to his compositions after attending a concert given by Liszt in Berlin on 6 December 1855: "Not for a long time have I known such bitter disappointment," he confided to Clara Schumann (Johannes Joachim and Moser 1911–13, vol. 1, 298); and in a letter to Liszt on 27 August 1857, he formally rejected his music. (They would not meet again for almost 25 years.) Finally, the rift between the two camps was publicly exposed in 1860 by the manifesto that Brahms and Joachim launched against the "New German School," whose compositions it castigated as being "contrary to the intrinsic spirit of music"; while Liszt was not actually named, there could have been little doubt that he was the prime target. However, any effect that such an attack on Liszt and his supporters might have had was spoiled by its premature publication in the *Berliner Musik-Zeitung Echo* on 6 May 1860, over the names of only Brahms, Joachim, **Julius Otto Grimm**, and **Bernhard Scholz** (whereas a number of other musicians had, in fact, indicated their willingness to sign it). Indeed, the potential impact of the manifesto had already been undermined even earlier, as a result of its being leaked to the *Neue Zeitschrift für Musik*, the very journal it singled out for criticism, which had brought out a parody of it on 4 May.

For the rest of his life Brahms expressed disdain for Liszt's music, and none of Liszt's works were presented at the regular concerts of the Gesellschaft der Musikfreunde during the three years when he was its artistic director. In 1879 he went as far as dismissing *Les Préludes* in a letter to **Julius Stockhausen**, as "Lisztschen Schwindel und Katzenjammer" [Lisztian swindle and caterwauling] (Brahms 1993, 139); and in 1887 he made a point of arriving late at the Tonkünstlerfest at Cologne so that, as he told **Robert Schnitzler**, he might "begin the music festival by not hearing *Saint Elisabeth* [the oratorio *Die Legende der heiligen Elisabeth*]" (Schnitzler 1935, 52). At the same time, if he did not waver in his opposition to Liszt's music, he consistently admired him as a pianist. He once said to **Klaus Groth**, referring to himself and some other well-known pianists, "Of course, we are also capable of playing the piano, but none of us possesses more than a few fingers of his two hands" (Lohmeier 1997, 190). In particular, Brahms must have thought highly of Liszt as an interpreter of **Chopin**, for when Breitkopf & Härtel were preparing a Chopin edition, he urged the firm in March 1878 to secure Liszt's contribution for more than just the preludes (which he was already scheduled to edit) and also gain his collaboration at least for the Mazurkas: "I would ask you to consider that there would be exceptional and widespread interest in the prospect of a [Chopin] edition by Liszt" (Brahms 1974/14, 285–86). Finally, despite his dislike of Liszt's compositions, Brahms remained all his life under the spell of his personality. Thus he once remarked to **Robert Freund**: "I wish we had many musicians with his nobility of character" (Freund 1951, 21), and Heuberger noted in his diary on 5 March 1888 that Brahms had "praised Liszt's character in the warmest possible terms, as, by the way, he always has" (Heuberger 1976, 36). In fact, as far as one can tell, none of Brahms's post-manifesto meetings with Liszt were ever marred by any unpleasantness. While in Budapest for a concert in April 1884, Brahms even went to call on Liszt, but he did not find him at home. (He may have felt somewhat uneasy, though, for he asked Freund to accompany him, as he "did not want to visit [Liszt] alone" (Freund 1951, 15; Freund mistakenly places this episode in the year 1885).

Three of Brahms's meetings with Liszt are of particular interest. On 11 January 1874 both took part in a charity concert in Vienna, at which star billing was accorded to Liszt, who came from Budapest to be the soloist in his own arrangement for piano and orchestra of **Schubert**'s "Wanderer" Fantasy and in his *Fantasy on Hungarian Folk Themes*; Brahms (one of the five participating conductors) directed performances of a short choral piece by Mendelssohn ("Richte mich Gott") and of **Bach**'s fugue for double chorus, orchestra, and organ, "Nun ist das Heil und die Kraft." Both Liszt and Brahms attended the banquet that followed the concert. (Brahms also attended the banquet in Liszt's honor in Vienna on 16 March 1877, following Liszt's participation in an all-**Beethoven** concert given in aid of the Beethoven monument fund; see Legány 1984, 204–5.)

On 2 February 1882, Liszt attended an all-Brahms recital given by Bülow in Vienna. (According to **Max Kalbeck**, Brahms had himself attended Bülow's all-Liszt recital in Budapest on 14 February 1881; if Kalbeck's information is correct, he had presumably met Liszt on that occasion, since Liszt had also been present.) Now, in Vienna, Liszt told Brahms that he would be interested to see his new (Second) Piano Concerto, and the next day Brahms wrote to **Fritz Simrock** asking him to send two copies to Liszt in Budapest. The reference is evidently to the two-piano arrangement that had appeared in print the previous month; its publication preceded that of the full score. (Liszt had not been in Budapest when Brahms had given the first performance of the concerto there on 9 November 1881.) A few weeks later Liszt reported to Brahms that the work had at first reading seemed somewhat colorless to him, but that he had gradually come to appreciate its considerable qualities; the concerto, he wrote, "has the richness of a striking masterpiece, in which ideas and feelings move forward in splendid harmony" (La Mara 1893–1905, vol. 8, 394). In his memoirs Freund relates that Liszt subsequently proposed that the concerto be performed at the Zurich music festival in July, with either Bülow or, if he declined, Freund as soloist; but Freund goes on to explain that it proved impossible to obtain the score and parts in time—as it turned out, they were only published in July—and that he performed Liszt's A Major Concerto instead (Freund 1951, 11).

On 17 April 1885, Brahms and Liszt were both present at a reception arranged by the newly constituted Viennese Tonkünstlerverein, on which occasion, according to Heuberger, they had a long and pleasant conversation (Heuberger 1976, 30). This meeting is likely to have been their final one. Liszt again spent several days in Vienna in March of the following year, but Brahms was not there at the time. A few months later Liszt died at Bayreuth.

As for Liszt's opinion of Brahms's compositions, it was presumably generally unfavorable, since, according to his biographer Alan Walker (1987–96), he never played a single one of them in his numerous recitals (vol. 2, 353); but see above concerning the Second Piano Concerto). When **Ludwig Bösendorfer** once found him playing one of Brahms's sets of variations for himself in private, Liszt explained rather enigmatically, in response to Bösendorfer's look of surprise, that one had to know everything before one was capable of making a proper appraisal and assessment of any music (Brahms Exhibition 1983, 35). (Brahms Exhibition 1983; Brahms 1974/5, 1974/14; Brahms 1993; Freund 1951; Goldhammer 1963; Heuberger 1976; Hinrichsen 1994; Johannes Joachim and Moser 1911–13; Kelley and Upton 1906; La Mara 1893–1905; Litzmann 1902; Lohmeier 1997; Mason 1901; Schnitzler 1935; A. Walker 1987–96)

LITOLFF, HENRY (CHARLES) (b. London, 7 August 1818; d. Bois-Colombes, 5 August 1891). Son of an Alsatian violinist and a Scotswoman. A pupil of Ignaz Moscheles, he became a highly successful pianist; he was also a prolific composer, but only one of his pieces, the Scherzo from his *Concerto symphonique* no. 4, has remained in the general repertoire of modern performers.

According to **Louise Japha-Langhans**, as reported by **Max Kalbeck**, Litolff gave the young Brahms support at a time when he needed all the encouragement he could get. In February 1852, or possibly in December 1851, while Litolff was in Hamburg for a concert appearance, Brahms called on him at his hotel and played his (still unpublished) Scherzo in E-flat Minor (op. 4) for him. Fearing that it might appear too long, he limited himself to the first trio and to one reprise of the principal section. He was highly gratified when Litolff advised him to write a second trio—which, since he had in fact already composed it, he was able to play straightaway. Litolff praised the piece, to the delight of Brahms, who promptly told Louise Japha, "beaming with pleasure" (Kalbeck 1976, vol. 1, 84–85).

According to Brahms's handwritten list of his compositions (preserved at the Stadt-und Landesbibliothek in Vienna and published by A. Orel in *Die Musik* in 1937), he had completed the Scherzo in August 1851. He first played it in public at a court concert at Hanover on 8 June 1853 (*see* GEORG V, KING OF HANOVER); it was published by **Breitkopf & Härtel** in February 1854.

LÜBKE, WILHELM (b. Dortmund, 17 January 1826; d. Karlsruhe, 5 April 1893). Historian of art and architecture. His numerous publications include surveys of architecture (*Geschichte der Architektur*) and of art (*Grundriss der Kunstgeschichte*), which exercised a considerable influence on contemporary cultural ideas. His teaching career started in Berlin and subsequently took him to the Technical University of Zurich (1861), to Stuttgart (1866), and finally to Karlsruhe (1885). In Zurich he formed a close friendship with **Theodor Billroth** that lasted until his death.

Like Billroth, Lübke made Brahms's acquaintance on the occasion of his first concert appearances in Zurich in November 1865. Together with Billroth and Otto Wesendonck, he arranged a private concert (on 26 November) so that he could hear Brahms play his First Piano Concerto and conduct his Serenade op. 16, works that would otherwise not have been heard in Zurich at that time. After Billroth moved to Vienna in 1867, he regularly corresponded with Lübke, and many of his letters contain informative remarks about his contacts with Brahms and about Brahms's latest compositions. Brahms had some correspondence with Lübke, and he also met him again—perhaps at Karlsruhe in November 1876 on the occasion of the premiere of the First Symphony, and definitely in Vienna in March 1881 when Billroth gave an all-Brahms concert at his house, at which both Brahms and Lübke were present. The printed program of this "Gemütlicher Brahmsabend" announced performances of the Violin Sonata op. 78 by Brahms and **Joseph Hellmesberger**; of the Klavierstücke op. 76 and Rhapsodien op. 79 by Brahms, and of the vocal quartets opp. 31, 64, 52, and 65 by Ferdinand Maas, Adolf von Schultner, Pauline Kner, and Frl. Ötzelt. Lastly, Brahms almost certainly saw Lübke once more when he was in Stuttgart later that same year for a concert on 22 November. Shortly before, Lübke had strongly praised Brahms's music in an article in the Stuttgart *Merkur*, which Billroth had brought to Brahms's notice. **Clara**

Schumann also knew Lübke personally and mentioned him in several of her letters to Brahms. "I like him very much and esteem him very highly," she wrote on 13 July 1884 (Litzmann 1970, vol. 2, 280). (Gottlieb-Billroth 1935; Litzmann 1970; Rohling 1957)

LUTHER, MARTIN (b. Eisleben, 10 November 1483; d. Eisleben, 18 February 1546). Theologian. Brahms set a stanza from one of Luther's songs as part of the Motet op. 74/1.

– M –

MACPHERSON, JAMES (b. Ruthven, near Kingussie, Scotland, 27 October 1736; d. Inverness, 17 February 1796). Historian; self-proclaimed "translator" of poems attributed by him to the legendary Gaelic warrior and bard Ossian (in reality, Macpherson was editing traditional Gaelic poems, into which he inserted passages of his own invention).

Brahms set two of Macpherson's "Ossianic" poems, in **Johann Gottfried Herder**'s German versions, in "Gesang aus Fingal" (op. 17/4) and "Darthulas Grabesgesang" (op. 42/3).

MAGNUS, HELENE: *see* HORNBOSTEL, (OTTO) ERICH VON.

MAHLER, GUSTAV (b. Kalischt [Kalište, Czech Republic], 7 July 1860; d. Vienna, 18 May 1911). Composer and conductor. Brahms made his acquaintance on the occasion of a performance of *Don Giovanni* that Mahler conducted at the Budapest Opera House on 16 December 1890. Brahms, who had been persuaded to attend against his inclination ("I have never heard a good performance of *Don Giovanni* yet"), was so delighted with the performance that he rushed to the stage after the first act to congratulate Mahler (K. Blaukopf 1976, 189). The memory of that experience remained in Brahms's mind, and he is usually credited with having later supported Mahler's efforts to secure a leading position at the Vienna Opera, even though there is no firm evidence that he actually intervened on his behalf; certainly his friend **Eduard Hanslick** played a considerably more active role in this respect. Mahler's appointment as a conductor at the opera was announced in the Viennese press on 8 April 1897, two days after Brahms's funeral, and the contract was signed a week later; he made his debut on 11 May, conducting *Lohengrin*. In July he was made deputy director, and on 8 October he succeeded Wilhelm Jahn as director.

Mahler was to see Brahms on various occasions after their initial meeting in Budapest, especially at Ischl, where Mahler visited him during several summers in the 1890s, cycling over from his own vacation quarters at nearby Steinach, on the Attersee. It appears that he was always well received, although their relationship remained a rather formal one—not surprisingly, given the difference in their ages and temperaments, not to mention their often-opposing views on musical matters. On 26 June 1896 Mahler wrote to Anna von Mildenburg, "Within the next few days I shall make a short excursion to Ischl, where I have been meeting Brahms for several years. In this connection I can really say, like Faust: 'From time to time I enjoy seeing the old man!' He is a gnarled, sturdy tree, but bearing ripe and sweet fruit, and it gives one pleasure to contemplate the mighty trunk and the rich foliage" (H. Blaukopf 1982, 161). In his autobiography *Theme and Variations* Bruno Walter relates Mahler's own account of this, his last, visit to Brahms. Mahler was particularly affected by the sight of the sick old man preparing his frugal supper of sausage and bread. Describing the scene to Walter, Mahler kept murmuring to himself, with deep emotion, "For all things are but vanity" (B. Walter 1947, 98).

Brahms, Mahler told Anna von Mildenburg, had been especially amiable on this occasion and had asked Mahler to send him his Second Symphony (of which Hermann Behn had published his own two-piano arrangement the previous December—the full score would not be issued until 1897; but the first three movements had, in fact, already been sent to Brahms the previous year). Mahler was later reportedly somewhat put out to learn that Brahms had said, after looking at the work: "I have thought until now that **Richard Strauss** was the chief of the iconoclasts, but I now realise that Mahler is the king of the revolutionaries" (Karpath 1912–13, 251). Yet the remark ought not to have greatly surprised Mahler, for he himself felt increasingly out of sympathy with most of Brahms's own compositions. Among those for which he is known to have expressed admiration are the String Sextet op. 18 (see below), the Clarinet Quintet, the Clarinet Sonatas, the Third Symphony, and the *Haydn Variations* ("he shows a superb mastery and unprecedented skill in this musical genre" [Killian 1984, 153]). Generally, though, even his appreciative remarks were qualified by reservations. He was especially put off by what he regarded as Brahms's emotional reserve, by his artistic "puritanism" that led him to avoid any "ornamentation, embellishment, or fantasy," and by his deliberate neglect of certain techniques and innovations in orchestration "merely out of obstinacy and opposition to **Richard Wagner**" (Killian 1984, 150). Mahler's harshest judgments are to be found in letters he wrote to his wife Alma in 1904: "For a change, I played the piano, some chamber music by Brahms, but unfortunately much of it is terribly barren music making, and if I had not unexpectedly chanced upon a delightful Sextet in B-flat Major [i.e. op. 18] I would have given him up in despair. . . . I have now gone pretty well through the whole of Brahms. All I can say is that he is a puny little man who quickly runs out of breath." Brahms greatest failing as a composer, Mahler concluded, was his inadequate handling of the "so-called development sections": "Only very rarely does he know what to do with his themes, which are often beautiful. To be sure, only **Beethoven** and **Wagner** truly possessed that art" (Mahler 1940, 299, 302). In another letter to Alma he described Brahms and **Anton Bruckner** as "an odd couple of second-raters" (Mahler 1940, 303). (Bauer-Lechner 1907; H. Blaukopf 1982; K. Blaukopf 1976; Brodbeck 1992; W. Ebert 1986; Karpath 1912/13; Killian 1984; La Grange 1994–99; Mahler 1940, 1978; McGuinness 1977; K.-J. Müller 1988; B. Walter 1947)

MAHO, J. Parisian music publisher who was active by 1852 at the latest (according to Cecil Hopkinson's *A Dictionary of Parisian Music Publishers, 1700–1950*). From 1859 until 1877, the business was located at 25 Rue du Faubourg St. Honoré; in the latter year it was taken over by J. Hamelle.

Maho was the French distributor for the first editions of the following of Brahms's compositions, published by **Jakob Melchior Rieter-Biedermann**: the *Variations on a Theme by Schumann* for piano duet (op. 23, 1863), the arrangement for piano duet of the First Piano Concerto (1864), the Piano Quintet (1865), the *Paganini Variations* (1866), and the arrangement for piano duet of the *Waltzes* op. 41 (1866).

Brahms was in contact with Maho, who tried unsuccessfully on more than one occasion to buy one of his latest compositions (see Brahms's correspondence with Rieter-Biedermann [Brahms 1974/14] and **Fritz Simrock** [Brahms 1974/9–12], and also the two letters by Maho preserved in the archive of the Gesellschaft der Musikfreunde in Vienna). (Brahms 1974/9–12, 1974/14)

MANDYCZEWSKI, EUSEBIUS (b. Czernowitz [Chernovtsy, Ukraine], 18 August 1857; d. Sulz, Lower Austria, 13 July 1929). Musicologist, composer, and teacher. The son of a Greek Orthodox priest of Ukrainian origin and a Romanian mother, he was educated at local German schools. In 1875 he enrolled at the University of Vienna, where, among other subjects, he studied the history of music under **Eduard Hanslick**; he also received private instruction in musical theory from **Gustav Nottebohm**. In 1887 he succeeded **Carl Ferdinand Pohl** as archivist of the Gesellschaft der Musikfreunde, and he also conducted some of that society's concerts; in 1896 he was appointed to the faculty of the conservatory. He is best known for his distinguished contributions to the editions of the collected works of **Beethoven**, **Franz Schubert**, **Haydn**, and Brahms. His work on the Schubert edition was highly appreciated, not least by Brahms (*see* SCHUBERT, FRANZ [PETER]); it was considered so outstanding that it earned Mandyczewski an honorary doctorate from the University of Leipzig. His own compositions were mainly of a religious nature and included 12 settings of the Mass. He was universally admired, as much for his personal qualities as for his exemplary scholarship. **Edward Speyer** (1937) described him as "one of the most lovable men that it has been my good fortune to meet" (211).

Mandyczewski met Brahms by 1879 at the latest. That year Brahms, in his capacity as a member of the committee responsible for proposing talented but impecunious composers for the award of state stipends (*see* DVOŘÁK, ANTONÍN [LEOPOLD]), strongly supported Mandyczewski's candidacy in a letter to his fellow adjudicators Hanslick and **Karl Goldmark**. (Hanslick later presented the letter to Mandyczewski, who gave it to the Gesellschaft der Musikfreunde.) However, it is quite possible that Brahms was by then already personally acquainted with Mandyczewski, for he was evidently not only familiar with Mandyczewski's earlier compositional efforts, over which the latest one, in his view, showed a most satisfactory and indeed unexpectedly impressive progress, but he was also aware of certain aspects of Mandyczewski's family life. Karl Geiringer, who published some of the correspondence exchanged by Brahms and Mandyczewski between 1882 and 1896 in the *Zeitschrift für Musikwissenschaft* in 1933, was informed by Mandyczewski's brother that Brahms had probably met the young composer at the house of **Arthur and Bertha Faber**, with whom Mandyczewski was on friendly terms. For many years he conducted a women's choir at their house (in this connection, see the remarks in the article on the Fabers about the first complete performances of Brahms's *5 Gesänge* [op. 104]).

It is clear from their correspondence, as well as from other evidence, such as **Richard Heuberger**'s diary, that Mandyczewski enjoyed increasingly friendly relations with Brahms during the final period of the latter's life. Brahms liked Mandyczewski; in one of his letters, in the spring of 1895, he describes himself as "someone who, as you know . . . has great affection for you" (Geiringer 1933, 364). Furthermore, he had a very high regard for Mandyczewski's musical knowledge and taste, and he followed with great interest the musicological research Mandyczewski undertook in connection with his various editorial projects; he was not even above seeking Mandyczewski's opinion on his own new compositions. For his part, Mandyczewski was devoted to Brahms and clearly considered it a privilege to render him numerous services of a professional as well as of a personal nature, the latter especially when Brahms was away from Vienna during his extended summer vacations; on one occasion, Brahms even asked him to settle a bill for some boots he had had made. In Vienna they met regularly—at the offices of the Gesellschaft der Musikfreunde (which were located close to the Karlsgasse and which Brahms moreover passed on his way to the inner city), in restaurants, and at the houses of mutual friends, such as the Fabers. Mandyczewski also frequently joined Brahms on his Sunday walking tours. In a rare expression of his personal feelings, he wrote to Brahms in April 1895: "I cannot refrain from confessing that your warm affection is the most precious thing in my life and that I wish for nothing more exquisite than that I may preserve it in all circumstances" (Geiringer 1933, 365).

In October 1899 Mandyczewski organized a Brahms exhibition at Meiningen on the occasion of the unveiling of the Brahms monument in that town. He was also responsible, together with Hans Gál, for publishing the collected edition of Brahms's works (Leipzig, 1926–27). (Gál 1961; Geiringer 1933; Heuberger 1976; Speyer 1937)

MANZ, GUSTAV (1868–1931). Journalist. In the Budapest newspaper *Pester Lloyd* on 11 April 1897, he recalled his various meetings with Brahms, whose acquaintance he had made at Thun in the spring of 1887. He had been invited to go there by **Gustav Wendt**, the director of the Gymnasium at Karlsruhe, which he had previously attended. Later that same year he was present at the private performance by Brahms, **Joseph Joachim**, and **Robert Hausmann**, of Brahms's new Double Concerto for Violin Cello at Baden-Baden on 23 September. His description of the event is of some interest, not least his statement that the work was played twice. Manz concludes his account of his personal contacts with Brahms with some recollections of a stay in Vienna in 1892, during which he repeatedly called on Brahms and also joined him for meals at the Roter Igel restaurant. (Manz 1897)

MARPURG, FRIEDRICH WILHELM (b. Seehof, near Wendemark, Brandenburg, 21 November 1718; d. Berlin, 22 May 1795). Theorist and composer. Given Brahms's intense interest in older music and musical technique, it is only natural that he should have eagerly studied and cherished the writings of the two most prominent German theorists of the 18th century, Marpurg and **Johann Mattheson**.

By the middle of the 1850s, Brahms was already familiar with some of their most important publications and probably also with some of their music (as a composer, Mattheson was by far the more wide ranging of the two, being the creator of many operas and oratorios, as well as various instrumental pieces, while Marpurg's output was restricted to a number of works for the keyboard and to songs). Brahms acquired much of his knowledge of their work during the many hours he spent at the Hamburg city library examining old music and writings, but he also purchased certain of their treatises. Writing to **Clara Schumann** from Hamburg in November 1855, he mentioned that he was spending half his days in secondhand bookshops, to which he added regretfully that he had not yet found any of Mattheson's works, nor Marpurg's "best book, the one on the fugue" (Litzmann 1970, vol. 1, 154). Both gaps in his growing private library were to be filled soon. For Christmas that year, **Joseph Joachim** presented him with Mattheson's most important book, *Der vollkommene Capellmeister* (1739), and for the New Year he received from Clara Schumann Marpurg's *Abhandlung von der Fuge*, in the revised edition published by **Simon Sechter** in 1843. He promptly offered to lend it to Joachim, with whom he was planning to exchange some contrapuntal exercises. In July 1956, in acceding to **Adolf Schubring**'s request that he become godfather of Schubring's newborn son Johannes Max, Brahms assured him that he was already looking forward to the time "when he can study Marpurg's and Mattheson's books with me" (Brahms 1974/8, 188).

At his death, Brahms's library contained the following works by Marpurg, in addition to the one mentioned above: *Historisch-kritische Beyträge zur Aufnahme der Musik* (1754), *Anleitung zum Clavierspielen* (1755), *Handbuch bey dem Generalbasse und der Composition* (1755), and *Versuch über die musikalische Temperatur* (1776); he also had in his possession Marpurg's *Zweyter Versuch in figurirten Chorälen* for organ or harpsichord (around 1792), and the collection *Berlinische Oden und Lieder* (1756), which contained 24 songs by Marpurg. (Brahms 1974/5, 1974/8; Litzmann 1970)

MARXSEN, EDUARD (b. Nienstädten, near Altona, 23 July 1806; d. Altona, 18 November 1887). Pianist, teacher, and composer. He was taught by his father, who was organist at Altona, and by Johann Heinrich Clasing in Hamburg, before going to Vienna where he studied theory with Ignaz Seyfried and the piano with Karl Maria von Bocklet. Later, in Hamburg, he gave a number of recitals and also became a highly respected piano teacher. His compositions include many pieces for the piano, as well as orchestral works, vocal and chamber music, and an operetta.

In 1843 Marxsen began to give lessons to the young Brahms, who until then had been taught by his pupil **Otto Friedrich Willibald Cossel**, and soon, at Cossel's request, he assumed sole responsibility for the boy's musical education; aware of the modest earnings of Brahms's father, he refused all payment. Under his guidance, Brahms's pianistic skills continued to develop very satisfactorily; in addition, Marxsen taught him some theory and supervised his early efforts at composition. In a letter to **Hermann Levi** on 9 October 1873, Marxsen claimed that, notwithstanding the imperfection of these pieces, he had quickly discerned the exceptional potential of his pupil and that, at the time of Mendelssohn's death (i.e., in 1847 when Brahms was 14), he had remarked to friends, "A master of the art has disappeared, an even greater one is blossoming in Brahms" (Kalbeck 1976, vol. 1, 32). This contradicts **Eduard Reményi**'s later assertion in an interview published in the *New York Herald* on 18 January 1879 (p. 10, and reprinted in Kelley and Upton 1906, 79–95), that he had himself been the first to recognize Brahms's genius, whereas Marxsen had said to him, "Well, well, I am sorry for your judgment. Johannes Brahms may have some talent, but he certainly is not the genius you stamp him." However, Reményi is hardly a reliable witness. (In Kelley and Upton 1906, 84, the wording of Marxsen's supposed statement appears in a slightly different form.)

There is no doubt that Marxsen showed considerable generosity toward the Brahms family—he also taught Johannes's brother **Fritz**, without a fee—and that Brahms acquired a great mastery of the piano under his tuition. For the rest of his life, Brahms would feel intensely grateful to Marxsen and think of him with deep affection (as mentioned below). On the other hand, it has been questioned—notably by **Gustav Jenner** (1912) in an article printed in the journal *Die Musik* in 1912—whether Marxsen was in fact the "right teacher" for the young composer (as opposed to the budding pianist). Well intentioned though Marxsen undoubtedly was, Jenner argues, he was incapable of instilling in Brahms the profound technical basis necessary to enable him to fully realize his innate gift for composition. In support of this judgment, and of his view that Brahms became well aware of the less than ideal situation, he cites the following observations that Brahms made to **Gustav Wendt** in later years:

> The composition teacher to whom my father entrusted me had, I'm sure, all the best intentions, and I will never forget that he refused the heavy purse of money my father had saved up to pay for my lessons—he would not accept it, but I was free to come to him four times a week. . . . And I faithfully went there; but I learnt absolutely nothing. . . . Mendelssohn had a great advantage over us: an excellent schooling. What endless efforts it has cost me to make that up when I was already a man. (Jenner 1912, 82–83)

To Jenner himself Brahms once remarked, in a similar vein, "What might I not have become if I had learnt in my youth what I had to acquire with great effort when I was already a man!" (Jenner 1912, 80).

After Brahms moved away from Hamburg, he remained in contact with Marxsen, mainly through his father, but sometimes also by direct correspondence; and he saw him, of course, during his later stays in Hamburg. Moreover, he regularly sent, or arranged for his publishers to send, copies of his published compositions to Marxsen, and even solicited the latter's comments on the Requiem before it was performed and printed. (He would have liked Marxsen to attend its performance at Bremen on 10 April 1868, but Marxsen was prevented by illness from making the journey; he was likewise unable to be present when it was performed there on 7 April 1871.) Brahms provided a particularly striking token of his devotion with the dedication of his Second Piano Concerto "to his dear friend and teacher Eduard Marxsen" in 1882; and the following year he gave further pleasure to Marxsen by secretly arranging for the publication, at his own expense, of Marxsen's *100 Variations on a folk song*, for piano. In thanking Brahms for this generous gesture that clearly moved him greatly, Marxsen called him "the pride of my life and of my artistic activity" (letter of 29 November 1883, now in the archive of the Gesellschaft der Musikfreunde in Vienna). Marxsen dedicated the work to Brahms. (Jenner 1912; Kelley and Upton 1906; Krause 1903)

MASON, WILLIAM (b. Boston, 24 January 1829; d. New York, 14 July 1908). Pianist, teacher, and composer; son of the prominent American composer and conductor Lowell Mason (1792–1872). Following studies in the United States, he received further tuition from Ignaz Moscheles, **Moritz Hauptmann**, and Ernst Friedrich Richter in Leipzig, Alexander Dreyschock in Prague, and **Liszt** at Weimar. During his stay at Weimar he witnessed Brahms's first meeting with Liszt, of which he gives an account in his *Memoirs of a Musical Life* (for details, *see* LISZT, FRANZ [FERENC]). According to his memoirs, he met Brahms again at **Ferdinand David**'s at Leipzig (in December of that same year) and in May 1880 during the music festival held at Bonn on the occasion of the unveiling of the monument at **Robert Schumann**'s tomb.

There is another reason why Mason merits the interest of Brahmsians. In 1855, the year following his return to America, he established a series of chamber music recitals in New York, and for this purpose formed a string quartet consisting of Theodore Thomas, Joseph Mosenthal, George Matzka, and Carl Bergmann. The program of their opening concert, on 27 November 1855, included a performance of Brahms's Piano Trio op. 8 (first version), given by Mason, Thomas, and Bergmann; Mason repeated the work a few weeks later in Boston "with the assistance of members of the Mendelssohn Quintet Club." He reports in his *Memoirs* that the work "received appreciation on both occasions and was listened to attentively, but without enthusiasm" (Mason 1901, 194–95). It was long believed that this performance was in fact the world premiere of the trio (M. McCorkle 1984, 24); but, as Michael Struck has shown, that honor belongs to the performance given by three musicians named Haupt (pianist), Braun (violinist), and Klahr (cellist) at Danzig [Gdansk] on 13 October 1855. On the other hand, Mason's claim that the performance in New York was the first time that the Trio was played in America appears to be correct (see Johnson 1979, 90). (H. Ehrlich 1893a; Johnson 1979; Struck 1991, 1997)

MATTHESON, JOHANN (b. Hamburg, 28 September 1681; d. Hamburg, 17 April 1764). Composer and theorist. Regarding Brahms's interest in Mattheson's writings, *see* MARPURG, FRIEDRICH WILHELM. At his death, Brahms's library contained the following works by Mattheson: *Exemplarische Organisten-Probe* (1719), *Kleine Generalbass-Schule* (1735), *Kern melodischer Wissenschaft* (1737), and *Der vollkommene Capellmeister* (1739). He also owned a set of fugues published by Mattheson, as well as a manuscript copy he had himself made at the Hamburg city library of the chorus of the Jews from Mattheson's oratorio *Das Lied des Lammes*.

MAY, FLORENCE (b. London, 6 February 1845; d. London, 29 June 1923). Pianist, teacher, and biographer; daughter of Edward Collett May, an organist and highly respected teacher. She first studied with her uncle Oliver May, a professor at the Royal Academy of Music, and she also received some instruction from **Clara Schumann** while the latter was in London for concerts in February–April 1871. As May (1948) recounted in her book on Brahms, Clara Schumann offered to continue the lessons at Baden-Baden, and she accordingly traveled there later that spring. On her very first day in the German spa, she made Brahms's acquaintance at Clara Schumann's house and subsequently saw him practically every day. When Clara Schumann left for a month's holiday in Switzerland in July, Brahms, at her request, taught May in her absence. May was so gratified by the progress she made under his tuition and so delighted to hear him play, as he frequently did at the end of the lessons, that, according to her own account, she asked him shortly before Clara Schumann's return whether he could continue to teach her, but he replied, "I don't think it can be done." However, Clara Schumann decided that he should remain her teacher for the few remaining lessons, "saying I had become more his pupil than hers" (vol. 1, 24). Brahms remembered the situation rather differently, for many years later he told **Richard Heuberger** that May had suggested to Clara Schumann that she might study technique ["das Technische"] with her and interpretation ["das Geistige"] with Brahms, whereupon Clara had "chased her away, and Brahms too" (Heuberger 1976, 90).

May met Brahms again a number of times: in January 1882 in Berlin, when he gave two concerts there with the Meiningen orchestra and **Hans von Bülow**, and later during her several visits to Vienna (starting in 1888) and her visits to Ischl in 1894 and 1895. During her first stay in Vienna, she greatly pleased Brahms by presenting him with a first edition of some of Rameau's compositions. (This was presumably the partial edition of the *Nouvelles Suites de pièces de clavecin* that was found among his books after his death.) It is not known whether he ever heard her perform in public. He was, at any rate, away from Vienna when she gave a recital at the Bösendorfer Saal on 10 January 1896, at which she played several of his compositions (a capriccio, some intermezzi, and the *Paganini Variations*); the program also included **Beethoven**'s "Appassionata" Sonata and **Franz Schubert**'s "Wanderer" Fantasia, as well as six "small waltzes" composed by May herself. According to R. Pascall, she was the first to play the *Handel Variations* in England, on 14 February 1891 at the Crystal Palace in London. She also gave two of the earliest English performances of the Second Piano Concerto, in December 1888 in the concert room of the piano manufacturers Broadwood, and in February 1891 at the Royal Academy of Music; on both occasions the orchestral accompaniment was replaced by an arrangement for two pianos, which on the first occasion were played by Otto Goldschmidt and Stephen Kemp, and on the second by Kemp and Septimus Webbe. (This should evidently not be confused with the two-piano version of the concerto made by Brahms himself, which he played with **Ignaz Brüll** in Ehrbar's concert hall in October 1881 and published the following January.) "The ensemble of the three Broadwood grands was not so dreadful as might have been expected," Corno di Bassetto [George Bernard Shaw] reported regarding the first performance, in a review in *The Star* on 12 December 1888 remarkable for its scathing denigration of Brahms's music in general. About the soloist he wrote, "All that can be said confidently of Miss May is that her technique is undeniable." When he reprinted the review in 1937 in a collection of his musical criticism, he admitted that his description of Brahms's music had been "hasty (not to say silly)," and he added, "I had not yet got hold of the idiosyncratic Brahms. I apologize" (Shaw 1937, 46–47).

May wrote books on **Bach** and on the young Clara Schumann, but she is almost exclusively remembered today as a writer for *The Life of Johannes Brahms* that she published in 1905; a German translation by Ludmilla Kirschbaum appeared at Leipzig in 1911. It is a very useful and well-researched book, during the preparation of which she was in contact with many people who had known Brahms well. Of particular interest is the opening section entitled "Personal Recollections," which, among other things, offers a detailed description of Brahms's teaching methods. In due course she planned a new edition of her book, which was to take account of the important biographical information brought to light as a result of the publication of some of Brahms's correspondence and Berthold Litzmann's *Clara Schumann: Ein Künstlerleben*, but she had to abandon the project owing to the difficulties of publishing during the First World War, and she never carried it out later. A revised edition incorporating her additions and corrections eventually appeared in 1948, 25 years after her death. In his introduction, the well-known English critic Ralph Hill, who had brought out a study of Brahms in 1933 (*Brahms: A Study in Musical Biography*), called May's biography "the most comprehensive single work on the composer yet published." Comparing it with **Max Kalbeck**'s *magnum opus*, he wrote: "If not as long and detailed as Kalbeck's monumental four-volume work, it gains by being considerably less flowery and 'imaginative' in style" (May 1948, xviii). (May 1948; Pascall 2001; Shaw 1937)

MAYER, ALOIS (1835–96). Viennese lawyer, and an excellent violinist; his wife Ernestine, née Dellazia (1835–1924), was a first-rate pianist. Mayer used to arrange quartet sessions with other amateur musicians of his acquaintance at his flat on Sundays, at which they played especially **Beethoven**'s later quartets; he normally took the second violin part. During the winter of 1864, Brahms was introduced to the couple by **Josef Gänsbacher**, and thereafter he became a frequent guest. In 1879 the Mayers moved to a flat in the Augustinerstrasse, which had a large music room. According to Ernestine's recollections, quoted by Wolfgang Ebert (1997) in *Brahms in Aussee*, the artists who performed there included such well-known musicians as **David Popper**, Ole Bull, and the Rosé Quartet, while **Theodor Billroth**, Brahms, and **Eduard Hanslick** were among the invited guests. Mayer and Brahms also used to meet at the home of **Moriz Kässmayer**. Ebert states that Brahms thought very highly of Mayer and that the two men addressed each other with the intimate "Du."

Mayer regularly spent his summer vacation with his family at Altaussee in the Austrian Salzkammergut and, while there, he was a member of Professor **Laszlo Wagner de Zólyom**'s quartet, in which, however, he played not the violin but the viola. It was therefore as a violist that he took part in the very first (private) performance of Brahms's String Quintet op. 88 at Wagner de Zólyom's villa on 25 August 1882 (for details, *see* WAGNER DE ZÓLYOM, LÁSZLÓ). (W. Ebert 1997a)

MEISSNER, ALFRED (b. Teplitz [Teplice, Czech Republic], 15 October 1822; d. Bregenz, 29 May 1885). Poet and novelist. Brahms set one of his poems in the song "Nachwirkung" (op. 6/3). (Jäger 1990; Steinecke 1990)

MENZEL, ADOLPH (FRIEDRICH ERDMANN) VON (b. Breslau [Wrocław, Poland], 8 December 1815; d. Berlin, 9 February 1905). Painter, lithographer, illustrator, and teacher. In 1830 his father Carl Erdmann Menzel, the owner of a lithographic printing works, settled in Berlin, which remained Adolph Menzel's residence for the rest of his life. He made his name primarily as a portrayer of historical subjects, especially events connected with Frederick the Great; in later life he was equally successful in depicting scenes from contemporary life, particularly as observed in Berlin.

His first major project was the creation of 400 drawings for woodcut illustrations to Franz Kugler's *Geschichte Friedrichs des Grossen* (Leipzig, 1840). When Brahms had an opportunity to consult the book in 1892, he greatly enjoyed both the illustrations and the text itself (even though the latter was by then generally regarded as being rather out of date). Subsequently, Menzel had produced some 200 woodcuts for a luxury multivolume set of Frederick the Great's works (1843–57), and these illustrations were published separately in two volumes in 1886. Brahms was absolutely delighted when **Fritz Simrock** offered him this latter edition at Christmas 1892. Between 1849 and 1858 Menzel also made eight large oil paintings depicting incidents in Frederick's reign.

Brahms's felt great admiration for Menzel's artistic productions, which he considered to be invariably of a very high standard; one had the impression, he told **Richard Heuberger** (6 April 1896), that Menzel worked on every one of his drawings or canvasses with total enthusiasm and undiminished power (Heuberger 1976, 102). During his stay in Berlin in December 1891, Brahms had struck up a close personal relationship with the artist, which was maintained over the following years, each finding the other's character highly congenial. Among the highlights of Brahms's visit to Berlin at that time were the world premieres of the Clarinet Trio and Clarinet Quintet at a concert given by the Joachim Quartet on 12 December, with Brahms taking the piano part in the trio and **Richard Mühlfeld** the clarinet parts in both works. Menzel was present on that occasion, and he commemorated it in a drawing of Mühlfeld, which he presented to Brahms ("not a close resemblance, but very flattering!" Brahms commented to Fritz Simrock [Brahms 1974/12, 68]). They were to meet on more than one further occasion, Menzel visiting Brahms at Ischl in 1894 (perhaps also already in 1893), and Brahms spending some time with Menzel during his visits to Berlin in January 1895 and January 1896. **Ludwig Karpath**, who made Brahms's acquaintance at Ischl in 1894, noticed how well the two got on, with Brahms constantly teasing the older man, and Menzel retaliating with gusto. (Brahms 1974/12; Brinkmann 1999; Heuberger 1976; Huschke 1939; Karpath 1934)

MEYSENBUG, VON, FAMILY. Prominent Detmold family at the time of Brahms's association with the town in 1857–59. **FRIEDRICH AUGUST KARL VON MEYSENBUG** (b. Kassel, 12 May 1807; d. Lauenau, near Nenndorf, 8 February 1866) was then the court marshal of **Leopold III, Prince zur Lippe**. He was the son of Ludwig Georg Karl Philipp Rivalier von Meysenbug (1779–1847), who had been a minister and close friend of the elector Wilhelm II of Hessen-Kassel and had been ennobled by him in 1825 and subsequently created an Austrian Freiherr by emperor Franz I in 1834. The court marshal's mother, **ERNESTINE DOROTHEE JEANETTE RIVALIER VON MEYSENBUG**, née Hansell (1784–1861), was living at Detmold when Brahms stayed there, together with two of her daughters, one of whom, Laura (1818–87), was a pupil of **Clara Schumann**. (Another daughter, Malwida [1816–1903], later famous for her friendship with **Richard Wagner** and **Friedrich Nietzsche** and for her book *Memoiren einer Idealistin*, was then living in London.)

Brahms made Laura's acquaintance at Düsseldorf in 1855, when he took over her piano lessons during Clara Schumann's absence. Quite probably he also, at that time, met her mother, who had reportedly accompanied her to Düsseldorf. Brahms was subsequently invited to visit Detmold, which he eventually did in the spring of 1857 (*see* LEOPOLD III, PRINCE ZUR LIPPE). On that occasion he was the guest of Laura and her mother; he also met Laura's brother, the court marshal, and his wife **META SOPHIE LUISE** (1819–1906), who later, after he had taken up his appointment at Detmold, lent him one of her pianos, an instrument made in Vienna by **Conrad Graf**, which stood in his hotel room during the three autumns he spent at Detmold. Although Meta Sophie Luise von Meysenbug was already an accomplished pianist (at a concert conducted by Brahms she performed the piano part in **Beethoven**'s *Choral Fantasia*), she nonetheless asked him to give her some tuition. Apparently, though, she did not greatly care for his manners, and after once playing duets with him, she absolutely refused to repeat the experience. However, he was a frequent visitor to her house, where he often participated in the music making, and he spent his last Christmas Eve in Detmold, in 1859, with the family. The couple's two sons, **HERMANN** (1847–1913) and **CARL** (1851–?1920), published their memories of Brahms in the Viennese newspaper *Neues Wiener Tagblatt* a few years after his death; their articles focused, above all, on the light-hearted side of his activities at Detmold. (Häntzschel 1994; C. Meysenbug 1902; H. Meysenbug 1901; Schramm 1983; Weech 1970)

MICHALEK, LUDWIG (b. Temesvar [Timisoara, Romania], 13 April 1859; d. Vienna, 24 September 1942). Painter, graphic artist, and etcher. In 1873 he enrolled at the Akademie der bildenden Künste [Academy of Plastic Arts] in Vienna, where his teachers included painters August Eisenmenger, Christian Griepenkerl, and Karl August Ludwig Wurzinger; subsequently, he traveled widely in Europe. He specialized in portrait painting.

Michalek, who had made Brahms's acquaintance at the Tonkünstlerverein, frequently called on him, and Brahms, in his turn, visited Michalek repeatedly in his studio. When Brahms was persuaded to sit for the sculptor **Victor Tilgner** in 1891, he gave Michalek permission to attend the sittings for the purpose of painting his portrait. Michalek, who was present at most of the sittings in Tilgner's studio, made a pastel painting as well as a charcoal drawing. Two years later, on the occasion of Brahms's 60th anniversary, he prepared an etching from the original pastel painting. Fifty copies were made of this etching, accompanied by remarque sketches showing Brahms's music room in Vienna (with the Karlskirche in the background), the harbor in Hamburg, a portrait of the young composer, and the house in which he was born. Brahms signed 18 of these copies. In a letter to Robert Gund, Michalek described in some detail the circumstances in which he painted Brahms in 1891 (see Hofmann and Hofmann 1997, 184–88).

This was not the only time Michalek portrayed Brahms. On 3 April 1897 he made a chalk and charcoal drawing of Brahms on his deathbed, and the following year he executed a nearly life-size chalk and charcoal portrait (dated 22 January 1898), based on a photograph that **Maria Fellinger** had taken of Brahms in November 1893. In 1908 Michalek provided an elaborate frontispiece for the special booklet *Zur Enthüllung des Brahms-Denkmals in Wien, 7 Mai 1908*, which was published on the occasion of the unveiling of **Rudolf von Weyr**'s Brahms monument; and in 1922, to mark the 25th anniversary of Brahms's death, he made an etching depicting the composer against the background of the Karlskirche, based on a photograph taken in 1892 by **Viktor von Miller zu Aichholz**'s son Eugen, though with a slightly altered view of the church. (*ÖBL* 1957–)

MILLER ZU AICHHOLZ, VIKTOR VON (b. Vienna, 21 October 1845; d. Vienna, 14 May 1910). Wealthy industrialist and banker. The youngest and most musical of the five sons of the industrialist Joseph Maria Miller

(1797–1871), who was ennobled in 1865. One of Viktor's brothers, August (1829–99), was for almost 30 years (1872–99) on the board of directors of the Gesellschaft der Musikfreunde; another, Eugen (1835–1919), became a celebrated patron of the arts and a noted collector, who, among his numerous treasures, owned several huge paintings by Giovanni Battista Tiepolo that were prominently displayed in the luxurious residence he built for himself in Vienna (at 30 Heugasse, now 28 Prinz-Eugen-Strasse; the mansion was demolished in 1961 and replaced by a nondescript modern building).

Viktor, a pupil of **Julius Epstein**, was an excellent pianist; his wife Olga, née Johanny (1853–1931), was gifted in other ways (she made an excellent chalk drawing of Brahms). The couple counted many leading musicians among their close acquaintances. Their friendship with Brahms appears to date from the winter of 1889–90; according to a statement made later by their son Eugen (1878–1963) to Maria Menczigar, when she was preparing her dissertation on Epstein, it was the latter who introduced them to Brahms. During the following years, Brahms was a frequent guest at the Millers' Viennese residence (13 Heumarkt) as well as in Gmunden, in Upper Austria, where they spent their summers from 1878 onward, at first in a rented house and from 1885 in their own villa. Brahms, who clearly liked the couple and greatly enjoyed their hospitality, for he did not hesitate to invite himself more than once, used to come over to Gmunden from his vacation quarters in Ischl for a meal and some music making, usually just for the day, but sometimes also staying the night. **Max Kalbeck** (1976) described Viktor von Miller as "without a doubt the most selfless, faithful, and devoted admirer of the Master, whom he loved tenderly" and his wife as "an angel of kind-heartedness, delicacy of feeling, and cheerfulness" (vol. 4, 167–68, 170). Others who knew them well, e.g., Emil Hess (1962), a musician in the service of ex-King **Georg V of Hanover**, have also paid tributes to Miller's innate goodness and modesty and to his wife's kind and gentle character. On occasion Miller, though reportedly with some trepidation, joined Brahms in performing two-piano arrangements of certain of his works. Thus, on 11 June 1893 they played the first two movements of the Piano Quintet op. 34, and on 26 September of the same year, the Fourth Symphony. It was at the Millers' house in Gmunden, that, at Brahms's suggestion, **Eduard Hanslick**'s 70th birthday was celebrated at a special dinner on 11 September 1895; the hosts had even arranged a fireworks display on the preceding evening. Brahms made the short journey from Ischl at least once more in the summer of 1896, and he dined with the Millers several times in Vienna during the following winter. His last visit took place little more than a week before his death, on 25 March, and he even intended to return the next day but was no longer able to do so. (Much interesting information concerning Brahms's visits to the Millers in Gmunden and Vienna may be gleaned from **Richard Heuberger**'s [1976] diary and also from that of Olga von Miller [which is frequently quoted in Spitzbart 1997a; see also Spitzbart 1997b and 2001].)

In September 1900 Viktor von Miller established a Brahms museum in a small building in the grounds of his Gmunden estate; in 1939 the collection was donated by the Millers' heirs to the town of Gmunden, where it is housed in the Kammerhof Museum (which had been founded by Miller). It contains, among other items, almost 100 letters and other communications by Brahms, addressed mainly to the Miller family, as well as portraits (including photographs taken by the Millers' son Eugen), musical scores, books and periodicals, and a very large number of concert programs. Furthermore, Viktor von Miller was instrumental in the formation of the Brahms Society in Vienna in April 1904, and he was elected its first president. He was also a member of the committee established to plan and collect funds for a Brahms monument in Vienna, and eventually succeeded **Arthur Faber** as president of its executive committee.

Lastly, he published a *Brahms-Bilderbuch* in 1905—a series of photographs illustrating various aspects of Brahms's life and activities, with explanatory comments by Max Kalbeck. Apart from music, his great passion was numismatics; his important coin collection was donated by his son Eugen to the department of coins of the Kunsthistorisches Museum in Vienna in 1913. (Haider 1984; Hess 1962; Heuberger 1976; Menczigar 1957; Prillinger 1985, 2001; Spitzbart 1997a, 1997b, 2001)

MÖRIKE, EDUARD (FRIEDRICH) (b. Ludwigsburg, 8 September 1804; d. Stuttgart, 4 June 1875). Poet and writer of short narrative tales. Brahms set three of his poems in the songs "An eine Aeolsharfe" (op. 19/5) and "Agnes" (op. 59/5), and the duet "Die Schwestern" (op. 61/1). (Gockel 1990)

MOSENTHAL, SALOMON HERMANN VON (b. Kassel, 14 January 1821; d. Vienna, 17 February 1877). Poet and dramatist who settled in Vienna in 1841–42 and achieved international success with his play *Deborah*, first produced in Hamburg in 1848 (with 400 performances in New York in 1862, and over 500 in London in 1863–64). He also wrote a number of opera librettos, including those for **Karl Goldmark**'s *Die Königin von Saba* and Nicolai's *Die lustigen Weiber von Windsor*. Furthermore, he was a member of the board of directors of the Gesellschaft der Musikfreunde (1868–71) and the society's vice president (1871–77). It was in the latter capacity that he arranged the amicable dissolution of Brahms's contract as artistic director of the society in 1875. Brahms, he reported to the board, had conducted himself like a "gentleman" in those discussions. The official *Protocoll* drawn up in this connection on 3 April 1875 bears the signatures of Mosenthal and Brahms.

In a note to his edition of Brahms's correspondence with **Heinrich** and **Elisabeth von Herzogenberg**, **Max Kalbeck** states that Brahms occasionally met Mosenthal at social gatherings and in restaurants. In his Brahms biography, he alleges that Mosenthal, whose temperament differed widely from that of Brahms, was in fact ill disposed toward him, above all because Brahms had wounded his pride and vanity by declining, with a joke, his offer to furnish Brahms with the text for an opera. Mosenthal is mainly remembered by Brahmsians for a bon mot that Brahms cited with evident amusement in a letter to Elisabeth von Herzogenberg in November 1879: "He complained that I was far too serious in my art, and when I remarked that I was also merry at times, he admitted that I was right: yes indeed, he said, and when things really warm up and you get truly merry, you sing 'Das Grab ist meine Freude' [The grave is my joy]" (Brahms 1974/1, 106). (Brahms 1974/1; *ÖBL* 1957–; Schug 1966)

MOZART, WOLFGANG AMADEUS (b. Salzburg, 27 January 1756; d. Vienna, 5 December 1791). Composer. Brahms was a great student and admirer of Mozart's music (see, for instance, **Max Kalbeck**'s [1976] and **Florence May**'s [1948] biographies, some of Brahms's letters, his conversations as reported by **Richard Heuberger** [1976], and especially Imogen Fellinger's recent articles [I. Fellinger 1983a, 1983b, 1990]). He was tremendously impressed by *The Marriage of Figaro*, *Don Giovanni*, and *Idomeneo* ("a marvellous work"); he encouraged **Clara Schumann** to play the concertos in public; he considered the C Minor Piano Concerto K. 491—which he performed at a concert in Hamburg on 26 January 1856—a "wonderful work of art," superior to **Beethoven**'s concerto in the same key (Heuberger 1976, 93); and he composed his own cadenzas to that concerto as well as to those in G major K. 453 and D minor K. 466 (M. McCorkle 1984, WoO 13–15). Brahms even published (anonymously) the first edition of the *Offertorium de venerabili sacramento "Venite populi"* (K. 260), shortly after conducting the work at the Musikverein in Vienna on 8 December 1872, and he later contributed an edition of the Requiem (M. McCorkle 1984, Anhang VI/7) to **Breitkopf & Härtel**'s collected edition of Mozart's works, in which it appeared without his name in 1877. His report [Revisionsbericht] was published two years later.

Yet, it is worth noting that during his three years as artistic director of the Gesellschaft der Musikfreunde (1872–75), Brahms presented none of

Mozart's concertos or symphonies and only three vocal compositions: the aria *Ch'io mi scordi di te* (K. 505), sung by **Marie Wilt** at his very first concert on 10 November 1872, the Offertorium *Venite populi* (K. 260) on 8 December 1872, and the cantata *Davide penitente* (K. 469) on 25 January 1874 (an aria from the cantata was also on the program of the concert of 28 February 1875). During the same period, the Philharmonic Orchestra, under **Felix Otto Dessoff**, offered performances of the "Haffner," G Minor (K. 550), and "Jupiter" Symphonies, of the C Major Piano Concerto K. 503, and of the Divertimento K. 334, the Adagio from the String Quintet K. 516, and also the quintet from Act I of *Cosi fan tutte*. Even if one bears in mind that the Philharmonic Society gave slightly more concerts in a year than the Gesellschaft gave, the comparison is not without interest. (I. Fellinger 1983a, 1983b, 1990; Heuberger 1976; Köchel 2005; Litzmann 1970; May 1948)

MUCHANOFF [REALLY: MUCHANOVA], MARIE, COUNTESS (b. Warsaw, 7 August 1822; d. Warsaw, 22 May 1874). Daughter of Count Friedrich Karl Nesselrode, Russian commandant in Warsaw (whose family was of German descent) and his Polish-born wife Thecla Natecz de Gorska, and niece of the famous statesman and diplomat Karl Robert Nesselrode. She married twice: in 1839 to a Greek by the name of Kalergis, from whom she separated soon after the birth of a daughter the following year, and in 1863 to the Russian Count Sergei Sergeievich Muchanov. Exceptionally beautiful and highly intelligent, she was a cherished member of the international high society, as well as a friend of writers, musicians, and artists, among them Eugène Delacroix, Théophile Gautier (who eulogized her in "Symphonie en blanc majeur," one of the poems of *Émaux et camées*), **Heinrich Heine**, **Hector Berlioz**, **Liszt**, and **Richard Wagner** (whom she supported financially on one occasion and who, in 1869, dedicated his anti-Semitic tract *Aufklärung über das Judentum in der Musik* to her). Moreover, she was an outstanding pianist, having been taught by **Chopin**, who described her playing as "truly admirable" (La Mara 1911, x). **Hans von Bülow** once praised her as "the best female Chopin player I know" (La Mara 1911, xi), and he further described her as "one of the most generous, most intellectually brilliant and most widely cultured women in the whole world" (M. von Bülow 1895–1908, vol. 5, 173); and Liszt, who likewise thought very highly of her musical talent, arranged a memorial concert at Weimar and even composed an elegy in her memory. In short, she fascinated all who met her. The English diplomat Sir Horace Rumbold (1902) refers to her in his memoirs as "this wonderfully brilliant woman" and considered her appearance to be "the perfection of northern beauty" (216).

Rumbold had made her acquaintance at Baden-Baden, where she frequently stayed in the summer, whereas she spent her winters in Paris. It was also at Baden-Baden that Brahms met her in the summer of 1866, at a time when she seems to have taken a particular interest in his music ("Brahms is still my consolation," she had written to her daughter, Countess Marie Coudenhove, from Dresden that June [La Mara 1911, 177]). On 23 August she informed Marie, "Brahms is spending a month here [i.e., Baden-Baden] before returning to Vienna. I had him to dinner this evening—an interesting character, with his natural and uninhibited directness. . . . As soon as I have regained some of my strength I shall study his music. I cannot forgive myself for having let ten years go by without getting to know it" (La Mara 1911, 182).

In fact, Brahms stayed at Baden-Baden from about mid-August until shortly after mid-October that year, and he and the countess are quite likely to have met again after that first evening, yet nothing certain is known about their further contacts. The statement in the countess's letter to her daughter on 12 September that "Brahms embellit ma vie" [Brahms enriches my life] (La Mara 1911, 184) could indeed refer to such contacts, or it might simply reflect her response to his music, which she was presumably studying by then. (La Mara 1911; Rumbold 1902)

MÜHLFELD, RICHARD (BERNHARD HERMANN) (b. Salzungen, 28 February 1856; d. Meiningen, 1 June 1907). Clarinettist. He was born into a musical family: his father Leonhard (1819–76), who taught himself to play several instruments, was appointed conductor of the Salzungen Orchestra in 1851, and Richard's three older brothers also became professional musicians. By the time he reached his early teens, he was proficient as a violinist, pianist, and clarinettist. He joined the second violins of the Meiningen Orchestra on a probationary basis in 1873 and in 1874 was promoted to the first violins. In 1875 he was among the 26 orchestra members who were recruited by **Richard Wagner** for his Bayreuth Festival Orchestra, and he accordingly played in the performances of the *Ring* with which the Festival Theatre was inaugurated in 1876. However, that year he switched increasingly to the clarinet, and it was as a performer on that instrument that he joined the military band during his army service.

On 28 October 1877 he made his first appearance as a soloist with the Meiningen Orchestra when he played Weber's Concertino for clarinet (Jähns 109), and two years later he was offered a formal contract as principal clarinettist. Highly regarded by **Duke Georg II** and greatly admired by the orchestra's conductors, notably **Hans von Bülow** and **Fritz Steinbach**, he was granted the title "Kammervirtuose" in 1885 and named "Musikdirektor" in 1890, the latter rank entitling him to deputize for the permanent conductor and also to direct music at the theater. He was to remain with the orchestra until his death. Long before then he had come to be regarded throughout Germany as a clarinettist of quite outstanding merit, and from 1884 to 1896 he was solo clarinettist in the Bayreuth orchestra. Moreover, his numerous concert appearances outside Germany gained him an international reputation, and nowhere was he more sincerely appreciated than in England. After his performances in Brahms's Clarinet Quintet in London in March–April 1892, the critic of the *Musical Times* hailed him as "an executant of the highest calibre," adding, "His tone in the lower register is superb, and his phrasing absolutely unsurpassable for finish and beauty of expression" (*Musical Times*, 1 May 1892, 277). In *The Times*, J. A. Fuller Maitland was no less enthusiastic: "Herr Mühlfeld is a superlatively fine artist, and not only his tone, but the perfection of his phrasing, the depth of his musical expression, and his absolute ease and finish mark him as a player altogether without parallel in England at least" (*The Times*, 29 March 1892, 11).

As for Brahms, four of his last works owed their composition to the impact that Mühlfeld's playing had made on him. Since Brahms repeatedly visited Meiningen during the 1880s and, while there, conducted the orchestra at rehearsal and in performance, he must have become quite well acquainted with Mühlfeld; yet, it was not until 1891 that he fully appreciated the exceptional quality of his playing and, in consequence, the rich potential of the clarinet. One particular event that helped to stimulate this awareness was Mühlfeld's rendition of Weber's Clarinet Concerto in F Minor (Jähns 114), which Brahms heard during his week's stay at Meiningen in March 1891. "One cannot play the clarinet more beautifully than does Herr Mühlfeld," he wrote to **Clara Schumann** on 17 March (Litzmann 1970, vol. 2, 447).

Still under the enchantment of Mühlfeld's playing, Brahms composed his Clarinet Trio and Clarinet Quintet during his stay at Ischl that summer. He then invited himself to Meiningen for private performances of the two new works: "Your Mühlfeld is the greatest master of his instrument and I cannot imagine a performance of these compositions anywhere else than at Meiningen," he wrote to **Baroness Helene Heldburg** in July 1891 (Brahms 1991, 114). To Clara Schumann, whom he tried to persuade to make the journey to Meiningen, he wrote in August, "To hear the clarinettist there would be a most joyful experience for you; you would revel in it" (Litzmann 1970, vol. 2, 459). The proposed private performances duly took place at Meiningen in November 1891, while the first public performances of the two works were given in Berlin on 12 December 1891, when the trio was played by Brahms, Mühlfeld, and **Robert Hausmann**, and the quintet by Mühlfeld and the Joachim Quartet. (In this connection, *see also* MENZEL, ADOLPH [FRIEDRICH ERDMANN] VON.) Subsequently, Mühlfeld took part in numerous other performances of the two works in various places, including in Vienna in mid-January 1892, (at the earliest Viennese performances, on 17 December 1891 and 5 January 1892, respectively, the clarinettist had been F. Steiner) and in London in March–April 1892. Joachim had prepared the ground for Mühlfeld's first concert appearances in England by informing his friend **Sir Charles Villiers Stanford** in December 1891 that "Brahms is willing to have it [the quintet] performed in England, if we engage the Clarinet player, who has done it in Berlin, a Mr. Mühlfeld from the Meiningen band, a stupendous fellow; I never heard the like of his variety of tone and expression" (original text in English; Johannes Joachim and Moser 1911–13, vol 3, 406). Mühlfeld was to return to England nine more times.(*See also* BEHRENS, ADOLPH.)

During his final years, Brahms saw Mühlfeld fairly regularly. In May 1894, when both Mühlfeld and Hausmann visited Vienna, there was, as Brahms happily reported to Clara Schumann and others, a good deal of music making. He must have found it particularly stimulating, for only a few weeks later he composed at Ischl the two clarinet sonatas (op. 120). After private performances at the villas of **Anna Franz** (*see* WITTGENSTEIN FAMILY) and Princess Marie of Sachsen-Meiningen at Berchtesgaden in September, at Clara Schumann's at Frankfurt in November, at Altenstein Castle, for the benefit of Duke Georg II and his wife, also in November, and a performance at the Tonkünstlerverein in Vienna on 7 January 1895, Brahms and Mühlfeld played the sonatas for the first time in public at concerts of the Rosé Quartet at the Bösendorfer Saal: the sonata in E-flat Major on 8 January, and that in F minor on 11 January 1895. Further public performances by Brahms and the clarinettist he affectionately called "his dear nightingale" (see, for instance, Lienau 1934, 43) followed at Leipzig (27 January), Frankfurt (15 February), and Meiningen (25 February); later that year, Mühlfeld performed the sonatas in Holland (with **Julius Röntgen**), in Switzerland (with **Robert Freund**), and in England (with **Fanny Davies**). In August 1895 Mühlfeld visited Brahms at Ischl. "Mühlfeld was also here, therefore Clarinet Quintet and Sonatas," Brahms reported to Clara Schumann (Litzmann 1970, vol. 2, 594; *see also* KNEISEL, FRANZ.) As a token of the enormous pleasure Brahms derived from his association with Mühlfeld, he presented him with the autographs of the two sonatas. Mühlfeld last met Brahms in Vienna in March 1897, when, during a five-day stay, he saw him each day. Two weeks later, with

Bram Eldering, he represented Duke Georg II and his family at Brahms's funeral; and on 7 May, in Berlin, he participated with **Heinrich Barth** and the Joachim Quartet in a Brahms Memorial Concert, which included a performance of the Clarinet Quintet.

During the last 15 years of his life Mühlfeld accepted, as far as his commitments in Meiningen permitted it, an increasing number of offers to concertize elsewhere in Germany, as well as in England, Denmark, Holland, France, Switzerland, and Austria. If he owed a major part of his fame to Brahms, he amply repaid this debt by championing Brahms's music for the clarinet wherever he went. Herta Müller has calculated that he appeared altogether at 645 concerts in 138 towns, and that he played in 54 performances of the Clarinet Trio (44 of them after Brahms's death), in 126 performances of the Clarinet Quintet (72 of them after Brahms's death), and in 48 performances of the Sonata op. 120/1, and 32 performances of the Sonata op. 120/2 (Herta Müller 2002, 141). (Brahms 1991; I. Fellinger 1981; Hofmann and Hofmann 2003; Johannes Joachim and Moser 1911–13; Lienau 1934; Litzmann 1970; Herta Müller 2002)

MÜNZ, SIGMUND (b. Leipnik [Lipnik, Czech Republic], 7 May 1859; d. Budapest, 7 September 1934). Writer and journalist. After studying history at the universities of Vienna and Tübingen, he took up journalism. From 1885 to 1888 he lived in Rome as a correspondent for various German and Austrian newspapers, then in Milan, Venice, and Florence (1889–91), and subsequently he worked until the First World War for the *Neue freie Presse* in Vienna, while also contributing to numerous foreign periodicals. Later (1920–34), he was employed as a correspondent by the Buenos Aires newspaper *La Nacion*. He was known in particular for his writings on politics and political figures.

Münz first met Brahms when the latter spent a few days in Rome with **Josef Viktor Widmann** in May 1888. They renewed their acquaintance later that same year in Vienna, met again at Ischl in the summer of 1890, and after Münz had settled in Vienna in the autumn of 1891 they saw each other quite frequently, especially at the houses of their mutual friends **Hugo Conrat** and **Ignaz Brüll**. On 23 November 1896 Münz reported to **Marie Renata Rückert**: "Yesterday I dined at the house of friends with Brahms. He was very lively and ate with very good appetite, yet he is said to be gravely and incurably sick" (R. Hofmann 2001, 411). In an article in the *Neue freie Presse* on 30 March 1898, and at much greater length in his book *Römische Reminiscenzen und Profile* (1900), he draws an interesting and largely convincing moral portrait of Brahms. He also tells of calling at Brahms's flat on the day before he died when, from the room adjoining the bedroom, he heard Brahms's voice for the last time, raised in irritation at some information he had just been given by his landlady, which he mistakenly believed to be wrong. In a general reference to Brahms's notoriously short temper, Münz (1900) observed, "The commonplace word 'amiability' could not be applied to this irascible, extraordinary man. He was amiable only inasmuch as, receptive to any novelty and any fresh knowledge, he was ready to follow his interlocutor along the most diverse paths" (150–51). (R. Hofmann 2001; Münz 1898, 1900)

– N –

NARATH, ALBERT (b. Vienna, 13 September 1864; d. Heidelberg, 14 August 1924). Surgeon. After graduating in 1890, he was employed as an assistant at the Anatomical Institute under Professor Emil Zuckerkandl (1889–91) and subsequently worked at the surgical clinic of the University of Vienna under **Theodor Billroth**. In 1896 he was appointed professor of surgery at Utrecht. During his stay in that city, he became very friendly with the physiologist **Wilhelm Engelmann** and his wife, and married their daughter Anna. In 1906 he took up a post at the University of Heidelberg, from which he retired for health reasons in 1910. However, he continued with his scientific work, and also acted as principal editor of the *Deutsche Zeitschrift für Chirurgie*.

In January 1897 he went to Vienna at Engelmann's request in order to examine Brahms. While he apparently gave the latter a reassuring diagnosis of his condition, he was evidently more candid in his remarks to Brahms's Viennese friends, for **Richard Heuberger** noted in his diary that Narath had reportedly expressed himself in very pessimistic terms (Heuberger 1976, 119). His report to his father-in-law also left little room for hope, but Engelmann, anxious to keep Brahms's spirits up, informed him in a letter on 18 January that he had been delighted to be told by Narath that, although his convalescence was likely to be a lengthy affair, there was no reason to believe that the illness could not be cured (Brahms 1974/13, 174). (Brahms 1974/13; Heuberger 1976; *ÖBL* 1957–)

NAUMANN, ERNST (b. Freiberg, 15 August 1832; d. Jena, 15 December 1910). Organist, conductor, composer, and music editor. He studied with **Moritz Hauptmann**, Ernst Friedrich Richter, and **Ernst Ferdinand Wenzel** at Leipzig and with the organist Johann Schneider at Dresden; in 1858 he obtained his doctorate at Leipzig University. In 1860 he settled at Jena, where he had been appointed director of music at the university and city;

he occupied these posts until 1906. It was at Jena that he conducted the first public performance of Brahms's *Alto Rhapsody* at a concert of the Jena Akademischer Gesangverein, with **Pauline Viardot** as soloist, on 3 March 1870.

Naumann wrote especially chamber music, songs, and sacred works. **Robert Schumann**, in his celebrated "Neue Bahnen" article in 1853, named him as one of the promising young composers of the time. In his later years Naumann devoted himself increasingly to the edition and arrangements of classical works (including two-piano versions of **Beethoven** symphonies and arrangements of **Mozart** quartets and quintets for piano duet). He made a major contribution to the great **Bach** edition published by **Breitkopf & Härtel**, and also worked on their **Haydn** edition.

According to Andreas Moser, the biographer of **Joseph Joachim** and editor of his correspondence with Brahms, the "E. Naumann" mentioned by Brahms in a letter to Joachim in early May 1860 as one of the musicians who had signed the manifesto against the "New German School" was Ernst's cousin Emil Naumann (1827–88), likewise a composer and musical scholar, who then held a prominent position in Berlin and later taught at the Dresden conservatory. (Brahms 1974/6; Stein 1910–11)

NAWRATIL, KARL (b. Vienna, 9 October 1836; d. Vienna, 6 April 1914). Civil servant; pianist and composer. Brahms reportedly arranged for him to study counterpoint with **Gustav Nottebohm**. He was one of two pianists accompanying the singers at the Viennese premiere of some of the *Liedeslieder-Walzer* (op. 52) on 5 December 1869. In 1871 Brahms presented him with the proofs of the score of the first edition of the Requiem (**Jakob Melchior Rieter-Biedermann**, 1869). The proofs, which bear a number of penciled corrections by Brahms himself, are now at the Brahms Institute at Lübeck. Nawratil dedicated his Piano Trio op. 9 to Brahms. (*See also* Nawratil's sister-in-law GRASSL VON RECHTEN, JOHANNA.)

NEUDA-BERNSTEIN, ROSA (b. Lemberg [Lwiw, Ukraine], 10 August 1856). Singer and teacher. As a child, she studied piano with **Carl Tausig** for a year. Some time before Tausig left Vienna in 1865, he introduced her to Brahms, who then taught her for a time. In his Brahms biography, **Max Kalbeck** (1976) cites some of her recollections of Brahms (vol. 2, 107–8). If the above date of her birth (as given in Kutsch-Riemens's [1987–94] *Grosses Sängerlexikon*) is correct, she must have been an infant prodigy, for according to her own account, when Brahms first heard her, during one of her last lessons with Tausig, she was playing **Chopin**'s First Piano Concerto. Nevertheless, Brahms hesitated to accept her as a pupil, because, he told her, she was playing with "iron fingers." However, when she quickly developed a more flexible and softer touch, he changed his mind. The lessons took place either at her home or in Brahms's rooms at the Haus des Deutschen Ritterordens (7 Singerstrasse). Neuda-Bernstein adds that Brahms "used to complain to my mother that he had so few friends among the Viennese musicians. Most of the time he was sad and gloomy."

Notwithstanding her pianistic skills, it was as a singer that Neuda-Bernstein made her name. Trained by Mathilde Marchesi, she began in Venice and Leipzig what promised to be a successful operatic career; but after her marriage she settled in Vienna and confined her artistic activities to the concert platform; she was known especially for her performances of religious music. She also enjoyed a considerable reputation as a singing teacher. On 3 February 1880 she took part in a concert at which Brahms conducted his Violin Concerto, with **Joseph Joachim** as the soloist. Among other items, she sang Brahms's song "Die Mainacht" (op. 43/2). (Kutsch and Riemens 1987–94)

NIETZSCHE, FRIEDRICH (b. Röcken, Saxony, 15 October 1844; d. Weimar, 25 August 1900). Philosopher. Brahms never met Nietzsche and only addressed one communication to him, but his music played a not unimportant role in Nietzsche's life.

It has been suggested (e.g., by David S. Thatcher) that Nietzsche probably first heard some of Brahms's compositions at the Lower Rhine Music Festival at Cologne in June 1865, at which **Julius Stockhausen** sang two of the *Magelone-Lieder.* (At the same festival, the 20-year-old Nietzsche sang in the choir at a performance of **Handel**'s oratorio *Israel in Egypt*.) Nietzsche's reaction to this first exposure to Brahms (if it indeed was the first) is not recorded, but he is known to have evinced considerable interest in Brahms's music during most of his 10-year stay at Basle, where he was appointed a professor at the university in 1869. He acquired a number of the scores, occasionally sang some of Brahms's songs at social gatherings and, above all, appears to have been profoundly impressed by the *Triumphlied*, of which he attended more than one performance, including that conducted by Brahms himself at Basle on 9 June 1874. Yet, despite the impression that the *Triumphlied* made on him, he confessed to a friend that his efforts to come to terms with the music posed a very difficult "test of [his] aesthetic conscience" (Thatcher 1973, 263). At the same time, his fascination with the work led to a confrontation with **Richard Wagner**. The incident, which was not lacking in comic overtones, took place at Bayreuth in August of that year. According to Wagner's own account, Nietzsche stubbornly persisted in his attempts to play the music for his host, in the face of Wagner's no less determined opposition, until he was finally ejected from the Villa Wahnfried (Thatcher 1973, 263). In another version of the incident, he excitedly proclaimed, "This is absolute music, yes indeed, absolute music!" before launching into a performance of the score with **Hans Richter**, who happened to be present; but after a short while, Wagner reportedly declared that he had heard quite enough of that absolute music (Thatcher 1973, 264). The occasion marked a turning point in their relations, and later, Wagner even went as far as to declare that his hostility toward Brahms dated from that episode, which had resulted in the loss of his devoted disciple Nietzsche (Thatcher 1973, 266). This is an assertion that is, at best, only partly true, not merely as an explanation of his dislike for Brahms (on this subject, *see* WAGNER, [WILHELM] RICHARD), but also, insofar as it applies to Nietzsche, whose reaction to the incident needs to be placed within the context of a more general shift in his aesthetics, as a result of which he changed from a fervent Wagnerite into an outright anti-Wagnerite. This development reached its climax in the tract *Der Fall Wagner* [*The Case of Wagner*], which he wrote in 1888, five years after his former idol's death, by which time he felt no less hostile toward Brahms than he did toward Wagner.

In fact, as well as featuring a fierce attack on the music of Wagner, *Der Fall Wagner* also contains, in its second postscript, a savage condemnation of Brahms, whose compositions, Nietzsche claims, display "the melancholy of impotence" and have as their primary quality a sense of yearning; they accordingly appeal to those who feel unfulfilled and, in particular, to unfulfilled women (Thatcher 1973, 277). This diatribe against Brahms's music drew a highly critical response from **Josef Viktor Widmann**, who, in a review entitled "Nietzsche's Abfall von Wagner" published in the Berne daily newspaper *Der Bund* (20–21 November 1888), asserted that he had never come across "such a ludicrously distorted spiritual portrait" and claimed that the author had "brought lasting shame upon himself" with his characterization of Brahms's admirers as essentially frustrated persons.

While the extremely hostile views concerning Brahms's music that Nietzsche advances in *Der Fall Wagner* are not inconsistent with certain sentiments expressed by him in private correspondence during the preceding years, the vehemence of the assault may nonetheless surprise, given that only a year earlier he had pronounced himself gratified on hearing that Brahms had shown interest in his writings; he had, in fact, subsequently arranged for copies of his *Zur Genealogie der Moral* and of his composition *Hymnus an das Leben* to be sent to Brahms. In a brief acknowledgement, written on one of his visiting cards, Brahms politely expressed his appreciation of the honor Nietzsche had done him, as well as his gratitude for the stimulus he had derived from what he had received; at the same time, he pointed out gleefully to **Max Kalbeck** how ingeniously he had avoided any reference to the music itself (Kalbeck 1976, vol. 4, 157). Later, some writers (Kalbeck, Widmann) alleged that Nietzsche had been greatly offended by Brahms's response (or lack of it) to his composition and that his resentment accounted for the nature and tone of his remarks about Brahms in *Der Fall Wagner*. There is, however, some contemporary evidence that Nietzsche had been quite pleased with Brahms's note, and this was confirmed by his intimate friend Peter Gast [Heinrich Köselitz] in his brief article "Nietzsche und Brahms," which appeared in the Berlin journal *Die Zukunft* in 1897 [Gast 1897]. Gast maintains that Nietzsche undoubtedly felt considerable respect for Brahms the composer and approved of certain aspects of his music, such as its North German seriousness, the sober, masculine manner, the abstention from any haphazard accumulation of melodies, and the sense of logic and construction. However, these positive reactions had long been outweighed by serious negative ones provoked by the absence of captivating, charming, or fantastic elements, of any well-sustained swell of emotion, of an adequate measure of imagination, and of sheer beauty of sound. Above all, Gast writes, Nietzsche found Brahms's compositions to be lacking the simplicity and comprehensibility that, in his judgment, were essential characteristics of works of true genius. Gast further explains that if Nietzsche focused so exclusively and forcefully on the negative features of Brahms's compositional style in *Der Fall Wagner*, he did so in order to discourage any conclusion that, having abjured Wagner, he now believed his musical ideal to have been realized by Brahms.

It is difficult to know what Brahms thought of Nietzsche's writings. He is known to have read some of them, and among the books in his private library were the aforementioned *Die Genealogie der Moral* and volume 8 (published in 1895) of the first collected edition of Nietzsche's works, which contained, among other items, *Der Fall Wagner*. In November 1888, **Elisabeth von Herzogenberg** described to him at some length her own attempts to come to terms with Nietzsche ("Reading him, one must constantly separate the wheat from the chaff and accept a good deal with patience; but what remains is nonetheless worth the effort, and there are some things, it seems to me, which only that eccentric is capable of saying" (Brahms 1974/2, 222). In reply, Brahms urged her not to spoil the precious sunshine too often with such reading matter and to keep always in mind the maxim "the opposite may also be true" (a motto once used by **Beethoven** and much cherished by Brahms). A few years later, Brahms warmly praised Widmann's play *Jenseits von Gut und Böse* [*Beyond Good and Evil*], in which the author took issue with Nietzsche's attack on contemporary morality in his identically titled book published in 1886. Brahms was present, as was Widmann, at the performance of the play at the Meiningen court theater on 29 January 1893. (Borchmeyer 1997; Borchmeyer and Salaquarda 1994; Brahms 1974/2; Gast 1897; Holinrake 1973; Janz 1978; Montsopoulos 1997; Reiber 1997; Thatcher 1973, 1978)

NIKISCH, ARTHUR (b. Lébényi Szent Miklós, 12 October 1855; d. Leipzig, 23 January 1922). Conductor. From 1866 to 1873 he studied at the Vienna conservatory, where his teachers included Wilhelm Schenner for piano, **Joseph Hellmesberger** for violin, and **Felix Otto Dessoff** for composition. In 1874 he joined the court opera orchestra as a violinist, and in 1878 he was engaged at the Stadttheater at Leipzig, initially as chorus master, but soon afterward as a conductor, and he became principal conductor the following year. In 1889 he was appointed conductor of the Boston Symphony Orchestra, with which he frequently toured throughout the United States (*see* KNEISEL, FRANZ). He returned to Europe in 1893 as musical director of the Budapest Opera, but he occupied that position only until 1895, when he accepted the conductorship of both the Leipzig Gewandhaus Orchestra and the Berlin Philharmonic Orchestra. It is a measure of the considerable renown he enjoyed by then that, whereas his long-serving predecessor at Leipzig, **Carl Reinecke**, received a salary of 5,000 marks until 1890 and 7,000 during the last five years of his appointment, Nikisch was from the outset paid a sum of 18,000 marks. In 1897 he also took charge of the philharmonic concerts in Hamburg, and among his numerous guest appearances elsewhere were frequent visits to London, where he first conducted some concerts in June 1895, even before he had taken up his post in Leipzig. A critic in the London *Musical Times* (1 July 1895) particularly praised his interpretation of Brahms's Second Symphony, declaring, in a rather curiously worded tribute, that "it is difficult to imagine a rendering of this noble work more calculated to silence criticism." Nikisch built up an especially close and fruitful association with the London Symphony Orchestra, which he even took to America.

Among the admirers of his performances of Brahms's music was the composer himself. Nikisch had invited him to attend one of his early concerts with the Gewandhaus Orchestra, on 16 January 1896 (not 16 February, as stated in Hofmann and Hofmann 1983, 230), at which the Fourth Symphony was to be played. After the performance, Nikisch later recalled, Brahms had come up to him, beaming with joy, and had said, "It's true that you have done everything quite differently, but you are right—this is how one must play it" (Pfohl 1925, 70). To **Fritz Simrock** Brahms wrote, equally enthusiastically, later that month, "The symphony was played in exemplary fashion, one cannot imagine a better performance" (Brahms 1974/12, 189). Altogether, in the relatively short period between his assumption of the conductorship of the Gewandhaus Orchestra and Brahms's death, Nikisch offered Leipzig music lovers performances of all four symphonies: the Requiem, the *Alto Rhapsody*, the two overtures, and the *4 ernste Gesänge*. The two men also met socially, in particular at Ischl (in this connection, *see* KNEISEL, FRANZ); and when the Berlin Philharmonic Orchestra arranged to give six concerts in Vienna in early April 1897, of which **Felix Weingartner** and Nikisch were to direct two each, Brahms, already fatally ill, let it be known that while he felt unable to receive a deputation from the orchestra, he would be ready to see Weingartner or Nikisch for a few minutes. However, he died before these visits could take place. The first concert, conducted by Weingartner on 5 April, then became a memorial concert for Brahms (*see* GUTMANN, ALBERT J.). At the two concerts Nikisch directed on 7 and 8 April, he conducted Brahms's First Symphony and the Violin Concerto, in which **Hugo Heermann** was the soloist. He also turned the opening concert of the 1897–98 season of the Gewandhaus Orchestra, on 7 October 1897, into another Brahms memorial concert, with a program consisting of the *Tragic Overture*, the *4 ernste Gesänge* (soloist: **Felix von Kraus**, accompanied by Nikisch on the piano), the first Piano Concerto (soloist: **Willy Rehberg**), two of the *Magelone-Lieder*, and the First Symphony. Finally, it may be mentioned as a matter of some interest that the *4 ernste Gesänge* were also on the program of the Gewandhaus concert held in Nikisch's own memory on 26 January 1822, when they were sung by the contralto Sigrid Onegin, accompanied by the pianist Günther Ramin.

On 1 July 1885 Nikisch married the soprano Amélie Heusner (1862–1938), who had been brought up in Brussels by her German parents. She began her stage career at the Stadttheater in Cologne before moving to Leipzig, where she appeared successfully in soubrette roles such as Papagena (in *Die Zauberflöte*) and Laura (in *Der Bettelstudent*). Amélie composed a burlesque opera, *Daniel in der Löwengrube*, which was produced at the Stadttheater in Hamburg in 1913, and several operettas. **Max Kalbeck** relates that when, at **Johann Strauss**'s house at Ischl, she sight read, to her husband's accompaniment, many of the folk songs that Brahms had arranged, he was so delighted by her singing that he presented her with the autographs of books 1–6 of the collection WoO 33 (Kalbeck 1976, vol. 4, 176). She is also credited with the first known public performances of "Erlaube mir, feins Mädchen," "Feinsliebchen, du sollst mir nicht barfuss gehn," and "Och Moder, ich well en Ding han" (WoO 33/2, 12, 33) at a concert given by **David Popper** in Vienna on 20 February 1895. (Brahms 1974/12; Chevalley 1922; Forner 1981; Pfohl 1925)

NOTHNAGEL, HERMANN (b. Alt-Lietzegöricke, Brandenburg, 28 September 1841; d. Vienna, 7 July 1905). Internist. He studied in Berlin (1859–63) and trained further under Ernst von Leyden at Königsberg [Kaliningrad]. His professional career began at the University of Freiburg im Breisgau (1872–74), continued at Jena (1874–82), and was crowned by his appointment as head of the First Medical Clinic in Vienna in 1882. He made a name for himself particularly through his publications on angina pectoris and on the physiology and pathology of the nervous system and the intestines.

Brahms's condition reached a critical stage on 2 April 1897. He had suffered a severe intestinal hemorrhage on 25 March and, in the view of his doctor, **Josef Breuer**, any further bleeding could precipitate his death. When more such bleeding occurred on the morning of 2 April, Dr. Breuer asked **Richard Fellinger** to bring Dr. Nothnagel to Brahms's rooms for a consultation. This was done, however, more in conformity with a well-established practice followed in such situations rather than in the hope of developing a new treatment, for it was clear that the end was near. (*ÖBL* 1957–)

NOTTEBOHM, (MARTIN) GUSTAV (b. Lüdenscheid, Westphalia, 12 November 1817; d. Graz, 29 October 1882). Musicologist, teacher, and composer. He studied with Siegfried Dehn in Berlin (1838–39) and during his subsequent stay in Leipzig (1840–45) was in close contact with both Mendelssohn and **Robert Schumann**. In 1846 he settled permanently in Vienna, where he received further instruction in musical theory from **Simon Sechter**. For the rest of his life he earned a rather meager living, deriving his income mainly from giving private piano lessons and instruction in theory. A confirmed bachelor, he was also well known for his uncompromising nature, which caused him often to be cantankerous and rude, especially toward strangers who seemed to threaten his privacy. At the same time, he was no recluse; at one time, he regularly joined the group of people, Brahms among them, who met in the evening at Gause's beer parlor in Johannesgasse.

Among his few close friends were **Robert Volkmann** and Brahms; with the latter he shared not only a North German origin but also certain character traits, which in his own case were, however, often developed to the point of eccentricity (**Max Kalbeck** [1976] described his clothes as "a model of perfect bad taste" [vol. 4, 57, n. 1]). Brahms greatly admired his mastery of musical theory, as well as his meticulous scholarship that enabled him to make important contributions, especially to the knowledge and understanding of **Beethoven**'s compositional process. Particularly enlightening in this respect was his analysis and partial publication of certain sketchbooks (1865, 1880). A collection of his articles on Beethoven, reprinted for the most part from the *Allgemeine musikalische Zeitung*, appeared in 1872 under the title *Beethoveniana*, and his illuminating study of the exercises that the young Beethoven had prepared for his teachers (*Beethoven's Unterricht bei J. Haydn, Albrechtsberger und Salieri*) was issued the following year. (A volume of his further essays on Beethoven was published by **Eusebius Mandyczewski** in 1887 as *Zweite Beethoveniana*.) Moreover, Nottebohm had in common with Brahms a strong interest in early music; six volumes of manuscript copies made by Nottebohm of such compositions were found in Brahms's library after his death.

Brahms struck up a lasting friendship with Nottebohm during his early years in Vienna and was quickly impressed by the quality of his research: "With his serious application, his sound knowledge, and his quiet diligence, Gustav Nottebohm reminds me agreeably of certain North German musicians and friends," he wrote to **Adolf Schubring** in January 1864 (Brahms 1974/8, 201). Moreover, he was soon recommending Nottebohm as an excellent teacher of musical theory, and would continue to do so until Nottebohm's death. "This autumn I have, as usual, sent several pupils to Nottebohm," Brahms informed **Joseph Joachim** in November 1879 (Brahms 1974/6, 185; *see also* BUSONI, FERRUCCIO [DANTE MICHELANGOLO BENVENUTO] and WOLF, HUGO [FILIPP JAKOB]). Furthermore, it was at his suggestion that **Jakob Melchior Rieter-Biedermann** published the above-mentioned books relating to Beethoven. "You may be certain that they are the result of immense application and will be of the greatest interest to musicians, scholars, and amateurs," he wrote to Rieter-Biedermann in October 1870 (Brahms 1974/14, 192). According to Kalbeck, Brahms even shared lodgings with Nottebohm for a short time (presumably in late 1868), before moving to the Hotel Zum Kronprinzen. Furthermore, Nottebohm was one of Brahms's companions on his second trip to Italy in the spring of 1881—or at any rate during a part of it, for he apparently did not set out from Vienna with the others as planned but joined them in Venice and later remained behind in Rome, while Brahms and **Theodor Billroth** moved on to Sicily (**Adolf Exner** was also in the party, at least for some of the time). In October 1882 Brahms responded to a pathetic call for help from Nottebohm, who was gravely ill at Graz. He arrived in time to spend Nottebohm's last days with him, and afterward made the arrangements for the funeral, for which, Kalbeck states,

Brahms paid, as Nottebohm had died in penury. (Antonicek 1988; Brahms 1974/6, 1974/8, 1974/14; Grasberger 1967b)

– O –

OCHS, SIEGFRIED (b. Frankfurt am Main, 19 April 1858; d. Berlin, 5 February 1929). Chorus master and composer. He studied with **Ernst Rudorff**, **Joseph Joachim**, Friedrich Kiel, and Adolf Schulze at the Hochschule für Musik in Berlin, and later privately with Kiel and Heinrich Urban. In 1882 he started a choir with just 11 singers, which became the Philharmonischer Chor in 1887 and eventually had some 400 members. It was dissolved in 1920, but a large part of it was absorbed by the choir of the Hochschule, whose faculty Ochs had joined.

Ochs made Brahms's acquaintance through **Hans von Bülow**. As he recalled in his memoirs *Geschehenes, Gesehenes*, he had numerous conversations with Brahms, who from the outset treated him with great cordiality. The reason for this immediate friendliness, according to Ochs, was that in dedicating his opera *Im Namen der Gerechtigkeit* to his wife, he had, on the title page of the score, printed below the dedication the opening bars of one of Brahms's compositions for women's chorus (op. 44/1), though without the words and without identifying the piece or its composer. Brahms had apparently come across the piano reduction of the opera in Bülow's rooms and, naturally recognizing the quotation at once, had been amused by Ochs's action. (Holde 1946; Ochs 1922)

OPHÜLS, GUSTAV (b. Krefeld, 4 June 1866; d. Frankfurt am Main, 24 March 1926). Lawyer. A close friend of the **Von der Leyen**s and **Von Beckerath**s and, like them, a great music lover; he was also an excellent pianist, having studied with **Richard Barth**. He made Brahms's acquaintance during the latter's visits to Krefeld in the early 1880s, and met him again in October 1892 in Berlin, where Brahms was participating in the inauguration of the Bechstein Saal (*see* WOLFF, HERMANN) and where Ophüls had gone to take his final law examination. In a letter to his parents (see *Brahms-Studien* 10) he gave a most interesting account of the concerts and social events he attended, in which Brahms was also involved.

The highpoint of Ophüls's personal relations with Brahms occurred at Whitsun 1896 when both were among the guests entertained by **Walther** and Emmy **Weyermann** at their villa at Bad Honnef. There he heard Brahms's moving performance—Ophüls later described it as a dramatic declamation rather than singing—of the recently composed *4 ernste*

Gesänge. Furthermore, he had several conversations with Brahms, during one of which Brahms asked him whether there was any risk, in his view, of the public performance of the *Gesänge* being forbidden for religious reasons (in a letter to **Fritz Simrock** in early May 1896 Brahms had characterized them as being "damnably serious and, at the same time, so impious that the police might well prohibit them—if the words weren't all in the Bible" (Brahms 1974/12, 195). Ophüls later recalled having declared that such a step, for which there were, in any case, no valid legal reasons, would be an outrage against art. Brahms had presumably sought Ophüls's opinion on the matter because he was a lawyer. At Whitsun 1896 he was temporarily employed as a judge at the Düsseldorf regional court, a position to which he would be permanently appointed in January 1897, at which time he moved his residence from Krefeld to Düsseldorf (where he founded a women's choir).

Ophüls mentioned to Brahms that he had at one time assembled all the texts used by Brahms in his compositions for solo voice, and this had greatly interested Brahms, who expressed a desire to see the collection. Ophüls promised to send it to him, once he had incorporated the texts of the works for several voices. During the following months he worked hard on the project, and in the process managed to identify in most cases the source Brahms had used. He even tried, though unsuccessfully, to enlist Brahms's help. (He also inserted various notes, which, however, he ultimately removed, fearing that they would displease Brahms, who, he knew, disliked such a scholarly apparatus.) In December 1896 he was finally able to send Brahms the result of his labors, presented in a handsomely bound manuscript of which the title page and certain initial letters on later pages had been decorated by his friend **Willy von Beckerath**. Brahms acknowledged the gift in a letter expressing the great pleasure it had given him, and he reportedly took much delight in showing it to his friends in Vienna. The collection appeared in print in 1898, and an augmented and corrected edition was published in 1908 and reissued in 1923. Finally, an extensively revised version, which included some three dozen additional texts and followed a somewhat different order, was published by Kristian Wachinger in 1983. The manuscript Brahms received from Ophüls is now at the Staats- und Universitätsbibliothek, Hamburg.

In 1917 Ophüls set down his recollections of his stay at Bad Honnef at Whitsun 1896 for the future benefit of his children and with no intention of presenting them to the general public. However, he was encouraged by others to do so, and his *Erinnerungen an Johannes Brahms* duly appeared in print in 1921. The little book was reissued in 1983, on the occasion of the 150th anniversary of Brahms's birth. It presents a fascinating and, in part, extremely moving account of those memorable days and of Brahms's state of mind and feelings immediately after the death of **Clara Schumann**, for he had gone to the Weyermanns straight from her funeral at Bonn. (Brahms 1974/12; E. Ophüls 1992; G. Ophüls 1983a, 1983b, 1994; Pieper 1937b)

OSER, BETTY, JOHANN, AND JOSEPHINE: *see* WITTGENSTEIN FAMILY.

OSSIAN: *see* MACPHERSON, JAMES.

OTTEN, GEORG DIETRICH (b. Hamburg, 8 February 1806; d. La Tour de Peilz, near Vevey, Switzerland, 28 July 1890). Conductor and teacher, active in Hamburg. He studied music with composer and piano teacher Johann Heinrich Clasing in Hamburg and with court Kapellmeister Friedrich Schneider at Dessau. His musical activities culminated in his foundation, in 1855, of a musical association that two years later became the Hamburger Musik-Verein and flourished under his direction until 1863. The concerts he conducted made a significant contribution to the musical activities of Hamburg, especially since he championed the leading romantic composers who were still being largely neglected at that time in the more classically oriented programs of the Philharmonic Orchestra under **Friedrich Wilhelm Grund**. Thus, Otten was the first to introduce Hamburg music lovers to certain works by Marschner, Spohr, and Weber, and especially Mendelssohn and **Robert Schumann**. (Already in 1847 he had conducted an ambitious memorial concert for Mendelssohn, and his performance of Schumann's music to Byron's *Manfred* on 21 April 1855 had been attended by **Clara Schumann**.)

Kurt Stephenson's assertion that Brahms made Otten's acquaintance no later than 1851 may well be correct, although he is on rather shaky ground in basing that conclusion simply on what he describes as a firm statement by Walter Hübbe that Otten was responsible for Brahms's giving piano lessons to Hübbe's brother that year. In reality, Hübbe's (1902) statement is a purely speculative one about what might have influenced his father to engage Brahms: "I can merely assume that his [my father's] attention could have been drawn to him [Brahms] only by Otten, who no doubt already knew Brahms by then" (4).

Brahms's correspondence indicates that he had frequent contact with Otten during the weeks he spent in Hamburg in late 1854 and late 1855; in particular, he mentions several invitations to Otten's home (Otten had an excellent private library, which Brahms admired). Brahms was further delighted when Otten praised some of his compositions. It was with Otten's orchestra that he made his first public concert appearance in Hamburg in several years on 24 November 1855, when he played **Beethoven**'s "Emperor" Concerto and some piano compositions by **Franz Schubert** and Schumann. On 26 January 1856, he performed **Mozart**'s D Minor Piano Concerto (K. 466) and on 25 October 1856 Beethoven's Fourth Piano Concerto at other concerts of the Musik-Verein. Thus, he had good cause to feel grateful to Otten, with whom, moreover, he was quickly on intimate "Du" terms; given the difference in their ages, the offer could only have come from Otten. Yet, while Brahms quite liked him as a person and even expressed his admiration to **Clara Schumann** regarding certain aspects of his character, he was soon irritated by Otten's considerable vanity; more seriously still, he came to judge Otten's musical capabilities with an increasingly critical eye, as did his friend **Joseph Joachim**.

Relations between Brahms and Otten grew somewhat strained when Otten, who nurtured the hope of outshining the Philharmonic Orchestra, was displeased that Brahms should have performed Schumann's Piano Concerto with Grund's band on 22 November 1856, and Brahms was forced to justify his action. On 9 February 1858 he played the piano part in Beethoven's *Choral Fantasia* at a concert conducted by Otten that, in a letter to Clara Schumann, he described as a "really crummy event" [Lumpen-Soiree] (Litzmann 1970, vol. 1, 217). His feelings toward Otten cooled further after a rather vague plan to present the first performance of his recently composed piano concerto at the Musik-Verein on 25 March 1858 was abandoned; he was convinced, as he told Joachim, that Otten had made the original proposal less out of any genuine interest in the work than from a desire to prevent its performance by the Philharmonic Orchestra (Brahms 1974/5, 203). Their next musical collaboration did not occur until 20 April 1860 when, with considerable misgivings (see letter to Joachim of 18 April)—for by now he was dismissing Otten scathingly as an "atrocious musician" (Litzmann 1970, vol. 1, 307)—Brahms finally did play his First Piano Concerto with the Musik-Verein. (But this was, of course, no longer its first public performance, which had taken place at Hanover on 22 January 1859, nor even its first performance in Hamburg, which Brahms had given with the Philharmonic Orchestra conducted by Joachim on 24 March 1859.) The performance on 20 April 1860 was not a success and marked the last joint appearance of Brahms and Otten at a concert. On 11 September of that year, he informed Clara Schumann that his contacts with Otten had practically ceased ("I don't call on him these days, unless it is necessary" (Litzmann 1970, vol. 1, 322); but there was no formal permanent break in their relations, as is shown by a letter couched in very friendly terms that Brahms addressed to Otten from Vienna in the spring of 1863, in which, among other matters, he expressed his thanks to his "dear friend" for regularly providing his parents with free tickets to his concerts (Stephenson 1962b, 515). The Musik-Verein closed down later that same year, but Otten remained active as a music teacher in Hamburg until 1883. (Brahms 1974/5; Callomon 1943; Hübbe 1902; Litzmann 1970; Sittard 1971; Stephenson 1928, 1962b; Zinnow 1992)

OTTIKER, OTTILIE (b. ?1847; d. Zurich, 16 April 1921). Soprano. After studying at the conservatory in Munich, she was engaged at the Munich Opera (1871–73) and subsequently at the Mannheim court theater (1873–79). While there, she sang the title roles at the premieres of **Hermann Goetz**'s operas *Der Widerspenstigen Zähmung* (11 October 1874) and *Francesca da Rimini* (30 September 1877). In 1880 she accepted a contract at the Cologne Opera, where she appeared for some 10 years. After retiring from the stage, she founded an opera school in Zurich. During her stay in Mannheim she became very friendly with **Ernst Frank**, the conductor at the court theater, and through him she met Brahms. She is frequently mentioned in the Brahms-Frank correspondence.

Ottilie Ottiker is credited in M. L. McCorkle's (1984) *Werkverzeichnis* with taking part in the first performance, at Mannheim on 13 February 1875, of the third of Brahms's *Drei Quartette* op. 64, and with having given the first performance of the eighth of the *Neun Gesänge* op. 69, at Karlsruhe on 22 October 1877. (Kutsch and Riemens 1987–94)

– P –

PASSY-CORNET, ADELE (b. Braunschweig, 22 January 1838 [?1834]; d. Nuremberg, 2 November 1915). Soprano; daughter of the tenor Julius Cornet (1793–1860) and the soprano **Franziska Cornet-Kiel**. She received her musical training in Hamburg, and after successful appearances at concerts there and in Vienna, Braunschweig, and Hanover, she settled in 1862 in Vienna, where she taught at the conservatory until 1870. Moreover, she was engaged at the Kärntnertor Theater in 1865, making her debut as the Queen of the Night in *Die Zauberflöte*. Her other most acclaimed roles included Isabelle in Meyerbeer's *Robert le Diable*, Rosina in Rossini's *Il barbiere di Siviglia*, and Elvire in Auber's *La Muette de Portici*. However, despite her very successful career in opera, she eventually devoted herself entirely to concert appearances and to teaching. In 1871 she founded her own school of singing in Vienna; from 1881 to 1892 she was on the faculty of the Budapest Academy of Music. Among her many pupils were her sons

Josef (1864–1934) and Anton (1868–1934), who both became opera singers; her daughter Anna (1857–1939) was active in Vienna as a concert singer and teacher under the name Prasch-Passy.

Together with her mother, Passy-Cornet took part in Brahms's concerts in Hamburg on 21 September 1848 and 14 April 1849. In 1862, the year in which both she and Brahms moved to Vienna, she sang at the first concert he gave there (on 29 November); he, in turn, performed at her own concert on 20 December, playing some pieces by **Robert Schumann** and, with **Joseph Hellmesberger**, **Bach**'s Violin Sonata in E Major. On 24 February 1875, at a concert of the Singakademie conducted by Rudolf Weinwurm, she sang in Brahms's quartets "An die Heimat" and "Der Abend" (op. 64/1–2); according to M. L. McCorkle's (1984) *Werkverzeichnis*, the performance of the latter composition was its first public one. (Kutsch and Riemens 1987–94)

PERGER, RICHARD VON (b. Vienna, 10 January 1854; d. Vienna, 11 January 1911). Conductor, composer, and teacher. Grandson of painter and etcher Sigismond Ferdinand von Perger (1778–1841) and son of painter and writer Anton Franz von Perger (1809–76). Richard studied cello with F. Schmidtler and composition with L. Zeller. On the recommendation of a jury composed of Brahms, **Karl Goldmark**, and **Eduard Hanslick**, he was awarded several state stipends to enable him to pursue his studies in composition. (In the *Neue freie Presse* on 29 June 1897, Hanslick published some letters in which Brahms had praised three quartets that Perger had submitted to the jury in different years.) Whether Brahms actually gave him any tuition, as has sometimes been stated (e.g., by Ch. Harten in *ÖBL* [1957–] and H. Jancik in Blume 1949–86), is uncertain. Perger was later director of the Rotterdam conservatory and conductor of the concerts of the Rotterdam section of the Maatschappij tot Bevordering van Toonkunst (1890–95). In 1895, probably with Brahms's help, he was appointed conductor of the concerts of the Gesellschaft der Musikfreunde in Vienna, which he directed until 1900; from 1899 to 1907 he served as principal of its conservatory.

By his own account, Perger first established personal contact with Brahms in 1877. Later, he came to know Brahms well and was among those who joined him on his Sunday walks. At Brahms's funeral on 6 April 1897, Perger, in his capacity as president of the Wiener Tonkünstlerverein, made a brief farewell speech at the graveside. Earlier, as the cortège stopped in front of the Musikverein, he had conducted the Singverein in Brahms's "Fahr wohl!" (op. 93a/4). On 11 April he conducted Brahms's Requiem at a memorial concert of the Gesellschaft der Musikfreunde.

Perger's compositions include the opera *Der Richter von Granada* and the Singspiel *Die vierzehn Nothelfer*, as well as choral and chamber music. In 1887 he dedicated one of his string quartets to Brahms, whose music considerably influenced his own. Furthermore, he contributed a short book on Brahms to the Reclam series of biographies of musicians in 1908. In the preface he wrote, "I owe almost everything I have achieved in my public activities to him" (Perger 1908, 5). The following year Perger was invited to write the history of the Gesellschaft der Musikfreunde. However, he only managed to cover the period 1812–70 before he died, and the account of the remaining years (1870–1912) was then entrusted to Robert Hirschfeld; the two parts were published together in 1912. (*ÖBL* 1957–; Perger 1908)

PETERS (music publishers): *see* ABRAHAM, MAX.

PETERSEN, CARL FRIEDRICH (b. Hamburg, 6 July 1809; d. Hamburg, 14 November 1892). Mayor of Hamburg, 1876–92; a lawyer by profession, he had earlier served as Hamburg's chief of police (1861–75). He presided over the city's fortunes at an important time in its economic development, for it was during this period that Hamburg, which had joined the North German confederation in 1866 and was made a constituent state of the German empire in 1871, became a member of the German *Zollverein*. Petersen was greatly admired for his intelligence, integrity, devotion to duty, and kindness.

His house was a favorite meeting place of Hamburg's musicians. His daughter Antonia [Toni] (b. 23 March 1840; d. 20 September 1909) was an admirer of **Richard Wagner** and knew his family. Her interest in Brahms's music is believed to have been greatly stimulated by **Hans von Bülow**, who played a prominent part in the musical life of Hamburg from 1886 onward. At Bülow's suggestion and with Toni's strong encouragement, Petersen proposed in 1889 that the city should confer honorary citizenship on Brahms. It was hoped that such a distinction would help to assuage any bitterness Brahms might still be feeling at having been twice passed over for the conductorship of the Hamburg Philharmonic.

Petersen's proposal obtained the approval of the senate and was, in due course, endorsed by the Bürgerschaft [parliament]. On 23 May 1889 he informed Brahms of the award by telegram. Brahms, who was then staying at Ischl, expressed to Petersen his great pleasure at the gesture, first in a telegram, and subsequently in a long letter on 30 May. The certificate, dated 14 June 1889, was presented to him by Petersen in Hamburg on 14 September. Toni later wrote, for **Max Kalbeck**'s benefit, a detailed account (now at the Staats-und Universitätsbibliothek Hamburg) of her own and her father's official and private contacts with Brahms during the week he spent in Hamburg on that occasion, as well as the contacts they enjoyed during Brahms's visits to Hamburg in late November–early December 1891. She herself had first met him at the 50th anniversary celebrations of the founding of the Hamburg Philharmonic Society in 1878, but she "had only seen him from a distance" when he came to perform at various concerts in Hamburg during the following decade (for the full text of her recollections, see K. Hofmann 1979a, 77–83).

After the presentation ceremony, the hand-decorated certificate of citizenship was exhibited in Hamburg for four weeks before being delivered to Brahms in Vienna (*see* DÜYFFCKE, PAUL). Brahms gave a tangible token of his gratitude to Petersen by dedicating to him the *Fest-und Gedenksprüche* (op. 109) that were first performed, in Brahms's presence, by **Julius Spengel** and the Cäcilienverein in Hamburg on 9 September 1889 and were published by **Fritz Simrock** in 1890. (The link established by some scholars between the composition of these vocal pieces and the conferment of the honorary citizenship is no longer considered a valid one, since Brahms is known to have already worked on them earlier.)

As already indicated, Brahms saw Petersen again in the autumn of 1891. He met Toni once more in February 1893, after her father's death, and they corresponded the following year on the occasion of Bülow's death. Brahms's correspondence with Carl Friedrich and Toni Petersen was published by K. Hofmann in 1979. (K. Hofmann 1979a; Wohlwill 1900)

PIENING, KARL THEODOR (b. Bielefeld, 14 April 1867; d. Bremen, 18 March 1942). Cellist. Son of the pianist, organist, and teacher Ludwig Piening (1838–1912). He studied cello with Carl Schröder at Sondershausen (1884–86) and subsequently with **Robert Hausmann** (1886–90) at the Hochschule für Musik in Berlin; there, he also received tuition in ensemble playing from **Joseph Joachim** and **Woldemar Bargiel**. From 1890 to 1892 he resided at Glasgow, where he was a member of the Glasgow Quartet led by Dutch violinist Maurice Sons and probably also played in the local orchestra. In 1893, after his period of military service, he was appointed principal cellist of the Krefeld orchestra. He did not, however, stay at Krefeld long; in the autumn of 1894, **Fritz Steinbach** engaged him, on Hausmann's recommendation, as principal cellist of the Meiningen orchestra, with which he was to be associated for the next 25 years.

During his stay at Krefeld, Piening, according to his biographer Klaus Reinhardt (1991), was invited to join in the musical activities of the **Beckerath** family, came to know Laura von Beckerath and her sons Kurt and

Willy, and taught the cello to **Alwin von Beckerath**'s son **Heinrich [Heinz]**. Piening's daughter Elisabeth Meyer-Piening (as quoted by Reinhardt) recalled later that it was as a result of his contacts with the Beckeraths that he made Brahms's acquaintance; but if the information is correct, it is not clear when and where their first meeting occurred (Brahms, in any case, is not known to have visited Krefeld or any of the Beckerath or **Von der Leyen** residences in 1893 or 1894). Elisabeth Meyer-Piening also stated that on one occasion Brahms was so delighted with Piening's performance of a solo passage that he gave him a kiss (Reinhardt 1991, 34). This event, true or not, had evidently become part of the Piening family's lore.

Piening may have had an opportunity to meet Brahms when the latter briefly stayed at Meiningen in November 1894. He definitely met Brahms three months later, when he was among the orchestral players who traveled with Brahms from Meiningen to Merseburg on 21 February 1895 for a "Brahms Evening," at which the Clarinet Quintet was performed. A few days later, on 25 February, at the Kasino at Meiningen, Piening played in a performance of the Piano Quartet op. 25, in which Brahms himself took the piano part. Brahms was also present at the music festival held at Meiningen in September of the same year, at which Piening, together with **Bram Eldering**, joined the Joachim Quartet in a rendition of the Sextet op. 18. He last saw Brahms in May 1896, when they were both guests of **Walther** and Emmy **Weyermann** at the Hagerhof, at Honnef on the Rhine. Many years later (on 4 June 1933), Piening published his recollections of his stay at the Hagerhof in the *Weser Zeitung* and the *Westfälische Zeitung*, under the title "Johannes Brahms' letztes Pfingstfest." There had been much music making, which had included the Piano Quintet op. 34 and the Piano Trio op. 101; in both works, Brahms had taken the piano and Piening the cello part. (Piening's article is reprinted in K. Reinhardt's biography. A far more detailed account of those memorable days appears in Gustav Ophüls's [1983b] *Erinnerungen an Johannes Brahms*.)

Piening remained at Meiningen until 1920. In addition to occupying the position of solo (i.e., principal) cellist in the orchestra, he played much chamber music (at one time forming a quartet with Bram Eldering, August Funk, and Alphons Abbas, later a trio with Wilhelm Berger and **Richard Mühlfeld**). Eventually, he also began to conduct, and in 1915 he became the orchestra's sole conductor, being granted the title Hofkapellmeister in 1917. However, the orchestra did not long survive Duke Bernard III's abdication in November 1918; the following year it was replaced by a new ensemble, which took the name "Meininger Musikverein," still with Piening as its conductor. But at the end of 1920, Piening left Meiningen and, after a period spent at Bielefeld (1920–22) where most of his time was taken up with teaching, he joined the piano manufacturing firm of L. W. Kretschmar at Bremen, of which he would become sole proprietor in 1931. At the same time he still occasionally conducted and also performed as a cello soloist. (Reinhardt 1991)

PLATEN, AUGUST, VON [in full: Platen-Hallermünde, Karl August Georg Maximilian, Count] (b. Ansbach, 24 October 1796; d. Syracuse, Sicily, 5 December 1835). Poet and dramatist. Brahms set five of his poems in the songs "Wie rafft ich mich auf in der Nacht," "Ich schleich umher betrübt und stumm," "Der Strom, der neben mir verrauschte," "Wehe, so willst du mich wieder," and "Du sprichst, dass ich mich täuschte" (op. 32/1, 3–6). (Dove 1991)

POHL, CARL FERDINAND (b. Darmstadt, 6 September 1819; d. Vienna, 28 April 1887). Music historian, organist, and composer. He was born into a musical family, his grandfather having been active as a maker of glass harmonicas at Kreibitz [Chřibská] in Bohemia, while his father was a chamber musician in the service of the duke of Hessen-Darmstadt; his mother was a daughter of Czech-born composer and piano teacher Antonín František Bečvařovsky. Pohl originally trained as an engraver at Darmstadt, but in 1841 he went to Vienna, where he studied with **Simon Sechter** and subsequently earned his living as a music teacher. From 1848 to 1855 he was organist at the protestant church in the Viennese suburb of Gumpendorf.

On the occasion of an international industrial exhibition held in London in 1862, he wrote a brief history of the glass harmonica (*Zur Geschichte der Glas-Harmonica*, entitled in the English version *Cursory Notices on the Origin and History of the Glass Harmonica*). He lived in London from 1863 to 1866, and as a result of the research he carried out there, in 1867 he published a two-volume study, *Mozart und Haydn in London*. The previous year he had been appointed archivist and librarian of the Gesellschaft der Musikfreunde in Vienna, a post he was to hold until his death. His other writings include, notably, a history of the Gesellschaft der Musikfreunde and its conservatory (1871) and, above all, an ambitious and important book on **Haydn**, of which he was able to publish only two volumes (1875, 1882); the final volume, edited by H. Botstiber, did not appear until 1927. As a composer, he wrote music for organ and piano, as well as some songs and a Mass.

An exceedingly modest and kind-hearted man, unfailingly thoughtful toward others and eager to help them, Pohl had many friends, none more appreciative or sincerely affectionate than Brahms, with whom he regularly lunched at the Roter Igel restaurant. He was particularly devoted to Brahms—"I would run through roses and thorns for Saint Johannes," he wrote to Brahms on 14 May 1873 (Geiringer 1935, 399); for a striking example of Pohl's generosity and of the trouble he was willing to take in order to please Brahms, see Kalbeck 1976, vol. 3, 180.) Moreover, he had a profound admiration for Brahms's music. "The work is marvelous," he reported to **Fritz Simrock** on 30 December 1872 after listening to rehearsals of the Second Symphony. "Every movement is pure gold" (Kalbeck 1976, vol. 3, 179). At the same time he valued Brahms's choral compositions even more highly than his symphonies and tried, unsuccessfully, to persuade him to write more. "You know how much I like our dear Pohl, but he has been tormenting me for years with the same story," Brahms told **Max Kalbeck** with some exasperation. "He says I ought, if possible, to compose another 'German Requiem'! If he wasn't such a wonderfully good fellow, I would have thrown him out long ago" (Kalbeck 1976, vol. 3, 180, n. 1).

Pohl was often in poor health, especially during the last year of his life. In August 1886 Brahms wrote to **Theodor Billroth**, who kept him informed of Pohl's medical condition while he was away in Switzerland: "The kind, wonderfully kind Pohl! How gladly I would do something for him, but one never could, either in small or large matters. He was only there for others" (Gottlieb-Billroth 1935, 393). Brahms even tried to induce Pohl to live in his own, more comfortable flat during his absence from Vienna, but in vain. After Pohl had died, Brahms remembered him fondly as "the kindest and most generous man in the world" (Kalbeck 1976, vol. 4, 46).

It was, incidentally, among the musical material that Pohl had collected in connection with his book on **Haydn** that Brahms came across the "St. Antony chorale" on which he afterward based his *Variations* op. 56. (Its attribution to Haydn is now considered doubtful.) (Geiringer 1935; Gottlieb-Billroth 1935; C. Pohl 1871, 1883)

POHL, RICHARD (b. Leipzig, 12 September 1826; d. Baden-Baden, 17 December 1896). Music critic and writer. In 1841 Pohl left Leipzig for Chemnitz, where, as he later wrote in an autobiographical sketch (1881), he spent "six years, the most wretched of my life" (R. Pohl 1881, 9), first studying engineering and subsequently employed in an engineering works. Later, he attended the Polytechnic at Karlsruhe, where he trained as a teacher, and the universities of Göttingen and Leipzig, where he studied physics and philosophy. Eventually, after an offer of a teaching post at Graz had been withdrawn and he failed to obtain employment in the Saxon state service, he resolved, at the age of 26, to follow his true inclination and earn his living as a freelance writer on music.

He had been attracted to music from a young age, and had, prior to his departure for Chemnitz, taken piano lessons from **Ernst Ferdinand Wenzel**. At Chemnitz he had continued to study piano, had acquired some knowledge of harmony, and had sung in a choir. Above all, Pohl had benefited from the numerous opportunities to listen to music that existed in Leipzig, Karlsruhe, Göttingen, and even Chemnitz. His earliest preference was for **Robert Schumann**, for whom he would later try to develop a subject suitable for an opera (*Die Braut von Messina*, based on **Friedrich von Schiller**'s play) or an oratorio (on Luther). Nothing came of these ideas, though Schumann composed an overture to the proposed opera; he did, however, set Pohl's text "Des Sängers Fluch" (based on Uhland's ballad).

Before long, Pohl discovered the three composers who were to remain his musical heroes for the remainder of his life: **Hector Berlioz** (whose overture to *Les Francs-juges* he first heard at Chemnitz), **Liszt** (whose presence at Weimar would be the reason for his moving there himself in 1854 and whose later departure from the town would cause him to leave it also), and **Richard Wagner** (under whose spell he fell on reading his essays *Kunst und Revolution* and *Das Kunstwerk der Zukunft*, even before he had heard any of his operas). He was to be their vociferous champion. Indeed, the belligerent tone in which he fought for the cause of the Weimar School and the "Music of the Future" is well reflected in the partly anagrammatical pseudonym "Hoplit" (recalling the heavily armed Greek infantrymen), under which he wrote for **Karl Franz Brendel**'s *Neue Zeitschrift für Musik*; in fact, his aggressive polemic nearly landed him in a duel with Karl August Krebs, who had replaced Wagner as Kapellmeister at the Dresden court opera. For some two years, Pohl reported on musical events in Dresden before moving to Weimar where he lived with his wife, harpist Johanna Eyth (1824–70), from 1854 to 1863. In the latter year the couple settled at Baden-Baden, where Pohl became editor and music critic of the *Badeblatt*, while his wife was engaged in the Karlsruhe court orchestra. (Two years after Johanna's death he married her niece Luise Eyth.) Apart from his contributions to the above-mentioned journals, he wrote during his career for a variety of other periodicals, published a German version of Berlioz's writings, translated the libretti of Berlioz's *Béatrice et Bénédict* and Saint-Saëns's *Samson et Dalila* and, furthermore, was the author of a volume of poetry, of a novel (*Richard Wiegand*), and of a comedy (*Musikalische Leiden*).

Pohl's initial attitude toward the music of Brahms, whom he first met during the latter's visit to Leipzig in December 1853, was unenthusiastic, and it remained essentially so, even if he was later to express an occasional measure of praise. In July and December 1855, in the *Neue Zeitschrift für Musik*, he wrote about the compositions that had so far appeared in print (i.e., opp. 1–9). Largely critical in tone but lacking a well-constructed exposition of the supposed shortcomings, the articles contain a number of rather vague statements, apparently none of them resulting from a close examination of the works in question, which lead the writer to the conclusion that it is as yet too early to decide whether Brahms is a composer of genius or merely one of talent. Pohl promised to shore up this assessment with a detailed analysis of the compositions in a further article in the same journal, but never did so.

Later, when he had settled at Baden-Baden, he abandoned his aggressively polemical stance, at any rate in his writings in the *Badeblatt*; as far as Brahms was concerned, he even printed a decidedly laudatory piece on the occasion of the latter's appearance there at a concert in August 1872. He also wrote a largely positive review of the First Symphony. But it would be wrong to deduce from this that his general opinion of Brahms's music had dramatically changed, and an incident described by Luise Pohl in the *Frankfurter Zeitung* (14 April 1907) and cited by **Max Kalbeck**, in which Pohl spoke disparagingly in private of the Piano Quartet op. 60, bears this out (Kalbeck 1976, vol. 2, 401). It is also noticeable that, in the autobiographical essay (*Autobiographisches*) that he published in 1881, he makes no mention of Brahms's music and only a very brief reference to the man.

Brahms was in any case not convinced by Pohl's seemingly more benign attitude, as is proved by an incident that occurred on the occasion of the private run-through of the Double Concerto at the Kurhaus in Baden-Baden on 23 September 1887. Pohl had not been invited but, having heard of the event, turned up nevertheless and vehemently reproached Brahms for not asking him. Brahms is reported to have told him calmly that he had not thought it necessary to invite him, since Pohl in any case always ran down his compositions. In the event, as if to prove him wrong, Pohl wrote in the *Badeblatt* the next day that while he did not think it appropriate to express a personal judgment of the work, since the performance had been a private one, it would have been a highly favorable one in every respect. In 1889 **Richard Heuberger** (1976) noted in his diary that Brahms did not like Pohl much and had described him as "a poor, wretched creature" (160). (Baser 1973; Heuberger 1976; R. Pohl 1855, 1881)

POPPER, DAVID (b. Prague, ?16 June 1843; d. Baden, near Vienna, 7 August 1913). Cellist and composer. He studied under Julius Goltermann at the Prague conservatory and in 1863 made very successful concert appearances in Germany. Later, he visited Holland, Switzerland, and England, and in 1867 he performed for the first time in Vienna; subsequently, for several years he occupied the post of principal cellist at the Vienna court opera; he also joined the Hellmesberger Quartet. In 1873 he resumed touring, but in 1886 he finally settled in Budapest, where he joined the faculty of the Academy of Music and also became a founding member of the Hubay Quartet. As a member of that ensemble, he played in numerous performances of Brahms's music and, notably, in the first public performances of Brahms's Piano Trio op. 101 (20 December 1886) and of the new version of his Piano Trio op. 8 (10 January 1890). Brahms took part in both performances, and at the former concert he also played his Cello Sonata op. 99 with Popper. (*See also* EIBENSCHÜTZ, ILONA.)

Popper composed music for cello (several concertos and numerous pieces for cello and piano). He liked to show his compositions to Brahms, who reportedly was not greatly impressed by them. In 1872 Popper married pianist Sophie Menter (1846–1918), and after their divorce in 1886, Olga Löbl, a Czech girl some 20 years his junior. (De'ak 1980)

PORUBSZKY, BERTHA: *see* FABER, ARTHUR (LUDWIG) AND (LOUISE MARIE) BERTHA.

PRECHEISEN, OLGA (b. Graz, 7 July 1853; d. Vienna, 26 July 1935). Actress. She began her career at the Stadttheater at Graz in 1869, was engaged at the Vienna Burgtheater in 1871, and appeared at the Deutsches Landestheater in Prague from 1873 to 1876. She then returned to Vienna but made numerous guest appearances elsewhere, and later she accepted full-time engagements at Kassel (1879–84) and Leipzig (1884–89). Even after she was given a new contract at the Burgtheater in 1889 and appointed a "Hofschauspielerin" in 1896, for two years she was a member of the Stuttgart court theater (1900–1902) and subsequently toured widely for several years. From 1906 until 1932 she performed regularly at the Burgtheater.

At the request of her fiancée **Josef Lewinsky** (whom she was to marry in 1875), Brahms composed for her the five Ophelia songs (WoO posthum 22) in November 1873; the text was taken from **August Wilhelm von Schlegel**'s German translation of *Hamlet*. She sang the songs for the first time at the Deutsches Landestheater in Prague, during a performance of *Hamlet*, on 22 December 1873. (*ÖBL* 1957–, under "Lewinsky-Precheisen")

PROHASKA, KARL (b. Mödling, near Vienna, 25 April 1869; d. Vienna, 27 March 1927). Composer, conductor, pianist, and teacher. His teachers included **Eugen d'Albert**, **Eusebius Mandyczewski**, and **Heinrich von Herzogenberg**. He taught at the Strasbourg Conservatory (1894–95), worked as an assistant at the Bayreuth Festival, and from 1901 to 1905 held the post of conductor of the Warsaw Philharmonic Orchestra. Thereafter, he devoted himself to composition and to teaching (from 1908, at the conservatory of the Gesellschaft der Musikfreunde and later at the Fachhochschule für Musik und darstellende Kunst [Academy of Music and the Performing Arts] in Vienna).

It was Brahms who recommended Prohaska to Herzogenberg (then living in Berlin) as a prospective pupil in 1890. He declared that he could do so unreservedly, even though he did not then know Prohaska at all well. By the mid-1890s Prohaska, with his friend **Felix von Kraus**, had joined the circle of closer acquaintances who accompanied Brahms on his Sunday walks and also met him elsewhere. In October 1895, the two young men attended the music festival at Meiningen—according to Kraus's daughter, at Brahms's invitation. On his return to Vienna, Brahms told **Richard Heuberger** how much he liked them both: they were intelligent and cultured young men, and good musicians (Heuberger 1976, 86).

Prohaska's compositions include songs and choral works, chamber and orchestral music, and works for the piano and organ. (Heuberger 1976; *ÖBL* 1957–)

– R –

RAFF, (JOSEPH) JOACHIM (b. Lachen, near Zurich, 27 May 1822; d. Frankfurt am Main, 24 June 1882). Composer and teacher. The son of a German father and a Swiss mother, he grew up in Switzerland. In 1845 he met **Liszt**, who took him under his wing. For the rest of his life Raff lived in Germany.

Brahms made his acquaintance in 1853 at Weimar, where Raff then belonged to Liszt's intimate circle. Over the next 30 years they would meet a number of times, but little is known about their contacts, apart from a few anecdotes. They would almost certainly have met in February 1863, when Raff, by then married to actress Doris Genast and living at Wiesbaden, went to Vienna to attend the final rehearsals and the performance (under **Joseph Hellmesberger**) of his programmatic symphony "An das Vaterland" [To the Fatherland], which had won first prize in a competition organized by the Gesellschaft der Musikfreunde; Brahms was reportedly present at one of the rehearsals and may well have attended the subsequent concert. Furthermore, they are known to have met in February 1876 at Wiesbaden, where Raff, dismayed at the unenthusiastic reception accorded to Brahms's performance of his First Piano Concerto, was seen to applaud so vigorously that the rest of the audience finally joined in; the next day Brahms humorously invited Raff to accompany him on his concert tour as his "claqueur." Brahms told **Sir George Henschel**, whom he took to see Raff: "I am really fond of the man, but can't help being amused at his good-natured loquacity" (G. Henschel 1978, 25). Brahms must also have met Raff more than once later at Frankfurt, where Raff served as the first director of the Hoch Conservatory from 1878 until his death (and where **Clara Schumann** also took up residence in 1879 on her appointment to the faculty). In her biography of her father, Raff's daughter Helene records his final meeting with Brahms, for which, however, she gives no precise date; it probably took place during Brahms's brief stay in Frankfurt in February 1882. As Brahms was leaving, Raff said to him, "If I should not see you again, Brahms—may God protect you" (Raff 1925, 248).

Raff was a startlingly prolific composer (as far back as 1846 Liszt had warned him, unavailingly, against the artistic and commercial risk of overproduction). His enormous output covered a wide range of genres, which included six operas (of which only two, *König Alfred* and *Dame Kobold* were produced), numerous works for solo voice or chorus, a dozen symphonies, much chamber music, and a mass of compositions for piano. "You will see that [Raff] is an extraordinary fellow," Brahms, who was rather amused by his productiveness, told Henschel (1978) at Wiesbaden in 1876. "He is not happy unless he composes a certain number of hours every day, and with all that he copies even the parts of his symphonies himself." When, during Raff's temporary absence from the room, his wife said how glad she was that he now went for a two-hours' walk each day, which kept him from composing for at least that much time, Brahms, Henschel noted in his diary, "looking as innocent as a new-born babe," promptly remarked, "Ah, that's good, that's very good" (25).

Raff's compositions were admired by many contemporary musicians, and by none more than **Hans von Bülow**, who revered both the man and the composer. To his fiancée Marie Schanzer he wrote on 28 June 1882, following Raff's death: "The great artist, the noble man—for once, how rare, indeed unique it is, the two were indivisible—served as my ideal" (Raff 1925, 197–98). However, his compositions did not appeal to everyone—certainly not to Clara Schumann, who thought them too tainted by Lisztian influences, and very little by Brahms. Writing to **Anna de Dobjansky**, Bülow observed that Raff's music was of the kind that only the composer's pupils, who had no choice but to listen to them, were likely to admire; and he added: "I am sorry for you that you have to be subjected to this experience" (Slonimsky 1954, 4). (M. von Bülow 1895–1908, vol. 6; G. Henschel 1978; Huschke 1939; Raff 1925; Slonimsky 1954)

REGER, (JOHANN BAPTIST JOSEPH) MAX(IMILIAN) (b. Brand, Bavaria, 19 March 1873; d. Leipzig, 11 May 1916). Composer and pianist. As a composer, he was profoundly marked by the influence of Brahms's music, for which he felt great admiration. In a letter to Hugo Riemann on 17 August 1895, he described himself as a musician "who has at all times served only his masters **Bach**, **Beethoven**, and Brahms, with the most unwavering and heart-felt enthusiasm" (Gurlitt 1937, 81). An interesting study of the main stylistic and technical correspondences between the compositions of Brahms and Reger will be found in Helmut Wirth's (1974) article "Johannes Brahms and Max Reger."

The two men never met, but they exchanged some letters. In the summer of 1896, Reger sent Brahms his organ suite op. 16 and at the same time asked permission to dedicate a future symphony to him, which Brahms granted in a cordial note. In a later letter, Brahms expressed the hope that he might have an opportunity to discuss Reger's work with him in person. He also sent a signed photograph of himself and suggested that Reger respond to his gesture in kind.

Brahms died before Reger had an opportunity to dedicate any work to him, but he was to mark the first anniversary of Brahms's death by citing the theme of the slow movement from the F Major Symphony in the fifth of his own *Fantasiestücke* (op. 26); he placed the inscription "Den Manen Johs. Brahms" [In memory of Johannes Brahms] over his Rhapsody in E Minor (op. 24/6), also composed in 1898. In 1914–15 he orchestrated the following six songs by Brahms: "Auf dem Kirchhofe" (op. 105/4), "Feldeinsamkeit" (op. 86/2), "Immer leiser wird mein Schlummer" (op. 105/20), "In Waldeinsamkeit" (op. 85/6), "Sapphische Ode" (op. 94/4), and "Wir wandelten, wir zwei zusammen" (op. 96/20). He also made piano reductions of the slow movements of Brahms's symphonies. All these arrangements were published by the firm N. Simrock (*see* SIMROCK, FRIEDRICH [FRITZ]). (Gurlitt 1937; Hase-Koehler 1928; Huschke 1939; Möller 1990; Reger 1928; Stockmann 1984; H. Wirth 1974)

REHBERG, WILLY (b. Morges, 2 September 1863; d. Mannheim, 21 April 1937). Pianist, teacher, and composer. He studied at the Zurich conservatory, and then at the Leipzig conservatory under **Carl Reinecke**. After teaching at the latter establishment (1884–90), he joined the faculty of the conservatory in Geneva in 1900 and of the Hoch Conservatory at Frankfurt am Main in 1907. In 1917 he became codirector of the Mannheim conservatory, subsequently director of the one at Basle (1921–26), and finally, director of the Mannheim conservatory (1927–33). He was also active as a conductor and, especially, as a pianist; in that capacity, he took part in the earliest performances in Germany of Brahms's opp. 99–101 (*see* JOACHIM, AMALIE) and later became a highly regarded interpreter of Brahms's music.

Rehberg made Brahms's personal acquaintance at Leipzig in January 1888, when his father-in-law **Ernst Wilhelm Fritzsch**, the publisher of the *Musikalisches Wochenblatt*, arranged for him to fetch Brahms from his hotel and escort him to the house of **Adolph Brodsky**, where the Piano Trio op. 101 was due to be rehearsed. To his delight, Brahms, knowing that he was familiar with the work, invited Rehberg to turn the pages for him. From Rehberg's "Brahms-Erinnerungen," it appears that he met Brahms on several later occasions.

Rehberg's son Walter (1900–1957), who was, like his father, a successful pianist and teacher, published, with his wife Paula, a book on Brahms in 1947. (W. Rehberg 1933; Rehberg and Rehberg, 1947)

REIMERS, C. H. CHRISTIAN (b. Altona, 27 October 1823). Cellist. **Robert Schumann** knew him, or at any rate knew about him, by the autumn of 1850 at the latest, for on 29 September of that year he informed **Wilhelm von Wasielewski**, who was about to leave Leipzig to take up the post of Konzertmeister at Düsseldorf, that there was regrettably no vacancy for Reimers in that orchestra. Nevertheless, Reimers went to Düsseldorf in February 1851, though still without any prospects of a permanent engagement. He appears to have earned his living by giving piano lessons, and he also played cello in trio recitals with Wasielewski and **Julius Tausch** at Düsseldorf (and, on at least one occasion, with Wasielewski and **Carl Reinecke** at Bonn). Furthermore, he participated in private music making at the Schumanns'. Thus, on 23 March 1851, he played there in a run-through of Schumann's Cello Concerto (presumably in one using Schumann's piano reduction of the orchestral score), and together with **Clara Schumann** and Wasielewski, he took part in a rehearsal (on 27 October of the same year) and subsequently in a private performance (on 15 November) of Schumann's Third Piano Trio. When Wasielewski moved to Bonn in 1852, Reimers went there too, having been invited to play in the orchestra of the Beethovenverein. In 1855–56 he taught the cello at the Cologne conservatory. Nothing definite seems to be known about his later life. Wasielewski states in his memoirs that Reimers died in Australia, while, according to O. Klauwell (1900), he died in America, where he is said to have moved after spending some time at Liverpool. His brother Johann Hermann Otto Reimers (1825–98) was active as a piano teacher at Bonn.

Brahms made Reimers's acquaintance, at the same time as Wasielewski's, at the **Deichmanns**' at Mehlem, near Bonn, in the late summer of 1853. In a letter to **Joseph Joachim** on 10 September, he described them as "delightful gentlemen" (Brahms 1974/5, 6). The following year he visited Schumann at the Endenich clinic at least twice with Reimers (on one of those occasions Wasielewski accompanied them). He also made music with him. Thus, he wrote to Joachim on 1 April 1854 from Düsseldorf: "Reimers is here at present. No doubt we shall have to play my trio [op. 8] again for Frau Schumann" (Brahms 1974/5, 36). He met Reimers once more at the Lower Rhine music festival at Düsseldorf in 1856 and appears to have remained in contact with him for at least a few more years, assuming that Clara Schumann, as seems likely, was referring to the same person when, on 5 August 1859 in a letter to Brahms, who was then in Hamburg, she wrote (with reference to a piano quartet [perhaps op. 25] on which he had apparently been working), "I hear that you are playing it with Reimers" (Litzmann 1970, vol. 1, 271). (Brahms 1974/5; Klauwell 1900; Litzmann 1970; Wasielewski 1897)

REINECKE, CARL (HEINRICH CARSTEN) (b. Altona, 23 June 1824; d. Leipzig, 10 March 1910). Composer, teacher, pianist, and conductor. Taught to play violin and piano by his father Johann Peter Rudolf Reinecke (1795–1883), a musical autodidact who became a highly regarded music teacher, he made his debut as a pianist at Altona in 1836. He traveled and concertized widely in Europe, living at different times at Leipzig, where he met Mendelssohn, **Ferdinand von Hiller**, and **Robert Schumann**; at Copenhagen (1846–48), where he held the position of court pianist; again at Leipzig (1848–49), where he met **Liszt**, who praised his pianistic skills and liked to play duets with him; at Bremen (1849–50), where he gave music lessons in addition to appearing at concerts; in Paris (1851), where he made the acquaintance of many prominent composers, including **Hector Berlioz**, played at concerts and in salons, and gave piano lessons to Liszt's daughters Blandine and Cosima; at Cologne (1851–54), where he was invited by Hiller to teach piano and, later, composition and counterpoint at the conservatory; at Barmen (1854–59), where he was active as a teacher, conductor, and director of choral societies; at Breslau [Wrocław, Poland] (1859–60), where he was in charge of the Singakademie, conducted symphony concerts, and acted as Musikdirektor at the university; and, finally again in Leipzig, where he was conductor of the Gewandhaus Orchestra (1860–95) and also taught at the conservatory (1860–1902), the last five years as its "Studiendirektor." As a pianist, he was known especially for his performances of **Mozart**'s music. As well as undertaking these manifold activities, he composed copiously—especially for piano, but also much vocal music, and even works for the stage (notably the opera *König Manfred*)—and he also made countless piano arrangements, for two and four hands, of works by other composers. Brahms did not think highly of him as a composer: "Reinecke's talent is a very, very small one," he once remarked to **Richard Heuberger** (Heuberger 1976, 99).

Reinecke met the then-20-year-old Brahms at Cologne in September 1853 and was apparently dazzled by his performance of his E-flat Minor Scherzo (op. 4). Before Brahms traveled on to Düsseldorf to call on the Schumanns, Reinecke introduced him to Hiller. Nothing is known about Brahms's initial impression of Reinecke, but the appearance in the *Süddeutsche Musikzeitung* in May 1854 of a highly negative assessment of his recently published opp. 1–4, coupled with a personal attack accusing the young composer of having made use of Schumann's influential position in a shameful effort of self-promotion, resulted, if **Max Kalbeck** is correct, in Brahms holding a lifelong grudge against Reinecke in the mistaken belief that he had been involved in the hostile article (see Kalbeck 1976, vol. 1, 207, 290). According to Kalbeck, Brahms never made Reinecke aware of the resentment he continued to feel on that account.

Reinecke's strong attachment to the Viennese classical composers, as well as to Mendelssohn and Schumann, inevitably made him less sympathetic to more modern trends in music, but this certainly did not make him neglect Brahms's music altogether, and he did in fact make various attempts to introduce Leipzig audiences to several of his most important works.

Thus, he conducted the first performance anywhere of the complete Requiem on 18 February 1869 (followed by another one on 13 November 1873), and he gave the world premiere, together with **Emil Hegar**, of the Cello Sonata op. 38 on 14 January 1871; in 1873 he conducted the first Leipzig performances of the *Schicksalslied* and *Triumphlied*. Moreover, he invited Brahms on several occasions to Leipzig, for the first time in 1874, and thus provided him with opportunities to direct the first local performances of certain of his works, such as the First Symphony (18 January 1877), Second Symphony (10 January 1878), Violin Concerto (1 January 1879, also its world premiere), the *Tragic* and *Academic Festival Overtures* (13 January 1881), Third Symphony (7 February 1884), and Fourth Symphony (18 February 1886). In addition, Reinecke also conducted some other performances of these works, but his renditions generally did little to enhance Brahms's reputation, in part perhaps because Reinecke was not really attuned to contemporary music, but essentially because he was a competent rather than an inspiring conductor; furthermore, he was hampered by the very limited time allowed for orchestral rehearsals, a restriction that also explains, at least to some extent, Brahms's reluctance to respond promptly to certain invitations to conduct the Gewandhaus Orchestra. His long-simmering dissatisfaction with the conditions in which his music was generally performed at the Gewandhaus and its often unenthusiastic reception by the audience reportedly drove him to declare, during his stay in Leipzig in January 1888, that he would not appear at the Gewandhaus again until there had been a change in the musical direction. He did, in fact, return once more while Reinecke was still in charge: at a concert on 31 January 1895, he conducted the *Academic Festival Overture* and the two piano concertos, which were played by **Eugen d'Albert**. By then, Reinecke's tenure at the Gewandhaus was approaching its end, and the final concert of the season on 28 March 1895 also turned out to be his last as conductor of the orchestra. Under pressure from the more progressive members of the board he was forced to quit his post in July, to be replaced by **Arthur Nikisch**.

When Reinecke spent some time in Vienna in 1896, he met Brahms repeatedly: they dined together at the Roter Igel restaurant and at the house of their mutual friend **Ignaz Brüll**. Reinecke last saw Brahms when, during his next stay in Vienna, he called on him on 13 March 1897. In the article "Meine letzten Begegnungen mit Johannes Brahms" printed in the periodical *Dur und Moll* later that year, he recalled their meetings in 1896 and 1897, as well as the first one in Cologne in 1853. Subsequently, he included this article in his book of recollections of famous musicians he had known, published in 1900. (Brahms 1974/3; H. Ehrlich 1888,1893a; Forner 1981; Heuberger 1976; C. Reinecke 1897, 1900; Sietz 1964a)

REINHOLD, C. [pseudonym of Christian Reinhold Köstlin] (b. Tübingen, 29 January 1813; d. Tübingen, 14 September 1856). Lawyer, from 1839 professor of criminal law at Tübingen University; **Maria Regina Fellinger**'s father. Under his pseudonym he published plays, novellas, and poetry (in 1853, a volume entitled *Gedichte*). In 1855 Brahms set four of his poems in the songs "Nachtigall" (op. 97/1; see also M. McCorkle 1984, Anhang IIa/26), "Auf dem Schiffe" (op. 97/2), "Auf dem See" (op. 106/2), and "Ein Wanderer" (op. 106/5). (Naucke 1980)

REINICK, ROBERT (b. Danzig [Gdańsk, Poland], 22 February 1805; d. Dresden, 7 February 1852). Poet. Brahms set texts by Reinick in the songs "Liebestreu" (op. 3/1) and "Juchhe" (op. 6/4). (Berbig 1991)

REINTHALER, KARL (MARTIN) (b. Erfurt, 13 October 1822; d. Bremen, 13 February 1896). Conductor, organist, and composer. After completing his theology studies, he received instruction in music from Adolf Bernhard Marx in Berlin, and in singing from Giulio Bordogni in Paris. He taught at the Cologne conservatory (1853–57), and subsequently held the positions of cathedral organist and director of the Singakademie at Bremen (1858–87).

He met Brahms, probably for the first time, at the Lower Rhine Music Festival at Cologne in May 1856. Nothing is known about any further contacts between them until October 1867, when they began a correspondence concerning Brahms's Requiem, the manuscript of which Reinthaler had, without Brahms's knowledge, been given by their mutual friend **Albert Dietrich**. Reinthaler was greatly impressed by the Requiem ("I would consider myself fortunate if I had written this work," he assured Brahms in his letter of 5 October 1867 [Brahms 1974/3, 9]), and he at once proposed a performance at Bremen Cathedral for Good Friday of the following year. This performance, on 10 April 1868, was the first given anywhere of the six-movement Requiem. It was highly successful, much of the credit being due to Reinthaler's meticulous preparation. "The work had been splendidly rehearsed by Reinthaler," **Clara Schumann** noted in her diary (Litzmann 1902, vol. 3, 219). This was evidently also the view taken by Brahms, who conducted the final rehearsal and the actual performance himself, for the two men were henceforth on "Du" terms.

In his above-mentioned letter of 5 October 1867, Reinthaler, while declaring his profound admiration for the Requiem, expressed nonetheless some regret at the absence of one, in his opinion, essential feature in such a work, namely any reference to man's redemption through Christ's death and resurrection, and he suggested that Brahms might either make a suitable insertion in one of the existing movements or even compose a new movement for that purpose. However, Brahms made no immediate changes in the score, but the performance at Bremen Cathedral was enriched by several other items. After the third movement, **Joseph Joachim**, accompanied by the organ, played the Andante from **Bach**'s Violin Concerto in A Minor (BMV 1041) and Tartini's Andante in F Major; and following the Requiem, **Amalie Joachim** sang, accompanied by her husband on violin, the aria "Erbarme dich, mein Gott" from the *St. Matthew Passion*. The concert concluded with the chorus "Seht, das ist Gottes Lamm," the aria "Ich weiss, dass mein Erlöser lebt" (sung by Amalie Joachim), and the *Halleluja Chorus*, from **Handel**'s *Messiah*. A second performance of the Requiem was conducted by Reinthaler in Brahms's presence, on 27 April, though not at the cathedral. Subsequently, Brahms composed a further movement, which became the fifth.

The performance of 10 April 1868 led to a lifelong friendship with Reinthaler and established for Brahms a useful link with Bremen. He returned for a further performance of the Requiem on 7 April 1871, and on that occasion he also conducted the opening movement of his *Triumphlied*, in what was the first performance anywhere of any part of that work; in the summer of the same year, he met Reinthaler again when both were staying at Baden-Baden. On 11 April 1879 Brahms conducted his recently composed Second Symphony at Bremen.

In a letter of condolence to Reinthaler's daughter Henriette, written shortly after her father's death, Brahms spoke of the "many beautiful memories" he retained of his contacts with his "dear friends," her parents, and of the great affection with which he thought of them (Brahms 1974/3, 86; Karl Reinthaler's wife Charlotte had died the previous year). Reinthaler dedicated his composition *In der Wüste*, based on the 63rd Psalm, for soloists, chorus, and orchestra (op. 26) to Brahms. (Brahms 1974/3; Dietrich 1898; Litzmann 1902; Sietz 1962)

REMÉNYI, EDE [EDUARD] (b. Miskolc, 17 January 1828; d. San Francisco, 15 May 1898). Hungarian violinist. (The date of birth given here seems to be the correct one, rather than the year "1829" or the date "17 July 1830" found in certain documents or publications. "Reményi" was a "magyarized" form of the family's original German name "Hoffman" [the latter spelling is cited according to the baptismal register]. Eduard, who was of Jewish descent, was baptized at Eger on 14 May 1836, together with some of his siblings and his parents Johann Heinrich and Josepha Rosina [Rozalia] Hoffman.)

Eduard began his musical education at Eger and later studied with Joseph Böhm (1842–45) at the Vienna conservatory, where, for a time, he was a fellow pupil of **Joseph Joachim**. He made his concert debut at Pest in 1846, and subsequently performed in Paris in 1846 and London in 1848. During the Hungarian uprising (1848–49), he was attached to General Artúr Görgey's headquarters and often played for the general's staff, an activity that led to his being considered a dangerous agitator by the Austrians, presumably a reference to his fiery performance of Magyar music, which was to be a prominent feature of his concerts throughout his career. Following the surrender of the Hungarian army to the Russian forces at Vilagos on 13 August 1849, Reményi fled the country, like many of his compatriots who had taken part in the revolution, and in due course he arrived in Hamburg, bound for America.

In his Brahms biography, **Max Kalbeck** mentions three events in November 1849 at which Reményi performed during his stay in Hamburg, one of them, on 19 November, being his own concert at the Tonhalle at which he played Bernhard Molique's *Souvenir de la Hongrie*, two movements from a violin concerto by Vieuxtemps, and a medley of "Hungarian National Melodies." By the beginning of the following year, he was in New

York, where he gave his first concert on 19 January 1850 (for details, see Kelley and Upton 1906, 243; Kalbeck [1976] is evidently mistaken in stating that he remained in Hamburg for at least another year before sailing for America). He did not stay in America more than six months (Kelley and Upton 1906, 11); in January and February 1851, according to Kalbeck, he performed at concerts in Hamburg. A report prepared by the Göttingen police in 1853 (and published in the *Göttinger Zeitung* by Joachim's son Johannes on 25 March 1911) states that Reményi traveled to America together with his brother at the end of 1849; spent at least a part of the summer of 1852 in Paris, where on 25 September he obtained a passport from the American Embassy; thereafter stayed in Brussels until November; and then went to Hamburg.

In her *Johannes Brahms: Life and Letters*, S. Avins (1997) writes that Brahms made Reményi's acquaintance while the latter was "on his way to America"—that is, in 1849—and that the meeting took place one evening at the house of a wealthy Hamburg businessman, where Reményi was performing and Brahms was engaged to play piano; and furthermore, that Reményi was so impressed by the unknown youth that they subsequently frequently played together on a casual basis until the Hungarian was forced to flee to America to escape arrest (Avins 1997, 10). On the other hand, Reményi, in an interview published in the *New York Herald* on 18 January 1879 (Reményi 1879, reprinted in Kelley and Upton 1906, 79–95), ascribed his first meeting with Brahms to January 1853, following his own return to Hamburg the previous month. According to his detailed, though quite likely considerably embroidered, account of the occasion, Brahms had been recommended to him by the owner of a music shop as a possible replacement for his usual accompanist, who had suddenly fallen ill on a day when they were due to perform at the house of "one of the great merchant princes of Hamburg, a Mr. Helmrich." In due course, Brahms presented himself at Reményi's hotel to rehearse for the concert, and afterward played some of his own compositions. By that time, Reményi recalled, he had become convinced that he was dealing with a "genius." In his intense enthusiasm ("I was electrified and sat in mute amazement") he forgot all about his evening engagement: "We did not separate until four o'clock in the morning." As a result of his failure to play for Helmrich's guests, he lost many similar opportunities, but "I clung to my Johannes Brahms through thick and thin." Reményi also claims in the interview that he maintained his belief in Brahms's genius against the skepticism expressed by Brahms's own father (*see* BRAHMS, JOHANN JAKOB) and by his teacher **Eduard Marxsen**, and to have "determined to take him away from Hamburg," where his exceptional gifts would never be recognized.

Brahms did in fact leave Hamburg with Reményi on 19 April 1853, on a journey that was to change his life. Whether Reményi deserves all the credit he later attributed to himself in that respect is open to question, but he undoubtedly merited Brahms's gratitude, if only for introducing him to Joseph Joachim in Hanover in late April. At the end of their short concert tour, they arrived toward the middle of June at Weimar, where Reményi may or may not have witnessed Brahms falling asleep while **Liszt** played his Piano Sonata (*see* LISZT, FRANZ [FERENC] and MASON, WILLIAM); and it was also at Weimar that he and Brahms parted company. In his 1879 interview, Reményi claimed to have persuaded Brahms that after the disagreeable incident with Liszt he would do well, in the interests of his future career, to find a more congenial place than Weimar, and that he had then furnished him with a letter to Joachim, in which he asked Joachim to send Brahms to **Robert Schumann**: "The visit to Schumann was most deliberately arranged by myself, and my letter to Joachim and the letter from Joachim to Schumann were simply stepping-stones in the career of Johannes Brahms."

This vainglorious account is contradicted by Brahms's own letter from Weimar to Joachim at the end of June 1853, which shows clearly that the separation occurred against Brahms's own wishes and was due to Reményi's disagreeable behavior ("it is his desire, my comportment could not have given him the slightest cause, even though I have had to suffer more every day under his ill-humour" [Brahms 1974/5, 3]). While their incompatibility of temperament and of artistic ideals may well have played a role in the break, Reményi's decision to distance himself from Brahms at that juncture was probably a largely opportunistic move, resulting from his eagerness to ingratiate himself with Liszt and from his awareness that Brahms's manifest reluctance to join in the prevalent hero worship was not likely to make him popular at Weimar. Reményi wished to ally himself with the music Liszt championed, to study with him and to gain his support. In fact, Liszt took a strong liking to his young compatriot and formed a very favorable opinion of his talent; he was particularly taken with Reményi's performance of what both regarded, not always correctly, as typical Gypsy music. In his book *Des bohémiens et de leur musique en Hongrie* (1859), Liszt went out of his way to extol Reményi as an exponent of the authentic tradition, true form, and esoteric meaning of that music. He and Reményi met repeatedly in later years. In Rome, in the spring of 1864, Reményi was in almost daily contact with Liszt over a period of several weeks; Liszt, who attended all his concerts, was moreover greatly impressed with the progress Reményi had made, and he informed his friend Agnes Street that Reményi was now an artist of the very first rank. It is surely symptomatic of the profound differences between the musical aesthetics of Liszt and Reményi, on the one hand, and Brahms on the other, that when Brahms heard Reményi at Karlsruhe just a few weeks later (in late August), he should, in a letter to Joachim, have dismissed his playing as "abominable," have called his performances of the *Fantasy on "Les Hugenots"* and the Rakoczy March "unbelievably brazen and ludicrous" (Brahms 1974/6, 33).

Reményi told his American interviewer in 1879 that he met Brahms just twice more after their separation at Weimar, and that their conversation on those occasions had been of a general character, no reference being made by either of them to the past (Reményi 1879). One such meeting is known to have taken place at Leipzig in December 1853; the second presumably occurred at Karlsruhe in August 1864, as mentioned above. The final part of the 1879 interview was devoted to remarks about the first 10 *Hungarian Dances* (WoO 1), which had appeared in Brahms's arrangement in 1869 and had since become immensely popular. While acknowledging that Brahms had not represented himself as the composer but only as a transcriber of the various melodies in the original edition, Remény complained that the distinction had not always been made so clear in later editions. He explained that during their concert tour in 1853 he had himself composed a number of "Hungarian" melodies, which he had shown to Brahms, sometimes without indicating that they were of his own invention but instead, "for the purpose of making an innocent deception," calling them "national airs." Now he claimed that he was in fact the composer of one of the 10 *Hungarian Dances*, as well as part of another one. Like many of Reményi's statements in that interview, these remarks are essentially self-serving.

Finally, it should be stressed that even though Reményi was regarded as something of a charlatan by certain contemporary musicians (Andreas Moser [1923], in his *Geschichte des Violinspiels*, asserts that "one could not, with the best will in the world, take him seriously" [527]), he enjoyed a highly successful career as a much admired violin virtuoso, excelling, as G. P. Upton observed in a biographical sketch, in "works which, unlike the classics, did not restrain him within limits, and which gave free rein to his fancies" (Kelley and Upton 1906, 24); in England he was even named violinist to Queen Victoria. Granted amnesty in 1860, he lived for a time in Hungary before setting out once more on his travels, which were to take him all over the world, leading Sir George Grove to label him "the wandering musician *par excellence*." Grove added that "at intervals, when the whim takes him, he will disappear from public view altogether"; but Grove went on to observe that "although somewhat of the nature of a comet, he is undoubtedly a star of the first magnitude in his own sphere" (Kelley and Upton 1906, 22).

Shortly before his death, Reményi began writing an account of his personal relations with Brahms for the Chicago periodical *Music*, but only an introductory fragment was ever published there (in November 1898, a few months after his death). It offered a generous tribute, though its subject might not have appreciated the implications of Reményi's statement that "since the death of Liszt, Brahms was undoubtedly the greatest composer left" (Reményi 1898, 43). (Avins 1997; Brahms 1974/5–6; Kelley and Upton 1906; A. Moser 1923; Stephenson 1962a; Reményi 1879, 1898; A. Walker 1987–96)

REUSS-KÖSTRITZ, HEINRICH XXIV, PRINCE (b. Trebschen, Saxony, 8 December 1855; d. Ernstbrunn, 2 October 1910). A son of Prince Heinrich IV (1821–94), he mostly resided at Ernstbrunn Castle, near Korneuburg, northwest of Vienna. He studied composition with his father and later with Wilhelm Rust and **Heinrich von Herzogenberg** in Leipzig, and was well acquainted with Brahms, who, while never giving him any formal instruction, agreed to examine and discuss some of his compositions. In his biography of Brahms, **Max Kalbeck** (1976) quotes at length from a statement he received from the prince in February 1900, in which he comments on Brahms's pedagogical ability and recalls Brahms's views on certain musical matters, as well as some remarks he made regarding his own compositional process (vol. 4, 88–89, n. 1). In a letter to Wilhelm Altmann in 1903, Reuss recalled that "in his extremely concise and clear manner" (Altmann 1903, 5, n. 3) Brahms often taught him more in 10 minutes than Herzogenberg did in several months.

It was apparently Reuss who convinced a very reluctant Brahms that he had to seek an audience with Emperor Franz Joseph in order to thank him in person for conferring on him the Commander's Cross of the Order of Leopold in 1889.

RICHTER, HANS (b. Raab [Györ], 4 April 1843; d. Bayreuth, 5 December 1916). Conductor. During the last quarter of the 19th century he was a central figure in the musical life of Vienna: principal Kapellmeister at the court opera (1875–1900), conductor of the philharmonic concerts (1875–98, except for the 1882–83 season); and conductor of the concerts of the Gesellschaft der Musikfreunde (1884–90).

Richter was a fervent Wagnerian (he conducted the first full *Ring* cycle at Bayreuth in 1876), as well as a stout champion of the music of **Anton Bruckner** (of whose fourth and eighth symphonies he conducted the premieres). But he also directed many performances of Brahms's orchestral and choral works, and he was, in fact, responsible for the world premieres, at philharmonic concerts in Vienna, of the Second Symphony (30 December 1877), the *Tragic Overture* (26 December 1880), and the Third Symphony (2 December 1883). **Eduard Hanslick**, writing about the very successful premiere of the Second Symphony in the *Neue freie Presse* on 3 January 1878, stated that Richter had conducted it at the composer's express wish. Furthermore, Richter conducted the first Viennese performance of the Fourth Symphony, on 17 January 1886 (for its world premiere, *see* GEORG II, DUKE OF SACHSEN-MEININGEN). His admiration for Brahms's music is well illustrated by the Philharmonic Orchestra's 1881–82 season, which offered the first Viennese performance of the Second Piano Concerto (with Brahms as soloist), as well as performances of the Violin Concerto (with **Hugo Heermann**), and the First Symphony. The performance of the latter work on 26 March 1882 was entirely due to Richter, who overrode objections voiced by more than half the orchestra and shared by certain members of the program committee. As it turned out, the concert, which also included **Beethoven**'s overture *Die Weihe des Hauses* and **Edvard Grieg**'s Piano Concerto, was by far the most poorly attended of the season, and part of the audience demonstratively walked out at the beginning of the symphony.

In addition, Richter was largely responsible for the acceptance and growing popularity of Brahms's music in England, which he regularly visited from 1877 onward. He conducted numerous concerts in London, was music director of the triennial Birmingham Festival (1885–1909), and conductor of the Hallé Orchestra (1897–1911). "The fact that [Brahms's symphonies] are listened to and loved by the few, and tolerated at all by the many is due, like so much else of what is good in English musical taste, very largely to the efforts of Hans Richter," William Strutt wrote in his *Reminiscences of a Musical Amateur* in 1915 (Strutt 1915, 109). According to R. Pascall, Richter directed the first English performances of *Gesang der Parzen* (5 May 1885), of the Third Symphony (12 May 1884), and of the Fourth Symphony (10 May 1886).

The very last concert Brahms attended was the philharmonic concert conducted by Richter in Vienna on 7 March 1897, which featured his Fourth Symphony. Encouraged by Richter, the enthusiastic audience obliged Brahms, after each movement, to come to the front of the box where he was seated discreetly out of sight, in order to receive the applause and cheers. At a concert that took place on the day following Brahms's death, Richter directed a performance of **Mozart**'s *Masonic Funeral Music* in his memory. (At a memorial concert for Queen Victoria in England in January 1901, he was to perform **Beethoven**'s *Missa solemnis* and two movements from Brahms's Requiem.)

According to Richter's biographer Christopher Fifield (1993), he conducted altogether, in his long career, 28 performances of Brahms's First Symphony, 18 of the Second, 19 of the Third, and 20 of the Fourth; he also directed seven performances of his Requiem. (Antonicek 1988; Fifield 1993; Kennedy 1960; Pascall 2001; Strutt 1915)

RIEDEL, CARL (b. Cronenberg, near Elberfeld, 6 October 1827; d. Leipzig, 3 June 1888). Chorus master and composer. Originally trained as a dyer, he later (1849–52) attended the Leipzig conservatory, where his teachers included C. F. Becker, **Karl Franz Brendel**, **Moritz Hauptmann**, Ignaz Moscheles, and **Julius Rietz**. Subsequently, he established a certain reputation in Leipzig as a piano teacher, but his main interest lay from the outset in choral music. What started out as a simple quartet of mixed voices in 1854, under the name Riedel-Whistling Verein (Frau Whistling was the wife of a local dealer in music), became the Riedel'sche Verein in 1855. That autumn its membership had already grown to 36, and it was to rise to 46 by the summer of 1856, to 80 by May 1857, and to 150 by April 1859; from 1863 until Riedel's death, it comprised some 250 men and women. The choir gave its first concert on 25 November 1855, and it soon became an important part of the musical life of Leipzig. While the Riedel'sche Verein paid particular attention to the church music of the 16th, 17th, and 18th centuries, it did not entirely neglect more modern sacred works. Thus, it offered, during the 33 years between its establishment and its founder's death, no fewer than 17 performances of **Beethoven**'s *Missa solemnis*, and it also presented compositions by, among others, **Hector Berlioz**, Brahms, **Liszt**, and Mendelssohn. After Riedel's death, his immediate successor as conductor of the choir (which then took the name Riedel Verein) was **Hermann Kretzschmar**, who directed it from 1888 until 1897.

On 14 March 1873, at the Thomas Kirche, the Riedel'sche Verein performed Brahms's Requiem. The performance made a far greater impact than the mediocre first public performance of the complete work, which had been given by the Gewandhaus choir and orchestra under **Carl Reinecke** on 18 February 1869, and it considerably enhanced Brahms's reputation in Leipzig as a serious composer. The Verein performed it again on 21 November of that year, eight days after Reinecke had directed it once more at the Gewandhaus. According to Johannes Forner, the Riedel Verein gave, altogether, seven performances of the Requiem under Riedel's and Kretschmar's direction at the Thomas Kirche in Brahms's lifetime. (Forner 1987; Göhler 1904)

RIETER-BIEDERMANN, JAKOB MELCHIOR (b. Winterthur, 14 May 1811; d. Winterthur, 25 January 1876). Music publisher. Like his father Heinrich, of whose cotton-spinning mill he became a part owner, he was keenly interested in music, and in 1835 he joined Winterthur's Musikkollegium, in which he was active as timpanist and librarian; he also played violin and viola. (His father, a clarinettist, was likewise a member of the Musikkollegium, while his mother was a competent pianist.) In 1849 Rieter-Biedermann opened a music shop, and subsequently he founded a publishing firm, which gradually gained an international reputation and by the time he died had issued some 900 works, including compositions by **Theodor Kirchner** (who was organist at Winterthur from 1843 to 1862), **Heinrich von Herzogenberg** (who was recommended to him by Brahms), **Hector Berlioz** (whom he had met while studying engineering in Paris in 1833), **Robert Schumann** (most of the posthumously published opp. 136–48), and Brahms. In 1853 he acquired a splendid property at Winterthur known as the Schanzengarten, where Brahms was a guest on several occasions. In 1862 Rieter-Biedermann opened a branch at Leipzig, which was eventually managed by his son-in-law Edmund Astor (1845–1918) and became the headquarters of the firm after the Winterthur office closed in 1884 following the death of Rieter-Biedermann's son Karl the previous year. Edmund Astor was eventually succeeded as director of the firm by his son Robert, who died in 1917. The following year the business was acquired by C. F. Peters (*see* ABRAHAM, MAX). Among Rieter-Biedermann's major achievements was the foundation of the *Allgemeine musikalische Zeitung*, which appeared in Leipzig from 1866 to 1882.

Max Kalbeck credits Kirchner with having aroused Rieter-Biedermann's interest in Brahms; more recently, Kurt Hofmann has speculated (in Brahms Exhibition 1997b) that it was probably **Clara Schumann** and **Carl Grädener** who established the contact between them. One might add that it was most likely Schumann's famous eulogy of Brahms in 1853 that first caused Rieter-Biedermann, a very great admirer of Schumann, to take an interest in the young composer. As for the initial contact, it is apparent from Brahms's first letter to Rieter-Biedermann, at the beginning of September 1856, that Rieter-Biedermann had written to him some time before, inviting him to send manuscripts to Winterthur. In his letter, Brahms, who was then staying with his sister Elise (*see* BRAHMS [LATER: GRUND], ELISABETH [ELISE] WILHELMINE) and Clara Schumann and two of her sons at Gersau on Lake Lucerne, mentioned that he was hoping to visit Winterthur on his return journey to Germany in order to make Rieter-Biedermann's acquaintance. That this may not have happened is suggested by a letter dated 28 February 1858, in which Brahms asked Clara, who was then on a concert tour of Switzerland, to give his regards to Rieter and Kirchner "unbekannterweise"—the adverb, which signifies that the writer has never met the person in question, may well be meant to apply to both names (Litzmann 1970, vol. 1, 220).

Brahms was slow to respond to Rieter-Biedermann's request for original compositions, but in November 1858 Rieter-Biedermann published, without mention of his name, a set of nursery songs (*Volks-Kinderlieder*, WoO 31) for which he had written the accompaniment. Their collaboration did not start in earnest until Brahms, in August 1860, offered Rieter-Biedermann the First Piano Concerto and certain other works that **Breitkopf & Härtel** had just turned down. Rieter-Biedermann immediately accepted them and thereby laid the basis for an association that lasted until 1873 and comprehended, among other items, the *Variations* on themes by Schumann and Paganini, the *Magelone-Lieder*, and, most notably, the Requiem. (The complete list of opus numbers published by Rieter-Biedermann is as follows: 12–15, 22–23, 32–35, 37, 39, 41, 43–45, and 57–59; without opus numbers: WoO 31 and 34.) Furthermore, Rieter-Biedermann issued Brahms's piano reduction of **Franz Schubert**'s Mass D 950 (M. McCorkle 1984, Anhang Ia/18), and his editions of works by **C. P. E. Bach** (Anhang VI/2), **W. Fr. Bach** (Anhang VI/3), Schubert (Anhang VI/12), and Schumann (Anhang VI/15–16).

Brahms is known to have visited Rieter-Biedermann repeatedly; he even stayed at the Schanzengarten for several weeks in 1866. They also met elsewhere—in Zurich, Baden-Baden, Vienna (November 1864), and Leipzig; in 1868 Rieter-Biedermann traveled to Bremen to attend the first performance of the Requiem. The business association soon developed into a friendship that extended to Rieter-Biedermann's wife Louise (1812–1902) and also to their youngest daughter Ida (1847–1931), a proficient amateur pianist who was taught by **Hermann Goetz**; she joined her father and Brahms on some walking trips in Switzerland. She was reportedly attracted to Brahms, and Clara Schumann suggested to him (in a letter on 4 September 1868) that she might make a very suitable wife for him: "I am told that she has become really lovely and she is, moreover, well off, an important asset for a composer" (Litzmann 1970, vol. 1, 594), but Brahms was apparently not interested in such an alliance, and in 1872 Ida married Edmund Astor.

After Rieter-Biedermann's death, Brahms wrote in his letter of condolence to the widow that he mourned "the loss of an exceptionally good and faithful friend" (Brahms 1974/14, 257). He kept in sporadic contact with her and in 1888, while staying at Thun, arranged to visit her at Bönigen, near Interlaken. Most of his letters to Rieter-Biedermann, his son Karl, and Edmund Astor were published by Wilhelm Altmann in 1920; a few further letters and postcards have since been published by Rudolf Hunziker and Peter Sulzer. (Brahms 1974/14; Hunziker 1927; Litzmann 1970; Sulzer 1973, 1974, 1985)

RIETZ, (AUGUST WILHELM) JULIUS (b. Berlin, 28 December 1812; d. Dresden, 12 September 1877). Cellist, composer, conductor, and editor. Son of Johann Friedrich Rietz (1767–1828), a violinist in the court Kapelle; brother of violinist and conductor Eduard Rietz (1802–32). He studied cello with Friedrich Schmidt, Moritz Ganz, and Bernhard Heinrich Romberg, and theory with Carl Friedrich Zelter. After playing in the orchestra of the Königsstädtisches Theater in Berlin (1828–34), he was engaged as assistant to Mendelssohn at Düsseldorf, and within a short time, upon Mendelssohn's departure in 1835, he became that city's music director. In 1847 he was appointed Kapellmeister at the Leipzig theater and the following year he succeeded **Niels Gade** as conductor of the Gewandhaus Orchestra, a position he held until 1852 and 1854–60. He also taught composition at the conservatory (1848–54) and directed the Singakademie. Finally, in 1860, he moved to Dresden to take up the post of Kapellmeister there, in succession to Carl Gottlieb Reissiger. He retired on pension in June 1877 and died soon afterward. His standing as a composer (he wrote a number of orchestral works, as well as chamber and sacred music) was outshone by the reputation he enjoyed as an editor, partly on account of his contributions to the collected editions of **Mozart** and **Beethoven**, but above all for the 41-volume edition of Mendelssohn's works for which he was solely responsible.

Until his final years, when his prestige declined, Rietz was regarded as a fine and conscientious conductor, though his dislike of the "Music of the Future" made him the target of attacks by adherents of the "New German School." **Robert Schumann** had a high opinion of him, both as a musician and a man; and **Clara Schumann** was once so thrilled with his interpretation of her husband's Second Symphony that she presented the autograph score to him. As for Brahms, he had a famous professional association with Rietz on the occasion of the performance of his First Piano Concerto at Leipzig on 27 January 1859, which Rietz conducted. Brahms's biographers usually acknowledge that the concerto's failure that day was by no means surprising, given current musical taste and practice. As **Max Kalbeck** (1976) concedes, the work made "more intense demands on the listener's attention than the average symphony" (vol. 1, 345). Even among his own circle of acquaintances, Brahms reported, only **Ferdinand David** had praised the concerto; the others had said nothing at all, and **Heinrich von Sahr** and Rietz, when questioned by him, had even admitted that they did not like it (Litzmann 1970, vol. 1, 242). As for the members of the orchestra, they had already made their feelings clear at the rehearsals, at the second and final of which "not a muscle moved in the musicians' faces" (Brahms 1974/5, 233). Yet Brahms appears to have borne the setback with equanimity, and in his letters to Clara Schumann and **Joseph Joachim** he expressed no criticism of either the players or their conductor; indeed, he appears to have been well satisfied with the quality of the performance: "The orchestra," he wrote, "played excellently" (Brahms 1974/5, 233). Nevertheless, at least one influential 19th-century critic, **Hermann Kretzschmar**, writing in the *Musikalisches Wochenblatt* in 1874, laid the blame for the hostile reception squarely on Rietz's shoulders. (However, he had not himself attended the concert; in any case, he was only 11 years old at the time.)

In a letter to Clara Schumann written a few days after the concert, **Livia Frege** reported that Conrad Schleinitz (a lawyer and a friend of Mendelssohn, who was for many years chairman of the board of management of the Leipzig conservatory) and Ignaz Moscheles had voiced unfavorable opinions about the concerto, and that Rietz had expressed his disapproval in particularly strong terms ("I have spoken to Schleinitz and Moscheles for several hours about Brahms's concerto—still, I believe that they are not the most unjust—but Rietz!!!" [Litzmann 1902, vol. 3, 53). In fact, Rietz, after studying the concerto, seems to have been genuinely puzzled by the high reputation that Brahms enjoyed in certain circles. He must have expressed his puzzlement to his friend **Pauline Viardot**, which would account for the following passage in one of her letters to him shortly after the concert: "Yes, I have often heard Clara Schumann speak of Brahms with the most profound conviction (on her part) of his *genius*. She has played me several compositions of his which neither pleased nor interested me" (Viardot 1915–16, *Musical Quarterly* 1 [1915]: 538; later Viardot's opinion of Brahms's music improved—*see* VIARDOT, [MICHELLE FERDINANDE] PAULINE.)

In 1860, the year following that disastrous concert, Brahms and Joachim hoped to obtain Rietz's signature to the manifesto they proposed to launch against the "New German School." On 15 May Joachim, who had perhaps traveled to Dresden to speak to Rietz in person, reported to Brahms that Rietz, though doubtful of the effectiveness of such a proclamation, was in principle willing to add his name to it but would prefer to wait until a particularly suitable occasion presented itself. However, although Joachim does not seem to have known it, the matter had by then become largely academic, for the document had already been leaked to the Berlin journal *Echo* and published by it with just the signatures of Brahms, Joachim, **Julius Otto Grimm**, and **Bernhard Scholz**.

During his three-year tenure of the post of artistic director of the Gesellschaft der Musikfreunde, Brahms conducted only one of Rietz's compositions, the *Arioso* for violin and orchestra (op. 48a), on 19 April 1874. (Brahms 1974/5; Forner 1981; Litzmann 1902, 1970; Sietz 1964b; Viardot 1915–16)

RIGGENBACH-STEHLIN [STÄH(E)LIN], FRIEDRICH (b. Basle, 11 September 1821; d. Schloss Bechburg, near Oesingen, Canton Solothurn, 3 March 1904). Banker; amateur singer, and music patron. In 1859, upon the death of his father Johannes Riggenbach, he assumed responsibility for the bank founded by the latter, and he directed its business until his retirement in 1893. A man of wide interests, he was a keen botanist and entomologist, as well as having an abiding love for music. While gaining experience in banking in Paris in 1842–44, he was a member of the local Swiss men's choir, which was conducted by **Julius Stern**, later founder of the Sternscher Gesangverein in Berlin and cofounder of the Berlin conservatory. He took part in the choir's performance of Mendelssohn's music for Sophocles' *Antigone* at the Odéon Theatre in 1844, and later in London in a performance of *Paulus* directed by Mendelssohn himself. His predilection for choral singing led him to form a mixed choir, which met at his house in Basle; conducted by **August Walter**, it gave performances before an invited audience, in which the host, a fine tenor, and his wife participated. Riggenbach's wife Margaretha, whom he married in 1849, was a widely admired contralto; she was a soloist in the first complete Swiss performance of **Beethoven**'s Ninth Symphony, which was conducted by Ernst Reiter at Basle in 1853, as well as in the first performance of **Bach**'s *St. John Passion* in 1861. Riggenbach also occupied a prominent position in several music societies, including the Konzertgesellschaft, of which he was president, and the Allgemeine Musikgesellschaft (founded in 1876), and he furthermore took a leading role in the project that led to the construction of the Basle Musikhalle.

Many visiting artists enjoyed the Riggenbachs' generous hospitality. Brahms stayed with them more than once, and he also took an active part in the private music making at their house. Brahms clearly felt comfortable there, for on one occasion, arriving unannounced with **Joseph Joachim** and at an inopportune moment for his hosts, he is reported to have assured them that he would rather live in their house, if need be on bread and water, than in any hotel. Another member of Brahms's circle who stayed with the Riggenbachs more than once was **Clara Schumann**. (Probst 1905)

RÖNTGEN, JULIUS (b. Leipzig, 9 May 1855; d. Bilthoven, near Utrecht, 13 September 1932). Composer, pianist, conductor, and teacher. He was born into a musical family: his father Engelbert Röntgen (1829–97), a violinist and a pupil of **Ferdinand David**, was a member of the Gewandhaus Orchestra from 1853 and its Konzertmeister for many years; his mother Pauline (1831–88) was a daughter of violinist Moritz Gotthold Klengel (1793–1870), who played in the Gewandhaus Orchestra for more than 50 years, and a sister of composer and singing teacher **Julius Klengel** (1818–79). (*See also* KLENGEL, JULIUS and KLENGEL, PAUL.) Wilhelm Conrad Röntgen (1845–93), the discoverer of X-rays, was a distant cousin.

Julius Röntgen was given his early music lessons by his grandfather Moritz Klengel and subsequently studied piano with Louis Plaidy and **Carl Reinecke**. Later, between 1871 and 1873, he received some instruction in composition from **Franz Lachner** in Munich. An infant prodigy, he was composing by the time he was nine, and in 1869 his Duet for Violin and Viola was played at the Lower Rhine Music Festival at Düsseldorf by his father and **Joseph Joachim**; in 1871 he took part in a performance of his first Cello Sonata (op. 3) at Leipzig. His first composition to be published, a Sonata for Violin and Piano, appeared in the same year, and he continued to write music throughout his life; its wide range covered operas, symphonies, concertos, chamber music, pieces for piano, songs, and choral compositions (the opus numbers of his published works extended to 100).

In 1873–74 he acted as accompanist to **Julius Stockhausen**, who then held the position of Kammersänger to King Karl I of Württemberg and was living at Cannstadt, near Stuttgart. They appeared together at concerts not only in Stuttgart, but also in various other German towns and even in Austria. The experience was no doubt very valuable for the young Röntgen, who in later years, in addition to his activities as soloist and conductor, had an extremely distinguished and satisfying career as an accompanist to Johannes Messchaert; he also enjoyed fruitful partnerships with Pablo Casals and Carl Flesch. (**Max Kalbeck** [1976] called him "the ideal accompanist" [vol. 4, 426].) Stockhausen is likely to have fostered his interest in Brahms, but Röntgen did not at once warm to his music; eventually, though, he became a fervent admirer.

In 1878 he was appointed a piano teacher at the music school of the Maatschappij tot Bevordering Toonkunst in Amsterdam and was a co-founder of the local conservatory (1884) and taught there until 1926 (from 1912 to 1924 as its director). In addition, he conducted the Excelsior choral society (1884–86) and the Toonkunstkoor (1886–98), as well as some of the "Felix Meritis" concerts, and not long before the First World War he formed the Röntgen Trio with the two sons from his first marriage, Julius (1881–1951), a violinist who had been a member of the Kneisel Quartet from 1907 to 1912, and Engelbert (1886–1958), a cellist. Röntgen was married twice: in 1880 to the Swedish violinist Amanda Maier (1853–94), who had studied with his father, and in 1897 to the Dutch pianist Abrahamina des Amorie van der Hoeven (1870–1940). Of the four sons of the second marriage, the oldest, Johannes, became a pianist, conductor, and composer, and the youngest, Joachim, a violinist.

Röntgen saw a good deal of Brahms when the latter spent a few days in Leipzig in January 1877 for the purpose of conducting his First Symphony. At a musical soiree at Raymund Härtel's, Röntgen played in a performance of Brahms's Piano Quintet op. 34 in his presence; at another one, at the house of **Paul Bernhard Limburger**, Brahms, who had evidently taken a great liking to him, even danced a waltz with him. The next morning Brahms attended a rehearsal of Röntgen's Serenade for Wind Instruments (op. 14) and afterward warmly complimented him. But it was during Brahms's several visits to Holland between 1878 and 1885 that Röntgen came to know him really well, and he felt increasing admiration for both the man and his music. On 27 February 1884 he played the Second Piano Concerto under Brahms's direction in Amsterdam. (However, Siegfried Kross is mistaken in stating in his Brahms biography that Röntgen thus became the first pianist other than Brahms to play the work in public [Kross 1997, 861]; the earliest such performance appears to be that given by Oscar Beringer in London on 14 October 1882, and the concerto was also played by **Heinrich Barth** in Berlin on 3 November 1882, and by **Sir Charles Hallé** at Manchester on 23 November 1882.) Later Röntgen was to see Brahms repeatedly on the occasion of his own frequent concert appearances in Vienna, mostly as accompanist to Messchaert.

In 1934 Röntgen's widow published a selection of his letters to various correspondents, among them his parents, his two wives, Brahms, and certain close friends, notably **Wilhelm Engelmann**, **Edvard Grieg**, **Heinrich von Herzogenberg**, and Johann Messchaert. These letters reflect a highly attractive character and, especially, an exceptionally warm and generous nature, which helps to explain why Röntgen inspired so much affection and devotion; his unwavering enthusiasm for music must also have been profoundly infectious. After Röntgen's death, Donald Tovey wrote to his widow: "I don't know any experience, which either at the moment or in retrospect seems to me more 'himmlisch' than my visits to Röntgenheim" (A. Röntgen 1934, 263). In a tribute to Röntgen in *The Times* on 19 September 1932, Tovey affirmed that "jealousy, intrigue and malice did not enter into his world."

Toward Brahms, Röntgen's attitude was inevitably more formal and his tone more guarded than toward those whose equal he felt himself to be—in a letter to Carl Flesch in 1907, he described his relationship with Brahms as having been "solely one of passive reverence" (A. Röntgen 1934, 244); but Brahms, like the others, was fully aware of Röntgen's innate goodness, and he expressed his feelings for him with quite unusual warmth to **Clara Schumann** in February 1896. That winter Röntgen was giving a number of recitals in Vienna with Messchaert, and Brahms spent some time in his company. After praising their performance of **Robert Schumann**'s *Dichterliebe*, in which, he told Clara, Röntgen's "every tone and every chord sounded as if it had been struck with special love," he added, "He is moreover a quite exceptional and most lovable man. He has remained a child, so innocent, pure, frank, enthusiastic. . . . Not for a long time have I taken such great pleasure in anyone" (Litzmann 1970, vol. 2, 616–17). Röntgen last met Brahms in January 1897, when he was in Vienna for a performance of the Piano Quintet op. 34 with the Rosé Quartet (on 26 January). "I have the most moving, the most beautiful memories of those days," he recalled in a letter to Herzogenberg on 12 April; and on the same day he wrote to Grieg: "In Brahms's case, the man and the artist were cast from the same great mould" (A. Röntgen 1934, 138 and 170). On 11 April, at a concert he arranged in Amsterdam in Brahms's memory, he played in the Piano Quartet op. 60; the program also included the Cello Sonata op. 38 and the String Sextet op. 18. The following year he directed a three-day Brahms Memorial Festival there, of which the highlight was a performance of the Requiem in the imposing Ronde Lutherse Kerk on the Singel Canal, on the first anniversary of Brahms's death. Among the other works performed were the Second Piano Concerto (in which Röntgen was soloist) and the *Liebeslieder-Walzer* (in which Röntgen and his wife accompanied the singers).

Brahms thought quite favorably of Röntgen's compositions. As already mentioned, he was most complimentary about the Serenade for Wind Instruments (op. 14), which, furthermore, he described as "altogether delightful" in a letter to Clara Schumann in January 1877 (Litzmann 1970, vol. 2, 90). Moreover, it was at his—entirely unsolicited—warm recommendation that **Fritz Simrock** undertook to publish Röntgen's *Norwegian Ballad* for orchestra (op. 36) in 1896. In his letter to Simrock, Brahms characterized Röntgen's talent as "light and pleasing" (Brahms 1974/12, 193). Röntgen dedicated his two-piano arrangement of the *Ballad* (op. 36b) to Brahms.

Brahms also had some contact with Julius Röntgen's father Engelbert, whom he most probably first met at Leipzig in late 1853. They collaborated musically on at least two occasions: on 1 February 1874 at Leipzig, they took part in a performance of Brahms's Piano Quartet op. 25; and on 20 January 1877, also at Leipzig, they both played in a performance of the Piano Quartet op. 60. In 1896 Brahms wrote to Engelbert Röntgen: "I hope your son has adequately sung the praises of Vienna to you. You will also, I hope, have read to your satisfaction how much we praised and loved him" (Kalbeck 1976, vol. 4, 396, n. 1). (Brahms 1974/12; Brooijmans 2001; Kross 1997; Litzmann 1970; A. Röntgen 1934; J. Röntgen 1920)

ROSÉ, ARNOLD [real name: Rosenblum, Arnold Josef] (b. Jassy [Iaszi, Romania], 24 October 1863; d. London, 25 August 1946). Violinist and teacher; brother-in-law of **Gustav Mahler** whose sister Justine (1868–1938) he married in 1902. He studied with Karl Heissler at the Vienna Conservatory (1874–77), and in 1881 became Konzertmeister of the Vienna Opera orchestra and a member of the Philharmonic Orchestra, positions he held until 1938; several times between 1888 and 1896 he was also Konzertmeister of the Bayreuth Festival orchestra. In addition, he taught at the Vienna conservatory (1893–1901, 1908–24). In 1938 he emigrated to London, where he performed in public until 1945.

In 1882 he founded the Rosé Quartet, together with Julius Egghard, Anton Loh, and his own brother Eduard (1859–1943). Their initial recital took place on 22 January 1883; the third and final concert of the first season offered Brahms's Piano Trio op. 87, with **Julius Epstein** as the pianist. The composition of the quartet underwent several changes during its first two decades, but from 1905 to 1920, during which period it attained a considerable international reputation, its membership remained constant: Rosé, Paul Fischer, Anton Ruzitska, and Friedrich Buxbaum. They excelled not only in the classical repertoire but also in contemporary chamber music (they did not, of course, confine themselves to playing quartets). Among the composers whose names frequently appeared on their programs was Brahms; they even offered "Brahms cycles." The following events merit special mention: on 22 February 1890 Brahms played his Piano Trio op. 8 (second version) with Rosé and **Reinhold Hummer**; on 11 November 1890 the Rosé Quartet (Rosé, August Siebert, Sigmund Bachrich, and Hummer), together with F. Jelinek, gave the first performance of Brahms's String Quintet op. 111; on 5 January 1892 it presented what was the first Viennese performance—and the second anywhere—of the Clarinet Quintet op. 115, with Franz Steiner as clarinettist (the Joachim Quartet and **Richard Mühlfeld** had given its first performance in Berlin on 12 December 1891, and were to play it again in Vienna on 19 January 1892); and the concerts of 8 and 11 January 1895 featured the world premieres of the Clarinet Sonatas op. 120/2 and op. 120/1, respectively, given by Brahms and Mühlfeld (who also took part in a performance of the Clarinet Quintet at the second concert).

Rosé's son Alfred (1902–75) was a pianist and composer, his daughter Alma (1906–44) a noted violinist. (Rosé 1932)

ROSENHAIN, JACOB [Jakob, Jacques] (b. Mannheim, 2 December 1813; d. Baden-Baden, 21 March 1894). Composer and pianist who undertook his first concert tours at the age of nine. He studied with Jakob Schmitt at

Mannheim, Johann Wenzel Kalliwoda at Donaueschingen, and Schnyder von Wartensee at Frankfurt. After living at Frankfurt (1828–37) and in Paris (1838–60), he settled in 1870 at Baden-Baden, where he played a prominent role in the local musical life.

Brahms was in contact with him there, and Rosenhain was among the invited guests who witnessed the first private performance of the Double Concerto on 23 September 1887. Of greater interest to Brahms scholars is no doubt the fact that the young Brahms opened his first public concert, in Hamburg on 21 September 1848, with two movements from Rosenhain's Piano Sonata in A Major.

RÖSING [ROESING], ELISABETH. Widow of the scholar Jakob Georg Hermann Rösing, and aunt of **Marie and Elisabeth [Betty] Völkers**. According to her daughter Elisabeth Proffen, Frau Rösing, who was then living at Hamm (a village between Hamburg and Wandseck, now part of Hamburg) made the acquaintance of Brahms one spring evening in 1861 at the Völkers' house.

In July he rented a large room in her house, which he kept until he set out for Vienna in September 1862. The period he spent there was one of the happiest and most productive of his life. The compositions he worked on during this time included the *Magelone-Lieder*, the three piano quartets, the *Variations on a Theme by Schumann* for piano duet, the *Handel Variations* for solo piano, the Cello Sonata op. 38, and the Piano Quintet. When he left, he wrote the opening bars of the latter work in the album belonging to Frau Rösing's daughter, and beneath them, "I shall not be able to hear this and much other music without thinking very warmly of the house in which it was composed, and of its dear occupants" (Roesing 1927). The genuineness of his gratitude to Frau Rösing is proved by his subsequent dedication to her of the Piano Quartet op. 26, published in 1863. The piano that he had used while staying with her—the **Schumanns**' Graf grand piano that **Clara** had given him after **Robert**'s death—remained in her house until she moved to Hanover in 1868 (on its later peregrinations, *see* GRAF, CONRAD). (Hübbe 1902; Roesing 1927)

ROUSSEAU, JEAN-JACQUES (b. Geneva, 28 June 1712; d. Ermenonville, 2 July 1778). Philosopher, writer, and composer. Brahms set a text by Rousseau, in a German version first published in 1826, in the song "Der Frühling" (op. 6/2).

RUBINSTEIN [RUBINSHTEYN], ANTON (GRIGOR'YEVICH) (b. Vikhvatinets, Podolsk district, 28 November 1829; d. Peterhof, near St.

Petersburg, 20 November 1894). Pianist, composer, and teacher. Having been taught by Alexander Villoing in Moscow, he made his public debut there in July 1839. At the end of the following year, he embarked on his first foreign tour, performing in France, England, Scandinavia, Holland, Germany, Austria, and France; in Paris he made the acquaintance of **Liszt** and **Chopin**. He then settled for a time (1844–46) in Berlin, where he studied with Siegfried Dehn, and subsequently lived in Vienna (1846–48) before returning to Russia. A further highly successful tour, starting in 1854, firmly established his international reputation as a mature pianist of quite outstanding quality, and the numerous tours he was to undertake throughout Europe in later years brought him ever-increasing renown. He had an extremely wide repertoire, which he played entirely from memory (but he did suffer some lapses in his later years). Moreover, he possessed quite remarkable mental and physical stamina; in the course of a tour of the United States, which he made with violinist Josef Wieniawski in 1872, he appeared at 215 concerts in 239 days. He was also active as a conductor, and from 1859 until 1867 he directed the concerts of the Russian Musical Society, which he had helped to found; in 1871–72 he was artistic director of the Gesellschaft der Musikfreunde in Vienna, preceding Brahms in that post. In addition to these activities, he enjoyed a distinguished career as a teacher, during which he served in 1862–67 and again in 1887–91 as director of the St. Petersburg conservatory, which owed its foundation to him. Lastly, he was a prolific and somewhat facile composer, which may help to explain why almost none of his compositions, with the glowing exception of the famous *Melody in F*, is widely known today.

A highly individualistic and temperamental performer, prone to follow the impulse of the moment, he was famous for rarely playing a piece the same way twice. His brilliant technique enabled him to produce well-contrasted and intensely dramatic performances that electrified his audiences. In Liszt's transcription of **Franz Schubert**'s "Erlkönig," according to Amy Fay (1965), "where the little child is so frightened, his hands flew all over the piano, and absolutely made it shriek with terror. It was enough to freeze you to hear it" (Schonberg 1965, 258). His hold over his listeners was spectacular; of his concerts in London in 1886 **Edward Speyer** (1937) wrote, "The fascination exercised by the gigantic power and originality of Rubinstein's playing was indescribable" (76). He was also widely admired for his beautiful touch, for he could play delicately when he wished, as **Bernhard Scholz** (1911) fondly recalled in his memoirs, "How his hefty fist could stroke the keys and coax from them the sweetest and softest sounds with his caresses!" (219).

Of course, he had his critics among the purists and the more academically inclined musicians. Among these was **Clara Schumann**, who witnessed his career almost from the beginning; in fact, they performed her husband's *Andante and Variations* for two pianos (op. 46) together at a concert in Vienna on 15 December 1846. As her diary and also her letters to Brahms show, she had many opportunities to hear him play in later years, both at concerts and in private, and her reaction was frequently unfavorable. "Above all he lacks the sacred seriousness [of the true artist], and one feels this when he composes, conducts, and plays," she wrote to Brahms in April 1864 (Litzmann 1970, vol. 1, 449–50). Elsewhere, she accuses Rubinstein of insensitiveness, of thumping, of exaggeratedly "whispering" with the soft pedal down (Litzmann 1902, vol. 3, 225); but even she was not always entirely untouched by the spell he so generally cast over his listeners: "He really is an astonishing man," she noted, evidently not wholly approvingly, in her diary in November 1881, after attending one of his concerts in Frankfurt, but added, "yet interesting in everything he does" (Litzmann 1902, vol. 3, 414). And, like everybody else who came into contact with Rubinstein, she greatly liked him as a person. "You are quite right," she told Brahms in the above-mentioned letter, "he has rare human qualities." Indeed, she speculated that Rubinstein got away with some bad performances just because he was so universally popular, a thought that prompted a highly interesting reflection: "How greatly Brahms would no doubt be fêted if he had just a small part of Rubinstein's amiability" (Litzmann 1902, vol. 3, 463).

Rubinstein made Brahms's acquaintance in 1856 at Hanover, where he played some of his own compositions at a concert on 9 February. By that time Brahms was already familiar with several of his works, but neither then or later could he muster much enthusiasm for them. The previous year he had taken part in a private performance in Hamburg, with **Georg Dietrich Otten** and **Alfred Jaëll**, of Rubinstein's G Minor Piano Trio (op. 15/2), which, he afterward reported to Clara Schumann, "is like all his other pieces—now insignificant, now awful, and now and then ingenious" (Litzmann 1970, vol. 1, 161). Some 20 years later he let himself be persuaded to place the overture to Rubinstein's opera *Dmitry Donskoy* on the program of one of his Gesellschaft der Musikfreunde concerts (8 November 1874), but not without first challenging **Felix Otto Dessoff** to "find eight attractive bars" in it (Brahms 1974/16, 138–39).

The initial contacts in Hanover did not lead to particularly close relations, but the two men did meet periodically—for instance, at Baden-Baden in 1862 and again in 1864, when Brahms very probably attended Rubinstein's private Sunday musical matinees. Rubinstein had even placed his house at Brahms's disposal during his absence, and Brahms briefly availed himself of the offer. That summer Rubinstein presented Brahms with a suitably inscribed musical autograph, and during the following winter he reportedly conducted the opening movement of Brahms's Serenade op. 11 at a concert at St. Petersburg. Their relations became, however, strained in 1872. An unsatisfactory performance in Vienna of the *Schicksalslied* on 21 January 1872, for which Brahms blamed Rubinstein ("He is a very mediocre conductor," he wrote to **Hermann Levi** [Brahms 1974/7, 97]), made him unwilling to entrust to Rubinstein what would have been the first performance of the complete *Triumphlied* at that year's Lower Rhine Music Festival at Düsseldorf, which Rubinstein was to direct. Indeed, Brahms made it clear that he would authorize the performance of the still unpublished work only if he could conduct it himself. Thereupon, Rubinstein declared that in that case he would merely conduct one of his own works at the festival but would not accept responsibility for the whole event. In the circumstances, the organizers decided to forego the performance of the *Triumphlied* rather than do without Rubinstein's overall participation. Brahms's attitude is likely to have irritated and even offended Rubinstein, who does not, however, seem to have borne him a lasting grudge, for **Richard Heuberger** relates that, at a dinner of the Tonkünstlergesellschaft in Vienna on 17 April 1885, Rubinstein, on entering the room, spotted Brahms and at once went to greet him (Heuberger 1976, 30).

There is no doubt, though, that in his later years Rubinstein felt increasingly jealous of Brahms's steadily growing renown as a composer, while his own works failed to make their mark. Brahms's works probably held little appeal for him, in any case, but his frustration at not being recognized as a creator of some genius certainly fed his resentment. On one occasion, at a concert at Cologne in which he took part together with **Antonia Kufferath**, who sang the seven songs of Brahms's op. 95, he asked her, "How can you sing such things?" (Speyer 1937, 76). Brahms's Violin Concerto he likened to a "decent, but ugly and uninteresting girl" (Stargardt-Wolff 1954, 67). Not surprisingly, his celebrated series of seven mammoth concerts, in which he purported to cover the whole history of piano music and which he presented in several prominent European music centers in 1885–86, did not include a single piece by Brahms. **Karl Goldmark** (1922) recalls in his memoirs how Rubinstein, discovering music by Brahms and **Richard Wagner** on **Julius Epstein**'s piano one evening, at once fulminated against both composers, and when Goldmark spoke up for them, angrily complained that Goldmark too was a more famous composer than he was himself, despite the fact that "in the time you finish one composition, I can write a hundred." Not surprisingly, Goldmark chided Rubinstein for being a "great child," but he also regarded him as "great and noble human being" (71).

As for Brahms, while he had little praise for Rubinstein the composer and scant regard for Rubinstein the conductor, he held him in extremely high esteem as a pianist. "When I hear Rubinstein play," he once told **Ottilie Ebner**'s daughter, "I always feel that it would be best for me to clasp my hands tightly behind my back and never touch the piano again" (Balassa 1933, 119); and Heuberger (1976) tells of attending a Rubinstein concert with Brahms in Vienna on 11 March 1894, at which Brahms exclaimed, "I could listen to Rubinstein all night. A fantastic fellow!" (65). To **Robert Freund** Brahms once remarked: "What [**Bülow, d'Albert**] can do, I can do too, but what Rubinstein can do, that I can't do. I no longer play certain pieces such as the last movement of Weber's A flat sonata or **Mozart**'s Rondo in A flat even to myself, since I have heard Rubinstein play them" (Freund 1951, 18). (Balassa 1933; Benningsen 1939; Bowen 1939; Brahms 1974/7, 1974/16; Droucker 1904; Fay 1965; Goldmark 1922; Heuberger 1976; Litzmann 1902, 1970; May 1948; McArthur 1889; Rubinstein 1969; Scholz 1911; Schonberg 1965; Speyer 1937)

RÜCKAUF, ANTON (b. Prague, 13 March 1855; d. Erlaa, Lower Austria [now part of Vienna], 19 September 1903). Composer, pianist, and teacher. He studied piano with M. Proksch, organ with F. Z. Skuherský́n, and theory with F. Blažek. In 1878 he moved to Vienna, where he received further instruction in counterpoint from **Gustav Nottebohm** and **Karl Nawratil**, and took some lessons with Theodor Leschetitzky. He became a successful piano (later, also singing) teacher and a prominent accompanist; in particular, he regularly concertized with **Gustav Walter**. On 9 November 1896 he accompanied **Anton Sistermans** in the first complete public performance of Brahms's *4 ernste Gesänge*. He was also **Alice Barbi**'s accompanist at her two all-Brahms recitals in Vienna on 30 March and 1 April 1898.

As a composer, Rückauf is especially noteworthy for his more than 100 songs; his opera *Die Rosentalerin* was produced at Dresden in 1897. He dedicated his Piano Quintet in F Major (op. 13) to Brahms. (*ÖBL* 1957–)

RÜCKERT, (JOHANN MICHAEL) FRIEDRICH (b. Schweinfurt, 16 May 1788; d. Neuses, near Coburg, 31 January 1866). Poet and dramatist. Brahms set texts by Rückert in the songs "Gestillte Sehnsucht" (op. 91/1) and "Mit vierzig Jahren" (op. 94/1); in "Fahr wohl!" (op. 93a/4), for a chorus of four mixed voices; in "Nachtwache I" and "Nachtwache II" (op. 104/1–2), for mixed choir; in the canons for women's voices op. 113/9–13; and in the canon for four voices WoO 30.

Brahms never met Rückert, but he knew his daughter **Marie** (*see* RÜCKERT, MARIE RENATA). In 1890 he had some correspondence with the mayor of Schweinfurt, Carl Schultes, as it was hoped that he might write a special composition for the festivities planned in connection with the unveiling of Rückert's statue in October of that year. For various reasons Brahms could not, or at any rate did not, accede to the request, although he assured Schultes that he would have been extremely happy "to have had an opportunity to offer the illustrious son of your city a token of my most profound admiration" (Kreutner 1997, 155). The monument, a joint work of the architect Friedrich von Thiersch and the sculptor Wilhelm von Rümann, was unveiled at Schweinfurt on 18 October 1890. (R. Hofmann 2005; Kreutner 1997)

RÜCKERT, MARIE RENATA (b. Erlangen, 26 June 1835; d. Coburg, 2 January 1920). Daughter of **Friedrich Rückert**. Brahms met Marie repeatedly, the first time in March 1861 while she was staying with the **Hallier** family in Hamburg, and for the last time probably in Vienna in March 1891; she visited him at Mürzzuschlag in 1885. For some particulars of their contacts, in person and by letter, and of her reactions to his music (enthusiastic) and to his personality (hostile, at any rate initially), see Renate Hofmann's (2001) study of their relations. As for Brahms, he seems to have been rather attracted to her, and he wrote for her the canon "Ich weiss nicht, was im Hain" (op. 113/11), to a text by her father. On a copy of the canon, made by Julie Hallier, Marie recorded, "Composed for me by the mulish Brahms at a time when I almost fell into his clutches" (R. Hofmann 2001, 399).

Marie does not appear to have been initially involved in any way in the effort to obtain from Brahms a musical contribution to the festivities that were being planned for the unveiling of the Rückert statue at Schweinfurt in 1890 (*see* RÜCKERT, [JOHANN MICHAEL] FRIEDRICH and R. Hofmann 2005). (R. Hofmann 2001, 2005; Kreutner 1997, 1999)

RUDORFF, ERNST (FRIEDRICH KARL) (b. Berlin, 18 January 1840; d. Berlin, 31 December 1916). Pianist, teacher, and composer. While still a teenager, he studied piano and composition with **Woldemar Bargiel** (1852–57) and violin with Louis Ries (1852–54), and also received some instruction in 1858 from **Clara Schumann**. Later, after studying theology, philosophy, and philology at Berlin University and attending lectures on history at Leipzig University, he enrolled at the Leipzig conservatory where his teachers included Ignaz Moscheles, L. Plaidy, and **Carl Reinecke** for piano, **Moritz Hauptmann** and **Julius Rietz** for composition, and **Ferdinand David** for conducting. In 1864 he conducted some concerts of the Hamburg Singakademie. Subsequently, he was on the faculty of the Cologne conservatory (1865–69) and the Hochschule für Musik in Berlin

(1869–1910); at the latter school he headed the department for piano and organ and conducted the students' orchestra in practice sessions and also occasionally at public concerts. While in Cologne, he had founded a **Bach** Choir; in Berlin he was, from 1880 to 1890, in charge of the Sternscher Gesangverein. He wrote numerous choral works, as well as compositions for orchestra, some chamber music, and pieces for piano. Furthermore, he collaborated in the editions of the complete works of **Mozart** and **Chopin** (see also below). He was a well-respected figure in the musical circles of his time; but if he is at all known to the general public in Germany today, it is as the founder of the national environmental movement—he was the original German "Green."

Rudorff first met Brahms at Clara Schumann's house in Berlin in 1859. His relationship with Brahms was a fairly formal one, based on mutual respect, and all but foundered over Brahms's declared sympathy for **Amalie Joachim** in the divorce proceedings opposing her to her husband, whom Rudorff supported unreservedly. His admiration for Brahms's music was slow in developing. After Clara Schumann had performed the Serenade op. 16 with Brahms for students of the Leipzig Conservatory on 30 November 1860, she noted in her diary, "Rudorff was quite enchanted by it, which pleased me especially, since I have had such difficulty making him appreciate Johannes's compositions" (Litzmann 1902, vol. 3, 90). In fact, Rudorff appears henceforth to have found Brahms's music increasingly appealing. Thus, he was delighted with the *Handel Variations* when he heard Clara play them in December 1861, and in November 1865 he wrote to Brahms to express his admiration for the *Magelone-Lieder*; in January 1867 Clara reported to Brahms that he had been greatly moved by the Requiem. In the summer of 1868 Rudorff saw Brahms frequently during the latter's stay at Bonn, and it was perhaps this temporarily closer contact that led him to dedicate his *Phantasie* for piano (op. 14) to Brahms in 1869. In January of that year, he wrote enthusiastically about the songs that **Fritz Simrock** had recently published (opp. 46–49) and, in particular, assured Brahms that he was "absolutely crazy" about his setting of Hölty's "An die Nachtigall" [op. 46/4] (Brahms 1974/3, 151).

By his own account, his almost daily conversations with **Joseph Joachim**, once he had moved to Berlin, further stimulated his interest in Brahms the composer and Brahms the man. On 19 March 1870 he conducted ten of the *Liebeslieder-Walzer* (op. 52/1, 2, 4–6, 8, 9, 11, and op. 65/9), with Amalie Joachim and Anna von Asten (*see* ASTEN, JULIE VON) among the soloists. This performance, although not mentioned in M. L. McCorkle's (1984) *Werkverzeichnis*, was the first of these songs with orchestral, instead of the original piano, accompaniment. (Brahms appears to have orchestrated them at Rudorff's request—see his letter to Rudorff in January 1870 [Brahms 1974/3, 155–56]). Moreover, Rudorff was tremendously impressed with the Third Symphony, on which he congratulated Brahms most enthusiastically, "You have completely conquered me with your music, to a degree such as has not happened to me in a long while on any first impression," he wrote on 5 January 1884, after the first Berlin performance conducted by Joachim the previous day (Brahms 1974/3, 179). Later that month he had several opportunities to speak to Brahms when the latter came to Berlin to direct two performances of the symphony. Their last meeting took place in 1889, also in Berlin, on the occasion of Joachim's artistic jubilee.

Brahms and Rudorff were both contributors to the editions published by **Breitkopf & Härtel** of Chopin's and Mozart's complete works. Their collaboration on these projects led to some interesting correspondence between them (in the case of Chopin, Rudorff contributed editions of the ballads, waltzes, Études, and songs; in the case of Mozart, he dealt with the concertos for string and wind instruments).

Rudorff's memories of his contacts with Brahms, as well as his assessment of certain of Brahms's works, were published posthumously in the *Schweizerische Musikzeitung* in 1957 under the title "Johannes Brahms: Erinnerungen und Betrachtungen." (Brahms 1974/3; I. Fellinger 1964; Litzmann 1902; Rudorff 1957)

RUPERTI, FRIEDRICH (1805–67). Poet. Brahms set one of his texts in the choral composition "Es tönt ein voller Harfenklang" (op. 17/1).

– S –

SACHSEN-MEININGEN: *see* GEORG II, DUKE OF SACHSEN-MEININGEN.

SAHR, HEINRICH SAHRER [SARRER] VON (b. Dresden, 2 November 1829; d. Munich, 6 December 1898). Composer and music teacher. When Brahms went to Leipzig in 1853, Sahr, a friend of **Albert Dietrich** and **Julius Otto Grimm**, was a student at the conservatory there. Aware, thanks to Dietrich and others, of the great impression Brahms had made on everyone—starting with **Robert** and **Clara Schumann**—at Düsseldorf, he looked forward eagerly to Brahms's arrival, and he and Grimm at once offered him hospitality in their rooms. Saar quickly fell under Brahms's charm. "He is a divine creature," he wrote to Dietrich. "The days since he has been here are among the most wonderful I have ever lived. He corresponds so exactly to the ideal I have fashioned for myself of the true artist. And also as a man!" (Dietrich 1908, 8).

Sahr proved invaluable to Brahms in opening many doors for him in Leipzig. "I have taken him to see the Härtels, Moscheles, **David**, and others. . . . This afternoon Marie Wieck and a few other persons are coming to see me, probably also **Rietz**, in order to make his acquaintance" (from the same letter to Dietrich). Nevertheless, grateful as he must have felt toward Sahr, Brahms did not altogether take to him, certainly not as much as to Grimm, who, he wrote to **Joseph Joachim**, "has such a lively, merry, and wholesome disposition, the opposite of Sahr" (Brahms 1974/5, 26).

It was not until several years later that Brahms found him a more congenial companion. "Sahr recently arrived here unexpectedly," he reported to Grimm from Hamburg in July 1858. "He plans to travel back home via Göttingen [where Grimm was then living]. You will be glad to see that he has changed (in certain respects) and become more human. In fact, he is very pleasant" (Brahms 1974/4, 64). The following year he may again have stayed with Sahr when he went to Leipzig for what turned out to be a disastrous performance of his First Piano Concerto (27 January 1859). In the summer of 1860 they met at Bonn, and in 1862 Sahr joined Brahms, Dietrich, and **Woldemar Bargiel** on a short walking tour that began at Münster am Stein, where they had visited Clara Schumann.

In 1863–64 Sahr replaced Dietrich as Kapellmeister at Oldenburg, and at a concert on 31 March 1864, he performed Brahms's Serenade op. 11. Brahms met Sahr once more in Munich in October 1864; nothing seems to be known about any later meetings, but he heard about Sahr occasionally from mutual friends. Thus, in February 1873 **Hermann Levi** wrote from Munich, where he had recently moved and where Sahr had settled in 1869: "**Allgeyer**, Sahr and myself spend almost every evening together most pleasantly. Sahr is an eccentric, but a fine and clever man. No fire, no coal can burn as fiercely as secret compositions, about which no one knows anything" (Brahms 1974/7, 133). The last sentence reflects Sahr's lack of confidence in his ability as a composer, which reportedly led him ultimately to burn his manuscripts and desist from creative work. He is even said to have given his piano away because he was no longer satisfied with the quality of his playing. Toward the end of his life he became a recluse. (Brahms 1974/4, 1974/5, 1974/7; Dietrich 1898; Grimm 1900/1; Linnemann 1956; Ludwig 1925)

SAUER, EMIL VON (b. Hamburg, 8 October 1862; d. Vienna, 27 April 1942). Pianist, composer, and teacher. He studied with Nicolas Rubinstein at the Moscow conservatory, with **Liszt** at Weimar, and with **Ludwig Deppe** in Hamburg. His highly successful concert career, which also took him to America, spanned over 50 years (1882–1936). In addition, he taught a master class at the Vienna conservatory for many years (1901–8, 1914–21, and again from 1931). He wrote a number of works for piano, including two concertos and two sonatas, and published editions of compositions by Scarlatti, Liszt, **Chopin**, and Brahms.

In his memoirs *Meine Welt* Sauer (1901) describes his contacts with Brahms, to whom he was first introduced at the Roter Igel restaurant in Vienna in 1889. After he started to give concerts in Vienna the following year, he regularly met Brahms, at the latter's flat, at his own hotel, at the Tonkünstlerverein, and at some of his concerts that Brahms attended. "It was the same with the man as with the composer," Sauer later recalled, "one grew more fond of him at each new encounter" (192–93). He last saw Brahms in early 1897, when Brahms, notwithstanding his enfeebled condition, climbed the three flights of stairs to Sauer's room at the Hotel Bristol to explain that his failing strength made it impossible for him to attend Sauer's concert the following day, although "I should have liked so much to hear you play my F Minor Sonata and the *Handel Variations* once more" (194). The next time Sauer traveled to Vienna was to attend Brahms's funeral. (Sauer 1901)

SCHACK, ADOLF FRIEDRICH, COUNT (b. Gut Brüsewitz, near Schwerin, 2 August 1815; d. Rome, 14 April 1894). Poet, dramatist, and historian. Brahms set three of his poems in the songs "Herbstgefühl" (op. 48/7), "Abenddämmerung" (op. 49/5), and "Serenade" (op. 58/8). (Schmitz 1991)

SCHARFF, ANTON (b. Vienna, 16 June 1845; d. Vienna, 6 July 1903). Medalist. A son of the coin engraver Johann M. Scharff (1806–55), he studied at the Vienna Akademie der bildenden Künste [Academy of Fine Arts] and at the Graveur-Akademie des Hauptmünzamtes [Academy of Engraving of the Mint]. In 1882 he became head of the latter institute and, in 1896, its director.

Scharff was one of the outstanding Austrian engravers of his time, specializing in portrait medals. His subjects included members of the imperial family and the nobility, as well as numerous scientists, artists, politicians, and industrialists, and other prominent citizens. The Gesellschaft der Musikfreunde commissioned him to create a Brahms medal to celebrate the composer's 60th birthday in 1893. Brahms willingly granted him some sittings, and the result was an excellent likeness. One medal, cast in gold, was presented to Brahms, who is reported to have been greatly moved. Several were cast in silver, and a larger number in bronze were placed at Brahms's disposal to be distributed as he wished. In this connection the archivist of the Gesellschaft der Musikfreunde, **Eusebius Mandyczewski**, drew up a provisional list of some 40 individuals, as well as museums, associations, and municipalities. This list was accepted by Brahms, with the somewhat cryptic comment, "Many thanks for your communication. I easily suppress any idea or thought of adding further names, as I must admit that I would on this occasion have thought of only very few of those listed" (Geiringer 1933, 355). The medal was issued in three sizes.

Scharff was later responsible for creating the memorial plaque that was affixed on 10 July 1898 to the house in the Hirschensprunggasse at Karlsbad [Karlovy Vary], where Brahms had stayed in September 1896. Later still, Scharff was a member of the jury entrusted with the task of choosing the sculptor for the proposed Brahms statue in Vienna (*see* WEYR, RUDOLF VON). (Geiringer 1933; *ÖBL* 1957–)

SCHARWENKA, (FRANZ) XAVER (b. Samter [Szamotuly, Poland], 6 January 1850; d. Berlin, 8 December 1924). Pianist, composer, and teacher. His principal teacher was Theodor Kullak. He enjoyed a brilliant international career, during which he repeatedly toured the United States and Canada. He also founded music schools in Berlin and New York.

Scharwenka was introduced to Brahms by Georg Henschel [later **Sir George Henschel**] in the summer of 1876, when all three were vacationing at Sassnitz on the island of Rügen. In his memoirs *Klänge aus meinem Leben*, he recalls this first meeting and also the expedition to catch flounders, which he and Brahms joined the following morning. Later that year Scharwenka dedicated to Brahms the *Romanzero* (op. 33) that he had composed at Sassnitz. (Leichtentritt 1931; Scharwenka 1922; Zobel 1950)

SCHENKENDORF, (GOTTLOB FERDINAND) MAX(IMILIAN GOTTFRIED) VON (b. Tilsit, 11 December 1783; d. Koblenz, 11 December 1817). Poet. Brahms set texts by Schenkendorf in the songs "Frühlingstrost," "Erinnerung," "An ein Bild," "An die Tauben," (op. 63/1–4), and "Todessehnen" (op. 86/6). (E. Weber 1991)

SCHILLER, (JOHANN CHRISTOPH) FRIEDRICH VON (b. Marbach am Neckar, 10 November 1759; d. Weimar, 9 May 1805). Poet, dramatist, and philosopher. Brahms set texts by Schiller in the vocal quartet "Der Abend" (op. 64/2), and in the choral compositions *Nänie* (op. 82) and "Dem dunkeln Schoss der heilgen Erde" (WoO 20).

SCHIRMER, JOHANN WILHELM (b. Jülich, 7 September 1807; d. Karlsruhe, 11 September 1863). Landscape painter, etcher, and lithographer. He was on the faculty of the Düsseldorf Academy from 1840 until 1854 and in the latter year was appointed director of the newly established art school at Karlsruhe. Brahms made his acquaintance during his visit to Düsseldorf in 1853 and evidently took to him, since in July 1855 he made a special trip from Heidelberg to Karlsruhe in order to see him, but Schirmer was out of town. He did, however, meet him there in the summer of 1862 (*see* SCHROEDTER, ADOLF (and ALWINE)).

SCHLEGEL, AUGUST WILHELM VON (b. Hanover, 8 September 1767; d. Bonn, 12 May 1845). Poet, translator, and critic. Brahms used Schlegel's German translations of Shakespeare in the choral composition "Komm herbei, komm herbei, Tod!" [Come away, come away, death] from *Twelfth Night*, ii: 4 (op. 17/2), and in the songs "Wie erkenn ich dein Treulieb" [How should I your true love know], "Sein Leichenhemd weiss wie Schnee zu sehn" [With his shroud as the mountain snow], "Auf morgen ist Sankt Valentins Tag" [To-morrow is Saint Valentine's day], "Sie trugen ihn auf der Bahre bloss" [They bore him barefac'd on the bier], and "Und kommt er nicht mehr zurück?" [And will he not come back again?] from *Hamlet*, iv: 5 (WoO 22/1–5). (Menhennet 1991)

SCHMALTZ, SUSANNE (b. Hamburg, 19 April 1838). Daughter of a Protestant clergyman, Moritz Ferdinand Schmaltz (d. 1860) and his wife Concordia, née Hensel (d. 1854). She took piano lessons with **Friedrich Wilhelm Grund** in Hamburg, and in 1854 and again in 1855–56 with **Ernst Ferdinand Wenzel** at Leipzig, where she also made the acquaintance of Moscheles and **Ferdinand David**. A great admirer of Brahms, she was delighted when a relative's generosity later (probably in early 1859) enabled her to receive some tuition from him in Hamburg. Moreover, she was a member of his women's chorus.

She met Brahms again some years later in Vienna (probably in 1867), when she spent two days seeing the sights of the city in his company. She was to recall her various contacts with him in her memoirs *Beglückte Erinnerung: Lebenslauf eines Sonntagskindes.* (Schmaltz 1926)

SCHMIDT, FELIX (b. Dresden, 11 May 1848; d. Berlin, 3 September 1927). Singer (bass baritone) and teacher. He studied singing with Eduard Mantius and theory with Karl Friedrich Weitzmann, and also attended the Hochschule für Musik in Berlin. From 1872 until 1920 he was on the teaching staff of that conservatory.

To Schmidt goes, apparently, the credit of having been the first to sing any of Brahms's *4 ernste Gesänge* in public. At a concert given at the Kaiser Wilhelm Gedächtnis Kirche in Berlin on 22 October 1896 to mark the birthday of Empress Auguste Viktoria, he sang the fourth of the *Gesänge*. (For a brief report of the concert, see the *Allgemeine Musik-Zeitung* for 30 October 1896; regarding the first semiprivate and public performances of the complete set, *see* KRAUS, FELIX VON and SISTERMANS, ANTON.) (Frank and Altmann 1983)

SCHMIDT, HANS (b. Fellin, 6 September 1854; d. Riga, 29 August 1923). Composer, organist, teacher, and critic. He studied at the Leipzig conservatory (1875–78) and in Berlin. Subsequently, he spent lengthy periods of the years 1879–81 in Vienna, where he had gone to study music theory with **Gustav Nottebohm**; previously he had tutored some of **Joseph Joachim**'s children. Brahms appears to have taken a liking to him. In a letter to **Theodor Billroth** in October 1879, he described him as "very amiable and cultured" (Gottlieb-Billroth 1935, 294). In 1881 Schmidt published a collection of original poems and translations, *Gedichte und Übersetzungen*, of which he sent a copy to Brahms who was staying at Pressbaum at the time. From there Brahms sent him a very pleasant letter of acknowledgement, which **Max Kalbeck** (1976) later printed in his Brahms biography (vol. 3, 299, n. 1). Brahms set four of the poems in "Sommerabend," "Der Kranz," "In den Beeren" (op. 84/1–3), and "Sapphische Ode" (op. 94/4). (Gottlieb-Billroth 1935; Lenz 1970)

SCHMIDT, JULIUS (b. Bückeburg, 1818; d. Detmold, 6 March 1906). Cellist who became a member of the Detmold court band in 1839, was named "Kammermusicus" in 1852, and played in the court Kapelle until 1875. He enjoyed an international reputation, giving concerts in Belgium, England, and Russia. He also composed songs and short instrumental works.

Brahms must have come to know him quite well while he was staying at Detmold, for Schmidt was one of the musicians who used to join him in the evenings in his room at the Hotel Stadt Frankfurt for impromptu music making. He was presumably also the (unidentified) cellist with whom, Brahms told **Joseph Joachim** in 1857, he and **Carl Bargheer** had been practicing **Beethoven**'s Triple Concerto (Brahms 1974/5, 192). In addition, Schmidt no doubt performed with Brahms in chamber music at court, for many of the works that, according to Bargheer, Brahms liked to play there contain a part for cello. (Brahms 1974/5; Müller-Dombois 1972; Schramm 1983)

SCHMITT, (GEORG) ALOYS (b. Hanover, 2 February 1827; d. Dresden, 15 October 1902). Composer, pianist, conductor. He belonged to a musical family: his grandfather (1757–1828) was active as an organist and teacher; his father Aloys Schmitt (1788–1866) was a well-known composer, pianist, organist, and teacher; and his uncle Jakob Schmitt (1803–53) became a piano teacher in Hamburg. After touring widely as a concert pianist in his youth, Aloys Schmitt served from 1856 until 1892 as director of music and Kapellmeister at the court of the grand duke of Mecklenburg-Schwerin at Schwerin. After his retirement he settled at Dresden, where, from 1896, he directed the **Mozart**-Verein. His compositions included an opera, *Trilby*, which was produced at Frankfurt am Main in 1845, and numerous orchestral works and pieces for piano, as well as some choral music.

Schmitt was an enthusiastic supporter of **Richard Wagner**'s operas—in 1878, at Schwerin, he staged the first performance of *Die Walküre* outside Bayreuth, and that same year he presented a production of *Siegfried*; but he was also an admirer of Brahms's works. According to **Max Kalbeck**, he came to appreciate them under the influence of his former pupil Emma Brandes/Engelmann (*see* ENGELMANN, [THEODOR] WILHELM). In October 1878 he introduced the Schwerin public to Brahms's Second Symphony, with such success that he gave another performance of it the following month. In the spring of 1880 he arranged what was virtually an all-Brahms concert (the only exception being Cherubini's *Anakreon* Overture), to which he invited the composer. At this concert, which took place on 10 April, Brahms conducted his Second Symphony and his *Schicksalslied*, was the soloist in the First Piano Concerto, and played one of the *Rhapsodies* from his op. 79 and some of the Hungarian Dances (WoO 1), while Karl Hill sang "Von ewiger Liebe" (op. 43/1) and "Wie bist du, meine Königin" (op. 32/9). In a letter to Kalbeck on 27 May 1897, Schmitt explained that his friendship with Brahms had dated from that concert. Brahms had been so delighted with the way Schmitt had studied the works with the orchestra that he henceforth addressed him with the familiar "Du." Schmitt added that Brahms had later returned to Schwerin on several further occasions and had stayed in his house (Kalbeck 1976, vol. 3, 239–40, n. 1). However, only two further visits by Brahms to Schwerin are known, both in 1883. On 9 February of that year, he conducted the *Gesang der Parzen* and the *Academic Festival Overture*, while on 8 April he directed a performance of the Requiem, in which Schmitt's wife Cornelia Schmitt-Czányi (1851–1906) was soprano soloist. (Stör 1892)

SCHNACK, FRIEDRICH [FRITZ] WILHELM (b. Hamburg, 22 April 1849; d. Pinneberg, Holstein, 18 January 1919). Son of Karoline Louise Schnack (*see* BRAHMS, KAROLINE LOUISE), and, as a result of her marriage to **Johann Jakob Brahms** in 1866, Johannes Brahms's stepbrother; within the family he was sometimes referred to as "Der kurze

Fritz" [Short Fritz], to distinguish him from Johannes's blood brother "Der lange Fritz" [Tall Fritz]. He was a clockmaker by trade, which he exercised from 1869 at St. Petersburg; but an injury to his spinal column forced him to return to Germany, where, for several years, he was unable to work. Eventually, however, thanks in part to Brahms's financial assistance, he largely regained his health and opened his own shop at Pinneberg, some 25 kilometers from Hamburg, in 1880. Brahms continued to provide periodic support, as he did to his stepmother, who went to live with Fritz at Pinneberg in 1883.

Brahms felt great affection for his stepmother and stepbrother, and in his will he bequeathed a life annuity of 5,000 marks to Karoline, with the legacy to pass to Fritz upon her death. For his part, Fritz always felt profound gratitude toward Brahms, and also immense admiration for his achievements. In October 1897 he traveled to Vienna to visit Brahms's tomb, and on this occasion he made the acquaintance of **Richard and Maria Fellinger**, with whom he thereafter maintained friendly contact. Maria Fellinger took a photograph of Schnack, which has been frequently reproduced. Her son Richard called on him at Pinneberg a few years before the First World War and found him living surrounded by Brahms memorabilia; for Schnack had made it his pious mission to assemble and preserve all the material connected with his illustrious stepbrother that he was able lay his hands on or could afford to purchase. This important collection, which eventually comprised numerous letters, documents, books, newspaper cuttings, and photographs, has since 1959 been housed in the "Johannes Brahms-Archiv" of the Staats-und Universitätsbibliothek, Hamburg. Furthermore, Schnack set up a "Brahms-Stiftung" [Brahms Foundation] for the purpose of assisting promising young musicians; it still exists today. (R. Fellinger 1997; Stephenson 1973)

SCHNITZLER, ROBERT (b. Cologne, 21 February 1825; d. Cologne, 27 September 1897). Son of the banker Eduard Schnitzler (1792–1864) and his wife Wilhelmine (1800–1865); married to Klara, née Schmidt (1830–1907). Robert Schnitzler became a senior civil servant [Geheimer Regierungsrat], and also served as secretary (1850–57) and later as first president of the Cologne Konzertgesellschaft (formed in 1827 as a result of the amalgamation of the local Musikalische Gesellschaft and the Singverein and, from 1857, responsible for organizing the so-called Gürzenich concerts). He also played a part in the establishment of the conservatory in 1850.

Both Robert and his wife Klara were excellent pianists, and their great interest in music was furthermore reflected in the musical afternoons that took place on Wednesdays at their home on 4 Bahnhofstrasse and that regularly brought together local luminaries (such as **Ferdinand Hiller**), as well as many visiting artists. Robert was an early supporter of Brahms, and when a vacancy occurred at the Cologne conservatory in 1858 as a result of Eduard Franck's resignation, he strongly encouraged Hiller to approach Brahms; but Brahms turned the offer down. The Schnitzlers remained his warm admirers all their lives, and their son **Viktor** (*see* SCHNITZLER, VIKTOR) remembered many years later how, only a year before his mother's death, he had played Brahms's symphonies with her as a piano duet, "and I can still feel to-day the youthful enthusiasm with which she performed even the final movements of those difficult works at a very lively pace" (Schnitzler 1935, 13). According to Viktor, Brahms's personal relations with the Schnitzlers did not become really close until after **Franz Wüllner** had succeeded Hiller as the city's Kapellmeister; thereafter he regularly stayed with them when he came to Cologne. Viktor also claims that several of Brahms's chamber music works—such as the Piano Trio op. 101, the Piano Trio op. 8 (in its revised form), and the Clarinet Quintet—received their first performance in Germany in the music room at 4 Bahnhofstrasse. After Hiller resigned his post for health reasons in April 1884, both he and Robert Schnitzler tried to persuade Brahms to accept it, but without success. In May of that year, Robert and Klara Schnitzler were present at the Villa Carlotta at Candenabbia when Brahms and **Rudolf von der Leyen** played the two-piano arrangement of the Third Symphony for **Duke Georg II** and **Baroness Helene Heldburg**.

SCHNITZLER, VIKTOR (b. Nachrodt, Westphalia, 19 July 1862; d. Mehlem, 26 July 1934). Son of **Robert Schnitzler**. Like his parents, he enjoyed friendly relations with Brahms, who agreed to become godfather to his second child, Olga Johanna (1890–1970). Viktor studied law and eventually attained the high rank of Justizrat in the civil service. At the same time he was, like his parents, an accomplished pianist (he had been taught by James Kwast, who was on the faculty of the conservatory); and, like his father, he assumed an important role in the musical life of Cologne. On his father's death, he was elected to the governing councils of the conservatory and the Konzertgesellschaft, and from 1897 until 1931 he served as first president of both.

In January 1888 Viktor married Ludowika [Wika] Andreae (1865–1955), who was a very fine pianist. After his death she recalled that "the last piece of music he heard me play was the Intermezzo in B Minor, op. 119, by Brahms which we both loved so much" (Schnitzler 1935, 115). At a commemorative ceremony in October 1934, Brahms's *Schicksalslied* was performed, a work of which Viktor had been particularly fond. His memoirs, *Erinnerungen aus meinem Leben*, were originally written for his family and friends and privately printed in 1921, but he later agreed to their wider publication; they appeared posthumously in 1935, with a supplement covering the period 1921–34 added by his widow. They present much valuable information on musical life in Cologne and the persons who animated it, and contain some interesting memories of Brahms. (Knierbein 1986; Schnitzler 1935)

SCHOLZ, BERNHARD (b. Mainz, 30 March 1835; d. Munich, 26 December 1916). Composer, conductor, pianist, and teacher. He studied harmony with Heinrich Esser and piano with Ernst Pauer at Mainz, and later theory with Siegfried Wilhelm Dehn in Berlin. In the course of a career spanning more than 50 years, he taught at the Munich conservatory (1856–57), spent brief periods as a conductor at theaters at Zurich (1857–58) and Nuremberg (1858–59), held the position of assistant Kapellmeister at Hanover (1859–65), conducted concerts of the Società Cherubini in Florence (1865–66), and later, in Berlin, concerts of the Cäcilia Choir, as well as orchestral concerts arranged by Emil Robert **Lienau** (and he also briefly taught at the Kullak and Stern Conservatories). From 1871 to 1883 he conducted the concerts of the Orchester-Verein at Breslau [Wrocław, Poland], and finally, he served as director of the Hoch Conservatory at Frankfurt (1883–1908); he also conducted the Rühl Choir there. As a composer, he covered a wide spectrum of genres, from operatic and choral compositions to orchestral works, chamber music, and pieces for piano.

His first contact with Brahms occurred in 1856, when he wrote to Brahms from Munich to ask for the address of **Clara Schumann**, to whom he wished to dedicate a piano concerto. A few years later he was introduced to Brahms by **Joseph Joachim**, with whom he had quickly established a friendly relationship after arriving in Hanover. He helped Joachim draft the manifesto against the "New German School," and his name was one of the four that appeared beneath the text when it was prematurely published in May 1860 (the others being those of Brahms, **Julius Otto Grimm**, and Joachim). Brahms saw a good deal of Scholz while staying at Hanover in early 1862, by which time Scholz had come to regard his compositions with a certain approval (writing to Brahms on 25 January 1862, Clara Schumann observed that she had been glad to hear that "Scholz is now, after all, at last beginning to appreciate your music" (Litzmann 1970, vol. 1, 392). Ten years later Scholz himself, in a letter to Brahms, expressed his admiration for the Requiem, and especially for its first two movements, and suggested that his highly favorable reaction ought to please Brahms particularly, since "as you know, I am not one of those who go into raptures over every note you write." Even so, he expressed some reservations on certain minor aspects of the Requiem, but there is no doubt that the work made a very deep impression on him. "You really are a devil of a fellow who gives me much pleasure," he concluded enthusiastically (Brahms 1974/3, 191–92).

Once he had taken up his appointment in Breslau, he lost little time in making Brahms's music better known to the local public. Thus, at a concert on 6 February 1872, he played some of the *Hungarian Dances* (WoO 1) with Emma Brandes (the future Emma Engelmann—*see* ENGELMANN, [THEODOR] WILHELM), and on 11 March 1872 he conducted a partial performance—movements 1, 2, 4, and 7—of the Requiem (it was this performance that prompted his above-mentioned letter to Brahms). He also directed performances of the *Schicksalslied* (19 March 1872), of the Sextet op. 36 (11 November 1873 and 17 February 1874), and of the *Haydn Variations* (10 February and 31 March 1874).

Furthermore, Scholz repeatedly invited Brahms to Breslau, and as a result Brahms made several concert appearances there while Scholz was in charge of the Orchester-Verein, the first on 29 December 1874 (when he performed his First Piano Concerto) and the last on 20 December 1881 (when he played his Second Piano Concerto). In between, he conducted the earliest Breslau performances of his First Symphony (23 January 1877) and of his Second Symphony (22 October 1878). On the latter occasion, the program also included the *Alto Rhapsody*, and two days later Brahms took part in a chamber music concert featuring his Piano Quartet op. 26, as well as a string quintet (op. 47) by Scholz, which the composer dedicated to him. Another notable date was 4 January 1881, when Brahms conducted the very first performance of the *Academic Festival Overture*, composed in appreciation of the honorary doctorate that Breslau University had granted him on 11 March 1879. No doubt Scholz had a hand in arranging that award.

A part of Brahms's correspondence with Scholz and his wife Luise, extending over the period 1872–82, has been published by Wilhelm Altmann. It bears witness to their growing friendship. "You must surely have felt yourself how much I enjoyed being with you," Brahms wrote to Scholz in January 1875, after his first visit (Brahms 1974/3, 199). Their next meeting, in 1876, led to the two men addressing each other with the intimate "Du." Altmann's collection of letters ceases with Scholz's move to Frankfurt, mainly no doubt because the correspondence had been essentially about activities arising from Scholz's position as director of the Breslau orchestra; in Frankfurt he had no further opportunity to invite Brahms's participation in any musical events. There is, however, evidence in Clara Schumann's diary that they continued to see one another during Brahms's later visits to that city. (Brahms 1974/3; Hanau 1903; Litzmann 1902, 1970; Scholz 1899, 1911)

SCHROEDTER, ADOLF (b. Schwedt an der Oder, 28 June 1805; d. Karlsruhe, 9 December 1875) and **ALWINE** (b. Gummersbach, 13 February 1820; d. Karlsruhe, 12 April 1892). Painters. Adolf, by far the better known of the two, studied with Ludwig Buchhorn in Berlin and, from 1829, with Wilhelm von Schadow at Düsseldorf, where he himself resided for the next 30 years, except for a spell (1848–54) at Frankfurt am Main. In 1859 he was appointed professor of decorative drawing and watercolor painting at the Polytechnikum (now Universität Fridericiana) at Karlsruhe. While he gained a certain reputation as a painter in oils, it was as a graphic artist that he achieved his greatest celebrity. The etchings and decorated borders he created for various literary works were highly appreciated, and he became known as the "König der Arabeske" [King of the Arabesque]. His wife Alwine, whom he married in 1840, also practiced this kind of decorative art, as well as excelling in floral painting.

Brahms made the Schroedters' acquaintance at Düsseldorf, probably through **Robert** and **Clara Schumann**. It was Adolf Schroedter who designed the original simple gravestone that was placed at Schumann's grave in Bonn on 8 June 1857. (It was replaced by Donndorf's much more elaborate and "poetic" funerary monument on 2 May 1880.)

In a letter to Brahms on 20 July 1859, Clara Schumann referred to his having given Alwine "a folk-song which she has decorated so charmingly" (Litzmann 1970, vol. 1, 268); presumably Brahms had sent her an autograph copy of one of the folk-song arrangements he had made the previous year (WoO 32). Clara added that Alwine proposed to use the sheet as the title page of a collection of songs and passed on Alwine's request for another, longer folk song that could be included in the collection, such as "Nachtgesang" (WoO 32/14) or "Scheiden" (WoO 32/16). On 10 September of the same year, Brahms informed Clara that he was "in lively correspondence" with Alwine, and he asked Clara to send Alwine his accompaniment to certain folk songs that Clara had in her possession (Litzmann 1970, vol. 1, 277). On 9 November he reported from Detmold that Alwine had sent him a pretty, evidently decorated, sheet for Clara.

In 1862 Brahms visited Karlsruhe, and on that occasion he saw the Schroedters again, as well as other acquaintances he had known in Düsseldorf, such as **Johann Wilhelm Schirmer** and the **Lessings**. It may be assumed that he visited the Schroedters on various further occasions while staying at Karlsruhe or Baden-Baden during later years.

In an undated letter to **Hermann Levi** that, from internal evidence, has been ascribed to the year 1865, Brahms stated that he was enclosing a sheet of music for Alwine, in response to her recent request for some "musical verses" (Brahms 1974/7, 25). This may well have been the autograph of the four canons op. 113/1, 10–11, and WoO 28, which is now at the Karlsruhe Stadtarchiv. In a note on the back of the sheet, Brahms had expressed the hope that these items would meet Alwine's purpose and that he would soon see them "handsomely illustrated." However, the sheet bears no ornamentation. Apart from its connection with the Schroedters, it holds a further interest for Brahmsians inasmuch as all four canons offer differences when compared with their other known versions. It was shown at the exhibition *Johannes Brahms in Baden-Baden und Karlsruhe* at Karlsruhe in 1983, and both sides of it were photographically reproduced in the catalog (see Draheim et al. 1983, 44–45 and 157). (Anon. 1906; Brahms 74/7; Litzmann 1970)

SCHRÖTTER VON KRISTELLI, LEOPOLD (b. Graz, 5 February 1837; d. Vienna, 22 April 1908). Laryngologist and internist. He belonged to a distinguished family, being a grandson of landscape painter Ludwig von Kristelli, a son of noted chemist Anton Schrötter von Kristelli (1802–75), who discovered red, amorphous phosphorus, and a stepbrother of painter and art teacher Alfred Schrötter von Kristelli (1856–1935).

He studied at the University of Vienna, where in 1861 he qualified as a doctor and surgeon. After working for some six years as an assistant to the well-known internist Joseph Skoda at the Allgemeine Krankenhaus [General Hospital], in 1870 he was appointed director of the recently established laryngology clinic, and he later also headed the department of internal medicine at the Rudolfsspital and a section of the Allgemeine Krankenhaus. In 1890 he was appointed director of a newly established university clinic. He also had interests outside medicine: from 1893 he served on the board of directors of the Gesellschaft der Musikfreunde. Among his patients was **Anton Bruckner**, who apparently expressed his gratitude by presenting his harmonium to him.

Given Schrötter's eminence as a physician, and his reputation of being an excellent diagnostician, it is not surprising that Dr. Hertzka, after he had examined Brahms at Ischl in July 1896 (and diagnosed jaundice, or an inflammation of the liver), should have availed himself of Schrötter's presence in the area to seek a second opinion. (Schrötter was vacationing at Rinnbach near Ebensee, on the Traunsee.) Schrötter duly visited Brahms, who was told that he had been summoned to Ischl by a member of the imperial court who was ill and, being in Ischl, had been asked to call on Brahms. That same day (2 August), Brahms informed **Richard Heuberger** gleefully that, after a thorough examination, Schrötter had reached the conclusion that there was not the slightest need for him to undertake a more severe cure or to go to Karlsbad [Karlovy Vary], as Heuberger had strongly recommended him to do (Heuberger 1976, 110). Subsequently, Schrötter corresponded with Hertzka about Brahms's illness, and on 28 August Brahms told Heuberger that Schrötter was against his going to Karlsbad because he suspected that jaundice (or hepatitis) was not the sole cause of his illness. But Brahms refused to undergo a joint examination by the two doctors; instead, he decided to return to Vienna on 31 August to consult Professor **Josef Toelg** (Heuberger 1976, 111; for the sequel, *see* TOELG, JOSEF.)

Heuberger, who had been surprised at Schrötter's original advice to Brahms, heard the explanation from the doctor himself when he happened to meet him in Vienna in September. His friend, Schrötter informed him, was doomed: "For Brahms's illness there is no Karlsbad. It is of no consequence where he spends his money" (Heuberger 1976, 110). (Heuberger 1976; *ÖBL* 1957–)

SCHUBERT, FRANZ (PETER) (b. Vienna, 31 January 1797; d. Vienna, 19 November 1828). Composer. Brahms was associated with Schubert's music in several different ways: as a performer (both solo pianist and accompanist), conductor, arranger, editor, and collector of autographs. He once told **Florence May** that he did not regard even the longest works, with all their repeats, as too long (May 1948, vol. 1, 22). He was probably made familiar with some of the compositions for piano by **Eduard Marxsen**, who had studied in Vienna with Karl Maria von Bocklet, an enthusiastic and excellent interpreter of those works. In February 1856 Brahms wrote to **Clara Schumann**, with reference to one of her recent concerts in Vienna: "I was so glad you played some Schubert. One must do so, if only for the sake of the beloved name. . . . If I were a moderately respected pianist and one worthy of respect, I would long ago have played one of the sonatas in public (for instance, the one in G [D 894]). It is bound to delight people, if played well" (Litzmann 1970, vol. 1, 176–77). Of course, opportunities to hear any of the orchestral works were no less rare in Hamburg than elsewhere in those days. The "Great" C-Major Symphony (D944) was actually performed twice at philharmonic concerts there in the 1840s (27 March 1841 and 11 March 1848), but Brahms did not hear the work until he attended a rehearsal of the Gewandhaus Orchestra in Leipzig in December 1853. "Few things have so enchanted me," he confided to **Joseph Joachim** (Brahms 1974/5, 21). His understanding of Schubert's songs was to be greatly enriched as a result of his friendship and artistic collaboration with **Julius Stockhausen**, with whom he partnered in numerous recitals. In April 1861 they performed the complete *Die schöne Müllerin* in Hamburg and at nearby Altona. (Stockhausen had been the first to sing the full cycle at a concert, on 4 May 1856 in Vienna.)

Brahms was afforded a further significant opportunity to extend his knowledge of Schubert's music when, during his first stay in Vienna (September 1862–May 1863), the publisher **C. A. Spina** permitted him to make copies of as yet unprinted manuscripts and, moreover, allowed him to take any Schubert edition already issued by his firm; Brahms was also able to consult some of the manuscripts owned by Schubert's nephew Eduard Schneider. In February 1863 he wrote to **Jakob Melchior Rieter-Biedermann**: "Altogether I owe my happiest hours here to unpublished works by Schubert, of which I have a large number at home in manuscript" (Brahms 1974/14, 77).

One of the scores he discovered at Spina's shop was that of the oratorio *Lazarus*, of which he copied out parts not available elsewhere at the time. According to **Max Kalbeck**, it was this copy that enabled **Johann von Herbeck** to conduct the entire work at a concert of the Gesellschaft der Musikfreunde on 27 March 1863. In addition, Brahms soon began buying Schubert autographs for his own collection (from Spina and others, including the son of Schubert's friend **Karl von Enderes**); among the compositions he thus acquired and was eventually to bequeath to the Gesellschaft der Musikfreunde were the *Quartettsatz* (D703), a number of dances, and various songs, including "Der Wanderer" (D489). He published the *Quartettsatz* anonymously (**Bartolf Wilhelm Senff**, 1870), as he did *12 Ländler* for piano (Spina, 1864), *Clavierstücke* (Rieter-Biedermann, 1868), and the song "Der Strom" (**Ernst Wilhelm Fritzsch**, 1877). Furthermore, he published, also anonymously, his own piano reduction of the Mass in E-flat Major (M. McCorkle 1984, Anhang Ia/18; Rieter-Biedermann, 1865); *20 Ländler* for solo piano, of which he had arranged nos. 17–20 from Schubert's piano duet version (Anhang Ia/6; **J. P. Gotthard**, 1869}; and *20 Ländler* in arrangements for piano duet, of which Nos. 17–20 had been prepared by Schubert himself and the remainder by Brahms (Anhang Ia/6; Gotthard, 1869). Finally, he prepared arrangements for voice and orchestra of the songs "An Schwager Kronos," "Ellens Gesang II" (first performed at a Gesellschaft der Musikfreunde concert under Brahms's direction on 23 March 1873), "Geheimes," "Greisengesang," "Gruppe aus dem Tartarus," and "Memnon" (Anhang Ia/12–17); these were not published in his lifetime, nor were the arrangements he made for solo piano of two marches and of the Scherzo from the Octet (Anhang IIb/3–4), which he is known to have performed at concerts and of which no manuscripts survive.

In addition, Brahms was a contributor to **Breitkopf & Härtel**'s *Gesamtausgabe* of Schubert's music. As is well known, he was highly skeptical of the usefulness of "complete" editions, even though he participated in several such projects. More specifically, he was generally reluctant to support the posthumous publication of previously unprinted compositions (though he clearly made some exceptions in Schubert's case) and, above all, he regarded the posthumous publication of fragments and sketches as unnecessary and even undesirable, and took care to destroy his own. Thus, it is not surprising that when Oskar von Hase, one of the partners of Breitkopf & Härtel, arrived in Vienna in 1882 for a meeting of the prospective editors of the proposed Schubert *Gesamtausgabe*, Brahms, who was among their number, tried to dissuade him from undertaking the project, contending that all the essential works had already been published and that all that was now needed was for Schubert's remaining works to be examined by a competent musician and for one copy to be deposited in a library in either Vienna or Berlin. However, when his arguments failed to sway Hase, he duly attended the meeting, which was held at Nikolaus Dumba's house, and agreed to collaborate in the project. Still, it was probably due to his objections that a number of works that had figured in the original plan were omitted in the published volumes (a full list of the missing items is given in O. E. Deutsch's [1951] article "Schubert: The Collected Works"). In the end, though, Brahms came to recognize the usefulness of complete editions, or at any rate of a complete edition of Schubert's songs. Meeting Hase again in Leipzig in February 1895, he told him that he had been mistaken and that especially **Eusebius Mandyczewski**'s edition of all the songs provided an entirely new insight into Schubert's creative process (Hase 1917–19, vol. 2, 629). Brahms was himself responsible for preparing the edition of the symphonies (divided into two volumes published in 1884–85), of which only the "Unfinished" and the "Great C Major" had previously appeared in print. His name did not appear on the title pages but was mentioned in the list of editors inserted into a later volume.

Given Brahms's intense, even passionate, devotion to Schubert's music, one may wonder why he did not take better advantage of his position of artistic director of the Gesellschaft der Musikfreunde in 1872–75 to promote performances of his works. It is true that the program of his very first concert, on 10 November 1872, included Joachim's orchestral arrangement of the Grand Duo (D812), in which Brahms had unsuccessfully tried to interest the Hamburg conductor **Friedrich Wilhelm Grund** years earlier. But apart from the Kyrie and Credo from the Mass in A-flat (D678), he offered only the overture to *Fierabras*, one song, and one aria by Schubert during the first two seasons, and no Schubert at all during the final one. Furthermore, when asked to conduct a special all-Schubert concert during the International Exhibition in 1873, he expressed reservations about devoting an entire concert to the works of a single composer and added that, as far as Schubert was concerned, there were in any case not enough major compositions that would justify such a concert on that special occasion. He accordingly declined the invitation. (At the concert on 4 May, **Felix Otto Dessoff** conducted the "Unfinished" Symphony and two marches by Schubert orchestrated by **Liszt**, Eduard Kremser directed performances of two of his choruses by the Singverein, and Bertha Ehnn and **Gustav Walter** sang several of his Lieder.)

In certain important respects, then, Brahms's contribution to the rekindling of interest in Schubert's music in Vienna in the second half of the 19th century, for much of which he is often given credit, pales in significance when compared to Herbeck's. For, in addition to retrieving the score of the "Unfinished" Symphony from obscurity and conducting its first-ever performance on 17 December 1865 (as well as some later ones), Herbeck gave the aforementioned first performance in more than 30 years of *Lazarus* on 27 March 1863 and a further performance of it on 7 April 1868, as well as one of the C Major Symphony on 27 November 1869, all at Gesellschaft der Musikfreunde concerts; and with the Hofkapelle, he directed performances of the Masses in G major (D167) on 25 December 1865, in E-flat major (D950) on 12 August 1866, and in A-flat major (D678) on 18 April 1869. Moreover, as choirmaster of the Männergesangverein, he was responsible for the first public performances of several of Schubert's part-songs for male voices, and he rescued others from the oblivion into which they had fallen. At the same time, he very actively encouraged the performance of Schubert's choral works elsewhere. "I am forever urging societies: Sing Schubert, more Schubert, and still more Schubert," he wrote in 1865 in his preface to Spina's edition of Schubert's choral music (Herbeck 1885, 155). He also published arrangements for voices and piano of certain choral works, including *Lazarus*. Last but not least, he was largely responsible for the decision to create a Schubert monument in Vienna, conducted a concert for the benefit of the monument fund on 19 March 1865, which included the C Major Symphony, and conducted the "Unfinished" Symphony at another special concert on the day it was unveiled (12 October 1868); in recognition of his outstanding role in the realization of the project, he was presented with a small bronze model of the statue. In short, while Brahms's contribution to the Schubert revival was by no means insignificant, its importance should not be exaggerated.

Lastly, the degree to which Brahms may have been indebted to Schubert in his own compositions has been frequently examined, both with regard to particular works and to more general aspects of form and tonality. Thus, some musicologists have recognized the influence of the "Wanderer Fantasia" (D760) in Brahms's Piano Sonata op. 1, and of the String Quintet in

C Major (D956) in his Sextet op. 36, while, in a wider sense, Donald Tovey (1949) concluded in his essay "Tonality in Schubert" that "upon Brahms the influence of Schubert is far greater than the combined influence of **Bach** and **Beethoven** (151). (Brahms 1974/5, 1974/14; Brahms Exhibition 1997; Clive 1997; Deutsch 1951; Hase 1917–19; Krones 1988a; Litzmann 1970; May 1948; Tovey 1949; Webster 1979)

SCHUBRING, ADOLF (b. Dessau, 3 March 1817; d. Dessau, 4 March 1893). Jurist; music critic. A man of considerable culture, he mastered a number of languages, including, according to **Max Kalbeck**, Sanskrit, Greek, Latin, and Hebrew; in addition, he was a competent pianist. He rose high in his profession, becoming a senior judge with the rank of "Oberlandesgerichtsrat" and later "Geheimer Justizrat." His stepbrother Julius, a clergyman, prepared the texts for Mendelssohn's oratorios *St. Paul* and *Elijah*. Brahms at one time examined one of Julius Schubring's as yet unused oratorio texts (possibly on St. Boniface) but concluded that it was not suitable for setting to music.

Schubring's earliest publication on musical matters was a review in the *Neue Zeitschrift für Musik* in 1847 of the opera *Das Kätchen von Heilbronn* by Friedrich Lux, the principal Kapellmeister at the Dessau court theater. Schubring's great admiration for **Robert Schumann** led him to publish in the same journal in the 1860s a series of articles under the collective title "Schumanniana," in which he discussed certain aspects of Schumann's works before turning his attention to the four composers whom he considered to be the leading members of what he termed the "Schumann'sche Schule," that is, Schumann's true successors: Carl Ritter, **Theodor Kirchner**, **Woldemar Bargiel**, and Johannes Brahms. The one he valued most highly was Brahms, to whose first 18 opus numbers (all the compositions in print at the time he prepared his study) he devoted a comprehensive examination that extended over five issues of the journal, from 21 March to 18 April 1862. Overwhelmingly positive, his careful and perceptive analysis nevertheless contained occasional reservations, for he was far from being a blinkered enthusiast. The last work Schubring (1862) examined, the String Sextet op. 18, he extolled as "the loveliest, most beautiful, and most mature" composition Brahms had yet written (128); but his delight with the Sextet as a whole did not prevent him from expressing doubts about the aptness of the tempo indicated for the Scherzo, nor from complaining about its brevity compared to the other movements. However, he had no doubts about Brahms's exceptional gifts and viewed his future with supreme confidence: "Why should I worry about Brahms? His genius will assuredly lead him in future along the proper path, as it has done until now," and he forecast that Brahms might well become the equal of **Bach**, **Beethoven**, and Schumann (Schubring 1862, 128).

Thus, he was one of the first critics to undertake a searching assessment, sympathetic but essentially objective, of Brahms's early compositions. In later articles in the *Allgemeine musikalische Zeitung* in 1868 and 1869, Schubring discussed the *Schumann Variations* (op. 23) and the Requiem. He had attended the Bremen performance of the latter work on 10 April 1868 and had already, in fact, prior to the publication of his article in the *Allgemeine musikalische Zeitung* in January 1869, given an account of the Requiem on 17 June 1868 in the *Little Musical Gazette/Kleine Musikzeitung*, a bilingual journal published by J. Schuberth & Co. in New York. For Schubring, the appearance of new compositions by Brahms were indeed red-letter days, and he promptly arranged performances of most of them at his house, often with the help of members of the local orchestra, and with himself conducting from the piano. A few weeks after the performance of the Requiem at Bremen, it was sung with great success at Schubring's before an audience of nearly a hundred guests.

In his edition of Brahms's letters to Schubring, Max Kalbeck states that it was in 1854 at Düsseldorf that Brahms first received a letter from Schubring, whom he did not know personally at the time. (Schubring's letters have not been published.) The earliest communication from Brahms that appears in Kalbeck's edition dates from January 1856 (it is a reply to a letter he had received from Schubring a year earlier); the last was written in March 1886. In this exchange, which reached its peak in the 1860s, Brahms, as he was to acknowledge himself, generally played the more passive role, namely that of the respondent to Schubring's remarks and questions regarding his compositions. It is clear, in any case, that Brahms came to respect Schubring's judgment, as expressed in Schubring's letters and publications. In April 1862 he invited Schubring's comments on his new Piano Quartets in G Minor and A Major, of which he sent him manuscript copies (these works were not published until more than a year later, as opp. 25 and 26), and he may well have taken some account of Schubring's observations regarding these and other compositions. The tone of Brahms's letters is very friendly, even warm, throughout, reflecting the fact that their relationship had assumed a personal note from the very outset, for in January 1856 Schubring had asked Brahms (whom he did not yet know personally) to become godfather to his second son Johannes Max. In the spring of 1863 Brahms readily accepted Schubring's proposal that they should address each other with the intimate "Du."

It is not certain how many times Brahms actually met Schubring, or even how many times he visited him at Dessau. In a letter of condolence to Luise

Schubring on 7 March 1893, he stated that he had visited her late husband "in his comfortable home" only once (Brahms 1974/8, 237)—presumably a reference to his stay with the Schubrings in September 1862, while on his way to Vienna. However, Brahms mentioned in a letter to **Fritz Simrock** in September 1875 that he had recently visited Dessau during his return journey from Heidelberg to Vienna (Brahms 1974/9, 204); but it is, of course, possible that Schubring was not there at the time. As for the statement made by Schubring's son Richard, in a letter to Kalbeck, that Brahms had attended the aforesaid baptism of his godson Johannes Max in 1856, it is likely to be wrong. On the other hand, it is known that Brahms met Schubring elsewhere on more than one occasion—for instance, in Hamburg in 1863 and at Bremen in 1868. Moreover, Brahms repeatedly urged his friend to join him in Leipzig when he concertized there. Thus, he wrote on 27 December 1877, in connection with the forthcoming performance there of his First Symphony: "Of course, the most important thing in Leipzig are the friends whom one sees on this occasion—and you are most certainly among them, and you will come, won't you?" (Brahms 1974/8, 231). It is more than likely that Schubring took the opportunity, then or later (1878, 1882), of joining Brahms during his visits to Leipzig.

Contacts between the two men appear to have ceased after 1886, and in his above-mentioned letter to Schubring's widow, Brahms expressed regret that he had never written to his old friend during those final years. Richard Schubring told Kalbeck that, when failing eyesight had made it hard for his father to read music and he had consequently given up playing piano and contributing to musical journals, his conscience did not allow him to accept any more free copies of Brahms's new compositions that Simrock was in the habit of sending him. Perhaps, Richard Schubring added, Brahms had heard of this and, misinterpreting his friend's delicacy of feeling, had let the correspondence lapse. For his father, he added, "the sun of his life set" when he lost contact with Brahms (Brahms 1974/8, 170). (Brahms 1974/8, 1974/9; W. Frisch 1983; Schubring 1862, 1868, 1869)

SCHUMANN, CLARA (JOSEPHINE), née Wieck (b. Leipzig, 13 September 1819; d. Frankfurt am Main, 20 May 1896). Pianist and composer; daughter of the music teacher Friedrich Wieck (1785–1873) and Marianne Wieck, née Tromlitz (they divorced in 1824). She married **Robert Schumann** on 12 September 1840; they had eight children—for details, *see* SCHUMANN FAMILY.

When she first met Brahms, probably on 1 October 1853 (*see* SCHUMANN, ROBERT [ALEXANDER]), she was 34 years old and the mother of seven children. Only the previous day she had, in her diary (as published by Berthold Litzmann), expressed dismay at being once again pregnant ("My last good years are slipping away, my strength also. . . . I feel so discouraged" [Litzmann 1902, vol. 2, 279]); her last child, Felix, would be born on 11 June 1854. This diary entry alone shows the absurdity of the allegation later made by Clara's grandson Alfred that Brahms was Felix's father (*see* SCHUMANN FAMILY). Further proof, if still needed, is surely provided by the letter Clara wrote to Brahms on 18 June 1854, in which, addressing him very formally as "Lieber, verehrter Herr Brahms," she describes the very painful days she is living through: "When I look at the beautiful little boy and think of the much loved father who is ailing, far from all those he holds dear, and does not even know of his existence, I feel my heart will break from melancholy and grief" (Litzmann 1970, vol. 1, 6).

The frequently discussed question whether Clara and Brahms became lovers during the two years following Felix's birth is less easily settled conclusively, especially since, with the exception of the above-mentioned letter, none of those addressed by Clara to Brahms prior to 1858 appear to have survived, primarily no doubt as a result of their later agreement to return each other's letters. Brahms sent Clara's letters back to her—without looking at them again, he wrote, because he assumed he would otherwise be unable to part with them—and she thereupon began to destroy them, before eventually yielding to her daughter **Marie**'s entreaty to preserve the rest for her children. As for Brahms's letters, Clara did read them again, and she even obtained his permission to keep those she particularly cherished; but, as he himself later told **Richard Heuberger**, he threw a bundle of those she did give back to him into the Rhine (Heuberger 1976, 60). It should also be added that the edition of their correspondence, originally published by Berthold Litzmann in 1927, may not have included all the then extant letters, nor did it reproduce the full text of every single one of those included. However, as far as the omissions from the included (and now still surviving) letters are concerned, they do not appear to have been motivated by any desire to suppress "delicate" evidence, and the omitted text is therefore unlikely to have thrown any fresh light on their personal relationship. The same may not, of course, apply to any excluded (and subsequently destroyed) letters. In the absence of Clara's letters to Brahms, the principal source available for assessing her feelings toward Brahms during that early period of their relationship is Berthold Litzmann's (1902) *Clara Schumann: Ein Künstlerleben*, which draws on her diaries (which were later destroyed) and on her letters to certain other persons. It is also occasionally possible to draw some conclusions regarding her attitude to Brahms from his surviving replies to her letters. As far as the possibility of a sexual connection is concerned, these sources—quite apart from other, more general, considerations—point to a negative answer. It is true that Clara decided in November 1854 to use the intimate "Du" in addressing Brahms (as, incidentally, Robert Schumann did quite independently at about the same time). But, as Clara explains in her diary: "He had asked me to do so in Hamburg and I could not refuse, since I love him so dearly, like a son (Litzmann 1902, vol. 2, 355). Significantly, she had written in the diary after bidding farewell to his mother upon leaving Hamburg on that occasion, "Who knows how long that estimable woman will still live—perhaps it will one day be my fate to assume the role of mother to him" (Litzmann 1902, vol. 2, 354). There is no doubt that Clara grew deeply attached to Brahms; in particular, she drew very great comfort, not least when she was away on concert tours, from his devotion to her: "Only one thing, that He, my dearest and truest friend, Johannes, is thinking of me and accompanying me with his good wishes . . . gives me strength again and again," she once noted; at another time she wrote, "I had longed immensely to be with Johannes! Only with him can I speak freely about everything that stirs my heart," and elsewhere she refers to him as "Johannes, the Faithful Friend" and as "Johannes, the Comforter in times of bitterest grief" (Litzmann 1902, vol. 2, 352, 360, 356, 357). In December 1855 she placed a room in the Schumanns' flat in Bilkerstrasse at his disposal, and when the family moved to a flat in Poststrasse the following August, he moved with them.

If Clara's feelings toward Brahms had a strong maternal element at that time, it is evident that his were soon far from filial. In June 1854 he confided to **Joseph Joachim** that he deeply loved her and was deeply in love with her, and that he had to restrain himself often from embracing her (he added, "and even—," the dash presumably standing for "kissing her"); he felt moreover that it seemed such a natural thing to do that he could not really imagine that she would be annoyed (Holde 1959, 314). At the same time, while Brahms's statement hardly suggests a son's feelings for his mother, his hesitation to give physical expression to his sentiments surely indicates the absence of any sexual relationship at that time. In January 1855 he wrote to Joachim: "Frau Schumann left for Holland over a week ago. . . . I followed her the next morning, I just couldn't help myself" (Brahms 1974/5, 86). By the autumn of that year, the words "kiss" and "kisses" regularly appear in the concluding lines of his letters. Thus, in October, "I greet and kiss you most tenderly. I think of you all day" (Litzmann 1970, vol. 1, 139); in November, "I kiss you tenderly, you whom I hold dear above all else" (vol. 1, 150); and in December, "A thousand greetings and kisses, my most beloved Clara" (vol. 1, 159). Yet it was not until January 1856 that the "Du" form first appeared in one of his letters, and then only in the final, particularly affectionate, paragraph (vol. 1, 169). The next, very long, letter in early February is characterized by the same restriction of the more intimate pronoun to the final lines: "Let me kiss you [still 'Sie']. I think of you ['Du'] always in old love and in ever newer and deeper love" (vol. 1, 172). After that, the "Du" disappears altogether from his letters until mid-May 1856, when it creeps back into the ending. A week later, doubtless in response to a remark of Clara's (who was in England at the time), Brahms finally explained why he had been so hesitant to use it: "I thought it better not to take advantage of your present kindness and love, it might displease you later. For this reason I am still using 'Sie' in writing to you" (vol. 1, 187). This clearly proves once again that their relationship was not a sexual one then. It was, however, the last time he would ever use the formal "Sie." The very next letter—in which he employs "Du" throughout—opens moreover with the most outspoken declaration of love to be found in the entire published correspondence: "My beloved Clara, I wish I could write to you as tenderly as I love you. . . .You are so infinitely dear to me that I cannot find words to express it. I want constantly to call you 'Darling.' . . . If this continues, I shall have to place you under glass later or save up to have you set in gold." (vol. 1, 188).

On 4 July 1856 Brahms met Clara at Antwerp on her return from her three-months' stay in England; they arrived at Düsseldorf on the 6th. Three weeks later he witnessed Clara's visit to her dying husband, the first time the couple had seen each other in more than two years; the scene profoundly moved Brahms (*see also* SCHUMANN, ROBERT [ALEXANDER]) and may have influenced his future attitude toward Clara, especially as it was soon to be followed by Robert's death.

In mid-August, two weeks after Robert's funeral, Brahms and Clara, accompanied by two of her sons and his sister Elise (*see* BRAHMS [LATER: GRUND], ELISABETH [ELISE] WILHELMINE), went on a five-week trip that took them to Gersau in Switzerland. On 21 October, a month after their return, Brahms left Düsseldorf and moved back to Hamburg. Clara was heartbroken over his departure: "I accompanied him to the station—going home, I felt as I was returning from a funeral," she wrote in her diary (Litzmann 1902, vol. 3, 15), and in her letters to friends she described her grief over the separation. One can only speculate about the reasons for his departure, especially at a time when she was still so greatly affected by Robert's death and, accordingly, particularly vulnerable and in need of his consoling and comforting presence. One of the principal reasons may well have been a desire for that independence that he regarded increasingly as an essential condition for the creative artist. (In this connection, *see also* SIEBOLD, [SOPHIE LUISE BERTHA] AGATHE VON.) If so, then the realization that Clara was now free to marry again, should she wish to, might even have made him more anxious to put some distance between them. The answers to the following questions might throw some further, and perhaps even a different, light on his conduct: Firstly, how had Clara reacted to that declaration of love he sent her in May? (Unfortunately, there is no way of guessing her response, for Litzmann quotes no pertinent entry from her diary, and the published as well as the now still extant correspondence contains no letters from Brahms dating from the month of June, although he almost certainly would have written some.) Furthermore, what, if anything, happened during their late summer trip? And if Clara would have liked Brahms to remain with her in Düsseldorf, as she evidently did, how did she view the future? In short, might Brahms have decided to leave because Clara did not envisage a change in their relations—or on the contrary, because she did?

It is true that Brahms returned to Düsseldorf at Christmas 1856 and even spent the early months of the following year there (during part of which period Clara was appearing at concerts elsewhere). But his return to Hamburg in October 1856 appears nevertheless to mark the end of a chapter in his life. While he would continue to assure Clara of his deep love for her, the passion that he had so eloquently expressed that spring would not surface again in his letters. However, although they would never again, after the spring of 1857, reside in the same town for very long, except during a number of summer vacations spent at Baden-Baden, they remained in close contact for most of the next 40 years, and their actions and correspondence offer convincing evidence that they continued to feel profound affection, admiration, and respect for one another. Moreover, they would always be linked intimately by the prominent role that music played in both their lives. For most of that period, Clara was the first person to whom Brahms sent his newly composed works, and he attached considerable importance to her comments. In her turn, Clara derived enormous satisfaction, as she had during her life with Robert, from her association with a creative artist whose music generally gave her immense pleasure.

She had from the outset done her best to further his career, trying to interest publishers in his compositions, occasionally concertizing with him, and above all, making his music known to concert audiences. On 23 October 1854 she played the Andante and Scherzo from his Sonata op. 5 at Leipzig, and she performed them again at Hamburg, Altona, Bremen, and Berlin soon afterward. (Styra Avins [1997] claims in *Johannes Brahms: Life and Letters* that the Leipzig performance marked "the first time his music was played in public" [65, n. 70]—meaning, presumably, by another musician, for he had, of course, played some of it on more than one occasion, including at Leipzig on 17 December 1853; but even so the statement is incorrect—*see* BÜLOW, HANS [GUIDO] VON.) On 16 November 1854 Clara played the middle movements of the Sonata op. 1 in Hamburg, and she performed them again on 12 February 1856 in Vienna where a few weeks earlier, on 20 January 1856, she had played one of the Gavottes from WoO 3 and one of the Sarabandes from WoO 5 (apparently the first time Brahms's music had been heard in Vienna). Later, she was to give, or take part in, the first public performances of the following works: the Piano Quartet op. 25 in Hamburg on 16 November 1861; the *Handel Variations* in Hamburg on 7 December 1861 (she played them again at Leipzig a week later and, during her visit to Paris in April 1862, at a private "Brahms-Séance," to which she invited a number of local musicians); and the complete *Liebeslieder-Walzer* in Vienna on 5 January 1870, which she accompanied together with Brahms. Earlier joint concert appearances by them included performances of Schumann's *Andante and Variations* for two pianos (op. 46) in Hamburg on 15 January 1861, of **Bach**'s Concerto for Two Pianos (BMV 106) and **Mozart**'s Sonata for Two Pianos in Hamburg on 22 January 1861, and another performance of Schumann's *Andante and Variations* in Vienna on 28 November 1868 (*see* KUPFER, [THEODOR] WILHELM). At her last appearance as a concert pianist, at Frankfurt on 12 March 1891, Clara played Brahms's *Haydn Variations*, in which she was partnered by James Kwast.

Furthermore, Clara could take credit for introducing Brahms to an English audience: at her recital at the Hanover Square Rooms on 17 June 1856, she included one of the Gavottes (WoO 3) and one of the Sarabandes (WoO 5) in her program, and even repeated them as encores. During later visits to England, she performed various other piano pieces by Brahms and took part in several performances of his chamber music. Thus, on 19 March 1888, on her last visit to London, she played the Piano Trio op. 101 with Wilma Neruda and Alfredo Piatti (she had previously performed it at Frankfurt with **Hugo Heermann** and Valentin Müller on 28 October 1887).

Profoundly satisfying from a musical point of view, Clara's association with Brahms was not without its up and downs at a personal level. In particular, his sometimes brusque manner, inconsiderate behavior, and tactless ways (such as when he urged her more than once, no doubt with the best of intentions, to abandon her concert activities and lead a more quiet and settled life) put an occasional strain on their relations; they were also in disagreement regarding the desirability of publishing the original version of Schumann's Fourth Symphony (*see* SCHUMANN, ROBERT [ALEXANDER] and WÜLLNER, FRANZ). But such temporary tensions did not shake the firm bond of friendship that united them, nor impair the deep devotion they felt toward each other. "I love you more than myself or anyone else or anything in this world," he assured her in March 1876, when she was greatly troubled by her son Felix's illness (Litzmann 1970, vol. 3, 332). In a conversation with **Sir George Henschel** later that same year he called Robert and Clara Schumann "two true and beautiful *Menschenbilder* [human beings]," adding, "Knowledge, achievement, power, position—nothing can outweigh this: to be a beautiful *Menschenbild*" (G. Henschel 1978, 48). To Richard Heuberger he confided in June 1895, "Apart from Frau Schumann, I am not attached to anyone with all my heart" (Heuberger 1976, 83). It was in October of that year that they met for the last time, during a brief visit Brahms paid to Frankfurt. Six months later, when Clara was known to be seriously ill, he wrote to Joachim: "When she has gone from us, will our faces not light up with delight whenever we think of her? Of that marvellous woman from whom it was our good fortune to derive so much pleasure throughout a long life—and to love and admire her ever more" (Brahms 1974/6, 303). At her funeral Brahms was observed by **Richard Barth** to be "weeping pitifully" (K. Hofmann 1979b, 62), and **Rudolf von der Leyen** was to recall how Brahms had thrown his arms around his neck, sobbing, and had gone on crying for a long time. The next day Brahms remarked to **Alwin** and Marie **von Beckerath**, "Now there is nothing more left to me to lose" (Beckerath 1958, 92).

It was during that weekend at the Hagerhof, the Weyermanns' estate at Bad Honeff, that Brahms presented his most recent compositions, the *4 ernste Gesänge*, to the friends assembled there. While he had not written them specifically with Clara in mind, he subsequently asked Marie and **Eugenie Schumann**, who received a copy, to regard them as a "funerary offering" for their mother (Kalbeck 1976, vol. 4, 943).

Brahms dedicated two early works to Clara—the Piano Sonata op. 2 and the *16 Variations on a Theme by Schumann* (op. 9), both published in 1854—and later his arrangement for piano of the Gavotte from **Christoph Willibald Gluck**'s *Iphigénie en Aulide* (M. McCorkle 1984, Anhang Ia/2), published in 1871/72. (Beckerath 1958; Brahms 1974/5–6; G. Henschel 1978; Heuberger 1976; K. Hofmann 1979b; Höft 1983; Holde 1959; Kühn 1998; Litzmann 1902, 1970; Munte 1977; Nauhaus 2001; Pascall 1988a; N. Reich 1985, 1990; Struck 1988)

SCHUMANN, ROBERT (ALEXANDER) (b. Zwickau, Saxony, 8 June 1810; d. Endenich, near Bonn, 29 July 1856). Composer; husband of **Clara Schumann**, by whom he had eight children (for details, *see* SCHUMANN FAMILY).

The days Brahms spent with Robert and Clara Schumann at Düsseldorf in the autumn of 1853 were without any doubt among the most memorable of his entire life. Three years earlier, in March 1850, he had taken advantage of their presence in Hamburg to ask Schumann to examine some of his compositions. According to **Max Kalbeck**, he sent them to Schumann; on the other hand, **Wilhelm von Wasielewski**, who claims to base himself on an account given to him by Brahms in 1853, states in his memoirs (published in 1897) that Brahms had handed them over personally. In any case, whether or not Brahms had actually briefly met Schumann on that occasion is of little significance; what matters is that Schumann had no time to look at the manuscripts during his stay in Hamburg and returned them unread to Brahms. As a result of this disappointing experience, the latter was reluctant to consult Schumann again, and it was probably only at the urging of **Joseph Joachim** and Wasielewski (who, indeed, claims sole responsibility for convincing him) that the 20-year-old Brahms traveled to Düsseldorf in late September 1853. At the same time, he may have welcomed an opportunity to contact Schumann once more just then, for he had only very recently, while staying with the **Deichmann**s at Mehlem, become better acquainted with his compositions and come to admire them. Until then his knowledge of Schumann's music had, by his own account, been superficial. As for the Schumanns, by the time Brahms arrived at Düsseldorf at the end of September 1853, they must have been highly curious and eager to meet him. In "Neue Bahnen" [New Paths] (see below), Schumann was to state that Brahms had recently been recommended to him by "an esteemed and well-known master"—evidently Joseph Joachim, who had stayed at Düsseldorf for three days at the end of August and had stopped off there again on 23 September on his way to the Karlsruhe Music Festival. Having spent a large part of that summer in the company of Brahms, whose musical talent had made such a profound impression on him, Joachim is certain to have described his accomplishments in glowing terms to the Schumanns. Moreover, his praise would have counted for a good deal, for the Schumanns greatly admired Joachim both as an artist and as a person. (Forty years later, Brahms told **Richard Heuberger** that he had no special letters of introduction to Schumann but that Joachim and others had written to Schumann about him (Heuberger 1976, 61). If he knew about Joachim's visits to Düsseldorf, he had evidently forgotten about them.)

According to **Marie Schumann**'s recollections, cited in **Eugenie Schumann**'s (1931) book about their father, Robert and Clara were out when Brahms first presented himself at 1032 (now 15) Bilker Strasse, and it was she who answered the door. Marie reports that she told him to come back the following morning, which he did (while Marie was at school), and that, at her father's invitation, Brahms played some of his compositions for him and Clara. That day, at their midday meal ("which has remained unforgettable for me") her parents, she recalled, were in a state of high excitement and "could speak of nothing but their brilliant visitor of that morning" (E. Schumann 1931, 357).

Two entries in Schumann's *Haushaltbuch*, very different in tone, refer to his first meetings with Brahms: on 30 September he simply noted, "Herr Brahms from Hamburg," whilst on 1 October he recorded, "Visit from Brahms (a genius)" (Nauhaus 1982, 637). The striking difference between the two entries—one cold and purely factual, the other so enthusiastic and even eulogistic—surely points to the following conclusion: Brahms did not play for the Schumanns until 1 October. In that case, how should one interpret the entry of 30 September? The most likely explanation, bearing in mind Marie's above-mentioned recollections, would seem to be that Brahms first called at Bilker Strasse on 30 September in her parents' absence, that she informed them of his visit on their return (perhaps he had left a visiting card), that Schumann simply recorded in his diary the bald fact of Brahms having called at the house that day, and that he and Clara first met Brahms the next day, 1 October, when he also played for them and dazzled them with his musical talent. (While Marie's recollections of her parents' relations with Brahms, written down many years after the events, may well contain some inaccuracies and even some deliberately embroidered statements, there appears no reason to doubt the accuracy of the sequence of Brahms's initial visits to Bilker Strasse as described by her.)

However, it might be objected that Schumann normally mentioned in his diary only persons he had just met, rather than those he was about to meet. In that case it could be argued that Brahms's first visit to Bilker Strasse had already taken place on 29 September, that he returned to present himself to the Schumanns on the following day, 30 September (hence Robert's entry in his diary that day), but that he did not actually *play* for them until his next visit, on 1 October. While this version seems less persuasive and evidently runs counter to Marie's statements, it nonetheless also offers a possible scenario. It has, incidentally, proved impossible so far to determine the precise day of Brahms's arrival at Düsseldorf, principally because he appears not to have stayed at a hotel but to have found private accommodations.

On 7 October Schumann wrote to Joachim: "Johannes is the true apostle, who will also produce revelations which many Pharisees . . . will not have comprehended many centuries from now; only the other apostles understand him" (Johannes Joachim and Moser 1911–13, vol. 1, 84). During the month Brahms spent at Düsseldorf, he was a frequent visitor to the Schumanns' home. There was a lot of music making, in which Joachim joined when he briefly stayed there on his return journey from Karlsruhe (14–15 October) and again when he came back to Düsseldorf for some concerts at the end of that month. In anticipation of his second visit, Schumann, Brahms, and **Albert Dietrich** (whose acquaintance Brahms had made at Düsseldorf) jointly wrote a violin sonata for him, with Schumann contributing two movements and the others one each. When Joachim played it with Clara, probably on 28 October, he correctly identified the composer of each part. (Subsequently, Schumann added two further movements to the two he had originally written, turning the whole into his Third Violin Sonata.)

It was on 9 October, little more than a week after his first meeting with Brahms, that Schumann began writing his celebrated article "Neue Bahnen." which subsequently appeared in the *Neue Zeitschrift für Musik* on 28 October (R. Schumann 1853). In it he announced that Brahms had fulfilled his expectation that a composer "would suddenly appear one day, who was destined to provide the perfect expression of our times in an ideal form" and who, moreover, would attain his mastery, not in gradual stages, but straight away, just as "Minerva sprang fully armed from the head of Chronos." (Schumann here mixes Greek and Roman mythologies and furthermore confuses Kronos, the grandfather of Athena/Minerva with her father Zeus.) This highly flattering article, which made Brahms famous overnight, placed him in a delicate position, particularly since he had not yet published a single composition. Schumann did his best to help remedy that situation by at once recommending him to **Breitkopf & Härtel**, who during the next few months brought out opp. 1–4. (Brahms consulted Schumann as to which works to publish first and in what order but did not entirely follow his advice.) It was also largely at Schumann's urging that Brahms went to Leipzig in November.

He met Schumann again in January 1854 at Hanover, where Robert and Clara spent the latter half of that month. Robert was to have directed a performance of *Das Paradies und die Peri*, which in the end, however, did not take place; but Joachim played Schumann's *Fantasie* and conducted his Fourth Symphony at a concert on 21 January, at which Clara was soloist in **Beethoven**'s "Emperor" Concerto. In private, there was again much music making. It was the last time Brahms was to see Robert, other than at Dr. Franz Richarz's clinic at Endenich. Four weeks after Schumann returned to Düsseldorf, he tried to commit suicide by throwing himself into the Rhine. Shortly afterward, on 3 March, a day before Schumann was taken to the clinic, Brahms arrived at Düsseldorf, anxious to give whatever help and moral support he could to Clara. Brahms visited the clinic at least twice that year to obtain progress reports on the patient's condition—on 29

March, together with Wasielewski and **C. H. Christian Reimers**, and on 19 August with Reimers (on the latter occasion he was even able to observe Schumann from a distance); but it was not until early the following year that he actually conversed with him (as mentioned below). By then they were in direct correspondence. Schumann had started the exchange on 27 November 1854, when he wrote to express his admiration for Brahms's newly published *Variations* (dedicated to Clara) on a theme taken from Schumann's *Bunte Blätter*. (In a letter to Clara that same day Robert fondly recalled the wonderful impression their brilliant young visitor had made on them that first time with his C Major Sonata and later the F Sharp Minor Sonata and the E-flat Minor Scherzo.) Brahms effusively thanked Schumann for "the first letter I have ever received from you—I treasure it immensely" (Litzmann 1970, vol. 1, 44). In his next letter, on 15 December, Schumann addressed him with the familiar "Du" and also mentioned with pleasure the fact that Clara had sent him Brahms's portrait (*see* LAURENS, JEAN-JOSEPH-BONAVENTURE). In both letters he noted with regret that they had not seen each other since Hanover. In response to this discreetly worded request for a visit, Brahms went to see him on 11 January 1855, and on 23 February he spent four hours with him. (For accounts of these and later visits by Brahms to the Endenich clinic, see his correspondence with Clara and Joachim [Litzmann 1970, Brahms 1974/5].) He was also present when Clara saw her husband on 27 July 1856 for the first time since he had been taken to the clinic more than two years earlier. "I am certain that I shall never experience anything so moving again," he wrote to **Julius Otto Grimm** (Brahms 1974/4, 44).

Schumann obviously felt deep affection for Brahms; he loved him "like a son," Joachim told **Liszt** after Schumann's death (Johannes Joachim and Moser 1911–13, vol. 1, 360). In a letter to Clara on 5 May 1855, Schumann called Brahms "unser Geliebter" [our beloved one] (Litzmann 1902, vol. 2, 374); for Brahms's birthday that month he gave him his autograph score of the Overture to **Friedrich von Schiller**'s tragedy *Die Braut von Messina*. As for Brahms, he revered Schumann all his life. "I hold Schumann's memory sacred," he wrote to **Friedrich Heimsoeth** in 1873. "That noble, pure artist always remains a model for me, and it is very unlikely that it will ever be granted to me to love a better person" (Brahms 1974/3, 121). Speaking to **Robert Kahn** and Ludwig Rottenberg in 1887, he remembered Schumann as "a wonderful, exquisite man—wonderful blue eyes—usually half closed, but when he looked at one lovingly, it was just marvellous!" (Laugwitz 1986, 645). It may seem a little surprising in the circumstances that Brahms (perhaps out of modesty) should not have dedicated any of his early compositions to Schumann, while during the 33 months between his first meeting with the Schumanns and Robert's death, he dedicated two works to

Clara, and Schumann dedicated the Concert-Allegro and Introduction (op. 134) to him in 1855. (The dedication to Brahms of the ballad *Des Sängers Fluch* [op. 139], which was not published until 1858, was due to Clara, Brahms having taken part in its first public performance at Elberfeld on 28 February 1857, when he had played the harp part on the piano.)

Brahms composed two sets of variations on themes by Schumann. One, for solo piano (op. 9), based on the first of the five "Albumblätter" from Schumann's *Bunte Blätter* (op. 99), was written and published, with a dedication to Clara, while Schumann was still alive. The other, for piano duet (op. 23), drew on a theme that Schumann believed he had invented at the clinic, but which he had in fact already used in his Violin Concerto; Brahms's variations were written in 1861 and published in 1863, with a dedication to **Julie Schumann**.

Brahms performed Schumann's Piano Concerto on several occasions, including the Hamburg Philharmonic concert given in Schumann's memory on 22 November 1856. Moreover, he made and published arrangements of the Scherzo from Schumann's Piano Quintet op. 44 (for solo piano, 1883) and of the Piano Quartet op. 47 (for piano duet, 1887); he also prepared a reduction for piano duet of the Piano Quintet op. 44, but it was never published and has apparently been lost. Furthermore, at Clara's request, he collaborated in the Breitkopf & Härtel edition of Schumann's collected works (1881–93), being in particular responsible for the Supplement, which contained nine posthumous compositions (some of which he had previously published anonymously). Last but by no means least, he published in 1891, together with **Franz Wüllner**, the original version of the Fourth Symphony, of which he possessed the autograph score. Clara, who wished to make available in print only what had been authorized by her late husband, did not approve of that particular publication; but Brahms found the original version altogether "delightful" and went ahead with it anyway: "It is a pleasure to see how what was invented in a light and merry mood is expressed in an equally light and natural manner," he wrote to **Heinrich von Herzogenberg** in October 1886; and he argued that it was only because he was faced with a mediocre orchestra at Düsseldorf that Schumann had decided to reorchestrate the work (Brahms 1974/2, 127; on his publication of this score, see especially his correspondence with Clara.) (Beller-McKenna 1995; Brahms 1974/2, 1974/3, 1974/4, 1974/5; Geiringer 1974; Heuberger 1976; Kahn 1994; Kross 1891b; Johannes Joachim and Moser 1911–13; Laugwitz 1986; Litzmann 1970; Munte 1977; E. Schumann 1931; Wasielewski 1897)

SCHUMANN FAMILY. Robert and Clara Schumann had eight children: Marie (1841–1929), Elise (1843–1928), Julie (1845–72), Emil (1846–47),

Ludwig (1848–99), Ferdinand (1849–91), Eugenie (1851–1938), and Felix (1854–79). In 1858 Brahms dedicated the *Volks-Kinderlieder* (WoO 31), his arrangements of 14 "folk songs for children," to "the children of Robert and Clara Schumann." Only Elise and Ferdinand married; Elise and her husband Louis Sommerhoff had four children, Ferdinand and his wife Antonie Deutsch seven. The following of Robert and Clara Schumann's children and grandchildren are of particular interest to Brahmsians:

ALFRED (1878–1944). Third child of their son Ferdinand. In 1926, angered by the flattering portrait of Clara drawn by Eugenie Schumann in her memoirs (as mentioned below), he launched a violent attack on his grandmother's reputation under the pseudonym "Titus Frazeni," alleging that the father of her last born, Felix, was in fact Brahms (*Johannes Brahms, der Vater von Felix Schumann: Das Mysterium einer Liebe*). The principal reason for Alfred's detestation of Clara lay in the hostility that she had persistently shown toward his mother Antonie, whom his father had married against Clara's wishes. This hostility had not only caused Clara to behave unfeelingly toward the dying Ferdinand, but it had continued after his death and materially affected his children. (Regarding the highly improbable allegation of Brahms's paternity, *see* SCHUMANN, CLARA [JOSEPHINE].)

EUGENIE. The Schumanns' youngest daughter is of interest principally by virtue of her memoirs (*Erinnerungen*, first published at Stuttgart in 1925), in which not only her mother, brothers and sisters, but also Brahms, figure prominently; she even devotes a separate chapter to him. (An English translation by Marie Busch appeared in London and New York in 1827.) A "racially purified" version, omitting notably various references to the Schumanns' Jewish friends, was published in 1942; the original text was reissued in 1995, with a postscript by Clara Schumann's biographer Eva Weissweiler. In 1931 Eugenie published a book on her father, *Robert Schumann: Ein Lebensbild meines Vaters*, in which she writes scathingly of **Wilhelm von Wasielewski**'s biography. (On Eugenie, *see also* FILLUNGER, MARIE.)

FELIX. The Schumanns' youngest son. In her memoirs, his sister Eugenie (1995) described him as possessing "brilliant intellectual gifts, a fine character, a noble mind, and a good and kind heart, together with an amiable disposition and an attractive appearance" (84). Brahms was one of his godparents, the others being the singer **Mathilde Hartmann** and a certain Fräulein Bölling. (**Joseph Joachim** could not become a godfather, as Clara would have liked, since he was Jewish.) Felix never knew his father, who was already being treated at the clinic at Endenich when he was born; and throughout his life he saw relatively little of his mother, partly due to the fact that she was very actively pursuing her professional career and relied on others to take care of her younger children, partly because his studies kept him elsewhere (Heidelberg, Zurich), and partly as a result of the tuberculosis that began to affect him in his teens and later increasingly obliged him to seek out climates considered more beneficial for his health, such as the Swiss mountain air and, finally, the balmy weather of Sicily. He was particularly drawn to music and poetry but received little support from his mother, who discouraged him from making music his career and urged him to publish his writings anonymously lest their failure should sully the family name. Joachim, after examining his musical talent at Clara's request, provided guarded encouragement, lent Felix his Guarnerius, and offered him a place at the Berlin Hochschule für Musik; but Felix, who after much hesitation, did finally opt for a musical career, was soon forced by illness to abandon any hopes of being able to pursue it. He never published anything, but Brahms set three of his poems to music: "Meine Liebe ist grün" (op. 63/5), "Wenn um den Holunder der Abendwind kost" (op. 63/6), and "Versunken" (op. 86/5), the first in Vienna in 1873, the second at Rüschlikon during the summer of 1874, and the third at Pörtschach in 1878.

Felix moved to Sicily in October 1877, and the following April he met Brahms, probably at Naples. **Theodor Billroth**, who accompanied Brahms on his journey, sent a vaguely optimistic report on Felix's condition to Clara, but any remaining illusions about the state of his health vanished the following year, and after a brief stay at Baden-Baden and a slightly longer one at a sanatorium at Falkenstein, he arrived at the beginning of November 1878 in a greatly enfeebled state at Clara's house in Frankfurt. There he died, some three months later, on 16 February 1879. It has been suggested that Brahms may have been influenced in the composition of his Violin Sonata op. 78 by the sadness he felt because of Felix's illness. At any rate, he sent a manuscript bearing the first 24 bars of the slow movement to Clara in early February, with the comment, "If you play [this music] slowly, it may tell you more clearly than I could do in any other way how affectionately I am thinking of you and Felix." Following Felix's death, a parcel of his poems was sent to Brahms, who, however, found nothing in it that he wished to use.

As aforementioned, fifty years after his death, Felix's name was thrust into the public limelight by his nephew Alfred.

FERDINAND (1877–1952). Second child of the Schumanns' son Ferdinand. Unlike his siblings (see the section on Alfred above), he retained fond memories of Clara, in whose house in Frankfurt he lived from 1894 until her death. He was thus well placed to observe Brahms's activities and comportment during his visits to the town during that period, and in 1915 he published in the *Neue Zeitschrift für Musik*, under the title "Erinnerungen an Johannes Brahms," a number of diary entries he had made during those visits. (A condensed version of this article, translated by Jacques Mayer, appeared in the *Musical Quarterly* in 1916.) In 1917 Ferdinand presented in the same German journal various diary entries relating to Clara ("Erinnerungen an Clara Schumann"). It is symptomatic of the affection and admiration he felt for her that he should also later have published a scathing rebuttal of his brother Alfred's allegation that their uncle Felix was the product of her adulterous relationship with Brahms.

JULIE. The Schumanns' third child was a pretty, gifted, and charming girl whose character endeared her to everyone. "I find her exuberant, effusive nature most appealing," Clara wrote to Brahms on 14 January 1868, "and when I am with her I always feel as if I was still a young girl myself" (Litzmann 1970, vol. 1, 573). Brahms declared that one could not think of Julie "other than with delight" (vol. 1, 575); and her sister Eugenie remembered her as "a child of the sun" (E. Schumann 1995, 73). But Julie's health was chronically fragile, although the doctors diagnosed her frequent coughing and other afflictions as being due to nervous rather of than organic disorders. Brahms, who had, of course, known her since she was a child, had an opportunity to get well acquainted with the teenage Julie when, in the autumn of 1861, she and her mother spent over a month in Hamburg where Clara had various concert engagements. It was at this time that he composed the *Variations on a Theme by Schumann* (op. 23) for piano duet. They were published by **Jakob Melchior Rieter-Biedermann** in 1863, with a dedication to Julie.

In late 1868, while spending some time at Divonne-les-Bains, a well-known French spa specializing in the treatment of nervous disorders, Julie received a proposal of marriage from Count Vittorio Amadeo Radicati di Marmorito (1831–1923), a widower with two young daughters. She was eager to accept it, but not until July 1869, at Baden-Baden, did Clara give her formal consent to the union. Clara then broke the news to her friends, beginning with Brahms, who was also staying at Baden-Baden and who, she wrote in her diary, "does not seem to have expected anything of that nature and appeared quite startled" (Litzmann 1902, vol. 3, 229). A few days later she noted that "Johannes has been a changed man, he calls rarely and says hardly a word, not even to Julie, to whom he had always been so very pleasant. Could he really have been in love with her? Yet he never thought of getting married, and Julie has never felt attracted toward him" (vol. 3, 230). Shortly afterward **Hermann Levi** told her that Brahms indeed deeply loved Julie ("dass Johannes Julie ganz schwärmerisch lieb habe"—vol. 3, 230, n. 1).

The nature of Brahms's true feelings about the marriage remains inevitably a matter for speculation, but it is tempting to regard it as more than coincidence that he should that summer have composed the *Alto Rhapsody*, with its stark portrayal of a grief-stricken man fleeing from the world that has caused him so much suffering, and with its appeal to the Father of Love to make the man aware (in **Johann Wolfgang von Goethe**'s text) of "the thousand springs which surround the thirst-plagued sufferer in the desert." Brahms's letter to **Fritz Simrock** at the end of August announcing this latest work is likewise of interest, if somewhat enigmatic: "I have written a bridal song here [i.e. in Baden-Baden] for the Schumann countess—but I write this kind of thing with an inward rage—with fury! How then can it turn out well?" (Brahms 1974/9, 78).

The marriage was celebrated at Lichtental (Baden-Baden) on 22 September 1869, after which the couple departed for Turin where the count and his daughters resided. (According to Clara's diary, "**Levi**, Brahms, and **Allgeyer** gave Julie some very beautiful presents" (Litzmann 1902, vol. 3, 232; in this connection, *see also* LEVI, HERMANN.) A few days later Brahms played for Clara his *Alto Rhapsody* on the piano, calling it once again "his bridal song." The words and the music, she confided to her diary, had moved her as no composition had for a long time: "I cannot interpret this work otherwise than as an expression of his own profound grief" (vol. 3, 232; in 1894 she told her grandson Ferdinand that she had been moved to tears.) Shortly afterward, Brahms sent a further message about the *Alto Rhapsody* to Simrock: "It is the best prayer I have ever intoned, and even if our worthy altos may not be eager to sing it straight away, there are many people who are in need of this kind of prayer" (Brahms 1974/9, 85).

Julie bore her husband two sons, Eduardo (1870–77) and Roberto (1871–1945). She died in Paris on 10 November 1872, aged 27, while expecting her third child.

MARIE. The Schumanns' first child devotedly and faithfully supported her mother throughout the four decades following her father's death. She often served as a surrogate mother to her own younger siblings, ran Clara's household, accompanied her on many of her tours, and assisted in her teaching. Clara loved her dearly and trusted her completely. It was to Marie that she left her diaries, and it was Marie who supervised Berthold Litzmann's biography of Clara and his edition of her correspondence with Brahms.

Marie, who evidently knew Brahms extremely well, last saw him during his fatal illness. **Max Kalbeck** (1976) wrote in his diary on 18 February 1897, "Marie Schumann is in Vienna, and Brahms wants to visit her tomorrow" (vol. 4, 503). On 5 March they both dined with the **Faber**s, and on 21 March, Marie was among the guests invited by **Karl Wittgenstein** to a rehearsal of the Soldat-Roeger Quartet (*see* SOLDAT, MARIE), at which Brahms was also present. Quite likely they also met elsewhere during this period. Marie attended his funeral on 6 April. (On Marie's later life, *see* FILLUNGER, MARIE.) (Brahms 1974/9; Litzmann 1902, 1970; A. Schumann 1926; E. Schumann 1931, 1995; F. Schumann 1915, 1917; Struck 1988)

SECHTER, SIMON (b. Friedberg [Frymburk, Czech Republic], 11 October 1788; d. Vienna, 10 September 1867). Theorist, composer, pianist, and organist; from 1851 until his death, he taught thoroughbass and counterpoint at the conservatory. In 1856 **Clara Schumann**, while in Vienna, bought for Brahms a copy of Sechter's 1843 revised edition of **Friedrich Wilhelm Marpurg**'s *Abhandlung von der Fuge*.

Brahms came into contact with Sechter during his first stay in Vienna and received from him an autograph of a canon Sechter had composed. This autograph, on which Brahms inscribed the date "February 1863," is now in the archive of the Gesellschaft der Musikfreunde in Vienna.

SENFF, BARTOLF WILHELM (b. Friedrichshall, near Coburg, 2 September 1815; d. Badenweiler, 25 June 1900). Music publisher at Leipzig, where he had gained his knowledge of the trade while working for Carl Friedrich Kistner (who had acquired Heinrich Albert Probst's firm in 1831). In 1843 he launched the periodical *Signale für die musikalische Welt*, which enjoyed considerable success and which he directed until his death (it continued to appear until 1941). He set up his own publishing firm in 1847.

Brahms made his acquaintance at Leipzig in November 1853 and, to judge from the tone of his early letters to Senff, quickly established amicable relations with him. Senff, he wrote to **Joseph Joachim**, was eager to take whatever compositions he had (Brahms 1974/5, 18). In the event, Senff published the *Sechs Gesänge* (op. 6) in December 1853 and the Piano Sonata op. 5 the following February. (Brahms had at first also proposed his Violin Sonata in A Minor [since lost], but Senff was not interested in violin music.)

The above were the only original compositions of Brahms that Senff was to publish, for he declined to take the four ballades for piano (op. 10), which Brahms offered him in 1855 (they were subsequently accepted by **Breitkopf & Härtel**). Not until 1868 did he contact Brahms again with a request for compositions. In his reply, Brahms pointed out that collaboration was difficult "between a lazy composer and such a silent publisher"

(Brahms 1974/14, 167). He also intimated that the composer in question might well have been hesitant to approach that particular publisher after the severe mauling he had received in *Signale für die musikalische Welt*—a reference to the highly critical review printed in that periodical following Brahms's performance of his First Piano Concerto in Leipzig on 27 January 1859. However, although Brahms would not offer Senff any further works of his own composition, he did make available to him over the next 10 years several piano arrangements he had prepared of works by other composers. Accordingly, in April 1869 Senff published Brahms's arrangements for piano duet of **Chopin**'s Étude in F Minor (op. 25/2) and of the Rondo from Carl Maria von Weber's Piano Sonata op. 24 (see M. McCorkle 1984, Anhang Ia/1/1–2), in December 1871 or January 1872 his arrangement for piano solo of the Gavotte in A Major from **Christoph Willibald Gluck**'s opera *Iphigénie en Aulide* (Anhang Ia/2), and in December 1878 his arrangements for piano duet of the Presto from **Bach**'s Violin Sonata BWV 1001 and his arrangement for the left hand of the Chaconne from Bach's Partita for Violin BWV 1004 (Anhang Ia/1/3–5), together with a reprint of the two arrangements of the pieces by Chopin and Weber already issued in 1869. Lastly, in 1870 Senff brought out the first edition (Anhang VI/10) of **Franz Schubert**'s *Quartettsatz* D703 at the suggestion of Brahms, who owned the autograph and checked the proofs.

After Senff's death, the business was managed by his niece Marie Senff; in 1907 it was acquired, together with the periodical *Signale für die musikalische Welt*, by the firm of Simrock, which was then directed by **Fritz Simrock**'s nephew Johann [Hans] Baptist Simrock. (Brahms 1974/5, 1974/14)

SEYFFARDT, ERNST H. (b. Krefeld, 6 May 1859; d. Garmisch-Partenkirchen, 30 November 1942). Composer, choirmaster, pianist, and teacher. He studied piano with **August Grüters** at Krefeld and **Heinrich Barth** in Berlin, and composition with **Ferdinand Hiller** in Cologne and Friedrich Kiel in Berlin. While in Cologne, he heard Brahms's First Symphony and his Requiem, and became a fervent admirer of his music. Therefore, he took advantage of a study trip to Vienna (October 1881 to April 1882) to call on Brahms and, provided with letters of introduction by Hiller and **Joseph Joachim**, was very cordially received. He subsequently met Brahms on quite a few occasions and even, at Brahms's suggestion, spent an entire afternoon playing his youthful compositions for him.

On his return to Berlin, he resumed his lessons with Kiel and produced some further compositions. One of these, *Schicksalsgesang*, a setting for alto solo, mixed chorus, and orchestra of **Emanuel von Geibel**'s poem

"Schicksalslied," he dedicated to Brahms. First performed at Krefeld on 13 November 1883, it was published by **August Cranz** the following year. (For his own *Schicksalslied*, composed between 1868 and 1871 and published in the latter year, Brahms had used a text by **Friedrich Hölderlin**.) In 1887 Seyffardt took up the post of conductor of the Liedertafel at Freiburg im Breisgau, and it was in that town that he saw Brahms once more, in September of that year, when Brahms spent a night there on his way from Thun to Baden-Baden. Among the many works Seyffardt performed with his choir at Freiburg was Brahms's Requiem. In 1892 he was appointed director of the Singverein and professor at the conservatory at Stuttgart, where he was to spend the next three decades. He last saw Brahms near Ischl during the summer of 1896.

Seyffardt composed some orchestral and chamber music, as well as numerous choral works and Lieder, and an opera, *Die Glocken von Plurs*, which was produced at Krefeld on 8 December 1912. He described his meetings with Brahms in his memoirs *Erinnerungen aus einem deutschen Musikerleben*. (Bach 1959; Graessner 1929; Seyffardt 1936)

SHAKESPEARE, WILLIAM: *see* SCHLEGEL, AUGUST WILHELM VON.

SIEBOLD, (SOPHIE LUISE BERTHA) AGATHE VON (b. Göttingen, 5 July 1835; d. Göttingen, 1 March 1909). Daughter of the gynecologist Eduard von Siebold (1801–61) and his wife Wilhelmine, née Nöldechen (1800–1892). The family counted, on the father's side, a number of distinguished men and women. Eduard's grandfather Carl Caspar von Siebold (1736–1807) was a celebrated professor of obstetrics in Berlin and was ennobled in 1801; Eduard's father Adam Elias (1775–1828) likewise taught obstetrics at Berlin University; Eduard's cousin Charlotte, who practiced obstetrics at Darmstadt, enjoyed so wide a reputation that she was asked to supervise the birth, at Kensington Palace in London on 24 May 1819, of the Duke of Kent's daughter (the future Queen Victoria); and his brother Karl Theodor Ernst was a professor of zoology at Erlangen, Freiburg, Breslau [Wrocław, Poland], and Munich, and an internationally known authority in his field.

Eduard von Siebold taught first at Marburg and, from 1833, at Göttingen University. He was also a passionate music lover who performed very competently on the piano, violin, and (his favorite instrument) the drum. Agathe's name was, in fact, a direct result of his enthusiasm for music, being taken from the heroine of Weber's opera *Der Freischütz*. There was naturally much music making at his house, and the Siebolds were also on very friendly terms with several other leading figures in local musical circles, among them the piano manufacturer Wilhelm Ritmüller. Eduard's daughters Josephine [Pemma] (1834–1907) and Agathe received their early musical instruction from his colleague **Arnold Wehner**, the university's director of music. Subsequently, Agathe studied singing, piano, and harmony with **Julius Otto Grimm**, and she would later sing at some concerts conducted by Grimm, at Göttingen and eventually also at Münster. Styra Avins (1997) states in *Johannes Brahms: Life and Letters* that she possessed "a fine alto voice" (799); yet her biographer Emil Michelman, who knew her very well and heard her sing on numerous occasions, writes more than once with admiration of her high soprano voice, which he calls clear, bell-like, and silvery. (Agathe herself, in a memoir she wrote in old age for her children's benefit, merely recalled that she had been blessed with a very pleasing voice and a dash of temperament.)

It was Grimm who introduced her to Brahms when the latter spent the months of August and September 1858 at Göttingen. This period remained forever etched in her memory as one of sublime happiness, when she had made music with **Clara Schumann**, **Joseph Joachim** and, above all, with Brahms, who spent much of his time with her and fell in love with her, as she did with him. After he left for Detmold, he wrote repeatedly, usually addressing his letters jointly to Julius and "Pine Gur" Grimm and Agathe, although on at least one occasion, he enclosed a letter meant exclusively for her. (Since he refers to it as a reply, she had evidently written to him.) He returned to Göttingen eagerly on New Year's Day 1859 and remained a week. Then, if not already the previous September, they exchanged rings as tokens of their love. The ring Brahms gave Agathe was still in the keeping of her descendants in the 1990s; as for the one he wore, which can be seen in a photograph reproduced by Michelman, it was in 1930 in the possession of Robert Fellinger, a son of his great friends **Richard and Maria Fellinger**.

The only source for what occurred between Agathe and Brahms after he left Göttingen in early January 1859 for Hanover—where he made arrangements for the premiere of his First Piano Concerto, which took place there on 22 January—is her above-mentioned memoir, *Allerlei aus meinem Leben* (Küntzel 1985, 89–98). In it she briefly mentions the summer of 1858, and that she had deeply loved Brahms and he had loved her "for a short time"; the first half of the month of January 1859 had brought their permanent separation, and "I did not see him again after that, nor would I have wished to." A separate short section entitled "In memoriam J. B." (Küntzel 1985, 99–101) tells their story in quasifictional form ("There once was a young girl.") and, while not naming any people or dates, furnishes a more detailed account of the growth and subsequent breakup of the loving relationship between that girl and a young man who was "one of those privileged human beings 'whom the Gods already love at their birth' . . . a genius and one of the greatest." When he returned after a three months' absence (i.e., in January 1859), their love, hitherto kept secret, became widely known. As a result, an "older, noble and faithful friend" of the girl, "who was also a friend of the young man and knew him better than she did" (i.e., Grimm), spoke "serious and well-meaning words to her" after the young man's departure and at the same time wrote to the young man, insisting that he ought not, in the new circumstances, come to Göttingen again unless he declared his intention to bind himself to her for life. Instead, the young man wrote to her assuring her of his love, of his desire to see her again, to embrace her, kiss her, and tell her that he loved her—but bind himself he could not. Whereupon the girl's sense of duty and honor obliged her to inform the young man that they must part. She grieved over her lost happiness for many long years, but in the end she recognized that he had been right to tear up the chains that threatened to shackle him, for, like every genius, he belonged to mankind.

This account of the steps that led to their breakup is likely to be essentially correct. It is in any case impossible to verify Agathe's statements, since the two key letters she mentions—Grimm's to Brahms, and Brahms's to her—were, if they ever really existed, evidently destroyed by the recipients. Various reasons were later put forward, not least by Brahms, to explain why he had persistently avoided matrimony. Thus he told **Joseph Viktor Widmann** that at the time when he most felt like marrying, his compositions were hissed or very coldly received, and he could not have faced reporting those defeats to a wife and be pitied by her (Widmann 1898, 52–53). One may, however, wonder whether this was really the sole reason for his reluctance to marry, or whether, as Agathe surmised, he had not instinctively, as a creative artist who "belonged to mankind," wished to avoid the "chains" of marriage. Perhaps the specter of his parents' less than happy union also influenced his views on marriage. In later life he liked to quip, "I never married, worse luck, and thank God, I am still not married."

Agathe's distress was intensified by the death of her father two years later; moreover, the family found itself reduced to more modest circumstances. Agathe helped by giving singing lessons, and in December 1863 she left to take up a post as governess in the west of Ireland, from where she did not return to Göttingen until June 1865. It was during her absence that Brahms, who had been informed about it (as well as about her unhappiness) by Grimm, paid his last visit to the town. For two-and-a-half years following her return, Agathe taught English, Italian, and singing at a local girls' school. On 28 April 1868 she married Dr. Carl Schütte (1831–87); they had five children, of which the first was stillborn. To please her husband, who apparently cared little for music and resented her music making, in which he was unable to take part, Agathe gave up singing in public, and even informally before friends. But after his death in 1887, she resumed her former activities and, in particular, very promptly joined a mixed choir founded by the new music director at the university, Otto Freiberg. As a member of that choir she sang, during the following years, in several of Brahms's major works, including the Requiem, *Gesang der Parzen*, and *Schicksalslied*. At home, his picture hung over her grand piano. Moreover, she gradually renewed contact with certain of her earlier acquaintances, including, eventually, in 1894, Joseph Joachim, whom she thereafter saw on several occasions. (By a strange coincidence, it fell to her daughter Antonie who, like Joachim, was in London at the time, to inform him of Brahms's death.) Agathe also maintained a close and loving relationship, until their deaths, with Grimm and his wife. She did not reveal her personal association with Brahms to her children for very many years, and her sense of discretion and propriety similarly made her refuse **Florence May**'s request for an interview in 1903, when May was working on her Brahms biography; but she consented a few years later to receive **Richard Barth**, when he was preparing the edition of the Brahms-Grimm correspondence, and she subsequently approved of the tactful way in which he dealt with her involvement in Brahms's life. (As already noted, the most intimate letters had not survived.) The memory of Brahms was always present in her mind; she once confided to her daughter-in-law Marie Schütte: "I live only in thoughts of *him*, as if my entire life was sinking behind me" (Michelmann 1930, 368). During her last years, she made a determined effort to renew acquaintance with those of his songs that she had sung in her youth, and to familiarize herself with all the rest. At her funeral Johannes Joachim, Joseph's first child and Brahms's godson, deposited a laurel wreath in the name of the German Brahms Society.

In the fictionalized account of their meeting (see above), Agathe wrote, "This girl came to know and love a young man, but his love was not as strong and profound as hers." Yet Brahms's feelings for Agathe left significant traces in his music. Thus it is a highly probable that most of the songs that he composed at Göttingen in September 1858 and at Detmold during the following months (published in opp. 14 and 19) were inspired by his love for her; of some of those that he wrote at Detmold, he sent her manuscript copies. Attention has also been drawn to the appearance of what has been labeled the "Agathe motif" in op. 44/10, a setting for women's chorus of a poem by **Paul Heyse**, and in the String Sextet op. 36. The former composition, ascribed in

M. L. McCorkle's (1984) *Werkverzeichnis* to the period between summer 1859 and spring 1860, opens with the notes a–g–a–b–e [in the German notation: "a–g–a–h–e"]; the text tells of a recently dug grave containing a beautiful heart that died as the result of having loved too ardently. The second example is even more striking: in the opening movement of the Sextet the sequence of the notes (in German) of a–g–a–d/h–e occurs three times in succession (the 'd' and 'h' sounding simultaneously). What makes the connection more obvious and convincing here is the fact that Brahms composed this movement at Lichtental in September 1864, shortly after his final visit to Göttingen. Reportedly, Brahms once told **Josef Gänsbacher** that in the Sextet he had freed himself from his last love (Neunzig 1973, 50). Yet he did not succeed in doing so altogether, for the memory of Agathe continued to haunt him for the rest of his life. In his "Erinnerungen an Johannes Brahms," **Heinz von Beckerath** recalls that during a conversation with his parents **Alwin** and Marie **von Beckerath** at the **Weyermanns**' in May 1896, Brahms remarked that he had behaved toward Agathe "wie ein Schuft" [like a cad] (Beckerath 1958, 92). (Beckerath 1958; Brahms 1974/4; Küntzel 1985; Michelmann 1930; Neunzig 1973)

SILLEM, JERÔME ALEXANDER (b. Amsterdam 1840/1; d. Amsterdam, 29 April 1912). Lawyer and music lover, residing at Amsterdam. Brahms presumably made his acquaintance during his first Dutch tour in 1876, and he met Sillem again regularly during his later visits to Holland. On several occasions he stayed at Sillem's house in Herrengracht, where, according to **Julius Röntgen**, he liked to browse through his host's private library and enjoyed playing chamber music in the evening with his friends. In 1880 he wrote to **Eduard Hanslick** who was about to visit Holland, "Herr Sillem (bachelor, most amiable and cultivated) will be the best and most congenial companion for you, from morning till evening, and wherever you may be inclined to go" (Hanslick 1897b, *Neue freie Presse*, 1 July 1897, 2).

Sillem was one of the prime movers in the project to build a new concert hall in Amsterdam. He was a member of the small committee formed for this purpose in September 1881, and also served on the first board of directors of the Concertgebouw, which was inaugurated on 11 April 1888 with a concert at which Henri Viotta conducted 500 singers and an orchestra of 120 players (the program included the "Autumn" section of **Haydn**'s *The Seasons* and **Beethoven**'s "Choral" Symphony). The board tried to engage **Hans von Bülow** as conductor of the permanent orchestra that was to be established later that year, and when he declined the offer, it appointed Willem Kes, but at the same time, at Sillem's suggestion, invited Brahms to assist in the establishment of the orchestra. However, Brahms declined.

The new orchestra's first concert, on 3 November 1888, included Brahms's *Haydn Variations*, and among the major works performed during its opening season were his Second and Fourth Symphonies. (Kes remained the orchestra's conductor until 1895, when he left to take charge of the Scottish Orchestra in Glasgow and was succeeded by Willem Mengelberg.)

Sillem continued to serve on the board of the Concertgebouw until his death; in 1903, following the death of P. A. L. van Ogtrop, he became its chairman. After his death, the "Eroica" Symphony was played in his memory at a concert on 2 May 1912. (Bottenheim 1948–50; Hanslick 1897b; J. Röntgen 1920)

SIMROCK, FRIEDRICH [FRITZ] (AUGUST) (b. Bonn, 2 January 1837; d. Ouchy, near Lausanne, 20 August 1901). Music publisher; son of **Peter Joseph Simrock**. He attended a private school at Ouchy, subsequently enrolled at a college of commerce at Lübeck, and finally studied jurisprudence, history, and modern languages at the University of Bonn. After fulfilling his military service obligations, he joined the family firm, but when his father disapproved of his engagement to Clara Heimann (1838–1928), he left Bonn and found employment in the music shop Timm & Co. in Berlin. He did extremely well in his new position, was able to marry Clara, and in 1864 bought the business, which he renamed "Simrock'sche Musikhandlung." In 1867, or perhaps early 1868, he was invited by his ailing father (who was to die in December 1868) to take charge also of the Bonn firm. In 1870 Fritz Simrock moved it to Berlin and merged it with the firm he had established there; from 1871 he concentrated entirely on publishing. His new firm, named "N. Simrock Musikverlag" (the "N" recalling its original founder, Nikolaus Simrock), prospered greatly over the years and in the process yielded him a considerable personal fortune, for he was an excellent, hardheaded businessman and possessed, moreover, excellent musical taste (he was himself a very good pianist) and the ability to recognize talent in still little-known composers. Fritz and Clara Simrock's splendid apartment at 3 Am Karlsbad, which was embellished by a number of outstanding paintings, became a well-known center of Berlin's cultural, and especially musical, life; they also owned a handsome residence at Pully, on Lake Geneva. Clara, with whom Brahms seems to have been on excellent terms, became a greatly admired and loved figure in Berlin society.

Fritz Simrock made Brahms's acquaintance at Bonn in 1860 and quickly recognized his great talent; he was reportedly responsible for persuading his father to publish the Serenade op. 16 (*see* SIMROCK, PETER JOSEPH). Their closer professional relationship began in 1868, following Brahms's first visit to Berlin, where he gave two concerts with **Julius**

Stockhausen on 2 and 7 March. In the fall of that year the Simrock'sche Musikhandlung published four sets of Brahms's songs (opp. 46–49), in 1869 the cantata *Rinaldo* (op. 50) and the *Liebeslieder-Walzer* (op. 52), and in 1870 the *Alto Rhapsodie* (op. 53). The later publications of Brahms's works for which Fritz Simrock was responsible, starting with the *Schicksalslied* (op. 54) in 1871, bore the imprint "N. Simrock in Berlin." They were extremely numerous; in fact, Simrock became Brahms's principal publisher. To say that, in his enthusiasm, he *encouraged* his favorite composer to produce new works, which his firm might then publish, would be an understatement. In 1870 Brahms warned him, "Stop driving your composers so hard, it could be as harmful as it generally is futile. Composing is not like spinning and sewing" (Brahms 1974/9, 92). Of Simrock's genuine profound admiration for Brahms's music there can be no doubt: "I *personally* treasure every note of yours," he assured Brahms in a letter on 12 April 1877, and in another letter on 11 February 1884 he characterized their association as "a relationship which comprises everything I feel proud of as a person and as a businessman" (Stephenson 1961, 97, 192). It was indeed his ambition to become *the* Brahms publisher (*see* BREITKOPF & HÄRTEL), and as early as 1870 he suggested a commitment on Brahms's part that would have tied him to Simrock's firm for life, but Brahms, then and later, refused any formal arrangement designed to curb his freedom of choice.

In order to avoid any possible dispute over money, as a result of which Brahms might have turned to another publisher, Simrock always insisted on Brahms fixing the fees for his compositions himself. Brahms, who felt uncomfortable with this arrangement, repeatedly tried to persuade Simrock to propose a figure himself, but Simrock persisted in his position: "Just believe what I said at the beginning of our association, and I can only go on repeating it: no demand of yours is ever too high for me" (Stephenson 1961, 97). While Brahms could thus hardly complain about the payments he received from Simrock, he did protest more than once about the prices the latter charged for his music, which, Brahms believed, were unduly high and beyond the means of many potential buyers. "As you know, I don't complain about anything and have indeed every reason to feel grateful," he wrote in December 1890, "except that you deprive me of the sole pleasure I could derive from writing music. For you can't convince me that I would not gain greater pleasure (and you more money) from my symphonies and my songs if they were more affordable, like those of all my colleagues" (Brahms 1974/12, 35–36). Despite these various quibbles, Brahms kept going back to Simrock, principally no doubt because he was well satisfied with the quality of the firm's productions, but also as a result of the personal friendship that developed between the two men over the years. Altogether, Fritz Simrock published the following compositions: opp. 46–56, 60–62, 65–81, 83–111, and 114–21, as well as some works without opus numbers, most notably the hugely successful *Hungarian Dances* (WoO 1). In other words, from the time Brahms first made contact with Simrock in Berlin, he sent him everything he wrote, with the exception of *Nänie* and some shorter vocal pieces; indeed, he might just as well have committed himself to the Berlin firm for life. In addition to issuing all these compositions, Simrock, in his ambition to be not only Brahms's principal publisher, but his only one, bought from **Breitkopf & Härtel** in 1888 the rights to the works that that firm had brought out (for details, *see* BREITKOPF & HÄRTEL). However, his negotiations with C. F. Peters (*see* ABRAHAM, MAX) regarding a joint collected edition of Brahms's works came to nothing.

As might be expected, given the extent of their association, Brahms and Fritz Simrock were in frequent and regular correspondence; about 900 letters by Brahms and some 160 by Simrock have been published. Moreover, the two men are known to have seen each other from time to time in Berlin (where Brahms stayed with the Simrocks), at Baden-Baden, and in Vienna, and they vacationed together in Italy in the company of **Theodor Kirchner** in the spring of 1887. Clearly certain reservations regarding Simrock's business habits in no way affected Brahms's very cordial personal relations with him. He liked Simrock, respected him, and trusted him; for quite a number of years until Brahms's death, Simrock managed his financial affairs. Further proof of the confidence Brahms placed in Simrock's integrity is the fact that, while staying at Ischl in May 1891, he wrote out his will in a letter to him, which is now generally referred to as his "Ischl Testament" (see Kalbeck 1976, vol. 4, 228–30). In April 1896 he asked for its return and made some changes, but he never sent the document back to Simrock, and it was found in a drawer of his desk after his death. It was at first officially recognized as his legally valid will but later declared void. (Concerning Brahms's wills, *see also* Biba 1987 and FELLINGER, RICHARD ALBERT AND MARIA REGINA.)

In view of these various tokens of what had evidently become a relationship transcending the bounds of a mere business association, it is rather surprising that it was not until 35 years after their first meeting, in January 1895, when the Simrocks were staying in Vienna, that the two men began to address each other with the intimate "Du." Shortly afterward Brahms lost 20,000 marks as a result of an unfortunate investment made on his behalf by Simrock, but he in no way allowed this misfortune to affect their friendship and refused Simrock's immediate offer to make good the loss.

Simrock met Brahms in Vienna in October 1896 and again, for the last time, in March 1897; he returned there soon afterward to attend the funeral.

Following Fritz Simrock's death in August 1901, the management of the business was taken over by his nephew Johannes [Hans] Baptist Simrock (b. Cologne, 17 April 1861; d. Berlin, 26 July 1910), who had become a partner at the beginning of that year. He strove to win a wider public for Brahms by reducing the prices charged for his compositions and issuing separate editions of various works as well as arrangements. He was also responsible, together with a number of other admirers of Brahms, for the establishment of the Deutsche Brahmsgesellschaft in 1906; in 1908 he founded the Vereinigung der Brahmsfreunde [Society of the Friends of Brahms]. He also played a major part in the organization of the highly successful Brahms Festival at Munich in 1909. (Anon 1992; Biba 1987, 1997a; Bock 1931; Brahms 1974/9–12; Döge 1991; Heuberger 1976; E. Müller 1928; Ottendorff-Simrock 1954, 1960a, 1960b; Plessing 1929; Stephenson 1961)

SIMROCK, PETER JOSEPH (b. Bonn, 18 August 1792; d. Cologne, 13 December 1868). Music publisher; son of Nikolaus Simrock (1751–1832), who founded the firm in 1793. Brahms first met Simrock and his son **Fritz** when he spent several weeks at Bonn after attending the Lower Rhine Music Festival held at Düsseldorf from 27 to 29 May 1860. The meeting led to the publication by the firm of the Serenade op. 16 later that year. (According to **Max Kalbeck**, Fritz persuaded his reluctant father to accept the work.) Simrock subsequently published the *4 Gesänge* (op. 17), the Sextet op. 18, *5 Gedichte* (op. 19), *3 Duets* (op. 20), and *21 Variations on an Original Theme* for piano (op. 21), all of which had appeared by March 1862. Peter Joseph Simrock further published the two Piano Quartets opp. 25–26 in 1863, and in 1866 he issued the String Sextet op. 36 (which **Breitkopf & Härtel** had rejected after accepting it and which he had himself initially refused), the Cello Sonata op. 38, and the Horn Trio op. 40. These were the last of Brahms's works to appear under the imprint "N. Simrock" in Bonn. (Brahms 1974/9; Ottendorff-Simrock 1954, 1960b)

SISTERMANS, ANTON (b. S'Hertogenbosch, Holland, 5 August 1867; d. The Hague, 6 March 1926). Baritone. After studying with **Julius Stockhausen** at Frankfurt, he settled in that city and later at Wiesbaden, while pursuing a highly successful international career as a concert singer; his large repertoire included oratorios and works such as **Bach**'s *St. Matthew* and *St. John Passions*, **Beethoven**'s *Missa solemnis*, and Verdi's Requiem. On 16 March 1896, in Berlin, he sang in the earliest known performance of **Gustav Mahler**'s *Lieder eines fahrenden Gesellen*. He frequently appeared at concerts in Berlin and also in Vienna, and his foreign travels took him as far as Moscow and St. Petersburg. His only venture into opera seems to have been his assumption of the role of Pogner in *Die Meistersinger* at Bayreuth in 1899. From 1904 to 1917 he was on the faculty of the Scharwenka Conservatory in Berlin, and after his return to Holland in 1919, he taught at the Blaauw Conservatory at The Hague.

By his own account (printed in Kalbeck 1976, vol. 4, 482–84), Sistermans first met Brahms through Stockhausen in Frankfurt in 1890 or 1891, and later visited him in Vienna more than once. He came to be regarded as one of the foremost Brahms singers of his generation, being particularly associated with the *4 ernste Gesänge*, of which he gave the first complete public performance at the Bösendorfer Hall in Vienna on 9 November 1896, accompanied by **Anton Rückauf**. A week later he presented the first complete Berlin performance of the songs, accompanied by Wilhelm Berger. (The final *Gesang* had first been sung in public by **Felix Schmidt** in Berlin on 22 October, and **Felix von Kraus** had sung all four at a semi-private performance at the Vienna Tonkünstlerverein on 30 October.) Brahms attended neither Kraus's nor Sistermans's performance. Moreover, Sistermans later recalled that when he subsequently offered to perform the *4 ernste Gesänge* for Brahms alone, the latter found a pretext to prevent the performance, and when, at Brahms's suggestion, he arranged a private performance before a small invited audience (*see* HORNBOSTEL, [OTTO] ERICH VON), Brahms stayed away. Sistermans finally realized that Brahms, for some particular reason (perhaps connected with his illness), simply did not wish to hear this work.

Sistermans also sang the entire set at a concert of the Berlin Philharmonic Orchestra in Vienna on 8 April 1897. Three days earlier, at the opening concert of the series, he had sung the last two *Gesänge* at what became in part a Brahms memorial concert (*see* GUTMANN, ALBERT J.). (Kutsch and Riemens 1987–94; Leichtentritt 1931)

SMYTH, DAME ETHEL (MARY) (b. London, 22 April 1858; d. Woking, 9 May 1944). Composer. Rather to the dismay of her family (her father was a major general in the Royal Artillery), she decided to make her career in music. In 1877 she enrolled at the Leipzig conservatory, where she studied composition with **Carl Reinecke**, and counterpoint and general theory with Samuel Jadassohn. Dissatisfied with the quality of the instruction, she abandoned her classes in 1878 to become a private pupil of **Heinrich von Herzogenberg**. During the following decades, she was to spend a considerable part of her life in Germany, especially at first at Leipzig. It was there that certain of her early compositions were first performed (a string quintet in 1884, a violin sonata in 1887); her first three operas were all initially produced in Germany. She was to write some vocal and orchestral works, as well as chamber and instrumental music; but she is best known today for her operas *The Wreckers* (produced at Leipzig and in Prague in 1906, and in London in 1909) and *The Boatswain's Mate* (first produced by Sir Thomas Beecham in 1916). She also published a number of fully or partly autobiographical books that give a lively and consistently entertaining account of her experiences and of her contacts with many of the persons who have entries in this dictionary (among them **Livia Frege**, **Edvard Grieg**, Heinrich and **Elisabeth von Herzogenberg**, **Adolf Hildebrand**, **Joseph Joachim**, **Clara Schumann**, and **Tchaikovsky**).

Smyth was introduced to Brahms by **Sir George Henschel** in January 1878, Brahms having come to Leipzig to conduct his new Second Symphony. She came to know him better when he returned there a year later for a performance of his Violin Concerto, with Joachim as the soloist, and again in January 1881, when he spent a week there (during which he conducted the *Academic Festival Overture* and the *Tragic Overture*). Since he was staying with the Herzogenbergs and Smyth was by then a constant visitor to their house, she had repeated opportunities to observe him and even to speak with him. In *Impressions that Remained* (1919) she draws a most interesting portrait of Brahms as seen by a young Englishwoman of independent mind who was a fervent admirer of his music, but nonetheless capable of appraising his behavior with greater objectivity than the starry-eyed members of his immediate circle. Thus, while fully appreciating his many good qualities, she was displeased by what she perceived to be his highly condescending attitude toward women in general and toward most artistically inclined women in particular (with the signal exceptions of Elisabeth von Herzogenberg and Clara Schumann); she especially disliked the derogatory and somewhat vulgar term "Weibsbilder" [wenches], which was "for ever on his lips" (Smyth 1919, vol. 1, 264). Summing up, she wrote: "I saw integrity, sincerity, kindness of heart, generosity to opponents, and a certain nobility of soul that stamps all his music; but on the other hand I saw coarseness, uncivilised-ness, a defective perception of subtle shades in people and things, lack of humour, and of course the inevitable and righteous selfishness of people who have a message of their own to deliver and can't run errands for others" (vol. 1, 269). But later in the same book, in discussing the great unhappiness she felt when her loving and intimate friendship with Elisabeth von Herzogenberg came to an abrupt end in the summer of 1885, she wrote: "During the two bereft winters I spent in Leipzig, anything more markedly kind, fatherly, and delicate than Brahms's manner to me cannot be imagined; but I had always known that with all his faults he had a heart of gold" (vol. 2, 152). By her own account she saw little of him in later years, but when she once called on him in Vienna she was cordially received. (Smyth 1919, 1936)

SOLDAT [SOLDAT-ROEGER, also **ROEGER-SOLDAT], MARIE** (b. Graz, 25 March 1863; d. Graz, 30 September 1955). Violinist and pianist; both her grandfather and her father were well-known organists and teachers in Graz. Soldat, who studied piano with Johann Lutzer and violin with Eduard Pleiner and August Pott in Graz, was a precocious musician who first performed in public as a pianist at the age of eight, at a concert presented by the pupils of Johann Wowa's music school. As a violinist, she made her public debut in 1874, playing Vieuxtemps's *Fantasie-Caprice* at a concert of the Steiermärkischer Musikverein. She gave her own first concert in Graz on 2 January 1876, when she performed **Max Bruch**'s G Minor Violin Concerto, H. W. Ernst's *Airs hongrois variés*, and a polonaise by **Ferdinand Laub**; her accompanist was the young **Richard Heuberger**.

In the summer of 1879 she undertook a short tour with pianist Adele Dirmayer, which took her as far south as Ljubljana and terminated at Pörtschach. It was there that she was introduced to Brahms, who was so impressed with her playing that he persuaded **Louise Dustmann-Meyer**, who also happened to be staying at Pörtschach, to take part in a concert that Soldat was due to give there on 12 August, and, moreover, he offered to accompany the singer himself, thus ensuring the success of the event. Soldat performed Mendelssohn's Violin Concerto and Ernst's *Airs hongrois variés*, as well as some piano pieces. Shortly afterward, at Brahms's suggestion and in his presence, she played for **Joseph Joachim** (whose acquaintance she had already made the previous year) at his summer quarters at Aigen, near Salzburg, and was promptly offered a place at the Hochschule für Musik in Berlin. She studied with Joachim there until 1882, and subsequently privately until 1889; she also received tuition from pianist **Ernst Rudorff**. (For a more authentic account than **Max Kalbeck**'s of her meetings with Brahms and Joachim in 1879, see Barbara Kühnen (2000), which draws on Soldat's personal diary.)

Once she had completed her studies at the Hochschule, Soldat's career soon flourished, initially mostly in Germany. Among her early engagements was one at the Cologne music festival in May 1883, which she apparently owed to Brahms. Moreover, she is certain to have met him again shortly afterward at Wiesbaden, where she played in a concert on 1 June and the following day took part in music making at the **Beckeraths**'

(Brahms was spending that summer at Wiesbaden and in almost daily contact with the Beckeraths). Over the next years she became one of Brahms's favorite interpreters of his own works, and particularly of his Violin Concerto. Indeed, Kalbeck (1976) relates that when she played it in Vienna under **Hans Richter** on 8 March 1885, he was so delighted with her performance that he exclaimed, "Isn't the little Soldat a splendid person? Isn't she a match for ten men? Whoever could do it better?" (Kalbeck 1976, vol. 3, 158, n. 1; in German "Soldat" means "soldier," and Brahms played upon that word association on more than one occasion.) However, Michael Musgrave (1990) is mistaken in stating (in his essay on Soldat in the *Festschrift* for Siegfried Kross) that Soldat "gave the Vienna premiere of the work under Richter . . . on March 8, 1855 [sic]" (Musgrave 1990, 321). The Viennese *premiere* had been given by Joachim on 14 January 1879, under **Joseph Hellmesberger**; what Brahms was witnessing on 8 March 1885 was Soldat's own first public performance of the concerto in Vienna. Six days earlier, at the house of **Richard and Maria Fellinger**, he had accompanied her in an informal performance of the work, playing his own piano reduction of the orchestral parts. She was to play the concerto once more with him at his summer flat at Mürzzuschlag on 23 August of that year.

Soldat was soon widely admired as an exceptionally gifted violinist, and especially as an inspired interpreter of Brahms's music. **Klaus Groth** described her performance of the Violin Sonata op. 78 at Altona in late 1885 as one of "surpassing beauty" (Lohmeier 1997, 260, n. 8); and **Clara Schumann** noted in her diary on 6 October 1887 that Soldat had given an "excellent" performance of the Violin Concerto at a Museum concert in Frankfurt (Litzmann 1902, vol. 3, 497). But Soldat was not content with her successful appearances as a solo violinist; as early as 1887 she formed a ladies' quartet in Berlin, of which the other members were Mary Schumann (second violin), Gabriele Roy (viola), and Lucy [Lucie] Campbell (cello). They gave recitals in Berlin and other German towns; for instance, they presented a "Streichquartett-Soirée" in Frankfurt on 4 November 1887, with a program consisting of quartets by **Haydn** and **Beethoven**, as well as violin and cello solos. (The information given by M. Musgrave, in his above-mentioned article on Soldat, about the original composition of Soldat's Berlin and Vienna quartets is incorrect.)

Following her marriage to Wilhelm Roeger, a senior police official, on 29 July 1889, Soldat left Berlin and moved to Vienna, and almost immediately afterward to Simbach (not Limbach, as stated by B. Kühnen) in Bavaria, where her son Joseph was born on 13 September 1890. However, by the spring of 1892, she was back in Vienna, having separated from her husband and, while it is not certain exactly when she resumed regular concert activities (a letter from Clara Schumann to her in January 1894 indicates that she was at that time considering the possibility of confining herself to teaching), she was back in the limelight by early 1895 at the latest, for on 11 March of that year her newly formed ladies' quartet gave its first concert at the Bösendorfer Saal. The original members of the new Soldat-Roeger Quartet were, apart from herself, Ella Finger-Bailetti (second violin), Natalie Bauer-Lechner (viola), and Lucy Campbell, cellist of the Berlin quartet; later Finger-Bailetti was replaced by Elsa von Plank, and Campbell by Leontine Gärtner. The quartet was to hold a prominent place among European quartets for the next 18 years (its final recital is believed to have been the one given in the same hall on 15 March 1913).

Soldat's close friendship with the Fellingers went back to the time when she was living in Berlin. Later, she was a frequent visitor to their Viennese home and, on more than one occasion, met Brahms there and also played some of his works with him. To cite a few examples, apart from their already mentioned run-through of the Violin Concerto: On 20 October 1886 they played the new Violin Sonata op. 100; one day in the spring of 1888, the Piano Trios opp. 87 and 101 with **Robert Hausmann**; and on 11 May 1895, the violin and piano version of the Clarinet Sonatas op. 120. Soldat must also have met Brahms repeatedly at the **Wittgenstein**s, to whom she was introduced by Joachim in 1884, for Kalbeck states that she frequently took part in music making at their house. In fact, one of Brahms's last outings, on 21 March 1897, was to attend a rehearsal of the Soldat-Roeger Quartet at the Wittgensteins' prior to a public concert.

A charming photograph showing Soldat with Brahms, taken by Maria Fellinger on 26 March 1894, suggests that he felt a particular affection for her. Soldat evidently returned his warm feelings, for she remained in regular contact with him until the end. When Kalbeck called at Brahms's flat on 13 March 1897, three weeks before his death, he found her there; moreover, he noted in his diary that it was the third or fourth time that he had met her at Brahms's recently. After Brahms's death she appeared at the memorial concert held at the Tonkünstlerverein on 13 April, playing the Violin Sonata op. 108 with **Karl Prohaska**. A year later, the Soldat-Roeger Quartet gave a recital in his memory at Graz (4 May 1898), in which **Richard Mühlfeld** participated. Furthermore, Soldat served on the ladies' committee formed to gather funds for the Brahms monument fund, to which she herself contributed 50 kronen, in addition to the not inconsiderable sum of 1,200 kronen derived from the proceeds of a recital given by the quartet.

Soldat was particularly popular in England, where she first performed in 1888. She scored a great success with her performances of the Brahms concerto and was hailed "a female Joachim" (Musgrave 1990, 324), and a critic in *The Musical Times* (1 July 1888, 410) declared that "Miss Soldat played Brahms's Violin Concerto in a manner which would have rejoiced the heart of her master Joachim." She was subsequently to make many more concert appearances in England, both in London and in various provincial music centers (in late 1896, for instance, she appeared at concerts in London, Manchester, Liverpool, Huddersfield, Cambridge, Glasgow, and Oxford). Especially well received was her participation in the famous visit of the Meiningen Orchestra under **Fritz Steinbach** in 1902, when she once more played the Brahms concerto (on 19 November, at the St. James's Hall). Among her other noteworthy appearances in London were several events organized by **Edward Speyer** on behalf of the Classical Concert Society; they included a concert on 25 November 1908, at which she played Brahms's Piano Quartet op. 25 with Frank Bridge, Robert Hausmann, and Leonard Borwick, and another one on 20 October 1909, at which she performed Brahms's Piano Trio op. 101 and **Franz Schubert**'s Trio D898 with Borwick and Pablo Casals.

A portrait of Marie Soldat by Fedor Encke is exhibited at the Brahms Museum at Mürzzuschlag. (Antonicek 1988; R. Fellinger 1997; Kühnen 2000; Litzmann 1902; Lohmeier 1997; Musgrave 1990; Suppan 1962–66)

SPEE, FRIEDRICH VON [really: F. Spe(e) von Langenfeld] (b. Kaiserswerth, near Düsseldorf, 25 February 1591; d. Trier, 9 August 1635). Professor of philosophy and theology at Paderborn, Cologne, and Trier; author of a controversial tract against the prosecution of witches; poet.

Brahms used texts by Spee in the motet "O Heiland, reiss die Himmel auf" (op. 74/2) and in three settings of "In stiller Nacht," for solo voice (WoO 33/42), mixed choir (WoO 34/8), and women's chorus (WoO 36/1). (Sieveke 1991)

SPENGEL, JULIUS (b. Hamburg, 12 June 1853; d. Hamburg, 17 April 1936). Chorus master and pianist. He studied the violin with Heinrich Ernst Kayser in Hamburg (1866–68), piano and harmony with **Ernst Rudorff** in Cologne and Berlin (1869–71), and composition with Friedrich Kiel in Berlin (1870–71). Subsequently, he enrolled at the Hochschule für Musik in Berlin (1872–77), where his teachers included **Joseph Joachim**, and later he studied counterpoint with **Carl Grädener** and organ with Karl F. Armbrust in Hamburg.

In 1877 Spengel succeeded Carl Voigt as conductor of the Hamburg Cäcilien-Verein, a choir Voigt had founded in 1843 (by 1870 its membership had risen from the initial handful to close to 130); one of the choir's main aims was the cultivation of a cappella singing, in which it soon had few, if any, rivals. While Brahms's music hardly ever appeared on the programs of the Cäcilien-Verein under Voigt's direction, the situation changed drastically once Spengel had taken over. During the first 10 years under his direction, the choir presented all of Brahms's major choral works, as well as a number of his pieces for a cappella singing. Moreover, Brahms conducted some of these compositions, and he would have conducted many more if he had accepted every invitation Spengel extended to him. As it is, he took part in three all-Brahms concerts given by the Cäcilien-Verein—on 6 April 1883, 9 December 1884, and 9 April 1886. At the first one, he conducted the *Gesang der Parzen*, as well as the *Academic Festival Overture*, was soloist in his Second Piano Concerto, and played the *Rhapsodies* op. 79; at the second, he conducted *Nänie*, his Second Symphony, the *Tragic Overture*, the opening movement of the *Triumphlied*, the Motet op. 74/2, and some of the *Lieder und Romanzen* of op. 93a; and at the third, he conducted the *Schicksalslied*, the Fourth Symphony, and the second movement of the *Triumphlied* (the concert also featured several other vocal compositions by Brahms). At the same time, Spengel's admiration for Brahms's music did not find expression only in his activities with the Cäcilien-Verein. Thus he gave a recital with Joachim in Hamburg on 30 October 1889 that included all three violin sonatas. In March 1892 Brahms was awarded honorary membership in the Hamburger Tonkünstlerverein, when Spengel was president of that society.

According to M. L. McCorkle's (1984) *Werkverzeichnis*, the first documented public performances of the following works took place at concerts of the Cäcilien-Verein, with Spengel either conducting or playing piano: op. 59/1, on 28 May 1894; op. 62/5, on 9 April 1886; op. 71/4, on 18 March 1878; op. 71/5, on 29 October 1877; op. 74/2, on 30 January 1880; op. 84/1, on 21 May 1895; op. 104/5 (the A minor version), on 25 March 1887, and op. 104/2 and 5 (C minor version), on 29 March 1889; *Fest-und Gedenksprüche* (op. 109), performed in Brahms's presence by an augmented choir of some 400 singers, on 9 September 1889; op. 110/3, on 15 January 1890; op. 112/3–6, on 21 November 1892; op. 117/3, on 27 November 1893; and WoO 1, book 4, on 12 May 1892.

Brahms took a personal liking to Spengel and had a high opinion of his musicianship, as is evident from a report he sent to **Franz Wüllner** in 1886:

> I cannot really appraise Spengel's competence as a singing teacher for you, since I am not qualified to do so. But he must be competent in the matter, for he directs a choral society in Hamburg quite excellently; it is the only choir

> there which sings superbly, also *a cappella*. . . . Sp[engel] is, moreover, an excellent and splendid person and musician, just the kind that appeals to you. You will like him very much. (Brahms 1974/15, 135)

Brahms was godfather of one of Spengel's children.

In 1898 Spengel gave an interesting lecture at a meeting of the Gesellschaft Hamburgischer Kunstfreunde, in which he discussed Brahms's personal qualities and musical achievements; it was published that same year in Hamburg under the title *Johannes Brahms: Charakterstudie*. The text of a shorter talk on his personal relations with Brahms, which he gave to the Hamburg Tonkünstlerverein in 1933, was printed in 1936–37 in the *Deutsche Musik-Zeitung*. Lastly, in 1959, Spengel's daughter Annemari published a number of letters that Brahms had written to her father between 1882 and 1897; they include the few already quoted by Spengel in his talk to the Tonkünstlerverein. (Spengel's letters to Brahms were not found among the papers left by Brahms, and only two letters were found from Spengel's wife, which her daughter also prints.) (Brahms 1974/15; Sittard 1971; A. Spengel 1959; J. Spengel 1898, 1937; Stephenson 1928; and information kindly supplied by Christiane Wiesenfeld)

SPERATUS, PAUL [really: P. Hoffer or Offer] (b. Rötlen, near Ellwangen, 13 December 1484; d. Marienwerder [Kwidzyn, Poland], 12 August 1551). Theologian; poet. Brahms set one of his text in the motet "Es ist das Heil uns kommen her" (op. 29/1). (Düwel 1991; Tschackert 1971)

SPEYER, EDWARD [EDUARD] (b. Frankfurt am Main, 14 May 1839; d. Shenley, Hertfordshire, 8 January 1934). Businessman and great music lover; son of violinist and composer Wilhelm Speyer [Speier] (1790–1878). He moved to England in 1859 but returned to Frankfurt in 1886 before permanently settling in England in 1891. His first wife having died in 1882, he married singer **Antonia Kufferath** on 2 June 1885. He was a close friend of **Joseph Joachim** and organized the concerts regularly given by the Joachim Quartet in London between 1901 and 1906; he was also instrumental in arranging the visit of the Meiningen orchestra to London in November 1902 (*see* STEINBACH, FRITZ). Furthermore, he was one of the founders and the first chairman of the Classical Concert Society; among the many notable concerts he arranged for the society were three in celebration of the centenary of **Robert Schumann**'s birth in April 1910 (*see also* EIBENSCHÜTZ, ILONA) and one on 20 October 1909, which served to establish the outstanding reputation thereafter enjoyed in England by Pablo Casals (the program consisted of **Bach**'s unaccompanied Suite in

C Major played by Casals, and Brahms's Piano Trio op. 101 and **Franz Schubert**'s Piano Trio D898, both performed by Leonard Borwick, **Marie Soldat**, and Casals). There was much music making at Speyer's house "Ridgehurst" near Shenley, where the guests included many well-known British and foreign performers.

Speyer made Brahms's acquaintance at **Clara Schumann**'s house in Frankfurt on 25 June 1887, when he was present at the informal run-through of Brahms's recently composed Cello Sonata op. 99, Violin Sonata op. 100, and Piano Trio op. 101, the executants being **Hugo Becker**, **Hugo Heermann**, and Brahms. (Regarding Antonia Speyer's earlier contacts with Brahms, *see* KUFFERATH, ANTONIA.) Speyer also attended the final rehearsal and the first public performance of the Double Concerto at Cologne on 18 October 1887, and he was to meet Brahms on several further occasions while still living in Frankfurt. In his memoirs *My Life and Friends*, of which two chapters are devoted to his recollections of Brahms, he recalls a party that he and his wife gave in Brahms's honor in January 1889; on that occasion Brahms played his Violin Sonata op. 108 with Heermann, and the Piano Quartet op. 60 with Heermann, Konink, and Becker; in addition, he accompanied Antonia in the recently published five songs of op. 105.

In September 1895 Speyer and his wife traveled from their home in England to Meiningen, collecting Antonia's father in Brussels on their way, in order to attend the music festival that featured works by Bach, **Beethoven**, and Brahms. The party given by Clara Schumann in Frankfurt a few days later (*see* KUFFERATH, ANTONIA) was almost certainly the last occasion on which Speyer saw Brahms. (Speyer 1937)

SPIES, HERMINE (b. Löhnbergerhütte, near Weilburg, Hessen, 25 February 1857; d. Wiesbaden, 26 February 1893). Contralto. Daughter of Friedrich Spies (1814–83), manager of an iron and steel works. She studied singing with Pauline Freudenberg at Wiesbaden, Ferdinand Sieber in Berlin, and **Julius Stockhausen** in Frankfurt. After making her first public appearance at a music festival at Mannheim in July 1880, in a performance of Mendelssohn's cantata *Die erste Walpurgisnacht*, she quickly established herself as an outstandingly gifted and delightful singer, with a beautiful, well-controlled voice and an intuitive ability to grasp and express the meaning and mood of any particular song. As **Max Kalbeck** (1976) was to write of her performances, "She seems to be a different singer in each song, or rather each song seems to be sung by a different person, so greatly does the nature of her rendition, including even the coloring of her voice, vary from one to another" (Spies 1905, 202). To an admirer who wondered how she could so convincingly perform both profoundly grave and light-hearted songs, she quipped, "The answer is simple: a serious voice and a jolly girl" (Spies 1905, 197). She was, in fact, an extremely gay and high-spirited young woman, whose pleasing manner and attractive looks greatly enhanced the beguiling effect produced by her voice. By January 1883, when she reportedly made Brahms's acquaintance at Krefeld, she had already performed in several other German towns as well as in Holland (very recently, on 2 December 1882, she had been highly acclaimed when she sang in **Max Bruch**'s *Odysseus* in Berlin).

Kalbeck quotes **August Grüters** as stating that she was introduced to Brahms at Krefeld after a performance of the *Gesang der Parzen*, which Brahms conducted there on 23 January 1883; in that case, they very likely met at the house of **Rudolf von der Leyen**, with whom Brahms was staying. Grüters, according to Kalbeck (1976), further relates that on that occasion Spies sang Brahms's "Vergebliches Ständchen" (op. 84/4) and that her rendition of the song drew from Brahms the comment "I think she'll let him in after all" (vol. 3, 375), which was evidently a tribute to Spies's charming and humorous interpretation. (He clearly much enjoyed the manner in which she performed that particular song, for when she sang it to his accompaniment later that year at the **Beckeraths**' (see below), he made her repeat it, saying, "Let's assume that some one has shouted *Da capo*" [Spies 1905, 95].)

It is not clear why Spies should have been at Krefeld at that time; the details of the program of the concert on 23 January, as given by Von der Leyen (1905) in his memoir *Johannes Brahms als Mensch und Freund*, indicate that she did not appear in it as a soloist, and since she later wrote in her diary that her performance in the *Alto Rhapsody* at Koblenz in July of that year (as mentioned below) was the first time she had sung under Brahms's direction, it seems clear that she could not have been a member of the six-voice chorus in the *Gesang der Parzen* when he had conducted the work at Krefeld. It is also a little strange, especially in view of Spies's subsequent celebrity, that Von der Leyen, who devotes four pages to the concert and Brahms's visit, should not have mentioned her presence. Lastly, her sister Wilhelmine [Minna], in the book she devoted to Hermine, makes no reference to any visit to Krefeld and describes her meeting with Brahms at the Cologne music festival in May 1883 as their first. According to Minna's first-hand account, the meeting took place in rather dramatic conditions: Hermine, having fled from the hall in tears during a public rehearsal after being reprimanded for a mistake by the conductor, **Ferdinand Hiller**, was consoled by Brahms, who led her back to the podium (Spies 1905, 76–78). For the aria from **Handel**'s *Hercules* that she had been engaged to perform she then substituted "Che farò" from **Christoph Willibald Gluck**'s *Orfeo*. Perhaps Grüters was mistaken regarding the circumstances of Hermine's introduction to Brahms.

On 16 July 1883 she sang in a performance of the *Alto Rhapsody* under Brahms's direction at a music festival at Koblenz; it was a work with which she would become very closely associated and which she would perform twice more under his baton the following year (on 5 March 1884 at Dresden and on 16 December 1884 at Bremen). About her experience at Koblenz, she wrote in her diary, "To sing under Brahms is marvellous. . . . He has such a calming effect on the singer" (Spies 1905, 88).

Brahms was to see more of Hermine later that year while staying at Wiesbaden, where he also accompanied her in some of his songs at the house of his friends **Rudolf** and **Laura von Beckerath**. Indeed, some of his biographers have suggested that her residence in that town was one of the reasons for Brahms's decision to spend the summer there, and, furthermore that his feelings for her provided the inspiration for at least some of the music he composed over the next few years, during which they met repeatedly. There is ample evidence that Brahms quickly formed a very high opinion of her as an artist, and he may have come to share the widely held view that she was a Brahms singer *par excellence*. In addition, he was greatly attracted to her as a person and there were some, such as **Maria Fellinger** and apparently even his own sister Elise (*see* BRAHMS, [LATER: GRUND], ELISABETH [ELISE] WILHELMINE), who thought that he might marry her, notwithstanding the 24-year age gap. How seriously Brahms ever envisaged that possibility, as some writers affirm that he did, remains, of course, open to question. As for Hermine, the thought expressed by Maria Fellinger in a letter to Minna in 1886, shortly after Hermine's first visit to Vienna, that Brahms "belonged" to her appears to have filled her with dismay:

> You are mistaken in what you write about Brahms in relation to myself. . . . No, in that you are most certainly mistaken! No doubt he quite likes me, for I sing his songs no worse than others and I am also, after all, a creature equipped with five healthy senses. . . . But—that he belongs to me . . . I absolutely refuse to accept that responsibility. I wouldn't know at all how to behave in that case. . . . He doesn't know at all how small I feel intellectually compared to him. (Spies 1905, 274)

In fact, the reverence she felt for him as an artist and a man made it difficult for her to feel completely at ease with him, much as she enjoyed the affectionate and mildly flirtatious manner in which he treated her. "How nice he was again," she wrote to the same correspondent after visiting

Vienna in March 1888. "If only I could tell him how happy it makes me that he is so kind to me; but one's courage fails one when one sees him" (Spies 1905, 281). Later that same year, a fresh element entered her emotional response toward him, which emphasized the difference in their ages. After seeing him in Berne, where they were both guests of **Josef Viktor Widmann**, she wrote to Maria Fellinger: "He met us at the station with Widmann, but, dear heart, how burnt out he is and, alas, alas, how white he has become! . . . If he did not have those splendid, youthful blue eyes and such a lively, pleasant manner, he would be an old man." However, making music with him filled her, as always, with profound happiness: "Wherever he is, one's life is twice as rich. . . . How grateful I am to my kind fate for having brought me into contact with him" (Spies 1905, 282).

Brahms met Hermine on various occasions between 1883 and 1889, appearing at concerts with her, acting as her accompanist in informal performances at private houses (at the Beckeraths' at Wiesbaden and Rüdesheim, at the Widmanns' in Berne, at the **Billroth**s', the Fellingers', and the **Hornbostel**s' in Vienna), and even seeing her during his holidays, at Wiesbaden and at Berne, as already indicated, and also at Hofstetten, where she visited Brahms with her sister, in 1886; in addition, he exchanged letters with her. Furthermore, there are a number of references to her in his correspondence with **Klaus Groth**, who had likewise fallen under the spell of her voice and her personality; each, addressing the other, refers to her teasingly as "your Herminchen." Brahms's setting (op. 97/5) of Groth's poem "Komm bald," of which he sent her a manuscript inscribed "To H . . . from Johannes Brahms" in June 1885, has been regarded as coming very close to a declaration of love. (Groth himself had addressed the poem to "A," i.e., Anna Huethe, a longstanding friend.) Other songs in op. 97, as well as those of op. 96, are also likely to have been written for her, and it may well be that several outstanding works dating from the years following his first meeting with Hermine likewise owed their composition to the powerful stimulation that his profound feelings for her exercised on his creative imagination.

In the latter half of the 1880s, Hermine Spies was regarded as the leading German contralto, with the possible exception of **Amalie Joachim**, whose prominence had, however, somewhat declined after her divorce in 1884. Like her teacher Julius Stockhausen, and perhaps influenced by his example, Spies confined her musical activities to the performance of Lieder and oratorios; she declined more than one offer to appear in opera. During those years, she toured widely in Germany and also appeared with great success in Holland, Denmark, Switzerland, Hungary, Russia, and, repeatedly, in Austria; in 1889 she gave two recitals in London. As already noted, she was regarded as an ideal interpreter of Brahms's music, but her repertoire also encompassed songs by various other contemporary composers, as well as some earlier ones, notably **Franz Schubert** and **Robert Schumann**; and Ernst Wolff, one of her accompanists, later recalled that "one could not imagine a more perfect interpreter of Bruch's contralto arias than Hermine Spies" (Wolff 1913/14, 126). Typical of her wide range are the programs of her recitals in London at the Prince's Hall on 13 June and at St. James's Hall on 2 July 1889, which offered music by **Eugen d'Albert**, **Bach**, **Georges Bizet**, Brahms, Emmerich, **Haydn**, **Sir George Henschel**, Loewe, Massenet, **Mozart**, Schumann, and Weber.

When she first went to sing in Vienna (at the Bösendorfer Saal on 26 and 27 November 1886), Brahms did his best to ease her path; it was no doubt at his suggestion that Billroth gave a musical soiree in her honor three days before her first concert, at which one of the invited guests was **Eduard Hanslick**. During the following years, she performed several times in Vienna. Thus she returned for more concert appearances in March 1887, and on 5 April she sang in a performance of Bach's *St. Matthew Passion* at a Gesellschaft der Musikfreunde concert conducted by **Hans Richter**. Early in March 1888, Brahms informed Groth, with evident pleasure, "Your Herminchen is arriving in a few days" (Lohmeier 1997, 117). Her recital on 19 March, so **Gustav Jenner** reported to Groth, evoked "unbelievable enthusiasm" (Lohmeier 1997, 266, n. 7). During her stay she was also present at the first private performance of Brahms's *Zigeunerlieder* (op. 103) at the Billroths' (see Gottlieb-Billroth 1935, 424); and she was back in Vienna in March 1889. On that occasion she again saw Brahms more than once. Thus, on 26 March, which she described as a "marvelous day," she met him in the morning at the Fellingers, where there was much music making; and in the evening, at the house of **Erich von Hornbostel**, Brahms accompanied her and their host's wife Helene, née Magnus (*see* HORNBOSTEL, [OTTO] ERICH VON) in some duets, presumably of his own composition (Spies 1905, 211). However, her visit to Vienna in March 1889 may have been the last time she met Brahms personally, although they still corresponded (see Spies 1905, 311–14). In 1892 Hermine married Walter Hardtmuth, a judge at Wiesbaden (in congratulating her on the engagement, Brahms had written that he was looking forward to seeing her during her honeymoon when she might be passing through Vienna [Spies 1905, 313], but it is not known whether he actually did.) On 26 February 1893, shortly after giving birth to a daughter who lived only briefly, she died at the age of 36. Stockhausen attended her funeral and afterward wrote to his brother Franz: "A fine woman, a beautiful voice, an inspired singer has disappeared" (J. Wirth 1927, 441).

According to M. L. McCorkle's (1984) *Werkverzeichnis*, Spies gave the first documented public performances of the following songs by Brahms: "Heimkehr" (op. 7/6) on 26 November 1886, "Bitteres zu sagen" (op. 32/7) on 22 March 1887, "O liebliche Wangen" (op. 47/4) on 26 March 1887, "Der Überläufer" (op. 48/2) and "Der Jäger" (op. 95/4) on 18 January 1890, "Vorschneller Schwur" (op. 95/5) on 26 March 1886, all in Vienna, and "Immer leiser wird mein Schlummer" (op. 105/2) and "Mädchenlied" (op. 107/5) in Frankfurt on 4 January 1889. In addition, she sang "Dämmrung senkt sich von oben" (op. 59/1) at the Beckeraths' in Wiesbaden on 5 September 1883, some nine months before the earliest recorded public performance of that song by Frl. Dugge in Hamburg on 28 May 1894. (However, Wolfgang Ebert [1997], in his article "Die von Hermine Spies gesungenen Brahms-Lieder," gives the date of the first public performance of op. 95/5 as 26 March 1887.)

The most important source of information on Hermine's life is the abovementioned memoir that her sister Minna, her constant companion on her travels, published in 1894. It is extremely valuable for the numerous extracts from Hermine's diary and letters, but the dates of different events are not always clearly established. Of particular interest is the third, revised edition (1905), since it includes correspondence between Hermine and Brahms, as well as letters from her to Maria Fellinger and some she received from Klaus Groth, which were not printed in the earlier editions. (W. Ebert 1997b; Gottlieb-Billroth 1935; Lohmeier 1997; Miesner 1933; Schuppener 1993; Spies 1905; J. Wirth 1927)

SPINA, C. A. (publishing firm). Music publishing business directed by Carl Anton Spina (b. Vienna, 23 January 1827; d. Vienna, 5 July 1906) from late 1851 until 1872. In December 1850 he had become a partner in the firm Anton Diabelli & Co., which was directed by Anton Diabelli and Carl's father Anton Spina from 1824 to 1851. Anton Diabelli retired in January 1851 and Anton Spina later that same year, whereupon Carl assumed sole charge of the business, which he renamed "C. A. Spina." In 1872 the firm was acquired by Friedrich Schreiber; it merged with the Hamburg publishing house **August Cranz** in 1876.

The firm C. A. Spina published first editions of numerous works by **Franz Schubert**, among them 16 songs, the part-song "Gesang der Geister über den Wassern," the Piano Sonata in A Minor (D537), *Thirteen Variations on a Theme by Anselm Hüttenbrenner*, the String Quartet in B-flat Major (D112), the String Quintet, the Octet (D803, but omitting the fourth and fifth movements), the "Unfinished" Symphony, and also piano arrangements of the oratorio *Lazarus* and of the overtures to several of Schubert's stage works.

Moreover, Carl Spina owned manuscripts of a considerable number of Schubert's compositions, including many still unpublished works.

After his first concert appearances in Vienna in late 1862, Brahms was approached by several publishers, including Spina, who were eager to add some of his compositions to their lists. However, as he wrote to his parents at the end of November, he preferred to deal with North German publishers, even if it meant forgoing the higher fees he might receive in Vienna. In a letter to **Jakob Melchior Rieter-Biedermann** on 18 February 1863, he mentioned that Spina had wished—but in vain—to publish the "quartets," that is, the Piano Quartets opp. 25–26, which he had presented to Viennese audiences on 16 and 29 November (in fact, he had already accepted **Peter Joseph Simrock**'s offer for the two works on 4 November). He added, however, that he "had to offer Herr Spina at least some items" (Brahms 1974/14, 77); and he did indeed, in that very same month, arrange for the publication by Spina of his setting of the 13th Psalm (op. 27) and of the 4 Duets (op. 28). According to **Max Kalbeck**, the arrangements were made with the help of **J. P. Gotthard** (who was then either working for Spina or at any rate had some connection with him, and with whom Brahms had already been in contact by letter prior to his arrival in Vienna—for further details, *see* GOTTHARD, J. P.). The duets were published in December 1863, the Psalm setting in 1864 (maybe in May—see M. L. McCorkle's [1984] *Werkverzeichnis*). Also in 1864, Spina issued Brahms's edition of 12 Ländler by Schubert (M. L. McCorkle 1984, Anhang VI/11); the editor's name was not indicated.

The relatively minor compositions opp. 27–28 constituted the sum total of Brahms's original works published by Spina, even though it is clear from Brahms's correspondence that Spina would gladly have accepted others. Moreover, as Brahms informed Rieter-Biedermann in February 1864, Spina was also very eager to publish his arrangements of *Volkslieder*, which had been performed at concerts of the Singakademie under his direction; but once again Brahms was disinclined to satisfy Spina's request, even though "this gentleman pays far more than I can receive in Germany or in your Republic" (Brahms 1974/14, 90). It is not altogether clear why Brahms took this line; but it is evident that he was far less interested in Spina as a prospective publisher than as the issuer of numerous Schubert editions and the owner of many Schubert manuscripts. To the latter he was granted full access, and moreover he was allowed to borrow them so that he could study and copy them at his leisure; as for the printed editions, Spina permitted him to take a copy of any Schubert work published by his firm, so Brahms was able to fill the gaps in his personal library. To his delight, Spina even gave him a Schubert manuscript. (Brahms 1974/14; Stephenson 1973)

SPITTA (JULIUS AUGUST) PHILIPP (b. Wechold, near Hoya, 7 December 1841; d. Berlin, 13 April 1894). Musicologist; son of theologian Carl Johann Philipp Spitta (1801–59) who published the well-known Protestant hymn collection *Psalter und Harfe*. As a classicist by training, Spitta taught Greek and Latin at secondary schools at Reval [Tallinn, Estonia] (1864–66), Sondershausen (1866–74), and Leipzig (1874–75), while increasingly devoting his free time to the study of the history of music, in particular that of earlier periods. In 1875 he settled in Berlin, where he held the posts of professor of the history of music at the Hochschule für Musik, professor of musicology at the university, and second permanent secretary of the Royal Academy of Arts and Sciences. These appointments testify to the recognition he had by that time attained as a leading and indeed pioneering figure in this relatively new area of research. A highly productive scholar, he was to enhance his reputation greatly during the following two decades.

Spitta's major achievement was his two-volume biography of **Johann Sebastian Bach** (1873–80), which is still highly regarded today. As well as publishing illuminating studies on a number of other composers, among them Heinrich Schütz and Brahms, he was active as an editor of early music. Thus, he was mainly responsible for the first collected edition of Schütz's works (16 vols., 1885–94; two supplementary volumes appeared later) and published the first comprehensive edition of Buxtehude's organ music (1875–76). Furthermore, he was a cofounder (with **Heinrich von Herzogenberg**, Franz von Holstein, and Alfred Volkland) of the Bach-Verein in Leipzig in 1874, a cofounder (with **Friedrich Chrysander** and Guido Adler) of the *Vierteljahrsschrift für Musikwissenschaft* in 1885, and one of the moving spirits behind the creation of the series *Denkmäler deutscher Tonkunst*.

Spitta made Brahms's acquaintance through **Julius Otto Grimm** at Göttingen in the summer of 1864. Many years later Brahms told **Richard Heuberger** that he had on that occasion suggested to Spitta that he should devote himself to the study of music rather than to composition and had told him that musicology would be his own "passion," if only he had Spitta's intelligence and learning (Heuberger 1976, 53). In 1868, under the profound impression made on him by the Requiem, Spitta wrote to Brahms, and from then on the two men remained in contact, mostly by correspondence, until Spitta's death, except for a lengthy period in the 1880s when Spitta broke off relations out of loyalty to his close friend and colleague **Joseph Joachim**, over Brahms's support for **Amalie** in the couple's divorce proceedings. They met occasionally, for instance in Berlin in June 1876 and probably also in December 1890. On the other hand, Brahms was away from Vienna when Spitta, at the invitation of the Tonkünstlerverein, gave a lecture there on 2 April 1886 on Carl Maria von Weber.

From the outset, Spitta felt profound admiration for Brahms's music, which he commented on and analyzed with considerable acumen, both in his letters and, especially and at some length, in the essay "Johannes Brahms" included in his book *Zur Musik* (Berlin, 1892). He proclaimed Brahms to be the greatest contemporary composer and laid particularly stress on the essential originality that, in his view, characterized each of his major works, even where these might, on first consideration, be thought to be set firmly in traditional paths. Brahms, in his turn, followed Spitta's research with much interest and pleasure, and highly appreciated his scholarship and insights. He dedicated the Motets op. 74 to Spitta.

Brahms was deeply moved when he learned of Spitta's death through a telegram from Joachim. In expressing his condolences to the widow some time later, he referred to Spitta as "that marvellous man" and declared that Spitta was irreplaceable for him both as a friend and a teacher (Brahms 1974/16, 18). (Brahms 1974/16; I. Fellinger 2001; Heuberger 1976; U. Schilling 1994; Spitta 1892)

SPITZER, DANIEL (b. Vienna, 3 July 1835; d. Merano, 11 January 1893). Feuilletonist. The son of a Jewish industrialist, he studied law and worked for several years at the Lower Austrian chamber of commerce before becoming a full-time journalist. His articles appeared in *Die Presse*, *Deutsche Zeitung*, and, from 1873, *Neue freie Presse*. Particularly appreciated was the series entitled *Wiener Spaziergänge* [*Walks through Vienna*], in which he commented, with humor and often with sarcasm, on different aspects of the contemporary artistic and social and political life in Vienna (and, occasionally, elsewhere). The articles proved so popular that he published six volumes of collected *Wiener Spaziergänge* between 1869 and 1886; four further volumes appeared posthumously in 1912 under the title *Letzte Wiener Spaziergänge*, edited by **Max Kalbeck**. Spitzer also wrote some novellas.

He was a leading member of a group consisting mainly, but by no means exclusively, of well-known journalists and writers (among them Ludwig Speidel and Hugo Wittmann) who had their "Stammtisch" in the evening at Gause's beer hall in Johannesgasse. Brahms regularly joined them, enjoying their witty conversation and the barbs that they aimed not only at absent victims, but even at each other. Kalbeck states that it was Spitzer to whom Brahms felt closest. According to Kalbeck (1976), Brahms went to Gause's for more than ten years and he met Spitzer also at the **Faber**s' and at the **Billroth**s', as well as at the houses of other mutual friends. Furthermore, he sometimes saw Spitzer in the summer at Ischl. In an article published on 18 August 1889, Spitzer writes about Brahms drinking his afternoon coffee on the terrace of the Café Walter there (Spitzer 1970, 249–52).

Brahms remained in contact with Spitzer even during the latter's long and painful final illness and visited him in the Viennese hospital where Spitzer was undergoing several operations. Brahms even brought him a gift of money, a gesture that surprised and pleased Spitzer, who later said to Kalbeck, "And I have always thought this man was one of the greatest egoists!" (Kalbeck 1976, vol. 2, 426, n. 1).

It is an indication of the high regard in which Spitzer continued to be held in Vienna long after his death that in 1925 a street should be named after him (in Pötzleinsdorf, in the 18th district). It was renamed after the sculptor Franz Barwig under the National Socialists but reverted to the name "Spitzergasse" after the Second World War. (Czeike 1992–97; Spitzer 1970)

STANDTHARTNER, JOSEPH (b. Troppau [Opava, Czech Republic], 4 February 1818; d. Vienna, 29 August 1892). Prominent Viennese physician, also a member of the board of directors of the Gesellschaft der Musikfreunde (1861–92). Moreover, he was a personal friend of **Richard Wagner**, and it was he who arranged (perhaps with the help of **Peter Cornelius** and **Carl Tausig**) the famous meeting between Wagner and Brahms on 6 February 1864. (For some details of that meeting, as later related by Standthartner's stepson Gustav Schönaich, *see* WAGNER, [WILHELM] RICHARD.) (Antonicek 1985; Biba 1983b; Schönaich 1897)

STANFORD, SIR CHARLES VILLIERS (b. Dublin, 30 September 1852; d. London, 29 March 1924). Composer, teacher, and conductor. He entered Queen's College, Cambridge, as a choral scholar in 1870 and later studied composition with **Carl Reinecke** in Leipzig and Friedrich Kiel in Berlin.

Stanford was actively involved in the three major efforts to bring Brahms to England. When the senate of Cambridge University decided on 18 May 1876 to offer honorary doctorates to Brahms and **Joseph Joachim**, Stanford was organist at Trinity College and also conductor of the Cambridge University Musical Society (CUMS), having been appointed to both positions even before he had graduated in the classical tripos in 1874. On 23 May 1876, five days after that decision was made, Stanford, who had been a fervent admirer of Brahms's music ever since he heard the *Handel Variations* at the age of 15, directed a performance of the Requiem by the CUMS, one of the earliest in England. In the circumstances, there can be little doubt that Stanford had some influence on the University Senate's decision to honor Brahms, whom he had met at a dinner hosted by **Ferdinand Hiller** in Cologne on 20 August 1873, on the day following the close of the **Schumann** Festival at Bonn. In late 1876, while staying in Berlin, he discussed with Joachim the concert that was to be given in Cambridge on the occasion of the conferment of the degrees. It was arranged that the program would include a work by each of the honorands, in Brahms's case, his First Symphony; and even though Brahms ultimately declined to travel to Cambridge and under the university's regulations could therefore not be awarded the degree, he agreed to send the manuscript of the then still unpublished work. As a result, the symphony duly received its first English performance, under Joachim, at Cambridge on 8 March 1877. (At the same concert Stanford conducted the *Schicksalslied*.) According to Stanford, Brahms had been on the verge of accepting the university's invitation but, fearful of being lionized by London society, had intended to visit only Cambridge; when he learned that the management of the Crystal Palace in London had publicly announced that they were hoping to secure his participation in a special concert of his works, he had promptly changed his mind about traveling to England. More recently, Karl Geiringer has suggested that Brahms's reluctance to undertake the journey may have stemmed from a more prosaic reason, namely a fear of seasickness.

In 1882 Stanford, with Brahms's permission, dedicated *Songs of Old Ireland*, his first collection of Irish songs, to him. Some time afterward, while on a visit to Vienna, he went to see Brahms with **Hans Richter**. He later recalled that he was rather coolly received, but eventually "the ice was broken and never froze again" (Stanford 1908, 112). After that he met Brahms again on more than one occasion; once he accompanied him to a rehearsal of **Christoph Willibald Gluck**'s *Alceste* at the opera house (this was presumably in 1885, in which year a new production of that opera was presented in Vienna on 4 and 7 October).

In 1889 Stanford, by then professor of music at Cambridge University (in addition to holding a professorship of composition and orchestral playing at the Royal College of Music in London since its foundation in 1883), tried to persuade Brahms to attend a performance of his Requiem that was to be given at the Leeds Festival that year: "I wrote and told him that if he would come to Cambridge *via* Harwich, I would go to Leeds and back with him, and conceal his identity from every one; but he was not to be stirred" (Stanford 1908, 113). Stanford was no more successful when, in connection with the CUMS's golden jubilee celebrations in 1893, offers of honorary degrees were, probably at his suggestion, extended to Brahms and Verdi; both declined. (The eventual recipients were Boito, **Max Bruch**, **Edvard Grieg**, Saint-Saëns, and **Tchaikovsky**, all of whom attended the ceremony with the exception of Grieg, whom was ill at the time.)

Stanford last met Brahms on 10 January 1896 in Berlin, at a dinner following an all-Brahms concert (see the chronology under that date). He later offered some interesting recollections of his contacts with Brahms in *Studies and Memories* (1908) and *Pages from an Unwritten Diary* (1914); he also wrote an introductory essay on Brahms's life and music for a small volume devoted to Brahms that was published in 1912 and also contained four of Brahms's songs and three pieces for the piano (two of the waltzes and the "Andante espressivo" from the Piano Sonata op. 5). (Geiringer 1982; Pascall 2001; Stanford 1908, 1912, 1914)

STEINBACH, FRITZ (b. Grünsfeld, 17 June 1855; d. Munich, 13 August 1916). Conductor and composer (of a number of songs and some chamber music). In 1873 he enrolled at the Leipzig conservatory, having during the previous two years been taught by his brother Emil (1849–1919), who was then Kapellmeister at the Mannheim theater. In 1877 he went to Vienna to study theory and composition with **Gustav Nottebohm** and the piano with **Anton Door**; subsequently, he received tuition in composition from **Vincenz Lachner** and in conducting from **Felix Otto Dessoff** at Karlsruhe. In 1880 he was appointed assistant Kapellmeister at Mainz, where he mainly conducted operas. (Emil held the position of principal Kapellmeister there from 1877 to 1909.) In 1886 he joined the Hoch Conservatory at Frankfurt as an instructor in counterpoint and composition, but later that same year he moved to Meiningen to become **Richard Strauss**'s successor as court Kapellmeister. In the course of the 17 years during which he was in charge of the Meiningen orchestra, he came to be regarded, in and outside Germany, as the foremost conductor of Brahms's music. This reputation outlasted his life; thus, Sir Adrian Boult, looking back in 1973 on six decades of listening to music, singled out Steinbach as the greatest Brahms conductor in his long experience. (Furthermore, he named him and Hugh Allen as the greatest **Bach** conductors he had ever heard.)

It is not known for certain when Steinbach first made Brahms's acquaintance, but he is believed to have called on him at Ziegelhausen in 1875, perhaps in an unsuccessful attempt to persuade Brahms to accept him as a pupil. It was reportedly Brahms who advised him to study with Nottebohm and Door in Vienna. No doubt these two friends of Brahms, and later Dessoff at Karlsruhe, exercised a considerable influence on Steinbach's attitude toward Brahms and his music, inspiring in him a deep affection for the man and a profound admiration for his compositions, sentiments he retained for the rest of his life. Brahms, for his part, was later to form a high opinion of Steinbach's musicianship, for it was mainly on his recommendation that **Duke Georg II** offered Steinbach the appointment at Meiningen. He was officially engaged from 1 July 1886, and took up his duties on 1 October. From 1 January 1894 he held the title of "Musikdirektor."

Steinbach lost no time in performing Brahms's music at his concerts in Meiningen: the first, on 9 November 1886, included the Serenade op. 16, the second, on 21 November, the Requiem. (Steinbach would altogether conduct six performances of the Requiem at Meiningen in Brahms's lifetime, as well as four of its movements in a memorial concert for **Hans von Bülow**.) He must have had opportunities to converse with Brahms during the latter's visits to Meiningen in December 1887 and January 1889. He is also known to have conducted the *Tragic Overture*, the *Haydn Variations*, and the First and Fourth Symphonies in Brahms's presence during the latter's stay at Meiningen in March 1891, and to have so moved Brahms with his performance of the First that Brahms asked for a repeat. In the late summer of 1894, Steinbach and his wife paid a visit to Brahms, who was at Ischl at the time, and while there he surprised Brahms by secretly copying out one night the clarinet part of the newly composed clarinet sonatas, for the benefit of **Richard Mühlfeld**. He subsequently traveled with Brahms and Mühlfeld to Berchtesgaden and was present when they tried out the new sonatas at **Anna Franz**'s villa Soletap and at Princess Marie von Sachsen-Meiningen's Villa Felicitas there (on Princess Marie, *see* GEORG II DUKE OF SACHSEN-MEININGEN).

In the following year, 1895, an event took place that profoundly marked Steinbach's relationship with Brahms. From 27 to 29 September he organized and directed a festival at Meiningen that, by celebrating the music of Bülow's "three Bs"—Bach, **Beethoven**, and Brahms—constituted in fact an act of profound homage to the latter. On the first day, Steinbach conducted the *St. Matthew Passion*; the second concert presented Brahms's vocal quartets "An die Heimat" (op. 64/1), "Nächtens" (op. 112/2), and "Wechsellied zum Tanze" (op. 31/1), the Concerto for Violin and Cello, the *Handel Variations* for piano, and the First Symphony (as well as Bach's Sixth Brandenburg Concerto and Beethoven's Fifth Piano Concerto); and the program of the final day's concert consisted of Beethoven's *Missa solemnis*, Brahms's *Triumphlied*, and a cantata by Bach. In addition, there were two chamber music matinees, at which Brahms was represented by the Clarinet Sonata op. 120/1, the Clarinet Quintet, and the String Quintet op. 111. The participants included the Joachim Quartet, **Eugen d'Albert**, and Richard Mühlfeld. As **Edward Speyer** (1937), who had traveled from England with his wife and daughter to attend the festival, later wrote in his memoirs *My Life and Friends*, "the Meiningen Festival of 1895 proved an apotheosis for Brahms and a crowning of his life's work" (101). Moreover, he quotes Brahms saying, when they first met him in the street, "You can't imagine how wonderful it is to do music here. The chorus, the orchestra and that incomparable Steinbach; everything is perfection" (101). Brahms was also profoundly moved by the performances of the works of Bach, another composer whom Steinbach, like Brahms, venerated. Before Brahms left for Vienna, he expressed his gratitude to Steinbach in a note written in what was for him a quite exceptionally effusive style (see Kalbeck 1976, vol. 4, 409). When Steinbach stayed in Vienna with his wife later that year, they saw a good deal of Brahms ("Meister Brahms spends almost the whole day with us, and he has finally found his true vocation, as a tourist guide," Steinbach informed **Baroness Helene Heldburg** [Herta Müller 1999, 103]). At Easter 1896 Brahms sent Steinbach the autograph of the Clarinet Trio op. 114 as a present (it is now at the Städtische Musikbibliothek, Munich). Steinbach was to see Brahms just once more, in tragic circumstances (as mentioned below).

After Brahms's death, Steinbach conducted his Requiem at a memorial concert at Meiningen on 14 April 1897. He continued to serve Brahms faithfully. Thus, when the Meiningen orchestra gave four concerts under his direction in Berlin in November of that year, he devoted the first one, on 12 November, entirely to Brahms's music. Above all, though, he strove to make Meiningen a Brahms center, and it was largely on his initiative that a committee was formed (with **Joseph Joachim** as its president) for the purpose of having a permanent memorial built in Brahms's honor. The unveiling of **Adolf von Hildebrand**'s monument in the Englischer Garten on 7 October 1899 was the occasion for the Second Meiningen Music Festival. The ceremony was preceded by a performance of the Requiem and followed by one of the *Triumphlied*, both conducted by Steinbach at the Stadtkirche. In addition, an all-Brahms concert offered the *Tragic Overture*, the *Vier ernste Gesänge* (soloist: **Felix von Kraus**), the Second Piano Concerto (soloist: Eugen d'Albert), the *Alto Rhapsody* (soloist: Adrienne Osborne), and the Second Symphony. Steinbach conducted another all-Brahms concert at Meiningen on 4 March 1901.

But Steinbach's plans went well beyond the erection of a monument; he was hoping to build a new concert hall—the "Brahmshalle"—and a conservatory adjoining it, to be staffed by himself (as director) and members of the orchestra. Eventually, the project had to be abandoned, and its failure may have been one reason why Steinbach later left Meiningen to become **Franz Wüllner**'s successor as conductor of the Gürzenich concerts and director of the conservatory at Cologne. However, before relinquishing his post at Meiningen, he took the orchestra on its first visit to London. The five concerts that he conducted at the St. James's Hall between 17 and 21 November 1902 included all four Brahms symphonies, as well as the Violin Concerto played by **Marie Soldat**. They were a great artistic as well as financial, success. The symphonies, the *Musical Times* (1 December 1902, 819) declared, were "rendered with such life and impulse, with such a spirit of romance, that one felt their power in quite unaccustomed degree." Steinbach reported to Duke Georg II, "The most important thing is that we have suddenly made Brahms popular in London" (Herta Müller 1999, 115). In later years Steinbach returned to England to conduct the newly established London Symphony Orchestra. In 1905, a critic in the *Musical Times* (1 January 1905, 41) particularly praised him and the orchestra for their rendition of Brahms's fourth symphony: "We cannot recall a performance of this great . . . work, in which its beauty and majesty were so luminously and thoroughly manifested." Finally, Steinbach bade farewell to Meiningen with the Third Meiningen Music Festival that was held on 14 and 15 April 1903 and featured, among other works, cantatas by Bach, Beethoven's Ninth Symphony, and, once again, Brahms's Requiem. Steinbach was to remain in contact with Duke Georg II and the Baroness Heldburg, and it was on his recommendation that Wilhelm Berger and later **Max Reger** were appointed conductors of the Meiningen orchestra.

As might have been expected, Steinbach continued his efforts on behalf of Brahms's music after settling at Cologne, not only in that city but also elsewhere. Thus, he organized and directed the first German Brahms Festival at Munich in September 1909, and also a four-day Brahms Festival at Wiesbaden in 1912, which counted **Fritz Kreisler** and Artur Schnabel among the participating musicians. He further championed Brahms's works as a guest conductor in Madrid, Paris, London, Moscow, St. Petersburg, and New York. In 1914, however, he was obliged to resign his posts at Cologne for health reasons.

In view of the signal services, Steinbach rendered Brahms and his music—second only or perhaps even equal to Bülow's—it is surprising that so little attention has been paid to him by so many Brahms biographers, notwithstanding the fact that Kalbeck already provided clear evidence of the important role he had played in this respect and also of Brahms's own awareness of the debt he owed him. To cite four recent examples of this unjust neglect: Malcolm Macdonald (1990), in his *Brahms*, makes just one glancing reference to Steinbach, and an inaccurate one at that; Jan Swafford's (1997) *Johannes Brahms: A Biography* has just two references to him, one of them incorrect; Styra Avins's (1997) *Johannes Brahms: Life and Letters*, in its 860 pages, does not, according to the index, cite his name even once; and Siegfried Kross, in his 1997 book, while according him several mentions, manifestly fails to do him full justice. However, an excellent and comprehensive survey by Herta Müller (1999) of Steinbach's activities at Meiningen and of his efforts on behalf of Brahms's music has at last redressed the balance ("Fritz Steinbach's Wirken in Meiningen und für Johannes Brahms von 1886–1903." In addition, an interesting study published by the same scholar elsewhere that year ("Die 'Musikalischen' Meininger auf Reisen," in *Die Meininger kommen!* [Kern and Müller 1999, 34–78]) examines Steinbach's concert tours with the orchestra within the overall history of the orchestra's many performances outside Meiningen under its different conductors. It is therefore to be hoped that future biographers of Brahms will accord Steinbach the importance he so clearly merits.

Herta Müller does not mention Steinbach's final meeting with Brahms, as related by **Gustav Ophüls**, who had heard the story from Steinbach. Knowing Brahms to be dying, Steinbach went to Vienna to see him in early 1897. He had already left the room at the end of his visit, after a falsely cheerful "Auf Wiedersehen," when Brahms, who had easily seen through the pretext invented by Steinbach to account for his presence in Vienna, called out that he still had something else to say to him. When Steinbach went back into the room, "Brahms, deeply moved, seized both his hands and, looking at him with indescribable sadness, said: 'I just wanted to press your hand once more!'" (Ophüls 1983b, 42). (Boult 1973; Brahms 1991; Erck, Kertscher, and Schaefer 1983; Erck, Müller, and Schneider 1987; I. Fellinger 1966; Kern and Müller 1999; Herta Müller 1999; E. Ophüls 1992; Speyer 1937)

STEINWAY. American firm of piano makers, established in New York in 1853 by Heinrich Engelhard Steinway [originally: Steinweg] (b. Wolfshagen, 15 February 1797; d. New York, 7 February 1871), who had emigrated to the United States in 1850 from Germany, where he had founded his original piano business at Seesen, in the Duchy of Braunschweig [Brunswick], in 1835. The new firm soon made its mark in the American market, and its reputation also spread internationally as a result of its success at various exhibitions (London, 1862; Paris, 1867; Vienna, 1873). Under the guidance of Heinrich Engelhard's sons C. F. Theodore Steinway (1825–89), a superb craftsman and technician who joined the firm in 1865 and devised some dramatic improvements, and William Steinway (1836–96), a man highly skilled in promotion and marketing, the firm prospered spectacularly during the last 30 years of the 19th century. The "Steinway system" came to be widely adopted also by European manufacturers, and Steinway pianos were acclaimed by many prominent musicians.

Following Heinrich Engelhard Steinweg's departure for America, his original factory at Seesen was managed by his eldest son, the aforementioned C. F. Theodor Steinweg, who in 1855 moved it to Wolfenbüttel. Three years later he entered into a partnership with Friedrich Grotrian, and the firm then moved once more, this time to Brunswick. When Theodor Steinweg left in 1865 for the New World (where he became Theodore Steinway), he sold his part of the business to Adolph Helfferich, H. G. W. Schulz, and Grotrian's son Wilhelm, granting them the privilege of trading as "Successors to C. F. Th. Steinweg" for the next 10 years. However, the firm retained the designation well beyond the stipulated period, thereby giving rise to legal disputes that were to extend over many decades. (The Grotrian family ultimately adopted the name "Grotian Steinweg" in 1919, and in a hyphenated form in 1926.)

In 1876 Brahms proposed having a "Steinweg" sent from Braunschweig for his concerts at Breslau [Wrocław, Poland] on 21 and 23 March, should no suitable piano be available locally. But when, in anticipation of forthcoming concert appearances in northern Germany, he wrote from Mürzzuschlag to **Julius Spengel** in Hamburg on 11 September 1884, asking him to arrange for Steinweg to place a small piano in his Hamburg hotel room and to provide fine grands for his chamber music recital with the Bargheer Quartet in Hamburg on 12 December and for his concert at Oldenburg (where he was due to play his Second Piano Concerto on 19 December), he presumably expected the instruments to be obtained from Steinway's Fabrik, the piano factory the American Steinway firm had opened in Hamburg in November 1880, mainly for the purpose of catering for the European market. According to Richard K. Lieberman (1995), the most authoritative chronicler of the firm's history, the new factory, which was legally independent of the New York business, "bought plates, action frames, lumber, and unfinished pianos from the New York factory" and "assembled the instruments in Hamburg" (Lieberman 1995, 97).

Brahms clearly had a high regard for the Steinway grand. Further evidence of his admiration for that instrument is provided by two of his friends. In his autobiography *My Life and Friends*, **Edward Speyer** (1937) recalls a party at his house in Frankfurt in 1889, at which both Brahms and **Clara Schumann** were present. Clara declined to play on her host's piano, because she found the Steinway action too hard, and, turning to Brahms, asked, "Is it not so, Johannes?" To which he replied, "You are right, Clara, but, for myself, I must say this is about the finest pianoforte my fingers have ever touched" (Speyer 1937, 90). The other story is related by **Ottilie Ebner**'s daughter Ottilie von Balassa (1933). When, as a young married woman (in 1892 or 1893), she caught scarlet fever, Brahms visited her and played the piano for a long time for her entertainment: "It gave him pleasure too," Balassa writes, "not only because he knew that it made me very happy, but also because he had never before played on such a wonderful grand piano. It was a Steinway of quite exceptional quality." When, more than 30 years later, Balassa made **Eusebius Mandyczewski**'s acquaintance, he said to her, "So you are the fortunate owner of the most marvelous Steinway. Brahms came to me in great excitement many years ago and told me that he had played on a fabulous instrument at your house. He said it was superb, and did not at all sound like an ordinary piano" (114). (Balassa 1933; Bozarth and Brady 2000; H. Ehrlich 1900; Lieberman 1995; Ratcliffe 1989; Speyer 1937)

STERN, JULIUS (Breslau [Wrocław, Poland], 8 August 1820; d. Berlin, 27 February 1883). Conductor, teacher, and composer. He studied the violin in Breslau and afterward in Berlin, where he also received instruction in conducting and composition, and later he studied singing with J. Miksch in Dresden; during a stay in Paris, he conducted the German Gesangverein. In 1847, in Berlin, he founded the Sternscher Gesangverein, which he directed until 1874, by which time it consisted of some 360 singers. In 1850, together with Th. Kullak and A. B. Marx, he established a conservatory in Berlin, and, after his partners had both retired (Kullak in 1855 and Marx in 1857), he directed it by himself until 1877 under the name "Sternsches Konservatorium für Musik." In a letter in January 1869, Brahms advised the young singer **Rosa Girzick** to go to Berlin to study with Stern, a "very competent and highly regarded gentleman" who would teach her the "necessary roles" and help her find a "suitable position" (Kalbeck 1976, vol. 2, 274). Girzick did not take his advice.

Like Berlin's music public in general in those days, Stern seems to have viewed Brahms's music with little enthusiasm. **Julius Stockhausen**, who succeeded Stern as conductor of his Gesangverein in April 1874, informed Brahms the following year that "Stern himself warned me against playing Brahmsian music when I took over the choir, and that no doubt for a good reason: he did not wish to see something which he himself was unable to produce, and perhaps also did not understand, to bloom right away in his garden" (Brahms 1993, 109). It was, in fact, not until Stockhausen had taken Stern's place that the choir began to tackle Brahms's great choral works: the *Triumphlied* on 17 December 1874 and 18 January 1875, the *Schicksalslied* on 10 May 1875, and the Requiem on 12 February 1876. (Stockhausen conducted the Gesangverein until September 1878, when the position was assumed by **Max Bruch**.) (Brahms 1993)

STERNAU, C. O. [pseudonym of Otto Inkermann]. Poet. Brahms set one of his texts in the vocal quartet "An die Heimat" (op. 64/1). Furthermore, he placed the opening lines of Sternau's poem "Junge Liebe" above the Andante of the Piano Sonata op. 5.

STOCKHAUSEN, JULIUS (FRANZ CHRISTIAN) (b. Paris, 22 July 1826; d. Frankfurt am Main, 22 September 1906). Singer (baritone), conductor, and teacher. Oldest child of harpist and composer Franz Stockhausen (1789–1868), who was born in Cologne and had settled in Paris by 1812, and of soprano Margarethe Stockhausen, née Schmuck (1803–77), who came from Gebweiler [Guebwiller] in Alsace. In addition to singing, he learned to play piano and several other instruments. Among his teachers were his own parents and the younger Manuel García, with whom he studied singing in Paris and London.

His first important public performance, in Mendelssohn's *Elijah* at Basle in 1848, marked the beginning of an outstanding career that was to make his name famous not only throughout Germany but also internationally. While he appeared with some success on the stage (notably at Mannheim in 1852–53 and at the Paris Opéra comique in 1856–59), he was to achieve renown principally as a singer of oratorios and of Lieder (especially those of **Franz Schubert**, **Robert Schumann**, and Brahms). A man of considerable intelligence and charm, and blessed with a very beautiful, though not particularly powerful, voice that he handled with supreme skill, he had a gift for communicating the meaning and mood of a song in a most effective and moving manner. In his *Dictionary of Music and Musicians* George Grove wrote: "The rich beauty of the voice, the nobility of the style, the perfect phrasing, the intimate sympathy, and, not least, the intelligible way in which the words were given . . . all combined to make his singing of songs a wonderful event" (Colles 1927, vol. 5, 141). Furthermore, Stockhausen also had some success as a choral and orchestral conductor—with the Philharmonische Konzertgesellschaft and the Singakademie in Hamburg (1863–67), and the Sternscher Gesangverein in Berlin (1874–78); and, lastly, he also became a highly regarded singing teacher who, after serving on the faculty of the Hoch Conservatory in Frankfurt, founded his own school in that city in 1880 (he had already established a similar school in Hamburg in 1865). Among his pupils were **Antonia Kufferath**, Johannes Messchaert, Karl Scheidemantel, **Anton Sistermans**, **Hermine Spies**, and Raimund von Zur Mühlen.

The young Stockhausen's reputation grew steadily throughout the 1850s. To cite some of his most noteworthy engagements during the period 1853–56: In 1853 he sang at Basle in the first Swiss performance of **Beethoven**'s Ninth Symphony; in early 1854 he performed at three concerts in Vienna, winning high praise from the critics, including **Eduard Hanslick**; in May of that year he sang in Mendelssohn's *Paulus* at Basle and Strasbourg; in March 1856 he sang at the Weimar court, accompanied by **Liszt**, and in April 1856 he performed before Friedrich Wilhelm IV in

Berlin; "il a eu un succès inouï" [he had an extraordinary success], **Hans von Bülow** reported to Liszt (J. Wirth 1927, 159). Subsequently, Stockhausen sang in Leipzig, Prague, and in Vienna (where, on 4 May 1856, he became the first singer to present the complete *Die schöne Müllerin*—a feat he was to repeat on several later occasions, including at Cologne on 28 October 1862 before an audience of two thousand); and, last but not least, he scored a personal triumph at the 34th Lower Rhine Festival, held on 11–13 May 1856 at Düsseldorf (not at Cologne, as S. Avins [1997] states in her *Johannes Brahms: Life and Letters*), where he was a soloist in *Elijah* on the first day and in **Handel**'s *Alexander's Feast* and Beethoven's Ninth Symphony on the second, and performed an aria and some songs on the third.

It was on the occasion of this music festival that Stockhausen first met Brahms, who was then living at Düsseldorf. Brahms was no doubt already well aware of Stockhausen's musical accomplishments, if only because **Clara Schumann** is certain to have extolled them to him. She had made Stockhausen's acquaintance at Ostend on 21 August 1854 and had been so intensely moved by his interpretation of certain Lieder he sang for her, especially some composed by her husband ("A wonderful singer," she noted in her diary [Litzmann 1902, vol. 2, 326]), that she had invited him to take part in a concert with her at the Belgian spa five days later. Writing to him the following year (13 April 1855), she expressed the wish that he might once visit Robert at Endenich, together with Brahms, and sing for him (however, Stockhausen never did). In March 1856, while staying at Weimar, he made a special trip to Leipzig in response to Clara's request that he should take part in a concert she was due to give at a private house; there she accompanied him in songs by Schumann. For his part, Stockhausen must have been eager to know the young Hamburg genius who had so impressed Schumann and about whom Clara, whom Stockhausen revered, spoke with such admiration and affection.

The two men evidently took to each other at once, for before the end of May 1856 they gave a concert at Cologne. It was the first of many joint artistic ventures. To mention but a few: In March 1859 they both took part in a concert with **Joseph Joachim** in Hamburg; in April 1861 they performed the complete *Dichterliebe* in Hamburg; in 1868, during a tour lasting several weeks, they performed together in Hamburg, Berlin, Dresden, Lübeck, Kiel, and Copenhagen; in 1869 they gave several concerts in Vienna and Budapest; and in March 1884 they took part in a performance of the *Liebeslieder Walzer* in Frankfurt. Moreover, Stockhausen became a champion of Brahms's vocal music, and he is credited with having given, or participated in, numerous first public performances of his songs and duets (for details, see M. L. McCorkle's [1984] *Werkverzeichnis*). Furthermore, he was the baritone soloist at the performance of the six-movement Requiem in Bremen on 10 April 1868. (He also conducted, and sang in, the first performance of the entire work in England, which took place on 7 July 1871 at the house of the surgeon Sir Henry Thompson, with the host's wife, the pianist Fanny Loder, and Cipriani Potter playing the accompaniment). In addition, he directed performances of the *Schicksalslied*, *Trumphlied*, and Requiem while in charge of the Sternscher Gesangverein in Berlin (*see* STERN, JULIUS). It was, incidentally, at Stockhausen's request that Brahms orchestrated a number of Schubert's Lieder; Stockhausen sang two of them at the concert at Karlsruhe on 18 October 1871, at which Brahms directed the first performance of the *Schicksalslied* (and also conducted the Schubert songs).

Stockhausen appears to have been genuinely surprised and dismayed on learning that Brahms was disappointed not to have been offered one or both of the abovementioned appointments that he himself accepted in Hamburg in 1862 (and took up the following year). He promptly wrote to Brahms, urging him to return to Hamburg where there would be many opportunities for joint music making, and, in particular, inviting him to conduct the works in which he himself would be singing. He even offered to leave the field open for Brahms: "If you wish, I will go on my way and look for a position elsewhere" (Brahms 1993, 31). Privately, however, he did not really think that Brahms was by experience or temperament suitable for the post. Brahms, he wrote to a friend at the time, "has never in his life been a 'conductor,' he is not practical enough, and not amiable enough with the orchestra musicians, one moment coldly disapproving, the next indulgent. Moreover, being so greatly gifted . . . he would never have the patience to make something from nothing" (Brahms 1993, 18).

Brahms does not seem to have borne Stockhausen a grudge as a result of the appointments, and their friendship suffered no serious decline. In any case, Stockhausen was able to be of service to him and his family while in Hamburg: he occasionally sent tickets for the concerts, he arranged for **Johann Jakob Brahms** to become a double-bass-player in the orchestra, he stored Johannes's books for him for a time, and when **Fritz** gave a concert of his own on 9 January 1864, Stockhausen not only offered him his own Érard piano but also tried to ensure the success of the concert by singing at it himself. Brahms and Stockhausen continued to correspond, to meet periodically, and to share the aforesaid concert platform. Brahms dedicated his *Magelone-Lieder* to Stockhausen (two books in 1865, three further books in 1869); in his turn, Stockhausen dedicated his *Vier Gesänge*, which **J. P. Gotthard** published in 1871, to Brahms. In 1877 Brahms agreed to become a godfather of Stockhausen's son Johann.

In the 1890s Stockhausen's health deteriorated; he had to undergo two eye operations and suffered increasingly from rheumatic pain. He last appeared in public as a singer on 20 January 1892, and as a conductor on 3 February 1901; in 1904 he was forced to close his singing school, but he still taught a few students at home. **Ferdinand Schumann** (1915), in his "Erinnerungen an Johannes Brahms," described a meeting between Stockhausen and Brahms that took place at Clara Schumann's house in Frankfurt on 13 February 1895. Stockhausen arrived while Clara was playing Robert Schumann's Piano Trio op. 80 with **Hugo Heermann** and **Hugo Becker**. "Brahms greeted him very warmly, led him to the table, and conversed with him in a whisper. He asked after little Julie [Julia] Stockhausen who has been confined to bed by a serious illness for three weeks. Stockhausen seemed to be in very low spirits" (F. Schumann 1915, 234). Three days later Brahms went to see him. At this time, Stockhausen was still grieving over the death of his daughter Margarethe the previous year and was no doubt afraid that he might lose Julia as well, but she recovered. He was also much troubled by his failing eyesight; however, an operation in October 1896 was to prove successful.

Stockhausen was greatly distressed when he learned of Brahms's fatal illness, but, as his wife explained to a Viennese friend (Helene Magnus-Hornbostel [*see* HORNBOSTEL, (OTTO) ERICH VON]), he was reluctant to travel to Vienna to see Brahms one last time, as he felt that the anguish of a reunion under such circumstances might be more than he could bear in his frail state of health. Apprised of Brahms's death, he wished to attend the funeral but was dissuaded from doing so by his wife and his doctor. On 9 May 1897 he arranged a memorial concert at his singing school, which consisted mainly of compositions by Brahms. For his 80th birthday in 1906 Helene Magnus-Hornbostel presented him with a marble bust of Brahms (see CONRAT, ILSE). Not long before his death, after looking at the bust for a long while, he was heard to remark, "He is already with the angels" (J. Wirth 1927, 445). (Brahms 1993; F. Schumann 1915; Stephenson 1928; J. Wirth 1927)

STOJOWSKI, ZYGMUNT [SIGISMOND] (DENIS ANTONI) (b. Strzelce, Poland, 14 May 1870; d, New York, 6 November 1946). Composer, pianist, and teacher. He studied composition with Léo Delibes and Jules Massenet, and piano with Louis Diémer and Ignazy Jan Paderewski. In 1905 he settled in New York, where he taught piano at the Institute of Musical Art (1906–11) and the Von Ende School of Music (1911–17); he also continued to perform in public. His compositions include a symphony, concertos for piano, violin, and cello, as well as chamber music.

According to his "Recollections of Brahms" (*Musical Quarterly*, 1933), he came to know Brahms while still in his teens. The article consists mainly of an account of conversations he had with Brahms in Vienna and Ischl, but its most interesting part relates to a description given to Stojowski by **Tchaikovsky** of one of his meetings with Brahms—not their first, as Stojowski mistakenly states, but a later one that occurred in Hamburg in March 1889 (*see* TCHAIKOVSKY, PYOTR IL'YICH). (Stojowski 1933)

STORM, (HANS) THEODOR (WOLDSEN) (b. Husum, 14 September 1817; d. Hademarschen, 4 July 1888). Poet and writer of novellas. Brahms set one of his poems in the song "Über die Heide" (op. 86/4). (Paulin 1991)

STRAUS, LUDWIG (b. Pressburg [Bratislava], 28 March 1835; d. Cambridge, 23 October 1899). Violinist. He studied at the Vienna conservatory (1843–48) with Joseph Böhm and Gottfried von Preyer. After making his professional debut at a concert at the Musikverein in 1850, he performed during the next 10 years as a soloist at various private and public concerts, and also as second violin in Joseph Mayseder's quartet; in addition, he made some concert tours outside Austria. In 1860 he became leader of the Frankfurt am Main theater orchestra and of the orchestra performing at the Museum concerts, as well as leader of the Frankfurt Quartet. Four years later he moved to England, where he had already appeared with some success in 1860 and 1861. Having been appointed leader of **Sir Charles Hallé**'s orchestra (a post he was to hold until 1888), he resided principally in Manchester, but he also made frequent concert appearances in London and was awarded the title of "solo violinist" to Queen Victoria. It is a measure of the great reputation he enjoyed in England that a writer in the *Musical Times* in June 1926 should have included him in his list of the leading instrumentalists who had performed there during the 1870s, 1880s, and 1890s.

Straus liked to spend his holidays in Austria. He was in contact with **Alois Mayer** and **László Wagner de Zólyom**, and led the quartet assembled by the latter at Altaussee. Thus it came about that he played in the first (private) performances of Brahms's Piano Trio op. 87 and the String Quintet op. 88, which took place at Wagner de Zólyom's villa there on 25 August 1882 (for details, *see* WAGNER DE ZÓLYOM, LÁSZLÓ).

STRAUSS, JOHANN (BAPTIST) (b. Vienna, 25 October 1825; d. Vienna, 3 June 1899). Composer, conductor, and violinist; eldest son of Johann Strauss (1804–49).

Brahms's admiration for his music, especially his waltzes, many of which he knew by heart, is well documented, as is the enchanting manner in which he himself played them on the piano. Emil Krause, who taught piano and theory at the Hamburg conservatory, recalled in 1899 that Brahms used to perform Strauss waltzes at his house with evident delight, sometimes for more than an hour; and he added, "Anyone who has heard Brahms play *An der schönen blauen Donau*, that most beautiful of all the waltzes composed by Strauss, will never forget the intense pleasure of the experience" (Würzl 2001, 555). Brahms reportedly did not miss an opportunity to hear a new work by Strauss; in May 1891 he delayed his departure for his summer vacation at Ischl for several days so that he could attend the concert in the Prater, at which Strauss was to present his new waltz *Gross-Wien (Tout Vienne)*, and his very last visit to the theater was to attend the premiere of Strauss's operetta *Göttin der Vernunft* at the Theater an der Wien on 13 March 1897.

Brahms marveled at the wealth of Strauss's melodic invention. "The man overflows with music," he observed to the German dramatist and novelist Paul Lindau (Lindau 1916–17, vol. 2, 174). But what Brahms particularly admired was the inspired use Strauss made of the different instruments, even in the later compositions that, in his view, lacked the power of invention and the skill in developing musical themes that had characterized Strauss's earlier works. Thus he said to **Richard Heuberger**, after hearing the *Gartenlaube* waltz (first performed on 6 January 1895), "Sure, it's all very Straussish, but there is nothing there any more. My pleasure is in the orchestra, which is marvellously handled" (Heuberger 1976, 75). And after attending the premiere of the operetta *Waldmeister* on 4 December 1895, Brahms exclaimed, "How magnificently Strauss orchestrates!" (Heuberger 1976, 89).

It is not known when Brahms made Strauss's personal acquaintance—maybe, as is sometimes stated, soon after his arrival in Vienna (an opportunity might, for instance, have arisen on 11 November 1862—see the chronology), or perhaps not until several years later at Baden-Baden, where Brahms regularly attended Strauss's concerts. It was from Baden-Baden, on 13 September 1872, that **Hans von Bülow** reported to his friend Louise von Welz Brahms's statement that Strauss was one of the few "colleagues" for whom he "felt total respect" (Mailer 1983–2002, vol. 2, 214). The earliest firm evidence of their social contact in Vienna dates to November 1874, when, according to Paul Lindau, Brahms attended a party at Strauss's Viennese villa and entertained the company with a brilliant rendition of the *Blue Danube* waltz. According to Lindau, Strauss was moved to tears, and he afterward tenderly embraced Brahms and kissed him on the cheek (Lindau 1916–17, vol. 2, 173; Lindau actually places the incident in 1875, but it is more likely to have taken place the previous year—see Mailer 1983–2002, vol. 2, 261–64.)

After that, there is no authentic record of any personal contacts between Brahms and Strauss for many years; but in April 1889 Brahms informed **Fritz Simrock** that he was "seeing Strauss more frequently at present" (Brahms 1974/11, 216; in the same letter, Brahms tried to persuade Simrock to take on some of Strauss's compositions, and for several years Simrock did indeed publish Strauss's latest works, including the "Emperor Waltz"). Thereafter Brahms and Strauss met fairly frequently. "Ah, the evenings with Strauss! and his wife! and the champagne! and the waltzes!" Brahms wrote to Simrock in November 1889 (Brahms 1974/12, 12). Yet, cordial as their contacts had become, they were never to be really intimate, which is hardly surprising, given their very different temperaments. Indeed, Strauss seems to have found Brahms's character decidedly unattractive at times, to judge by a letter he wrote to his friend **Victor Tilgner** in 1890, in which he refers to Brahms's "cold North-German soul" and, scathingly, to his aptitude for self-promotion ["alle Achtung vor seiner Mache"] (Würzl 2001, 559). Two years later, however, Strauss dedicated the waltz *Seid umschlungen, Millionen* (op. 443) to Brahms.

It was also in 1892 that Strauss began to spend his summers at Ischl. As a result, the two men now had further opportunities for socializing. During the summer of 1894, Brahms was a regular guest at Sunday dinner at the Villa Erdödy, the splendid house that Strauss was then renting at Ischl for the season (and would eventually buy). A fellow guest, cellist Sigmund Bürger, later related that Brahms was usually in a very jovial mood by the end of the meal and would, even without being asked, sit down at the piano and play Strauss waltzes and melodies from his operettas. On one memorable occasion he and Strauss even played duets. It was at this time that the court photographer Rudolph von Krziwanek took the celebrated photograph of Brahms and Strauss standing together on the veranda of the Villa Erdödy, as well as one of Brahms and Adèle. Furthermore, there is evidence of closer contact between them in Vienna. Stauss and Adèle were present at a rehearsal of Brahms's clarinet sonatas at the Tonkünstlerverein on 7 January 1895, when Adèle even turned the pages of the manuscript for Brahms. They also attended the concert of the Rosé Quartet on 11 January 1895, at which Brahms and **Richard Mühlfeld** gave the very first performance of the Clarinet Sonata op. 120/1.

At Ischl that summer Brahms was invited to the engagement party at the Villa Erdödy of Strauss's stepdaughter Alice and the **Marquis de Bayros** (*see* BAYROS, FRANZ WILHELM, MARQUIS DE) (On this occasion his Piano Quartet op. 25 was performed by **Ilona Eibenschütz**, **Franz Kneisel**, Louis Svečenski, and Sigmund Bürger). Moreover, he was asked by Alice to be a witness for her at the wedding on 27 February 1896: "It would mean so much to me to welcome to the ceremony not only the Zeus-like Master revered by all, but also my dear Papa's kind friend who is so greatly esteemed by my family and by myself" (Mailer 1983–2002, vol. 8, 197). Brahms accepted but subsequently changed his mind because, as he told Richard Heuberger, he could not bear the idea of having to wear a "horrible" dress suit, white gloves, and top hat (Heuberger 1976, 94). However, he did attend the wedding and afterward was a guest at the wedding meal at Strauss's house in Igelgasse. (Alice's marriage to Bayros soon broke down; her subsequent marriage to **Julius Epstein**'s son Richard likewise ended in divorce.)

According to an article on Brahms in the *Neue freie Presse* on 6 April 1897, Brahms last visited the Strauss's house on 23 January of that year. There was to be a posthumous link between him and Strauss: his Requiem was performed at a memorial concert for Strauss arranged by the Gesellschaft der Musikfreunde on 25 October 1899; it was conducted by **Richard von Perger**. (Brahms 1974/11–12; M. Bülow 1895–1908; Heuberger 1976; Huschke 1939; Krause 1903; Lamb 1975; Lindau 1916–17; Mailer 1983–2002; Würzl 1995, 2001)

STRAUSS, RICHARD (GEORG) (b. Munich, 11 June 1864; d. Garmisch-Partenkirchen, 8 September 1949). Composer and conductor. He owed his first contacts with Brahms—initially by letter and then in person—to **Hans von Bülow**, who greatly assisted him in his early musical career. Thus Bülow included his Serenade for 13 Wind Instruments (op. 7) among the works he conducted during a tour of the Meiningen Orchestra in the winter of 1883–84, and when he first met Strauss in Berlin in February 1844 (not in January, as stated in Blume 1949–86), he asked him to write a similar piece specially for that orchestra. This new composition, the Suite for 13 Wind Instruments (op. 4), was first played by the Meiningen orchestra in Munich on 18 November 1884, in a performance that Strauss, at Bülow's invitation, conducted himself; and Bülow subsequently took the suite on another tour of the Meiningen ensemble in March 1885. Moreover, it was as a result of Bülow's strong recommendation that Strauss became assistant Musikdirektor at Meiningen on 1 October 1885 (in succession to Franz Mannstädt, who was moving to Berlin).

By early 1884 Strauss was well on his way to becoming a great admirer of Brahms's music. During a stay in Berlin, he heard his new Third Symphony no fewer than four times (twice conducted by Brahms), and with ever-increasing enjoyment. In a letter to his father on 1 February he wrote enthusiastically, "The symphony is really most beautiful. Clear in form and construction, splendidly worked out, it has delightful themes, and a force and drive which reminds one of **Beethoven**" (Schuh 1954, 38). To his friend Ludwig Thuille he described it as "not only his

[Brahms's] most beautiful symphony, but undoubtedly the most important one which has recently been written" (Ott 1969, 190). It may be assumed that Bülow did his best to stimulate Strauss's growing interest in Brahms's music still further.

On 19 November 1884, the day following the above-mentioned first performance of the Suite op. 4, Strauss, at Bülow's suggestion, sent the score to Brahms, with a request for his comments (for the text of this letter, see Grasberger 1967a, 21–22). It is not known how Brahms responded to Strauss, but according to **Max Kalbeck** (1976), he thought quite highly of the work (vol. 3, 496). Strauss did not make his personal acquaintance for almost another year—to be precise, not until 18 October 1885, when he called on Brahms at his rooms in the Meiningen palace (Brahms had arrived the previous evening). Brahms, he wrote to his father later that day, had been "very friendly and pleasant" (Schuh 1954, 620). That evening Strauss made his first appearance at a concert at Meiningen since assuming the position of assistant director of music two weeks earlier; he was the soloist in **Mozart**'s Piano Concerto K. 491 and also conducted the first performance of his own Symphony (op. 12). Brahms, asked for his opinion of the work, pronounced it "quite good," but added some useful advice on what not to do the next time (Schuh 1954, 63; Kalbeck 1976, vol. 3, 496–97). During the following week, Strauss saw him every day and on one occasion even spent some time alone with him ("all of which was, of course, tremendously interesting," he told his father [Schuh 1954, 63]). He was present at the rehearsals and at the world premiere (on 25 October) of Brahms's new Fourth Symphony, which deeply impressed him: "It is difficult to define all the magnificent aspects of this work in words, one can only listen again and again in reverence and admire," he wrote to his father on 24 October (Schuh 1954, 64); and in a letter to **Franz Wüllner** on 31 October he described it as "one of the most magnificent achievements in the sphere of instrumental music . . . entirely new and original, and yet from start to finish true Brahms" (Kämper 1963b, 7). He was also enchanted by the Violin Concerto that **Adolph Brodsky** played at the same concert. The next day he heard Brahms conduct his "splendid Haydn Variations" (Schuh 1954, 64), as well as the *Academic Festival Overture*, for which Bülow handled the cymbals and Strauss beat the big drum. That afternoon Strauss accompanied Brahms, Bülow, and a few others to Weimar, where they all spent two days together, after which Strauss returned to Meiningen with Bülow while Brahms went on to Frankfurt.

Strauss, who replaced Bülow as Musikdirektor at Meiningen in late 1885, met Brahms once more there at the beginning of April 1886. When he left the town later that month to take up an appointment as third

Kapellmeister at the Munich Hofoper (effective from 1 August), he was clearly still "ein wütender Brahmsianer" [a fanatical Brahmsian], as his father, who did not share his enthusiasm, had labeled him in a letter on 3 October 1885 (Grasberger 1967a, 27). But as he fell increasingly under the spell of **Liszt** and **Richard Wagner**, he turned away from Brahms. Due to conduct Brahms's Requiem at a music festival at Wiesbaden in June 1889, he replaced it with Liszt's symphonic poem *Héroïde funèbre*. In a letter to Cosima Wagner on 26 November of the same year, he compared the Requiem very unfavorably with that of **Hector Berlioz**, calling Brahms "musikalisch enthaltsam" [deficient in music] and a mediocrity (Trenner 1978, 11). His new hostility to Brahms also determined his actions on the occasion of the memorial concert arranged in connection with Bülow's funeral in Hamburg in March 1894. When invited to conduct the concert, he telegraphed that he wished to perform "serious music, therefore no Brahms," and proposed a program comprised of Liszt's *Héroide funèbre*, Bülow's *Nirwana*, **Beethoven**'s "Eroica" Symphony, and the preludes to *Tristan und Isolde* and *Die Meistersinger*. It was pointed out to him that Bülow had particularly disliked Liszt's composition and had in his last years turned away from Wagner (who, in any case, seemed an unsuitable choice for more personal reasons), but Strauss would not change his mind and ultimately declined to participate. Toni Petersen, who appears to have been among those responsible for discussing the matter with Strauss by telephone and telegraph, reported to Luise Wolff, "Strauss does not want Brahms, he hates him, despises his music and is afraid of Bayreuth, where Brahms is held in contempt and where Strauss is to conduct next season." (For a detailed account of these discussions with Strauss, see Stargardt-Wolff 1954, 87–88; Strauss, who had already worked as a musical assistant at Bayreuth in 1889, did in fact conduct *Tannhäuser* there in 1894.) The music eventually chosen for the memorial concert (Beethoven and **Franz Schubert**) was conducted by **Gustav Mahler**. (On Toni Petersen, *see* PETERSEN, CARL FRIEDRICH; on Louise Wolff, *see* WOLFF, HERMANN.) (Erck, Kertscher, and Schaefer 1983; Erck, Müller, and Schneider 1987; Grasberger 1967a; Kämper 1963b; Ott 1969; Schuh 1954, 1976; Schuh and Trenner 1954; Stargardt-Wolff 1954; Trenner 1978)

STREICHER, JOHANN BAPTIST (b. Vienna, 3 January 1796; d. Vienna, 28 March 1871) and **STREICHER, EMIL** (b. Vienna, 24 April 1836; d. Vienna, 9 January 1916). Piano manufacturers. Johann Baptist was the grandson of the famous Augsburg piano manufacturer Johann Andreas Stein and a son of Viennese piano makers (and **Beethoven**'s friends) Johann Andreas and Maria Anna Streicher; Emil, Johann Baptist's son, became his partner in 1857 and, after his father's death, ran the business by himself until he was obliged to liquidate the firm in 1896.

The first documented occasion on which Brahms played on a Streicher piano in Vienna was at a soiree at the firm's recital hall on 12 April 1863 (at his first two public appearances in Vienna, on 16 and 29 November 1862, he had performed on a **Bösendorfer** piano). During almost all his years in Vienna, Brahms had a **Streicher** piano in his music room. The earliest evidence of this can be found in a letter to **Clara Schumann** written in October 1864, at which time he was living at 1 Singerstrasse: "I have a beautiful grand piano from Streicher. With it he wanted to bring his latest improvements to my notice, and I believe that if he were to make a similar one for you, you would be pleased with it" (Litzmann 1970, vol. 1, 471). Clara knew the Streichers quite well. While staying in Vienna in December 1858, she had written to Brahms: "I know no one here whom I specially wish to see regularly; only at the Streichers' do I feel at home" (vol. 1, 232).

It appears from the above letter by Brahms, and the fact is confirmed by later references in his correspondence to the Streicher pianos that he had in his different flats in Vienna, that he did not purchase or rent any of them, but that they were placed at his disposal by the manufacturer. In 1872 he was provided with a piano made four years earlier that was to remain in his possession until his death. The firm even transported it to his summer quarters at Pörtschach when he vacationed there in the late 1870s.

In April 1873 Brahms wrote to **Adolf Schubring**, for whose brother he had just ordered a Streicher piano, "I consider Streicher to be good and reliable." But he added, "I hope that [the piano] will please your brother and that he will long derive enjoyment from it. I would ask you, though, not to spoil his pleasure! You are used to different pianos, and the German action will seem strange to you. I like it well enough in my room, only I cannot yet get used to the local grand pianos in the concert hall" (Brahms 1974/8, 224–25). The last time he performed on a Streicher piano in public was probably at a quartet evening given by the Hellmesberger Quartet in November 1880 (according to G. S. Bozarth's and S. H. Brady's [2000] article "Johannes Brahms and his Pianos," which also contains much fascinating technical information about the various types of pianos used by Brahms during his career).

After Brahms's death, his Streicher piano remained at first in his rooms at 4 Karlsgasse, where it was planned to set up a permanent memorial to him; but when the house was demolished in 1906, the furnishings were initially placed in the care of the Gesellschaft der Musikfreunde and later moved to the Historisches Museum der Stadt Wien. Nearly all the furniture was destroyed during the Second World War, and the Streicher piano was severely damaged. (Bolte 1917; Bozarth and Brady 2000; Brahms 1974/8; Cai 1989; Good 2001; Lepel 1936; Litzmann 1970)

SUK, JOSEF (b. Křečovice, 4 January 1874; d. Benešov, 29 May 1935). Composer and violinist. From 1885 to 1892 he studied at the Prague conservatory where his teachers included Antonín Bennewitz for violin, Hanuš Wihan for chamber music, and, during his final year, his future father-in-law **Antonín Dvořák** for composition. In 1892 he joined with Karel Hoffmann, Oskar Nedbal, and Otto Berger—all then, like himself, aged under 20—to form the Czech Quartet (with Hoffmann as its leader). On 19 January 1893, under the name "Das Böhmische Streichquartett," they made their highly successful Viennese debut with a concert devoted to the music of Smetana. Three further concerts followed. At the final one, on 27 February, they played Brahms's Piano Quintet, together with Joseph Jiránek. The Czech Quartet became one of the leading chamber music ensembles in Europe; it performed until 1933, when Suk retired. (Berger had been replaced by Wihan in 1894, and Wihan by Ladislav Zelenka in 1914; Nedbal was replaced by Jiří Herold in 1906).

In an article published in the Austrian periodical *Der Merker* in 1910, Suk related that he took advantage of his stay in Vienna in January 1893 to call on Brahms, on whose recommendation he had been awarded a state scholarship for composition. He was received with Brahms's typical mixture of kindness and gruffness: "So you are the scholarship holder Suk? Let me tell you something: next time your composition must be more competent or you won't get anything!" (Suk 1910, 147). By his own account (which is, however, rather confused in its chronology), Suk had various further conversations with Brahms during the quartet's later visits to Vienna; but he is also likely to have met with him at Leipzig in 1895 on the occasion of a concert there on 29 January, at which the quartet delighted Brahms with another performance, this time with **Eugen d'Albert**, of his Piano Quintet. According to **Max Kalbeck**, they wished to present an all-Brahms evening but had to be content, at his insistence, with just one of his compositions. Finally, Suk states that he last saw Brahms when he called on him together with Dvořák and his wife. This visit appears to have taken place on 27 March 1896, on which day the Czech Quartet presented Brahms's String Sextet op. 18 at their evening concert. Suk attended Brahms's funeral.

It was on Brahms's recommendation that **Fritz Simrock** decided to publish Suk's *Serenade for Strings* (op. 6), which appeared in 1896. Suk showed his gratitude for Brahms's support by dedicating his Piano Quintet op. 8 to him. (Boleška 1902; Suk 1910)

– T –

TAUSCH, JULIUS (b. Dessau, 15 April 1827; d. Bonn, 11 November 1895). Conductor, pianist, and composer. After studying at the Leipzig conservatory (1844–46), he moved to Düsseldorf, where he resided until 1890. There he was in charge of several local choirs, and from 1853 he also deputized for the ailing **Robert Schumann**, whom he succeeded in 1855 as municipal director of music. Between 1853 and 1887 he directed 10 Lower Rhine Music Festivals; certain of his own compositions were performed on those occasions.

Tausch appears to have been a fairly competent but rather uninspired conductor, and he was increasingly held responsible by many at Düsseldorf for the declining quality of the musical performances and the lower attendance at concerts. Accordingly, it was proposed in 1876 to replace him by a more distinguished figure, namely Brahms. Among the prominent people favoring that idea were the head of the Düsseldorf administration, Regierungspräsident **Karl Hermann Bitter**, and its legal adviser, Dr. Steinmetz. The two men were in contact with Brahms during the autumn of 1876 and the early weeks of 1877, both before and after the municipal council dismissed on 19 December a motion to maintain Tausch's appointment as municipal director of music and instead endorsed one calling for the appointment of a more eminent musician, each time by a majority of 17 to 7 (*see* BITTER, KARL HERMANN for some particulars of the negotiations with Brahms). However, from the outset, Brahms was wary of accepting the post, and in the end Bitter was obliged to inform the administration on 27 January 1877 that he had declined the offer.

One of the main reasons cited by Brahms for his decision was his unwillingness to oust a colleague who, notwithstanding the criticism voiced in some quarters, could evidently still count on the support of a significant part of the Düsseldorf population. In reaching that conclusion, Brahms was clearly influenced by the above-mentioned divided vote in the municipal council, but he was doubtless also aware that at the beginning of December leaflets had been distributed in Düsseldorf containing an "appeal to the sense of justice of our citizens and their representatives" that argued strongly for the retention of Tausch and also expressed some doubts that Brahms, if he were to accept the position, would keep it for more than a year or two (Kalbeck 1976, vol. 3, 125–27). Brahms accordingly suspected that he might land in a hornets' nest, and, as he told Bitter in a letter on 24 December, he had no taste for quarrels, fighting, or intrigue. Indeed, the uncertainty he felt regarding the conditions he might encounter at Düsseldorf strengthened his growing conviction that he would be wise to preserve the complete independence he had only fairly recently attained as a result of the dissolution of his contract with the Gesellschaft der Musikfreunde in Vienna.

Tausch remained director of music at Düsseldorf for 13 more years. He last conducted there on 27 March 1890. (Du Mont 1962)

TAUSIG, CARL [KAROL] (b. Warsaw, 4 November 1841; d. Leipzig, 17 July 1871). Pianist and composer; son of piano teacher and composer Aloys Tausig (1820–85), who was a pupil of **Sigismond Thalberg** (it is sometimes, but apparently erroneously, stated that Carl also received instruction from Thalberg). From 1855 to 1857 Tausig studied with **Liszt** at Weimar, and subsequently he became one of the most widely acclaimed pianists of his generation, even if it was not until the final years of his short life that he was accepted by the critics as a truly great musician, rather than simply as a brilliant virtuoso with a fiery temperament. (In 1864, **Clara Schumann** observed in a letter to Brahms that she had so far always heard Tausig described as a mere "Pauker" [thumper] (Litzmann 1970, vol. 1, 450).

Tausig settled in Vienna some time before Brahms arrived there in the autumn of 1862, at which period he was sharing accommodation with **Peter Cornelius** (who, in his diary, affectionately refers to him as "Carlo"). After the concert given by the Hellmesberger Quartet on 16 November 1862, at which Brahms presented himself to the Viennese public both as a pianist and as the composer of a piano quartet (op. 25), Tausig wrote to him expressing profound admiration for the work. By the end of that year Brahms was seeing Tausig and Cornelius regularly, and he evidently not only took to Tausig as a person but was also fascinated by his pianistic skills, for the difficult *Paganini Variations*, which he composed that winter, was a tribute to Tausig's technical brilliance. **Max Kalbeck** (1976) regarded it as "a lasting monument to the friendship of the two musicians" (vol. 2, 40). Kalbeck states that Brahms first played the work in Vienna on 17 March 1867, and that Tausig first played it in Berlin on the 25th of the same month. In actual fact, the very first performance of the *Variations* was given by Brahms from the manuscript in Zurich on 25 November 1865; they were published by **Jakob Melchior Rieter-Biedermann** in January 1866.

When Brahms returned to Vienna in the late summer of 1863 after an absence of several months, he quickly resumed his contacts with Tausig. They visited each other and sometimes played duets together; and on 17 April 1864, at a concert of the Singakademie, of which Brahms was then the director, they gave the first public performance of the Sonata for Two Pianos op. 34 bis (which Brahms later turned into the Piano Quintet op. 34). Two weeks earlier Brahms had written to Clara Schumann about Tausig: "He is a strange little fellow and a very extraordinary pianist, who, moreover, as much as any man can, is constantly changing to his advantage. The compositions of **Rubinstein**, of **Chopin**, and, of course, especially of Liszt he often plays quite wonderfully" (Litzmann 1970, vol. 1, 445). In May 1864 Brahms and Cornelius went with Tausig to visit the Vrabély family at Bratislava, and there on 8 November of that year they both attended Tausig's marriage to one of the daughters, Seraphine (1841–1931), who was also a talented pianist. According to Kalbeck, her sister Stephanie (later Countess Wurmbach-Stuppach) received some tuition from Brahms.

Before long Tausig and his wife moved to Berlin, where he opened a school for advanced piano instruction. It closed, however, within a few years, as he did not really enjoy teaching. The marriage ended in divorce, and the last period of Tausig's life seems to have been marked by increasing personal unhappiness and frail health. When Brahms went to Berlin in March 1871, he met Tausig once more, and perhaps even stayed with him. That summer Tausig died of typhoid, at the age of 29. In later years Brahms would look back on his association with Tausig with some pleasure (*see* CORNELIUS, [CARL AUGUST] PETER; on his contacts with Tausig, *see also* WAGNER, (WILHELM) RICHARD). (H. Ehrlich 1893a; Fay 1965; La Mara 1875b; Litzmann 1970)

TCHAIKOVSKY, PYOTR IL'YICH (b. Kamsko-Votkinsk, Vyatka province, 7 May 1840; d. St. Petersburg, 6 November 1893). Composer. Given their different temperaments, cultural backgrounds, and musical ideals, it is hardly surprising that Tchaikovsky and Brahms were unable to warm to the each other's compositions. In his letters and other writings, Tchaikovsky repeatedly stated his distaste for Brahms's music, pronouncing it dry, pretentious, devoid of individuality, lacking in beauty, and second-rate ("It vexes me that this self-conscious mediocrity should be recognised as a genius" [P. Tchaikovsky 1969, 203]). He particularly disliked the symphonies, which he found too long and colourless. Nevertheless, he recognized in Brahms a serious and committed artist and, after meeting him, even expressed some liking for the man.

Tchaikovsky might have introduced himself to Brahms during his first brief stay in Vienna in December 1877, if his pride and a distaste for hypocrisy had not stopped him. As he explained to Nadezhda von Meck, Brahms's support would be invaluable, since Brahms was famous and he himself a nonentity. But he added, "Yet without false modesty I have to say that I think I am better than Brahms. What am I to say to him? 'I do not rate you at all highly and regard you with the greatest condescension. But I need you and so I have come to you.' If, however, I am dishonest and untruthful, then I will say the exact opposite. I can do neither one thing nor the other" (Orlova 1990, 119).

Thus, he did not make Brahms's acquaintance for another 10 years, and then by chance, when, on New Year's Day 1888 (not 2 January, as indicated in R. and K. Hofmann's *Zeittafel*), he called on **Adolph Brodsky** in Leipzig and found him in the middle of a rehearsal of Brahms's Piano Trio op. 101, with Brahms himself at the piano. (The cellist was **Julius Klengel**.) That evening Tchaikovsky attended a performance of Brahms's Double Concerto, which, notwithstanding his appreciation of the excellent playing of **Joseph Joachim** and **Robert Hausmann**, left him quite unmoved. On 2 January Brahms was, in his turn, present at Tchaikovsky's rehearsal with the Gewandhaus Orchestra of his First Suite for Orchestra (op. 43) in preparation for its public performance on 5 January. Tchaikovsky had some further conversation with Brahms that day; however, as he wrote to his brother Modeste, "we are ill at ease, because we do not really like each other, but he takes great pains to be kind to me" (M. Tchaikovsky 1906). Tchaikovsky found **Edvard Grieg**, who was also in Leipzig at the time, far more congenial company. Nonetheless, he later drew an agreeable enough portrait of Brahms when describing this visit to Leipzig in the *Diary of My Tour in 1888*: "Brahms is rather a short man, suggests a sort of amplitude and possesses a very sympathetic appearance. His fine head—almost that of an old man—recalls the type of a handsome, benign, elderly Russian priest. . . . Brahms's manner is very simple, free from vanity, his humour jovial, and the few hours spent in his society left me with a very agreeable recollection" (M. Tchaikovsky 1906, 541, n. 2).

Tchaikovsky met Brahms once more, in Hamburg in March 1889, on which occasion he was gratified to learn that Brahms had decided to delay his departure so that he could attend the rehearsal of Tchaikovsky's Fifth Symphony. Afterward Brahms expressed his opinion of the work. According to Modeste Tchaikovsky, he had liked it on the whole, though not the final movement. On the other hand, Sigismond Stojowski (1933) (*see* STOJOWSKI, ZYGMUNT [SIGISMOND] (DENIS ANTONI)), in his "Recollections of Brahms," recalls being told by Tchaikovsky that Brahms had "proceeded to a sharply derogatory critique of subject-matter, form, orchestration and what not" (149). Stojowski also quotes Tchaikovsky as remarking that he would have been deeply hurt by Brahms's comments, had he not himself hated Brahms's symphonies so much. At the same time, Tchaikovsky's esteem for Brahms as an honest and straightforward man appears to have been heightened by his candor. At any rate, the incident did not prevent him from inviting Brahms to Moscow to conduct a symphony concert, an offer Brahms declined. (Biba 1983/84; Orlova 1990; Stojowski 1933; M. Tchaikovsky 1906; P. Tchaikovsky 1945, 1969)

THALBERG, SIGISMOND (b. Pâquis, near Geneva, 8 January 1812; d. Posillipo, near Naples, 27 April 1871). Pianist and composer. His compositions for piano provided bravura pieces for himself and other virtuosos. Brahms clearly appreciated their brilliance, for he resorted to them repeatedly in his early efforts to dazzle Hamburg audiences. Thus, at his very first public appearance as a pianist, at Carl Birgfeld's concert in Hamburg on 20 November 1847, his contribution consisted of Thalberg's Fantasia on Bellini's opera *Norma*, while at his next public appearance, at Therese Meyer's concert a week later, he took part in a duet for two pianos by Thalberg. At a concert given by the tenor Theodor Wachtel on 1 March 1849, he performed Thalberg's Fantasia on *Don Giovanni*, and he played it once more at his own concert on 14 April. Furthermore, he performed Thalberg's *Variations* on a theme from Donizetti's *Lucia di Lammermoor* at a concert by the singer Rudolf Lohfeldt on 5 December of the same year, and parts of the same variations at a concert of the violinist Antoine de Kloot on 4 March 1850.

THIERIOT [?THIERRIOT], FERDINAND (b. Hamburg, 7 April 1838; d. Hamburg, 4 August 1919). Composer and teacher. He reportedly studied piano with **Eduard Marxsen** in Hamburg and composition with Joseph Rheinberger in Munich. Subsequently, he was active as a teacher and musician in Hamburg, Leipzig, and Glogau. In 1870 he was appointed artistic director of the Steiermärkischer Musikverein at Graz on the recommendation of Brahms, who had known him for many years; apart from his other duties, he taught piano and musical theory. He was obliged to relinquish his position in 1885, a fact that Brahms regretted, since, as he told **Richard Heuberger**, Thieriot was "a decent and excellent man, capable of producing good results by his teaching and example, as well as by his personal qualities" (Heuberger 1976, 29). Heuberger also mentions in his diary spending the evening of 11 April 1885 with Brahms, Thieriot, and others at a Viennese restaurant and café.

There seems to be no evidence of any later meetings between Brahms and Thieriot. On the other hand, there is a record of earlier ones, and even of a musical association between them, provided that Werner G. Zimmermann (1983) is correct in identifying, in *Brahms in der Schweiz: Eine Dokumentation*, the cellist "Thierriot" (as his name is given in the printed programs) who played in Brahms's concerts in Zurich on 25 and 28 November 1865, with Thieriot (Zimmermann 1983, 21). On the first occasion, "Thierriot" took part with **Friedrich Hegar**, Oskar Kahl, and Brahms in a performance of the Piano Quartet op. 25, while on the second he assumed the cello part in **Beethoven**'s String Quartet in E-flat Major (op. 127). Moreover, on 4 May 1866 **Theodor Billroth** reported to Brahms, who was then at Winterthur, that he had the previous evening played his "new Cello Sonata" [op. 38] with "Thieriot" (Gottlieb-Billroth 1935, 180). It would therefore appear that the Thierriot/Thieriot in question either visited Switzerland on more than one occasion or that he spent at least several months at Zurich in 1865–66. If he was still there during the summer of 1866 when Brahms spent several weeks at nearby Fluntern, they will almost certainly have met again and may well have shared in some further music making at Billroth's or at Hegar's.

Ferdinand Thieriot's published compositions include a Sinfonietta, a Serenade for String Orchestra, a violin concerto, and a concerto for three violins, so his interest in string instruments is manifest, even if he may not have written specifically for the cello. He dedicated his Piano Trio op. 14 to Brahms. (Gottlieb-Billroth 1935; Heuberger 1976)

TIECK, (JOHANN) LUDWIG (b. Berlin, 31 May 1773; d. Berlin, 28 April 1853). Poet, novelist, and critic. He was the author of the poems set by Brahms in his *Romanzen aus L. Tieck's 'Magelone'* (op. 33). The poems had originally appeared in *Wundersame Liebesgeschichte der schönen Magelone und des Grafen Peter aus der Provence* in *Volksmärchen herausgegeben von Peter Leberecht* (1797)—"Peter Leberecht" being a pseudonym adopted by Tieck—and had later been published in his *Phantasus* (1812). (Michael Neumann 1991)

TILGNER, VICTOR (OSKAR) (b. Pressburg [Bratislava], 25 October 1844; d. Vienna, 16 April 1896). Sculptor. He studied at the Academy of Fine Arts in Vienna (1859–71), and was subsequently pointed toward the Baroque Revival by the French sculptor Gustave Deloye, who lived in Vienna in 1872–73. He first attracted attention with his bust of the celebrated actress Charlotte Wolters, which was awarded a gold medal at the Vienna World Exhibition of 1873.

Tilgner's enormous output comprised large figures for several state buildings (Neue Hofburg, Naturhistorisches Museum, Kunsthistorisches Museum, Burgtheater), funerary monuments, ornamental fountains, and busts (of royalty, aristocrats, artists, and musicians). In addition, he designed a number of important statues in Vienna, several of which were not unveiled until after his death. Among the statues are those of **Mozart**, unveiled on the Albrechts-Platz on 21 April 1896 (and moved to its present site in the Burggarten in 1953); of the painter Hans Makart in the Stadtpark, made by the elder Fritz Zerritsch after a sketch by Tilgner and unveiled in 1898; of **Anton Bruckner**, unveiled in the Stadtpark in 1899 (and now in the garden of the former Bourgoing Palais, currently used by the Hochschule für Musik, in Metternichgasse); and one of **Eduard Hanslick** at the university, which was not unveiled until 1913.

In January 1891 Tilgner modeled a bronze bust of Brahms, whom he is likely to have already met socially on various occasions, if only because they had several friends and acquaintances in common, among them **Viktor von Miller zu Aichholz** and **Johann Strauss** (both Tilgner and Brahms appear in the **Marquis de Bayros**'s (*see* BAYROS, FRANZ WILHELM, MARQUIS DE) painting *Ein Abend bei Johann Strauss*). According to **Max Kalbeck** (1976), it was Viktor von Miller who persuaded Brahms to sit for Tilgner (vol. 4, 268), and a similar statement can be found in the catalog of the 1997 Hamburg Brahms exhibition. Curiously though, the very next page of that catalog carries an extract from a letter by **Ludwig Michalek**, which states that Brahms was influenced by a request made by Viktor's brother Eugen (Brahms Exhibition 1997b, 67–68). Since Michalek was present at some of the sittings (while Tilgner was modeling the bust, Michalek was painting Brahms's portrait), his testimony has some force. He also mentions that the sittings took place at Tilgner's studio at the Schwarzenberg Palais (2 Rennweg). There were apparently some six or seven sittings, with Brahms getting increasingly impatient for them to end. The finished bust did not please everyone. Kalbeck (1976), for one, found its style too "ornate" and "Rococo," and soon banished his plaster copy to the top of one of his bookcases (vol. 4, 269, n. 1), while one of the sons of Brahms's friend **Richard Fellinger** complained that Tilgner's "dandyish" Brahms evoked neither the man nor his genius (R. Fellinger 1997, 136). An interesting discussion of the bust, relating its features to the artistic trends then prevailing in Vienna, will be found in the above-mentioned exhibition catalog.

In 1892, the year following its creation, the bust was presented to the Kunsthalle in Hamburg as a gift by the Austro-Hungarian consul general Baron Friedrich von Westenholz. (Brahms Exhibition 1997b; R. Fellinger 1997)

TOELG, JOSEF (b. Braunau, 1852). Physician. He qualified at the University of Vienna in 1878 and was employed as an assistant at Professor Heinrich von Bamberger's clinic in Vienna until 1885. In 1891 he was appointed director of the Wilhelminenspital.

On 28 August 1896 Brahms, who had been examined by Dr. Hertzka and Professor **Leopold Schrötter von Kristelli** during his stay at Ischl, informed **Richard Heuberger** that Schrötter was of the opinion that he should not go to Karlsbad [Karlovy Vary], because he believed that there might be another cause for Brahms's illness apart from jaundice (or hepatitis); Brahms had therefore decided to return to Vienna to consult Professor Toelg "who knows him well and for whom he has a high regard" (Heuberger 1976, 111). Brahms duly traveled back to Vienna from Ischl on 31 August, and on 1 September, at an evening meal at the Goldene Kugel restaurant he told a group of friends, Heuberger among them, that he was leaving for Karlsbad the following day (i.e., 2 September). On that day **Richard Fellinger** wrote to Heuberger that Toelg regarded Brahms's condition as grave but not incurable, that he attributed it to a disorder of the biliary tract, and that a cure at Karlsbad was likely to be successful (Heuberger 1976, 169). It is accordingly evident that Brahms must have consulted Toelg on 1 September, and that his decision to take the cure at Karlsbad was taken on the latter's advice. According to **Max Kalbeck**, however, it was not until the evening of 3 September that Brahms, accompanied by Fellinger, took the train to Karlsbad (Kalbeck 1976, vol. 4, 465).

On 20 October, some three weeks after Brahms's return to Vienna, Heuberger noted in his diary that Toelg was in favor of operating "if there is still time" (Heuberger 1976, 113). (Heuberger 1976)

TRUXA, CELESTINE [CÖLESTINA] (b. Verona, 4 August 1858 [according to Nigg 1893 and Pataky 1898]; d. Vienna, 20 May 1935). Brahms's landlady at 4 Karlsgasse from 1887 until his death. When Ludovika **Vog(e)l** died in November 1886, Brahms was most anxious not to lose the comfortable accommodations to which he had grown accustomed over the past 15 years, and he even considered renting the flat himself, though only as a last solution. His friends, in the meanwhile, tried to find someone who might wish to rent the flat and at the same time be a congenial landlord for him, and it was apparently through **Maria Fellinger** that Celestine Truxa's attention was drawn to the matter. After she had inspected the flat and met Brahms, she decided to rent and to accept him as her lodger, an arrangement to which he readily agreed and which seems to have worked out extremely well for him.

She was then a recent widow, her husband, Dr. Robert Truxa having died in an accident at Interlaken on 17 August 1886, leaving her with two young boys. He had been a journalist and owner of the *Verkehrs-Zeitung*, for the publication of which Celestina assumed responsibility after his death. She proved to be a person of tact and discretion who respected Brahms's privacy completely. According to **Max Kalbeck** (1976), who came to know her quite well, she was a "cultured, sensitive, and intelligent lady" (Kalbeck 1976, vol. 4, 56). She was at any rate intelligent enough to rescue some of Brahms's music autographs that he had torn up and thrown into the wastepaper basket.

Brahms treated her with courtesy and took a kindly interest in the two boys, to whom he regularly gave presents at Christmas. But although he was on cordial terms with Celestine Truxa and her sons, he hardly ever discussed private matters with her; it was, for instance, only after his death that she learned of the existence of his stepmother. During his final illness she looked after him with devotion, and it was she who was with him when he died and who closed his eyes. She described his final hours in a brief article ("Am Sterbebette Brahms'"), which was printed in the *Neue freie Presse* on 7 May 1903. She later related some of her memories of Brahms in an interview published in the *Neues Wiener Journal* on 4 May 1933 ("Besuch bei Cölestine Truxa, der Hausfrau von Johannes Brahms"), and she described in greater detail her early contacts with Brahms in a conversation with Gustav Fock, an account of which appeared in volume 3 of *Brahms-Studien* in 1979; the same issue of that periodical also offers the text of a brief letter addressed to Truxa on 1 May 1902 by her former maid Anastasia [Anna] Tettinek, recalling some events that happened on the day Brahms died.

A number of items of correspondence between Celestine Truxa and Brahms are preserved at the Stadt-und Landesbibliothek, Vienna. (Fock 1979; K. Hofmann 2001; M. 1933; Nigg 1893; Pataky 1898; Truxa 1903, 1972)

TURGENEV, IVAN SERGEYEVICH (b. Orel, 9 November 1818; d. Bougival, near Paris, 3 September 1883). Russian novelist and poet. Through **Pauline Viardot** and **Clara Schumann**, Turgenev made Brahms's acquaintance at Baden-Baden, where he lived from 1863 until late 1870. At some point he offered to write an opera libretto for Brahms, but when he eventually sent an outline for one, Brahms was not impressed. The autograph manuscript was found among Brahms's papers after his death; in 1981 it was auctioned at Sotheby's and acquired by the Pierpont Morgan Library of New York (in the auction catalog it was dated "*c*.1868").

The text was reproduced by P. Waddington in *The New Zealand Slavonic Journal* in 1982. The plot, which is set in Switzerland or the Tyrol, contains various Romantic features that, as Waddington (1982) rightly observes, "one might expect to find in an opera by Marschner or Konstantin Kreutzer rather than in one by Brahms" (6). They include the presence of a mysterious stranger patently nursing a guilty secret, and a duel in which the contestants have to draw lots, the one taking the death lot being expected to kill himself within six months—only he doesn't. The story, Brahms later told **Max Kalbeck**, was just "too silly" (Kalbeck 1976, vol. 2, 169; concerning Turgenev, *see also* VIARDOT, [MICHELLE FERDINANDE] PAULINE.) (Keefer 1966; Waddington 1982, 1983)

– U –

UHLAND, (JOHANN) LUDWIG (b. Tübingen, 26 April 1787; d. Tübingen, 13 November 1862). Poet, dramatist, scholar, and politician. Brahms set poems by Uhland for solo voice in "Heimkehr" (op. 7/6), "Scheiden und Meiden" (op. 19/2), "In der Ferne" (op. 19/3), "Der Schmied" (op. 19/4), "Sonntag" (op. 47/3); for women's choir in "Die Nonne" (op. 44/6), "Märznacht" (op. 44/12), and "Brautgesang" (M. McCorkle 1984, Anhang III/12); and for soprano and contralto in the canon "Wann" (WoO 29). (Fröschle 1991)

ULRICH VON WÜRTTEMBERG, DUKE (b. Reichenweiher, 8 February 1487; d. Tübingen, 6 November 1550). His reign covered a particularly turbulent period in the history of the duchy, during which he was more than once expelled from it; he was responsible for establishing Protestantism there.

Ulrich may be the author of the poems set by Brahms in the songs "Ich schwing mein Horn" (op. 41/1) and "Ich schell mein Horn ins Jammertal" (op. 43/3). (Schneider 1971; Taddey 1983)

UNGER, WILLIAM (b. Hanover, 11 September 1837; d. Innsbruck, 5 March 1932). Painter and etcher. After studying in Düsseldorf and Munich, he led a peripatetic existence until settling in 1872 in Vienna, where he lived and worked (and, for many years, taught) until 1919; he then moved to Innsbruck. He executed several portraits, his subjects including Emperor Franz Joseph and Pope Pius IX; but his magnum opus was probably the reproduction of pictures from the Belvedere Gallery (*Die k.k. Gemäldegalerie in Wien*: 100 sheets with 77 additional marginal etchings, published by H. O. Miethke between 1876 and 1885).

In February 1897 he received a commission from the London Philharmonic Society to make a portrait of Brahms, whom he had first seen at Göttingen in 1853. Brahms declined to sit for him on the grounds of his ill health; but after his death Unger executed his portrait in an etching, which was published by H. O. Miethke in October 1897. Although it seems a good enough likeness, the portrait is said to have been frequently criticized by those who had known Brahms; yet for Richard Fellinger (the son of Brahms's great friends **Richard and Maria Fellinger**), it was the only one that did full justice to Brahms the inspired musician, to "the spiritual kinsman of **Bach** and **Beethoven**" (R. Fellinger 1997, 136). (R. Fellinger 1997; Unger 1929)

– V –

VERHULST, JOHANNES (JOSEPHUS HERMANUS) (b. The Hague, 19 March 1816; d. The Hague, 17 January 1891). Composer and conductor. He studied violin, theory, and orchestration with J. H. Lübeck and C. J. Lechleitner and, subsequently, received further instruction in orchestration from C. Hansen, conductor of the orchestra of the Théâtre français, where he had been engaged as a violinist; he also played in the orchestra of the royal chapel. Later he studied briefly with Josef Klein at Cologne, and in 1838 he went to Leipzig where he conducted the "Euterpe" choral society. He formed a close friendship with **Robert Schumann** and was also on good terms with Mendelssohn, whom he had first met in 1836. After his return to Holland in 1842, he came to occupy an increasingly dominant position in Dutch musical life. Until 1863 (except for the years 1845–48) he was in charge of the choirs of the royal chapel at The Hague and of the Rotterdam section of the Maatschappij tot Bevordering der Toonkunst; in addition, he conducted the Diligentia concerts at The Hague from 1860. In 1863 he took over the direction of the Felix Meritis concerts at Amsterdam, and he also conducted the choir of the Amsterdam section of the Maatschappij; furthermore, he assumed in 1864 responsibility for the Caecilia concerts, likewise in Amsterdam.

Brahms made Verhulst's acquaintance in January 1855 when he joined **Clara Schumann** in Rotterdam. During his first tour of Holland in January 1876 he played his First Piano Concerto at Amsterdam and The Hague, with Verhulst conducting. They met again two years later, when Brahms presented his Second Symphony to Dutch audiences. "It was delightful to see how Verhulst behaved towards Brahms," Emma Engelmann (*see* ENGELMANN, [THEODOR] WILHELM) reported to Clara Schumann.

> At the first rehearsal of the D major [Symphony] he is said to have wept like a child; and at the Felix Meritis [concert] he was so blissfully happy during the symphony that he ran over to a lady he did not know, pressed her hands, and told her "Be sure never to forget how fortunate you are to hear this mu-

> sic." You could also see how fond he is of Brahms; no bride could have treated him with more tender and profound affection than Verhulst showed him. (Litzmann 1902, vol. 3, 368

In September 1878 they saw each other again at the music festival at Hamburg, and in January 1882 Verhulst conducted when Brahms played his Second Piano Concerto in Amsterdam.

Brahms amply returned Verhulst's affection and admiration. In January 1878 he wrote to Clara Schumann from Amsterdam: "I like Verhulst very much indeed, he reminds me so much of your husband" (Litzmann 1970, vol. 2, 133), and in the spring of 1880 he told **Eduard Hanslick**, who was about to leave Vienna on a visit to Holland: "If at all possible, don't fail to get to know *Verhulst*. . . . An outstanding musician, a friend of Mendelssohn and Schumann, a highly original person, extremely kind, with a childlike gentleness. You will, I am sure, find him most interesting—and also his songs, which are sometimes, as they should be, a very attractive likeness of himself" (Hanslick 1897b, *Neue freie Presse*, 1 July 1897, 2). Verhulst composed, in fact, numerous songs and choral works, apart from some chamber music and compositions for orchestra alone. He was very strongly influenced by Mendelssohn and Schumann, and entirely hostile to the "New German School." In the end his extreme conservatism provoked public irritation, and he was forced to resign from the Diligentia concerts in 1886. Soon afterward he withdrew entirely from his public musical activities. According to **Julius Röntgen**, Brahms at first considered that Verhulst had been unjustly treated but later recognized that he had been mistaken. (Hanslick 1897b; Litzmann 1902; J. Röntgen 1920)

VIARDOT, (MICHELLE FERDINANDE) PAULINE (b. Paris, 18 July 1821; d. Paris, 18 May 1910). Mezzo-soprano, composer, and teacher; daughter of the celebrated tenor Manuel García (1775–1832), and sister of the great mezzo-soprano Maria Malibran (1808–36) and of the younger Manuel García (1805–1906), a well-known baritone and teacher. She first performed at a concert in Brussels on 13 March 1837, made her operatic debut as Desdemona in Rossini's *Otello* in London on 9 May 1839, and thereafter enjoyed a brilliant international career that in 1843 took her to St. Petersburg. There she met the 25-year-old **Ivan Sergeyevich Turgenev**, who fell head over heels in love with her and would be her intimate friend for most of the remainder of his life. By the early 1860s, the quality of her voice had declined, and after a farewell appearance in Paris on 24 April 1863 in the title role of **Christoph Willibald Gluck**'s *Orfeo* (in which she had excelled and which she had performed some 150 times), she settled at Baden-

Baden with her husband Louis (1800–83), a well-known French writer whom she had married in 1840. Thereafter, she still made occasional appearances at concerts and in opera, but concentrated mainly on teaching. She also composed several operettas to librettos provided by Turgenev, who had followed the Viardots to Baden-Baden, and she staged performances of these, with the help of her children and pupils and of Turgenev himself, in her imposing concert room, which contained not only a piano, but also an organ. She was herself a very competent pianist and had originally intended to become a professional one; among her teachers was **Liszt**.

In the 1860s the spa town of Baden-Baden attracted the cream of European society, from royalty and aristocrats to the luminaries of the artistic world. In this international "jet set" Pauline Viardot shone brightly, highly respected and an enthusiastic promoter of the manifold public and private cultural activities that flourished there, especially during the summer season. Her Sunday matinees were among the highlights of these activities. Among those with whom she was in close contact at Baden-Baden was **Clara Schumann**, whom she had come to know well many years before at Leipzig. It was probably through Clara that Viardot met Brahms during one of his repeated visits to the spa during the 1860s. (It is evidently impossible to attach any credence to the bizarre story told by Viardot's former pupil Anna Eugénie Schoen-René (1941) in her memoirs (even though she claims to have heard it from Viardot herself), according to which Brahms, "a young man of about twenty-one years of age," had presented himself to Viardot at Baden-Baden, armed with a letter of introduction that Liszt had given him during his visit to Weimar in "about the year 1852." Viardot had invited him to stay at Baden-Baden as accompanist to her pupils, and he himself had often later attributed his success as a composer of Lieder to his "studies" with Viardot [151–52].)

Clara's earliest efforts to interest Viardot in Brahms's compositions had been unsuccessful, as is proved by the negative judgment she expressed in 1859 (*see* RIETZ, [AUGUST WILHELM] JULIUS). However, during her years at Baden-Baden, she must have heard quite a few performances of his works, in some of which he no doubt participated, and her opinion of his music changed. Most striking of all, it was she who gave the first public performance of the *Alto Rhapsody*, at Jena on 3 March 1870, with the Akademischer Gesangverein conducted by **Ernst Naumann**. (She had probably attended the private performance of the *Rhapsody* that **Hermann Levi** had conducted in Brahms's presence at Karlsruhe on 6 October 1869, for Clara Schumann's benefit, when the soloist had been Amalia Boni.) How the Jena performance came about is not certain; perhaps it was, as **Florence May** (1948) believed, "the outcome of a friendly chat" that Viardot had early in 1870 with Liszt's friend Dr. Carl Gille at Weimar (vol. 2, 442). Gille, who occupied a senior position at the Jena High Court of Appeal, was a guiding spirit of the "Akademische Konzerte."

By that time Brahms was evidently on friendly terms with Viardot, although their relations were never close. In 1865, or perhaps 1869, he composed a serenade, which was sung by her pupils, under his direction, on her birthday. He and Viardot are also known to have both participated in at least one musical event: in a performance of **Bach**'s *St. Matthew Passion* at Karlsruhe on 30 March 1864, in which she was one of the soloists and he played the organ part. On 24 August 1869 he conducted, from the piano, a performance of her operetta *Le Dernier Sorcier*, which was staged in her music room at Baden-Baden.

The outbreak of the Franco-Prussian war in 1870 drove the Viardots to seek refuge in London, from where they later returned to Paris. There is no evidence of any later contacts between Pauline and Brahms. (Baser 1973; Brand 1931; Fitzlyon 1964; May 1948; Schoen-René 1941; Viardot 1915–16; Waddington 1983)

VIOTTI, GIOVANNI BATTISTA (b. Fontanetto da Po, 12 May 1755; d. London, 3 March 1824). Violinist and composer. Brahms was a great admirer of Viotti ever since he heard **Carl Louis Bargheer** perform his Violin Concerto in A Minor (no. 22) at Detmold—"it was new to me and highly interesting," he reported to **Joseph Joachim** in December 1858 (Brahms 1974/5, 225). In June 1878 he wrote to **Clara Schumann**: "Viotti's A minor Concerto is a very special favourite of mine. . . . It is a marvellous work, with its remarkable free-flowing invention. It sounds as if he were improvising, but everything is conceived and composed in a masterly fashion" (Litzmann 1970, vol. 2, 145). In a letter to **Richard Barth** on 19 December 1903, Joachim referred to it as "Brahms's favourite composition" (Johannes Joachim and Moser 1911–13, vol. 3, 507).

Joachim, who was also very fond of the concerto, played it repeatedly in public, including at the concert of 14 January 1879 in which he introduced Brahms's Violin Concerto to a Viennese audience. Moreover, he believed that the passage leading to the coda of the first violin solo in Brahms's concerto was an "unconscious echo" of the transition from the first to the second main theme in Viotti's (Joseph Joachim and Moser 1902–5, vol. 3, 27). When Joachim was once asked to rank the most important concertos ever written for the violin, he named **Beethoven**'s, Viotti's 22nd, and Mendelssohn's; Brahms, he added, had agreed with that order (Moser 1908, vol. 2, 243). (Joachim clearly placed Viotti's A Minor Concerto above Brahms's; in fact, he was inclined to prefer Brahms's Double Concerto to his Violin Concerto.) (Brahms 1974/5; Johannes Joachim and Moser 1911–13; Joseph Joachim and Moser 1902–5; Litzmann 1970; A. Moser 1908)

VOG(E)L. Principal tenants of a third-floor flat at 4 Karlsgasse in Vienna, in which Brahms rented two rooms in late 1871; in 1877 he rented a third room, mainly to accommodate his personal library. Some time after the death on 10 November 1886 of Ludovika Vog(e)l, the last member of the family to occupy the flat, **Celestine Truxa** became its main tenant and thus Brahms's landlady. (While the family's name is persistently spelled "Vogl" by **Max Kalbeck** and later Brahms biographers, the register of deaths actually gives Ludovica's name as "Vogel.")

VÖLKERS, ELISABETH [BETTY] and **MARIE** (b. Hamm, 16 May 1836). Members of Brahms's Hamburg Frauenchor and also, with Laura Garbe and Marie Reuter, of the quartet that evolved from it. **Max Kalbeck** (1976) states that their father Karl Ludwig Völkers, a Hamburg insurance broker, was an accomplished amateur singer who frequently took part in public oratorio performances and "even in old age was so skilled in sight reading that Brahms often made music with him" (vol. 1, 441). Brahms came to know the family particularly well in 1861–62 when he rented a room at Hamm, near Hamburg, at a house occupied by the girls' aunt **Elisabeth Rösing**, which stood close to the Völkers' summer villa. Brahms visited them almost every day during his stay there and, as Marie recalled in a letter to Kalbeck many years afterward (vol. 1, 442), often played for them well into the night, readily fulfilling all their wishes. The Frauenchor held its choir practices and the girls' quartet met there. Moreover, some of Brahms's distinguished friends, notably **Clara Schumann** and **Joseph Joachim**, were among the Völkers' occasional guests. He himself appears to have had a closer relationship with Marie than with her sister, perhaps because, as she told Kalbeck, she "had the good fortune to be his pupil" (vol. 1, 442); whether the lessons had started before Brahms moved to Hamm is not known. According to the Völkers' family lore, he even proposed marriage to her.

After he left for Vienna in September 1862, the Völkers maintained friendly relations with his sister Elise (*see* BRAHMS [LATER: GRUND], ELISABETH [ELISE] WILHELMINE) and with his parents (including **Johann Jakob**'s second wife). In April 1868 Johann Jakob Brahms traveled with them to Bremen to attend the performance of his son's Requiem. Brahms was to correspond with Marie in later years. A number of his letters to her were published by Siegfried Kross in "Der Nachlass der Schwestern Völkers" in 1964; the earliest letter dates from September

1872, a year before her marriage to **John Böie** on 23 September 1873, the final two from the last year of Brahms's life. His letters are affectionate and filled with fond memories of the happy days at Hamm. He also met Marie and her husband on various occasions, and he saw Marie for the last time at Clara Schumann's funeral. She later remembered him with great tenderness: "He was a most wonderful man, unwavering in his love and loyalty," she wrote to Kalbeck (1976, vol. 1, 442). As for Betty, she married in 1862 violinist Otto von Königslöw (1824–98), who was Konzertmeister of the Gürzenich Orchestra at Cologne (1858–81) and also taught at the conservatory there.

Marie was not the only Völkers girl to receive musical instruction from Brahms. Minna Völkers (later Stone), a niece of Marie and Betty, became his pupil early in 1861 when she was 11; the lessons continued until the summer of the following year. Unlike her aunts, she was to publish her recollections of him (in the *Hamburger Nachrichten* on 3 April 1922). Above all, she considered him an excellent, kind, and patient teacher. She evidently became a highly proficient pianist herself and must have become well known in Hamburg musical circles, for in Johann Jakob's letters to Brahms there are several references to her concert appearances, at which, moreover, she did not forget her former teacher. Thus she played his Scherzo op. 4 at Franz Abt's concert on 8 December 1868, and the following autumn she began a series of concerts with violinist Henry Schradiek, during which she played the Andante from the Piano Sonata op. 5 and took part in performances of the Piano Quartets opp. 25–26. There was talk of a prospective marriage between her and Schradiek, but nothing came of it. (Styra Avins [1997], in *Johannes Brahms: Life and Letters*, mistaken links the rumors to Betty Völkers instead of to Minna, whom she does not mention at all.) (Kross 1964)

VOLKMANN, (FRIEDRICH) ROBERT (b. Lommatsch, near Dresden), 6 April 1815; d. Budapest, 29 October 1883). Composer, pianist, and teacher. He studied composition at the Leipzig conservatory with C. F. Becker (1836–39). In 1841 he settled in Budapest, where he lived for the remainder of his life, except for the years 1854–58, which he spent in Vienna. He became a well-known figure in musical circles in Budapest and was a frequent visitor to the house of Edward and **Ottilie Ebner**; he used to accompany Ottilie on piano, and even dedicated some of his songs to her. From 1875 he taught harmony and counterpoint at the new Royal Hungarian Academy of Music; his best-known student was Ilka Horovitz-Barnay (who also studied piano with **Liszt**).

Gustav Nottebohm, who was a close friend of his, informed Volkmann on 26 November 1864 that Brahms, "whom you do not know yet," was contemplating visiting Budapest (Volkmann 1912, 5). However, Brahms eventually gave up the idea of such a trip at that time. On 26 December 1866 Nottebohm inquired, no doubt at Brahms's request, whether Volkmann would advise Brahms, who was still eager to see Budapest, to give a concert there. Presumably Volkmann's response was positive; but he was, of course, not the only person whose views Brahms sought on the matter (see Gádor and Ebert 1993). Encouraged by the replies he received, Brahms decided to try his luck in Budapest and gave two concerts there on 22 and 26 April 1867; they were followed by numerous other concert appearances in the Hungarian capital during the next 24 years.

Very likely, then, Brahms made Volkmann's acquaintance in April 1867. He had a further opportunity to meet Volkmann in December of that year, when he returned to Budapest for two concerts with **Joseph Joachim**. Thereafter, they met on several occasions, not only in Budapest but also in Vienna, which Volkmann visited from time to time. They also engaged in correspondence, and a few of the letters were published by Volkmann's great-nephew Hans Volkmann in an article on their relations in *Die Musik* in 1912. Furthermore, they acted as joint judges at a competition for the composition of a new quartet, arranged by the Florentine String Quartet in 1876 (the winners, announced the following year, were **Bernhard Scholz**, Friedrich Lux, and August Bungert). The last letter from Brahms published by Hans Volkmann concerns Nottebohm's death in 1882.

Volkmann's output, in addition to songs, includes two symphonies, works for piano, and string quartets and other chamber music. Brahms was familiar with certain of his compositions long before he met him. Thus he wrote to **Clara Schumann** in February 1856: "Volkmann is very talented. Do you know his B minor Trio and A minor Quartet?" (Litzmann 1970, vol. 1, 174). During his tenure as artistic director of the Gesellschaft der Musikfreunde concerts, Brahms presented Volkmann's *Konzertstück* for piano and orchestra (op. 42) on 7 December 1873; the pianist was Emil Smietanski. Furthermore, Brahms planned to conduct Volkmann's Cello Concerto at the concert on 28 February 1875 with **Reinhold Hummer** as soloist and, in that connection, even consulted the composer regarding possible cuts in the score; but the performance never took place. (Litzmann 1970; Perger and Hirschfeld 1912; Volkmann 1912)

VORWERK, ANNA (b. Königslutter, 12 April 1839; d. Braunschweig, 18 November 1900). Daughter of Justizrat Wilhelm Vorwerk. She was for a time Brahms's pupil in Hamburg in 1862 and subsequently studied for a short period with **Hans von Bülow** in Berlin, where she also became friendly with **Clara Schumann**. Later she played a seminal role at Wolfsbüttel in the promotion of the education for young girls and the training of women teachers. She briefly recalled her memories of Brahms in 1897 in *Blätter aus dem Schlosse*, a periodical she had founded in 1887 largely for the dissemination of her pedagogical ideas. (Vorwerk 1897)

VOSS, JOHANN HEINRICH (b. Sommersdorf, Mecklenburg, 20 February 1751; d. Heidelberg, 29 March 1826). Poet, translator, and philologist. Brahms set one of his poems for four-voice women's chorus in "Minnelied" (op. 44/1). (E. Voss 1992)

VOSS, RICHARD (b. Neugrape, near Pyritz, 2 September 1851; d. Berchtesgaden, 10 June 1918). Narrative writer and dramatist. From 1877 to 1902 he divided his time mainly between Berchtesgaden and Frascati, near Rome, where he lived in the historic Villa Falconieri. It was there that Brahms visited him in May 1888, in the company of **Josef Viktor Widmann**. They had an opportunity to renew their acquaintance in March 1891, when both spent several days at Meiningen on the occasion of the production there of Widmann's play *Oenone* (Voss entertained very friendly relations with **Duke Georg II** and **Baroness Helene Heldburg**). Soon afterward they met again, this time in Vienna, where Voss had gone to attend the premiere of his drama *Schuldig!* at the Volkstheater. During his stay in Vienna, Voss had a hand in arranging a meeting between Brahms and **Heinrich Johann Ibsen**, at which, according to Voss's memoirs, Brahms behaved boorishly, both toward Ibsen and toward his hostess, Baroness Sophie Todesco (*see* IBSEN, HENRIK JOHAN). However, Brahms's unpleasant comportment on that occasion does not appear to have lessened Voss's high regard for him, for in July 1891 Baroness Heldburg wrote to Brahms from her chalet near the Königssee, in Bavaria: "Voss, who is going to post this letter, sends you a thousand greetings and insists on my telling you that you are a marvellous man [ein Prachtmensch]! There, I've said it"; and later that same month she again transmitted "many, many greetings" from Voss to Brahms (Brahms 1991, 111, 116). The two men met once more at Meiningen in November of that year.

Brahms did not regard Voss very highly as a writer. "It is true that he began better than he is now," he remarked to **Richard Heuberger** in 1895, "but he never really showed great talent even at the beginning. Now nobody pays any attention to him any more. In fact, he is finished" (Heuberger

1976, 84–85). In reality, Voss's career was then very far from finished; some of his most successful novels, such as *Zwei Menschen* (1911) were still to come. A selection of his works was published after his death (5 vols., 1922–25). (Brahms 1991; Göttsche 1992; Heuberger 1976; R. Voss 1920)

– W –

WAGNER, FRIEDERIKE [FRIEDCHEN] (b. Hamburg, 9 October 1831; d. Hamburg, 22 January 1917). Oldest of the three daughters of the Hamburg auctioneer Hermann Wagner. She received musical instruction from **Theodor Avé-Lallemant** and from her cousin **Georg Dietrich Otten**, and according to her memoirs (of which some passages were later printed in Sophie Drinker's [1952] *Brahms and His Women's Choruses*), it was during a piano lesson at Otten's house in 1855 that she made Brahms's acquaintance. When she asked him to teach her himself he readily agreed, and he did so over the next few years whenever he was staying in Hamburg for a longer period. Furthermore, Friedchen recounts that at her request he composed some folk songs for her to sing with her sisters Thusnelda and Olga. This vocal trio was, in a sense, a forerunner of the Hamburg Frauenchor, in the establishment of which, in 1859, Friedchen played a key role. The practice sessions of this women's choir, to which Brahms furnished three- and four-part compositions, were at first held at Friedchen's house; the very first session took place there on 6 June of that year. Writing to **Clara Schumann** the following month, Brahms called her his "favourite pupil" and described her as "a most charming, modest, and musical girl" and "the principal founder of my choir" (Litzmann 1970, vol. 1, 264).

In her memoirs, Friedchen states that she often played duets with Brahms, and also frequently **Bach**'s Concerto for Three Pianos with him and his brother **Fritz**; once she even played it with Brahms and Clara Schumann. One day in November 1861, Brahms played his arrangement for piano duet of the Serenade op. 11 with Clara Schumann at the Wagners', and also his *Handel Variations*. Over the years Friedchen was to form very friendly relations with Clara, who more than once stayed with the Wagners while in Hamburg and whose guest Friedchen was herself on more than one occasion. As for Brahms, his correspondence with Clara Schumann shows that over the years she sometimes provided him with news of Friedchen, who married Kurt Sauermann in 1869, and that he himself called on her during some of his visits to Hamburg. The last mention of such a meeting occurred in February 1893, when he reported spending an enjoyable hour at Friedchen's house. (Albrecht 1933; Drinker 1952; Hübbe 1902; Litzmann 1970)

WAGNER, (WILHELM) RICHARD (b. Leipzig, 22 May 1813; d. Venice, 13 February 1883). Composer. On 6 February 1864 Brahms was invited to the villa at Penzing that Wagner was then renting from Baron Rochow. (Penzing, then a suburb of Vienna, is now its 14th district; the location of the house corresponds to the present 72 Hadikgasse.) The meeting, postponed from an earlier date as the result of Wagner's indisposition, had been arranged by **Joseph Standthartner**, perhaps with the help of **Peter Cornelius** and **Carl Tausig**. Among the other guests that evening was Standthartner's stepson Gustav Schönaich, later a well-known journalist, who was to publish an account of the occasion in the Viennese daily *Reichswehr* on 4 April 1897. Everyone, he recalled, had been in the best of moods. Wagner asked Brahms to play, and he began with several pieces by **Bach**, after which, at Wagner's special request, he performed his own *Handel Variations*. "I still remember as if it had happened yesterday," Schönaich (1897) wrote, "with what sincere enthusiasm Wagner, who was incapable of praising any piece that did not please him, expressed his warmest appreciation to the young composer and how expertly he discussed all aspects of the composition. 'One sees what can still be done in the old forms by someone who knows how to handle them,' he remarked at the end" (2).

This has been frequently described by commentators as the only personal meeting between Wagner and Brahms; furthermore, it is regularly stated that they never met again afterward. The first statement is definitely incorrect, while the second is questionable. Regarding the first, in December 1862 Brahms was one of the persons (others being Cornelius, Tausig, and Wendelin Weissheimer) who copied out the orchestral parts of excerpts from some of Wagner's operas in preparation for his Viennese concerts on 26 December 1862, 1 January, and 8 January 1863. (Brahms attended all three.) In *Mein Leben* Wagner (1976) recalled that Brahms, who had been assigned an excerpt from *Die Meistersinger*, showed himself to be "modest and good-natured," but that he was so quiet that "he was often barely noticed at our meetings" (722). Surely Brahms must have "personally met" Wagner at that time. Moreover, Brahms later told **Richard Heuberger**, "Wagner was immensely talkative. He used to lecture incessantly, no one else could get a word in. But it was most interesting. I was frequently in his company. When there were only four or five of us, he spoke marvellously well" (Heuberger 1976, 55). It is not clear, however, whether Brahms was here referring to the period December 1862–January 1863 or to the early part of 1864, that is, to a time before or after that evening at Penzing; in either case, though, his remarks prove conclusively that the latter occasion was not the only time they met. As for any contacts subsequent to Wagner's hurried departure from Vienna on 23 March 1864 to escape from his creditors, they may well have met at least once more, namely at a concert given in Vienna by the Hellmesberger Quartet on 18 November 1875, at which Brahms took part in the first performance of his Piano Quartet op. 60 and which Richard and Cosima Wagner (1976) attended. In fact, Cosima noted in her diary that she had made Brahms's acquaintance at that concert: "A coarse-looking man with a florid complexion, his opus very dry and contrived" (C. Wagner 1976, vol. 2, 949). The introduction took place in the directors' box at the Musikverein; it is surely quite likely that her husband was also present.

The question why Wagner, who had apparently behaved so pleasantly on that day in February 1864, should in later years have shown such unyielding hostility toward Brahms has naturally greatly intrigued anyone interested in both composers. There is not a reference to Brahms's person or to his music in Cosima's diary that does not contain a sneering and disparaging remark, most often attributed by her to her husband, but it is clear that she fully shared his opinions. Thus she records on 3 February 1879 that they found a symphony by Brahms (either the first or the second), of which Richard had played the piano duet version with Josef Rubinstein, "quite nauseating," and adds, "R[ichard] criticizes its vulgarity, and we find relief in the conclusion of Plutarch's *Garrulousness* [i.e., the treatise *De garrulitate*]" (C. Wagner 1976, vol. 2, 303). Moreover, Wagner's own writings, whether in such polemical essays as the one on conducting (1869) or in contributions to his own journal *Bayreuther Blätter*, contain various disparaging allusions to both Brahms the man and Brahms the composer. Schönaich, in his previously cited article, attributed the worsening relations between them simply to the bitterness engendered by the biased and often malicious agitations of their respective partisans. These were, to be sure, liable to affect their attitudes to each other; but if so, they provoked Wagner far more than they did Brahms.

Styra Avins (1997) has argued, in *Johannes Brahms: Life and Letters*, that the matter of Wagner's hostility to Brahms needs above all to be examined in the context of their respective relations with **Mathilde Wesendonck** and, more precisely, in the light of the cessation of her contacts with Wagner and her growing personal interest in Brahms (370–71). It is indeed quite plausible to conclude that Wagner may have deeply resented this situation and that this resentment could well have been a factor in his intense dislike of Brahms; but it is unlikely to have been the only one. In fact, one might be tempted to think that Wagner was perhaps prejudiced against Brahms even before he met him, supposing that he believed himself to have been among the targets of the manifesto drawn up by

Brahms and **Joseph Joachim** and others against the "New German School" and the "Music of the Future" in 1860 (*see* LISZT, FRANZ). Yet such speculation would probably be false, for the document was aimed at Liszt and his followers, and Brahms had tried to ensure that no one reading it would think of Wagner (see Brahms 1974/5, 273). Furthermore, Richard Heuberger (1976) quotes Brahms as telling him in 1888 that they had even received letters from "**Berlioz**, Wagner, etc." on that occasion ("evidently supportive," Heuberger comments [38]). If this is true, Wagner's correspondent at the time was probably Joachim, with whom he had been friendly for several years.

However, given their very different character and outlook, Wagner and Brahms were never destined to enjoy easy relations. Fiercely dedicated to his self-assigned mission of creating a new German art form in the face of whatever obstacles might arise, and possessing a highly combative temperament, Wagner, unlike Brahms, was incapable of taking a tolerant view of a conception of the nature and role of music that was diametrically opposed to his own. There is much unconscious irony in a letter Cosima wrote to **Hans Richter** after Brahms's death, in which, referring to Brahms's attitude toward "our art," she observes approvingly that "his intelligence was too great to underestimate what was perhaps alien to him, and his character too noble to engage in hostile actions" (Kalbeck 1976, vol. 2, 128); these qualities do not appear to have been shared by her late husband. In the circumstances, as Brahms's reputation rose slowly but steadily and as he gained more and more admirers, not only in Vienna but also throughout Germany (some of whom were moreover decidedly unenthusiastic about Wagner's operas), it was only to be expected that Wagner would take an increasingly jaundiced view of the younger man's compositions and, given his character, extend his attacks to his rival's person. (In this connection, *see also* NIETZSCHE, FRIEDRICH.)

Brahms, for his part, maintained a characteristically detached and strikingly lucid attitude where Wagner's personality and musical achievements were concerned. All his friends are emphatic in declaring that, despite much provocation, they never heard him make any derogatory personal remarks about Wagner. Nor does his judgement appear to have been influenced by Wagner's attacks—which is not to say that he felt equal admiration for all of Wagner's works or for all parts of any of them. In the first place, he had a profound knowledge and clear understanding of them. (On this point, *see also* GUTMANN, ALBERT J.) "I once said to Wagner himself," Brahms told his future biographer Richard Specht (1928), "that I am to-day the best Wagnerian;" and he added, "Do you really believe I am so narrow-minded that I cannot take delight in the humour and the greatness of *Die Meistersinger*? Or so dishonest as to conceal the fact that I consider a few bars of this work worth more than all the operas which have been composed since?" (286). To **Anton Door** (1903) Brahms once said, "Wagner, he is now the very first one—no one even comes close to him. Everything else pales at present before his importance, which very few comprehend and appreciate as I do, least of all the Wagnerians!" (220). The operas of the *Ring* tetralogy Brahms ranked as follows, in descending order: *Götterdämmerung*, *Die Walküre*, *Siegfried*, and *Das Rheingold* (Heuberger 1976, 16). As for *Tristan und Isolde*, he praised the "splendidly orchestrated" Prelude (Stargardt-Wolff 1954, 141) and the love duet in Act II but once pronounced the remainder to be "unausstehlich" [unbearable] (Heuberger 1976, 39). Above all, though, he admired Wagner for his mastery of the theatrical craft.

In 1870 Brahms went to Munich to attend performances of *Das Rheingold* and *Die Walküre*, conducted by his friend **Franz Wüllner**. He never visited Bayreuth, though not for lack of interest in the operas—in 1876 he said to **Sir George Henschel**, who was about to attend one of the first *Ring* cycles there, "You *will* write me from Bayreuth, won't you? I know you will rave about it, and I don't blame you" (Henschel 1907, 51). But, as he told **Hans von Bülow** in 1882, he preferred to avoid the "Wagnerians," who were capable of spoiling his pleasure in the best of Wagner's music (Kalbeck 1976, vol. 2, 127). He would nonetheless have gone to Bayreuth that year to hear *Parsifal* if **Theodor Billroth** or **Fritz Simrock** had been able to accompany him. (The world premiere of *Parsifal* took place 26 July 1882; it was promptly followed by a number of further performances.)

Lastly, Brahms's relations with Wagner were for several years strained by another matter that was eventually settled in a more or less amicable fashion. Carl Tausig had at one time given Brahms the autograph of the Bacchanale that Wagner had composed for the performances of *Tannhäuser* in Paris in 1861. Tausig had apparently obtained the autograph from Cornelius, who had it in his possession for the purpose of copying it. The circumstances in which it passed from Cornelius to Tausig, and from the latter to Brahms, are unclear; but Brahms was evidently of the opinion that he had received it as a gift from Tausig and that he accordingly had a right to its ownership. He was therefore surprised when Cornelius wrote to him in September 1865, asking him to return it to Cosima (who, though still married to Bülow at the time, was already emotionally involved with Wagner—their daughter Isolde was born that year). Brahms did not reply to Cornelius at once, nor did he respond to several letters addressed to him by Cosima. When eventually he did answer Cornelius's letter, it was to express his reluctance to part with the autograph, not least because most of the various reasons given to him in justification of the request for its return no longer applied; moreover, he had formed the impression that the principal motive had been none other than a simple desire to remove it from his possession. There the matter rested until Wagner took a hand in the affair in June 1875. In a brief and firmly worded letter, he informed Brahms that he required the manuscript for the preparation of a revised edition of the score and that, in any case, Cornelius had been in no position to present it to a third party, since it had only been loaned to him. (Wagner did not mention Tausig.) The gist of Brahms's lengthy reply to this letter was that although he was still not convinced of the sincerity of the arguments advanced to justify the demand for the return of the autograph, he would comply; but he would greatly appreciate it if Wagner, as compensation for depriving his manuscript collection of one treasure, would enrich it with another, "perhaps *Die Meistersinger*." Wagner, who was reportedly much incensed by Brahms's letter, did not send a further manuscript, but instead an inscribed copy of the printed luxury edition of *Das Rheingold* that had been displayed at the Vienna World Exhibition of 1873. It is now in the archive of the Gesellschaft der Musikfreunde in Vienna. (For a detailed account of this whole affair, including the text of the correspondence exchanged, see Kalbeck 1976, vol. 2, 122–27.) (Aldrich 1928; H. Bauer 1988; Biba 1983b; Brahms 1974/5; Geiringer 1936; Glasenapp 1905; Henschel 1907; Heuberger 1976; Huschke 1939; Istel 1902; Kapp 1932; Schönaich 1897; Specht 1928; C. Wagner 1976; R. Wagner 1976; Weidemann 1922)

WAGNER DE ZÓLYOM, LÁSZLÓ (b. Pest [Budapest], 28 March 1841; d. Gossensass, South Tyrol [Colle Isarco, Italy], 2 July 1888). A professor of agriculture and forestry at the Joseph Polytechnic Institute in Budapest, he was also an accomplished amateur violinist, whose apartment at 19 Elisabethplatz was frequented by prominent local and visiting musicians. He arranged regular quartet sessions, in which he played first violin. It was in his music room that Brahms reportedly made the acquaintance of **Viktor von Herzfeld**, **Jenö Hubay**, and **Hans Koessler**, among others.

From 1875 on, Wagner de Zólyom spent his summer vacations at Altaussee in the Austrian Salzkammergut, at first in rented accommodation, but later in a villa especially built for him, which he first occupied in 1881. At Altaussee he also formed a regular quartet, in which, this time, he played second violin. It was led by **Ludwig Straus**, the violist was **Alois Mayer**, and the cellist a young man named Rudolf Lutz. Their informal concerts attracted an increasing audience, but when Wagner de Zólyom moved into his new villa, he found that its music room could accommodate only a small number of people so that he was obliged to limit invitations to his closest friends. In 1882, therefore, he had a larger music room built adjoining the villa. The series of concerts presented there was inaugurated on 25 August 1882 with a "Brahms Matinée," for which Brahms came over from his vacation quarters at nearby Ischl. The program opened with the Rhapsody op. 79/1, played by **Ignaz Brüll** (who was then also staying at Ischl), and this was followed by the very first performances anywhere, from manuscript, of the Piano Trio op. 87 (played by Brahms, Straus, and Lutz) and the String Quintet op. 88 (in which the host's regular quartet was joined by **Moritz von Kaiserfeld** as second violist). Among the audience was painter Baron Carl Binzer (1824–1902), to whom we owe a delightful drawing showing **Alois Mayer**, Wagner de Zólyom, and Rudolf Lutz rehearsing a trio.

Wagner de Zólyom was to spend only two more summers at Altaussee, for ill health prevented his return in 1885. That year he sold his villa to Viennese university professor Dr. Josef Seegen (who had attended the Brahms concert in August 1882). The house was eventually demolished, and the Hotel Seevilla opened on the site in 1979. To mark the centenary of the historic 1882 concert, a commemorative tablet was affixed to the building on 25 August 1982, on which occasion the trio and the quintet, as well as the Rhapsody and the Cello Sonata op. 38, were performed in the dining room of the hotel, which had been temporarily converted into a concert hall. In 1983, the year celebrating the 150th anniversary of Brahms's birth, an exhibition *Brahms and his Circle of Friends at Altaussee* was presented in the foyer of the Hotel Seevilla, and the lakeside promenade leading to the hotel was named "Johannes-Brahms-Weg." (W. Ebert 1982, 1997)

WALLISCH, FRIEDRICH (Mährisch-Weisskirchen [Hranice, Czech Republic], 31 May 1890; d. Vienna, 7 February 1969). Physician, writer, dramatist, and poet. In September 1963 he published a short article entitled "Symphonie in e-moll" in *Deutsche Rundschau* [Wallisch 1963], in which he presented a charming account of how Brahms had found the inspiration for completing the final movement of his Fourth Symphony by watching Wallisch's mother—a beautiful and highly musical lady who had studied with **Anton Bruckner**—as she was enjoying a meal at the Gause restaurant with the author, then a young child. Brahms had afterward found out where she lived and had even written her a letter (which Wallisch prints in full), in which he explained what had happened and invited her to visit him so that he might play for her the symphony "which has been completed with your help." However, having been warned by a close friend of the family, who was a judge, that she would be compromising her good name if she so much as replied to this "impertinent letter," she made no response. Years later she attended a performance of the symphony at which Brahms, already mortally ill, was present in a box (apparently a reference to the concert of 7 March 1897). When, at the end, Brahms stood up to acknowledge the frenetic applause of the audience, in which the author's mother, who was seated in the stalls not far from his box, joined ostentatiously, he recognized her, whereupon she looked at him and "with her eyes asked his forgiveness and expressed her gratitude" (Wallisch 1963, 64).

Unfortunately, although described by the journal's editor as "a personal memory of Johannes Brahms," the story is historically impossible, since Brahms completed his Fourth Symphony in 1885 and published it in 1886, several years before Wallisch was born. (Wallisch 1963)

WALLNÖFER, ADOLF (b. Vienna, 24 April 1854; d. Munich, 9 June 1946). Baritone, later tenor; composer. He studied composition and singing with **Felix Otto Dessoff**, Franz Krenn, and Hans von Rokitansky at the Vienna Conservatory. Soon after making his operatic debut as a baritone in the role of Count di Luna in *Il Trovatore* at Olmütz [Olomouc] in 1878, he switched to tenor parts and became one of the best-known heroic tenors of his time. He appeared with Angelo Neumann's touring Wagner-Theater (1882–83) and sang in Bremerhaven (1882–85), Prague (1885–95), New York (1895–96), Russia (1896), Stettin [Szczecin] (from 1896), and later at Breslau [Wrocław, Poland], Nuremberg (1902–6), and the Vienna Volksoper (1906–8). From 1908 he lived in Munich, teaching and composing. Altogether he wrote over 400 songs and ballads, choral works and other vocal music, as well as pieces for piano, chamber music, and an opera, *Eddystone*.

His earliest recorded association with Brahms's music occurred in 1876 when he sang in a performance of the *Triumphlied* at the Lower Rhine Music Festival at Aix-la-Chapelle. At a concert in Vienna in November of the same year, he performed two of the *Magelone-Lieder*. His admiration for Brahms's music prompted Wallnöfer to dedicate his first major work, *Die Grenzen der Menschheit*, for soloist, chorus, and orchestra, to Brahms. This led to some personal contact with Brahms, in the course of which Brahms, at Wallnöfer's request, brought him to the attention of **Fritz Simrock** in May 1879, though in terms more guarded than the young composer might have wished (Brahms 1974/10, 116).

On 24 April 1880 Wallnöfer presented an "all-Brahms" concert at the Ehrbar Saal in Vienna. The program contained a wide range of vocal numbers for one and more voices, as well as the Violin Sonata op. 78, played by **Joseph Hellmesberger** and **Julius Epstein**. At the time of the concert Brahms was away in Germany. (Brahms 19784/2; Kutsch and Riemens 1987–94; E. Müller 1930/34)

WALTER, AUGUST (b. Stuttgart, 12 August 1821; d. Basle, 22 January 1896). Conductor, pianist, violinist, and composer. A pupil of Bernhard Molique (in Stuttgart) and **Simon Sechter** (in Vienna), he was originally engaged at Basle in 1846 as a temporary replacement for Ernst Reiter, who was taking a leave of absence. He remained there for the rest of his life, and during those 50 years made a very significant contribution to the musical life of the city, conducting private and public concerts and directing numerous choral works. His two wives, Josefine Walter-Fastlinger (d. 1866), who created the part of Ortrud at the premiere of *Lohengrin* at Weimar on 28 August 1850 and whom he married in August 1855, and Anna Walter-Strauss (1846–1936), whom he married in September 1869 and who enjoyed a very successful international career, were both excellent singers.

At a concert at Basle on 9 November 1862, Walter accompanied Josefine in Brahms's song "Nachtigallen schwingen / Lustig ihr Gefieder" (op. 6/6). According to Werner G. Zimmermann, this is the earliest documented public performance of any of Brahms's compositions in Switzerland (Zimmermann 1983, 9). Brahms made Walter's acquaintance when he traveled to Basle in June 1865 to attend a performance of **Bach**'s *St. Matthew Passion*, after which they met regularly during Brahms's later visits to Basle. When there was a possibility that the first performance of the complete Requiem might take place at Basle, under Brahms's own direction, in early 1869, Walter hoped that the soprano solo would be entrusted to Anna Strauss. In the event, the work was first presented at Leipzig on 18 February 1869, with Emilie Bellingrath-Wagner as female soloist. (It was, however, given at Basle just nine days later under Ernst Reiter with Magdalena Reiter as soprano.) Walter included several other compositions by Brahms in his concerts. Moreover, on 9 June 1874, Brahms accompanied Anna in two of his own songs at **Friedrich Riggenbach-Stehlin**'s house, and one is no doubt justified in assuming that this was not the only occasion on which they made music together. (R. Hofmann 1999a, 1999b; Merian 1920; Niggli 1893; Zimmermann 1983)

WALTER, GUSTAV (b. Bilin [Bilina, Czech Republic], 11 February 1834; d. Vienna, 31 January 1910). Tenor. He trained as a singer under Franz Vogl in Prague and made his operatic debut as Edgardo in *Lucia di Lammermoor* at Brünn [Brno] in 1855. The following year he was engaged at the court opera in Vienna, where he first appeared as Gomez in Conradin Kreutzer's *Das*

Nachtlager von Granada on 14 July 1856. He became the leading lyric tenor of the company and was especially celebrated for his beautiful singing of **Mozart** roles, such as Don Ottavio (which he sang at the opening performance of the new opera house on 25 May 1869) and Tamino; he also excelled as the duke in *Rigoletto* and Manrico in *Il trovatore*. Following his retirement from the stage in 1887, he enjoyed a distinguished career on the concert platform, greatly admired as an interpreter of Lieder, particularly those of **Franz Schubert**. He was also much sought after as a teacher.

According to **Richard Heuberger**, Walter was Brahms's favorite tenor (Heuberger 1976, 132). He frequently accompanied Walter at public and private concerts, and on one occasion took him to Budapest where they performed some of his most recent songs at a concert of the Hubay Quartet (21 December 1888). Walter took part in the first performance of the cantata *Rinaldo* (28 February 1869) and was one of the soloists at the first complete performance of *Liebeslieder* (op. 52) on 5 January 1870. In addition, he gave, between 1874 and 1894, the first public performances of a considerable number of Brahms's other songs (for details, see M. L. McCorkle's [1984] *Werkverzeichnis*). (Antonicek 1988; Heuberger 1976; Kutsch and Riemens 1987–94)

WASIELEWSKI, WILHELM JOSEPH VON (b. Gross-Leesen, near Danzig [Gdansk], 17 June 1822; d. Sondershausen, Thuringia, 13 December 1896). Violinist, conductor, and writer on music. He studied composition with Mendelssohn and **Ferdinand Hiller**, theory with **Moritz Hauptmann**, and violin with **Ferdinand David** at the Leipzig Conservatory (1843–45), and subsequently played first violin in various local orchestras, including the Gewandhaus. In 1850 he was invited by **Robert Schumann**, whose acquaintance he had made in Leipzig in 1843, to become leader of the Düsseldorf Orchestra. His relations with the Schumanns had become increasingly close over the years, and he partnered with **Clara** on several occasions both in public recitals and private music making. In 1852 he moved to Bonn, where he conducted a choral society and the **Beethoven**-Verein orchestra, but with no prospect of a permanent engagement, he left after three years and settled at Dresden, where he did some writing, teaching, and research. In 1869 he returned to Bonn to take up the post of municipal director of music, which had been created during the intervening years; however, he failed to obtain a position at the university, as he would have liked. Soon after retiring in 1884, he settled at Sondershausen; there he taught at the conservatory and continued with his writing. Among his publications were the first biography of Schumann (1858), books on the violin and on the cello, and an autobiography that appeared posthumously. He also contributed to a number of journals.

According to his memoirs, Wasielewski first met Brahms when the latter called on him in Bonn in the late summer of 1853. In fact, though, he had apparently already met him a short while earlier at the house of **Wilhelm Ludwig** and Elisabeth **Deichmann** at Mehlem, where Brahms had arrived on 2 September. In a letter to **Arnold Wehner** dated the next day he conveyed greetings from Wasielewski "whose acquaintance I have made today" (R. Hofmann 1997, 30). A few days later he informed **Joseph Joachim** that he had met at Mehlem two "delightful" gentlemen, Wasielewski and **C. H. Christian Reimers**, who, moreover, he was pleased to say, visited his hosts frequently (Brahms 1974/5, 6). He had therefore seen Wasielewski more than once while at Mehlem. Wasielewski adds that Brahms stayed with him for several days at Bonn. Furthermore, he states that he urged Brahms to call on Schumann on his return journey to North Germany and even offered to furnish him with a letter of introduction. Brahms apparently left without having definitely committed himself to the idea; but when Wasielewski later read Schumann's eulogistic article in the *Neue Zeitschrift für Musik*, he realized that Brahms had after all "let himself be persuaded by my arguments" (Wasielewski 1897, 145). While it is, of course, quite possible that Wasielewski's encouragement helped to influence Brahms's decision, a major reason for it was doubtless his newly acquired admiration for Schumann's music, thanks to the Deichmanns.

Though Brahms and Wasielewski were never to enjoy an intimate relationship, they maintained a certain contact for the rest of their lives (they were to die within four months of one another). Renate Federhofer-Königs has published a few pieces of correspondence, relating to projected appearances by Brahms at concerts in Bonn in 1880 and 1883. She has also shown that Wasielewski did his share of promoting Brahms's music, directing or arranging the first performances in Bonn of a number of Brahms's most important works while he was director of music there. As for Clara Schumann's friendship with Wasielewski, once so cordial, it cooled off during the last period of her husband's life—perhaps, as Federhofer-Königs speculates, because she felt that he had not shown sufficient interest in Robert's unhappy situation and in her own anguished position. Federhofer-Königs also believes that Clara's changed attitude owed a good deal to Brahms's influence, but this is necessarily mere speculation. What is certain is that once Robert had died, Clara's previous encouragement for Wasielewski's plan to write a book on her husband ceased. (Robert himself had also been supportive.) She now informed Wasielewski that a biographical study appeared premature to her, and she declined to provide him with any documentation. When the book was published some 18 months after Robert's death, it met with a good deal of criticism, not least from Brahms who wrote to Clara in January 1858: "It is impossible to derive any pleasure from it. . . . In my view a biography can only be written by a close friend or an admirer. Impartiality is commendable (if also difficult), but it must not turn into coldness. And narrow-mindedness is assuredly unproductive wherever it occurs, and it does so very amply here, so there is really no point in quarrelling about other, more lofty, matters" (Litzmann 1970, vol. 1, 213). A very detailed review of the book by **Hermann Deiters**, which appeared in the *Allgemeine musikalische Zeitung* in 1869, following the publication of its second edition, expressed some serious reservations. In a letter on 26 December 1869 Clara thanked Deiters for pointing out certain shortcomings in Wasielewski's biography in his review and explained that she had not herself read the book, as she had been well aware of the author's "inadequacy as a human being as well as a critic" in relation to her husband (Litzmann 1902, vol. 3, 14; in this connection, see also her letter of 19 January 1859 to **Eduard Hanslick** following the original publication of the book [Federhofer-Königs 1975, 54, n. 149]). The general tone of Deiter's review is, however, mild compared to that which animates the fierce attack directed against Wasielewski's book by **Eugenie Schumann** (1931) in her own biography of her father. In 1888 Wasielewski brought out *Schumanniana*, a collection of essays dealing with both the man and his music.

When Brahms learned in 1884 that Wasielewski was leaving Bonn, he wrote to **Laura von Beckerath**: "W. has been a bad director of music, and now he is giving up the post to become an even worse scribbler" (Stephenson 1979, 41). (Brahms 1974/5; Federhofer-Königs 1974, 1975; R. Hofmann 1997; Litzmann 1902, 1970; E. Schumann 1931; Stephenson 1966, 1979; Wasielewski 1897, 1972)

WEHNER, ARNOLD (b. Hanover, 9 June 1820; d. Leipzig, 16 November 1880). Musician; pupil of Mendelssohn. When Brahms made his acquaintance through **Joseph Joachim** at Göttingen in the summer of 1853, he had been director of music at the university since 1846, and his house was an important center for local music making. He was also the music teacher of **Agathe von Siebold**, whose father Eduard was his colleague on the university faculty.

During his stay at Göttingen, Brahms seems to have been a frequent visitor to Wehner's house, and on one occasion (22 July 1853) he performed a concerto for two pianos by **Bach** (?BMV 1061) with Wehner at a public concert at the Zur Krone inn. After leaving Göttingen, Brahms undertook a walking tour along the Rhine that ended at Mehlem on 2 September, and the very next day he sent a detailed and enthusiastic account of his experiences to Wehner; in the same letter Brahms expressed his gratitude for the kindness that Wehner and his wife had shown him. For some time thereafter he remained in correspondence with Wehner, who evidently took a cordial interest in his professional activities, for in a letter to Joachim from Düsseldorf a few weeks later, Brahms mentioned that in each of his letters Wehner was urging him to go to Leipzig (Brahms 1974/5, 12).

Such direct contact between them does not, however, appear to have continued for very long. Perhaps Brahms was gradually influenced in his attitude by the fact that two of his closest friends, Joachim and **Julius Otto Grimm**, were by 1855 on rather strained terms with Wehner, who became Kapellmeister at the Schlosskirche at Hanover that year (he also directed the concerts of the Neue Singakademie there). His relations with Joachim, previously so amicable that they addressed each other with the intimate "Du," soured to the point where Joachim, in December 1857, described having to ask "our *cher ami* Wehner" for a certain piece of music as a highly distasteful task that was hurtful to his pride (Brahms 1974/5, 194). As for Grimm, who in 1855 exchanged Hanover for Göttingen, mainly in the hope of succeeding the departing Wehner in his position at the university, he did not take to Wehner, who may or may not have been at least partly responsible for his not receiving the anticipated offer. What other, more personal, reasons Brahms may have had for mistrusting Wehner is not known, but **Max Kalbeck** alleges in his edition of the Brahms-Herzogenberg correspondence that Wehner, who had originally been very well disposed toward Brahms, had later become one of his "silent enemies" (Brahms 1974/1, 14, n. 3). Kalbeck was commenting on a letter from **Elisabeth von Herzogenberg** to Brahms on 29 January 1877 in which, after reporting that Wehner, who was then living in Leipzig, had recently suffered a stroke that had left him blind in one eye, she remarked, "You must admit that, whatever he may have done in the past, this is a cruel Finale." It has not been possible to determine to what unpleasant past actions of Wehner's she was referring. (Wehner, who had retained his post at Hanover until 1869, except for a break in 1867, had resided there until 1875, when he had moved to Leipzig.) (Brahms 1974/1, 1974/5; R. Hofmann 1997)

WEINGARTNER, (PAUL) FELIX (b. Zara, Dalmatia, 2 June 1863; d. Winterthur, 7 May 1942). Conductor and composer. Though a great admirer of **Liszt** and **Richard Wagner**, the young Weingartner endeared himself to Brahms when, on 3 April 1895 in Vienna, he conducted the Berlin Philharmonic Orchestra in a performance of his Second Symphony, which

Brahms, writing to **Fritz Simrock**, acclaimed as "quite wonderful" (Brahms 1974/12, 169). Weingartner had made Brahms's acquaintance earlier that same day, when **Richard Heuberger** had taken him to Brahms's rooms in Karlsgasse. Brahms was so delighted with the performance that he tried to interest Weingartner in finding an appointment in Vienna, but that proved to be impossible then. (It was not until 1908 that Weingartner assumed the direction of the Vienna Opera and the Vienna Philharmonic concerts.)

As it happened, the Second Symphony was one of the few works by Brahms for which Weingartner felt wholehearted admiration at the time. Later, he was to revise his initially largely unfavorable opinion of Brahms's music, and he even publicly proclaimed his conversion, notably in the third edition of his essay *Die Symphonie nach Beethoven* (Leipzig, 1909; the original version had appeared in 1897); see also his article "Brahms, ein Meister der Instrumentationskunst" in the *Allgemeine Musik-Zeitung* in January 1905. (Brahms 1974/12; Heuberger 1976; Weingartner 1905, 1909, 1928–29)

WEISS, AMALIE: *see* JOACHIM, AMALIE.

WEISSE, MICHAEL (b. Neisse, Silesia [Nysa, Poland], about 1488; d. Landskron [Lanškroun, Czech Republic], March 1534). Preacher and author of church songs. He became a student at Krakow University in 1504 and later entered a monastery at Breslau [Wrocław, Poland], which he left in 1518. He then joined the Moravian Brethren at Leitomischl [Lytomišl], and sometime afterward became head of the community at Landskron. Between 1522 and 1524 he paid five visits to **Martin Luther** to discuss theological questions. He was ordained in 1531, and that same year he published a collection of hymns for the Moravian Brethren at Jungbunzlau [Mladá Boleslav] under the title *Ein neu Gesengbuchlen* [*A New Songbook*]. He had written or revised the text of 137 of the 157 hymns appearing in the volume; in addition, he had translated 16 from the Czech and four from Latin. The music was for single voice, without instrumental accompaniment; some 90 of the melodies were taken over from a hymnbook published by the Moravian Brethren in 1519.

Weisse's hymns found their way into most Protestant hymnbooks. His *Begräbnislied* [*Funeral Song*] that Brahms set for chorus and wind instruments (op. 13) had, according to K. Düwel, been praised by Luther as having been "written by a good poet." (Düwel 1992)

WENDT, GUSTAV (b. Berlin, 24 January 1827; d. Karlsruhe, 6 March 1912). Classicist and educator. In 1867, while head of the gymnasium at

Hamm in Westphalia, he accepted an invitation to become director of the Grand Ducal Gymnasium (now Bismarck Gymnasium) at Karlsruhe, a post he occupied with distinction until 1907. (The dates relating to this appointment that are given in the biographical sketch on Wendt in S. Avins's [1997] *Johannes Brahms: Life and Letters* are incorrect.)

Wendt was highly respected for both personal and professional reasons. Among his publications was an excellent translation of the plays of Sophocles, which appeared at Stuttgart in 1884 with a dedication to Brahms, who was delighted with the compliment and expressed his appreciation in what were for him unusually effusive terms. By that time the two men had known each other for some 20 years. The precise date of their first meeting is, however, uncertain. In his memoirs *Lebenserinnerungen eines Schulmanns*, Wendt (1909) relates that he became acquainted with Brahms—then "about 30 years old"—at the house of **Julius Otto Grimm** at Münster, on the occasion of one of the concerts given annually by the Cäcilienverein (a local choral society conducted by Grimm) on St. Cecilia's Day (i.e., 22 November), and he adds that among others attending was **Joseph Joachim**, who had come over from Hanover, as well as his future wife, **Amalie Weiss** (75). If this statement is entirely accurate, the meeting would have taken place no later than November 1862, since Joachim married Amalie (*see* JOACHIM, AMALIE) on 10 June 1863. In November 1862, however, Brahms was busy making a name for himself in Vienna and almost certainly did not travel to Münster, but he might conceivably have gone there in 1861 between his concerts with **Clara Schumann** in Hamburg on 16 November and 3 December; yet it is for other reasons unlikely that he would have met Joachim there at that time. Wendt's memory may well have failed him when he wrote this account of what happened some 45 or more years earlier (the book appeared in 1909). Perhaps he actually became acquainted with Brahms on the occasion of the latter's concert at Münster on 19 January 1862, in which, moreover, Joachim took part (*see* GRIMM, JULIUS OTTO).

In any case, more important than the exact date of their initial meeting is the fact that it laid the basis for what was to be a warm friendship that lasted until Brahms's death; it also extended to Wendt's wife, who was a fine pianist (she used to play duets with **Hermann Levi**). After Wendt had moved to Karlsruhe, he was to meet Brahms repeatedly there and at Baden-Baden (on 23 September 1887, he was among the people invited by Brahms to the private performance of his new Double Concerto), and he also spent some time with Brahms while the latter was staying at Heidelberg, at Thun in Switzerland, and finally at Ischl, where Wendt regularly visited him. It was there that Wendt saw him for the last time, in August

1896. On that occasion Brahms greeted him with the words, "This time you've come to see a sick man" (Wendt 1909, 167).

Brahms once confided to friends that he had been attracted to one of Wendt's daughters: "She might have had me if she hadn't chattered so much," he told them (according to **Laura von Beckerath**'s diary, see Stephenson 1979, 31). It is not known which of the three daughters had caught his eye. One of them, Adelheid, married archaeologist Adolf Furtwängler; the conductor Wilhelm Furtwängler was her son.

Wendt and his wife were also on cordial terms with Clara Schumann, who was moreover a close friend of his sister Mathilde. (Martin Neumann 1986; Stephenson 1979, Wendt 1909)

WENZEL, ERNST FERDINAND (b. 1808; d. 16 August 1880). Piano teacher from 1843 at the Leipzig Conservatory. He was a pupil of Friedrich Wieck and on friendly terms with Mendelssohn and **Schumann**. Brahms frequently met with Wenzel when the former first went to Leipzig in 1853. "I like Wenzel best of all. He has such a handsome head and splendid forehead," he wrote to **Joseph Joachim** on 20 November (Brahms 1974/5, 18). He dedicated the Scherzo op. 4, which **Breitkopf & Härtel** published in February 1854, to "his friend Ernst Ferdinand Wenzel." (Brahms 1974/5)

WENZIG, JOSEPH (1807–76). Poet. Brahms set Wenzig's German versions of certain Bohemian and Slovakian folk songs (published in his collections *Slawische Volkslieder* and *Westslawischer Märchenschatz*) in the following compositions: in the songs "Der Gang zum Liebchen" (op. 48/1), "Gold überwiegt die Liebe" (op. 48/4), "Sehnsucht" (op. 49/3), "Klage I," "Klage II," "Abschied," and "Des Liebsten Schwur" (op. 69/1–4); in the duets "Die Boten der Liebe" (op. 61/4) and "So lass uns wandern!" (op. 75/3); in the quartets "Neckereien" and "Der Gang zum Liebchen" (op. 31/2–3); and in the choral composition "Verlorene Jugend" (op. 104/4).

WESENDONCK, MATHILDE, née Agnes Luckemeyer (b. Elberfeld, 23 December 1828; d. near Altmünster, Salzkammergut, Austria, 31 August 1902). Poet. In 1848 she married Otto Wesendonck (b. Elberfeld, 16 March 1815; d. Berlin, 18 November 1896). The couple moved to Zurich in 1851 and built a splendid villa overlooking Lake Zurich; **Richard Wagner**, inspired by his passionate love affair with Mathilde, composed much of *Tristan und Isolde* in a cottage that was rented to him by her husband and was situated close to their house.

Styra Avins (1997) states in *Johannes Brahms: Life and Letters* that Mathilde heard Brahms's music "for the first time" on 10 November 1863, when she attended a concert in Zurich at which his Serenade op. 11 was performed and "very well received," and that the experience had turned her into an ardent admirer of Brahms (371). It seems very likely, however, that the Wesendoncks had already discovered his music earlier, for as keen music lovers and concert goers they might be expected to have been present at one or the other, if not both, of the performances of the Sextet op. 18, which were given in Zurich on 20 January and 3 February of that year—the second, according to the printed program, "in response to numerous requests" (Zimmermann 1983, 12). As for the statement that the Serenade was "very well received" at the concert of 10 November 1863, it rather clashes with the complaint made by Gerold Eberhard in his generally very favorable article in the *Neue Zürcher Zeitung* on 18 November that "Brahms's composition would surely have merited a warmer reception on the part of the audience" (Zimmermann 1983, 13).

Brahms's personal acquaintance with the Wesendoncks appears to date from his earliest concert appearances in Zurich in November 1865, when they (or, at any rate Otto), together with **Theodor Billroth** and **Wilhelm Lübke**, arranged an additional, private, concert so that they might hear more of his compositions. But they had already the previous year extended an invitation to him through **Theodor Kirchner** (who had transmitted it to **Julius Stockhausen**) to spend the summer at their villa, where he could work undisturbed. Similar offers were made, with just as much success, in later years (once Mathilde suggested that he might occupy what was in fact Wagner's old house, which the latter had by then vacated). Brahms was indeed in contact with the Wesendoncks and came to their villa on several occasions while staying at nearby Fluntern in the summer of 1866; but he was careful to preserve his independence. He was equally unmoved by Mathilde's efforts to induce him to set some of her poetry to music; her final attempt consisted in sending him on 24 November 1774 the text for a cantata to be performed during cremation, a funeral method for which she was trying to win his support and which she described as a "beautiful ancient custom" far more in accord with modern views than "the ugly and unpleasant Semitic practice of burial" (E. Müller 1943, 109–14). Brahms passed her text on to Billroth, suggesting that it might offer delightful entertainment for him and his wife, and Billroth, in his turn, reported Mathilde's initiative to Lübke, who lost no time in gleefully informing the Stockhausens. Evidently, the news evoked hilarity and head shaking all around. Mathilde was then among a very small minority of Christians who favored cremation. The matter was brought into particular prominence that very year by a congress held in Milan that recommended that cremation should be permitted, subject to proper supervision by the local authorities.

It would be quite some time, however, before such permission was granted. (In England, the first cremation took place at Woking, in March 1885.)

As far as is known, Brahms never replied to Mathilde's letter of November 1874, and according to E. H. Müller von Asow, who in 1943 published what he could find of their correspondence (the letters fall into the periods 1867–69 and 1873–74), this was the final documented episode in their relationship. Yet, notwithstanding the derision with which Brahms reacted to her letter, it must have planted a seed that was to grow with time; for among the testamentary instructions he conveyed to **Fritz Simrock** in May 1891 was one expressing his preference for being cremated. However, his wish was ignored. (Bissing 1942; Erismann 1974; Gottlieb-Billroth 1935; E. Müller 1943; J. Wirth 1927; Zimmerman 1983)

WEYERMANN, WALTHER. Banker. In 1880 he married Emilie [Emmy] Franziska von der Leyen (1861–1924), a half sister of **Rudolf von der Leyen**. During his trip to Italy with Rudolf in May 1884, Brahms met the couple at Genoa, where they were then living. They were well known for their cultural interests (Emmy was an excellent pianist), and in the 1890s they used to arrange private music sessions at Whitsun at their villa "Hagerhof" at Bad Honeff, some 17 kilometers outside Bonn, to which they invited various members of the Von der Leyen and **Von Beckerath** families, as well as a number of professional musicians of their acquaintance.

After attending **Clara Schumann**'s funeral at Bonn on Whit Sunday, 24 May 1896, Brahms accepted an invitation to join the Weyermanns' other guests at the Hagerhof. These included **Richard Barth**, **Bram Eldering**, **Leonhard Wolff**, and **Karl Theodor Piening**, who joined forces to form a string quartet. During the several days he spent there, Brahms participated in the musical activities, playing, among other items, the piano part in his Quintet op. 34. Even more memorable for those privileged to hear it was his presentation—**Gustav Ophüls** characterized it as a dramatic declamation rather than singing—of his recently completed *4 ernste Gesänge*, which acquired a special poignancy because of Clara's death. Ophüls gives a detailed and fascinating account of those memorable days in his *Erinnerungen an Johannes Brahms*. (G. Ophüls 1983b)

WEYR, RUDOLF VON (b. Vienna, 22 March 1847; d. Vienna, 30 October 1914). Sculptor. He studied from 1864 to 1872 at the Academy of Fine Arts, where his principal teacher was Franz Bauer (1798–1872); afterward he attended the Polytechnic Institute for two years, while at the same time working in the studio of Josef Cesar (1814–76). He is known particularly for the sculptures he created for several of the monumental buildings on the new Ringstrasse; among his other notable works is the Brahms statue on the Karlsplatz.

Plans for its construction were first discussed at a meeting arranged by wealthy industrialist and prominent patron of the arts Nikolaus Dumba on 19 December 1897. It was attended by Baron Josef Bezecny (president of the Gesellschaft der Musikfreunde), piano manufacturer **Ludwig Bösendorfer**, **Hugo Conrat**, **Arthur Faber**, **Richard Fellinger**, **Josef Gänsbacher**, **Eduard Hanslick**, **Richard Heuberger**, **Max Kalbeck**, Ludwig Koch (secretary of the Gesellschaft der Musikfreunde), **Eusebius Mandyczewski**, **Viktor von Miller zu Aichholz**, **Richard von Perger**, and **Hans Richter**. At this meeting it was decided to form a large committee that would be made up of representatives of the major music centers in Austria and other countries. On 3 April 1898, the anniversary of Brahms's death, an appeal for contributions drawn up by Kalbeck was launched by this Johannes-Brahms-Denkmal-Kommittee; it was signed by its president (Bezecny), its vice presidents (**Gustav Mahler** and Richter) and its secretaries (Koch and Mandyczewski), as well as by several hundred members representing a multitude of European cities from Moscow in the East to London, Edinburgh, and Glasgow in the West, and even by representatives from Boston, New York, and Chicago. A separate Ladies' Committee was also formed, presided over by Bertha Faber, with Karoline von Gomperz-Bettelheim and Olga von Miller zu Aichholz as its vice presidents.

When sufficient funds had been collected, designs for the proposed statue were invited from six well-known sculptors: the Austrians Johannes Benk, Edmund Heller, **Karl Kundmann** (who took Brahms's death mask and had created the **Franz Schubert** statue in Vienna), and Rudolf Weyr, and the Germans **Adolf von Hildebrand** and **Max Klinger**. Heller and Hildebrand declined the invitation, while Kundmann and Klinger later withdrew from the competition. The jury, which included Gustav Klimt, **Anton Scharff**, and Caspar von Zumbusch (the creator of the **Beethoven** statue unveiled in Vienna in 1880), as well as Arthur Faber and Max Kalbeck, chose in the end the model submitted by Weyr, subject to his making certain alterations. His modified version was finally approved in 1904, and the statue was unveiled on 7 May 1908. It stood in the Karlsplatz, approximately on a line running from Brahms's rooms in Karlsgasse to the Musikverein. On the preceding evening a "Festkonzert" had taken place at the Musikverein, the program including the *Fest-und Gedenksprüche* (op. 109) and the Requiem. On the evening of 7 May the *Magelone-Lieder* were performed at another "Festkonzert" at the Bösendorfer Hall. A "Brahms Exhibition" was held at the Musikverein from 6 to 11 May. (On the history of the monument, see especially the brochure *Zur*

Enthüllung des Brahms-Denkmals in Wien: 7 May 1908, prepared on the occasion of the unveiling, and also pp. 23–24, 36–41 of Brahms Exhibition 1997b.)

In connection with the construction of the Viennese U-Bahn, the statue was taken down in 1977 and re-erected the following year on a site a few meters to the southwest of the original one. (Brahms Exhibition 1997b; Brahms Monument 1908)

WIDMANN, JOSEF VIKTOR (b. Nennowitz [Brněnské Ivanovnice, Czech Republic], 20 February 1842; d. Berne, 6 November 1911). Journalist, literary critic, poet, dramatist, librettist, author of novels, stories, and travel books. Although he was born in Moravia, both his parents were of Viennese origin. His father, Josef Otto Widmann (1816–73), became a novice at the Heiligenkreuz Monastery in 1835, but later converted to Protestantism; in 1845 he was appointed pastor at Liestal, near Basle. Josef Viktor's mother Charlotte (1814–67), the daughter of a Viennese bookseller named Franz Winner, was very musical and the proud owner of a **Conrad Graf** piano that had once stood in **Beethoven**'s room. (It was sold by Josef Viktor in 1889 to the Verein Beethoven-Haus, Bonn.)

Widmann grew up at Liestal and later studied theology at the Universities of Basle, Heidelberg, and Jena. For a time he undertook auxiliary church duties as a "Pfarrhelfer," but he never became a pastor himself, as S. Avins (1997) mistakenly states in *Johannes Brahms: Life and Letters* (802). In fact, he declared later that the year's work as an assistant had made him realize that he had no desire to become a cleric for life. From 1868 he served as principal of a girls' school in Berne, a function he fulfilled with some distinction; however, his opposition to rigid religious orthodoxy made him enemies in conservative circles, and his appointment was terminated in 1880. He was thereupon awarded an honorary doctorate by the University of Berne and appointed editor of the "Feuilleton" of the Berne daily newspaper *Der Bund*, a position he held for more than 30 years, until his death. While his articles dealt primarily with literary matters, he also took a lively interest in social, political, and other topical subjects; he adopted, in particular, an enlightened attitude regarding women's suffrage and the environment.

Avins's (1997) statement that Widmann and Brahms first "met casually in 1866" (802) does not accord with the account that Widmann gave of their relations in his *Erinnerungen an Johannes Brahms*, published in 1898. There he recalls that when he first "saw and heard" Brahms at a concert at Winterthur during the winter of 1865 he made no attempt to meet him in person at that time. The concert in question is almost certainly the one in which Brahms, as well as **Theodor Kirchner** and **Friedrich Hegar**, took part on 29 November 1865. Later that evening Widmann made a drawing from memory of the three musicians, which was later reproduced by Elisabeth Widmann in her partial biography of her father. Even more importantly, Widmann was to draw in *Erinnerungen* a striking portrait in words of the young Brahms as he appeared to him on that occasion, "displaying an artistic personality which seemed to throb with genius down to his very fingertips" (J. Widmann 1898, 27).

Widmann has himself stated that he owed his first personal contact with Brahms to **Hermann Goetz** (28). On 11 July 1874 he and Brahms, together with Hegar, were asked to lunch by Hermann Goetz and his wife at their house near Zurich. (Goetz, who had been taken ill, listened to the conversation from an adjoining room.) That day marked the beginning of Widmann's friendship with Brahms, which continued, though not entirely untroubled, until the latter's death. The mutual attraction must have been strong from the outset, for Widmann mentions in *Erinnerungen* that they spent most of the following three days together, and a few weeks later Brahms visited him in Berne. Not long afterward they met once more, this time at Mannheim where, on 11 October 1874, they both attended the premiere of Goetz's opera *Der Widerspenstigen Zähmung*, for which Widmann had written the libretto. The possibility of his also writing a libretto for Brahms was discussed on this occasion, as well as later, and in 1778 Widmann sent Brahms a sketch for a scenario based on Gozzi's play *Il re cervo* (*see* ALLGEYER, JULIUS), but the project eventually died a quiet death.

Over the next 21 years they were to meet numerous times, mainly in Switzerland. Indeed, Brahms's choice of a village on Lake Thun for his summer quarters in the years 1886–88 was largely due to its proximity to Berne, which enabled him to spend many weekends with the Widmanns. In addition, he visited Italy three times in Widmann's company: in 1888, in 1890, and again in 1893. A fairly detailed account of the last journey, on which they were joined by Hegar and **Robert Freund**, can be found in Widmann's book *Sizilien und andere Gegenden Italiens: Reisen mit Johannes Brahms*. Published in 1903, it was dedicated to "Johannes Brahms dem Unsterblichen [Immortal]."

"A more agreeable companion than you I cannot imagine or wish for," Brahms had assured him in a letter on 7 January 1888, before their first joint trip (Brahms 1974/8, 72). Yet it was in that year that their relations came under serious strain, from which, Widmann feared at the time, they might never recover. The immediate cause was an article published by Widmann in *Der Bund* on 18 August to which Brahms took exception. In it Widmann criticized certain jingoistic remarks made by the new emperor Wilhelm II, who at a banquet at Frankfurt an der Oder two days earlier had proclaimed his fierce determination not to give up "a single stone" of Alsace and Lorraine, even if millions of Germans should have to die defending those conquered lands. What Widmann especially deplored as being unacceptably callous and brutal was the emperor's reported use, in referring to the soldiers who might thus be sacrificed, of a term signifying the displaying of animals killed in a hunt. (In *Erinnerungen* Widmann admitted that he had gone too far in his criticism.) The article greatly angered the extremely patriotic Brahms who, in a long letter, defended the young emperor and accused Widmann of anti-German prejudice (Brahms 1974/8, 88–90). Worse was to follow, for while he did not suspend his regular journeys to Berne, his visits now produced angry exchanges about the relative merits of monarchism and republicanism, on which the two men held diametrically opposed views. On one occasion, Widmann subsequently reported to **Henriette Feuerbach** that Brahms "spoke such harsh words to me as I would not have tolerated from anyone else," and the visits, formerly so enjoyable, became "real nightmares for the entire family" (Widmann and Widmann 1922–24, vol. 2, 338). Eventually, by tacit mutual consent, they avoided political discussions, and by the time Brahms left Switzerland in September, relations were once more sufficiently cordial for them to plan a further joint trip to Italy for the following spring (later postponed until 1890). Yet the quarrels were not so easily forgotten: "I feel that a block of ice lies between us, which is his incredibly chauvinistic German standpoint," Widmann wrote in the aforementioned letter to Henriette Feuerbach. As for Brahms, their profound differences of opinion and the acrimonious discussions that they had provoked may well have provided one of the reasons why he did not return to Switzerland the following summer.

In the long run, though, this quarrel had no adverse effect on their friendship. As already indicated, they made two further trips to Italy (and would have made more, if Widmann had not declined Brahms's proposals for health reasons), and they also saw each other elsewhere on several other occasions. In September 1889 they met at Baden-Baden, and in March 1891 at Meiningen, where Brahms attended the first performance of Widmann's tragedy *Önone*, which Brahms had brought to the attention of **Baroness Helene Heldburg**. In a letter to her two months earlier, he had referred to Widmann as "this quite exceptionally delightful and splendid man" and had also warmly praised his excellent journalistic work (Brahms 1991, 104). Lastly, Brahms and Widmann continued to correspond. An edition by **Max Kalbeck** of 138 letters and postcards from Brahms to Widmann was published in 1915; the earliest dated from November 1877, and the last one from December 1896. They testify to Brahms's warm feelings for Widmann as a person, as well as to his admiration for Widmann's writings, of which the latter frequently sent him copies. Unfortunately, Widmann's own numerous letters to Brahms are lost; when they were returned to him after Brahms's death, he apparently destroyed them.

The two men met for the last time in Zurich in October 1895 at the inauguration of the new Tonhalle. When Widmann learned from Kalbeck in February 1897 about Brahms's fatal illness, he was deeply distressed. "My heart is full of tears" he told Friedrich Hegar on 26 February, "above all at the thought of that splendid Jupiter-like figure being destroyed and crumbling away little by little" (Widmann and Widmann 1922–24, vol. 2, 340). Widmann promptly wrote to Brahms, pretending not to know how things really stood and offering his company, should Brahms wish to recuperate in the south. After receiving Kalbeck's telegram announcing Brahms's death, he declared that he now comprehended better than ever before "the exaltation felt by a great hero's faithful vassals as they killed themselves at his bier, so that they might follow their beloved master to the realm of shades" (Kalbeck 1976, vol. 4, 526). On 6 April he devoted an article in *Der Bund* to Brahms. Two years later, at the unveiling of the Brahms monument at Meiningen on 7 October 1899, the principal speech, given by **Joseph Joachim**, was preceded by a prologue written by Widmann and spoken by the actor Franz Nachbaur. (Brahms 1974/8, 1991; Frei 1914; Geiser 1976; Reiber 1997; E. Widmann and M. Widmann 1922–24; J. Widmann 1897a, 1897b, 1898, 1903, 1992; Zimmermann 1983)

WILT, MARIE, née Liebenthaler (b. Vienna, 30 January 1833; d. Vienna, 24 September 1891). Soprano. She had a distinguished career on the stage and in concert, and was regarded as an outstanding interpreter of Brahms's *Lieder*. Held back by a chest ailment that obliged her to whisper for several years, she did not realize her wish to become an opera singer until the age of 32 when, after studying with **Josef Gänsbacher**, she made her debut in 1865 at Graz as Donna Anna in *Don Giovanni*. In 1866–67 (and again later in 1874–75) she sang with great success at Covent Garden under the name "Maria Vilda," making her first appearance there on 1 May 1866 in the title role of Bellini's *Norma*. Her singing took the house by storm, but her appearance and acting aroused less enthusiasm (see Rosenthal 1958, 148).

Wilt was indeed unattractive and very stout; but she conquered all with her magnificent and extremely powerful voice, which, allied with a superb technique, allowed her to tackle an exceptionally wide range of works with dazzling and often very moving effect.

From 1867 to 1877 she was a member of the Vienna Opera. She appeared as Elvira in *Don Giovanni* at the opening of the new opera house on 25 May 1869, was the first Viennese Aida (in a German version, on 29 April 1874), and created the part of Sulamith at the premiere of **Karl Goldmark**'s *Die Königin von Saba* (10 March 1875). In 1878 she joined the Leipzig Opera and the following year sang Brünnhilde there in one of the earliest complete *Ring* cycles, which was conducted by Anton Seidl. From 1880 to 1882 she was a member of the Frankfurt company (on 20 October 1880 she sang Donna Anna at the opening of the new opera house), and she also made guest appearances at Budapest, Brünn [Brno], and Vienna, before finally returning permanently to Vienna in 1886.

Her association with Brahms began soon after his arrival in Vienna (*see* ASTEN, JULIE VON). At his second concert, on 6 January 1863, she sang four of his songs to his accompaniment: "Liebestreu" (op. 3/1), "Juchhe" (op. 6/4), "Treue Liebe" (op. 7/1), and "Parole" (op. 7/2); the last three songs were receiving their first public performances. Among other instances of Wilt's association with Brahms were the following: on 15 November 1863 she sang at his first concert with the Singakademie; at another Singakademie concert on 17 April 1864 she took part in the quartets "Wechsellied zum Tanze" (op. 31/1) and "Neckereien" (op. 31/2); at a concert of the Gesellschaft der Musikfreunde on 12 November 1870 she gave the first performances of "Die Trauernde" (op. 7/5) and "Sehnsucht" (op. 14/8), and, according to one source, also of "Ständchen" (op. 14/7); at another Gesellschaft concert on, 5 March 1871, she was soprano soloist in the first performance of the complete Requiem to be directed by Brahms; and on 7 April 1871 she took part in another performance of the Requiem, again conducted by Brahms, this time at Bremen Cathedral. Furthermore, she performed at several concerts of the Gesellschaft der Musikfreunde conducted by Brahms while he was its artistic director. At the very first concert, on 10 November 1872, she sang **Mozart**'s concert aria *Ch'io mi scordi di te?* (K. 505), accompanied by **Julius Epstein**; on 6 December 1874 she was a soloist in a performance of **Beethoven**'s *Missa solemnis*; and on 28 February 1875 she was once more the soprano soloist in the Requiem. It may be also assumed that she performed various Brahms songs at some of her own concerts and at others in which she participated. There is no indication that her relationship with Brahms was at any time other than purely professional. (The information given above concerning first performances of Brahms's songs is mainly based on M. L. McCorkle's [1984] *Werkverzeichnis*.)

Wilt's private life was an unhappy one. Her marriage to the engineer Franz Wilt ended in divorce, while a later relationship with a much younger man apparently brought her great distress. When close to sixty, she committed suicide by leaping from a fourth-floor window into the courtyard of a house on the Stephansplatz. (Kutsch and Riemens 1987–94)

WITTGENSTEIN FAMILY. Hermann Christian Wittgenstein (b. Korbach, Hesse, 12 September 1802; d. Vienna, 19 May 1878), a wealthy banker, married Franziska [Fanny] Christiane Figdor (b. Vienna, 7 April 1814; d. Vienna, 21 October 1890), a cousin of **Joseph Joachim**, in 1839 in Vienna. They resided in Leipzig until 1851, when they settled in Vienna. They had 11 children: Anna (1840–96), Marie (1841–1931), Paul (1842–1928), Josefine (1844–1933), Ludwig (1845–1925), Karl (1847–1913), Bertha (1848–1909), Clara (1850–1935), Lydia (1851–1920), Emilie (1853–1939), and Clothilde (1854–1937). Brahms, who became acquainted with the family through Joachim, enjoyed very friendly relations with several of the children, and notably with the following:

ANNA, who studied piano with **Clara Schumann** at Düsseldorf and was also for a time a pupil of Brahms. She became a sufficiently proficient pianist to play **Mozart**'s D Minor Piano Concerto with the Wiener Orchester-Verein at a concert in 1860. Furthermore, she sang in the ladies' choir that Brahms conducted at **Julie von Asten**'s home in Vienna. After Anna's marriage in 1867 to a prominent lawyer, Emil Franz (1839–84), Brahms was a frequent guest at their Viennese residence, where there was much music making, and he also met them regularly during the vacations he spent at Pörtschach (1877–79), where they owned a villa. After her husband's death, Anna remained in contact with Brahms. In 1892 she commissioned **Karl Kundmann** to make a bust of him, and it was at her house at Berchtesgaden that he first rehearsed his new clarinet sonatas with **Richard Mühlfeld** in September 1894.

BERTHA, who married the lawyer Karl Kuppelwieser (1841–1925), a son of **Franz Schubert**'s close friend Leopold Kuppelwieser, in 1869. Like Emil and **Anna Franz**, they owned a property at Pörtschach and entertained Brahms there. In 1877 Bertha made a marble bust of Brahms, which has been exhibited in the grounds of Schloss Leonstein (now a hotel), near Pörtschach, ever since.

EMILIE [MILLY], who married **Theodor von Brücke** (1853–1918), a grandson of the well-known physiologist Ernst Wilhelm von Brücke, in 1878. Brahms knew the latter and had friendly contacts with Milly and her husband.

JOSEFINE, who studied singing with **Josef Gänsbacher** and for several years sang at concerts at the Musikverein. In 1872 she married **Johann Nepomuk Oser** (1833–1912), a scientist who became a distinguished professor at the Technische Hochschule. Brahms was on excellent terms with the couple, as was Clara Schumann, who stayed with them on several occasions when she gave concerts in Vienna. Moreover, Johann Oser's sister **Betty** (1837–1922) had studied piano with Clara and became a close friend. Brahms knew Betty Oser very well, and there are repeated references to her in the Brahms–Clara Schumann correspondence.

KARL, who, being a less than enthusiastic high school student, ran off to America at the age of 17 and during his two-year stay there earned his living partly as a violin and language teacher. After his return he attended some lectures at the Technische Hochschule in Vienna before embarking on a career that, in a relatively short time, propelled him into the leading position in the Austrian iron and steel industry and made him one of the richest men in the country. As well as being a brilliant—and, in the eyes of some of his competitors, ruthless—businessman, he took a passionate interest in music and the fine arts. His splendid Viennese residence at 16 Alleegasse, where he lived from the early 1890s, was a well-known center of the city's musical life. It had a magnificent staircase and a beautiful music room, which, like other parts of the house, was sumptuously decorated. (Photographs of both are reproduced in Edgard Haider's [1984] splendid book *Verlorenes Wien: Adelspaläste vergangener Tage*.) Furthermore, Karl owned an important art collection and also possessed a considerable number of musical autographs (see E. F. Flindell's [1969] article "Ursprung und Geschichte der Sammlung Wittgenstein im 19. Jahrhundert").

Brahms's rooms in Karlsgasse were was within a few minutes' walk from Karl Wittgenstein's house, and he was a frequent visitor; his music (e.g., the Clarinet Quintet and the Clarinet Sonatas) were performed there. He last visited it on 21 March 1897, two weeks before his death, when he attended a rehearsal of the Soldat-Roeger Quartet (*see* SOLDAT, MARIE), prior to a public concert. In 1921, Alleegasse was renamed "Argentinierstrasse." The house was sold after the Second World War by Karl's daughter Hermine (1874–1950) to a bank, which demolished it and replaced it with a nondescript modern apartment building.

In 1874 Karl married Leopoldine Kallmus (1850–1926). Among their eight children were pianist **Paul Wittgenstein** (1887–1961) and philosopher Ludwig Wittgenstein (1889–1951). One of the daughters, Margarethe (1882–1958), married in 1905 an American, Jerome Stonborough (1873–1936), who acquired many Brahms autographs (for some details, see M. L. McCorkle's [1984] *Werkverzeichnis*).

PAUL, who painted an excellent portrait of Brahms (which is reproduced in Gustav Jenner's [1930] *Johannes Brahms als Mensch, Lehrer und Künstler* [2nd ed.] and in E. F. Flindell's abovementioned article). According to his aforementioned niece Hermine, Paul had been able to observe Brahms unnoticed while the latter was listening to music at her father's house. (Bramann 1974; Flindell 1969; Gaugusch 2001; Haider 1984; Otruba 1969)

WOLF, HUGO (FILIPP JAKOB) (b. Windischgraz, Styria [Slovenj Gradec, Slovenia], 13 March 1860; d. Vienna, 22 February 1903). Composer. He enrolled at the Vienna conservatory in September 1875 but returned home in March 1877, having been expelled "for offences against discipline" (F. Walker 1968, 44). By November of that year he was back in Vienna, where the tried to earn a living as a music teacher, a profession for which he was ill suited by temperament. Thus, he relied mainly on the help of friends and sympathizers. One of these, the jeweler Heinrich Köchert, arranged for him to become music critic for the fashionable weekly *Wiener Salonblatt*, where his reviews of musical events appeared from 20 January 1884 until 24 April 1887. A fervent admirer of **Richard Wagner** and **Anton Bruckner**, he chose Brahms as his favorite bête noire and rarely missed an opportunity to hurl abuse at his music.

Yet he must have felt some respect for him at one time, for he once sought Brahms's opinion regarding some of his own early compositions. The story of his unannounced visit to Brahms was told, no doubt in a somewhat embroidered version, by **Max Kalbeck** in his review of *Ein Musikbuch aus Österreich* (edited by **Richard Heuberger**) in the *Neues Wiener Tagblatt* on 9 March 1904, and again later in his Brahms biography (Kalbeck 1976, vol. 3, 410–11); however, it almost certainly took place in early 1879 and not in 1881 or 1882, as he states (see F. Walker 1968, 83–84). Exactly which songs the 19-year-old Wolf showed Brahms is not known—perhaps the Heine settings he had composed the previous summer. After discussing the compositions with him and pointing out what he regarded as their shortcomings, Brahms urged him to study counterpoint with **Gustav Nottebohm**, and, according to Wolf's own account, he said to him, "First you must learn something, then one will see if you have any talent" (Kalbeck 1976, vol. 3, 411, n. 1). Wolf, who despite his youth already considered himself a mature composer, was outraged, but nonetheless appears to have approached Nottebohm (or at any rate to have made inquiries about his fees), for on 7 April he informed his father that there was no question of taking lessons with him, as he charged three gulden an hour; in any case, Wolf added, this recommendation was "merely a piece of North-German pedantry" on Brahms's part (Grasberger 1960, 68).

While it is obviously impossible to determine what role Wolf's hurt pride subsequently played in his relentlessly furious attacks on Brahms's works, there can be little doubt that his hostility stemmed essentially from a profound difference in their temperaments and musical aesthetics. On one occasion Wolf declared that a composer's greatness could only be judged by whether or not he was capable of jubilating: "Wagner is able to jubilate, Brahms is not" (Grasberger 1960, 69). The most profound factor in the shaping of his musical outlook was, in fact, his discovery of Wagner's music at performances of *Lohengrin* and *Tannhäuser*, which were given under the composer's own direction at the Vienna Opera in late 1875. (He even called on Wagner in his Viennese hotel room and tried to show him his first piano pieces, but Wagner, anxious to get rid of his young visitor as soon as possible, declined to do so and merely made some polite and conventional remarks.)

Years later Wolf was to state that he had, in truth, at one time admired Brahms's music, but that was before he had come to know Wagner's. On the evidence of this statement, he was no longer very sympathetic to Brahms's music by the time he went to see him. Such commendation of it as he could bring himself to express in his critical writings in the *Wiener Salonblatt* was largely reserved for Brahms's chamber music, in particular for the String Sextet op. 36, which he called "delightful" (23 March 1884), and, on one occasion, for the String Quintet op. 88; he also praised the *Alto Rhapsody*. For the rest, especially for the symphonies and the concertos, he felt nothing but contempt, which he moreover pronounced in the most extravagant and offensive terms. Particularly famous are his onslaughts on the Fourth Symphony and the Second Piano Concerto. Of the former he wrote: "No other work of Brahms has revealed such nothingness, hollowness, and hypocrisy. . . . Let Herr Brahms be content with having found in his E minor symphony . . . the language which gives the most eloquent expression to his mute despair: the language of the most acute musical impotence" (24 January 1886); and concerning the concerto: "Anyone capable of swallowing this piano concerto with relish can face any famine with equanimity: one may assume that he enjoys an enviable digestion, and in time of famine will be able to manage splendidly on a nutritious diet of window panes, cork stoppers, stove screws, and the like" (7 December 1884).

Such a shower of abuse from an unknown young man in his 20s was hardly designed to trouble a man enjoying the prestige that Brahms had attained internationally by the mid-1880s, nor could the *Wiener Salonblatt* compete in importance with the *Neue freie Presse*, where his prominent supporter **Eduard Hanslick** occupied such an influential position. (Not surprisingly, Hanslick was also high on Wolf's blacklist.) In fact, Brahms apparently derived a good deal of amusement from Wolf's diatribes, which he liked to read aloud to his friends; but later he would appreciate that Wolf could not simply be dismissed as a "närrischer Davidsbündler," a crazy anti-Philistine, but that his music showed that he was in fact a serious-minded person, with serious intentions (Grasberger 1960, 69). When Wolf's "Der Feuerreiter" and "Elfenlied," both settings of poems by Eduard Mörike, were performed at a concert of the Gesellschaft der Musikfreunde in Vienna on 2 December 1894, Brahms was seen to applaud warmly. (Eckstein 1936; Fleischer 1918; Grasberger 1960; Höslinger 1988; Huschke 1939; Kahler 1999; Pleasants 1979; F. Walker 1968)

WOLFF, HERMANN (b. Cologne, 4 September 1845; d. Berlin, 3 February 1902). Concert impresario and writer on music. In his youth he studied harmony with Richard Wüerst, a pupil of Mendelssohn, and piano with Franz Kroll, a pupil of **Liszt**. In 1878 he married the former actress Aloysia [Louise] Schwarz (b. Brünn [Brno], 25 March 1855; d. Berlin, 25 June 1935), who had grown up in Vienna.

The concert agency "Konzertdirektion Hermann Wolff," which he founded in Berlin at the beginning of the 1880s, played a significant role in the musical life of the German capital. In addition to representing many already well-established musicians, such as **Anton Rubinstein**, for whom he arranged tours in Germany and elsewhere, and other as yet largely unknown artists for whom he perceptively foresaw a splendid international career, he was closely associated with the Berlin Philharmonic Orchestra and, moreover, was responsible for the construction in 1892 of the Bechstein Saal, which quickly became a favorite venue for music making in Berlin. From 1880 he was in regular contact with **Hans von Bülow**, and from 1882 he organized the tours of the Meiningen orchestra, and later also Bülow's subscription concerts in Hamburg.

Brahms was frequently in professional contact with Wolff, who offered him various engagements and also invited him to take part in the inauguration of the Bechstein Saal, which was marked by three concerts: a recital each by Bülow and Rubinstein and, between them, on 5 October 1892, an all-Brahms evening (String Sextet op. 18, Clarinet Quintet, and Violin Sonata op. 108) with the participation of Brahms, **Joseph Joachim** and his quartet, and **Richard Mühlfeld**. Furthermore, Brahms was a guest of Wolff and his wife in their Berlin home on several occasions, and he also met Wolff more than once in Vienna—for instance on the occasion of the concerts given there by the Berlin Philharmonic Orchestra in April 1895. Wolff last saw Brahms a few weeks before his death. In his diary, **Max Kalbeck** records meeting him and **Albert J. Gutmann** on 2 March 1897 outside the house where Brahms lived. They had just called on him, and the previous day had even walked with him in the Prater for an hour. Wolff was then probably in Vienna for discussions with Gutmann regarding another visit by the Berlin Philharmonic Orchestra that was to take place the following month. In the event, the first concert, on 5 April, was to turn into a memorial concert for Brahms (*see* GUTMANN, ALBERT J.). Wolff was among the mourners at Brahms's funeral.

After Wolff's death in 1902, his widow Louise assumed charge of the agency, and she managed it with supreme competence and a good deal of panache for more than 30 years. An imposing person endowed with a rather imperious character, she was known widely and affectionately as "Queen Louise." It was not until she was approaching her 80th birthday that she decided to close down the business; she died shortly afterward. (Stargardt-Wolff 1954; Louise Wolff 1990)

WOLFF, LEONHARD (b. Halberstadt, 14 May 1848; d. Bonn, 18 February 1934). Conductor, violinist, and teacher. Cousin of **Rudolf von Beckerath**, and son of Hermann Wolff (1815–75), who conducted the Singverein and the subscription concerts at Krefeld for some 15 years until 1870 and during his tenure directed the first (and not very successful) performance at Krefeld of Brahms's Requiem, on 14 April 1870.

Leonhard Wolff attended the Cologne conservatory, where he studied composition with **Ferdinand Hiller**, piano with Isidor Seiss, and violin with Otto von Königslöw. Later, he received further instruction from Henri Vieuxtemps in Frankfurt, Hubert Léonard in Paris, and **Joseph Joachim** in Berlin. For several years he was a member of a quartet that during the winter played at the Silesian residence of Count Bolko von Hochberg. After serving as director of music at Marburg an der Lahn from 1875 until 1880 (during which period he also played in the orchestra at the Museum concerts in Frankfurt), he became conductor of the Cäcilien-Verein and the Männerverein at Wiesbaden (1880–84); finally, he moved to Bonn, where he held the posts of Musikdirektor (1884–98) and director of music at the university (1884–1915).

Wolff came to know Brahms particularly well during the several months that the latter spent at Wiesbaden in 1883. In his memoirs *Meine musikalischen Erinnerungen*, he relates that he and Rudolf von Beckerath helped Brahms find suitable accommodations, and that they frequently played chamber music with him at Beckerath's flat in the evenings, with Brahms at the piano, Beckerath on violin, and Wolff on viola (and with the occasional help of a cellist). On one such occasion, Wolff (1932) recalled in his memoirs, he suggested substituting the viola, rather than the cello, for the horn in Brahms's Trio op. 40 (the title of the first edition in 1866 had been

Trio für Pianoforte, Violine & Waldhorn oder Violoncello); and he added that Brahms was so pleased with the result that "he immediately instructed **Simrock** to publish the horn trio with the viola" (90). In fact, though, it was not until March 1884 that Brahms brought the matter to Simrock's attention: "My horn trio ought really to be accompanied by a part for the viola instead of the cello! For it sounds horrible with the cello, but quite splendid with the viola. The title could state explicitly: horn or viola" (Brahms 1974/11, 53). Two weeks later he wrote, "The viola part for the horn trio would have to be written, respectively printed, separately. [Herr] **Keller** can easily do that" (Brahms 1974/11, 55). Simrock did not drop the reference to the cello but added the viola as a further alternative instrument.

A somewhat different story was told by **Heinz von Beckerath** in his article "Erinnerungen an Johannes Brahms: Brahms und seine Krefelder Freunde" in the journal *Heimat* in 1958. In it he quotes his father **Alwin von Beckerath** as attributing Brahms's ready acceptance of the viola as a substitute for the horn in this trio to his positive reaction to some private performances using that instrument, in which Alwin took part, together with **Richard Barth** and **Rudolf von der Leyen**, at Krefeld in January 1885. Moreover, Alwin had explained that he had himself, at Wolff's suggestion, arranged for the horn part to be rewritten for the viola; he had then reportedly practiced it diligently prior to Brahms's arrival. "Brahms was very pleasantly surprised by the beautiful new sound. We had to repeat [the trio] straightaway [at our house] and later played it twice more at the von der Leyens" (Beckerath 1958, 84). Furthermore, according to Alwin von Beckerath, Brahms wrote to Simrock then and there to ask for the viola part to be printed. Clearly there are certain inaccuracies in this version, especially in view of the fact that Brahms had already raised the matter with Simrock in the spring of 1884. But Wolff's role in persuading Brahms to accept the viola as an alternative to the cello, and as a substitute for the horn in op. 40, is well documented in both accounts.

In May 1896 Wolff was responsible for supervising the musical offerings on the occasion of **Clara Schumann**'s funeral. Afterward he was among the visitors to the "Hagerhof," the **Weyermanns**' property at Honnef, and he can be seen in the group photograph that was taken there. This was no doubt the last time he saw Brahms. (Brahms 1974/11; Kross 1988; Rembert 1933; Schwabe 1984; Leonhard Wolff 1932; Stephenson 1961)

WÜLLNER, FRANZ (b. Münster, 28 January 1832; d. Braunfels an der Lahn, 7 September 1902). Conductor, pianist, composer, and teacher. He reportedly learnt to play violin at the age of five and piano at six. His principal music teacher was **Beethoven**'s one-time factotum Anton Schindler, with whom he studied piano and composition from 1846, first at Münster and later in Frankfurt am Main. From 1854 to 1858 he lived in Munich, where he was active both as a pianist and a piano teacher (from 1856 at the conservatory). In 1858 he was appointed municipal music director at Aachen, which he left in 1865 to take up the post of court Kapellmeister in Munich. There he was initially responsible only for church music at the court church (at first together with **Franz Lachner**, from 1866 on his own), but the range of his activities soon grew to include classes in choral singing at the new Musikschule, as well as conducting at concerts and at the opera. Thus, he directed the very first performances of *Das Rheingold* (22 September 1869) and *Die Walküre* (26 June 1870). From the beginning of 1871, he held the rank of principal Kapellmeister, but **Hermann Levi**'s arrival the following year gradually undermined his position, and in 1877 he accepted an offer to succeed **Julius Rietz** as court Kapellmeister at Dresden; soon afterward he was, in addition, appointed director of the conservatory there.

But in Dresden he also became increasingly embroiled in a rivalry, this time with Ernst von Schuch, who succeeded in gaining control of all operatic performances, much to Wüllner's chagrin. Though feeling more and more frustrated in his position, he conscientiously carried out the duties allotted to him. It is an indication of his by then well-established reputation as a conductor that he was invited to direct a series of concerts of the Berlin Philharmonic Orchestra in 1882–85. Before the end of that period he had (in 1884) been chosen to succeed **Ferdinand Hiller** as music director and head of the conservatory at Cologne, and he served in those posts with distinction until his death; during that period he also directed six Lower Rhine Music Festivals. While the programs of his concerts were built primarily around the great German classical composers, he by no means neglected his contemporaries, including **Anton Bruckner**, though he felt little affinity with the latter's music (and even less with **Liszt**'s—he had been prepared to sign the Brahms-**Joachim** manifesto against it in 1860). Above all, he admired Brahms's compositions. He was also a notable supporter of the young **Richard Strauss**, of whose Serenade for Wind Instruments (op. 7) he gave the world premiere (Dresden, 27 November 1882), as he did later, at Cologne, of the tone poems *Till Eulenspiegels lustige Streiche* (5 November 1895) and *Don Quixote* (8 March 1897); furthermore, he directed performances of many of Strauss's other works. Wüllner's own compositions include orchestral works, chamber music, piano pieces, songs, and numerous choral works. He also made important contributions to the **Bach** edition prepared under the auspices of the Bach Society, and to **Breitkopf & Härtel**'s editions of the complete works of **Haydn** and **Mozart**.

The earliest documented meeting between Wüllner and Brahms took place at the house of **Wilhelm Ludwig** and Elisabeth **Deichmann** at Mehlem, near Bonn, in September 1853, but contrary to a statement by Ernst Wolff, the editor of their correspondence, this was not their first meeting, for in the first letter that Brahms wrote from there to Joseph Joachim, he named Wüllner among the "many acquaintances I have already found here" (Brahms 1974/5, 6). Early the following year Wüllner spent a few days at Hanover, during which he saw a good deal of Brahms, Joachim, and **Julius Otto Grimm**. By then he had already formed a high opinion of Brahms as a person and of his great potential as a composer: "Brahms is an uncommonly important and amiable man," he informed Schindler (Kämper 1963, 14). Their relations remained extremely cordial, if not particularly intimate, until Brahms's death; they were nourished not only by correspondence but also by numerous meetings (including several during Brahms's summer vacations in Germany, Switzerland, and Austria) and through repeated appearances by Brahms at concerts directed by Wüllner, who was all his life a devoted champion of Brahms's music. Reporting on a very well-received performance of the *Triumphlied* in Munich on 14 December 1872, he assured Brahms that he had "rehearsed and conducted it with the warmest, sincerest, and most heart-felt enthusiasm," adding, "I personally hold you in ever deeper affection with each new work of yours which I have come to know these past years" (Brahms 1974/15, 14). Among other works by Brahms to which he introduced Munich audiences were the Requiem (10 March 1872) and the *Haydn Variations* (10 December 1873); and it was at one of his concerts there that Brahms, on 15 November 1876, conducted the first Munich performance of his First Symphony, 11 days after its premiere at Karlsruhe. They celebrated the event by adopting the intimate "Du" in addressing each other.

It seems surprising that it should have taken them 23 years to reach that stage in the relations, for there is good evidence that Brahms liked Wüllner and enjoyed his company. In August 1877, after they had spent some days together at Pörtschach, he wrote to **Clara Schumann**: "Wüllner's visit gave me great pleasure" (Litzmann 1970, vol. 2, 122). Moreover, he had great respect for Wüllner's musicianship. In a later letter to Clara, in October 1891 (vol. 2, 467), he described Wüllner as "one of our most competent and erudite musicians" and as an excellent editor who would be eminently suitable to undertake the publication of the original version of **Robert Schumann**'s Fourth Symphony, a project in which Brahms was greatly interested at that time. (Wüllner had conducted the original version at a concert at Cologne on 22 October 1889. The eventual realization of the project temporarily strained Brahms's relations with Clara, who had not been in favor of it and had, in any case, been doubtful of Wüllner's ability to carry it out.) Brahms's opp. 102 and 110 provided other important links between the two men: the Double Concerto was first performed, under Brahms's direction, at one of Wüllner's concerts at the Gürzenichsaal on 18 October 1887; and Wüllner himself conducted the world premiere of the full set of the three Motets at the Cologne conservatory on 13 March 1890 in Brahms's presence. It was also at the conservatory that Wüllner conducted, on 2 May 1897, a Brahms memorial concert consisting of the *4 ernste Gesänge* (*see* WÜLLNER, LUDWIG), the Clarinet Quintet, the Violin Sonata op. 78, and three small choral pieces. The music was preceded by an address in which Wüllner paid tribute to Brahms the composer, "the greatest we possessed since **Wagner**'s death," and to Brahms the man, "the most faithful of friends" (Brahms 1974/15, 186, 190).

Wüllner's younger daughter Anna (later name: Anna Wüllner-Hoffmann) had a fine soprano voice. She once delighted Brahms when she sang his songs "Das Mädchen spricht" and "Mädchenlied" (op. 107/3, 5) to his accompaniment, at the house of **Robert Schnitzler**. In the autumn of 1889 Anna, together with **Amalie Joachim**, Raimund von Zur Mühlen, a bass called Schmalfeld, and pianist Ernst Wolff, undertook a concert tour to Danzig [Gdansk], Königsberg [Kaliningrad], and Riga, during which they repeatedly performed Brahms's *Zigeunerlieder* (op. 103). Later, Anna taught singing at the Stern Conservatory in Berlin. Wüllner's son **Ludwig** had a distinguished career as a singer, actor, and reciter (see WÜLLNER, LUDWIG). (Brahms 1974/5, 1974/15; Kämper 1963a, 1963b; Litzmann 1970; Sietz 1960d; Wüllner 1942)

WÜLLNER, LUDWIG (b. Münster, 19 August 1858; d. Kiel, 19 March 1938). Tenor, reciter, and actor; son of **Franz Wüllner**. He learned to play violin and piano at an early age, studied philology at the Universities of Munich and Berlin and obtained his doctorate in that subject at the University of Strasbourg. From 1884 to 1887 he lectured at the University of Münster, and during his stay in that town he also frequently appeared at concerts as violinist and singer (at a concert on 8 March 1884, he sang three of the *Magelone-Lieder*); furthermore, he made his debut as a reciter in a performance of Byron's *Manfred*, with **Robert Schumann**'s music, on 25 February 1885. He next trained as a singer at the Cologne conservatory and then joined the court theater company at Meiningen (1889–95). Later, he enjoyed a brilliant international career as a singer, which took him to all parts of Europe and three times to America; his first American concert, at New York on 14 November 1908, included Brahms's "Auf dem Kirchhofe" and "Verrat" (op. 105/4–5).

It was at Meiningen that Brahms, a long-standing friend of Ludwig's father, had repeated opportunities to admire him both as an actor and a singer; moreover, he seems to have taken a great liking to him as a person. "Imagine three shouts of 'hurrah' about the man, the singer, and the actor, and you will know more or less what I have to say about him," he wrote to Franz Wüllner on one occasion—probably after his stay at Meiningen in March 1891, during which Ludwig had appeared in the part of Thersites in **Josef Viktor Widmann**'s tragedy *Önone* and had sung the *Magelone-Lieder* at a concert at the palace (Brahms 1974/15, 178). After his visit to Schloss Altenstein in November 1894, on which occasion he and **Richard Mühlfeld** had played his new cello sonatas before **Duke Georg II** and his wife, Brahms wrote to **Fritz Simrock**: "Apart from Mühlfeld, it was especially the young Wüllner who gave me enormous pleasure, particularly by his excellent singing. I cannot imagine hearing a better performance of the folk songs [WoO 33]" (Brahms 1974/12, 154). He was also impressed by Wüllner's violin playing (he may on this occasion have played one or both of his earlier violin sonatas with Wüllner), and he asked Simrock to send Wüllner a copy of his Violin Sonata op. 108. A year later, in response to a letter from Simrock reporting some highly successful concert appearances by Wüllner in Berlin, Brahms wrote, "I don't know anyone to-day whose interpretation of songs gives me anything like as much pleasure . . . yet he does not really possess a singer's voice!" (Brahms 1974/12, 182). In fact, Wüllner seems to have owed his success principally to a profound sensitivity, allied with a superb technique that enabled him to communicate in striking fashion the meaning of a text and the mood evoked by the music. While his celebrity rested above all on his compelling rendition of Lieder, he did not confine himself to that genre but also successfully assumed operatic parts (most notably the title role in *Tannhäuser*) and sang in oratorio and certain other works (e.g., **Beethoven**'s Ninth Symphony, in which, in 1888, he made his concert debut as one of the soloists in a performance directed by his father). The above-mentioned sensitivity and splendid vocal control also help to account for his renown as a reciter.

At the Brahms memorial concert conducted by his father in Cologne on 2 May 1897, Ludwig Wüllner sang the *4 ernste Gesänge*. (Brahms 1974/12, 1974/15; Ludwig 1931)

– Z –

ZEMLINSKY, ALEXANDER (VON) (b. Vienna, 14 October 1871; d. Larchmont, New York, 15 March 1942). Composer and conductor. He studied piano, violin, theory, and composition at the Vienna conservatory (1887–92) and may well have first come to Brahms's attention when, on 26 June 1890, he won a grand piano as best pianist with his performance of the *Handel Variations*. (Although Brahms was at Ischl at the time, news of the event may well have reached him there.) Regarding his first meeting with Brahms, Zemlinsky has provided conflicting accounts, of which the more plausible is the one given in the journal *Musikblätter des Anbruch* in 1922, where he identifies the performance of a symphony he had written while still a student as the event on which he was presented to Brahms. The opening movement of his D minor symphony was in fact performed at an end-of-term concert at the conservatory on 11 July 1892; according to Zemlinsky's biographer Antony Beaumont, Brahms was present at the concert. (When the entire work was played, again by the conservatory orchestra, on 10 February 1893, Brahms was in Hamburg.) In any case, he is likely to have come into contact with Zemlinsky at the Tonkünstlerverein, which Zemlinsky joined in the 1893–94 season and whose meetings Brahms rarely missed; on 20 November 1893 Zemlinsky made his debut there as a composer and pianist with a performance of his Piano Quartet in D Major. On 18 March 1895 he even shared the rostrum with Brahms at a conservatory concert celebrating the 25th anniversary of the inauguration of the new Musikverein building: Brahms conducted his *Academic Festival Overture*, and Zemlinsky, his Suite for Orchestra.

It was apparently the performance by the augmented Hellmesberger Quartet of Zemlinsky's D Minor Quintet on 5 March 1896 that brought him into closer contact with Brahms, who told **Richard Heuberger** that it showed considerable talent. Zemlinsky later recalled that Brahms invited him to his rooms for a discussion of the work, which became increasingly critical. At the end of it, however, Brahms offered to pay him a monthly subsidy in order to free him at least partially from the need of giving private lessons and thus allow him more time for composing; it is not clear if the offer was accepted. (The quintet was, incidentally, repeated at the Tonkünstlerverein concert of 30 October 1896, at which the first complete performance of Brahms's *4 ernste Gesänge* took place—*see* KRAUS, FELIX VON and SISTERMANS, ANTON; Brahms was not present that evening.)

Also in 1896, Zemlinsky won third prize in a competition organized by the Tonkünstlerverein for a new chamber music work using at least one wind instrument; Brahms had given some of his own money to increase the value of the prizes and had also served on the jury. He subsequently recommended the winning entry, a clarinet quartet by Walter Rabl, and Zemlinsky's clarinet trio to **Fritz Simrock**, who published both. In his first compositions, Zemlinsky was strongly influenced by Brahms's music; later, he deliberately distanced himself from his early model. However, he never lost—or perhaps he lost and later regained—his admiration for Brahms's music. "To-day, when I conduct one of his symphonies or play one of his marvellous chamber works," Zemlinsky wrote in *Musikblätter des Anbruch* in 1922, "I fall once again unreservedly under the spell of the memories of those times and each bar becomes a profound experience for me" (70).

From 1896–97 Zemlinsky composed *Frühlingsbegräbnis* [*The Funeral of Spring*], for solo, chorus, and orchestra, to a poem by **Paul Heyse**. He dedicated the work to the memory of Brahms and conducted its first performance at a concert of the Gesellschaft der Musikfreunde on 11 February 1900. Later, he revised it for a larger orchestra. (Brahms 1974/12; Beaumont 2000; Clayton 1988; Heuberger 1976; Zemlinsky 1922)

ZITTEL, EMIL (b. Lörrach, 14 August 1831; d. Karlsruhe, 23 January 1899). Protestant cleric; from 1863 Stadtpfarrer [chief pastor] at Karlsruhe. Like his father Karl Zittel (1802–71), who in 1847 became Stadtpfarrer of Heidelberg, Emil Zittel was a prominent champion of Protestant liberalism. His influence went far beyond the confines of the Grand Duchy of Baden; from 1876 until 1892 he represented his diocese on the General Synods. He was also involved in translations of the New Testament and the author of various writings on the Bible.

In 1871 he worked, with **Hermann Levi**'s encouragement and in consultation with him, on an opera libretto for Brahms, inspired by the *Song of Songs*. Levi sent the text (or, at any rate, a fairly detailed sketch) of the first two acts of *Sulamith* to Brahms on 28 December 1871; but Brahms made it clear, in his reply, that he did not consider the subject suitable for the purpose. Levi, in a letter on 15 January 1872, did not hide his disappointment at Brahms's reaction and promised not to "torment" him again with such projects in the future (Brahms 1974/7, 95). However, he did later that year ask Brahms to call on Zittel during his next visit to Karlsruhe: "After all, he went to a great deal of trouble, and only wished to please you" (Brahms 1974/7, 114). Whether Brahms ever contacted Zittel is not known. (Brahms 1974/7; Hönig 1906)

ZUCCALMAGLIO, ANTON WILHELM FLORENTIN VON (b. Waldbröl, 12 April 1803; d. Nachrodt, Westphalia, 22/23 March 1869). Painter, poet, dramatist, writer on music and many other subjects, editor of folk songs; he was, in W. Wiora's (1953) words, "a universal genius, or rather, a universal dilettante" (Wiora 1953, 154). Residing in Warsaw and at different localities in Germany, he earned his living mostly as a private tutor.

His interest in folk songs, developed during his school and student days at Cologne and Heidelberg, led him to publish in 1829, with E. Baumstark, a collection of such songs drawn from various countries. In 1838 he published, with A. Kretzschmer, the first volume of *Deutsche Volkslieder mit ihren Original-Weisen* [*German Folk songs with their Original Melodies*], and, Kretzschmer having died in 1839, he issued the second volume by himself in 1840. Some years later he revised and even expanded the collection, but he never published his ultimate version, which is still preserved today at the Deutsche Staatsbibliothek, Berlin.

The Kretzschmer-Zuccalmaglio anthology did not meet with universal acclaim (*see* BÖHME, FRANZ MAGNUS and FRIEDLAENDER, [FRIEDLÄNDER], MAX); in particular, Zuccalmaglio was suspected of having composed many of the songs himself. The accusation did not trouble Brahms, who greatly admired the anthology and much preferred it to those issued by **Ludwig Erk** and **Franz Magnus Böhme**. "Less authentic? But whatever could be less authentic and, moreover, less delectable than so much in Böhme?" he wrote to **Franz Wüllner** in 1888, adding, "On the other hand, I have long regarded Kr[etzschmer's] and Z[uccalmaglio's] collection as a real treasure" (Brahms 1974/15, 155). The pleasure he derived from the Kretzschmer-Zuccalmaglio collection (of which he had even given a copy to **Agathe von Siebold**) is also strikingly reflected in the fact that some four-fifths of the 49 folk songs he published in 1894 (*see* BÖHME, FRANZ MAGNUS) were taken from it. Since then, Zuccalmaglio has been largely exonerated, for it has been shown that, while he did make some alterations, the folk songs themselves were generally authentic (see W. Wiora [1953], *Die rheinisch-bergischen Melodien bei Zuccalmaglio und Brahms*). (Brahms 1974/15; Friedlaender 1918; Günther 1967; Wiora 1953)

Bibliography

The following is a select list of the publications consulted during the preparation of this book. Most of those included are mentioned in abbreviated form among the sources cited at the end of individual entries in the dictionary (but see the note on encyclopedias in the preface). Abbreviations used in the dictionary are in bold.

Abert, Hermann. 1924. "Zum Gedächtnis Hermann Kretzschmars." *Jahrbücher der Musikbibliothek Peters*, 9–23.

ADB *Allgemeine deutsche Biographie*. 1967–71. 56 vols. Leipzig, Germany: Duncker & Humblot, 1875–1912. Reprint Berlin: Duncker & Humblot.

Adler, Guido. 1906. "Hanslick, Eduard." In *Biographisches Jahrbuch und Deutscher Nekrolog*, vol. 9 (1904), edited by A. Bettelheim, 342–47. Berlin: Reimer.

——. 1933. "Johannes Brahms: His Achievement, His Personality, and His Position." *Musical Quarterly* 19, no. 2 (April): 113–42.

Akad Gesangverein. 1908. *100 Semester Akademischer Gesangverein in Wien 1858–1908. Festschrift herausgegeben aus Anlass des 50. Stiftungsfestes des Akademischen Gesangvereines in Wien, 29. Mai bis 1. Juni 1908*. Vienna, Austria: Akademischer Gesangverein.

Albrecht, Otto E. 1933. "Johannes Brahms und Hans von Bülow." *University of Pennsylvania Library Chronicle* 1, no. 3 (October): 39–46.

Aldrich, Richard. 1928. *Musical Discourse*. From *The New York Times*. London: Oxford University Press. See "Wagner and Brahms on Each Other" (pp. 85–102) and "Franz Kneisel" (pp. 266–81).

Alf, Julius. 1940–41. *Geschichte und Bedeutung der Niederrheinischen Musikfeste in der ersten Hälfte des neunzehnten Jahrhunderts*. Düsseldorf, Germany: *Düsseldorfer Jahrbuch* 42/43.

——. 1952. "Das Düsseldorfer Musikleben under Julius Buths." In *Beiträge zur Musikgeschichte der Stadt Düsseldorf*, edited by K. G. Fellerer, 54–63. Cologne, Germany: Staufen-Verlag.

Allgeyer, Julius. 1872. "Anselm Feuerbach." *Oesterreichische Wochenschrift für Wissenschaft und Kunst*, new series, 2: 641–52.

——. 1904. *Anselm Feuerbach*. 2nd edition. 2 vols. Berlin: Spemann.

Alth, Minna von, and Gertrude Obzyna. n.d. *Burgtheater 1776–1976. Aufführungen und Besetzungen von zweihundert Jahren*. 2 vols. Vienna, Austria: Ueberreuter.

Altmann, Wilhelm. 1903. *Heinrich von Herzogenberg. Sein Leben und Schaffen.* Leipzig, Germany: Rieter-Biedermann.

——. 1912. "Brahmssche Urteile über Tonsetzer." *Die Musik* 12, no. 1 (October): 46–55.

——. 1929. "Antonin Dvořák im Verkehr mit Fritz Simrock." *N. Simrock Jahrbuch* 2: 85–151.

Ambrose, Jane P. 1987. "Brahms and the Hamburg Frauenchor: An American Footnote." *American Brahms Society Newsletter* 5, no. 2 (Autumn): 3–5.

Anon. 1905. "Miss Fanny Davies: A Biographical Sketch." *Musical Times* 46: 365–70.

Anon. 1906. "Alwine Schroedter." In *Badische Biographien*, part 5 (1891–1901), vol. 1, edited by F. Von Weech and A. Krieger, 710–14. Heidelberg, Germany: Winter's Universitätsbuchhandlung.

Anon. 1935. "Prof. Bram Eldering in Köln 70 Jahre alt" and "Bram Eldering und Joh. Brahms." *Neue Zeitschrift für Musik* 192, no. 8 (August), 894–95.

Anon. 1992. "The Brahms-Simrock Correspondence." *American Brahms Society Newsletter* 10, no. 2 (Autumn), 5.

Antonicek, Theophil. 1985. "Aus dem gemeinsamen Freundeskreis." In *Bruckner Symposion: Johannes Brahms und Anton Bruckner . . . 8.–11. September 1983*, edited by O. Wessely, 115–22. Linz, Austria: Anton Bruckner-Institut Linz.

——. 1988. "Aus dem Wiener Brahmskreis." In *Brahms-Kongress Wien 1983: Kongressbericht*, edited by S. Antonicek and O. Biba, 21–43. Tutzing, Germany: Schneider.

Arro, Elmar. 1935. "Ferdinand David und das Liphart-Quartett in Dorpat." *Baltische Monatshefte* 1: 19–30.

Auer, Leopold. 1923. *My Long Life in Music.* New York: Stokes.

Avé-Lallemant, Theodor. 1878. *Rückerinnerungen eines alten Musikanten. Die Philharmonischen Concerte in Hamburg, 1828–1878.* Hamburg, Germany.

Avins, Styra. 1992. "Brahms the Cellist." *Violoncello Society Newsletter* 10 (Summer): 1–3, (Winter): 4–5.

——. 1993. "The Young Brahms: Another View." *American Brahms Society Newsletter* 11, no. 2 (Autumn): 5.

——. 1997. *Johannes Brahms: Life and Letters.* Selected and annotated by Styra Avins. Translations by Josef Eisinger and Styra Avins. Oxford, UK: Oxford University Press.

——. 2001. "The Young Brahms: Biographical Data Reexamined." *19th Century Music* 24, no. 3 (Spring): 276–89.

——. 2003. "Brahms Observed: Carl Georg Peter Grädener with Brahms in Vienna." Translations by Styra Avins and Josef Eisinger. *American Brahms Society Newsletter* 21, no. 1 (Spring): 1–5, no. 2 (Autumn): 5–8.

Avins, Styra, and Josef Eisinger. 2002. "Six Unpublished Letters from Johannes Brahms." In *For the Love of Music: Festschrift in Honor of Theodore Front on His 90th Birthday*, edited by D. F. Scott, 105–35. Lucca, Italy: Lim antiqua. (Letters to Guido Adler, Theodor Avé-Lallemant, Adolph Brodsky, and Carl Georg Peter Grädener.)

Bach, Roman. 1959. "Ernst H. Seyffart zur 100: Wiederkehr seines Geburtstages am 6. Mai 1959." *Die Heimat* [Krefeld, Germany] 30: 87–92.

Bachrich, S[igmund]. 1914. *Aus verklungenen Zeiten: Erinnerungen eines alten Musikers*. Vienna, Austria: Knepler.

Bahr-Mildenburg, Anna. 1921. *Erinnerungen*. Vienna, Austria: Wiener literarische Anstalt.

Balassa, Ottilie von. 1933. *Die Brahmsfreundin Ottilie Ebner und ihr Kreis*. Vienna, Austria: Bondy.

Bamberger, Richard, et al., eds. 1995. *Österreich-Lexikon*. 2 vols. Vienna, Austria: Verlagsgemeinschaft Österreich-Lexikon.

Barth, Richard. 1904. *Johannes Brahms und seine Musik*. 2 vols. Hamburg, Germany: Meisner.

Bary, Helene de. 1937. *Museum: Geschichte der Museumsgesellschaqft zu Frankfurt a. M*. Frankfurt, Germany: Brönner.

Baser, Friedrich. 1973. *Grosse Musiker in Baden-Baden*. Tutzing, Germany: Schneider.

Bauer, Hans-Joachim. 1988. *Richard Wagner Lexikon*. Bergisch Gladbach: Lübbe.

Bauer, M. 1916. *Iwan Knorr: Ein Gedenkblatt*. Frankfurt, Germany: Reitz & Köhler.

Bauer, Werner M. 1989. "Anastasius Grün." In *Literatur Lexikon: Autoren und Werke deutscher Sprache*, vol. 4, edited by W. Killy, 389–90. 15 vols. Gütersloh, Germany: Bertelsmann Lexikon Verlag, 1988–93.

Bauer-Lechner, Natalie. 1907. *Fragmente: Gelerntes und Gelebtes*. Vienna, Austria: Lechner & Sohn.

Beaumont, Antony. 2000. *Zemlinski*. New York: Cornell University Press.

Beck, Ludwig. 1980. "Von Beckerath." *Die Heimat* [Krefeld, Germany] 51: 152–53. In Beck's "Krefelder Familien." *Die Heimat* 50 (1979): 189–92; 51 (1980): 151–58.

Beckerath, Heinz von. 1956. "Die Familie von der Leyen in Krefeld." *Der Mennonit* 9, no. 3 (March); no. 4 (April).

——. 1958. "Erinnerungen an Johannes Brahms." *Die Heimat* [Krefeld, Germany] 29: 81–93.

Beckermann, Michael. 1986. "Dvořák and Brahms: A Question of Influence." *American Brahms Society Newsletter* 4, no. 2 (Autumn): [6–8].

——, ed. 1993. *Dvořák and His World*. Princeton, N.J.: Princeton University Press.

Beller-McKenna, Daniel. 1995. "Brahms, the Bible, and Robert Schumann." *American Brahms Society Newsletter* 13, no. 2 (Autumn): 1–4.

——. 1998. "How *deutsch* a Requiem? Absolute Music, Universality, and the Reception of Brahms's *Ein deutsches Requiem*, op. 45." *19th Century Music* 22, no. 1 (Summer): 3–19.

——. 2004. *Brahms and the German Spirit*. Cambridge, Mass.: Harvard University Press.

Benningsen, Olga. 1939. "The Brothers Rubinstein and Their Circle." *Musical Quarterly* 25: 407–19.

Berbig, Roland. 1990. "Kugler, Franz (Theodor)." In *Literatur Lexikon: Autoren und Werke deutscher Sprache*, vol. 7, edited by W. Killy, 80–81. 15 vols. Gütersloh, Germany: Bertelsmann Lexikon Verlag, 1988–93.

——. 1991. "Reinick, Robert." In *Literatur Lexikon: Autoren und Werke deutscher Sprache*, vol. 9, edited by W. Killy, 374–75. 15 vols. Gütersloh, Germany: Bertelsmann Lexikon Verlag, 1988–93.

Berl, Heinrich. 1981. *Baden-Baden im Zeitalter der Romantik*. Baden-Baden, Germany: Schmidt.

Berlioz, Hector. 1972. *Correspondance générale*, vol. 4 (1851–55), edited by P. Citron, Y. Gérard, and H. J. Macdonald. Paris: Flammarion.

Beveridge, David. 1993. "Dvořák and Brahms: A Chronicle, an Interpretation." In *Dvořák and His World*, edited by M. Beckermann, 56–91. Princeton, N.J.: Princeton University Press.

Biba, Otto. 1978/79. "Brahms und Dvořák." *Musikblätter der Wiener Philharmoniker* 33: 197–201.

——. 1982/83. "Richard Strauss und Johannes Brahms." *Musikblätter der Wiener Philharmoniker* 37: 195–97.

——. 1983a. "Brahms–Gedenkstätten in Wien." *Österreichische Musikzeitschrift* 38: 245–47.

——. 1983b. "Brahms, Wagner und Parteiungen in Wien." *Musica* 37: 18–22.

——. 1983/84. "Tschaikowsky über Brahms oder: Brauchen wir ein neues Brahms-Bild?" *Musikblätter der Wiener Philharmoniker* 38: 169–72.

——. 1984a. "Brahms in Wien." In *Brahms und seine Zeit: Symposium Hamburg 1983*, edited by C. Floros, H. J. Marx, and P. Petersen, 259–71. [n.p.]: Laaber. (*Hamburger Jahrbuch für Musikwissenschaft* 7.)

——. 1984b. "Beobachtungen zum Wirken von Johannes Brahms in Wien." In *Johannes Brahms—Leben, Werk, Interpretation, Rezeption. Kongressbericht zum III. Gewandhaus-Symposium anlässlich der "Gewandhaus-Festtage 1983,"* 42–49. Leipzig, Germany.

——, ed. 1984c. *Johannes Brahms: Mit den Gedanken in Wien/With My Thoughts in Vienna. 5 Briefe/5 Letters*, translated by E. Hartzell. Vienna, Austria: Doblinger. (Letters to Franz Flatz, Johann Peter Gotthard, Johann von Herbeck, and the Gesellschaft der Musikfreunde.)

——. 1985. "Brahms, Bruckner und die Orgel." In *Bruckner Symposion: Johannes Brahms und Anton Bruckner . . . 8.–11. September 1983*, edited by O. Wessely, 191–96. Linz, Austria: Anton Bruckner-Institut Linz.

——. 1987. "New Light on the Brahms *Nachlass*." In *Brahms 2: Biographical, Documentary and Analytical Studies*, edited by M. Musgrave, 39–47. Cambridge, UK: Cambridge University Press.

——. 1988. "Brahms und die Gesellschaft der Musikfreunde in Wien." In *Brahms-Kongress Wien 1983: Kongressbericht*, edited by S. Antonicek and O. Biba, 45–65. Tutzing, Germany: Schneider.

——. 1997a. "Die Simrocks—Verleger für Beethoven wie für Brahms." In *Johannes Brahms und Bonn*, edited by M. Gutiérrez-Denhoff, 89–94. Bonn, Germany: Stadt Bonn.

——. 1997b. *"'Es hat mich noch Weniges so entzückt": Johannes Brahms and Franz Schubert*. Catalog of an exhibition at the Archives of the Gesellschaft der Musikfreunde, Vienna, Austria.

——. 1997c. "William Kupfer, ein Hamburger Musiker im Wiener Brahms-Kreis." *Österreichische Musikzeitschrift* 52: 41–45.

——. 2001. "Johannes Brahms und Ignaz Brüll: Zwei Künstlerfreunde im Salzkammergut." In *Internationaler Brahms-Kongress Gmunden 1997: Kongressbericht*, edited by I. Fuchs, 571–82. Tutzing, Germany: Schneider.

Billroth, Theodor. 1894–95. "Wer ist musikalisch?" *Deutsche Rundschau* 1: 107–33.

Bischoff, Ferdinand. 1890. *Chronik des Steiermärkischen Musikvereines: Festschrift zur Feier des fünfundsiebzigjährigen Bestandes des Vereines*. Graz, Austria: Verlag des Steiermärkischen Musikvereines.

Bissing, Friedrich Wilhelm, Freiherr von. 1942. *Mathilde Wesendonck: Die Frau und Dichterin*. Vienna, Austria: Scholl & Co.

Blaukopf, Herta, ed. 1982. *Gustav Mahler: Briefe*. Vienna, Austria: Zsolnay.

Blaukopf, Kurt. 1976. *Mahler: Sein Leben, sein Werk und seine Welt in zeitgenössischen Bildern und Texten.* Vienna, Austria: Universal Edition. (English version: *Mahler: A Documentary Study*, with contributions from Zoltan Roman. New York: Oxford University Press, 1976.)

Blès, Adrien. 1989. *Dictionnaire historique des rues de Marseille: Mémoire de Marseille*. Marseille, France: Jeanne Laffitte.

Bloesch, Hans. 1915. *Die Bernische Musikgesellschaft 1815–1915*. Berne, Switzerland: Grunau.

Blom, Eric, ed. 1954. *Grove's Dictionary of Music and Musicians.* 9 vols., with a supplementary volume, 1961. London: Macmillan.

Blum, Klaus. 1975. *Musikfreunde und Musici: Musikleben in Bremen seit der Aufklärung*. Tutzing, Germany: Schneider.

Blume, Friedrich, ed. 1949–86. *Die Musik in Geschichte und Gegenwart: Allgemeine Enzyklopaedie der Musik*. 17 vols. Kassel, Germany: Bärenreiter. (A second, revised edition, edited by Ludwig Finscher, began to appear in 1994.)

Bock, Alfred. 1931. "Erinnerungen an Clara Simrock und Johannes Brahms." *Zeitschrift für Musik* 98: 477–78.

Bodsch, Ingrid. 1997. "Johannes Brahms und die Bonner Schumannfeiern von 1873 und 1880." In *Johannes Brahms und Bonn*, edited by M. Gutiérrez-Denhoff, 62–79. Bonn, Germany: Stadt Bonn.

Boeck, Dieter. 1998. *Johannes Brahms: Lebensbericht mit Bildern und Doumenten*. Kassel, Germany: Wenderoth.

Böhler, Otto. 1941. *Geschichte der Gebrüder Böhler & Co. Ag. 1870–1940*. Berlin: Volk und Reich Verlag.

Böhm, August, Edler von Böhmersheim. 1908. *Geschichte des Singvereines der Gesellschaft der Musikfreunde in Wien*. Vienna, Austria: Holzhausen.

Bohn, Emil. 1887. *Festschrift zur Feier des 25jährigen Bestehens des Breslauer Orchester-Vereins*. Breslau: Hainauer.

Boleška, J. 1902. *Deset Let Českého vartetta, 1892–1902*. Prague, Czech Republic: Nákladem Mojmíra Urbánka.

Bolt, Karl Fritz. 1937."Ludwig Erk in den Briefen berühmter Zeitgenossen." *Die Tonkunst* 41, no. 18 (20 June): 277–78.

Bolte, Theodor. 1917. *Die Musikerfamilien Stein und Streicher*. Vienna, Austria: Ludwig Schönberger.

Borchard, Beatrix. 2001. "Amalie Joachim und die gesungene Geschichte des deutschen Liedes." *Archiv für Musikwissenschaft* 58: 265–99.

——. 2005. *Stimme und Geige: Amalie und Joseph Joachim. Biographie und Interpretationsgeschichte*. Vienna, Austria: Böhlau.

Borchmeyer, Dieter. 1997. "'Ich habe ihn geliebt und Niemanden sonst': Nietzsches Wagnerkritik zwischen Passion und Polemik." In *Nietzsche und die Musik*, edited by G. Pöltner and H. Vetter, 93–114. Frankfurt, Germany: Lang.

Borchmeyer, Dieter, and Jörg Salaquarda, eds. 1994. *Nietzsche und Wagner: Stationen einer epochalen Begegnung*. Frankfurt, Germany: Insel Verlag.

Botstein, Leon. 1990a. "Time and Memory: Concert Life, Science, and Music in Brahms's Vienna." In *Brahms and His World*, edited by W. Frisch, 3–22. Princeton, N.J.: Princeton University Press.

——. 1990b. "Brahms and Nineteenth-Century Painting." *19th Century Music* 14, no. 1 (Summer): 154–68.

——. 1999. "Brahms and His Audience: The Later Viennese Years, 1875–1897." In *The Cambridge Companion to Brahms*, edited by M. Musgrave, 51–77. Cambridge, UK: Cambridge University Press.

Bottenheim, S. A. M. 1948–50. *Geschiedenes van het Concertgebouw*. 3 vols. Amsterdam, The Netherlands: Joost van den Vondel.

Bottge, Karen M. 2005. "Brahms's 'Wiegenlied' and the Maternal Voice." *19th Century Music* 28, no. 3 (Spring): 185–213.

Böttger, Fritz. 1990. *Bettina von Arnim: Ihr Leben, ihre Begegnungen, ihre Zeit*. Berne, Switzerland: Scherz.

Boult, Adrian Cedric. 1973. *My Own Trumpet*. London: Hamish Hamilton.

Bouws, J. 1968. "Ein ungarischer Violinmeister in Südafrika (Ein Beitrag zur Biographie von Ede Reményi). *Studia musicologica Academiae Scientiarum Hungaricae* 10: 353–60.

Bowen, Catherine Drinker. 1939. *"Free Artist": The Story of Anton and Nicholas Rubinstein*. Boston: Little, Brown & Co.

Bozarth, George S. 1983a. "Brahms's Duets for Soprano and Alto, Op. 61." *Studia Musicologica* 25: 191–210.

——. 1983b. "The First Generation of Brahms Manuscript Collections." *Notes* 40, no. 2 (December): 239–62.

——. 1984. "Brahms Societies, Past and Present." *American Brahms Society Newsletter* 2, no. 2 (Autumn): [3–6].

——. 1985. "Leider nicht von Johannes Brahms." *American Brahms Society Newsletter* 3, no. 1 (Spring): [3–5].

——. 1986. "Klinger's Brahms." *American Brahms Society Newsletter* 4, no. 2 (Autumn): [8–9].

——. 1987. "Brahms on Record." *American Brahms Society Newsletter* 5, no. 1 (Spring): [5–9].

——. 1989. "In Memoriam Karl Geiringer." *American Brahms Society Newsletter* 7, no. 1 (Spring): 4–5.

——. 1990a. "Brahms's B major Trio: An American Première." *American Brahms Society Newsletter* 8, no. 1 (Spring): 1–4.

——. 1990b. "Brahms First Piano Concerto Op. 15: Genesis and Meaning." In *Beiträge zur Geschichte des Konzerts: Festschrift Siegfrid Kross zum 60. Geburstag*, edited by R. Emans and M. Wendt, 211–47. Bonn, Germany: Schröder.

——. 1994. "Brahms at Auction." *American Brahms Society Newsletter* 12, no. 2 (Autumn): 7–8.

——. 1995. "Brahms at Auction." *American Brahms Society Newsletter* 13, no.1 (Spring): 9.

——, ed., with Wiltrud Martin. 1996. *The Brahms–Keller Correspondence*. Lincoln, Nebr.: University of Nebraska Press.

——. 2001. "Synthesizing Word and Tone: Brahms's Setting of Hebbel's 'Vorüber.'" In *Internationaler Brahms-Kongress Gmunden 1997: Kongressbericht*, edited by I. Fuchs, 77–98. Tutzing, Germany: Schneider.

Bozarth, George S., and Stephen H. Brady. 2000."Johannes Brahms and His Pianos." *Piano Technicians' Journal* 42, no. 7 (July): 42–55. For an earlier version of this study, see the authors' "The Pianos of Johannes Brahms," 49–64 in W. Frisch 1990.

Brahms, Johannes. 1900. "Ungedruckte Briefe von Johannes Brahms [an Elise Denninghoff, née Giesemann]." *Allgemeine Musikzeitung* 27, no. 32/33 (10/17 August): 473–74.

——. 1924. *Johannes Brahms an Max Klinger*. Leipzig, Germany.

——. 1958. "Ein Brief von Johannes Brahms an Friedrich Hegar." *Schweizerische Musikzeitung* 98: 202.

——. 1974. *Briefwechsel*. Berlin: Deutsche Brahmsgesellschaft, 1910–22. Reprint Tutzing, Germany: Schneider. 16 vols., as follows:

1–2. *Johannes Brahms im Briefwechsel mit Heinrich und Elisabet von Herzogenberg*, edited by M. Kalbeck. 4th edition. 2 vols. 1921. (English translation by H. Bryant, *Johannes Brahms: The Herzogenberg Correspondence*. London: Murray, 1909. Reprint New York: Da Capo Press, 1987.)

3. *Johannes Brahms im Briefwechsel mit Karl Reinthaler, Max Bruch, Hermann Deiters, Friedrich Heimsoeth, Karl Reinecke, Ernst Rudorff, Bernhard und Luise Scholz*. 2nd revised edition by Wilhelm Altmann, 1912.

4. *Johannes Brahms im Briefwechsel mit Julius Otto Grimm*, edited by R. Barth, 1912.

5–6. *Johannes Brahms im Briefwechsel mit Joseph Joachim*, edited by A. Moser. 2 vols. Vol. 5: 3rd revised edition, 1921. Vol. 6: 2nd revised edition, 1912.

7. *Johannes Brahms im Briefwechsel mit Hermann Levi, Friedrich Gernsheim sowie den Familien Hecht und Fellinger*, edited by L. Schmidt, 1910.

8. *Johannes Brahms an Joseph Victor Widmann, Ellen und Ferdinand Vetter, Adolf Schubring*, edited by M. Kalbeck, 1915.

9–12. *Johannes Brahms: Briefe an P. J. Simrock und Fritz Simrock*, edited by M. Kalbeck. 4 vols., 1917–19.

13. *Johannes Brahms im Briefwechsel mit Th. Wilhelm Engelmann*, edited by J. Röntgen, 1918.

14. *Johannes Brahms im Briefwechsel mit Breitkopf & Härtel, Bartholf Senff, J. Rieter-Biedermann, Max Abraham, E. W. Fritzsch und Robert Lienau*, edited by W. Altmann, 1920.

15. *Johannes Brahms im Briefwechsel mit Franz Wüllner*, edited by E. Wolff, 1922.

16. *Johannes Brahms im Briefwechsel mit Philipp Spitta, Otto Dessoff*, edited by C. Krebs, 1920.

A new series of the Brahms *Briefwechsel*, edited by O. Biba, and K. Hofmann, and R. Hofmann, was launched in 1991. So far three volumes have appeared (see Brahms 1991, 1993, 1995).

——. 1985. "Johannes Brahms—Leander Schlegel." In *Brieven en Opdrachten van beroemde Musici / Briefe und Widmungen berühmter Musiker / Letters and Dedications from Famous Musicians*, introduced and annotated by W. Lievense, 57–66. Buren, The Netherlands: Knuf.

——. 1991. *Johannes Brahms im Briefwechsel mit Herzog Georg II. von Sachsen-Meiningen und Helene Freifrau von Heldburg*, edited by H. Müller and R. Hofmann. Tutzing, Germany: Schneider.

——. 1993. *Johannes Brahms im Briefwechsel mit Julius Stockhausen*, edited by R. Hofmann. Tutzing, Germany: Schneider.

——. 1995. *Johannes Brahms im Briefwechsel mit Ernst Frank*, edited by R. Münster. Tutzing, Germany: Schneider.

Brahms Exhibition. 1983. *Johannes Brahms in Wien*. Vienna, Austria: Gesellschaft der Musikfreunde in Wien. Catalog (by Otto Biba) of a Brahms exhibition at the Archives of the Gesellschaft der Musikfreunde.

Brahms Exhibition. 1997a. *"Es hat mich noch weniges so entzückt": Johannes Brahms und Franz Schubert*. Vienna, Austria: Gesellschaft der Musikfreunde. Catalog (by Otto Biba) of an exhibition at the Archives of the Gesellschaft der Musikfreunde.

Brahms Exhibition. 1997b. *"In meinen Tönen spreche ich": Für Johannes Brahms, 1833–1897*. Hamburg, Germany: Edition Braus. Catalog (by Otto Biba et al.) of a Brahms exhibition at the Museum für Kunst und Gewerbe in Hamburg.

Brahms-Institut an der Musikhochschule Lübeck: Die Sammlung Hofmann. 1992. Berlin: KulturStiftung der Länder. Contains a concise description of the collection, and articles by Carmen Debrin ("'und plötzlich hatte mich das Sammelfieber gepackt.' Der Sammler Kurt Hofmann und die Entstehung der 'Sammlung Hofmann'") and Michael Struck ("Struktur, Inhalte und Bedeutung der 'Sammlung Hofmann'").

Brahms Monument. 1908. *Zur Enthüllung des Brahms-Denkmals in Wien, 7. Mai 1908*. Brochure published on the occasion of the unveiling of Rudolf Weyr's Brahms monument in Vienna on 7 May. It contains, among other items, an article "Brahms und Wien" by Max Kalbeck.

Brahms Symposium. 1984a. *Brahms und seine Zeit: Symposium Hamburg 1983*, edited by C. Floros, H. J. Marx, and P. Petersen. [n.p.]: Laaber. (*Hamburger Jahrbuch für Musikwissenschaft* 7.)

——. 1984b. *Johannes Brahms—Leben, Werk, Interpretation, Rezeption. Kongressbericht zum III. Gewandhaus-Symposium anlässlich der "Gewandhaus-Festtage 1983."* Leipzig, Germany.

——. 1988. *Brahms-Kongress Wien 1983: Kongressbericht*, edited by S. Antonicek and O. Biba. Tutzing, Germany: Schneider.

——. 1999. *Johannes Brahms: Quellen—Text—Rezeption—Interpretation. Internationaler Brahms-Kongress Hamburg 1997*, edited by F. Krummacher and M. Struck, in collaboration with C. Floros and P. Petersen. Munich, Germany: G. Henle.

——. 2001. *Internationaler Brahms-Kongress Gmunden 1997: Kongressbericht*, edited by I. Fuchs. Tutzing, Germany: Schneider.

Bramann, Jorn K. 1974. "Karl Wittgenstein—ein Amerikaner in Wien." *Zeitgeschichte* 2: 29–40.

Brand, Erna. 1931. *Aglaja Oregni: Das Leben einer grossen Sängerin*. Munich, Germany: Beck'sche Verlagsbuchhandlung.

Brill, Franz. 1957. "Deichmann, Wilhelm Ludwig." In ***NDB***, vol. 3, 567–68. Berlin: Duncker & Humblot, 1952–.

Brinkmann, Reinhold. 1989. "Die 'heitre Sinfonie' und der 'schwer melancholische' Mensch: Johannes Brahms antwortet Vincenz Lachner." *Archiv für Musikwissenschaft* 46, 1st quarter: 296–306.

——. 1999. "Zeitgenossen: Feuerbach, Böcklin, Klinger und Menzel." In *Johannes Brahms: Quellen—Text—Rezeption—Interpretation. Internationaler Brahms-Kongress Hamburg 1997*, edited by F. Krummacher and M. Struck, in collaboration with Constantin Floros and Peter Petersen, 71–94. Munich, Germany: G. Henle.

Brodbeck, David. 1992. "Mahler's Brahms." *American Brahms Society Newsletter* 10, no. 2 (Autumn): 1–5.

Brodsky, Anna. 1904. *Recollections of a Russian Home (A Musician's Experiences)*. Manchester, UK: Sherratt & Hughes.

Brooijmans, Katja. 2001. "Brahms in The Netherlands. Concerts, Friendship, Irritation and Fun, 1876–1885." In *Internationaler Brahms-Kongress Gmunden 1997: Kongressbericht*, edited by I. Fuchs, 413–21. Tutzing, Germany: Schneider.

Brown, Maurice J. E. 1947. "Schubert's Grand Duo." *Monthly Musical Record* 77: 98–101.

Brücke, E. Th. 1928. *Ernst Brücke*. Vienna, Austria: Springer.

Bryan, George B. 1984. *An Ibsen Companion: A Dictionary-Guide to the Life, Works, and Critical Reception of Henrik Ibsen*. Westport, Conn.: Greenwood Press.

Buchholtz, Arend. 1909. *Die Geschichte der Familie Lessing*, edited by C. R. Lessing. 2 vols. Berlin.

Buek, F. Georg. 1828. *Handbuch der hamburgischen Verfassung und Verwaltung*. Hamburg, Germany: Hoffmann & Campe.

Bülow, Hans von. 1894. "Hans von Bülows Briefe an Richard Pohl." *Neue Deutsche Rundschau* 5: 446–76, 578–94, 783–801.

Bülow, Marie von, ed. 1895–1908. *Hans von Bülow: Briefe und Schriften*. 8 vols. Leipzig, Germany: Breitkopf & Härtel.

——. 1912. "Hans v. Bülow im Lichte zeitgenössischer Biographie." *Neue freie Presse*, 7 July: 31–34.

——. 1914. "Hans von Bülow und der Brahmsbiograph." *Musikpädagogische Blätter* 37: 366–67, 379–81.

——. 1925. *Hans von Bülow in Leben und Wort*. Stuttgart, Germany: J. Engelhorns Nachfolger.

Buschbell, Gottfried. 1953–54. *Geschichte der Stadt Krefeld*. Edited and enlarged by Karl Heinzelmann. 2 vols. Krefeld, Germany: Staufen.

Busoni, Ferruccio. 1929. "Jugenderinnerungen an berühmte Musiker," translated by F. Schnapp. *Westermanns Monatshefte* 177 (September): 82–84.

Cai, Camilla. 1989. "Brahms's Pianos and the Performance of His Late Piano Works." *Performance Practice Review* 2: 58–72.

Caillet, Robert. 1929. "Les Portraits des musiciens par Bonaventure Laurens à la bibliothèque de Carpentras." In *Les Trésors des bibliothèques de France*, fasc. 10, 64–70. Paris: Van Oest.

Caillet, Robert, and Erhard Göpel. 1933. "Ein Brahmsfund in Südfrankreich." *Zeitschrift für Musikwissenschaft* 15, no. 8 (May): 371–73.

Callomon, Fritz. 1943. "Some Unpublished Brahms Correspondence," translated by A. Mendel. *Musical Quarterly* 29: 32–44. (Letters to Adolph Kaufmann, founder of the Breslau Orchester-Verein, and to Georg Dietrich Otten; postcards to Gustav Dömpke and Bernhard Scholz.)

Caty, R., G. Reynaud, E. Richard, and C. Thomas. 2001. *La Campagne Castré: Du domaine privé à l'espace public*. Aix-en-Provence, France: Édisud.

Chevalley, Heinrich, ed. 1922. *Arthur Nikisch: Leben und Wirken*. Berlin: Bote & Bock.

Clapham, John. 1958. "Dvořák and the Philharmonic Society." *Music & Letters* 39: 123–34.

——. 1971. "Dvořák's Relations with Brahms and Hanslick." *Musical Quarterly* 57: 241–54.

Claus, Albrecht. n.d. *Geschichte des Singvereines der Gesellschaft der Musikfreunde 1858–1933: Zur Feier des 75jähringen Bestandes*. [Vienna].

Clayton, Alfred. 1988. "Brahms und Zemlinsky." In *Brahms-Kongress Wien 1983: Kongressbericht*, edited by S. Antonicek and O. Biba, 81–93. Tutzing, Germany: Schneider.

Clive, Peter. 1997. *Schubert and His World: A Biographical Dictionary*. Oxford, UK: Clarendon Press.

Colles, H. C., ed. 1927. *Grove's Dictionary of Music and Musicians.* 3rd edition. 5 vols. London: Macmillan.

Comini, Alessandra. 1984. "Ansichten von Brahms—Idole und Bilder." In *Johannes Brahms—Leben, Werk, Interpretation, Rezeption. Kongressbericht zum III. Gewandhaus-Symposium anlässlich der "Gewandhaus-Festtage 1983,"* 58–65. Leipzig, Germany.

——. 1987. "Johannes Brahms." In *The Changing Image of Beethoven: A Study in Mythmaking*, 305–14. New York: Rizzoli.

Conrat, Hugo. 1903. "Brahms, wie ich ihn kannte." *Neue Musik-Zeitung* 24, no. 1 (27 November 1903): 4–5; no. 2 (11 December): 17–18.

——. 1904. "Johannes Brahms. (Souvenirs personnels.)" *Revue musicale* 4, no. 21 (1 November): 314–20. Essentially an adaptation of Conrat 1903.

Cornelius, Carl Maria, ed. 1904–5. *Cornelius, Peter: Ausgewählte Briefe nebst Tagebuchblättern und Gelegenheitsgedichten*. 2 vols. Leipzig, Germany: Breitkopf & Härtel.

Cornelius, Carl Maria. 1925. *Peter Cornelius: Der Wort-und Tondichter*. 4 vols. Regensburg, Germany: Bosse.

Crowthers, Dorothy. 1924. "Franz Kneisel Recalls Some Yesterdays: Recollections of Brahms, Sarasate, Joachim, Dvořák." *Musical Observer* 23, no. 7 (July): 15, 31.

Crum, Margaret. 1987. "The Deneke-Mendelssohn Collection." *Bodleian Library Record* (April): 208–320.

Curtiss, Mina. 1959. *Bizet and His World.* London: Secker & Warburg.

Czeike, Felix. 1992–97. *Historisches Lexikon Wien*. 5 vols. Vienna, Austria: Kremayr & Scheriau.

Dane, Jeffrey. 1994. "Remembering Brahms: The Austrian Town of Mürzzuschlag is Home to the Only Museum Devoted Exclusively to Brahms Memorabilia." *Classical Music* (April/May): 18–22.

Danek, Victor B. 1962. "A Historical Study of the Kneisel Quartet." PhD diss., Indiana University.

Davies, Fanny. 1963. "Some Personal Recollections of Brahms as Pianist and Interpreter." In *Cobbett's Cyclopedic Survey of Chamber Music*, edited by W. W. Cobbett, 182–84. 2nd edition. London: Oxford University Press.

De'ak, Steven. 1980. *David Popper*. Neptune City, N.J.: Paganiniana Publications.

Deiters, Hermann. 1880. *Johannes Brahms*. Leipzig, Germany. (English version: *Johannes Brahms: A Biographical Sketch*, translation and additions by R. Newmarch; edited by J. A. Fuller Maitland. London: Fisher Unwin, 1888.)

De Lara, Adelina. 1955. *Finale*. London: Burke.

Dent, E. J. 1974. *Ferruccio Busoni*. 2nd edition. London: Eulenburg Books.

Deutsch, Otto Erich. 1951. "Schubert: The Collected Works." *Music and Letters* 32: 226–34.

——. 1960. "Die Brotarbeiten des jungen Brahms." *Österreichische Musikzeitschrift* 15: 522–23.

Dietrich, Albert. 1898. *Erinnerungen an Johannes Brahms in Briefen besonders aus seiner Jugendzeit*. Leipzig, Germany: Wigand.

Döge, Klaus. 1991. *Dvořák: Leben, Werke, Dokumente*. Mainz, Germany: Schott. (Numerous references to Brahms; in particular, see "Brahms und die Folgen," 167–79. See also "Simrock and Dvořák," 359–402.)

Dömpke, G. 1883a. "Johannes Brahms und seine neuesten Werke." *Die Gegenwart*, 374–77, 396–98.

——. 1883b. "Musik. (Zweites Philharmonisches Concert)." *Wiener allgemeine Zeitung*, 5 December, 1–3.

Door, Anton. 1903. "Persönliche Erinnerungen an Brahms." *Die Musik* 2: 216–21.

Dove, Richard. 1991. "Platen, August von." In *Literatur Lexikon: Autoren und Werke deutscher Sprache*, vol. 9, edited by W. Killy, 176–79. 15 vols. Gütersloh, Germany: Bertelsmann Lexikon Verlag, 1988–93.

Downes, Olin. 1942. "Talk with Kreisler: Violinist Discusses His Early Days and Some Contemporary Problems. " *New York Times*, 8 November, X7.

Draheim, Joachim. 1983. "Johannes Brahms und Otto Dessoff." In *Johannes Brahms in Baden-Baden und Karlsruhe*, edited by J. Draheim et al., 103–20. Karlsruhe, Germany: Badische Landesbibliothek. Exhibition catalog.

———. 1997a. "'Eine musikalische Versöhnung?' Das 'Concert für Violine und Violoncell mit Orchester von Johannes Brahms Op. 102' und seine Uraufführung in Baden-Baden." In *Johannes Brahms in den Bädern Baden-Baden—Wiesbaden, Germany—Bad Ischl—Karlsbad*, edited by J. Draheim and U. Reimann, 42–56. Baden-Baden, Germany: Stadt Baden-Baden.

———. 1997b. "Johannes Brahms in Baden-Baden: Eine Dokumentation, aus Briefen und Tagebuchaufzeichnungen." In *Johannes Brahms in den Bädern Baden-Baden—Wiesbaden, Germany—Bad Ischl—Karlsbad*, edited by J. Draheim and U. Reimann, 10–42. Baden-Baden, Germany: Stadt Baden-Baden.

———. 1997c. "Johannes Brahms in Bad Ischl." In *Johannes Brahms in den Bädern Baden-Baden—Wiesbaden, Germany—Bad Ischl—Karlsbad*, edited by J. Draheim and U. Reimann, 78–100. Baden-Baden, Germany: Stadt Baden-Baden.

———. 2001a. "'Ein guter Freund, guter Capellmeister.' Otto Dessoff—ein Portrait des Komponisten, Dirigenten und Brahms-Freundes." In *Otto Dessoff (1835–1892): Ein Dirigent, Komponist und Weggefährte von Johannes Brahms*, edited by J. Draheim and A. Jahn, 13–22. Munich, Germany: Katzbichler.

———. 2001b. "Otto Dessoff in Karlsruhe (1875–1880)." In *Otto Dessoff (1835–1892): Ein Dirigent, Komponist und Weggefährte von Johannes Brahms*, edited by J. Draheim and A. Jahn, 62–135. Munich, Germany: Katzbichler.

Draheim, Joachim, et al. 1983. *Johannes Brahms in Baden-Baden und Karlsruhe*. Karlsruhe, Germany: Badische Landesbibliothek. Exhibition catalog.

Draheim, Joachim, and Albert Jahn, eds. 2001. *Otto Dessoff (1835–1892): Ein Dirigent, Komponist und Weggefährte von Johannes Brahms*. (Contains, in addition to several articles, which are listed elsewhere in this bibliography under their authors' names, a "Zeittafel" presented by Draheim and Jahn, and a "Werkverzeichnis—Diskografie" compiled by Draheim.) Munich, Germany: Katzbichler.

Draheim, Joachim, and Ute Reimann. 1997. *Johannes Brahms in den Bädern Baden-Baden—Wiesbaden, Germany—Bad Ischl—Karlsbad*. Baden-Baden, Germany: Stadt Baden-Baden. (Catalog published on the occasion of the Brahms exhibition at Baden-Baden, 23 March–17 April 1997.)

Drinker, Sophie. 1952. *Brahms and His Women's Choruses*. Merion, Pa.: Drinker. ("Franziska Meier's Diary, 1859," 24–41.)

Droucker, Sandra. 1904. *Erinnerungen an Anton Rubinstein: Bemerkungen, Andeutungen und Besprechungen (mit vielen Notenbeispielen) in seiner Klasse im St. Petersburger Konservatorium*. Leipzig, Germany: Senff.

Dümling, Albrecht, ed. 1990. *Verteidigung des musikalischen Fortschritts: Brahms und Schönberg*. Hamburg, Germany: Argument. Includes Dümling's "Warum Schönberg Brahms für fortschriftlich hielt," 23–49.

Du Mont, Wolfgang. 1962. "Tausch, Julius." In *Rheinische Musiker*, edited by K. G. Fellerer, 2nd series: 104–8. Cologne, Germany: Arno Volk.

Dunkel, Nobert. 1933. "Unbekannte Briefe von Brahms." *Die Musik* 25: 612–13. (Four letters to his father János Nepomuk Dunk(e)l, later printed as nos. 10, 6, 16,

8 in *"In fliegender Eile möchte ich ihnen sagen." Johannes Brahms: 22 Briefe nach Ungarn*, edited by A. Gádor and W. Ebert. Mürzzuschlag, Austria: Österreichische Johannes Brahms Gesellschaft, 1993, where the first three are dated differently.)

Dunkl, J[ános] N[epomuk]. 1876. *Aus den Erinnerungen eines Musikers*. Vienna, Austria: Rosner.

Düwel, Klaus. 1991. "Speratus, Paul." In *Literatur Lexikon: Autoren und Werke deutscher Sprache*, vol. 11, edited by W. Killy, 99. 15 vols. Gütersloh, Germany: Bertelsmann Lexikon Verlag, 1988–93.

———. 1992. "Weisse, Michael." In *Literatur Lexikon: Autoren und Werke deutscher Sprache*, vol. 12, edited by W. Killy, 226–27. 15 vols. Gütersloh, Germany: Bertelsmann Lexikon Verlag, 1988–93.

Ebert, H. 1907. "Briefe von Anselm Feuerbach und Johannes Brahms." *Süddeutsche Monatshefte* 4, vol. 1 (January–June): 301–12.

Ebert, Wolfgang. 1982. *Johannes Brahms in Altaussee*. Unpublished manuscript.

———. 1984. *Johannes Brahms und Budapest*. Unpublished manuscript.

———. 1986. "Brahms in Ungarn: Nach der Studie 'Brahms Magyarorsagón' von Lajos Koch." *Studien zur Musikwissenschaft* 37: 103–64.

———. 1991. "Brahms und Joachim in Siebenbürgen." *Studien zur Musikwissenschaft* 40: 185–204.

———. 1997a. *Brahms in Aussee*. Altaussee, Austria: Verein "Kulturtreffpunkt Ausseer Land."

———. 1997b. "Die von Hermine Spies gesungenen Brahms-Lieder." *Brahms-Studien* 11: 73–81.

Eckardt, Julius. 1888. *Ferdinand David und die Familie Mendelssohn-Bartholdy*. Leipzig, Germany: Duncker & Humblot.

Eckstein, Friedrich. 1936. *"Alte unnennbare Tage!" Erinnerungen aus siebzig Lehr- und Wanderjahren*. Vienna, Austria: Reichner.

Eglinger, G. 1897. *Selmar Bagge: Biographische Skizze*. Basel, Switzerland: Werner-Riehm.

Ehinger, Hans. 1954. *E. T. A. Hoffmann als Musiker und Musikschriftsteller*. Olten, Switzerland: Walter.

Ehlert, Louis. 1884. "Brahms." In *Aus der Tonwelt: Essays*, 213–48. New series. Berlin: Behr.

Ehrismann, Sibylle. 2001. "Engagierte Verehrung und kühles Befremden: Die Brahms-Rezeption in der Schweiz bis 1900." In *Internationaler Brahms-Kongress Gmunden 1997: Kongressbericht*, edited by I. Fuchs, 175–98. Tutzing, Germany: Schneider.

Ehrlich, Cyril. 1990. "Steinway and the New Technology." In *The Piano: A History*, 47–67. London: Dent, 1976. Revised edition Oxford: Oxford University Press.

Ehrlich, Heinrich. 1888. *Aus allen Tonarten: Studien über Musik*. Berlin: Brachvogel & Ranft. Contains a chapter on Brahms.

———. 1893a. *Berühmte Klavierspieler der Vergangenheit und Gegenwart*. Leipzig, Germany: Payne. Includes articles on d'Albert, Karl Heinrich Barth, Baumayer, Brahms, Bronsart von Schellendorf, Brüll, Bülow, Davies, Door, Eibenschütz, Hiller, Jaëll, Kirchner, Mason, Reinecke, Rubinstein, and Tausig.

——. 1893b. *Dreissig Jahre Künstlerleben*. Berlin: Steinitz.

Ehrmann, Alfred von. 1933. *Johannes Brahms: Weg, Werk und Welt*. Leipzig, Germany: Breitkopf & Härtel.

——. 1937. "The 'Terrible' Brahms," translated by G. R. *Musical Quarterly* 23: 64–76.

Eibenschütz [Derenburg], Ilona. 1926. "My Recollections of Brahms." *Musical Times* 67: 598–600.

Eke, Norbert. 1989. "Halm, Friedrich." In *Literatur Lexikon: Autoren und Werke deutscher Sprache*, vol. 4, edited by W. Killy, 487–89. 15 vols. Gütersloh, Germany: Bertelsmann Lexikon Verlag, 1988–93.

Elvers, Rudolf. 1977. "Die Brahms-Autographen in der Musikabteilung der Staatsbibliothek Preussischer Kulturbesitz, Berlin." *Brahms-Studien* 2: 79–83.

Emans, Reinmar, and Matthias Wendt. 1990. *Beiträge zur Geschichte des Konzerts: Festschrift Siegfrid Kross zum 60. Geburstag*. Bonn, Germany: Schröder.

Enthoven, H. E. 1954. "Eldering, Bram." In *Grove's Dictionary of Music and Musicians*, vol. 2, edited by E. Blom, 904. 5th edition. 9 vols. London: Macmillan.

Erck, A., H.-J. Kertscher, and M. Schaefer. 1983. *Kunst und Künstler in Meiningen, 1871–1945*. Meiningen, Germany: Kulturfund der DDR.

Erck, A., H. Müller, and H. Schneider. 1987. "Zur Musikentwicklung in Meiningen Ende des 19. / Anfang des 20. Jahrhunderts." In *Zur Entwicklung Meiningens—Ende des 19. / Anfang des 20. Jahrhunderts. Kolloquium der Bezirksleitung Suhl, 14 Juni 1986, Meiningen*, 10–44. Suhl, Germany: Kulturfund der DDR.

Erck, Alfred, and Hannelore Schneider. 1997. *Georg II. von Sachsen-Meiningen: Ein Leben zwischen ererbter Macht und künstlerischer Freiheit*. Meiningen, Germany: Zella-Mehlis.

Erismann, Hans. 1974. *Johannes Brahms und Zürich*. Zürich, Switzerland: Fretz.

Esche-Braunfels, Sigrid. 1993. *Adolf von Hildebrand (1847–1921)*. Berlin: Deutscher Verlag für Kunstwissenschaft.

Ettlinger, Anna. 1913. "Johannes Brahms und Hermann Levi." *Neue Musik-Zeitung* 34, no. 2: 29–32.

——. 1920. *Lebenserrinerungen, für ihre Familie verfasst*. Leipzig, Germany.

Ewen, David. 1942. *Music Comes to America*. New York: Thomas Y. Cromwell Co.

Fay, Amy. 1965. *Music-Study in Germany in the Nineteenth Century*. Chicago: McClurg & Co., 1880. Reprint New York: Dover Publications.

Federhofer-Königs, Renate. 1974. "Der Briefwechsel von Wilhelm Joseph von Wasielewski (1822–1896) in seiner Bedeutung für die Schumann-Forschung." In *Convivium Musicorum: Festschrift Wolfgang Boetticher zum sechzigsten Geburtstag am 19. August 1974*, edited by H. Moser and D.-R. Moser, 52–67. Berlin: Merseburger.

——. 1975. "Briefe von und an Clara Schumann (1819–96)" and "Briefe von und an Johannes Brahms (1833–1897)." In Federhofer-Königs's *Wilhelm Joseph von Wasielewski (1822–1896) im Spiegel seiner Korrespondenz*, 29–80, 163–78. Tutzing, Germany: Schneider.

Fellerer, Karl Gustav. 1960–67. *Rheinische Musiker*. Cologne, Germany: Arno Volk. 1st series, 1960; 2nd series, 1962; 3rd series, 1964; 4th series, 1966; 5th series, 1967.

Fellinger, Imogen. 1964. "Rudorff, Ernst Friedrich Carl." In *Rheinische Musiker*, edited by K. G. Fellerer, 3rd series: 77–81. Cologne, Germany: Arno Volk.

———. 1965. "Das Brahms-Bild der *Allgemeinen Musikalischen Zeitung* (1863 bis 1882)." In *Beiträge zur Geschichte der Musikkritik*, edited by H. Becker, 27–54. Regensburg, Germany: Bosse.

———. 1966. "Steinbach, Fritz." In *Rheinische Musiker*, edited by K. G. Fellerer, 4th series: 158–60. Cologne, Germany: Arno Volk.

———. 1969. "Brahms und die Musik vergangener Epochen." In *Die Ausbreitung des Historismus über die Musik: Aufsätze und Diskussionen*, edited by W. Wiora, 147–63 (followed by a discussion, 164–67). Regensburg, Germany: Bosse.

———. 1981. "Johannes Brahms und Richard Mühlfeld." *Brahms-Studien* 4: 77–93.

———. 1983a. "Brahms's View of Mozart." In *Brahms: Biographical, Documentary and Analytical Studies*, edited by R. Pascall, 41–57. Cambridge, UK: Cambridge University Press.

———. 1983b. "Brahms und Mozart." *Brahms-Studien* 5: 141–68.

———. 1984. "Brahms und die Neudeutsche Schule." In *Brahms und seine Zeit: Symposium Hamburg 1983*, edited by C. Floros, H. J. Marx, and P. Petersen, 159–69. [n.p.]: Laaber. (*Hamburger Jahrbuch für Musikwissenschaft* 7.)

———. 1988. "Brahms' beabsichtigte Streitschrift gegen Erk-Böhmes *Deutscher Liederhort*." In *Brahms-Kongress Wien 1983: Kongressbericht*, edited by S. Antonicek and O. Biba, 139–53. Tutzing, Germany: Schneider.

———. 1989. "Das Händel-Bild von Brahms." *Göttinger Händel Beiträge* 3: 235–57.

———. 1990. "Brahms und die Gattung des Instrumentalkonzerts." In *Beiträge zur Geschichte des Konzerts: Festschrift Siegfrid Kross zum 60. Geburstag*, edited by R. Emans and M. Wendt, 201–9. Bonn, Germany: Schröder.

———. 2001. "Brahms und Philipp Spitta." In *Internationaler Brahms-Kongress Gmunden 1997: Kongressbericht*, edited by I. Fuchs, 437–57. Tutzing, Germany: Schneider.

Fellinger, Maria. 1911. *Johannes Brahms: Bilder*. Vienna, 1900. 2nd, enlarged edition, Leipzig, Germany: Breitkopf & Härtel.

Fellinger, Richard. 1997. *Klänge um Brahms: Erinnerungen*. Berlin: Deutsche Brahms-Gesellschaft, 1933. New edition by Imogen Fellinger, Mürzzuschlag, Austria: Österreichische Johannes Brahms-Gesellschaft.

Feuerbach, Anselm. 1902. *Ein Vermächtnis*. 5th edition. Vienna, Austria: Carl Gerold's Sohn.

Fifield, Christopher. 1988. *Max Bruch: His Life and Works*. London: Gollancz.

———. 1993. *True Artist and True Friend: A Biography of Hans Richter*. Oxford, UK: Oxford University Press.

Finck, Henry T. 1971. *Grieg and His Music*. London, 1910. Reissued New York: Blom.

Fischer, Georg, ed. 1897. *Briefe von Theodor Billroth*. 4th enlarged edition. Hanover, Germany: Hahn'sche Buchhandlung.

———. 1903. *Musik in Hannover*. 2nd, enlarged edition. Hanover, Germany: Hahn'sche Buchhandlung.

Fitzlyon, April. 1964. *The Price of Genius: A Life of Pauline Viardot*. London: John Calder.

Fleischer, Hugo. 1918. "Der Brahmsgegner Hugo Wolf." *Der Merker* 9, no. 24 (15 December): 847–56.

Flindell, E. Fred. 1969. "Ursprung und Geschichte der Sammlung Wittgenstein im 19 Jahrhundert." *Musikforschung* 22, no. 1 (January–March): 298–314.

Frank, Paul, and Wilhelm Altmann. 1983. *Kurzgefasstes Tonkünstler-Lexicon für Musiker und Freunde der Musik*. Founded by Paul Frank and enlarged by Wilhelm Altmann. 15th ed., 1936. Part 1. Reprint Wilhelmshaven, Germany: Heinrichshofen's Verlag.

Franken, Franz Hermann. 1991. "Johannes Brahms (1833–1897)." In *Die Krankheiten grosser Komponisten*, vol. 2, 245–89. 2nd edition. 2 vols. Wilhelmshaven, Germany: Florian Noetzel, *Taschenbücher zur Musikwissenschaft* 104–5.

Franzeni, Titus. See A. Schumann 1926.

Frei, Adolf. 1914. "Josef Viktor Widmann." In *Schweizer Dichter*, 151–59. Leipzig, Germany: Quelle & Meyer.

Freund, Robert. 1951. *Memoiren eines Pianisten*. Zurich, Switzerland: Gebruder Hug & Co.

Frevel, Stefan. 1989. "Geibel, (Franz) Emanuel (August) von." In *Literatur Lexikon: Autoren und Werke deutscher Sprache*, vol. 4, edited by W. Killy, 98–99. 15 vols. Gütersloh, Germany: Bertelsmann Lexikon Verlag, 1988–93.

Friedl, Hans. 1992. "Dalwigk zu Lichtenfels: Reinhard Ludwig Gustav Freiherr von." In *Biographisches Handbuch zur Geschichte des Landes Oldenburg*, edited by H. Friedl et al., 139–40. Oldenburg, Germany: Isensee Verlag.

Friedlaender, Max. 1902. "Brahms' Volkslieder." *Jahrbuch der Musikbibliothek Peters*, 9: 66–88.

———. 1918. "Zuccalmaglio und das Volkslied: Ein Beitrag zur Stilkritik des deutschen Volkslied." *Jahrbuch der Musikbibliothek Peters* 25: 53–80.

———. 1922. *Brahms' Lieder: Einführung in seine Gesänge für eine und zwei Stimmen*. Berlin: Simrock.

———. 1923. "Brahms' deutsche Volkslieder." *Deutsche Rundschau* 193: 177–82.

Frisch, Hans, ed. 1981. *Aus Gottfried Kellers glücklicher Zeit: Der Dichter im Briefwechsel mit Marie und Adolf Exner*. Vienna, Austria: Speidel'sche Verlagsbuchhandlung, 1927. New, enlarged edition by Irmgard Smidt, Stäfa (Zurich), Switzerland: Gut & Co.

Frisch, Walter. 1983. "Brahms and Schubring: Musical Criticism and Politics at Mid-Century." *19th Century Music* 7, no. 1 (Summer): 271–81.

———. 1986. "Brahms and the Herzogenbergs." *American Brahms Society Newsletter* 4, no. 1 (Spring): 1–3.

———, ed. 1990. *Brahms and His World*. Princeton, N.J.: Princeton University Press.

Fröschle, Hartmut. 1990. "Kerner, Justinus (Andreas Christian)." In *Literatur Lexikon: Autoren und Werke deutscher Sprache*, vol. 6, edited by W. Killy, 300–302. 15 vols. Gütersloh, Germany: Bertelsmann Lexikon Verlag, 1988–93.

———. 1991. "Uhland, (Johann) Ludwig." In *Literatur Lexikon: Autoren und Werke deutscher Sprache*, vol. 11, edited by W. Killy, 464–66. 15 vols. Gütersloh, Germany: Bertelsmann Lexikon Verlag, 1988–93.

Frühwald, Wolfgang. 1989. "Brentano, Clemens." In *Literatur Lexikon: Autoren und Werke deutscher Sprache*, vol. 2, edited by W. Killy, 201–17. 15 vols. Gütersloh, Germany: Bertelsmann Lexikon Verlag, 1988–93.

Fuchs, Ingrid. 1988. "Zeitgenössische Aufführungen der ersten Symphonie Op. 68 von Johannes Brahms in Wien: Studien zur Wiener Brahms-Rezeption." In *Brahms-Kongress Wien 1983: Kongressbericht*, edited by S. Antonicek and O. Biba, 167–86, 489–515. Tutzing, Germany: Schneider.

——. 1999. "*De mortuis nil sine bene*—oder doch nicht? Das Brahmsbild in den Nachrufen." In *Johannes Brahms: Quellen—Text—Rezeption—Interpretation. Internationaler Brahms-Kongress Hamburg 1997*, edited by F. Krummacher and M. Struck, in collaboration with C. Floros and P. Petersen, 495–509. Munich, Germany: G. Henle.

——. 2001. "Das Brahmsbild des ausgehenden 19. Jahrhunderts im Ausland am Beispiel ausgewählter Nachrufe." In *Internationaler Brahms-Kongress Gmunden 1997: Kongressbericht*, edited by I. Fuchs, 161–73. Tutzing, Germany: Schneider.

Fusner, Henry. 1983. "Brahms and the von Beckerath Family." *American Organist* 17, no. 5 (May): 47–48.

Gade, Dagmar, ed. 1894. *Niels W. Gade: Aufzeichnungen und Briefe*, translated from Danish. Basel, Switzerland: Geering.

Gádor, Ágnes, and Wolfgang Ebert. 1993. *"In fliegender Eile möchte ich ihnen sagen." Johannes Brahms: 22 Briefe nach Ungarn*. Mürzzuschlag, Austria: Österreichische Johannes Brahms Gesellschaft.

Gál, Hans. 1961. *Johannes Brahms: Werk und Persönlichkeit*. Frankfurt, Germany: Fischer. (English version: *Johannes Brahms: His Work and Personality*, translated by J. Stein. New York: Knopf, 1963.)

Gárdonyi, Zoltán. 1963. "Rózsavölgyi, Mark" and "Rózsavölgyi és Társa." In *Die Musik in Geschichte und Gegenwart: Allgemeine Enzyklopaedie der Musik*, vol. 11, edited by F. Blume, 1030–31. 17 vols. Kassel, Germany: Bärenreiter, 1949–86.

Gast, Peter. 1897. "Nietzsche und Brahms." *Die Zukunft* 19: 266–69.

Gaugusch, Georg. 2001. "Die Familien Wittgenstein und Salzer und ihr genealogisches Umfeld." *Adler* 21 [35], no. 4 (October/December): 120–45.

Gay, Peter. 1978. *Freud, Jews and Other Germans: Masters and Victims in Modernist Culture*. New York: Oxford University Press. See, in particular, "Hermann Levi: A Study in Service and Self-Hatred," 189–232; "Aimez-vous Brahms? On Polarities in Modernism," 231–56; "For Beckmesser: Eduard Hanslick, Victim and Prophet," 257–75.

Geiringer, Karl. 1933. "Johannes Brahms im Briefwechsel mit Eusebius Mandyczewski." *Zeitschrift für Musikwissenschaft* 15, no. 8 (May): 337–70.

——. 1935. "Der Brahms-Freund C. F. Pohl: Unbekannte Briefe des Haydn-Biographen an Johannes Brahms." *Neue Zeitschrift für Musik* 102, no. 4 (April): 397–99.

——. 1936. "Wagner and Brahms, With Unpublished Letters," translated by M. D. Herter Norton. *Musical Quarterly* 22: 178–89.

——. 1937–38. "Brahms and Chrysander." *Monthly Musical Record* 67 (1937): 97–99, 131–32, 178–80; 68 (1938): 76–79.

——. 1938. "Brahms und Henschel: Some Hitherto Unpublished Letters." *Musical Times* 79: 173–74.

——. 1974. "Schumanniana in der Bibliothek von Johannes Brahms." In *Convivium Musicorum: Festschrift Wolfgang Boetticher zum sechzigsten Geburtstag am 19. August 1974*, edited by H. Hüschen and D.-R. Moser, 79–82. Berlin: Merseburger.

——. 1982. *Brahms: His Life and Work*. In collaboration with Irene Geiringer. 2nd edition. New York: Oxford University Press, 1947. Reprint New York: Doubleday, Anchor Books, 1961; and New York: Da Capo.

——. 1988. "Das Bilderbuch der Geschwister Ettlinger: Zur Jugendgeschichte Hermann Levis und seiner Freunde Johannes Brahms und Julius Allgeyer." *Musik in Bayern* 37: 41–68.

Geiser, Samuel. 1976. "Josef Viktor Widmann." In *Beethoven und die Schweiz. Zum 150: Todestag Beethovens*, 178–213. Zurich, Switzerland: Rotapfel-Verlag.

Glasenapp, Carl F. 1905. *Das Leben Richard Wagners*. 6 vols. 4th edition. Leipzig, Germany: Breitkopf & Härtel.

Gleisberg, Dieter, ed. 1992. *Max Klinger, 1857–1920*. Leipzig, Germany: Edition Leipzig.

Gockel, Heinz. 1990. "Mörike, Eduard (Friedrich)." In *Literatur Lexikon: Autoren und Werke deutscher Sprache*, vol. 8, edited by W. Killy, 186–89. 15 vols. Gütersloh, Germany: Bertelsmann Lexikon Verlag, 1988–93.

Göhler, Albert, ed. 1904. *Der Riedel-Verein zu Leipzig: Eine Denkschrift zur Feier seines fünfzigjährigen Bestehens*. Leipzig, Germany: Riedel-Verein.

Goldhammer, O. 1963. "Liszt, Brahms und Reményi." *Studia Musicologica Academiae Scientiarium Hungaricae* 5: 89–100.

Goldmann, Bernd. 1989. "Bodenstedt, Friedrich (Martin) von." In *Literatur Lexikon: Autoren und Werke deutscher Sprache*, vol. 2, edited by W. Killy, 44–45. 15 vols. Gütersloh, Germany: Bertelsmann Lexikon Verlag, 1988–93.

Goldmark, Karl. 1922. *Erinnerungen aus meinem Leben*. Vienna, Austria: Ricola.

Göllerich, August. 1908. *Franz Liszt*. Berlin, Germany: Marquardt & Co.

——. 1974. *Anton Bruckner: Ein Lebens- und Schaffens-Bild*. Expanded and edited after Göllerich's death by M. Auer. 4 vols. Regensburg, Germany: Bosse, 1922–37. Reprint Regensburg, Germany: Bosse.

Golther, Wolfgang, ed. 1907. *Robert Franz und Arnold Freiherr Senfft von Pilsach: Ein Briefwechsel 1861–1888*. Berlin: Duncker.

Gomperz, Theodor. 1905. *Essays und Erinnerungen*. Stuttgart, Germany: Deutsche Verlags-Anstalt.

Good, Edwin M. 2001. *Giraffes, Black Dragons, and Other Pianos: A Technological History from Cristofori to the Modern Concert Grand*. 2nd edition. Stanford, Calif.: Stanford University Press.

Gottlieb-Billroth, Otto, ed. 1935. *Billroth und Brahms im Briefwechsel*. Berlin: Urban & Schwarzenberg.

Göttsche, Dirk. 1992. "Voss, Richard." In *Literatur Lexikon: Autoren und Werke deutscher Sprache*, vol. 12, edited by W. Killy, 66–67. 15 vols. Gütersloh, Germany: Bertelsmann Lexikon Verlag, 1988–93.

Graedener, Karl Paul Felix. 1920. *Meine Jugenderinnerungen*. Libau, Latvia: Gottl. D. Meyer.

Graessner, Franz. 1929. "Erinnerungen an Ernst H. Seyffardts Jugendzeit." *Die Heimat* [Krefeld, Germany] 8: 48–49.

Graf, Max. 1945. "Recollections of Johannes Brahms." In *Legend of a Musical City*, 97–114. New York: Philosophical Library. (Slightly reworked in "Erinnerungen an Johannes Brahms," In the German version *Legende einer Musikstadt*, 155–83. Vienna, Austria: Österreichische Buchgemeinschaft, 1949.)

Grasberger, Franz. 1960. "Johannes Brahms und Hugo Wolf." *Österreichische Musikzeitschrift* 15: 67–69.

——, ed. in collaboration with Franz Strauss and Alice Strauss. 1967a. *"Der Strom der Töne trug mich fort": Die Welt um Richard Strauss in Briefen*. Tutzing, Germany: Schneider.

——. 1967b. "Gustav Nottebohm: Verdienste und Schicksal eines Musikgelehrten." *Österreichische Musikzeitschrift* 22: 730–41.

Grasberger, Renate, and Erich Wolfgang Partsch, with Uwe Harten. 1991. *Bruckner skizziert: Ein Portrait in ausgewählten Erinnerungen und Anekdoten*. Vienna, Austria: Musikwissenschaftlicher Verlag.

Grimm, Julius Otto. 1900/91. "Erinnerungen aus meinem Musikerleben." *Jahresbericht des Westfälischen Provinzialvereins für Wissenschaft und Kunst* 29: 151–60.

Gruber, Gernot. 1995. "Johannes Brahms (1833–97) and Anton Bruckner (1824–96)." In *Musikgeschichte Österreichs*, vol. 3, edited by R. Flotzinger and G. Gruber, 62–73. 2nd enlarged edition. Vienna, Austria: Böhlau.

Grunsky, Peter. 2002. "Im Bannkreis von Johannes Brahms." In *Richard Heuberger: Der Operettenprofessor*, 51–68. Vienna, Austria: Böhlau.

Günther, Robert. 1967. "Zuccalmaglio, Anton Wilhelm Florentin von." In *Rheinische Musiker*, edited by K. G. Fellerer, 5th series: 138–46. Cologne, Germany: Arno Volk.

Gurlitt, Wilibald. 1937. "Aus den Briefen Max Regers an Hugo Riemann." *Jahrbuch der Musikbibliothek Peters* 43: 68–83.

Gutiérrez-Denhoff, Martella, ed. 1997a. *Johannes Brahms und Bonn*. Bonn, Germany: Stadt Bonn.

——. 1997b. "Johannes Brahms' Aufenthalte in Bonn, nach Briefen und zeitgenössischen Dokumenten." In *Johannes Brahms und Bonn*, edited by M. Gutiérrez-Denhoff, 9–24. Bonn, Germany: Stadt Bonn.

Gutmann, Albert. 1914. *Aus dem Wiener Musikleben. Künstlererinnerungen 1873–1908*. Vienna, Austria: Gutmann.

Haas, Frithjof. 1995. *Zwischen Brahms und Wagner: Der Dirigent Hermann Levi*. Zurich, Switzerland: Atlantis Musikbuch-Verlag.

——. 2001. "Die Uraufführung der Ersten Sinfonie von Johannes Brahms." In *Johannes Brahms in Baden-Baden und Karlsruhe*, edited by J. Draheim et al., 121–32. Karlsruhe, Germany: Badische Landesbibliothek, 1983. Exhibition catalog. Revised version in *Otto Dessoff (1835–1892): Ein Dirigent, Komponist und Weggefährte von Johannes Brahms*, edited by J. Draheim and A. Jahn, 136–48. Munich, Germany: Katzbichler.

Haberland, Detlef. 1988. "Alexis, Willibald." In *Literatur Lexikon: Autoren und Werke deutscher Sprache*, vol.1, 105–6, edited by W. Killy. 15 vols. Gütersloh, Germany: Bertelsmann Lexikon Verlag, 1988–93.

Haeussermann, Ernst. 1975. *Das Wiener Burgtheater*. Vienna, Austria: Fritz Molden.

Haider, Edgard. 1984. *Verlorenes Wien: Adelspaläste vergangener Tage*. Vienna, Austria: H. Böhlau's Nachfolger. In particular, see "Palais Miller-Aichholz" [the mansion owned by Eugen von Miller zu Aichholz], 152–57; and "Palais Wittgenstein," 158–62.

Haine, Malou. 2001. "Did Nineteenth Century Belgium Like Brahms?" In *Internationaler Brahms-Kongress Gmunden 1997: Kongressbericht*, edited by I. Fuchs, 227–79. Tutzing, Germany: Schneider.

Hallé, C. E., and Marie Hallé, eds. 1896. *Life and Letters of Sir Charles Hallé, Being an Autobiography (1819–1860) with Correspondence and Diaries*. London: Smith, Elder & Co.

Hamann, Johann, et al. 1986. *Rund um die Gängeviertel: Hamburg 1889–1930*. Photographs selected by W. Uka (Edition Photothek 14). Berlin: Dirk Nishen.

Hanau, Heinrich. 1903. *Dr. Hoch's Conservatorium zu Frankfurt am Main: Festschrift zur Feier seines fünfundzwanzigjährigen Bestehens (1878–1903)*. Frankfurt, Germany.

Hancock, Virginia. 1984. "Brahms's Performances of Early Choral music." *19th Century Music* 8, no. 1 (Summer): 125–41.

——. 1988. "Brahms' Aufführungen früher Chormusik in Wien," translated by B. Gross. In *Brahms-Kongress Wien 1983: Kongressbericht*, edited by S. Antonicek and O. Biba, 199–228. Tutzing, Germany: Schneider.

Hanslick, Eduard. 1869. *Geschichte des Concertwesens in Wien*. Vienna, Austria: Braumüller.

——. 1886. *Concerte, Componisten und Virtuosen der letzten fünfzehn Jahre, 1870–1885*. 2nd edition. Berlin: Allgemeiner Verein für Deutsche Litteratur.

——. 1894. *Aus meinem Leben*. 2 vols. 3rd edition. Berlin: Allgemeiner Verein für Deutsche Litteratur.

——. 1897a. "Aus Johannes Brahms' letzten Tagen." *Neue freie Presse*, 4 April, 1–2.

——. 1897b. "Johannes Brahms (Erinnerungen und Briefe)." *Neue freie Presse*, 27 June 1897, 1–3; 29 June 1897, 1–2; 1 July 1897, 1–4; 6 July 1897, 1–4. (Italian version by Paola Tonini in *Il Convegno musicale* 2 [1965], no. 3/4: 3–21; English version by Susan Gillespie in *Brahms and His World*, edited by W. Frisch, 163–84. Princeton, N.J.: Princeton University Press, 1990.)

——. 1899. *Am Ende des Jahrhunderts (1895–1899): Musikalische Kritiken und Schilderungen*. Berlin: Allgemeiner Verlag für Deutsche Litteratur.

——. 1900. *Aus neuer und neuester Zeit*. 2nd edition. Berlin: Allgemeiner Verein für Deutsche Litteratur.

Häntzschel, Hiltrud. 1990. "Heyse, Paul." In *Literatur Lexikon: Autoren und Werke deutscher Sprache*, vol. 5, edited by W. Killy, 306–7. 15 vols. Gütersloh, Germany: Bertelsmann Lexikon Verlag, 1988–93.

——. 1994. "Meysenbug . . . Malwida." In ***NDB***, vol. 17, 4407–9. Berlin: Duncker & Humblot, 1952–.

Harten, Uwe. 1985. "Max Kalbeck." In *Bruckner Symposion: Johannes Brahms und Anton Bruckner . . . 8.–11. September 1983*, edited by O. Wessely, 122–32. Linz, Austria: Anton Bruckner-Institut Linz.

Hase, Oskar von. 1917–19. *Breitkopf & Härtel: Gedenkschrift und Arbeitsbericht.* 4th edition. 2 vols. Leipzig, Germany: Breitkopf & Härtel.

Hase-Koehler, Else von, ed. 1928. *Max Reger: Briefe eines deutschen Meisters. Ein Lebensbild.* Leipzig, Germany: Koehler & Amelang.

Hauch, Gunnar, ed. 1922. *Breve fra Grieg*. Copenhagen, Denmark: Gyldendalske.

Hausmann, Friedrich Bernhard. 1987. "Brahms und Hausmann." *Brahms-Studien* 7: 21–39.

Heermann, Hugo. 1935. *Lebenserinnerungen*. Leipzig, Germany: Brockhaus.

Heinen, Jeannot. 1983. "Das Brahmshaus in Baden-Lichtental." In *Johannes Brahms in Baden-Baden und Karlsruhe*, edited by J. Draheim et al., 10–16. Karlsruhe, Germany: Badische Landesbibliothek. Exhibition catalog.

Heldburg, Ellen Franz. 1926. *Freifrau von Heldburg (Ellen Franz): Fünfzig Jahre Glück und Leid. Ein Leben in Briefen aus den Jahren 1873–1923*, edited by J. Werner. Leipzig, Germany: Koehler & Amelang.

Heller, Friedrich C. 1985. "Der Musiker in seiner gesellschaftlichen Stellung in Wien in der zweiten Hälfte des 19. Jahrhunderts: Am Beispiel Brahms und Bruckner." In *Bruckner Symposion: Johannes Brahms und Anton Bruckner . . . 8.–11. September 1983*, edited by O. Wessely, 41–47. Linz, Austria: Anton Bruckner-Institut Linz.

Hellsberg, Clemens. 1992. *Demokratie der Könige: Die Geschichte der Wiener Philharmoniker*. Zurich, Switzerland: Schweizer Verlagshaus.

——. 2001. "Otto Dessoff und die Wiener Philharmoniker." In *Otto Dessoff (1835–1892): Ein Dirigent, Komponist und Weggefährte von Johannes Brahms*, edited by J. Draheim and A. Jahn, 41–60. Munich, Germany: Katzbichler.

Helms, Siegmund. 1971. "Johannes Brahms und Johann Sebastian Bach." *Bach-Jahrbuch* 57: 13–81.

Henschel, George. 1978. *Personal Recollections of Johannes Brahms: Some of His Letters to and Pages from a Journal Kept by George Henschel*. Boston: Badger, 1907. Reprint New York: AMS Press.

Henschel, Helen. 1944. *When Soft Voices Die: A Musical Biography*. London: Westhouse.

Herbeck, Ludwig. 1885. *Johann Herbeck: Ein Lebensbild*. Vienna, Austria: Gutmann.

Hermann, Arthur. 1932. "Bronislav Huberman." *The Strad* 42: 530–32.

Herttrich, Ernst. 1988. "Brahms-Aufführungen in Wien—Rezensionen und Materialen." In *Brahms-Kongress Wien 1983: Kongressbericht*, edited by S. Antonicek and O. Biba, 229–43. Tutzing, Germany: Schneider.

——. 1997. "Brahms' Beziehungen zu den drei 'Bonnern,' Albert Dietrich, Hermann Deiters und Otto Jahn." In *Johannes Brahms und Bonn*, edited by M. Gutiérrez-Denhoff, 80–88. Bonn, Germany: Stadt Bonn.

Hess, Emil. 1962. *Der fröhliche Musikant*, edited by M. Hess. Vienna, Austria: Europäischer Verlag.

Heuberger, Richard. 1976. *Erinnerungen an Johannes Brahms: Tagebuchnotizen aus den Jahren 1875 bis 1897*, edited by K. Hofmann. Tutzing, Germany: Schneider.

Heussner, Horst. 1988. "Der Brahmsschüler Gustav Jenner." In *Brahms-Kongress Wien 1983: Kongressbericht*, edited by S. Antonicek and O. Biba, 247–57. Tutzing, Germany: Schneider.

Hevesi, Ludwig. 1903. "Max Klinger's Entwurf zu einem Brahmsdenkmal." *Zeitschrift für bildende Kunst*, new series 14, no. 9 (September): 236–38.

Hiller, Ferdinand, ed. 1876. *Briefe von Moritz Hauptmann, Kantor und Musikdirektor an der Thomasschule zu Leipzig, an Ludwig Spohr und andere*. Leipzig, Germany: Breitkopf & Härtel.

Hinrichsen, Hans-Joachim, ed. 1994. *Hans von Bülow: Die Briefe an Johannes Brahms*. Tutzing, Germany; Schneider.

Hirschfeld, Robert. See Perger and Hirschfeld 1912.

Hitschmann, Eduard. 1933. "Johannes Brahms und die Frauen." *Psychoanalytische Bewegung* 5, no. 2 (March/April): 97–129.

Hoffmann von Fallersleben, August Heinrich. 1868. *Mein Leben: Aufzeichnungen und Erinnerungen*. 6 vols. Hanover, Germany: Rümpler.

Hofmann, Kurt. 1973. *Johannes Brahms und Kiel: Ein Beitrag zur Musikgeschichte Kiels*. Hamburg, Germany: Brahms-Gesellschaft.

——. 1974. *Die Bibliothek von Johannes Brahms. Bücher- und Musikalienverzeichnis*. Hamburg, Germany: Karl Dieter Wagner.

——. 1975. *Die Erstdrucke der Werke von Johannes Brahms: Bibliographie*. Tutzing, Germany: Schneider.

——. 1979a. "Brahmsiana der Familie Petersen: Erinnerungen und Briefe." *Brahms-Studien* 3: 69–105.

——. 1979b. *Johannes Brahms in den Erinnerungen von Richard Barth: Barths Wirken in Hamburg*. Hamburg, Germany: Schuberth & Co.

——. 1981a. "Die Beziehungen zwischen Johannes Brahms und Theodor Kirchner, dargestellt an den überlieferten Briefen." In *Festschrift Hans Schneider zum 60: Geburtstag,* edited by R. Elvers and E. Vögel, 135–47. Munich, Germany: Vögel.

——. 1981b. "Ein neuaufgefundener Brief von Johannes Brahms an seine Stiefmutter." *Brahms-Studien* 4: 94–96.

——. 1983. "Marginalien zum Wirken des jungen Johannes Brahms." *Österreichische Musikzeitschrift* 38: 235–44.

——. 1984. "Johannes Brahms' Wirken in Hamburg bis zum Jahre 1862: Eine biographische Standortbestimmung." In *Johannes Brahms—Leben, Werk, Interpretation, Rezeption. Kongressbericht zum III. Gewandhaus-Symposium anlässlich der "Gewandhaus-Festtage 1983,"* 14–25. Leipzig, Germany.

——. 1986. *Johannes Brahms und Hamburg. Neue Erkenntnisse zu einem alten Thema, mit 29 Abbildungen.* 2nd, revised edition. Reinbek, Germany: Dialog-Verlag. (Contains text of Brahms' mother's last letter to him.)

——. 1999. "Brahms the Musician, 1833–1862," translated by M. Musgrave. In *The Cambridge Companion to Brahms*, edited by M. Musgrave, 3–30. Cambridge, UK: Cambridge University Press.

——. 2001. "Johannes Brahms' letzte Lebenszeit: Unveröffentliche Dokumente im Brahms-Institut Lübeck." In *Internationaler Brahms-Kongress Gmunden 1997: Kongressbericht*, edited by I. Fuchs, 531–51. Tutzing, Germany: Schneider.

——. 2002. "Ein Brahms-Denkmal für Hamburg? Zur Geschichte ds Modells von Reinhold Felderhoff." *Brahms-Studien* 13: 117–28.

——. 2003. *"Sehnsucht habe ich immer nach Hamburg": Johannes Brahms und seine Vaterstadt. Legende und Wirklichkeit*. Reinbek, Germany: Dialog-Verlag.

Hofmann, Kurt, and Renate Hofmann. 1983. *Johannes Brahms: Zeittafel zu Leben und Werk*. Tutzing, Germany: Schneider.

——. 1985. "Frauen um Johannes Brahms, von einer Freundin im Adressen-Buch des Komponisten vermerkt: Eine erste Bestandaufnahme." In *Festschrift Rudolf Elvers zum 60. Geburtstag*, edited by E. Herttrich and H. Schneider, 257–70. Tutzing, Germany; Schneider.

——. 1996. *Johannes Brahms in Baden-Baden*. Karben, Germany: CODA Verlag.

——, eds. 1997. *Über Brahms: Von Musikern, Dichtern und Liebhabern. Eine Anthologie*. Stuttgart, Germany: Philipp Reclam.

——. 2002. *Johannes Brahms privat: Tafelfreuden und Geselligkeit*. Heide, Germany: Boyens.

——. 2003. *Johannes Brahms auf Schloss Altenstein*. Altenburg, Germany: Kamprad.

Hofmann, Renate. 1984. "Johannes Brahms im Spiegel der Korrespondenz Clara Schumanns." In 1984. *Brahms und seine Zeit: Symposium Hamburg 1983*, edited by C. Floros, H. J. Marx, and P. Petersen, 45–58. [n.p.]: Laaber. Also in *Hamburger Jahrbuch für Musikwissenschaft* 7 (1984): 45–58.

——. 1986. *Clara Schumanns Briefe an Theodor Kirchner, mit einer Lebensskizze des Komponisten*. Tutzing, Germany: Schneider.

——. 1997. "Johannes Brahms' erste Reise an den Rhein: Ein unbekannter Brief von Johannes Brahms an Arnold Wehner." In *Johannes Brahms und Bonn*, edited by M. Guitiérrez-Denhoff, 25–431. Bonn, Germany: Stadt Bonn.

——. 1999a. "Aus dem Umkreis von Johannes Brahms: Der Schweizer Komponist August Walter und seine Korrespondenz." *Brahms-Studien* 12: 60–84.

——. 1999b. "Die Briefsammlung August Walter: Die Beziehungen zwischen August Walter und Johannes Brahms dargestellt auf der Grundlage der Korrespondenz August Walters und seiner Erinnerungen aus seinem Nachlass im Brahms-Institut Lübeck." In *Johannes Brahms: Quellen—Text—Rezeption—Interpretation. Internationaler Brahms-Kongress Hamburg 1997*, edited by F. Krummacher and M. Struck, in collaboration with C. Floros and P. Petersen, 267–78. Munich, Germany: G. Henle.

——. 2001. "Die Beziehungen zwischen Marie Rückert (1835–1920) und Johannes Brahms." In *Internationaler Brahms-Kongress Gmunden 1997: Kongressbericht*, edited by I. Fuchs, 393–411. Tutzing, Germany: Schneider.

——. 2002. "'Das nöthige Salz zur grossen Wassersuppe': Ein unbekanntes Schreiben von Johannes Brahms an Elisabeth von Herzogenberg." *Brahms-Studien* 13: 51–65.

——. 2005. "Eine Brahms-Komposition für die Enthüllungsfeier des Rückert-Denkmals in Schweinfurt?" *Brahms-Studien* 14: 47–54.

Höft, Brigitte. 1983. "Clara Schumann und Johannes Brahms in Baden-Baden." In *Johannes Brahms in Baden-Baden und Karlsruhe*, edited by J. Draheim et al., 17–34. Karlsruhe, Germany: Badische Landesbibliothek. Exhibition catalog.

——. 2001. "'Ein Feldherr, der einem Heer von Tönen gebietet'—Otto Dessoff in Frankfurt am Main (1880–1892)." In *Otto Dessoff (1835–1892): Ein Dirigent, Komponist und Weggefährte von Johannes Brahms*, edited by J. Draheim and A. Jahn, 149–78. Munich, Germany: Katzbichler.

Holde, Artur. 1946. "Unpublished Letters by Beethoven, Liszt, and Brahms." *Musical Quarterly* 32: 278–88. (Includes letters by Brahms to the Viennese book dealer Julius Grosser and to Siegfried Ochs.)

——. 1959. "Suppressed Passages in the Brahms-Joachim Correspondence Published for the First Time," translated by W. Wager. *Musical Quarterly* 45: 312–24.

Holinrake, Roger. 1973. "Wagner und Nietzsche: The *Triumphlied* Episode." *Nietzsche-Studien* 2: 196–201.

Holl, Karl. 1928. *Friedrich Gernsheim: Leben, Erscheinung und Werk*. Leipzig, Germany: Breitkopf & Härtel.

Hönig, Carl. 1906. "Emil Zittel." In *Badische Biographien*, part 5 (1891–1901), edited by F. von Weech and A. Krieger, 853–57. Heidelberg, Germany: Carl Winter.

Hopfner, Rudolf. 1999. *Wiener Musikinstrumentenmacher 1766–1900: Adressenverzeichnis und Bibliographie*. Tutzing, Germany: Schneider.

Horstmann, Angelika. 1984. "Die Rezeption der Werke op. 1 bis 10 von Johannes Brahms zwischen 1853 und 1860." In *Brahms und seine Zeit: Symposium Hamburg 1983*, edited by C. Floros, H. J. Marx, and P. Petersen, 33–44. [n.p.]: Laaber. (*Hamburger Jahrbuch für Musikwissenschaft* 7.)

Höslinger, Clemens. 1988. "Hugo Wolf's Brahms-Kritiken: Versuch einer Interpretation." In *Brahms-Kongress Wien 1983: Kongressbericht*, edited by S. Antonicek and O. Biba, 259–68. Tutzing, Germany: Schneider.

Hubay, Eugène de. 1930. "My Memories of Brahms, Liszt, and Massenet." *Musical Times* 71: 316–17.

—— [as Eugen v. Hubay]. 1933. "Erinnerungen an Brahms: Zur hundertsten Jahreswende seines Geburtstages." *Pester Lloyd* (Morgenblatt), 5 May, 1–3.

Hübbe, Walter. 1902. *Brahms in Hamburg*. Hamburg: Lütcke & Wulff.

Huber, Arnold. 1924. *Theodor Billroth in Zurich, 1860–1867*. Zurich, Switzerland: Füssli.

Huberman, Bronislaw. 1912. *Aus der Werkstatt des Virtuosen*. Leipzig, Germany: Heller & Co.

Hunziker, Rudolf. 1909. *Zur Musikgeschichte Winterthurs*. Winterthur, Switzerland: Geschwister Ziegler.

——. 1927. "Ein Brief von Johannes Brahms an seinen Verleger Rieter-Biedermann in Winterthur." *Schweizerisches Jahrbuch für Musikwissenschaft* 2: 107–9.

Hüschen, Heinrich, ed. 1962. *Festschrift Karl Gustav Fellerer zum sechzigsten Geburtstag am 7. Juli 1962*. Regensburg, Germany: Bosse.

Hüschen, Heinrich, and Dietz-Rüdiger Moser, eds. 1974. *Convivium Musicorum: Festschrift Wolfgang Boetticher zum sechzigsten Geburtstag am 19. August 1974*. Berlin: Merseburger.

Huschke, Konrad. 1927. "Johannes Brahms und Elisabeth v. Herzogenberg." *Die Musik* 19: 557–73.

——. 1931. "Anselm Feuerbach und Johannes Brahms." *Die Kunst* 65, no. 5 (February): 154–55, no. 6 (March): 179–81.

——. 1933. "Max Klinger und Johannes Brahms: Ein Gedenken zu Brahms' 100. Geburtstag." *Kunst für Alle* 48, no. 9 (June): 257–62.

——. 1939. *Musiker, Maler und Dichter als Freunde und Gegner*. Leipzig, Germany: Helingsche Verlagsanstalt. Contains chapters "Wagner und Brahms," "Brahms—Feuerbach und Menzel," "Hebbel, Brahms und Cornelius," "Joachim Raff—Bülow, Wagner, Brahms und Cornelius," "Brahms, Bruckner und Hugo Wolf," "Johann Strauss, Brahms und Bülow," and "Max Klinger—Beethoven, Brahms, Reger und Wagner."

Istel, Edgar. 1902. *Richard Wagner im Lichte eines zeitgenössischen Briefwechsels (1858 bis 1872)*. Berlin: Schuster & Loeffler.

Jacob, Gustav. 1971. "W. H. Ladenburg & Söhne: Aus der Geschichte eines Mannheimer Privatbankhauses." *Mannheimer Hefte* 2: 20–38.

Jacobi, Erwin R. 1969. "'Vortrag und Besetzung Bach'scher Cantaten- und Oratorienmusik': Ein unbekannter Brief von Moritz Hauptmann an Johannes Brahms (13. Februar 1859)." *Bach-Jahrbuch* 55: 78–86.

Jacobson, Christiane, ed. 1983. *Johannes Brahms: Leben und Werk*. Wiesbaden, Germany: Breitkopf & Härtel. The book contains studies of Brahms's life and works by many authors, and a section "Biographische Daten" by Renate and Kurt Hofmann.

Jaffé, Walther. 1913. *Alexander Baumann (1814–1857): Ein Beitrag zum Wiener lieterarischen Vormärz und zum volkstümlichen Lied in Österreich*. Weimar, Germany: Duncker.

Jäger, Hans-Wolf. 1980. "Kopisch, August." In ***NDB***, vol. 12, 564–66. Berlin, Germany: Duncker & Humblot, 1952–.

—— 1990. "Meissner, Alfred." In ***NDB***, vol. 16, 694–95. Berlin, Germany: Duncker & Humblot, 1952–.

Jahn, Albert. 2001. "Die Künstlerfamilie Dessoff—ein genealogischer Überblick—die Geschichte einer Wiederentdeckung." In *Otto Dessoff (1835–1892): Ein Dirigent, Komponist und Weggefährte von Johannes Brahms*, edited by J. Draheim and A. Jahn, 24–40. Munich, Germany: Katzbichler.

Jahn, Otto. 1866. "Das vierunddreissigste niederrheininische Musikfest in Düsseldorf, den 11., 12. und 13. Mai 1856." In *Gesammelte Aufsätze über Musik*, 199–223. Leipzig, Germany: Breitkopf & Härtel. (Article reprinted from *Die Grenzboten*, 1856.)

Janz, Curt Paul. 1978. "Friedrich Nietzsches Verhältnis zur Musik seiner Zeit." *Nietzsche-Studien* 7: 308–26. (Followed by a discussion, 327–38.)

Jenkins, D. T. 2004. "Behrens, Sir Jacob (1806–1889)." In *Oxford Dictionary of National Biography*, vol. 4, edited by C. G. Matthew and Brian Harrison, 851–52. 60 vols. Oxford, UK: Oxford University Press.

Jenner, Gustav. 1912. "War Marxsen der rechte Lehrer für Brahms?" *Die Musik* 12, no. 2 (October): 77–83.

———. 1930. *Johannes Brahms als Mensch, Lehrer und Künstler: Studien und Erlebnisse*. 2nd edition. Marburg an der Lahn, Germany: Elwert'sche Verlagsbuchhandlung, G. Braun. English version by Susan Gillespie in *Brahms and His World*, edited by W. Frisch, 185–204. Princeton, N.J.: Princeton University Press, 1990.

Joachim, Johannes, ed. 1911. *Joseph Joachims Briefe an Gisela von Arnim, 1852–1859*. Göttingen, Germany.

Joachim, Johannes, and Andreas Moser, eds. 1911–13. *Briefe von und an Joseph Joachim*. 3 vols. Berlin: Bard.

Joachim, Joseph. 1899. "Festrede Prof. Dr. Joachims zur Enthüllung des Brahms-Denkmals in Meiningen." *Allgemeine Musik-Zeitung* 26: 622–23.

Joachim, Joseph, and Andreas Moser. 1902–5. *Violinschule*. 3 vols., Berlin: Simrock.

Johnson, H. Earle. 1979. "Brahms, Johannes (1833–97)." In *First Performances in America to 1900: Works with Orchestra*, 72–90. Detroit: Information Coordinators Inc.

Kabel, Rolf, ed. 1964. *Eduard Devrient: Aus seinen Tagebüchern*. 2 vols. Weimar, Germany: Hermann Böhlaus Nachfolger.

Kahl, Willi. 1933. "Hermann Deiters. Zu seinem 100. Geburtstag." *Zeitschrift für Musikwissenschaft* 15: 394–403.

———. 1960a. "Deiters, Hermann." In *Rheinische Musiker*, edited by K. G. Fellerer, 1st series, 72–81. Cologne, Germany: Arno Volk.

———. 1960b. "Heimsoeth, Friedrich." In *Rheinische Musiker*, edited by K. G. Fellerer, 1st series, 111–15. Cologne, Germany: Arno Volk.

———. 1962. "Otto Jahn und das Rheinland." In *Festschrift Karl Gustav Fellerer zum sechzigsten Geburtstag am 7. Juli 1962*, edited by H. Hüschen, 264–81. Regensburg, Germany: Bosse.

———. 1964. "Gernsheim, Friedrich." In *Rheinische Musiker*, edited by K. G. Fellerer, 3rd series. 30–32. Cologne, Germany: Arno Volk.

Kahler, Otto-Hans. 1981. "Billroth und Brahms in Zürich." *Brahms-Studien* 4: 63–76.

———. 1985. "Brahms' Wiegenlied und die Gebirgs-Bleamln des Alexander Baumann." *Brahms-Studien* 6: 65–70.

———. 1999. "Zu Hugo Wolfs Brahms-Kritiken." *Brahms-Studien* 12: 23–28.

Kahn, Robert. 1994. "Erinnerungen an Johannes Brahms." *Brahms-Studien* 10: 43–51. See also Laugwitz 1986.

Kaiserfeld, Antonie. 1932. *Aus den Erinnerungen einer 85jährigen*. Vienna, Austria.

Kaiserfeld, Hans. 1996. "Oekonomen, Beamte, Advokaten—Eine bürgerliche Familie in Österreich-Ungarn Mitte 18. bis Anfang 20. Jahrhundert. Ein Fallbeispiel für die bürgerliche Epoche." PhD diss., University of Vienna, Austria.

Kaiserfeld, Moritz. 1898. "Eine Brahms-Erinnerung." *Neue Musik-Zeitung* 19, no. 16: 193.

Kalbeck, Max. 1898. "Neues über Brahms." *Neues Wiener Tagblatt*, 2 April, 1–3; 5 April, 1–3.

———. 1976. *Johannes Brahms*. 4 vols. 4th edition. Berlin: Deutsche Brahms-Gesellschaft, 1912–21. Reprint Tutzing, Germany: Schneider.

Kamen, Martin D. 1986. "On Creativity of Eye and Ear: A Commentary on the Career of T. W. Engelmann." *Proceedings of the American Philosophical Society* 130: 232–46.

Kämper, Dietrich. 1963a. *Franz Wüllner: Leben, Wirken und kompositorisches Schaffen*. Cologne, Germany: Volk.

——, ed. 1963b. *Richard Strauss und Franz Wüllner im Briefwechsel*. Cologne, Germany: Volk.

Kapp, Julius. 1932. *The Women in Wagner's Life*. London: Routledge & Sons.

Karell, Viktor. 1937. "Johannes Brahms als Karlsbader Kurgast." *Sudetendeutsche Monatshefte*, 197–202.

——. 1971. *Karlsbad von A bis Z: Ein Stadtlexikon*. Munich, Germany: Aufstieg-Verlag.

Karner, Peter, ed. 1986. *Die evangelische Gemeinde H.B. in Wien*. Vienna, Austria: Franz Deuticke.

Karnes, Kevin C. 2004. "Eduard Hanslick's History: A Forgotten Narrative of Brahms's Vienna." *American Brahms Society Newsletter* 22, no. 2 (Autumn): 1–5.

Karpath, Ludwig. 1912/13. "Persönliches von Gustav Mahler." *Der Merker* 4: 251–56.

——. 1934. "Bekanntschaft mit Johannes Brahms." In *Begegnung mit dem Genius: Denkwürdige Erlebnisse*, 325–37. 2nd edition. Vienna, Austria: Fiba-Verlag. (See also "Richard Wagner," 209–48.)

Kaufmann, Ludwig. 1979. "Berühmte Musiker in Wiesbaden: Komponisten, Instrumentalisten, Sänger und ihr Wirken in der Kurstadt. Ein musikalischer Beitrag zur Heimatkunde." Typescript at the Hessische Landesbibliothek, Wiesbaden, Germany.

Kaufmann, Paul. 1933. "Brahms-Erinnerungen." *Die Musik* 25, no. 10 (July): 749–54.

Keefer, Lubov. 1966. "The Operetta Librettos of Ivan Turgenev." *Slavic and East European Journal* 10, no. 2 (Summer): 134–54.

Keller, Werner. 1990. "Hebbel, (Christian) Friedrich." In *Literatur Lexikon: Autoren und Werke deutscher Sprache*, vol. 5, edited by W. Killy, 85–90. 15 vols. Gütersloh, Germany: Bertelsmann Lexikon Verlag, 1988–93.

Kelley, Gwendolyn Dunlevy, and George Upton. 1906. *Edouard Remenyi: Musician, Litterateur, and Man. An Appreciation*. Chicago: McClurg & Co.

Kelly, Elaine. 2004. "An Unexpected Champion of François Couperin: Johannes Brahms and the *Pièces de clavecin*." *Music & Letters* 85, no. 4 (November): 576–601.

Kempski, Jürgen von. 1966. "Gruppe, Otto Friedrich." In ***NDB***, vol. 7, 235–36. Berlin: Duncker & Humblot, 1952–.

Kempter, Lothar, ed. 1959. *Musikkollegium Winterthur: Festschrift zur Feier des dreihundertjährigen Bestehens, 1629–1929, vol. 2: Das Musikkollegium Winterthur 1837–1933*. Winterthur, Switzerland: Verlag des Musikkollegiums Winterthur.

Kendall, Raymond. 1941. "Brahms's Knowledge of Bach's Music." *Papers of the American Musicological Society, Annual Meeting 1941*, edited by G. Reese: 50–56.

Kennedy, Michael. 1960. *The Hallé Tradition: A Century of Music*. Manchester, UK: Manchester University Press.

——. 1971. *The History of the Royal Manchester College of Music, 1893–1972*. Manchester, UK: Manchester University Press.

Kern, Volker, and Herta Müller, eds. 1999. *Die Meininger kommen! Hoftheater und Hofkapelle zwischen 1874 und 1914 unterwegs in Deutschland und Europa*. Meiningen, Germany: Kulturstiftung Meiningen. Contents: Alfred Erck and Volker Kern, "Die Meininger in Europa." and "Die Meininger Prinzipien. 12 Neuerungen, die das Herzoglich Sachsen-Meiningensche Hoftheater in das europäische Theaterleben einbrachte.," and Herta Müller, "Die 'Musikalischen' Meininger auf Reisen."; also a statistical presentation of the performances given by the court theater and the court orchestra outside Meiningen.

Kersten, Ursula. 1993. *Max Klinger und die Musik*. 2 vols. Frankfurt, Germany: Lang.

Khittl, Christoph. 1992. "Eduard Hanslicks Verhältnis zur Ästhetik." In *Biographische Beiträge zum Musikleben Wiens im 19. und frühen 20. Jahrhundert*, edited by M. Permoser, 81–109. Vienna, Austria: VWGÖ.

Kienzl, Wilhelm. 1909. *Betrachtungen und Erinnerungen: Gesammelte Aufsätze*. Berlin: Allgemeiner Verlag für Deutsche Literatur. On Brahms, see 296–302.

——. 1926. "Johannes Brahms, 1833–1896 [sic]." In *Meine Lebenswanderung: Erlebtes und Erschautes*, 234–39. Stuttgart, Germany: J. Engelhorns Nachfolger. Contains account of first meeting with Brahms already given in Kienzl 1909.

Killian, Herbert. 1984. *Gustav Mahler in den Erinnerungen von Natalie Bauer-Lechner*. Notes by Knud Martner; revised and enlarged edition. Hamburg, Germany: Karl Dieter Wagner.

Killy, W., ed. 1988–93. *Literatur Lexikon: Autoren und Werke deutscher Sprache*. 15 vols. Gütersloh, Germany: Bertelsmann Lexikon Verlag.

Kindermann, Jürgen. 1980. *Thematisch-chronologisches Verzeichnis der musikalischen Werke von Ferruccio B. Busoni*. Regensburg, Germany: Bosse.

Kittel, Erich. 1957. *Geschichte des Landes Lippe: Heimatchronik der Kreise Detmold und Lemgo*. Cologne, Germany: Archiv für Deutsche Heimatpflege.

Kitzler, Otto. 1904. *Musikalische Erinnerungen mit Briefen von Brahms, Bruckner und Rich. Pohl.* Brünn, Czech Republic: Winiker. Contains texts of six letters from Brahms dating from 1874, 1882, and 1886.

Klauwell, Otto. 1900. *Das Konservatorium der Musik in Köln*. Cologne, Germany.

Kleinpass, Hans. 1975. "Die Strassennamen der Gemarkung Lannesdorf." *Godesberger Heimatsblätter* 13: 102–36.

Kluncker, Karlhans. 1984. *Georg Friedrich Daumer: Leben und Werk, 1800–1875*. Bonn, Germany: Bouvier.

Klusen, Ernst, Hermann Stoffels, and Theo Zart. 1979–80. *Das Musikleben der Stadt Krefeld, 1780–1945*. 2 vols. Cologne, Germany: Volk.

Knierbein, Ingrid. 1986. "'Solche Medizin lobe ich mir': Unveröffentliche Briefe von und an Johannes Brahms aus dem Besitz der Familie Justizrat Dr. Viktor Schnitzler." *Neue Zeitschrift für Musik* 147, no. 3 (March): 4–7.

Köbler, Gerhard. 1999. *Historisches Lexikon der deutschen Länder: Die deutschen Territorien und reichsunmittelbaren Geschlechter vom Mittelalter bis zur Gegenwart*. 6th, completely revised edition. Munich, Germany: Beck.

Köchel, Jürgen. 2005. "Brahms und Mozart." *Brahms-Studien* 14: 101–37.

Kohlweyer, Gerhard. 2002. "Elise Denninghoff—Johannes Brahms: Der Briefwechsel der 1880er Jahre." *Brahms-Studien* 13: 81–109.

Koht, Halvdan. 1971. *Life of Ibsen*. New York: Blom.

Komorn, Maria. 1928. *Johannes Brahms als Chordirigent in Wien und seine Nachfolger bis zum Schubertjahr 1928*. Vienna, Austria: Universal-Edition.

——. 1933. "Brahms, Choral Conductor," translated by W. O. Strunk. *Musical Quarterly* 19: 151–57.

Konold, Wulf. 1984. *Felix Mendelssohn und seine Zeit*. Regensburg, Germany: Laaber.

Kopitsch, Franklin, and Daniel Tilgner, eds. n.d. *Hamburg Lexikon*. Hamburg, Germany: Zeiseverlag.

Kowar, Helmut. 1985. "Johannes Brahms und sein Freundeskreis." In *Bruckner Symposion: Johannes Brahms und Anton Bruckner . . . 8.–11. September 1983*, edited by O. Wessely, 219–24. Linz, Austria: Anton Bruckner-Institut Linz.

Kowar, Helmut, Franz Lechleitner, and Dietrich Schüller. 1984. "On the Re-issue of the Only Existing Sound Recording of Johannes Brahms by the Phonogrammarchiv." *Phonographic Bulletin* 39 (July): 19–22.

Krafft, Alfred. 1957. "Candidus, Carl August." In ***NDB***, vol. 3, 121. Berlin, Germany: Duncker & Humblot, 1952–.

Kranefuss, Annelen. 1990. "Hölty, Ludwig Christoph Heinrich." In *Literatur Lexikon: Autoren und Werke deutscher Sprache*, vol. 5, edited by W. Killy, 391–92. 15 vols. Gütersloh, Germany: Bertelsmann Lexikon Verlag, 1988–93.

Kraus, Felicitas von. 1961. *Begegnungen mit Anton Bruckner, Johannes Brahms, Cosima Wagner, aus den Lebenserinnerungen von Dr. Felix von Kraus (1870–1937)*. Vienna, Austria: Franz Hain.

Krause, Emil. 1903. "Zu Johannes Brahms' 70. Geburtstag. Würdigung seiner Schöpfungen. Die Brahms-Literatur. Eigene Erlebnisse." *Musikalisches Wochenblatt* 34: 257–62.

Kretschmann, Theobald. 1910. "Johannes Brahms." In *Tempi passati: Aus den Erinnerungen eines Musikanten*, 148–53. Vienna, Austria: Prochaska.

Kretzschmar, Hermann. 1874. "Neue Werke von J. Brahms." *Musikalisches Wochenblatt* 5: 5–7, 19–21, 31–32, 43–45, 58–60, 70–73, 83–85, 95–97, 107–11, 147–50, 164–66.

——. 1884. "Johannes Brahms." *Die Grenzboten* 43, 3rd quarter: 123–32, 167–79, 276–84, 314–24, 324–28. Reprinted in *Gesammelte Aufsätze über Musik und Anderes aus den Grenzboten*, 151–207. Leipzig, Germany: Breitkopf & Härtel, 1910 (1911).

Kretzschmer, A., and Anton Wilhelm von Zuccalmaglio, eds. 1840. *Deutsche Volkslieder und ihre Original-Weisen*. 2 vols. Berlin: Vereins-Buchhandlung.

Kreutner, Rudolf. 1997. "'Ich wäre hochbeglückt gewesen, auch meinerseits dem grossen Sohn Ihrer Stadt ein Zeichen höchster Verehrung geben zu können': Oder ein Brahms-Brief im Stadtarchiv Schweinfurt." *Brahms-Studien* 11: 55–71.

——. 1999. "Marie Renate Rückert." In *Die "Sammlung Rückert." Part II: Die Familie Rückert*, 28–32. Schweinfurt, Germany: Stadtarchiv Schweinfurt.

Kreutziger-Herr, Annette. 1999. "Hölderlin, Brahms und das *Schicksalslied*." In *Johannes Brahms: Quellen—Text—Rezeption—Interpretation: Internationaler*

Brahms-Kongress Hamburg 1997, edited by F. Krummacher and M. Struck, in collaboration with C. Floros and P. Petersen, 343–73. Munich, Germany: G. Henle.

Kroll, Erwin. 1966. *Musikstadt Königsberg: Geschichte und Erinnerung*. Freiburg im Breisgau, Germany: Atlantis Verlag. In particular, see "Musikkritik in Königsberg," 153–79, and "Königsberg als Brahmsstadt," 212–17.

Krones, Hartmut. 1988a. "Der Einfluss Franz Schuberts auf das Liedschaffen von Johannes Brahms." In *Brahms-Kongress Wien 1983: Kongressbericht*, edited by S. Antonicek and O. Biba, 309–24. Tutzing, Germany: Schneider.

——. 1988b. "'der schönste und wichtigste Zweck von allen': Das Conservatorium der 'Gesellschaft der Musikfreunde des österreichischen Kaierstaates.'" *Österreichische Musikzeitschrift* 43: 66–88.

Kross, Siegfried. 1964. "Brahmsiana. Der Nachlass der Schwestern Völkers." *Musikforschung* 17: 110–36.

——. 1981a. "Brahms and E. T. A. Hoffmann." *19th Century Music* 5, no. 1 (Spring): 193–200.

——. 1981b. "Brahms und Schumann." *Brahms-Studien* 4: 7–44.

——. 1988. "Leonhard Wolff. Städtischer und Universitätsmusikdirektor in Bonn." *Bonner Geschichtsblätter* 37: 153–73.

——. 1997. *Johannes Brahms. Versuch einer kritischen Dokumentar-Biographie*. 2 vols., Bonn, Germany: Bouvier.

Kruse, Georg Richard. 1920. *Hermann Goetz*. Leipzig, Germany: Philipp Reclam jun.

Kühn, Dieter. 1998. *Clara Schumann, Klavier: Ein Lebensbuch*. Frankfurt, Germany: Fischer, 1996. New, enlarged edition. Frankfurt, Germany: Fischer Taschenbuch Verlag.

Kühnen, Barbara. 2000. "Marie Soldat-Roeger (1863–1955)." In *Die Geige war ihr Leben: Drei Geigerinnen im Portrait*, edited by K. Dreyfus, M. Engelhardt-Krajanek, and B. Kühnen, 13–98. Strasshof: Vier-Viertel Verlag.

Kuna, Milan, ed. 1987–89. *Dvořák: Korespondence a dokumenty. Kritické vydání*. 3 vols. Prague, Czech Republic: Editio Supraphon.

——. 1992. "Umělecká stipendia Antonína Dvořáka." *Hudebni věda*, new series, 4: 293–315.

Küntzel, Hans. 1985. *Brahms in Göttingen: Mit Erinnerungen von Agathe Schütte, geb. von Siebold*. Göttingen, Germany: Edition Herodot.

Kurschat, Wilhelm. 1933. *Das Haus Friedrich & Heinrich von der Leyen: Zur Geschichte der Rheinlande in der Zeit der Fremdherrschaft 1794–1814*. Frankfurt, Germany: Klostermann.

Kurz, Gerhard. 1990. "Hölderlin (Johann Christian) Friedrich." In *Literatur Lexikon: Autoren und Werke deutscher Sprache*, vol. 5, edited by W. Killy, 379–89. 15 vols. Gütersloh, Germany: Bertelsmann Lexikon Verlag, 1988–93.

Kutsch, K. J., and Leo Riemens. 1987–94. *Grosses Sängerlexikon*. 4 vols. Berne, Switzerland: Francke.

Ladenburger, Michael. 1997. "Johannes Brahms und das Beethoven-Haus." In *Johannes Brahms und Bonn*, edited by M. Gutiérrez-Denhoff, 95–113. Bonn, Germany: Stadt Bonn.

——. 2001. "Johannes Brahms als Beethoven-Forscher oder: Archivare und Musikwissenschaftler als Lehrer/Schüler/Kollegen berühmter Komponisten." In *Interna-*

tionaler Brahms-Kongress Gmunden 1997: Kongressbericht, edited by I. Fuchs, 459–86. Tutzing, Germany: Schneider.

La Grange, Henri Louis de. 1994–99. *Gustav Mahler: Chronique d'une vie.* 3 vols. Paris: Fayard. (English version: *Mahler*. Translated from the French. 4 vols. Oxford, UK: Oxford University Press, 1994–99.)

La Mara. 1875a. "Johannes Brahms." In *Musikalische Studienköpfe aus der Jüngstvergangenheit und Gegenwart: Charakterzeichnungen*, 233–97. Leipzig, Germany: Schmidt & Günther. (Reprinted, with minor differences and a list of Brahms's compositions to date, from *Illustrierte Deutsche Monatshefte* [December 1874]: 292–316.)

——. 1875b. "Carl Tausig." In La Mara's *Musikalische Studienköpfe aus der Jüngstvergangenheit und Gegenwart: Charakterzeichnungen*, 299–328. Leipzig, Germany: Schmidt & Günther.

——, ed. 1886. "Johannes Brahms . . . An Marie Lipsius." In *Musikerbriefe aus fünf Jahrhunderten: Nach den Urhandschriften erstmalig herausgegeben*, vol. 2, 348–50. Leipzig, Germany: Breitkopf & Härtel.

——, ed. 1893–1905. *Franz Liszts Briefe*. Leipzig, Germany: Breitkopf & Härtel.

——, ed. 1911. *Marie von Mouchanoff-Kalergis, geb. Gräfin Nesselrode, in Briefen an ihre Tochter. Ein Lebens- und Charakterbild.* 2nd, revised edition. Leipzig, Germany: Breitkopf & Härtel.

Lamb, Andrew. 1975. "Brahms and Johann Strauss." *Musical Times* 116: 869–71.

Lamond, Frederic. 1949. *The Memoirs of Frederic Lamond*. Glasgow, UK: Maclellan.

Langer, Wolfhart. 1973. "Johannes Brahms in Krefeld. Eine ergänzende Randbemerkung." *Die Heimat* [Krefeld, Germany] 44: 100–101.

Langner, Martin M. 1990. *Brahms und seine schleswig-holsteinischen Dichter*. Heide, Germany: Westholst. In particular, see "Das Verhältnis von Musik und Text: Begegnung mit Friedrich Hebbel," 53–69; "'Das Schöne muss gemacht werden': Die Freundschaft mit Klaus Groth," 70–11; and "'Ich nenne Sie natürlich immer unsern Landsmann': Brahms und das Schleswig-Holsteinische Musikfest," 100–111.

Laugwitz, Burkhard. 1986. "Robert Kahn erinnert sich." *Das Orchester* 34: 640–48. Includes an annotated reproduction of Kahn's recollections of Brahms (see Kahn 1994, where the same text is printed without any notes).

Laux, Karl. 1944. *Der Einsame: Johannes Brahms. Leben und Werk*. Graz, Austria: Pustet.

Lederer, Josef-Horst. 1977. "Cornelius und Johannes Brahms." In *Peter Cornelius als Komponist, Dichter, Kritiker und Essayist. Vorträge, Referate und Diskussionen*, edited by H. Federhofer and K. Oehl, 57–63. Regensburg, Germany: Bosse.

Legány, Dezső. 1984. *Franz Liszt: Unbekannte Presse und Briefe aus Wien 1822–1886*. Vienna, Austria: Böhlau.

Leichtentritt, Hugo. 1931. *Das Konservatorium der Musik Klindworth-Scharwenka Berlin 1881–1931: Festschrift aus Anlass des fünfzigjährigen Bestehens*. Berlin: Flock.

Leinburg, Mathilde von. 1905. "Johannes Brahms in Baden-Baden. Unveröffentliches." *Neue Musik-Zeitung* 26, no. 14 (20 April): 309–12.

——. 1907. "Johannes Brahms in Tutzing: Ein Beitrag zur Brahms-Biographie." *Neue Musik-Zeitung* 28, no. 13 (4 April): 286–87.

Leipzig Konservatorium. 1918. *Festschrift zum 75-jährigen Bestehen des Königl, Konservatoriums der Musik zu Leipzig*. Leipzig, Germany: C. F. W. Siegel's Musikalienhandlung.

Lentz, (née Meier), Franziska. 1902. "Brahms-Erinnerungen. Aus dem Tagebuch von Frau Wasserbaudirektor." *Jahrbuch der Gesellschaft Hamburgischer Kunstfreunde* 8: 41–60. See Drinker 1952.

Lenz, Wilhelm, ed. 1970. *Deutschbaltisches biographisches Lexikon 1710–1960*. Cologne, Germany: Böhlau.

Lepel, Felix von, ed. 1936. "Sieben unbekannte Briefe von Brahms." *Signale für die musikalische Welt* 94, no. 36/37 (2 September): 509–10. (Seven letters to Emil Streicher.)

Leyen, Rudolf von der. 1905. *Johannes Brahms als Mensch und Freund. Nach persönlichen Erinnerungen*. Düsseldorf, Germany: Langewiesche.

Lieberman, Richard K. 1995. *Steinway & Sons*. New Haven: Yale University Press.

Lienau, Robert. 1934. *Unvergessliche Jahre mit Johannes Brahms*. Berlin: Lienau.

Lindau, Paul. 1916–17. *Nur Erinnerungen*. 2 vols. Stuttgart, Germany: J. G. Cotta'sche Buchhandlung.

Lindlar, Heinrich. 1967. *C. F. Peters Musikverlag, 1800 – 1867 – 1967*. Frankfurt, Germany: Peters.

Linnemann, Georg. 1956. "Albert Dietrich (1861–1890)." In *Musikgeschichte der Stadt Oldenburg*, 230–78. Oldenburg, Germany: Stalling.

Linsmayer, Charles. 1989. "Frey, Adolf." In *Literatur Lexikon: Autoren und Werke deutscher Sprache*, vol. 3, edited by W. Killy, 107–8. 15 vols. Gütersloh, Germany: Bertelsmann Lexikon Verlag, 1988–93.

Liszt, Franz. 1872. *Robert Franz*. Leipzig, Germany: Leuckart.

Litzmann, Berthold. 1902. *Clara Schumann. Ein Künstlerleben*. 3 vols., Leipzig, Germany: Breitkopf & Härtel.

——, ed. 1970. *Clara Schumann—Johannes Brahms. Briefe aus den Jahren 1853–1896*. 2 vols. Leipzig, Germany: Breitkopf & Härtel, 1927. Reprint Hildesheim, Germany: Olms.

Lo, Kii-Ming. 1985. "Johannes Brahms in Heidelberg." In *Musik in Heidelberg 1775–1885*, 189–206. (Catalog of an exhibition held at Heidelberg Castle, 2 June–4 August 1985 [Heidelberg].)

Lochner, Louis P. 1950. *Fritz Kreisler*. New York: Macmillan.

Lockspeiser, Edward. 1962–65. *Debussy: His Life and Mind*. 2 vols. London: Cassell.

Lohmeier, Dieter, ed. 1997. *Johannes Brahms—Klaus Groth. Briefe der Freundschaft*. Heide, Germany: Boyens & Co. (New version of edition published by Volquart Pauls at Heide in 1956.) The supplement contains the following texts by Groth: "Notizen über Johannes Brahms," "Musikalische Erinnerungen," "Musikalische Erlebnisse," and "Erinnerungen an Johannes Brahms."

Lorenz, Michael. 2000. "Karl Enderes—eine biographische Studie." *Schubert durch die Brille* 24 (January): 31–80.

Losch, Philipp. 1937. *Der letzte deutsche Kurfürst Friedrich Wilhelm I. von Hessen*. Marburg, Germany: Elwert.

——. 1972. *Geschichte des Kurfürstentums Hessen, 1803 bis 1866*. Marburg, Germany: Elwert, 1922. Reprint Kassel, Germany: Hamecher.

Lübke, Wilhelm, and Eduard Hanslick. 1869. *Wilhelm Lübke und Eduard Hanslick über Wagner*. Berlin: Gerschel. Reprint of articles by Lübke on *Die Meistersinger* and Hanslick on *Das Judenthum in der Musik*, originally published in Vienna in *Neue freie Presse* on 5 March and 9 March 1869 respectively.

Ludwig, Franz. 1925. *Julius Otto Grimm: Ein Beitrag zur Geschichte der musikalischen Spätromantik*. Bielefeld, Germany: Velhagen & Klasing.

——. 1931. *Ludwig Wüllner: Sein Leben und seine Kunst. Mit vierzehn Beiträgen zeitgenössischer Persönlichkeiten*. Leipzig, Germany: Erich Weibezahl.

Lukoschik, Rita Unfer. 1993. *Der erste deutsche Gozzi. Untersuchungen zu der Rezeption Carlo Gozzis in der deutschen Spätaufklärung*. Frankfurt, Germany: Lang.

M., C. 1933. "Besuch bei Frau Cölestina Truxa, der Hausfrau von Johannes Brahmsz: Erinnerungen an die kleinen Alltagsbegegnungen mit einem Unsterblichen." *Neues Wiener Journal*, 4 May, 5–6.

MacDonald, Malcolm. 1990. *Brahms*. London: Dent.

Mahler, Alma. 1940. *Gustav Mahler: Erinnerungen und Briefe*. Amsterdam, The Netherlands: Allert de Lange. (English version: *Gustav Mahler: Memories and Letters*, translated by B. Creighton. London: John Murray, 1946. 2nd, enlarged and revised edition by Donald Mitchell. London: John Murray, 1968.)

——, ed. 1978. *Gustav Mahler: Briefe 1879–1911*. Berlin: Zsolnay, 1925. Reprint Hildesheim, Germany: Olms.

Maier, Elisabeth. 1979. "Die Brahms-Autographen der Österreichischen Nationalbibliothek." *Brahms-Studien* 3: 7–34.

Mailer, Franz, ed. 1983–2002. *Johann Strauss (Sohn): Leben und Werke in Briefen und Dokumenten*. 9 vols. Tutzing, Germany: Schneider.

Manz, Gustav. 1897. "Brahms-Erinnerungen, nach eigenen Erlebnissen erzählt." *Pester Lloyd*, 11 April.

Martin, Michael, ed. 1983. *Johannes Brahms: Briefwechsel mit dem Mannheimer Bankprokuristen Wilhelm Lindeck, 1871–1882*. Heidelberg, Germany: Heidelberger Verlagsanstalt.

Mason, William. 1901. *Memories of a Musical Life*. New York: Century Co.

Massin, Brigitte. 1999. *Les Joachim: Une famille de musiciens*. Paris: Fayard.

Matthew, C. G., and Brian Harrison, eds. 2004. *Oxford Dictionary of National Biography*. 60 vols. Oxford, UK: Oxford University Press.

May, Florence. 1948. *The Life of Johannes Brahms*. 2nd revised edition. 2 vols. London: William Reeves.

Mayer-Pasinski, Karin. 1981. *Max Klingers Brahmsphantasie*. Frankfurt, Germany: R. G. Fischer.

Mayr, Anton. 1934. *Erinnerungen an Robert Fuchs*. Graz, Austria: Leuschner & Lubensky.

McArthur, Alexander. 1889. *Anton Rubinstein: A Biographical Sketch*. Edinburgh, UK: Adam and Charles Black.

McCorkle, Donald M. 1973. *The N. Simrock Thematic Catalog of the Works of Johannes Brahms [Thematisches Verzeichniss sämmtlicher im Druck erschienenen Werke von Johannes Brahms].* New Introduction, incl. Addenda and Corrigenda, by Donald M. McCorkle. New York: Da Capo Press.

McCorkle, Margit L. 1984. *Johannes Brahms: Thematisch-bibliographisches Werkverzeichnis*. Munich, Germany: Henle.

McGuinness, Rosamond. 1977. "Mahler and Brahms: Gedanken zu 'Reminiszenzen' in Mahlers Sinfonien." *Melos/Neue Zeitschrift für Musik* 3, no. 3 (May/June): 215–24.

McKay, Elisabeth Norman. 1989. "Brahms and Scarlatti." *Musical Times* 130: 586–88. See also Klaus Häfner's letter regarding this article and McKay's reply in *Musical Times* 131 (1990): 10.

Meid, Volker. 1989. "Fleming (Flemming[ius]), Paul." In *Literatur Lexikon: Autoren und Werke deutscher Sprache*, vol. 3, edited by W. Killy, 413–16. 15 vols. Gütersloh, Germany: Bertelmanns Lexikon Verlag, 1988–93.

Meisner, Robert. 1977. "Aus Johannes Brahms' Schulzeit. Zur Kritik der Darstellung von Max Kalbeck—Der Schullehrer Johann Friedrich Hoffmann." *Brahms-Studien* 2: 85–94.

Melsbach, Heinrich. 1925. "Crefelder Brahmserinnerungen." *Heimat* 4: 26–30.

Menczigar, Maria. 1957. "Julius Epstein. Sein Leben und Wirken unter besonderer Erforschung seiner Beziehung zu Johannes Brahms." PhD diss., University of Vienna.

Menhennet, Alan. 1991. "Schlegel, August Wilhelm." In *Literatur Lexikon: Autoren und Werke deutscher Sprache*, vol. 10, edited by W. Killy, 257–59. 15 vols. Gütersloh, Germany: Bertelsmann Lexikon Verlag, 1988–93.

Merian, Wilhelm. 1920. *Basels Musikleben im XIX: Jahrhundert*. Basel, Switzerland: Helbing & Lichtenhahn.

Meurs, Norbert. 1996. *Neue Bahnen? Aspekte der Brahms-Rezeption 1853–1868*. Cologne, Germany: Studio Verlag Schewe.

Meyer, Michael. 1971. *Henrik Ibsen*. 2 vols. London: Hart-Davis.

Meysenbug, C[arl] von. 1902. "Aus Johannes Brahms' Jugendtagen." *Neues Wiener Tagblatt*, 3 April, 102–3; 4 April, 1–3.

Meysenbug, Hermann von. 1901. "Aus Johannes Brahms' Jugendtagen." *Neues Wiener Tagblatt*, 9 May, 1–3.

Meysenbug, Malwida von. 1903. *Memoiren einer Idealistin*. 7th edition. 2 vols. Berlin: Schuster & Loeffler.

Michaelis, Adolf, and Eugen Petersen. 1913. *Otto Jahn in seinen Briefen, Mit einem Bilde seines Lebens*. Leipzig, Germany: Teubner. (Prepared by A. Michaelis and published after his death by E. Petersen.)

Michelmann, Emil. 1930. *Agathe von Siebold, Johannes Brahms' Jugendliebe*. Stuttgart, Germany: J. G. Cotta'sche Buchhandlung Nachfolger.

Miesner, Heinrich. 1933. *Klaus Groth und die Musik: Erinnerungen an Johannes Brahms. Briefe, Gedichte und Aufzeichnugen nebst einem Verzeichnis von Vertonungen Grothscher Dichtungen*. Heide, Germany: Westholsteinische Verlagsanstalt. In particular, see "Erinnerungen an Johannes Brahms," 30–67; "Groth und Brahms im Briefwechsel," 68–77; "Hermine und Minna Spies," 78–97.

Mila, Massimo. 1994. *Brahms e Wagner*. A cura di Alberto Batisti. Turin, Italy: Einaudi.

Miller zu Aichholz, Viktor von. 1905. *Ein Brahms-Bilderbuch*. Explanatory text by Max Kalbeck. Vienna, Austria: Lechner.

Misch, Ludwig. 1922. *Johannes Brahms*. Bielefeld, Germany: Velhagen & Klasing.

Möller, Martin. 1990. "Max Reger—ein Brahms-Epigone? Zum Klavierkonzert Op. 114." In *Beiträge zur Geschichte des Konzerts: Festschrift Siegfrid Kross zum 60. Geburstag*, edited by R. Emans and M. Wendt, 343–52. Bonn, Germany: Schröder.

Moser, Andreas. 1908. *Joseph Joachim: Ein Lebensbild*. 2nd revised and expanded edition. 2 vols. Berlin: Verlag der Deutschen Brahms-Gesellschaft.

———. 1923. *Geschichte des Violinspiels*. Berlin: Max Hesses Verlag.

Moser, Dietz-Rüdiger, ed. 1990. *Clara Schumann: "Mein liebes Julchen." Briefe von Clara Schumann an ihre Enkeltochter Julie Schumann, mit Auszügen aus Julie Schumanns Tagebüchern und einem Bericht über ihre Begegnung mit Johannes Brahms*. Munich, Germany: Nymphenburger.

Moutsopoulos, Evanghelos. 1997. "'Der Fall Brahms' in der Musikphilosophie Nietzsches." In *Nietzsche und die Musik*, edited by G. Pöltner and H. Vetter, 81–91. Frankfurt, Germany: Lang.

Mühlfeld, Christian. 1910. *Die herzogliche Hofkapelle in Meiningen: Biographisches und Statistisches*. Meiningen, Germany: Brückner & Renner.

Müller [von Asow], Erich H. 1928. "Zur Geschichte des Hauses Simrock." *Simrock Jahrbuch* 1: 3–22.

———. 1930/34. "Der erste Brahms-Abend in Wien." *Simrock Jahrbuch* 3: 87–89.

———, ed. 1943. *Johannes Brahms und Mathilde Wesendonck: Ein Briefwechsel*. Vienna, Austria: Officina Vindobonensis.

Müller, Harald. 1997. "Johannes Brahms in Celle." In *Johannes Brahms und die Aufnahme seiner Werke in Celle, Ein Beitrag zur Rezeptionsgeschichte der Kompositionen von Johannes Brahms*, 13–25. Bielefeld, Germany: Verlag für Regionalgeschichte.

Müller, Herta. 1999. "Fritz Steinbach's Wirken in Meiningen und für Johannes Brahms von 1886–1903." *Südthüringer Forschungen* 30: 87–121.

———. 2002. "Richard Mühlfeld—der Brahms-Klarinettist." *Brahms-Studien* 13: 129–48.

Müller, Karl-Josef. 1988. *Mahler: Leben—Werke—Dokumente*. Mainz, Germany: B. Schott's Söhne.

Müller-Dombois, Richard. 1972. *Die fürstlich Lippische Hofkapelle: Kulturhistorische, finanzwirtschaftliche und soziologische Untersuchung eines Orchesters im 19. Jahrhundert*. Regensburg, Germany: Bosse.

Münster, Robert. 1974. "Frank, Ernst." In *Musik und Musiker am Mittelrhein: Ein biographisches, orts- und landesgeschichtliches Nachschlagewerk*, vol. 1, edited by H. Unverricht, 55–60. Mainz, Germany: Schott's Söhne.

———. 1984. "Brahms und Paul Heyse: Eine Künstlerfreundschaft." In *Land und Reich, Stamm und Nation. Probleme und Perspektiven bayerischer Geschichte. Festgabe für Max Spindler zum 90. Geburtstag*, vol. 3, 339–57. Munich, Germany: Beck'sche Verlagsbuchhandlung. (Reprinted in *Brahms Studien* 7 [1987]: 51–76.)

——. 1992. "Brahms und Joachim in Berlin: Eine neuentdeckte Originalzeichnung aus dem Jahre 1892." In *De editione musices: Festschrift Gerhard Croll zum 65. Geburtstag*, edited by W. Gratzer and A. Lindmayr, 411–19. Regensburg, Germany: Laaber.

——, ed. 1995. *Johannes Brahms im Briefwechsel mit Ernst Frank*. Tutzing, Germany: Schneider.

Munte, Frank. 1977. "Robert und Clara Schumann in Hamburg." *Brahms-Studien* 2: 7–46.

Münz. Sigmund. 1898. "Erinnerungen an Brahms." *Neue freie Presse*, 30 March, 1–3.

——. 1900. "Johannes Brahms." In *Römische Reminiscenzen und Profile*, 42–59. Berlin: Allgemeiner Verein für deutsche Litteratur.

Musgrave, Michael. 1883. "The Cultural World of Brahms." In *Brahms: Biographical, Documentary and Analytical Studies*, edited by R. Pascall, 1–26. Cambridge, UK: Cambridge University Press.

——. 1979. "*Frei aber Froh*: A Reconsideration." *19th Century Music* 3, no. 1 (July): 251–58.

——. 1985. *The Music of Brahms*. London: Routledge & Kegan Paul.

——, ed. 1987a. *Brahms 2: Biographical, Documentary and Analytical Studies*. Cambridge, UK: Cambridge University Press.

——. 1987b. "Brahms and England." In *Brahms 2: Biographical, Documentary and Analytical Studies*, edited by M. Musgrave, 1–20. Cambridge, UK: Cambridge University Press.

——. 1988. "Brahms und Kalbeck: Eine missverstandene Beziehung?" In *Brahms-Kongress Wien 1983: Kongressbericht*, edited by S. Antonicek and O. Biba, 397–404. Tutzing, Germany: Schneider.

——. 1990. "Marie Soldat, 1863–1955: An English Perspective." In *Beiträge zur Geschichte des Konzerts: Festschrift Siegfrid Kross zum 60. Geburstag*, edited by R. Emans and M. Wendt, 319–30. Bonn, Germany: Schröder.

——. 1999a. "Years of Transition: Brahms and Vienna 1862–1875." In *The Cambridge Companion to Brahms*, edited by M. Musgrave, 31–50. Cambridge, UK: Cambridge University Press.

——, ed. 1999b. *The Cambridge Companion to Brahms*. Cambridge, UK: Cambridge University Press.

——. 2000. *A Brahms Reader*. New Haven, Conn.: Yale University Press.

——. 2001. "Brahms-Rezeption in den USA bis 1900." In *Internationaler Brahms-Kongress Gmunden 1997: Kongressbericht*, edited by I. Fuchs, 343–55. Tutzing, Germany: Schneider.

Nagel, Martin, Karl-Ludwig Schober, and Günther Weiss. 1994. *Theodor Billroth, Chirurg und Musiker*. Regensburg, Germany: ConBrio Verlag.

Naucke, Wolfgang. 1980. "Köstlin, Reinhold." In ***NDB***, vol. 12, 408–9. Berlin: Duncker & Humblot, 1952–.

Nauhaus, Gerd. 1982. *Robert Schumann: Tagebücher*. Vol. 3: *Haushaltbücher 1837–56*. Leipzig, Germany: VEB Deutscher Verlag für Musik.

——. 2001. "Brahms und Clara Schumann. Aspekte einer Lebens- und Arbeitspartnerschaft." In *Internationaler Brahms-Kongress Gmunden 1997: Kongressbericht*, edited by I. Fuchs, 377–91. Tutzing, Germany: Schneider.

NDB *Neue deutsche Bibliographie.* 1952–. Berlin: Duncker & Humblot.

Neubacher, Jürgen. 1999. "Das Brahms-Archiv der Staats- und Universitätsbibliothek Hamburg: Ein Überblick über dessen Geschichte und Bestände." In *Johannes Brahms: Quellen—Text—Rezeption—Interpretation. Internationaler Brahms-Kongress Hamburg 1997*, edited by F. Krummacher and M. Struck, in collaboration with C. Floros and P. Petersen, 279–88. Munich, Germany: G. Henle.

Neumann, Martin. 1986. "Die Freundschaft zwischen Gustav Wendt und Johannes Brahms." In *Bismarck-Gymnasium Karlsruhe: Festschrift*, 332–43. Karlsruhe, Germany.

Neumann, Michael. 1990. "Hoffmann, E(rnst) T(heodor) A(madeus)." In *Literatur Lexikon: Autoren und Werke deutscher Sprache*, vol. 5, edited by W. Killy, 413–17. 15 vols. Gütersloh, Germany: Bertelsmann Lexikon Verlag, 1988–93.

——. 1991. "Tieck, (Johann) Ludwig." In *Literatur Lexikon: Autoren und Werke deutscher Sprache*, vol. 11, edited by W. Killy, 366–71. 15 vols. Gütersloh, Germany: Bertelsmann Lexikon Verlag, 1988–93.

Neumayr, Anton. 1989. "Johannes Brahms." In *Musik und Medizin: Am Beispiel der deutschen Romantik*, 211–59. Vienna, Austria: J&V Edition.

Neunzig, Hans A. 1973. *Johannes Brahms in Selbstzeugnissen und Bilddokumenten*. Reinbek, near Hamburg, Germany: Rowohlt.

Nigg, Marianne, ed. 1893. *Biographie der österreichischen Dichterinnen und Schriftstellerinnen: Ein Beitrag zur deutschen Literatur in Österreich*. Korneuburg: Kühlkopf.

Niggli, Arnold. 1893. *Das Künstlerpaar August und Anna Walter-Strauss: Ein biographisch-kritischer Essay*. Zurich, Switzerland: Gebrüder Hug.

——. 1900. *Adolf Jensen*. Berlin: Harmonie.

Ninck, Martin. 1959. "Hermann Goetz und Johannes Brahms in Winterthur." In *Das Musikkollegium Winterthur 1837–1933*, edited by L. Kempter, 76–80. Winterthur, Switzerland: Verlag des Musikkollegiums Winterthur.

Nolthenius, Hugo. 1904. *Richard Hol*. Haarlem, The Netherlands: H. D. Tjeenk Willink & Zoon.

Norris, Gerald. 1980. *Stanford, the Cambridge Jubilee and Tchaikovsky*. Newton Abbott, Devon, UK: David & Charles.

Nouza, Zdeněk. 1988. "Beobachtungen zu Brahms' Stellung im tschechischen Musikleben seiner Zeit." In *Brahms-Kongress Wien 1983: Kongressbericht*, edited by S. Antonicek and O. Biba, 405–23. Tutzing, Germany: Schneider.

ÖBL *Österreichisches biographisches Lexikon 1815–1950*. 1957–. Vienna, Austria: Verlag der Österreichischen Akademie der Wissenschaften.

Ochs, Siegfried. 1922. *Geschehenes, Gesehenes*. Leipzig, Germany: Grethlein & Co.

Ollendorff, Paul. 1931. "Max Abraham." *Jahrbuch der Musikbibliothek Peters* 38: 69–77.

Ophüls, Erika, ed. 1992. *Willy von Beckerath—Gustav Ophüls: Briefwechsel 1896–1926. Zeugnisse einer geistigen Freundschaft*. Berlin: Merseburger.

Ophüls, Gustav, ed. 1983a. *Brahms-Texte*. Leipzig, 1898. Completed and newly edited by K. Wachinger. Ebenhausen, near Munich, Germany: Langewiesche-Brandt.

——. 1983b. *Erinnerungen an Johannes Brahms: Ein Beitrag aus dem Kreis seiner rheinischen Freunde*. Berlin: Verlag der Deutschen Brahms-Gesellschaft, 1921. Reprint Ebenhausen, Germany: Langewiesche-Brandt.

——. 1994. "'Ein schöneres Geschenk als das Ihre aber gibt es nicht': Zwei Briefe aus dem Nachlass Gustav Ophüls." *Brahms-Studien* 10: 33–37.

Ordenstein, Heinrich. n.d. *Musikgeschichte der Haupt- und Residenzstadt Karlsruhe bis zum Jahre 1914*. Karlsruhe, Germany.

Orel, Alfred. 1937. "Ein eigenhändiges Werkverzeichnis von Johannes Brahms. Ein wichtiger Beitrag zur Brahmsforschung." *Die Musik* 29, no. 8 (May): 529–41.

——. 1964. *Johannes Brahms und Julius Allgeyer. Eine Künstlerfreundschaft in Briefen*. Tutzing, Germany: Schneider.

Orlova, Alexandra. 1990. *Tchaikovsky: A Self-Portrait*, translated by R. M. Davison. Oxford, UK: Oxford University Press.

Osborne, Harold, ed. 1970. *The Oxford Companion to Art*. Oxford, UK: Oxford University Press.

O[truba, G.]. 1969. "Wittgenstein." In *Altösterreichische Unternehmer: 110 Lebensbilder*, edited by R. Granichstaedten-Cerva, J. Mentschl, and G. Otruba, 134–38. Vienna, Austria: Bergland Verlag.

Ott, Alfons, ed. 1969. *Richard Strauss und Ludwig Thuille: Briefe der Freundschaft 1877–1907*. Munich, Germany: Walter Ricke.

Ottendorff-Simrock, Walther. 1954. *Das Haus Simrock: Ein Beitrag zur Geschichte der kulturtragenden Familien des Rheinlandes*. Ratingen: Aloys Henn.

——. 1960a. "Simrock, Fritz." In *Rheinische Musiker*, edited by K. G. Fellerer, 1st series, 243–48. Cologne, Germany: Arno Volk.

——. 1960b. "Simrock, Peter Joseph." In *Rheinische Musiker*, edited by K. G. Fellerer, 1st series, 240–43. Cologne, Germany: Arno Volk.

Otto, Eberhard. 1980. "Georg Friedrich Daumer und Johannes Brahms: Ein fränkischer Dichter und sein Komponist." *Musik in Bayern* 21: 11–18.

Pascall, Robert, ed. 1883. *Brahms: Biographical, Documentary and Analytical Studies*. Cambridge, UK: Cambridge University Press.

——. 1988a. "Die erste in Wien aufgeführte Musik von Brahms und deren Nachklang im Brahms'schen Schaffen." In *Brahms-Kongress Wien 1983: Kongressbericht*, edited by S. Antonicek and O. Biba, 439–48. Tutzing, Germany: Schneider.

——. 1988b. "Robert Fuchs: Eine kritische Würdigung." In *Brahms-Kongress Wien 1983: Kongressbericht*, edited by S. Antonicek and O. Biba, 449–53. Tutzing, Germany: Schneider.

——. 2001. "Frühe Brahms-Rezeption in England." In *Internationaler Brahms-Kongress Gmunden 1997: Kongressbericht*, edited by I. Fuchs, 293–342. Tutzing, Germany: Schneider. (A supplement contains the text of five letters from Brahms to Charles Villiers Stanford.)

Pastille, William. 1987. "Schenker's Brahms." *American Brahms Society Newsletter* 5, no. 2 (Autumn): [1–2].

Pataky, Sophie, ed. 1898. *Lexikon deutscher Frauen der Feder: Eine Zusammenstellung der seit dem Jahre 1840 erschienenen Werke weiblicher Autoren nebst Bio-*

graphien der lebenden und einem Verzeichnis der Pseudonyme. 2 vols. Berlin: H. Lang.

Paulin, Roger. 1991. "Storm, (Hans) Theodor." In *Literatur Lexikon: Autoren und Werke deutscher Sprache*, vol 11, edited by W. Killy, 227–30. 15 vols. Gütersloh, Germany: Bertelsmann Lexikon Verlag, 1988–93.

Paumgartner, Bernhard. 1959. *Erinnerungen*. Salzburg, Austria: Residenz Verlag.

Peham, Heinrich. 1903. "Chrobak, Rudolf." In *Biographisches Jahrbuch und Deutscher Nekrolog, 1. Januar bis 31. Dezember 1900*, 47–49. Berlin.

Perger, Richard von. 1908. *Brahms*. Leipzig, Germany: Philipp Reclam jun.

Perger, Richard von, and Robert Hirschfeld. 1912. *Geschichte der k.k. Gesellschaft der Musikfreunde in Wien*. Vienna, Austria: Gesellschaft der Musikfreunde.

Pessenlehner, Robert. 1943. "Alexander Friedrich von Hessen. Zum 80. Geburtstag." *Zeitschrift für Musik* 110, no. 2: 51–55.

——. 1958. "Anna Landgräfin von Hessen. Zur 40. Wiederkehr ihres Todestages (12.6.1918). *Fuldaer Geschichtsblätter* 34, no. 9/12: 81–128.

Petersen, Peter. 1984. "Brahms und Dvořák." In *Brahms und seine Zeit: Symposium Hamburg 1983*, edited by C. Floros, H. J. Marx, and P. Petersen, 125–46. [n.p.]: Laaber.

Pfohl, Ferdinand. 1925. *Arthur Nikisch: Sein Leben, seine Kunst, sein Wirken*. Hamburg, Germany: Alster-Verlag.

——. 1973. *Gustav Mahler: Eindrücke und Erinnerungen aus den Hamburger Jahren*, edited by K. Martner. Hamburg, Germany: Verlag der Musikalienhandlung.

Pfordten, Hermann Freiherr von der. 1923. *Robert Franz*. Leipzig, Germany: Quelle & Meyer.

Pieper, Karl. 1938a. "Niederrheinische Komponisten." *Die Heimat* [Krefeld, Germany] 17: 47–52.

——. 1938b. "Johannes Brahms und sein Freundeskreis: Nach einem Briefe von Gustav Ophüls vom 6. Oktober 1892." *Die Heimat* [Krefeld, Germany] 17: 398–400.

Pilipczuk, Alexander. 1990. "Die Hamburger Pianoforte-Fabrik C. H. Schröder und Johannes Brahms." *Das Musikinstrument* 39, no. 9 (September): 22–32.

Plaschke, Olga. 1899. *Amalie Joachim: Blätter der Erinnerung*. Berlin: Harmonie.

Platt, Heather. 2003. *Johannes Brahms: A Guide to Research*. New York: Routledge.

Pleasants, Henry, ed., trans., and ann. 1979. *The Music Criticism of Hugo Wolf*. New York: Holmes & Meier.

Plessing, C. Th. 1929. "Clara Simrock zum Gedächtnis." *Simrock Jahrbuch* 2: 3–8.

Pohl, C[arl] F[erdinand]. 1871. *Die Gesellschaft der Musikfreunde des österreichischen Kaiserstaates und ihr Conservatorium*. Vienna, Austria: Braumüller.

——. 1883. *Denkschrift aus Anlass des fünfundzwanzigjährigen Bestehens des Singvereines der Gesellschaft der Musikfreunde in Wien*. Vienna, Austria: Singverein.

Pohl, Richard [Hoplit]. 1855. "Johannes Brahms." *Neue Zeitschrift für Musik* 43, no. 2 (6 July): 13–15; no. 24 (7 December): 253–55; no. 25 (14 December): 261–64.

——. 1881. *Autobiographisches*. Leipzig, Germany: Fritzsch.

Pollens, Stewart. 2006. "The Schumann/Brahms Conrad Graf Piano." *American Brahms Society Newsletter* 24, no. 1 (Spring): 1–4.

Porter, Cecelia Hopkins. 1979. "The New Public and the Reordering of the Musical Establishment: The Lower Rhine Music Festivals, 1818–67." *19th Century Music* 3, no. 1 (July): 211–24.

Possart, Ernst von. 1901. *Hermann Levi: Erinnerungen*. Munich, Germany: Beck'sche Verlagsbuchhandlung.

Prahács, Margit, ed. 1966. *Franz Liszt: Briefe aus ungarischen Sammlungen 1835–1886*. Kassel, Germany: Bärenreiter.

Prillinger, Elfriede. 1985. "Johannes Brahms und Gmunden (Die Sammlung Miller-Aichholz im Gmundner Kammerhofmuseum)." *Brahms-Studien* 5 (1983): 181–204; 6: 75–87.

———. 2001. "Brahmsportraits. Aspekte der Datierung und Zuschreibung anhand der Sammlung Miller-Aichholz im Kammerhofmuseum Gmunden." In *Internationaler Brahms-Kongress Gmunden 1997: Kongressbericht*, edited by I. Fuchs, 503–29. Tutzing, Germany: Schneider.

Probst, Emanuel. 1905. "Friedrich Riggenbach-Stehlin, 11. September 1821–3. März 1904." *Basler Jahrbuch*: 1–46.

Prosl, Robert Maria. 1947. *Die Hellmesberger: Hundert Jahre aus dem Leben einer Wiener Musikerfamilie*. Vienna, Austria: Gerlach & Wiedling.

Pross, Wolfgang. 1990. "Herder, Johann Gottfried." In *Literatur Lexikon: Autoren und Werke deutscher Sprache*, vol. 5, edited by W. Killy, 232–38. 15 vols. Gütersloh, Germany: Bertelsmann Lexikon Verlag, 1988–93.

Pulver, Jeffrey. 1925. "Brahms and the Influence of Joachim." *Musical Times* 66: 25–28.

———. 1933. "Brahms and the Doctorate." *The Sackbut* 14, no. 2 (December): 127–29.

Purver, Judith. 1989. "Eichendorff, Joseph (Karl Benedikt), Frhr." In *Literatur Lexikon: Autoren und Werke deutscher Sprache*, vol. 3, edited by W. Killy, 198–203. 15 vols. Gütersloh, Germany: Bertelsmann Lexikon Verlag, 1988–93.

Rackwitz, Werner. 1999. "Anmerkungen zum Verhältnis Friedrich Chrysanders zu Johannes Brahms und Joseph Joachim." *Brahms-Studien* 12: 41–59.

Raff, Helene. 1925. *Joachim Raff: Ein Lebensbild*. Regensburg, Germany: Bosse.

Raupp, Wilhelm. 1930. *Eugen d'Albert. Ein Künstler- und Menschenschicksal.* Leipzig, Germany: Koehler & Amelang.

(Reger, Max). 1928. "Max Reger über seine Bearbeitungen Brahms'scher Werke: Aus Briefen an den Verlag N. Simrock." *Simrock Jahrbuch* 1: 65–71.

Rehberg, Walter, and Paula Rehberg. 1947. *Johannes Brahms*. Zurich, Switzerland: Atlantis.

Rehberg, Willy. 1933. "Brahms-Erinnerungen." *Der Weihergarten*, 19–20, 25–26.

Reiber, Joachim. 1997. "'Auch das Gegenteil kann wahr sein': Johannes Brahms, Josef Viktor Widmann und Friedrich Nietzsche." In *Nietzsche und die Musik*, edited by G. Pöltner and H. Vetter, 57–79. Frankfurt, Germany: Lang.

———. 2001. "Suche, Versuche, Versuchungen. Brahms und die Oper." In *Internationaler Brahms-Kongress Gmunden 1997: Kongressbericht*, edited by I. Fuchs, 13–30. Tutzing, Germany: Schneider.

Reich, Nancy B. 1985. *Clara Schumann: The Artist and the Woman*. Ithaca, N.Y.: Cornell University Press.

——. 1990. "Clara Schumann and Johannes Brahms." In *Brahms and His World*, edited by W. Frisch, 37–47. Princeton, N.J.: Princeton University Press.

Reich, Willi, ed. 1975. *Johannes Brahms in Dokumenten zu Leben und Werk*. Zurich, Switzerland: Manesse Verlag.

Reicke, Emil. 1911. *Malwida von Meysenbug: Die Verfasserin der "Memoiren einer Idealisten."* Berlin: Schuster & Loeffler.

Reinecke, Carl. 1897. "Meine letzte Begegnung mit Johannes Brahms." *Dur und Moll* 1: 128–30. (Reprinted, with minor changes and under the title "Johannes Brahms" in *"Und manche liebe Schatten steigen auf": Gedenkblätter an berühmte Musiker*, 109–19. Leipzig, Germany: Gebrüder Reinecke, 1900.)

Reinecke, Franz, ed. 1889. *Verzeichnis der bis jetzt in Druck erschienenen Compositionen von Carl Reinecke.* Leipzig, Germany: Breitkopf & Härtel.

Reinhardt, Klaus. 1991. *Ein Meininger Musiker an der Seite von Brahms und Reger: Das Wirken des Cellisten und Dirigenten Karl Theodor Piening (1867–1942).* Hanover, Germany: Jan Reinhardt.

Reismann, August. 1876. *Die königliche Hochschule für Musik in Berlin*. Berlin: J. Guttentag.

Rembert. 1933. "Die Krefelder Familie Wolff, ein Beitrag zur Musikgeschichte unserer Stadt und zur Vererbungslehre." *Die Heimat* [Krefeld, Germany] 12: 149–54.

(Reményi, Eduard). 1879. "A Twenty-five Years' Secret. Revelations That Will Stir the Musical World. Remenyi and Johannes Brahms. Who Composed 'Brahms' Celebrated Hungarian Dances?" *New York Herald*, 18 January, 10. (Reprinted in Kelley, Gwendolyn Dunlevy, and George Upton. 1906. *Edouard Remenyi. Musician, Litterateur, and Man. An Appreciation*, 79–95. Chicago: McClurg & Co.)

Reményi, Eduard. 1898. "Johannes Brahms Dead," translated by J. Rosenberg. *Music* (Chicago) 15, no. 1 (November): 43–46.

Richter, Kurt W. 1973. "Brahms und Klinger: Drei unveröffentliche Briefe Max Klingers an Johannes Brahms aus dem Brahms-Archiv." *Mitteilungen der Brahms-Gesellschaft Hamburg* 4 (April): 3–6.

Rieger, Eva, ed. 2002. *Mit 1000 Küssen Deine Fillu: Briefe der Sängerin Marie Fillunger an Eugenie Schumann 1873–93*. Cologne, Germany: Dittrich.

Riemann, Hugo. 1967. *Musik Lexikon*. 3 vols. New York: Schott Music. Supplement: 2 vols. Mainz, Germany: Schott, 1972–75.

Rienäcker, Gerd. 1997. "Auseinandersetzung unter Gleichgesinnten? Hanslick über Brahms." *Brahms-Studien* 11: 9–17.

Rilling, Helmuth. 1975. "From Johannes Brahms to Robert Kahn. 1887." *Bach* 6, no. 4 (October): 20–22.

Ringer, Alexander. 1980/81. "Friedrich Gernsheim (1839–1916) and the Lost Generation." *Musica Judaica* 3, no. 1: 1–12.

Roesing, Elizabeth. 1927. "Aus der Zeit des jungen Brahms: Nach Erinnerungen von Elisabeth Proffen, née Roesing." *Zeitschrift für Musik* 94: 416–18. (The same text, except for the final lines, is reproduced in "Erinnerungen an Johannes Brahms," *Die Heimat* [Krefeld, Germany] 25 (1954): 32–34.)

Roggenkamp, Peter. 1999. "Von einigen Berührungspunkten zweier grosser Meister: Brahms und Busoni." *Brahms-Studien* 12: 29–40.

Rohling, Ludwig. 1957. "Wilhelm Lübke." In *Westfälische Lebensbilder*, vol. 6, edited by R. Stupperich, 147–65. Münster, Germany: Aschendorff.

Rohnacher, Ilse. 1985. "Brahms in Ziegelhausen." In *Musik in Heidelberg 1775–1885*, 207–22. (Catalog of an exhibition held at Heidelberg Castle, 2 June–4 August 1985 [Heidelberg].)

Romeyk, Horst. 1994. *Die leitenden staatlichen und kommunalen Verwaltungsbeamten der Rheinprovinz 1816–1945*. Düsseldorf, Germany: Publikationen der Gesellschaft für Rheinische Geschichskunde, 69.

Röntgen, A., ed. 1934. *Brieven van Julius Röntgen*. Amsterdam, The Netherlands: H. J. Paris.

Röntgen, Julius. 1920. "Johannes Brahms in Holland." *Neue Musikzeitung* 41, no. 15 (29 April): 236–38.

——. 1930. *Grieg*. Gravenhage, The Netherlands: Krusman.

Rosé, Arnold. 1932. *Das Rosé Quartett: Fünfzig Jahre Kammermusik in Wien. Sämtliche Programme vom 1. Quartett am 22. Januar 1883 bis April 1932*. Vienna, Austria: Hofmeister-Figaro-Verlag.

Rosendahl, Erich. 1928. *König Georg V. von Hannover: Mit einem Abriss der Geschichte des Hannoverlandes. Ein Gedenkbuch*. Hanover, Germany: Helwingsche Verlagsbuchhandlung.

Rosenthal, Harold. 1958. *Two Centuries of Opera at Covent Garden*. London: Putnam.

Roses, Daniel F. 1986. "Brahms and Billroth." *Surgery, Gynecology and Obstetrics* 163: 385–98.

——. 1987. "Brahms and Billroth." *American Brahms Society Newsletter* 5, no. 1 (Spring): 1–5.

Rountree, Kathleen. 1994. "The Short-Lived Career of Ilona Eibenschütz." *American Music Teacher* 43, no. 5 (April/May): 14–17.

Roux, Jules-Charles. 1892. *Vingt ans de vie publique*. Paris: Guillaumin.

Rubinstein, Anton. 1969. *Autobiography, 1829–1889*, translated by A. Delano. Boston: Little, Brown,1890. Reissued New York: Haskell House Publishers.

Rudorff, Ernst. 1957. "Johannes Brahms. Erinnerungen und Betrachtungen." *Schweizerische Musikzeitung* 97: 81–85, 139–45, 182–87.

Ruhbaum, Antje. 2002a. "Ein Talent 'als Sängerin, Pianistin, vielleicht sogar als Komponistin in der Öffentlichkeit zu glänzen': Elisabeth von Herzogenberg als Musikförderin." In *Geschlechterpolaritäten in der Musikgeschichte des 18. bis 20. Jahrhunderts*, edited by R. Grotjahn and F. Hoffmann, 197–207. Herbolzheim, Germany: Centaurus Verlag.

——. 2002b. "Von Eisbergen und Unterwasserlandschaften: Elisabeth und Heinrich von Herzogenberg und der Brahmskreis." In *musik netz werke: Konturen der neuen Musikkultur. Dokumentation des 16. Internationalen Studentischen Symposiums für Musikwissenschaft in Berlin 2001*, 140–64. Bielefeld, Germany.

Rumbold, Horace. 1902. *Recollections of a Diplomatist*. London: Arnold.

Sadie, Stanley, ed. 1992. *The New Grove Dictionary of Opera*. 4 vols. New York: Grove's Dictionaries.

——, ed. 2001. *The New Grove Dictionary of Music and Musicians*. 2nd edition. 29 vols. New York: Grove's Dictionaries.

Sauer, Emil. 1901. *Meine Welt: Bilder aus dem Geheimfache meiner Kunst und meines Lebens*. Stuttgart, Germany: Spemann.

Saur. 1992. *Allgemeines Künstler-Lexikon: Die bildenden Künstler aller Zeiten und Völker*. Munich, Germany: K. G. Saur.

Schardig, Waltraut. 1986. *Friedrich Chrysander: Leben und Werk*. Hamburg, Germany: Karl Dieter Wagner.

Scharwenka, Xaver. 1922. *Erinnerungen eines Musikers*. Leipzig, Germany: Koehler.

Schauffler, Robert Haven. 1972. *The Unknown Brahms. His Life, Character and Works; Based on New Material*. New York: Dodd, Mead & Co., 1933. Reprint Westport, Conn.: Greenwood Press.

Scheible, Heinz. 1989. "Eber, Paul." In *Literatur Lexikon: Autoren und Werke deutscher Sprache*, vol. 3, edited by W. Killy, 139. 15 vols. Gütersloh, Germany: Bertelsmann Lexikon Verlag, 1988–93.

Scheman, Ludwig. 1955. "Bülow und Brahms." In *Hans von Bülow im Lichte der Wahrheit*, 65–93. Regensburg, Germany: Bosse.

Schenker, Heinrich. 1897. "Johannes Brahms." *Die Zukunft* 19 (May): 261–65. English version by William Pastille in *American Brahms Society Newsletter* 9, no. 1 (Spring 1991): 1–3.

Schilling, Jörg. 1988. "Allmers, Hermann." In *Literatur Lexikon: Autoren und Werke deutscher Sprache*, vol. 1, edited by W. Killy, 107–8. 15 vols. Gütersloh, Germany: Bertelsmann Lexikon Verlag, 1988–93.

Schilling, Ulrike. 1994. "Johannes Brahms." In *Philipp Spitta: Leben und Wirken im Spiegel seines Briefwechsels*, 175–82. Kassel, Germany: Bärenreiter. (The book also contains sections on Spitta's relations with, among others, Joseph Joachim, and Heinrich and Elisabeth von Herzogenberg.)

Schloenbach, Arnold. 1853. "Ein offener Brief an Franz Brendel." *Neue Zeitschrift für Musik* 39, no. 24 (9 December): 256–58.

Schlossmacher, Norbert. 1997. "'Er gab dem musikalischen Leben in Bonn einen mächtigen Schwung' Der Bonner Musikmäzen Carl Gottlieb Kyllmann (1803–1878)." In *Johannes Brahms und Bonn*, edited by M. Gutiérrez-Denhoff, 44–61. Bonn, Germany: Stadt Bonn.

Schmaltz, Susanne. 1926. *Beglückte Erinnerung: Lebenslauf eines Sonntagkindes*. Dresden, Germany: Verlag Deutsche Buchwerkstätten.

Schmelzer, Hans-Jürgen. 1983. *Johannes Brahms—Zwischen Ruhm und Einsamkeit: Eine Biographie*. Tübingen, Germany: Heliopolis Verlag.

Schmitz, Walter. 1990. "Hoffmann von Fallersleben, August Heinrich." In *Literatur Lexikon: Autoren und Werke deutscher Sprache*, vol. 5, edited by W. Killy, 421–23. 15 vols. Gütersloh, Germany: Bertelsmann Lexikon Verlag, 1988–93.

——. 1991. "Schack, Adolf Friedrich, Graf." In *Literatur Lexikon: Autoren und Werke deutscher Sprache*, vol. 10, edited by W. Killy, 144–45. 15 vols. Gütersloh, Germany: Bertelsmann Lexikon Verlag, 1988–93.

Schnabel, Artur. 1961. *My Life and Music, and Reflections on Music*. New York: St. Martin's Press.

Schnapp, Friedrich, ed. 1935. *Busoni: Briefe an seine Frau*. Zurich, Switzerland: Rotapfel Verlag. (English version: *Ferruccio Busoni: Letters to His Wife*, translated by R. Ley. London: Edward Arnold, 1938.)

Schneider, Eugen. 1971. “Ulrich von Württemberg.” In ***ADB***, vol. 39, 237–43. 56 vols. Berlin: Duncker & Humblot, 1967–71.

Schnitzler, Viktor. 1935. *Erinnerungen aus meinem Leben*. Cologne, Germany: Tischer & Jagenberg. (The text had been privately printed at Cologne in 1921.)

Schoen-René, Anna Eugénie. 1941. *America’s Musical Inheritance: Memories and Reminiscences*. New York: G. P. Putnam’s Sons.

Schönaich, Gustav. 1897. “Johannes Brahms.” *Reichswehr* (Vienna), 4 April, 1–2.

Scholz, Bernhard. 1899. “Hector Berlioz. Franz Liszt. Johannes Brahms.” In *Musikalisches und Persönliches*, 206–20. Berlin: Spemann.

——. 1911. *Verklungene Weisen: Erinnerungen*. Mainz, Germany: Jos. Scholz.

Schonberg, Harold C. 1965. *The Great Pianists*. London: Gollancz.

Schramm, Willi. 1983. *Johannes Brahms in Detmold*. New, annotated edition by R. Müller-Dombois. Hagen, Germany: Kommissionsverlag v. d. Linnepe.

Schubring, Adolf [DAS]. 1862. “Die Schumann’sche Schule. IV: Johannes Brahms.” *Neue Zeitschrift für Musik* 56: 93–96, 101–4, 109–12, 117–19, 125–28.

——. 1868. “Die Schumann’sche Schule. Schumann und Brahms: Brahms’ vierhändige Schumann-Variationen.” *Allgemeine musikalische Zeitung* 3: 41–42, 49–51.

——. 1869. “Ein deutsches Requiem.” *Allgemeine musikalische Zeitung* 4: 9–11, 18–20.

Schug, Karl. 1966. “Salomon Hermann Mosenthal: Leben und Werk in der Zeit. Ein Beitrag zur Problematik der literarischen Geschmacksbildung.” PhD diss., University of Vienna.

Schuh, Willi, ed. 1954. *Richard Strauss: Briefe an die Eltern, 1882–1906*. Zurich, Switzerland: Atlantis.

——. 1964. *Schweizer Musiker-Lexikon/Dictionnaire des musiciens suisses*, edited by Willi Schuh et al. Zurich, Switzerland: Atlantis Verlag.

——. 1976. *Richard Strauss: Jugend und frühe Meisterjahre. Lebenschronik 1864–1898*. Zurich, Switzerland: Atlantis.

Schuh, Willi, and Franz Trenner, eds. 1954. “Hans von Bülow / Richard Strauss Briefwechsel.” *Richard Strauss Jahrbuch*: 7–45.

Schultz, Hartwig. 1988. “Arnim, Bettine von.” In *Literatur Lexikon: Autoren und Werke deutscher Sprache*, vol. 1, edited by W. Killy, 214–16. 15 vols. Gütersloh, Germany: Bertelsmann Lexikon Verlag, 1988–93.

Schumann, Alfred [pseudonym Titus Frazeni]. 1926. *Johannes Brahms der Vater von Felix Schumann: Das Mysterium einer Liebe. Eine sehr ernste Parodie auf die “Erinnerungen” von Eugenie Schumann*. Bielefeld, Germany: Manfred-Verlag, Schumann & Steinau.

Schumann, Eugenie. 1931. *Robert Schumann: Ein Lebensbild meines Vaters*. Leipzig, Germany: Koehler & Amelang.

——. 1995. *Claras Kinder: Erinnerungen*. With a postscript by Eva Weissweiler. Cologne, Germany: Dittrich.

Schumann, Ferdinand. 1915. "Erinnerungen an Johannes Brahms. 1894, 1895, 1896." *Neue Zeitschrift für Musik* 82: 225–28, 233–36, 341–43. (Extracts, translated by Jacques Mayer, *Musical Quarterly* 2 (1916): 507–15.

———. 1917. "Erinnerungen an Clara Schumann: Tagebuchblätter ihres Enkels." *Neue Zeitschrift für Musik* 84: 69–72, 77–80, 85–88, 93–96, 101–4.

Schumann, Robert. 1853. "Neue Bahnen." *Neue Zeitschrift für Musik* 39, no. 18 (28 October): 1–2.

Schumann-Reye, Irmgard. 1990. "'Johannes Brahms im Leben unserer Mutter und Grossmutter' berichtet von Gertrud Reye." *Brahms-Studien* 8: 61–70.

Schuppener, Ulrich. 1993. "Hermine Spies und ihre Beziehungen zu Johannes Brahms. Zum 100. Todestag der berühmten Altistin aus Löhnberg." *Nassauische Annalen* 104: 197–216.

Schwabe, Günter. 1984. "Wolff." In "Krefelder Familien," 172. *Die Heimat* [Krefeld, Germany] 56: 167–72.

Schwarz, Hermine. 1922. *Ignaz Brüll und sein Freundeskreis: Erinnerungen an Brüll, Goldmark und Brahms*. Vienna, Austria: Rikola Verlag.

Schwarz, Werner. 1966. "Eine Musikerfreundschaft des 19. Jahrhunderts: Unveröffentliche Briefe von Ferdinand David an Robert Schumann." In *Zum 70: Geburtstag von Joseph Müller-Blattau*, edited by C.-H. Mahling, 282–303. Kassel, Germany: Bärenreiter.

Schwitzgebel, Bärbel. 1997. "Johannes Brahms in Wiesbaden." In *Johannes Brahms in den Bädern Baden-Baden—Wiesbaden, Germany—Bad Ischl—Karlsbad*, edited by J. Draheim and U. Reimann, 57–77. Baden-Baden, Germany: Stadt Baden-Baden.

Seelig. Geert. 1924. *Klaus Groth: Sein Leben und Werden*. Hamburg, Germany: Alster-Verlag.

Seewöster, Felix. 1992. "Wallisch, Friedrich." In *Literatur Lexikon: Autoren und Werke deutscher Sprache*, vol. 12, edited by W. Killy, 116. 15 vols. Gütersloh, Germany: Bertelsmann Lexikon Verlag, 1988–93.

Selbmann, Rolf. 1990. "Lingg, Hermann, Ritter von." In *Literatur Lexikon: Autoren und Werke deutscher Sprache*, vol. 7, edited by W. Killy, 303–4. 15 vols. Gütersloh, Germany: Bertelsmann Lexikon Verlag, 1988–93.

———. 1989. *Friedrich Rückert und sein Denkmal: Eine Sozialgeschichte des Dichterkults im 19. Jahrhundert*. Würzburg, Germany: Königshausen & Neumann.

Seyffardt, Ernst H. 1936. "Aus den Lebenserinnerungen des Krefelder Komponisten Prof. Ernst H. Seyffardt." *Die Heimat* [Krefeld, Germany] 15: 160–67.

Shaw, George Bernard. 1937. *London Music in 1888–89 as Heard by Corno di Bassetto (Later Known as Bernard Shaw) with Some Further Autobiographical Particulars*. London: Constable & Co.

Siedentopf, Henning. 1973. "Der Nachlass des Musikgelehrten Josef Sittard." *Musikforschung* 26: 350–52.

———. 1979. "Brahms und die Oper oder: Ein lautes Geheimnis." In *Musiker der Spätromantik: Unbekannte Briefe aus dem Nachlass von Josef und Alfred Sittard*, 13–23. Tübingen, Germany: Studio 74.

Siegmund-Schultze, Walther. 1983. "Händel und Brahms." *Händel-Jahrbuch* 29: 75–83.

Sietz, Reinhold, ed. 1958–70. *Aus Ferdinand Hillers Briefwechsel: Beiträge zu einer Biographie Ferdinand Hillers*. 7 vols. Cologne, Germany: Volk.

———. 1960a. "Bargiel, Woldemar." In *Rheinische Musiker*, edited by K. G. Fellerer, 1st series, 5–7. Cologne, Germany: Arno Volk.

———. 1960b. "Dietrich, Albert Hermann." In *Rheinische Musiker*, edited by K. G. Fellerer, 1st series, 5–7. Cologne, Germany: Arno Volk.

———. 1960c. "Hiller, Ferdinand." In *Rheinische Musiker*, edited by K. G. Fellerer, 1st series, 115–22. Cologne, Germany: Arno Volk.

———. 1960d. "Wüllner, Franz." In *Rheinische Musiker*, edited by K. G. Fellerer, 1st series, 271–75. Cologne, Germany: Arno Volk.

———. 1960e. "Johannes Brahms und Theodor Kirchner: Mit ungedruckten Briefen Th. Kirchners." *Musikforschung* 13: 396–404.

———. 1962. "Reinthaler, Karl Martin." In *Rheinische Musiker*, edited by K. G. Fellerer, 2nd series: 76–78. Cologne, Germany: Arno Volk.

———. 1964a. "Reinecke, Carl Heinrich Carsten." In *Rheinische Musiker*, edited by K. G. Fellerer, 3rd series: 68–73. Cologne, Germany: Arno Volk.

———. 1964b. "Rietz, Julius." In *Rheinische Musiker*, edited by K. G. Fellerer, 3rd series: 73–77. Cologne, Germany: Arno Volk.

———. 1971. *Theodor Kirchner: Ein Klaviermeister der deutschen Romantik*. Regensburg, Germany: Bosse.

Sieveke, Franz Günter. 1991. "Spee, Friedrich." In *Literatur Lexikon: Autoren und Werke deutscher Sprache*, vol. 11, edited by W. Killy, 91–93. 15 vols. Gütersloh, Germany: Bertelsmann Lexikon Verlag, 1988–93.

Sittard, Josef. 1971. *Geschichte des Musik—und Concertwesens in Hamburg vom 14. Jahrhundert bis auf die Gegenwart*. Altona, Germany: A. C. Reher, 1890. Reprint Hildesheim, Germany: Olms.

Slonimsky, Nicolas. 1954. "Musical Oddities." *Etude* 72, no. 10 (October): 4.

Smyth, Ethel. 1919. *Impressions That Remained: Memoirs*. 2nd edition. 2 vols. London: Longmans, Green & Co.

———. 1936. *As Time Went On*. London: Longmans, Green & Co.

Šourek, Otakar. 1984. *Antonín Dvořák: Letters and Reminiscences*, translated by R. F. Samsour. Prague, Czech Republic: Artia, 1954. Reprint New York: Da Capo Press.

Specht, Richard. 1928. *Johannes Brahms: Leben und Werk eines deutschen Meisters*. Hellerau, Germany: Avalun-Verlag.

Spengel, Annemari, ed. 1959. *Johannes Brahms und Julius Spengel: Unveröffentliche Briefe aus den Jahren 1882–1897*. Hamburg, Germany: Gesellschaft der Bücherfreunde.

Spengel, Julius. 1898. *Johannes Brahms: Charakterstudie*. Hamburg, Germany: Gesellschaft Hamburgischer Kunstfreunde.

———. 1936–37. "Erinnerungen an Johannes Brahms." *Deutsche Musik-Zeitung* 12 (1936): 95–96; 13 (1937): 2–3. Contains a few letters from Brahms to Spengel that are also included in A. Spengel 1959.

Speyer, Edward. 1937. *My Life and Friends*. London: Cobden-Sanderson.

Spielmann, Heinz. 1981. "Brahms in der bildenden Kunst." In *Johannes Brahms, geboren 7. Mai 1833 zu Hamburg, gestorben 3. April 1897 zu Wien*, 19–28. (Brochure published by the Deutsche Bank, Hamburg, on the occasion of its Brahms exhibition, 19 October to 6 November.)

[Spies, Minna]. 1905. *Hermine Spies: Ein Gedenkbuch für ihre Freunde von ihrer Schwester*. 2nd edition. Leipzig, Germany: G. J. Göschensche Verlagshandlung.

Spitta, Philipp. 1892. "Johannes Brahms." In *Zur Musik: Sechzehn Aufsätze*, 385–427. Berlin: Gebrüder Paetel.

Spitzbart, Ingrid. 1997a. *Johannes Brahms und die Familie Miller-Aichholz in Gmunden und Wien*. Gmunden: Kammerhofmuseum.

———. 1997b. *Johannes Brahms und die Familie Miller-Aichholz in Gmunden*. Vol. 4 of *Gmunden in alten Ansichten*. Zaltbommel, the Netherlands: Europäische Bibliothek.

———. 2001. "Brahms-Besuche bei der Familie Miller-Aichholz in Gmunden. Nach Quellen der Brahms-Sammlung des Kammerhofmuseums der Stadt Gmunden." In *Internationaler Brahms-Kongress Gmunden 1997: Kongressbericht*, edited by I. Fuchs, 487–501. Tutzing, Germany: Schneider.

Spitzer, Daniel. 1970. *Hereinspaziert ins alte Wien: Heiter Satirisches aus der Donaumonarchie*, edited by H. Hakel. Munich, Germany: Deutscher Taschenbuch Verlag.

Stahmer, Klaus. 1979. "Brahms auf Rügen. Der Sommeraufenthalt eines Komponisten." *Brahms-Studien* 3: 59–68.

Stanford, Charles Villliers. 1908. "A Few Memories of Johannes Brahms." In *Studies and Memories*, 107–16. London: Constable & Co. The book also contains a section "Ernst Frank" (99–106).

———. 1912. *Brahms*. New York: Frederick A. Stokes. In *Masterpieces of Music Series.* Contains "Brahms and His Music," 8–30.

———. 1914. *Pages from an Unwritten Diary*. London: Edward Arnold.

Stange, Hermann. 1906. "Die schleswig-holsteinischen Musikfeste." *Die Heimat* (Monatsschrift des Vereins zur Pflege der Natur- und Landeskunde in Schleswig-Holstein, Hamburg, Lübeck und dem Fürstentum Lübeck) 16, no. 6 (June): 135–53.

Stargardt-Wolff, Edith. 1954. *Wegbereiter grosser Musiker: Unter Verwendung von Tagebuchblättern, Briefen und vielen persönlichen Erinnerungen von Hermann und Louise Wolff, den Gründern der ersten Konzertdirektion, 1880–1935*. Berlin: Bote & Bock.

Stein, Fritz. 1910–11. "Ernst Naumann." *International Musical Society Zeitschrift* 12: 158–59.

Steinecke, Hartmut. 1990. "Meissner, Alfred." In *Literatur Lexikon: Autoren und Werke deutscher Sprache*, vol. 8, edited by W. Killy, 82–83. 15 vols. Gütersloh, Germany: Bertelsmann Lexikon Verlag, 1988–93.

Steiner, A[dolf]. 1898–99. *Johannes Brahms*. Allgemeine Musik-Gesellschaft in Zurich, Switzerland. *Neujahrsblatt* 86 and 87. Zurich: Druck von Zurcher & Furrer.

——. 1928. *Friedrich Hegar: Sein Leben und Wirken*. Allgemeine Musik-Gesellschaft in Zurich, Switzerland. *Neujahrsblatt* 116. Zurich: O. Fussli.

Stemplinger, Eduard. 1955. "Bodenstedt, Friedrich Maritn von." In ***NDB***, vol. 2, 355–56. Berlin, Germany: Duncker & Humblot, 1952–.

Stengel, Frida. 1958. "Richard Barth." In *Lebensbilder aus Kurhessen und Waldeck, 1830–1930*, vol. 6, edited by I. Schnack, 21–30. Marburg an der Lahn, Germany: Elwert.

Stephenson, Kurt. 1928. *Hundert Jahre Philharmonische Gesellschaft in Hamburg*. Hamburg, Germany: Philharmonische Gesellschaft.

——, ed. 1961. *Johannes Brahms und Fritz Simrock: Weg einer Freundschaft. Briefe des Verlegers an den Komponisten*. Hamburg, Germany: Augustin.

——. 1962a. "Der junge Brahms und Reményis 'Ungarische Lieder.'" *Studien zur Musikwissenschaft* 25: 520–31.

——. 1962b. "Johannes Brahms und Georg Dietrich Otten." In *Festschrift Karl Gustav Fellerer zum sechzigsten Geburtstag am 7. Juli 1962*, edited by H. Hüschen, 503–18. Regensburg, Germany: Bosse.

——. 1966. "Wasielewski, Wilhelm Joseph von." In *Rheinische Musiker*, edited by K. G. Fellerer, 4th series: 189–91. Cologne, Germany: Arno Volk.

——. 1972. "Wohnungen der Familie Brahms 1830 bis 1883." *Mitteilungen der Brahms-Gesellschaft Hamburg* 3: 5–7.

——, ed. 1973. *Johannes Brahms in seiner Familie: Der Briefwechsel, mit den Lebensbildern der Hamburger Verwandten*. Hamburg, Germany: Hauswedell & Co.

——. 1979. *Johannes Brahms und die Familie von Beckerath: Mit unveröffentlichen Brahmsbriefen*. Hamburg, Germany: Christians Verlag.

Stern, Adolf, ed. 1903. *Franz Liszts Briefe an Carl Gille: Mit einer biographischen Einleitung*. Leipzig, Germany: Breitkopf & Härtel.

Sternberg, Thomas. 1988. "Arnim, (Ludwig) Achim von." In *Literatur Lexikon: Autoren und Werke deutscher Sprache*, vol. 1, edited by W. Killy, 210–14. 15 vols. Gütersloh, Germany: Bertelsmann Lexikon Verlag, 1988–93.

Stockhem, Michel. 1993. "Armand Parent, Brahms et La France." *Revue belge de musicologie/Belgisch Tijdschrift voor Muziekwetenschap* 47: 177–88.

Stockmann, Bernhard. 1984. "Brahms—Reger oder Von der Legitimation des religiösen Liberalismus." In *Brahms und seine Zeit: Symposium Hamburg 1983*, edited by C. Floros, H. J. Marx, and P. Petersen, 211–22. [n.p.]: Laaber. (*Hamburger Jahrbuch für Musikwissenschaft* 7.)

Stojowski, Sigismond. 1933. "Recollections of Brahms." *Musical Quarterly* 19: 143–50.

Stör, Albrecht. 1892. "Alois Schmitt und das Hoftheater zu Schwerin." *Neue Berliner Musikzeitung* 46: 475–77, 491–93, 503–6, 522–24, 538–39, 559–60.

Strauss, Richard. 1957. *Betrachtungen und Erinnerungen*, edited by W. Schuh. 2nd, enlarged edition. Zurich, Switzerland: Atlantis.

Strobel, Gertrud, et al., eds. 1967–. *Richard Wagner: Sämtliche Briefe*. Leipzig, Germany: Deutscher Verlag für Musik, later Wiesbaden, Germany: Breitkopf & Härtel.

Struck, Michael. 1988. "Revisionsbedürftig: Zur gedruckten Korrespondenz von Johannes Brahms und Clara Schumann. Auswirkungen irrtümlicher oder lückenhafter Überlieferung auf werkgenetische Bestimmungen (mit einem unausgewerteten Brahms-Brief zur Violinsonate op. 78)." *Musikforschung* 41: 235–41.

——. 1991. "*Noch einmal* Brahms's B major Trio: Where Was the Original Version First Performed?" translated by V. Hancock. *American Brahms Society Newsletter* 9, no. 2 (Autumn): 8–9.

——. 1997. "Zwischen Alter und Neuer Welt: Unbekannte Dokumente zur Uraufführung und frühen Rezeption des Klaviertrios op. 8 von Johannes Brahms in der Erstfassung." In *Tradition—Neuansätze: Für Anna Amalie Abert (1906–1996)*, edited by K. Hortschansky, 664–76. Tutzing, Germany: Schneider.

Strutt, William M. 1915. *The Reminiscences of a Musical Amateur*. London.

Stuckenschmidt, H. H. 1967. *Ferruccio Busoni: Zeittafel eines Europäers*. Zurich, Switzerland: Atlantis. (English version: *Ferruccio Busoni: Chronicle of a European*, translatedby S. Morris. London: Calder & Boyans, 1970.)

Suk, Josef. 1910. "Aus meiner Jugend: Wiener Brahms-Erinnerungen." *Der Merker* 2, no. 4 (25 November): 147–50.

Sulzer, Peter. 1973. "Das verlegerische Werk J. M. Rieter-Biedermanns." *Winterthurer Jahrbuch*: 67–73.

——. 1974. "Johannes Brahms und Ida Rieter." *Winterthurer Jahrbuch*: 47–53.

——. 1985. "13 neu aufgefundene Postkarten und ein Brief von Johannes Brahms an Jakob Melchior Rieter-Biedermann." *Brahms-Studien* 6: 31–60.

Sumner, W. L. 1966. *The Pianoforte*. London: Macdonald, & Co.

Suppan, Wolfgang. 1962–66. *Steirisches Musiklexikon*. Graz, Austria: Akademische Druck- und Verlagsanstalt.

Swafford, Jan. 1997. *Johannes Brahms: A Biography*. New York: Knopf.

——. 2001. "Did the Young Brahms Play Piano in Waterfront Bars?" *19th Century Music* 24, no. 3 (Spring): 268–75.

Taddey, Gerhard, ed. 1983. *Lexikon der deutschen Geschichte: Personen, Ereignisse, Institutionen. Von der Zeitwende bis zum Ausgang des 2. Weltkrieges*. 2nd, revised edition. Stuttgart, Germany: Alfred Kröner.

Tchaikovsky, Modeste. 1906. *The Life & Letters of Peter Ilich Tchaikovsky*, edited by R. Newmarch. London: John Lane.

Tchaikovsky, Peter. 1945. *The Diaries of Tchaikovsky*, translated and annotated by W. Lakond. New York: Norton & Co.

——. 1969. "On Brahms." In *The Critical Composer: The Musical Writings of Berlioz, Wagner, Schumann, Tchaikovsky, and Others*, edited by I. Kolodin, 202–5. New York: Howell, Soskin & Co., 1940. Reissued Port Washington, N.Y.: Kennikat Press.

Ternant, Andrew de. 1924. "Debussy and Brahms." *Musical Times* 65: 608–9.

Tessier, André. 1930. "Bonaventure Laurens ou l'antiquaire musical XIXe siècle." *Revue musicale*, 11: 17–37, 132–44.

Thatcher, David S. 1973. "Nietzsche and Brahms: A Forgotten Relationship." *Music and Letters* 54, no. 3 (July): 261–80.

——. 1978. "Nietzsches Totengericht über Brahms." *Nietzsche-Studien* 7: 339–56. (Followed by a discussion, 357–61.)

Thiel, Rudolf. 1951. "Umgang mit Brahms." In *Der Himmel voller Geigen: Das Leben der grossen Symphoniker*, 597–668. Vienna, Austria: Paul Neff Verlag.

Thieme, Ulrich, and Felix Becker et al., eds. 1907–47. *Allgemeines Lexikon der bildenden Künstler von der Antike bis zur Gegenwart*. 36 vols. Leipzig, Germany: E. A. Seemann.

Thoene, Walter. 1960. "Buths, Julius Emil Martin." In *Rheinische Musiker*, edited by K. G. Fellerer. 1st series: 52–61. Cologne, Germany: Arno Volk.

Tovey, Donald Francis. 1935–39. *Essays in Musical Analysis*. 6 vols. London: Oxford University Press.

——. 1949. "Tonality in Schubert." In *Essays and Lectures on Music*, 134–59. London: Oxford University Press. (Originally published in *Music and Letters* 9, no. 4 [October 1928].)

Trenner, Franz, ed. 1978. *Cosima Wagner—Richard Strauss: Ein Briefwechsel*. Tutzing, Germany: Schneider.

Truxa, Celestina. 1903. "Am Sterbebett Brahms'." *Neue freie Presse*, 7 May, 8.

——. 1972. "Brief von Frau Celestina Truxa, der Hauswirtin von Johannes Brahms, an Frau Marie Böie anlässlich seines Todes am 3. April 1897—aus dem Besitz von Herrn Gerhard Maass, Ronco s. Ascona." *Mitteilungen der Brahms-Gesellschaft Hamburg* 3: 4–5.

Tsareva, Ekaterina. 1999. "Brahms-Rezeption in Russland: Zugänge zu Brahms in der russischen Musikkultur vom Ende des 19. bis zum Anfang des 20. Jahrhunderts." In *Johannes Brahms: Quellen—Text—Rezeption—Interpretation. Internationaler Brahms-Kongress Hamburg 1997*, edited by F. Krummacher and M. Struck, in collaboration with C. Floros and P. Petersen, 511–24. Munich, Germany: G. Henle.

——. 2001. "Brahms' Kammermusik in Russland 1870–1900." In *Internationaler Brahms-Kongress Gmunden 1997: Kongressbericht*, edited by I. Fuchs, 215–26. Tutzing, Germany: Schneider.

Tschackert, Paul. 1971. "Speratus." In ***ADB***, vol. 35, 123–35. 56 vols. Berlin: Duncker & Humblot, 1967–71.

Turner, Jane, ed. 1996. *Grove Dictionary of Art*. 34 vols. London: Macmillan.

Uhde-Bernays, Hermann, ed. 1907. *Briefe von und an Michael Bernays*. Berlin: Behr.

——, ed. 1912. *Anselm Feuerbachs Briefe an seine Mutter*. Berlin: Meyer & Jessen.

——, ed. 1913. *Henriette Feuerbach: Ihr Leben in ihren Briefen*. Berlin: Meyer & Jessen.

Unger, William. 1929. *Aus meinem Leben*. Vienna, Austria: Gesellschaft für vervielfältigende Kunst.

Viardot, Pauline. 1915–16. "Pauline Viardot-Garcia to Julius Rietz. (Letters of Friendship)," translated by T. Baker. *Musical Quarterly* 1 (1915): 350–80, 526–59; 2 (1916): 32–60.

Vignal, Marc. 2001. "Brahms und Frankreich." In *Internationaler Brahms-Kongress Gmunden 1997: Kongressbericht*, edited by I. Fuchs, 281–92. Tutzing, Germany: Schneider.

Vinant, Gaby. 1976. *Un esprit cosmopolite au XIXe siècle: Malwida de Meysenbug (1816–1903). Sa vie et ses amis*. Paris: Honoré Champion, 1932. Reprint Geneva, Switzerland: Slatkine Reprints.

Volkmann, Hans. 1912. "Johannes Brahms' Beziehungen zu Robert Volkmann." *Die Musik* 11, no. 13 (April): 3–13.

V[orwerk], A[nna]. 1897. "Meine Erinnerungen an Johannes Brahms." *Blätter aus dem Schlosse* [Wolfenbüttel] 40 (August): 1057–59.

Voss, E. Theodor. 1992. "Voss, Johann Heinrich." In *Literatur Lexikon: Autoren und Werke deutscher Sprache*, vol. 12, edited by W. Killy, 63–65. 15 vols. Gütersloh, Germany: Bertelsmann Lexikon Verlag, 1988–93.

Voss, Richard. 1920. *Aus einem phantastischen Leben: Erinnerungen*. Stuttgart, Germany: J. Engelhorns Nachfolger.

Waddington, Patrick. 1982. "Turgenev's Scenario for Brahms." *New Zealand Slavonic Journal* 1982: 1–16.

———. 1983. "Some Gleanings on Turgenev and His International Connections, with Notes on Pauline Viardot and Her Family." *New Zealand Slavonic Journal* 1983 (*Ivan Sergeyevich Turgenev: 1818–1883–1983*, edited by P. Waddington): 175–221. See especially "Turgenev and Brahms," 182–83.

Wagner, Cosima. 1976. *Die Tagebücher*, edited by M. Gregor-Dellin and D. Mack. 2 vols. Zurich, Switzerland: Piper & Co.

Wagner, Manfred. 1979. *Geschichte der österreichischen Musikkritik in Beispielen*. Tutzing, Germany: Schneider.

Wagner, Richard. 1976. *Mein Leben*, edited by M. Gregor-Dellin. Munich, Germany: List Verlag.

Walker, Alan. 1987–96. *Franz Liszt*. 3 vols. Vol. 1: *The Virtuoso Years, 1811–1847*, revised edition. Ithaca, N.Y.: Cornell University Press, 1987. Vol. 2: *The Weimar Years, 1848–1861*. Ithaca, N.Y.: Cornell University Press, 1993. Vol. 3: *The Final Years, 1861–1886*. New York: Knopf, 1996.

Walker, Ernest, and John Jones. 2004. "Farmer, John (1835–1901)." In *Oxford Dictionary of National Biography*, vol. 19, edited by H. C. G. Mathew and B. Harrison, 163–64. 60 vols. Oxford, UK: Oxford University Press.

Walker, Frank. 1968. *Hugo Wolf: A Biography*. London: Dent.

Wallisch, Friedrich. 1963. "Symphonie in e-moll." *Deutsche Rundschau* 89, no. 9 (September): 63–66.

Walter, Bruno. 1947. *Theme and Variations: An Autobiography*, translated by J. A. Galston. London: Hamish Hamilton.

Walter, Friedrich, ed. 1931. *Briefe Vincenz Lachners an Hermann Levi*. Mannheim.

Walter, Horst. 1960. "Erk, Ludwig Christian." In *Rheinische Musiker*, edited by K. G. Fellerer, 1st series, 5–7. Cologne, Germany: Arno Volk.

Wasielewski, Wilhelm Josef von. 1897. *Aus siebzig Jahren: Lebenserinnerungen*. Stuttgart, Germany: Deutsche Verlags-Anstalt.

———. 1920. *Die Violine und ihre Meister*. 6th, enlarged edition. Leipzig, Germany: Breitkopf & Härtel.

———. 1972. *Robert Schumann: Eine Biographie*. 4th, revised and considerably enlarged edition by Waldemar von Wasielewski. Leipzig, Germany: Breitkopf

& Härtel, 1906. Reprint Wiesbaden, Germany: Martin Sändig. For a contemporary review of the 2nd, enlarged edition (Dresden, Germany: Kuntze, 1869), see H. Deiters's in *Allgemeine musikalische Zeitung* 4 (1869): 364–67, 370–3, 378–80.

Watzinger, Karl Otto. 1984. "Ladenburg, Wolf Hajum." In *Geschichte der Juden in Mannheim, 1650–1945, mit 52 Biographien*, 109–10. Stuttgart, Germany: Kohlhammer.

Weber, Ernst. 1991. "Schenkendorf, (Gottlob Ferdinand) Max(imilian Gottfried) von." In *Literatur Lexikon: Autoren und Werke deutscher Sprache*, vol. 10, edited by W. Killy, 192–93. 15 vols. Gütersloh, Germany: Bertelsmann Lexikon Verlag, 1988–93.

Weber, Hildegard. 1958. *Das "Museum": Einhundertfünfzig Jahre Frankfurter Konzertleben, 1808–1958*. Frankfurt, Germany: Waldemar Kramer.

Webster, James. 1978–79. "Schubert's Sonata Form and Brahms's First Maturity." *19th Century Music* 2, no. 1 (July 1978): 18–35; 3, no. 1 (July 1979): 52–71.

Wecker, Hartmut. 1988. "'Der liebenswürdige Komponist des *Goldenen Kreuzes*': Eine kritische Würdigung Ignaz Brülls." In *Brahms-Kongress Wien 1983: Kongressbericht. Tutzing*, edited by S. Antonicek and O. Biba, 471–80. Germany: Schneider.

Weech, [Fr. von]. 1970. "Meysenbug: Wilhelm Freiherr Rivalier von M." In ***ADB***, vol. 21, 660–61. Leipzig, Germany: Duncker & Humblot, 1967–71.

Wehnert, Martin, Johannes Forner, and Hansachim Schiller. n.d. *Hochschule für Musik Leipzig, gegründet als Conservatorium der Musik*. Leipzig, Germany.

Weidemann, Alfred. 1922. "Brahms und Wagner." *Neue Musikzeitung* 43: 200–205, 217–20, 235–39.

Weigl, Bruno. 1907. "Johannes Brahms und Hermann Goetz." *Neue Musik-Zeitung* 28: 284–86.

Weingartner, Felix. 1905. "Brahms, ein Meister der Instrumentationskunst." *Allgemeine Musik-Zeitung* 32, no. 1 (6 January): 3–6. (English translation in *The New Music Review and Church Music* [March 1905]: 137–40. Reprinted in *American Brahms Society Newsletter* 12, no. 1 [Spring 1994]: 6–10.)

———. 1909. *Die Symphonie nach Beethoven*. 3rd, revised edition. Leipzig, Germany: Breitkopf & Härtel.

———. 1928–29. *Lebenserinnerungen.* 2nd, revised edition. 2 vols. Zurich, Switzerland: Orell Füssli.

Weinmann, Alexander. 1979. *J. P. Gotthard < Bohumil Pazdirek > 1839–1919: Biographisch-bibliographische Skizze*. Vienna, Austria: Krenn.

———. 1981. *Verzeichnis der Verlagswerke J. P. Gotthard*. Vienna, Austria: Krenn.

Weissheimer, W[endelin]. 1898. *Erlebnisse mit Richard Wagner, Franz Liszt und vielen anderen Zeitgenossen, nebst ihren Briefen*. Stuttgart, Germany: Deutsche Verlagsanstalt.

Weissweiler, Eva. 1990. *Clara Schumann: Biographie*. Hamburg, Germany: Hoffmann & Campe.

Wendler, Eugen, ed. 1996. *Clara Schumann: "Das Band der ewigen Liebe." Briefwechsel mit Emilie und Elise List*. Stuttgart, Germany: Metzler.

Wendt, Gustav. 1909. *Lebenserinnerungen eines Schulmanns*. Berlin: G. Grot'sche Verlagsbuchhandlung.

Wessely, Othmar, ed. 1985. *Bruckner Symposion: Johannes Brahms und Anton Bruckner . . . 8.–11. September 1983*. Linz, Austria: Anton Bruckner-Institut Linz.

——. 1988. "Johannes Brahms und die Denkmäler der Tonkunst Österreich." In *Brahms-Kongress Wien 1983: Kongressbericht*, edited by S. Antonicek and O. Biba, 481–88. Tutzing, Germany: Schneider.

Whyte, Deborah. 1984. "The Pianos of Conrad Graf." *Early Music* 12: 447–60.

Widmann, Elisabeth, and Max Widmann. 1922–24. *Josef Viktor Widmann: Ein Lebensbild*. Vol. 1: *Erste Lebenshälfte* by Elisabeth Widmann. Vol. 2: *Zweite Lebenshälfte* by Max Widmann. Frauenfeld, Switzerland: Huber & Co.

Widmann, Josef Viktor. 1897a. "Der Musenhof zu Meiningen." In *Sommerwanderungen und Winterfahrten*, 312–34. Frauenfeld, Switzerland: J. Huber.

——. 1897b. "Johannes Brahms." *Der Bund* (Berne, Switzerland), 6 April, 1–2.

——. 1898. *Erinnerungen an Johannes Brahms*. Berlin: Gebrüder Paetel.

——. 1903. *Sizilien und andere Gegenden Italiens: Reise mit Johannes Brahms*. 2nd edition. Frauenfeld, Switzerland: Huber & Co.

——. 1992. "Johannes Brahms in Zurich." In *"Ein Journalist aus Temperament": Josef Viktor Widmann, Ausgewählte Feuilletons*, edited by E. Pulver and R. Käser, 145–48. Berne, Switzerland: Zytglogge Verlag. (This is a reprint of an article published in the Berne newspaper *Der Bund* on 16 December 1881.) The book also contains "Eine Biographie in Texten und Bildern," a biographical study of Widmann by E. Pulver.

Wiechert, Berns. 1997. *Heinrich von Herzogenberg (1843–1900): Studien zu Leben und Werk*. Göttingen, Germany: Vandenhoeck & Ruprecht.

Wiora, Walter. 1953. *Die rheinisch-bergischen Melodien bei Zuccalmaglio und Brahms: Alte Liedweisen in romantischer Färbung*. Bad Godesberg, Germany: Voggenreiter Verlag.

Wirth, Helmut. 1974. "Johannes Brahms und Max Reger." *Brahms-Studien* 1: 91–112.

——. 1984. "Richard Wagner und Johannes Brahms." In *Brahms und seine Zeit: Symposium Hamburg 1983*, edited by C. Floros, H. J. Marx, and P. Petersen, 147–57. [n.p.]: Laaber. (*Hamburger Jahrbuch für Musikwissenschaft* 7.)

Wirth, Julia. 1927. *Julius Stockhausen, der Sänger des deutschen Liedes: Nach Dokumenten seiner Zeit.* Frankfurt, Germany: Englert & Schlosser.

Witkowski, Georg. 1926. "Michael Bernays." In *Badische Biographien*, Part 5: 1891–1901, vol. 1, edited by F. von Weech and A. Krieger, 72–77. Heidelberg, Germany: Winter.

Wohlwill, Adolf. 1900. *Bürgermeister Petersen: Ein hamburgisches Lebensbild*. Hamburg, Germany: Lütcke & Wulff.

Wolff, Ernst. 1913/14. "Erinnerungen an Amalie Joachim." *Almanach für die musikalische Welt* 10: 123–35.

Wolff, Leonhard. 1932. *Meine musikalischen Erinnerungen*. Bonn, Germany.

Wolff, Louise. 1990. "Begegnung mit Brahms." In *Verteidigung des musikalischen Fortschritts: Brahms und Schönberg*, edited by A. Dümling, 109–10. Hamburg, Germany: Argument.

Wood, Hugh. 1999. "A Photograph of Brahms." In *The Cambridge Companion to Brahms*, edited by M. Musgrave, 268–86. Cambridge, UK: Cambridge University Press.

Wüllner, Josepha. 1942. "Johannes Brahms in seiner Lebensfreundschaft mit Franz Wüllner." *Die Musik* 34, no. 6 (May): 192–97.

Würzl, Eberhard. 1995. "*Seid umschlungen Millionen* op. 443. Johann Strauss' Abschied vom Walzerkönigtum." In *Johann Strauss: Zwischen Kunstanspruch und Volksvergnügen*, edited by L. Finscher and A. Riethmüller, 97–114. Darmstadt: Wissenschaftliche Buchgesellschaft.

——. 2001. "Johannes und Johann—keine Künstlerfreundschaft." In *Internationaler Brahms-Kongress Gmunden 1997: Kongressbericht*, edited by I. Fuchs, 553–69. Tutzing, Germany: Schneider.

Wyklicky, Helmut. 1993. *Unbekanntes von Theodor Billroth: Eine Dokumentation in Fragmenten*. Vienna, Austria: Verlag der Österreichischen Wissenschaften.

Zagiba, Franz. 1955/56. "Johannes Brahms als 'Dirigenten-Promotor.'" *Musikerziehung* 9: 238–39.

Zapperi, A. 1960. "Barbi, Alice." In *Dizionario biografico degli Italiani*, directed by Alberto M. Ghisalberti, vol. 1, 188–90. Rome: Istituto della Enciclopedia italiana.

Zemlinsky, Alexander von. 1922. "Brahms und die neuere Generation: Persönliche Erinnerungen." *Musikblätter des Anbruch* 4, no. 5/6 (1 and 8 March): 69–70. (English version by Walter Frisch in *Brahms and His World*, edited by W. Frisch, 205–7. Princeton, N.J.: Princeton University Press, 1990.)

Zenker, Markus. 1990a. "Kopisch, August." In *Literatur Lexikon: Autoren und Werke deutscher Sprache*, vol. 6, edited by W. Killy, 493–94. 15 vols. Gütersloh, Germany: Bertelsmann Lexikon Verlag, 1988–93.

——. 1990b. "Lilienkron, Detlev von." In *Literatur Lexikon: Autoren und Werke deutscher Sprache*, vol. 7, edited by W. Killy, 290–91. 15 vols. Gütersloh, Germany: Bertelsmann Lexikon Verlag, 1988–93.

Zimmermann, Werner G. 1983. *Brahms in der Schweiz: Eine Dokumentation*. Zurich, Switzerland: Atlantis.

Zingel, Hans Joachim. 1963. *Das Kölner Gürzenichorchester—Werden und Sein*. Cologne, Germany: Hans Gerig.

Zinnow, Ingrid. 1992. "'Hochverehrter Herr!—Lieber Freund!' Unveröffentliche Briefe an Georg Dietrich Otten." *Brahms-Studien* 9: 36–45.

Zobel, Bertha. 1950. "Brahms on the Baltic: A Romance and a Dedication. Birth Centennials of Xaver Scharwenka and George Henschel Recall a Summer's Idyl." *Musical Courier* 141, no. 5 (1 March): 6–7.

Zwart, Frits. 2001. "'Herzlich willkommen, Herr Brahms!' Brahms-Rezeption in den Niederlanden bis etwa 1900." In *Internationaler Brahms-Kongress Gmunden 1997: Kongressbericht*, edited by I. Fuchs, 199–213. Tutzing, Germany: Schneider.

Index of Brahms's Works

BRAHMS'S ARRANGEMENTS OF OTHER COMPOSERS' COMPOSITIONS

(as listed in Anhang Ia of M. L. McCorkle's *Thematisch-bibliographisches Werkverzeichnis*)

Index of Names

Note: Page numbers in italic denote separate dictionary entries.

About the Author

Peter Clive is a specialist in French literature of the Renaissance and later 19th century and also has a strong interest in music. His doctoral dissertation (portions later published in the journal *Bibliothèque d'Humanisme et Renaissance*) examined the sources and literary aspects of the Calvinist attitude to music in the 16th century. Now retired, he has held posts at universities in England, the United States, and Canada, where he taught for 22 years.

His previous books include *Pierre Louÿs (1870–1925): A Biography* (1978), *Mozart and His Circle: A Biographical Dictionary* (1993), *Schubert and His World: A Biographical Dictionary* (1997), and *Beethoven and His World: A Biographical Dictionary* (2001).